ALGORITHMS, PROGRAMMING, PASCAL

BARBARA LI SANTI

LYDIA MANN

FRED ZLOTNICK

MILLS COLLEGE
OAKLAND, CALIFORNIA

WADSWORTH PUBLISHING COMPANY
Belmont, California
A Division of Wadsworth, Inc.

Computer Science Editor: Frank Ruggirello
Editorial Assistant: Reita Kinsman
Production Editor: Andrea Cava, Deborah McDaniel
Managing Designer: Andrew Ogus
Print Buyer: Barbara Britton
Designer: Vargas/Williams/Design
Copy Editor: Steven Hiatt
Technical Illustrator: Perfect Plot
Cover Designer: Vargas/Williams/Design
Cover Photograph: Francisco Hidalgo/The Image Bank West
Signing Representative: John Strohmeier

Printed in the United States of America   34

1 2 3 4 5 6 7 8 9 10---91 90 89 88 87

Library of Congress Cataloging-in-Publication Data

Li Santi, Barbara.
   Algorithms, programming, Pascal.

   Includes index.
   1. PASCAL (Computer program language)
I. Mann, Lydia.   II. Zlotnick, Fred.   III. Title.
QA76.73.P2L53   1987   005.13'3   86–24711
ISBN 0–534–06678–X

To

Micah Noe, Benjamin Summer

Elizabeth Li Santi, Winifred Asprey,
Mildred Campbell, Evalyn Clark

Katheryn Mann, Richard Mann,
Randall Bechler, Michael Bechler,
Leilani Tharp, George Mann

CONTENTS IN BRIEF

CONTENTS

PREFACE

By now it is generally accepted that an introductory computer science course should teach more than just the details of a programming language. The report of the ACM Curriculum Committee's Task Force for CS1[1] describes a number of objectives of such a course. These objectives include the introduction of a disciplined approach to problem solving and algorithm development. Perhaps in response to the committee's report, the latter two topics have recently gained greater emphasis in textbooks.

This text covers the material in the recommended curriculum for CS1, as well as some material that is recommended for CS2. In particular, we emphasize problem solving and algorithm development. However, the inclusion of these topics in a course does not automatically guarantee that students will understand how to apply them to programming. To aid in this application, we emphasize the correspondence between basic algorithm structures and the corresponding statement types in Pascal.

Pedagogical Approach

In this book we teach the structure and design of algorithms before we teach the details of Pascal. Our classroom experience shows that when students are first exposed to a programming language, they concentrate on the details of the language's syntax. Although this is quite natural, it is unfortunate; the fundamental ideas of programming are more deserving of emphasis. They form the basis for further study in computer science and are independent of any particular language.

These fundamental ideas also help a student understand how to use the features Pascal provides. Pascal is not just a random collection of statement types; rather, it is designed around the basic control structures out of which all algorithms are built. When a student who understands these structures is faced with a new Pascal construct, she has a context in which to understand it. At that point, the syntax is all that is new to her. A student without such an understanding, when faced with a new Pascal construct, has too many things to learn at once: How do I form these statements? Why are they in the language? Under what circumstances do I use them?

Much of this material has been taught implicitly in programming courses for a long time. Some students just pick it up, and some—particularly those who have mathematical or science backgrounds, where algorithmic thinking is used con-

---

1. Printed in the October 1984 issue of the *Communications of the ACM.*

stantly—may already have an informal understanding of how algorithms are put together. However, we think that understanding the fundamental ideas of programming is essential for students of computer science and that these ideas should be explicitly taught. We cover this material in the first part of the text.

The focus of Part I is the idea of an algorithm. It presents the ideas that all algorithms are built up from the building blocks of sequence, selection, iteration, and recursion and that the purpose of an algorithm is to manipulate data to reach a solution to a problem. This part is completely independent of any programming language. Studies have shown that expert programmers have a mental database of fundamental algorithms they can use as modules for the solution of most programming problems. Therefore, in addition to algorithm structure, we include two chapters on fundamental algorithms and present many examples. We also discuss the analysis of algorithms and the nature of data and its representation in the computer.

In our classes, we teach the material in Part I as part of the course. Some instructors may wish to have the students read these chapters independently or even treat this section as reference material. It is true that covering this material in class delays the start of student programming, by as much as three weeks. (It does not delay students' use of the computer, however. At Mills, our students use the early part of the semester to get computer accounts and learn how to log on and use the editor, how to compile and execute Pascal programs, how to use the electronic mail facility, and how to use the *script* command for submitting assignments.) In our experience, students who only start to program after having been introduced to the basic ideas of programming become much more accomplished programmers much more quickly than students who learn these ideas as they learn a programming language.

Part II of the text teaches the ISO Standard version of Pascal. The order of topics has been chosen to allow the student to write programs with visible results as soon as possible. We introduce procedures early, with parameters, to encourage the use of modular program style. We use data flow diagrams to illustrate the flow of data between program modules. Our introduction of Pascal flow-of-control constructs parallels the order in which the corresponding ideas are introduced in Part I. All flow-of-control constructs are introduced using only the data types *char* and *integer*.

This text assumes that the student will work in an interactive environment. Although we discuss batch processing of files, the bulk of our example programs display a dialogue with the user. We believe this is in accord with modern computing practice. In our experience, the extra generality gained by introducing the idea of batch processing is more than offset by the confusion it causes students who work in an interactive environment.

Special Features
Special features of our book include:

- Part I, a language-independent introduction to the basic ideas of computer science.

- Two chapters on fundamental algorithms:
  Chapter 6 deals with algorithms that manipulate simple data items. These include such basic algorithms as interchanging two values, finding the maximum or the minimum of a sequence of values, and finding the average of a sequence of values.
  Chapter 7 deals with algorithms that manipulate structured data items, and particularly data that in a programming language would be represented by an array. These algorithms include sorting, merging, and sequential and binary search.

- Tracing. We carefully trace the execution of many algorithms and programs and teach tracing.

- Early introduction of procedures, with parameters. We emphasize modular design of programs based on the flow of data.

- Typography to illustrate program elements. Programs, program fragments, and sample input and output are displayed in a special font that is `nonproportionally spaced` to correspond to the way most computer screens and printers display text. Pascal reserved words are shown in **boldface**, both in programs and in the text. Identifiers are typed in *italics,* in the same nonproportional typeface. A separate typeface is used to display algorithms.

- Exercises in the body of the text, as well as supplemental problems at the end of each chapter. The exercises are designed to reinforce each idea as it is introduced. The supplemental problems are designed to test knowledge of the chapter material as a whole.

- A chapter summary after each chapter.

- A section on common errors after each Pascal chapter. We describe syntax, semantic, and logical errors that students commonly make with the constructs introduced in that chapter.

- Debugging hints, after chapters where specific hints are useful.

How to Use This Book

There are a number of alternative paths you can take through this text, depending on your taste, pace, and the ability or background of your students. We recommend that you teach Part I first. The following is one suggested path through the book:

Cover in class	*Optional topic*
Chapters 1–4	Chapter 5
Chapters 6–7	
Chapter 9	Chapter 8
Chapters 10–23, in sequence	
Selections from Chapters 24–31, in any appropriate order.	

If you follow such a path, keep these points in mind:

- Chapter 5 consists only of examples. It is optional and can be read independently by students.

- Chapters 6 and 7 can be covered in class or can simply be read by students. You may prefer to postpone Chapter 7 until you reach arrays.

- The material in Chapter 8 is not referred to anywhere else in the book and is not necessary in a course for nonmajors. We recommend that potential CS majors cover this chapter.

- Chapters 10 through 20 cover the basic control structures and data structures of Pascal. They should be covered roughly in sequence, although variations are possible. (For instance, Chapter 18 can be moved up to follow 15, or it can be postponed.)

- Chapter 21, on ordinal types, can be postponed. We introduce ordinal types before arrays to describe index types in general, but it is also reasonable to introduce arrays with integer subrange indices only and to discuss other index types later.

After Chapter 23, you can cover the remaining material in many possible permutations. However, there are obvious limitations; records must precede dynamic data structures, for instance. We have had success covering these topics in the sequence given.

A different approach to the text involves making most of Part I supplementary reading for which students are responsible, but to which little lecture time is dedicated. You can have the students read chapters 1, 2, and 4 at the start of the semester and then jump straight to Part II. As appropriate, you can assign readings from chapters 3 and 5 through 9 in parallel with the material on Pascal. Here is one possible multitasking path that follows this approach through the book.

Cover in class	*Have students read concurrently*	*Optional topic*
Chapters 1, 2, 4		Chapters 5, 8
Chapter 10		
Chapter 11	Chapter 9	
Chapters 12 and 13		
Chapter 14		
Chapters 15 to 21, in order	Chapter 6	
Chapter 22	Chapter3	
Chapter 23	Chapter 7	
Selections from Chapters 24–31, in any appropriate order		

You may prefer this approach if you wish your students to begin writing programs as quickly as possible.

You can also use this text for a very traditional Pascal course. Such a course starts out by introducing elements of the language immediately. In this case, you can start directly with Part II, treating Part I as a reference. However, it is our experience that students in such a course only succeed if they are particularly apt or if they have particularly strong backgrounds in subjects where algorithmic thinking plays a role.

Cover in class	*Have students read as required*
Chapters 10–23, in order	Chapters 1–4, 8, 9
Selections from Chapters 24–31, in any appropriate order	

We discuss these options more fully in the Instructor's Guide. In this guide you will also find answers to all the exercises and problems in the book, masters for overhead transparencies that you may find useful, and teaching hints for each chapter.

Acknowledgments

The efforts, advice, assistance, and support of many people have helped us create this book. We would like to thank the members of the Department of Mathematics and Computer Science at Mills College for their support and encouragement. Particular thanks go to Professor Diane McEntyre, not only for her personal support but also for her doctoral dissertation[2], which provided early encouragement for our approach. We must also thank the staff of the Mills Academic Computer Center, who provided us with many of the electronic resources we needed. We are greatly indebted to our best critics, our students, who lived through many versions of the text and offered many helpful suggestions. We also owe much to the teaching assistants who worked with us and the students. In particular, Karina Assiter, Wai-Yee Chin, Sharon Flanagan, Judy Ko, Pek-Yew Ng, Andrea Silvestri, Chun-Hua Wang, and especially Lisa Lemon provided valuable insights. We had help from many others: Karina Assiter and Marianne Launay typed large portions of the manuscript. Nancy Campagna volunteered her time to help edit and proofread the manuscript, and Kathleen Costello spent part of her vacation drawing artwork for it. We are grateful to the reviewers who read and criticized various incarnations of the manuscript: Richard H. Austing, University of Maryland; Arthur Clarke, Montgomery College; Robert J. Del Zoppo, Jamestown Community College; Billy W. Denton, Itawamba Junior College; Clarence O. Durand, Henderson State University; A. Zoe Leibowitz, Central Connecticut State University; Blaise W. Liffick, Millersville University; Robert R. Little, Clemson University; John S. Mallozzi, Iona College; J. R. Rinewalt, University of Texas at Arlington; Charles N. Winton, University of North Florida; and Henderson Yeung, California State University, Fresno.

All authors know how important is the support of their publishers. We have been particularly fortunate in our associations at Wadsworth. We must thank Andrea Cava, Rhondal Jeong, Debbie McDaniel, Ev Sims, John Strohmeier, and especially our editor, Frank Ruggirello, who encouraged us, drove us, compelled us, and at crucial moments provided us with tickets to San Francisco Giants' games.

---

2. *Structures and Strategies for Teaching Programming in the Introductory Course,* Diane McEntyre, SESAME program, University of California at Berkeley, 1977.

ALGORITHMS, PROGRAMMING, PASCAL

PART

I

The purpose of this book is to help you learn how to solve problems using a computer and the programming language Pascal. To do that, you will need to master the rules of the Pascal language. These rules won't be very meaningful, however, until you become familiar with the problem-solving techniques and rules of abstract programming for which Pascal was designed. Once you have learned these techniques and rules, Pascal itself will make more sense. All too often, students who study programming find themselves memorizing an apparently random collection of facts. If they can figure out how to combine these facts, they succeed; otherwise, they remain confused. But there are methods and ideas underlying these facts. These can also be taught, and they can make the apparently random collection of facts fit into a coherent pattern. Our goal in this book is to teach you those methods and ideas first. Then, when you study Pascal, we hope that it will seem a natural extension of what you've already learned.

You may have heard someone say, "This problem was solved by a computer." They mean that a computer arrived at an answer to the problem. But computers are only tools; they do nothing by themselves. To solve a problem with a computer, you must provide it with precise instructions for solving the problem. This point may seem strange, so we'll restate it: If a computer is to solve a problem for you, you (or someone who has programmed the computer for you) must already know how to solve it, and must be able to articulate, with precision, the method of solution. And before you can do that, you must understand the problem completely.

Here's an example. Figure I.1 lists the Top 10 hit records (singles) in the United States for three consecutive weeks in 1964. You are asked to solve this problem:

INTRODUCTION: COMPUTERS AND PROBLEM SOLVING

> List alphabetically all the performers who had a record in the Top 10 for each of the three consecutive weeks ending on May 16, May 23, and May 30, 1964.

Can you tell from the statement of the problem what solution you are supposed to come up with? Is there just one way to interpret the statement? Or are there several ways? Try to think of at least two different ways in which you might interpret the problem statement.

Figure I.2 gives two possible solutions to the problem, either of which provides what the problem, as stated, seems to demand. The statement of the problem is ambiguous; it does not define the problem adequately. Does the problem ask you to give the names of performers as they are listed in Figure I.1—that is, a mixture of groups and individuals? Or does it ask you to give the names of the individual performers who make up the groups? If this is the case, where can you get that information? And suppose a group had one record on the charts for the first two weeks, and a second record that made the charts the third week. Should you include that group?

Before you can solve this problem properly, you must first be able to define it—that is, you must understand completely what information is given and what answer is asked for. Here is a restatement of the problem with the ambiguities removed:

> List alphabetically the names, as they appear on the charts shown in Figure I.1, of all the performing individuals or groups who, during each of the three consecutive weeks ending on May 16, May 23, and May 30, 1964, had some record on the lists of Top 10 singles shown in Figure I.1.

Figure I.1   **Top 10 songs from three weeks in 1964.** (Data from *The Gold of Rock &*
Roll 1955–1967, edited by H. K. Rhode.)

Top 10 for the week of May 16, 1964	Top 10 for the week of May 23, 1964	Top 10 for the week of May 30, 1964
1. "My Guy" M. Wells	1. "My Guy" M. Wells	1. "Chapel of Love" The Dixie Cups
2. "Hello Dolly" L. Armstrong	2. "Love Me Do" The Beatles	2. "Love Me With All Your Heart" Ray Charles Singers
3. "Love Me Do" The Beatles	3. "Hello Dolly" L. Armstrong	3. "Love Me Do" The Beatles
4. "Bits & Pieces" Dave Clark 5	4. "Chapel of Love" The Dixie Cups	4. "My Guy" M. Wells
5. "Do You Want to Know a Secret?" The Beatles	5. "Love Me With All Your Heart" Ray Charles Singers	5. "Romeo & Juliet" The Reflections
6. "Ronnie" The 4 Seasons	6. "Bits & Pieces" Dave Clark 5	6. "Little Children" B. J. Kramer & The Dakotas
7. "Don't Let the Rain Come Down" Serendipity Singers	7. "Romeo & Juliet" The Reflections	7. "A World Without Love" Peter & Gordon
8. "Dead Man's Curve" Jan & Dean	8. "A World Without Love" Peter & Gordon	8. "Hello Dolly" L. Armstrong
9. "White on White" D. Williams	9. "Ronnie" The 4 Seasons	9. "Walk on By" D. Warwick
10. "It's Over" R. Orbison	10. "It's Over" R. Orbison	10. "It's Over" R. Orbison

Figure I.2   **Two possible solutions to the Top 10 problem**

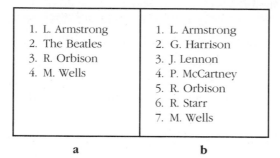

1. L. Armstrong	1. L. Armstrong
2. The Beatles	2. G. Harrison
3. R. Orbison	3. J. Lennon
4. M. Wells	4. P. McCartney
	5. R. Orbison
	6. R. Starr
	7. M. Wells

      a   **b**

Now can you solve the problem? You should come up with a list identical to one of the lists shown in Figure I.2.

Again, you can't begin to solve a problem until you understand it completely. And you can't understand it until it has been adequately defined. In Chapter 1, we'll discuss ways to define problems.

Now, can you describe how you solved the problem? Can you specify each step you took in coming up with your list? Here's a description of one method you may have followed.

I. Label a sheet of paper *Temporary List.*

II. For each of the songs numbered 1 through 10 on the *first list* (for May 16, 1964) in Figure I.1, do the following steps:
   A. Call the song we're doing this step for the *current song.* Look at the name of the performer of the *current song.* Search the *second list* to see if that name appears there as a performer of a song.
   B. If the performer's name was found on the *second list,* then,
      1. Search the *third list* for the same name.
      2. If the performer's name appears on the *third list* as well, then,
         a. Write the name on the sheet labeled *Temporary List.*

III. On another piece of paper, rewrite the names from the *Temporary List* in alphabetical order. Eliminate any duplicate names. This list is your answer.

Following the above sequence of steps is not the only way to solve the problem. But it will produce the list shown in Figure I.2a. Now we turn to a similar, but more complicated, problem:

You are provided with the Top 10 singles charts from *The Gold of Rock & Roll 1955–1967* for every week from January 1, 1955, to December 31,

1967. List alphabetically the names, as they appear on the charts, of all the performing individuals or groups who had a record on these charts during any three consecutive weeks between January 1, 1955, and December 31, 1967. If an individual or group qualifies more than once for your list, list the name only once.

By applying this procedure repeatedly to each consecutive triplet of weeks in the relevant period, you will come up with a list. And by alphabetizing and eliminating duplicate names you will arrive at a solution. However, coping with all the data involved is an overwhelming chore. This is a job for a computer.

Of course, you can't just present the computer with the problem statement and expect it to deliver the solution. You must first describe to the computer your exact method of solving the problem.

Actually, you have to do a bit more. You must give the computer all the relevant data needed for the solution—the 678 different lists of top 10 songs spanning the 13-year period. In general, if you want a computer to solve a problem you must provide

■ The relevant data (information) in some machine-understandable form (for example, tape, disk, or keystrokes)

■ A description of the steps the computer must carry out to get from the available data to the solution

You can't express these descriptions in English, however, because computers don't understand English. In any event, English is often ambiguous. Pascal and other programming languages provide a precise way of writing such descriptions in a form that the computer can understand.

To recap: To use a computer to solve a problem we must

■ Completely understand and describe the problem

■ Completely describe the steps necessary to arrive at a solution, and the information (data) required for the solution

■ Write a correct computer program that embodies all these descriptions in a form the computer can use

CHAPTER

1

1.1 UNDERSTANDING THE PROBLEM

The first step in solving a problem is to define it. That is, you have to understand the meaning of each part of the problem. To do so, you must answer these three questions:

- What do you need to solve the problem? Available information? Raw materials? If raw materials, where are they located?

- What constitutes a solution? A number? A list of names? An object?

- What restrictions are there on the problem or on the solution? For example, if the answer is a number, must it be a whole number? A positive number? If a list of names, must they be last names? Full names?

Answering these questions helps to ensure that you understand the problem. In addition, you may generate good ideas about how to approach the problem. Alternatively, you may identify roadblocks to a solution.

In defining a problem, it is often helpful to restate it, using English (or any other language), symbols, diagrams, pictures, tables, or any other means that enable you to describe the problem completely as you understand it. This step is particularly useful when someone else is posing the problem. Restating the problem to the person who is posing it may reveal misunderstandings, alternative solutions, or more obstacles to a solution.

Here are some examples. How would you define the following problems?

1. How can I bake a chocolate cake?
2. What was Rod Carew's batting average for the 1977 baseball season?

PROBLEM
DEFINITION

3. Someone in Paris must make a business trip to London, Amsterdam, Frankfurt, Lisbon, and Rome, returning to Paris. What is the best route?

4. How can I get from New York City to Boston?

5. What is the sum of all the whole numbers from 1 to 1,000,000?

Notice that these problems are of different types. Some are more formal than others. In some, it's clear what is asked for, even if we don't know how to get the answer, while in others it's not clear what the question means. For example, what exactly is meant by the phrase *a chocolate cake?* There are thousands of possible solutions to that problem. In the second problem, you may not know what a batting average is, or you may not have access to the information needed to compute the one requested.

The fifth problem seems well defined, even though working out a solution promises to be tedious.[1] We know that the solution will be a number, and the statement of the problem gives us all the information we need. Moreover, no restrictions are inherent in the problem statement.

Despite this problem's apparent clarity, it's useful for us to restate it. Here are two different restatements of problem 5:

5.A If we add all the numbers from 1 to 1,000,000, what answer will we get?

5.B How much is $1 + 2 + 3 + \ldots + 1,000,000$?

Notice that the phrase *from . . . to . . .* in the original problem statement makes it unclear whether the solution should include 1 and 1,000,000. Problem statement

---

1. It's tedious to actually carry out the summation. There is a formula, however, that quickly yields the answer.

9

5.A leaves this point unclear, while 5.B clearly indicates that 1 and 1,000,000 are to be included.

It may be, however, that the person who posed this problem meant for the solution to be the sum $2 + 3 + \ldots + 999,999$. Restating the problem may reveal that your conception of the problem is inaccurate. Two common sources of confusion in interpreting a problem are ambiguities and extraneous constraints.

Ambiguities are words or phrases that can be interpreted in more than one way. The phrase *from . . . to . . .* is ambiguous because it fails to specify the boundary values. In the fourth problem above, the word *best* is ambiguous. Does it mean the shortest route? The cheapest route? The fastest route? Or perhaps the most scenic route?

Natural languages like English are highly ambiguous. And yet people communicate well enough in natural languages because they can resolve the ambiguities by making "reasonable" assumptions based on context. Programming languages, by contrast, are unambiguous. A single statement means one thing and only one thing.[2] When you write programs, each statement you write will have a precise meaning. To ensure that these statements correctly reflect the problem you're solving, your problem statement must be precise.

Extraneous constraints are restrictions that are not evident in the original statement of the problem but are introduced by the problem solver. The effect of such restrictions is usually to make the problem harder. Suppose you were trying to define the fourth problem above: "How can I get from New York City to Boston?" If someone asked you this question in the course of a conversation, you would probably think it meant one of two things:

- What is the best route for driving from New York to Boston?
- What public transportation is available between the two cities?

In a conversation, the context constrains the meaning of a question. When a question is asked out of context, we tend to assume a context anyway. Thus, we might eliminate answers like "walking, cycling, or flying to London and then sailing to Boston." It doesn't usually matter if we don't consider these possibilities, but sometimes we fail to see the most creative solutions to problems by limiting our understanding of what's being asked. Restating the problem makes it less likely that extraneous constraints will arise:

What modes of public transportation will get me from New York to Boston within the next 24 hours?

---

2. Strictly speaking, this isn't quite true. There may be different versions of the same programming language on different computers, which may interpret the same program statement in slightly different ways. Each version of a programming language is referred to as an implementation of that language. Each implementation of a programming language is strictly unambiguous.

Most real-life problems, of course, are presented in some context. When we try to solve them, we draw on an enormous amount of contextual knowledge. We don't articulate this knowledge—that's hardly possible—but we make constant use of it. In solving problems with computer programs, however, we can't rely on contextual knowledge; the only information available to the computer is the information we explicitly provide.

Exercise 1.1: Restate problem 3 unambiguously. Specify what information is needed to solve the problem, what constitutes a solution, and what (if any) restrictions there are upon the solution. ■

1.2 AN EXAMPLE

To illustrate the ideas of the previous section, we'll do an example in some detail. The initial problem statement is

> You are given a sample of English text. You must provide a count of the number of times each letter of the alphabet occurs in the text.

To solve the problem we certainly need the sample of text. That seems to be all we need; the text sample contains all the information necessary to provide a solution. The solution itself will consist of a list of numbers, one number for each letter, indicating how many times each letter occurs in the text. There seem to be no restrictions in the problem statement, although we may spot some later on. This is a tentative problem definition.

It may seem that such a brief problem needs no restatement. Still, it's worth restating:

> Given a sample of text written in English, produce a list of the number of A's, the number of B's the number of C's,. . ., the number of Y's, and the number of Z's that appear in the sample.

In this statement, we've used an ellipsis (the three dots) instead of writing out a string of repetitive statements that follow an obvious pattern. You might argue that this practice introduces an ambiguity, since we don't say precisely what the ellipsis stands for. However, ambiguity is unlikely since the sequence of the Roman alphabet is well established.

A more serious criticism might be made of the way in which we have written the letters in the problem statement. Although the original problem statement makes no distinction between uppercase and lowercase letters, we chose to use uppercase letters. So there is a possible ambiguity here: You might interpret the problem restatement as requesting only a count of the uppercase letters.

Actually, this ambiguity may motivate us to ask other questions. For instance, what should we do about numerals or other special characters in the text? Should we ignore them? Should we count uppercase and lowercase letters separately? Let's settle for the simplest interpretations: We will make no distinction between uppercase and lowercase letters, and we will count only the 26 letters of the alphabet, not numerals or other characters.

What about the form of the output? The problem statement requests only numbers. Should the letter corresponding to each number appear to the left of the number? We tend to assume that the problem statement is asking us to list the letters, even though it doesn't. Such an assumption is a good example of an extraneous constraint.

We have looked at a number of possible interpretations of the original problem statement. Here is a final restatement of the problem:

> You are given a sample of English text. You must produce a list consisting of 26 numbers, of which the *n*th number in the list is the number of times the *n*th letter of the Roman alphabet occurs in the text, in either uppercase or lowercase form. Nothing else should appear on the list. Any nonletter characters in the text are to be ignored.

You may be thinking that this is a very complicated way of developing the problem definition. Actually, the simple approach you might use to solve this problem by hand doesn't work well for computer programs. (When we present this problem again as an exercise for you to solve with a computer program, you will see that the questions regarding uppercase and lowercase letters are essential to a correct computer solution.) To recap: In defining a problem, we must identify precisely

- What we know to start with
- What we are to end up with
- What restrictions apply to the solution

To identify these things, we have to resolve any ambiguities and remove any extraneous constraints we've placed on the problem.

1.3 ALGORITHMS

The ultimate purpose of defining problems is to solve them. Most problems for computer solution start with information and produce other information as the result. You can solve such a problem by figuring out how to transform the information you start with into the information you need, subject to the restrictions of the problem. Here are two useful definitions:

- *Input:* The information available to solve a problem.
- *Output:* The information required as the answer to a problem.

Simply put, solving the problem is a matter of transforming input into output. Computer programs describe how the computer is to make that transformation by setting down a finite sequence of steps to be followed in a prescribed order. Such a sequence is called an *algorithm*[3]:

> An *algorithm* is a precise, finite sequence of steps, in a prescribed order, that when carried out will lead to the solution of a specific problem.

Algorithms are common in science, mathematics, business, and other aspects of everyday life. For example, the steps to follow for computing one's income tax constitute an algorithm (a very complex one!). Algebraic formulas, knitting instructions, musical scores, and directions for getting to a party at a friend's house are all algorithms. And every computer program describes an algorithm. Such an algorithm consists of steps that manipulate information, or data[4]. The art of computer programming consists largely of designing algorithms to solve problems, and then, by means of a programming language, instructing computers to carry them out. In the next chapter, we'll talk about how one designs algorithms and discuss several fundamental building blocks of algorithms.

When the steps in an algorithm become too numerous or too complex to be carried out by hand, or involve more data than a human can effectively handle, a computer is useful. Computers routinely carry out algorithms that consist of many thousands, or even millions, of steps. Programming languages are a means of writing algorithms that computers can understand and execute.

CHAPTER SUMMARY

1. The first step in solving a problem is to define it. To do this, you must
   - Identify the *input* and *output* from the problem statement
   - Identify any *restrictions* on the solution imposed by the problem statement
   - Identify and resolve any *ambiguities* in the problem statement
   - Identify any *extraneous constraints* that do not appear in the problem statement but that you have imposed by your understanding of the problem

---

3. The term *algorithm* is derived from the name of the ninth-century Arabic mathematician al-Khowarizmi.

4. Thus, computer programming is sometimes referred to as *data processing*.

A useful step in this process is to *restate the problem*.

2. *Input* is the information available to solve a problem.
   Output is the information required as an answer to a problem.
   Data is the information used in any part of a problem solution.

3. An *algorithm* is a precise, finite sequence of steps, in a prescribed order, that will lead to the solution of a specific problem.

SUPPLEMENTAL PROBLEMS

For problems 1, 2, and 3, (a) find at least two interpretations of the problem; (b) restate the problem to eliminate all but one interpretation.

1. What are the five largest cities in the United States?

2. How many words are there on this page?

3. How many of the shapes below have six sides?

In problems 4, 5, and 6, identify the input and the output.

4. What is the last name in the Manhattan telephone directory?

5. Which letters of the alphabet do not occur in the last name of any U.S. president?

6. Given the academic records of all the seniors at a college, find the senior with the highest grade point average.

7. Consider the following problem: There are 20 people in a room. Identify the person having the most change in her or his pocket.
   a. Restate the problem. If you find the original statement to be ambiguous, make sure your restatement resolves the ambiguities.
   b. Describe the input and the output for this problem.

Problems 8, 9, and 10 contain sketches of purported algorithms to solve the indicated problems. Each of them is defective (that is, does not satisfy the definition of *algorithm*). Explain why.

8. To make pancake batter: Mix 1½ cups of flour with 1 teaspoon of baking powder and ½ teaspoon of salt. Add 2 eggs, 1 cup of milk, and 2 tablespoons of oil. Mix well.

9. To shampoo your hair: Wet hair. Lather, rinse, repeat.

10. To find out if there are 100 consecutive 7s anywhere in the decimal representation of pi (pi is an infinite, nonrepeating decimal): Repeatedly examine each sequence of 100 digits (the 1st through the 100th, the 2nd through the 101st, . . .) until you find 100 consecutive 7s. If you don't find them, there is no such sequence.

CHAPTER

2

Programming algorithms are written to specify ways of manipulating data. These algorithms have certain features in common: data manipulation, sequencing, selection, iteration, and recursion. These features enable you to develop algorithms that you can easily translate into any programming language. This chapter covers all topics except recursion, which is covered in Chapter 3.

2.1 MEMORY ALLOCATION

We begin by describing some of the ways in which computers deal with data. When someone asks you to add two numbers together, you listen for the numbers, make the calculation, and automatically store the sum somewhere in your head. You give the number when it is asked for, and after a while you may forget it. Similarly, when someone tells you his name you store it in your memory, along with some of the person's physical features, so that you can recall the name when you need it. You perform such functions automatically. You don't consciously store each piece of information in some particular place, nor do you refer to specific places when you wish to remember something. You never say, for example, "Someone is going to ask me to add two numbers. I must set aside a space to store each number and a space to store the sum of the numbers," or "I must take the number the person just told me and store it in that space in my memory." Computers, however, don't have this automatic facility for storing information.

Variable Data and Memory

Data whose values are determined during the execution of instructions are *variable data*. Whenever you want a program to have continued access to data it has

PIECES OF
ALGORITHMS

computed or data it has received from an outside source, you must explicitly indicate where that data should be stored. For example, if you write a general algorithm for taking two numbers and for printing their sum, you must have a space for each number so that the program can access the numbers when it calculates the sum. When you write programming algorithms, you should deal explicitly with the fact that programs store data in memory and that they need to be told when and how to manipulate that data.

In the computer algorithms we will be writing, we will include a specific *setup* stage and a specific *instruction* stage. The purpose of the setup stage is to reserve spaces in the computer's memory to store the data that must be available throughout the program. The pieces of paper we use as storage devices in our algorithms correspond to the memory spaces that programs use. Here is an example:

Setup

I. Label a piece of paper *first initial*.

II. Label a piece of paper *second initial*.

III. Label a piece of paper *last initial*.

Instructions

I. Ask someone for her first initial.

II. Write the letter she gives you on the piece of paper labeled *first initial*.

III. Ask the person for her second initial.

IV. Write the letter she gives you on the piece of paper labeled *second initial*.

V. Ask the person for her last initial.

VI. Write the letter she gives you on the piece of paper labeled *last initial.*

VII. Say, "Your initials backwards are."

VIII. Say the letter written on the paper labeled *last initial.*

IX. Say the letter written on the paper labeled *second initial.*

X. Say the letter written on the paper labeled *first initial.*

Constant Data

Some algorithms already contain certain data called *constant data.* You do not need to set aside storage space for constant data. Each constant data item is written into a particular instruction. For example, an algorithm might have this type of statement:

> If the value on the piece of paper marked *sum* is greater than 3, then say, "The number is too high."

Since the number 3 is data that cannot be changed without changing the algorithm, no space need be set aside for it.

Expressions

A third type of data used in algorithms is data created by expressions. The term *expression* is taken from mathematics. It describes something that has a value. The arithmetic expression $3 + 5$, for example, has the value 8. When you decide what the value of an expression is, you are said to be evaluating the expression. Arithmetic expressions evaluate to a numeric value. The arithmetic expression $4 + 7$ evaluates to 11. Often within an algorithm we don't wish to store the data created by an expression, but only to show its value or use it in a computation. For example, an instruction might read

> Write out the value of 5×5.

This instruction would cause the value 25 to be written somewhere, but the value would not be stored anywhere and would be inaccessible to further instructions in the algorithm.

As we proceed, you will notice that each algorithm contains explicit steps specifying what spaces are needed in memory and when and how the data in those spaces is to be manipulated. You should include such steps when you write your own programming algorithms.

2.2 SEQUENCING

When you are given a set of instructions for assembling some object, you usually start with the instruction labeled *1,* continue on to the instruction labeled *2,* and so on. You have been taught to perform instructions in a particular sequence or order.

When you read a page of English, you start at the top left-hand corner and move your eyes across to the top right-hand corner. You then go to the next line and read from left to right. Finally you reach the bottom of the page. If you are reading a page of Arabic, however, you start at the top right-hand corner and move your eyes to the left, and so on. In either case, you must understand the sequence in which the words appear to understand what you are reading. Similarly, when you write, you must observe the sequencing conventions of the language you are using.

Different programming languages have different rules regarding the sequence in which the computer will perform instructions. Algorithms, however, are usually written in a natural language (French, English, Japanese), so that they may easily be interpreted by their author. At the outset, all the algorithms we present are meant to be read similarly to English text. We shall give a precise definition of how those English sentences should be interpreted. Later on, we will introduce other ways of writing and reading algorithms.

You may ask at this point why sequencing is important. When you write an algorithm you must be aware that the instructions you give will be performed in a certain order. Sometimes it doesn't make any difference if one instruction is performed before another, but usually it does. It is important to identify whether the sequence of instructions in an algorithm will affect the outcome of the algorithm.

Consider the following algorithm, which demonstrates the importance of sequencing:

Setup

I. Have a blue piece of paper ready.

II. Have a red piece of paper ready.

III. Have a green piece of paper ready.

Instructions

I. Ask person #1 to write down a number on the blue piece of paper.

II. Ask person #1 to write down a number on the red piece of paper.

III. Ask person #1 to hand the red and blue pieces of paper to person #2.

IV. Ask person #2 to sum the numbers on the red and blue pieces of paper and write the total on the green piece of paper.

V. Ask person #2 to say out loud the number on the green piece of paper.

Here you could give instruction I before giving instruction II without affecting the output. But if you gave instruction IV before instruction I, someone trying to follow your instructions would become confused and be unable to finish the algorithm. In other words, the sequencing is important at some points and unimportant at others.

Let's look at another example:

Setup

I. Label a piece of paper with *1.*

II. Label a piece of paper with *2.*

III. Label a piece of paper with *3.*

IV. Label a piece of paper with *4.*

Instructions

I. Write the words "Twinkle twinkle little star" on the piece of paper labeled *1.*

II. Write the words "How I wonder where you are" on the piece of paper labeled *2.*

III. Write the words "Up above the world so high" on the piece of paper labeled *3.*

IV. Write the words "Like a diamond in the sky" on the piece of paper labeled *4.*

V. Hand someone the four pieces of paper.

VI. Ask the person to read the words written on the paper labeled *1.*

VII. Ask the person to read the words written on the paper labeled *2.*

VIII. Ask the person to read the words written on the paper labeled *3.*

IX. Ask the person to read the words written on the paper labeled *4.*

If we gave instruction VII before instruction II, a person would be unable to perform this task. If, however, we gave instruction VII before instruction VI, the person could complete the task but the outcome would not be what we intended. Unless he was familiar with the poem, the person performing the task would be unaware that anything was wrong.

Exercise   2.1: (a) Follow the above algorithm and write down what the person has read. (b) Change the instructions by switching instruction VII and instruction VI. Follow your new set of instructions and write down what the person has read. (c) How do the outcomes of the two sets of instructions differ?   ∎

2.3 TRACING AND DEBUGGING

It is important that you verify as much as possible that the solution produced by the algorithm is correct. In this chapter, we introduce a type of verification called *tracing*. Tracing is the monitoring of data throughout every instruction of an algorithm.

Tracing is an essential step in problem solving. Although it may seem time-consuming, it saves time, energy, and agony. If you encode an incorrect solution in the formal syntax of a programming language, you will have tremendous difficulty trying to get the program to work.

The first step in tracing an algorithm is to think of all the values that might possibly be input to the problem. Then you need to see if your solution works for each of those sets of input. Some situations are similar enough to be ignored even if they are not identical. For example, if we had an algorithm to add together two numbers, we would not have to test it with every pair of numbers in existence: A very small subset would be sufficient.

The second step in tracing is to follow the instructions with the test data you have chosen. You should keep some record of the values being manipulated after every step of the algorithm. Figure 2.1 shows an algorithm. Figure 2.2 shows a trace of that algorithm with the numbers 5, 6, and 7 used as data for the pieces of paper labeled **number one**, **number two**, and **number three**, respectively. Notice that it is clear when each space gets a value and what happens when each instruction is performed.

Exercise   2.2: (a) Describe the task the algorithm given in Figure 2.1 performs. (b) Rearrange the instructions in five ways. Two ways should affect the output of the problem; three ways should make it impossible to perform the instructions. Give your sequences simply by stating the numbers of the instructions (for example, I, II, IV, V, III . . .). (c) Trace the algorithms you have created, indicating the step where the instructions can no longer be followed or the step that makes the output of the algorithm different from that of the original algorithm. Explain why the traces differ.   ∎

Figure 2.1   **Sample algorithm**

Setup

   I. Label a piece of paper *solution.*

  II. Label a piece of paper *number one.*

 III. Label a piece of paper *number two.*

 IV. Label a piece of paper *number three.*

  V. Label a piece of paper *intermediate result.*

Instructions

   I. Ask a friend for a number.

  II. Write the number on the piece of paper labeled *number one.*

 III. Ask a friend for another number.

 IV. Write the number on the piece of paper labeled *number two.*

  V. Ask a friend for another number.

 VI. Write the number on the piece of paper labeled *number three.*

 VII. In your head, multiply the number found on the piece of paper labeled *number one* by the number on the piece of paper labeled *number two.* Find the paper labeled *intermediate result.* Erase any value you find there and write the number you just calculated.

VIII. In your head, add the number on the paper labeled *intermediate result* to the number on the paper labeled *number three.* Erase any value on the paper labeled *solution* and replace it with the number you just calculated.

 IX. Read out loud the number on the piece of paper labeled *solution.*

If we discover that some part of an algorithm does not work, then we must figure out what is wrong with it. This is an extremely important step. Never make a change before you know the cause of the trouble.

Correcting the mistakes in a faulty algorithm is called *debugging.*[1] Once we

---

1. The term *debugging* arose in the early days of computers, when real bugs such as spiders sometimes got into the wiring and affected the machines.

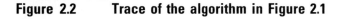

Figure 2.2   **Trace of the algorithm in Figure 2.1**

Step	Memory					Output
	solution	*number one*	*number two*	*number three*	*intermediate result*	
	?	?	?	?	?	
I.	?	?	?	?	?	number please?
II.	?	5	?	?	?	
III.	?	5	?	?	?	number please?
IV.	?	5	6	?	?	
V.	?	5	6	?	?	number please?
VI.	?	5	6	7	?	
VII.	?	5	6	7	30	
VIII.	37	5	6	7	30	
XI.	37	5	6	7	30	37

have corrected the algorithm, we must go back and retest it in all possible situations. We repeat this process until we are confident that the algorithm works correctly. As we introduce you to more complex algorithms we will show examples of debugging.

2.4   SELECTION

Often an algorithm will ask a question. Depending on the answer, certain instructions may be performed or skipped. Such instructions allow some form of choice to take place. For example, the instruction, **If you want to make the steak well-done, then cook an extra five minutes,** gives the cook an optional instruction depending on how he wanted the steak cooked. Such instructions are called *selection instructions* or *conditional instructions*. They make it possible to break the regular sequence in which the instructions are performed by "jumping over" or skipping some instructions.

Here is another example of a slightly different type of selection instruction: **If my dog is good, then take him for a walk; otherwise, put him in the dog house.** This instruction will tell the dogsitter either to take the dog for a walk or to put the dog in the dog house. Since the two instructions will not both be performed, regular sequencing is broken.

Single-Option Selection Instructions

Consider the following algorithm:

Setup

I. Get a piece of paper.

Instructions

I. Write your name on the piece of paper.

II. Write your age below your name on the same piece of paper.

III. If the number you put down as your age is greater than 16 and you can drive,
      then
         A. Put a comma by your age.
         B. Leave a space after the comma.
         C. Write the word "drive" after the space.

IV. Write your address below your age.

Instruction III implicitly asks a question. Depending on the answer, it instructs the person either to perform or not to perform the subset of instructions that follow within instruction III. In other words, it instructs the person to perform certain steps of the algorithm only if that person is older than 16 and can drive.

The option in a selection instruction is presented in what is called a *conditional expression*. We have seen that arithmetic expressions evaluate to numbers. Conditional expressions[2] evaluate to either the value *true* or the value *false*. Look again at our example: **If the number you put down as your age is greater than 16 and you can drive.** We can take the expression out of the instruction and decide whether it is true or false: **The number you put down as your age is greater than 16 and you can drive.** If this conditional expression evaluates to *true*, the following subset of instructions within the **then** clause will be performed. If the conditional expression evaluates to *false*, the subset of instructions will not be performed. No matter what happens, the instruction following the selection construct will be performed next.

When creating algorithms, the subset of instructions in a selection instruction should be marked off in some way—the usual method is to change the numbering/lettering system and indent the subset.

Here is another example of an algorithm that uses a selection instruction.

---

2. They are also called *Boolean expressions* after the British logician George Boole.

I. Get up at 8:00 am.

II. Brush your teeth.

III. If your hair is messy,
     then
         A. Brush your hair.

IV. Get dressed.

V. Eat breakfast.

IV. Go to class.

In this case, the conditional expression is **your hair is messy**. If this expression evaluates to true, the person would follow the subset of instructions by brushing his hair and then going on to step IV. If this expression evaluates to false, he would go directly to step IV.

Notice that no specific instruction is needed for proceeding to step IV. It is assumed that the reader will continue in a sequential manner, starting at the top and going to the bottom unless otherwise instructed. This is a *default rule* concerning sequencing. A default rule is one that is followed if no other instructions specify what to do. If a break in sequence occurs, it is assumed the reader will perform the necessary subset of instructions and will return to the regular sequence of the algorithm when he or she is done.

In a well-written algorithm, the sequence resumes smoothly after it has been interrupted by some operation. There should be no need for instructions directing the reader to pick up the sequence again. The following algorithm fails in that respect; it is badly written.

Setup

I. Get a piece of paper.

Instructions

I. Write your name at the top of the piece of paper.

II. Write your age below your name.

III. If you are older than 16 and can drive,
     then
         A. Go to step VI.

IV. Write your address on the line below your age.

V. STOP.

VI. Write a comma after your age.

VII. Leave a blank space after the comma.

VIII. Write the word "drive."

IX. Write your address on the line below your age.

This algorithm is unclear and hard to follow. Once the sequencing has been broken, the reader must search for the next instruction. The use of **go to** in an algorithm is almost always unnecessary and confusing. Any algorithm or program that you write will probably be looked at by another person. The way in which you write your algorithm or program should make it as easy as possible for that person to read and understand it.

Some algorithms contain more than one selection instruction. Here is an example:

Setup

I. Get a piece of paper.

Instructions

I. Write your name at the top of the piece of paper.

II. Write your age below your name.

III. If you are older than 16 and you can drive,
    then
    A. Put a comma after your age.
    B. Leave a space after the comma.
    C. Write the word "drive."

IV. Write your street address on the line below your age.

V. If your mailing address is different from the address given above,
    then
    A. Write your mailing address on the line below your street address.

Algorithms may have one selection instruction contained within another selection instruction. This arrangement is called *nesting:* One instruction is said to be nested within the other. Here is an example:

Setup

I. Get a piece of paper

Instructions

I. Write your name at the top of the piece of paper.

II. Write your age below your name.

III. If you are older than 16 and you can drive,
then
    A. Put a comma after your age.
    B. Leave a space after the comma.
    C. Write the word "drive".
    D. If you have a car,
      then
        1. Put a comma after the word "drive."
        2. Leave a space after the comma.
        3. Write the word "car."

IV. Write your street address on the line below your age.

V. If your mailing address is different from the one given in step IV,
then
    A. Write your mailing address on the line below your street address.

Notice that if you are not older than 16 or if you can't drive, you will not be asked whether you have a car.

Tracing Conditional Expressions

To trace an algorithm involving a conditional expression, you should include a column in your tracing form labeled *conditional expressions* just as you include a column labeled *output*. When an instruction involves a conditional expression, you should write the value of that conditional expression in the spot corresponding to the row of your instruction and the column for conditional expressions. Consider the following algorithm:

Setup

I. Label a piece of paper *capital*.

Instructions

I. Ask a friend for the name of the capital of California.

II. Write her reply on the paper labeled *capital*.

III. If the word on the paper labeled *capital* is "Sacramento,"
then
    A. Tell your friend that she is correct.
else
    A'. Tell your friend that she is incorrect.

A trace of this algorithm with *Los Angeles* as input, would look like this:

Instructions	Conditional expressions	Memory	Output
		Capital	
Setup		?	
I.		?	What is the capital of California?
II.		Los Angeles	
III.	False	Los Angeles	
III. A′		Los Angeles	You are incorrect.

Multioption Selection Instructions

The selection instructions we have discussed so far perform a subset of instructions if the conditional expression evaluates to true. If the conditional expression evaluates to false, the subset of instructions is skipped and the succeeding instructions are followed. Figure 2.3a shows the optional paths that can be taken with this type of instruction. Often we would like to perform one subset of instructions if a conditional expression evaluates to true, and an alternative subset of instructions if the conditional expression evaluates to false. The diagram in Figure 2.3b shows the optional paths we might want performed. Here is an example of an algorithm that contains a selection instruction of this type:

Setup

I. Get a piece of paper.

Instructions

I. Write your name at the top of the piece of paper.

II. Write your age below your name.

III. If you are older than 16,
    then
        A. Write "old enough to drive" after your age.
    else
        A′. Write "too young to drive" after your age.

IV. Write your address below your age.

Figure 2.3   **Flow of single-selection and two-option-selection instructions**

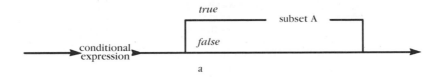

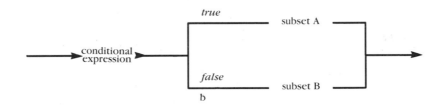

Everyone who follows these instructions will write her name, age, and address on the piece of paper. However, only those who are older than 16 will write the words **old enough to drive**, and only those who are 16 or younger will write the words **too young to drive**. If the instructions are followed correctly, it will be impossible for both **old enough to drive** and **too young to drive** to appear on the same piece of paper.

This type of instruction has two options because the conditional expression can be either true or false. The **then** specifies what happens if the conditional expression evaluates to true. The **else** specifies what happens if the conditional expression evaluates to false.

Figure 2.4 shows an algorithm for solving the following problem:

Compare two numbers and state which is larger.

Figure 2.4   **Setup**

I. Get a blue piece of paper.

II. Get a green piece of paper.

(continued)

Figure 2.4
Continued

Instructions

I. Write a number on the blue piece of paper.

II. Write a number on the green piece of paper.

III. If the number on the blue piece of paper is greater than the number on the green piece of paper,
   then
      A. Say, "The first number is larger."

   else
      B. Say, "The second number is larger."

Exercise   2.3: Trace the above instructions with each of the following sets of numbers: (a) 11, 12; (b) 15, 10; (c) 7, 7. Do not forget to show what happens at each step of the algorithm. Do the above instructions work correctly for the given problem statement? Why or why not?   ■

Notice that if the inputs to this algorithm are two different numbers, the instructions work perfectly well. If, however, the inputs are the same two numbers, the instructions do not work. There is an ambiguity in the problem statement because it does not accommodate the fact that the numbers may be the same. Let's add to the problem statement so that it reads

Compare two numbers. State which is larger, or if they are equal.

We can change the algorithm to fit this problem statement by nesting a single-option selection instruction within the multioption selection instruction. In general, you may nest any instruction within any type of selection instruction.
   Here is the new algorithm:

Setup

I. Get a blue piece of paper.

II. Get a green piece of paper.

Instructions

I. Write a number on the blue piece of paper.

II. Write a number on the green piece of paper.

III. If the number on the blue piece of paper is greater than the number on the green piece of paper,
  then
    A. Say, "The first number is larger."
  else
    A'. If the number on the green piece of paper is greater than the number on the blue piece of paper,
      then
        1. Say, "The second number is larger."
      else
        1'. Say, "The numbers are equal."

Notice that this is not the only possible solution to this problem. We could rearrange this algorithm as follows and still get the same output:

Setup

  I. Get a blue piece of paper.

  II. Get a green piece of paper.

Instructions

  I. Write a number on the blue piece of paper.

  II. Write a number on the green piece of paper.

  III. If the number on the blue piece of paper is greater than the number on the green piece of paper,
    then
      A. Say, "The first number is larger."
    else
      A'. If the number on the green piece of paper is equal to the number on the blue piece of paper,
        then
          1. Say, "The numbers are equal."
        else
          1'. Say, "The second number is larger."

As long as the input is the same, these last two algorithms will produce the same output.

Exercise 2.4: Rearrange this algorithm in yet another way that will work as well as the two versions above. ■

It may have occurred to you that we could have written the algorithm above with just single-selection instructions. For example:

Setup

I. Get a blue piece of paper.

II. Get a green piece of paper.

Instructions

I. Write a number on the blue piece of paper.

II. Write a number on the green piece of paper.

III. If the number on the blue piece of paper is greater than the number on the green piece of paper,
   then
      A. Say, "The first number is larger."

IV. If the number on the green piece of paper is equal to the number on the blue piece of paper,
   then
      A. Say, "The numbers are equal."

V. If the number on the green piece of paper is greater than the number on the blue piece of paper,
   then
      A. Say, "The second number is larger."

The last three algorithms perform the same task. Which way is best? In writing programming algorithms, the multioption selection instructions are more efficient and make better sense. If the first conditional expression is **the number on the blue piece of paper is greater than the number on the green piece of paper,** and it evaluates to true, none of the other conditional expressions are evaluated. With the single-option selection instructions, even if the first conditional expression evaluated to true, we would have to keep checking conditional expressions even though we know they would all evaluate to false.

Notice that single-option selection instructions and multioption selection instructions cannot always be interchanged. Consider these two algorithms, which perform operations with two numbers.

Setup

I. Get a red piece of paper.

II. Get a yellow piece of paper.

Instructions

  I. Write a number on the red piece of paper.

  II. Write a different number on the yellow piece of paper.

  III. If the number on the red piece of paper is greater than the number on the yellow piece of paper,
>then
>>A. In your head, add 5 to the number on the yellow piece of paper. Erase the number on the yellow piece of paper, and write the number you just calculated on the yellow piece of paper.

  IV. If the number on the yellow piece of paper is greater than the number on the red piece of paper,
>then
>>A. In your head, add 5 to the number on the red piece of paper. Erase the number on the red piece of paper and write the number you just calculated on the red piece of paper.

  V. Say the number on the red piece of paper.

  VI. Say the number on the yellow piece of paper.

Setup

  I. Get a red piece of paper.

  II. Get a yellow piece of paper.

Instructions

  I. Write a number on the red piece of paper.

  II. Write a different number on the yellow piece of paper.

  III. If the number on the red piece of paper is greater than the number on the yellow piece of paper,
>then
>>A. In your head, add 5 to the number on the yellow piece of paper. Erase the number on the yellow piece of paper and write the number you just calculated on the yellow piece of paper.
>else
>>A'. In your head, add 5 to the number on the red piece of paper. Erase the number on the red piece of paper and write the number you just calculated on the red piece of paper.

  IV. Say the number on the red piece of paper.

  V. Say the number on the yellow piece of paper.

Trace these two algorithms with the same inputs—the numbers 55 and 54 for the red and yellow pieces of paper, respectively. You will find that the outputs are different.

Exercise 2.5: Trace the above algorithms with the same inputs—the numbers 55 and 54 for the red and yellow pieces of paper, respectively. What are the outputs of the two algorithms? Why are they different? ■

Two conditional expressions are evaluated in the algorithm with the single-option selection instructions. If the first expression evaluates to true, it can change the values written on the pieces of paper. Because of this, when the second conditional expression is evaluated, it can also be true. This would cause the subset of instructions within the second single-option selection instruction to be performed.

In the algorithm with the multioption selection instruction, only one conditional expression is evaluated. If that conditional expression evaluates to true, the instructions in the first part of the instruction will be performed, and the instructions in the second, or **else,** part will not be performed.

2.5 ITERATION

Sometimes we want a subset of instructions to be followed a certain number of times. For example, your aerobics teacher might ask you to "run around the gym five times" or to "run around the gym until you are exhausted." In the first case, you simply need to keep track of the number of times you have run around the gym and then stop after the fifth circuit. In the second case, you must keep asking yourself if you are exhausted yet, and then quit when your answer is yes. Both instructions are examples of *iteration*. Iterative instructions are instructions that contain a subset of instructions that may be performed a given number of times. For this reason, iterative structures are often called loops. In the first case, some sort of counter is used to keep track of when the iteration has ended. This form of iterative instruction is called *definite iteration*. In the second case, a conditional expression is evaluated to determine when the loop is over. This form is *indefinite iteration*. We shall examine both types of instructions and see how they expand the variety of algorithms that we can describe.

Indefinite Iteration

Indefinite iterative instructions use conditional expressions to determine the number of times a subset of instructions will be performed. They are the most versatile type of iteration, because they can be used, if necessary, like definite iterative instructions. Here is a problem statement for a guessing game for which we shall proceed to write an algorithm:

> Think of a number between 1 and 100 inclusive. Ask a friend to guess what the number is until she has guessed correctly. Tell her when her guess is incorrect.

We must use an indefinite iterative instruction in this algorithm because we cannot know how long it will take the friend to guess the correct number. We shall use the word **while** to indicate that we must continue to perform the subset of instructions as long as the person has not guessed the correct number.

Setup

  I. Label a piece of paper *answer.*

 II. Label a piece of paper *guess.*

Instructions

  I. Write a number between 1 and 100 inclusive on the paper labeled *answer.*

 II. Ask a friend to name a number between 1 and 100 inclusive.

III. Write the number your friend says on the paper labeled *guess.*

IV. While the number on the paper labeled *answer* is not the same as the number on the paper labeled *guess,* do the following:
 A. Tell your friend her guess is incorrect.
 B. Ask your friend to name a number between 1 and 100 inclusive.
 C. Erase any number on the paper labeled *guess* and write the number your friend says on the paper labeled *guess.*

 V. Tell your friend she has guessed the correct number.

Exercise 2.6: Write an algorithm for a game you know that repeats a given set of instructions an indefinite number of times. ■

The subset of instructions within a loop is called *the body of the loop.* Sequencing plays an important role in determining when the body of this loop is performed and when the conditional expression that controls the loop is evaluated. Following the normal sequence in which instructions are read, the conditional expression is the first part of the instruction that is viewed. It is evaluated to decide whether the body of the loop will be performed. If the conditional expression evaluates to false, the body of the loop is skipped entirely.

If, however, the conditional expression evaluates to true, the body of the loop is performed. Once you start the body of a loop, you must do it all, even if the conditional expression changes value. This is a sequencing rule concerning iterative instructions. When writing programming algorithms, you should have only loops that can be left upon evaluation of their conditional expression.

Let's look at another problem whose solution includes a loop:

Given some text, you must provide a count of the number of vowels (a, e, i, o, and u) that appear in the first sentence. The end of the sentence will be indicated by a period, a question mark, or an exclamation point.

The input here is some text of unspecified length that contains at least one sentence that ends with a period, a question mark, or an exclamation point. The output is the number of vowels in the first sentence of the text. We need to use an indefinite iterative instruction, because the problem statement does not indicate the number of characters in the first sentence. We must use a looping instruction so that we can look at an indefinite number of characters. Here is an algorithm for the problem:

Setup

I. Label a piece of paper *number of vowels.*

II. Label a piece of paper *character.*

Instructions

I. Write the value 0 on the paper labeled *number of vowels.*

II. Find the first letter of the text. Write it on the paper labeled *character.*

III. While the character written on the paper labeled *character* is not a period, a question mark, or an exclamation point do:
    A. If the character on the paper labeled *character* is an "a", "e", "i", "o", or "u",
        then
            1. In your head, add 1 to the number found on the paper labeled *number of vowels.* Erase the number on the paper labeled *number of vowels,* and write the number you just calculated on the paper.
    B. Find the next character in the text. Erase the character on the paper labeled *character,* and write down the character you just found there.

IV. Say, "The number of vowels is."

V. Say the number written on the paper labeled *number of vowels.*

This loop contains a conditional expression something like the piece of paper labeled *character* doesn't have a period, a question mark, or an exclamation point written on it. For the conditional expression to be evaluated the first time the loop is reached, the piece of paper labeled *character* must already have some value written on it. Any value that appears in the conditional expression of a loop must be specified before the conditional expression can be tested.

Notice that this loop contains an instruction that is capable of changing the value on the piece of paper labeled *character.* This is necessary so that at some point the conditional expression can be reevaluated in such a way that the iteration stops. The conditional expression of a loop must contain some value that has the potential of being changed within the body of the loop. Otherwise, the loop will go on being performed indefinitely until some outside intervention stops the action.

Also notice that one of the first steps in the algorithm was to write the value 0 on the paper labeled *number of vowels*. We needed to do this so that the person following the instructions could perform step III. A.1. This is called *initialization* because we are giving *number of vowels* an initial value.

Exercise 2.7: A list of numbers is given as input to a problem. The last number will be a 0 (the only 0 in the list). Write an algorithm that will count the number of times the number 55 is found in the list. Be explicit about how you get the next number and where the total of 55s is being stored, as you have seen done in the example algorithms. ■

The type of iterative instruction we have seen so far causes a possible break in sequencing, as shown in Figure 2.5a. Figure 2.5b shows another way in which an iterative instruction might change sequencing. Notice that both types of loop can finish only immediately after the evaluation of the loop's conditional expression. Here is a problem to solve using this new type of iterative instruction:

The score must be kept for a game. A player must keep playing the game until she makes over 100 points. When a player has made over 100 points, she should be informed of how many points she has made.

The input to this problem consists of points. The output is the final score, reached by adding up the points. A constraint is that no more points can be entered once the score has exceeded 100. Since we don't know how many times points will be entered, we need an indefinite iterative instruction. Since we know points must be entered at least once, the second type of iterative instruction is useful. Here is an algorithm for the problem:

Setup

I. Label a piece of paper *score.*

II. Label a piece of paper *points.*

Instructions

I. Write the value 0 on the paper labeled *score.*

II. Repeat
    A. Ask for the points.
    B. Write the number you hear on the paper labeled *points.*
    C. In your head, add the number on the paper labeled *points* to the number on the paper labeled *score.* Erase any number on the paper labeled *score,* and write down the number you just calculated on the paper labeled *score.*
   Until the number on the paper labeled *score* is greater than 100.

III. Say, "The score is."

IV. Say the number on the paper labeled *score.*

This algorithm makes it clear that the conditional expression is not tested until the body of the loop has been performed at least once. Moreover, the iteration is over when the conditional expression is reached in the sequence and it evaluates to *true.*

There are two differences between the first loop we saw and the loop to which you have just been introduced. One, the first loop evaluated the conditional expression before performing the body of the loop. The second loop evaluated

Figure 2.5 **The flow through an algorithm using different iterative instructions**

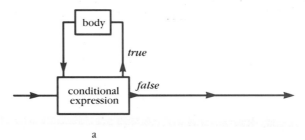

a

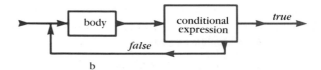

b

the conditional expression after performing the body of the loop. Two, the first loop ended when the conditional expression evaluated to false. The second loop ended when the conditional expression evaluated to true. The choice of which type of loop to choose depends on the problem and on the particular style of the author.

Let's look again at a problem we solved earlier using an iterative instruction that checked the conditional expression before performing the body of the loop. We shall write a solution to the problem using the new iterative instruction. Here is the problem:

> Think of a number between 1 and 100 inclusive. Ask a friend to guess what the number is until she guesses correctly. Tell her when her guess is incorrect.

We must ask for a number at least once, and we may have to ask an indefinite number of times. After each guess we must decide if we need to tell the person that her guess was incorrect. With a loop that has the conditional expression first, the player gets this message automatically as soon as she enters the loop, and the only way to enter the loop is to guess incorrectly. With a loop that evaluates the conditional expression after performing the body of the loop, the player is inside the loop before the algorithm can tell whether or not the guess is correct. Therefore, we must have some way of making a decision within the loop as to whether or not her guess is correct. We will have to put a selection statement within the loop. Here is an algorithm for the problem:

Setup

  I. Label a piece of paper *answer*.

  II. Label a piece of paper *guess*.

Instructions

  I. Write the number you have thought of on the paper labeled *answer*.

  II. Repeat
     A. Ask for a guess.
     B. Erase any number that is on the paper labeled *guess* and write the number that has been guessed on the piece of paper labeled *guess*.
     C. If the number on the paper labeled *guess* is not equal to the number on the paper labeled *answer*,
       then
         1. Say, "That's not the correct answer."
   Until the number on the paper labeled *guess* is equal to the number on the paper labeled *answer*.

  III. Say, "You got the correct answer!"

Exercise 2.8: Compare the algorithm for the last problem with the algorithm given earlier that uses a loop that evaluates the conditional expression before performing the body of the loop. What are the advantages and disadvantages of each algorithm compared to the other? ■

Exercise 2.9: Write two algorithms for the following problem, one for each type of iterative instruction you have seen.

A person is asked for a number between 5 and 25. You would like to make sure that he gives a valid number. Use a loop to check for valid data. Inform the person every time he enters invalid data. ■

Again, as with the selection instruction, the use of *goto's* within an iterative instruction should be avoided. They are unnecessary and confusing.

Definite Iteration

Definite iteration is used when a subset of instructions is to be performed a predefined number of times. That number must be known before the body of the definite iterative construct is undertaken, and it cannot be changed while the instructions within the body of the loop are being followed.

Here is an algorithm for counting the number of times the letter "a" appears in a text that contains 500 letters.

Setup

   I. Write the word *total* on a piece of paper.

   II. Write the words *current character* on a piece of paper.

Instructions

   I. Write down the number 0 on the piece of paper labeled *total*.

   II. Do the following for each of the 500 letters in sequence:
      A. Find the current character in the text and write it on the piece of paper labeled *current character*.

B. If the letter on the piece of paper labeled *current character* is an "a," then

    1. In your head, add 1 to the number on the sheet of paper labeled *total*. Erase the number written on the sheet of paper labeled *total* and write the number you just calculated on the piece of paper labeled *total*.

III. Say the number written on the piece of paper marked *total*.

Since the number of letters in the text is given in the instructions, a definite iterative instruction is used to describe the actions of the algorithm. However, this algorithm is only useful with texts of 500 letters. To make the solution more general, we could add a step to the algorithm that asked for the number of letters in the text before reaching the loop.

The following algorithm is similar to the one above, but it is more general because it can be used to process texts of different sizes.

Setup

I. Label a sheet of paper *how many times*.

II. Label a sheet of paper *total*.

III. Label a sheet of paper *current character*.

Instructions

I. Ask how many characters there are to read.

II. Write the response on the paper labeled *how many times*.

III. Write the number 0 on the paper labeled *total*.

IV. Do the following for each of the letters in the sequence. The number of letters in the sequence is indicated on the paper labeled *how many times*:

    A. Write the current character on the piece of paper labeled *current character*.

    B. If the letter written on the paper labeled *current character* is an "a", then

        1. In your head add 1 to the number on the paper labeled *total*. Erase any number written on the paper labeled *total* and write down the number you just calculated on the paper labeled *total*.

V. Say the number on the paper labeled *total*.

A definite iterative instruction can only be used when the number of times its body is to be performed can be specified before the instruction is reached. That number of times cannot be changed after the instruction is reached.

CHAPTER SUMMARY

This chapter introduced the main features of programming algorithms. They are

- *Memory allocation:* Setting aside specific spaces to store data so that it may be manipulated throughout the algorithm
- *Sequencing:* The order in which the instructions are performed
- *Selection:* The ability to choose which instructions will be executed
- *Iteration:* The ability to repeat a given subset of instructions

Most programming languages support these features. Computer programs will be easier to write if they are based on algorithms designed with these features.

This chapter also introduced *tracing,* which is a special way of performing algorithms to see if and how they work. The chapter also briefly introduced the concept of *debugging,* the process of correcting errors in algorithms by means of tracing.

SUPPLEMENTAL PROBLEMS

1. Identify the inputs, outputs, and constraints in the following problem. Restate the problem and write an algorithm to solve it.

   Given a list of 20 numbers, determine and report if they are in order from smallest to largest.

2. Identify the inputs, outputs, and constraints in the following problem. Restate the problem and write an algorithm to solve it.

   You are given a list of numbers. The list is of unspecified length; however, the end of the list is indicated by -1, which should not be considered part of the list. Determine and report if the numbers are in order from smallest to largest.

3. Identify the inputs, outputs, and constraints in the following problem. Restate the problem and write an algorithm to solve it.

   You are given a list of numbers. The list is of unspecified length; however, the end of the list is indicated by -1, which should not be considered part of the list. The numbers in the list should be either in the form smaller, larger, smaller, larger. . ., or in the form larger, smaller, larger, smaller. Determine and report whether the list fits either of these criteria.

4. Consider the algorithm given below. Can the if-then instructions be replaced by an if-then-else instruction? Why or why not?

Setup

I. Label a piece of paper *correct.*

Instructions

I. Ask for a letter of the alphabet between "a" and "e," inclusive.

II. Write the letter you hear on the paper labeled *correct.*

III. If the value on the paper labeled *correct* is not between "a" and "e," inclusive,
   then
       A. Inform the person that he or she doesn't follow instructions well.

IV. If the value on the paper labeled *correct* is between "a" and "e," inclusive,
   then
       A. Inform the person that he or she has done well.

For problems 5, 6, and 7, determine whether the problem can best be solved by using definite or indefinite iteration. If you determine that indefinite iteration is best, what type of indefinite iteration should be used? Explain your answers.

5. Determine the average of 2000 numbers.

6. A group bank account has the password "riches." You are to write a program that asks a person for the account password. You should give the person three tries at entering the correct password. If the person knows the correct password, the program should give a greeting message. If the person does not guess the password correctly after three tries, a warning message should be given.

7. Determine whether a list of 20 numbers is in order from largest to smallest.

8. Explain, in your own words, when it is appropriate to use each of the three different types of looping instructions.

9. The algorithm below should do the following:

Get two numbers from some person. Determine which of the two numbers is smaller. Put the smaller number on the paper labeled **smallnum,** and the larger number on the paper labeled **largenum.** Write the missing piece of the algorithm that switches the two numbers if they are on the incorrect pieces of paper. Add any pieces of paper that you think are necessary.

Setup

I. Label a piece of paper *smallnum.*

II. Label a piece of paper *largenum.*

Instructions

I. Ask for a number.

II. Write the number on the paper labeled *smallnum.*

III. Ask for another number.

IV. Write the number on the paper labeled *largenum.*

V. If the value on the paper labeled smallnum is greater than the value on the paper labeled *largenum,*
   then

   [fill in this part here]

10. Below is an algorithm that searches a list of names and heights to find the tallest person in the list. Trace the algorithm with the following list. What's your output?

Joe Blow	180
Jane Doe	180
Mighty Mo	180

I. Repeat the following steps until there is only 1 name left on the list:
   A. Place a mark next to the name of the first student on the list.
   B. Repeat the following step for every name on the list from the second through the last inclusive.
      1. Call the name we're doing this step for the *current name.* If the height next to the *current name* is less than the height next to the marked name, then erase the mark and place a mark next to the *current name.*
   C. [After repeating step I.B.1 as specified] Cross off the marked name. (Consider it no longer on the list.)

II. You have one name on the list. That is the name of the tallest student.

11. Change the Tallest Person algorithm as follows: Replace the words **less than** in step I.B.1 with **less than or equal to.** Trace this modified algorithm with the list in problem 10. What's your output?

CHAPTER

3

Recursion is a method for writing algorithms or parts of algorithms. It is a style of writing algorithms in which one instruction invokes the portion of instructions in which it is written. The easiest way to explain recursion is to give an example.

3.1 A RECURSIVE EXAMPLE—FACTORIAL

Let's look at the mathematical function called *factorial,* whose definition is often stated recursively. Here are some examples of the factorial function. (The factorial of a number, *n,* is traditionally written as *n* followed by an exclamation point. So 5 factorial would be written as 5!)

$$5! = 5 \times 4 \times 3 \times 2 \times 1$$
$$9! = 9 \times 8 \times 7 \times 6 \times 5 \times 4 \times 3 \times 2 \times 1$$
$$2! = 2 \times 1$$
$$1! = 1$$

This description of the factorial function works only with numbers greater than 0. A simple nonrecursive definition of *factorial* is that the factorial of a given number is the product of every whole number from that number down to 1.

The factorial of any number except 1 can easily be described in terms of another factorial. For example:

$$5! = 5 \times 4!$$

46

RECURSIVE ALGORITHMS

because 4! equals

$$4 \times 3 \times 2 \times 1.$$

Because of this feature of factorial, we could make a statement such as

$$4! = 4 \times 3! \text{ and } 3! = 3 \times 2! \text{ and } 2! = 2 \times 1! \text{ and } 1! = 1,$$
$$\text{so, } 4! = 4 \times 3 \times 2 \times 1.$$

A recursive definition of the factorial function is written in mathematical notation below:

$$\text{If } n > 1 \text{ then } n! = n \times (n-1)!;$$
$$\text{If } n = 1 \text{ then } n! = 1.$$

The first part of the definition is recursive. It states that if you have some number greater than 1, you must reuse the recursive definition to figure out the factorial of the number. For example, if you wish to find 5!, the definition states that you must multiply 5 times 4!. To get an actual number for the factorial of 5 you must compute the factorial of 4. The definition is reused to determine the value of 4!. Eventually n is no longer greater than 1, and the definition no longer reuses itself.

Let's use the formula written above and see how it works. Let's figure out the value of 4!. If n equals 4, $n-1$ equals 3. Let's fit these numbers into the formula and go on from there. We start with

$$4! = 4 \times 3!.$$

Since we actually want a single number describing 4! we must figure out the value

47

of 3!. We should now use the definition of factorial to figure out 3!. Because n equals 3, $n - 1$ equals 2:

$$3! = 3 \times 2!.$$

To get a single number describing 3! we must figure out the value of 2!. If n is 2, $n - 1$ equals 1:

$$2! = 2 \times 1!.$$

We must use the definition of factorial a last time to find the value of 1!. The definition states that the value of 1! is 1:

$$1! = 1.$$

We have finally reached a step where we no longer have to refer to the definition of factorial. All we need to do is go back and fill in the values we were missing originally. We know that

$$2! = 2 \times 1!.$$

We also now know that

$$1! = 1.$$

From this we can deduce that

$$2! = 2 \times 1,$$

which equals 2. Using this and the fact that

$$3! = 3 \times 2!,$$

we can deduce that

$$3! = 3 \times 2,$$

which equals 6. Using this and the fact that

$$4! = 4 \times 3!,$$

we can deduce that

$$4! = 4 \times 6,$$

which equals 24. We have found the answer.

Notice that we had to reuse the definition of factorial several times to reach a place where we could actually figure out the value of 4!. We could not compute the value of 4! without first computing the value of 3!: Recursive instructions often work this way.

Let's write an algorithm for this recursive definition. We will actually find that part of the algorithm is recursive and part of it is not. To make it clear which part is recursive, we will give those steps a title. In this case, the recursive portion will include its own setup stage. You can think of the recursive portion as a subalgorithm.

Setup

  I. Label a piece of paper *factorial*.

  II. Label a piece of paper *old factorial*.

Instructions

  I. Compute Factorial
    Setup
      A. Label a piece of paper *current number*.

    Instructions
      A. Write the number whose factorial you are trying to calculate on the paper labeled *current number*.
      B. If the number on the paper labeled *current number* is greater than 1, then
          1. Use the subalgorithm Compute Factorial to find the value of (*current number* − 1)! and write that value on the piece of paper labeled *old factorial*.
          2. In your head, calculate the product of the number written on the piece of paper labeled *old factorial* and the number written on the piece of paper labeled *current number*. Erase the number written on the piece of paper labeled *factorial* and put the number you just calculated there.
        else
          1'. Write the number 1 on the paper labeled *factorial*.

  II. Say, "The factorial of."

  III. Say the number written on the paper labeled *current number*.

  IV. Say, "is."

  V. Say the number written on the paper labeled *factorial*.

Let's trace this algorithm with *n* equal to 3.

The first step in the setup stage is to label a piece of paper *factorial*. The second step in the setup stage is to label a piece of paper *old factorial*. We then enter the subalgorithm Compute Factorial. Upon entering Compute Factorial, we set up a piece of paper labeled *current number.*

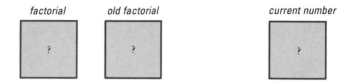

The next instruction, I.A, is to write on *current number* the value of the number whose factorial we are trying to compute. That value is 3:

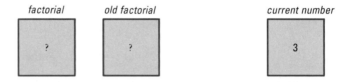

We evaluate the conditional expression in step I.B. The value on *current number* is greater than 1, so we proceed to instruction I.B.1. It directs us to figure out the factorial of 2 and write the value on the piece of paper labeled *old factorial.* We must start the subalgorithm Compute Factorial again.

If we were to list the instructions we have performed at this point, we would have a list that looks like this (note that the starred instructions are in the setup stages):

- *I.   (setup of *factorial*)
- *II.   (setup of *old factorial*)
- I.   (instruction to enter Compute Factorial)
- *I.A (setup of *current number*)
- I.A. (instruction to write value 3 on *current number*)
- I.B. (instruction to evaluate conditional expression *current number* > 1, which is true)
- I.B.1. (instructions to find the value of 2! and write that value on *old factorial*)

We cannot finish set I.B.1 until we have performed the subalgorithm Compute Factorial at least one more time.

Performing the subalgorithm Compute Factorial again, we label a piece of paper *current number,* step I.A in the setup. This is the second piece of paper we have labeled in this way:

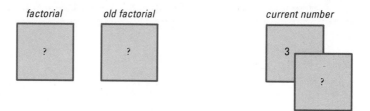

We then write the number whose factorial we are currently trying to compute on *current number* (step I.A in the instructions). In this case, it is 2.

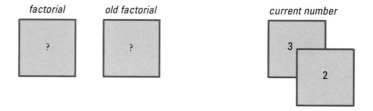

We evaluate the conditional expression in step I.B. Since the number written on the most recent *current number* is greater than 1, we proceed to instruction I.B.i. This step tells us to compute the factorial of *current number* minus 1 and write the value on the piece of paper labeled *old factorial.* We must start the subalgorithm Compute Factorial a third time. Here is a list of the instructions we have followed so far.

- ■ *I. (setup of *factorial*)
- ■ *II. (setup of *old factorial*)
- ■ I. (instruction to enter Compute Factorial)
- ■ *I.A (setup of *current number*)
- ■ I.A (instruction to write value 3 on *current number*)
- ■ I.B (instruction to evaluate conditional expression *current number* > 1, which is true)
- ■ I.B.1 (instruction to find the value of 2! and write that value on *old factorial*)
  - ■ *I.A (setup of second *current number*)
  - ■ I.A (instruction to write value 2 on second *current number*)
  - ■ I.B (instruction to evaluate conditional expression *current number* > 1, which is true)
  - ■ I.B.1 (instruction to find the value of 1! and write that value on *old factorial*)

The last four instructions are necessary so that we can complete the first instruction I.B.

We again begin Compute Factorial. We label a piece of paper *current number*. This is the third piece of paper we have labeled in this way:

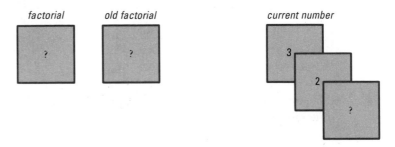

Following instruction I.A, we write the value 1 on the piece of paper labeled *current number*.

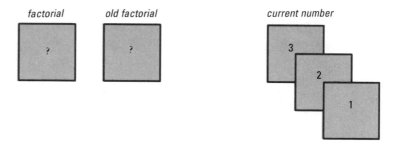

Evaluating the conditional expression in instruction I.B, we see that the number written on the piece of paper labeled *current number* is now no longer greater than 1. We now perform step I.B.1' of the algorithm. We write the value 1 on the piece of paper labeled *factorial.*

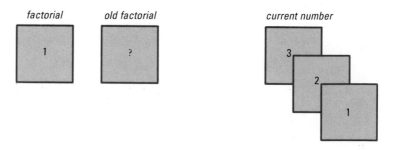

This finishes one complete run through Compute Factorial, the run that began most recently. Since it is over, we can discard the most recent *current number:*

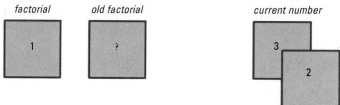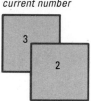

In addition to the instructions in the preceding list, we have now traced the following instructions:

- *I.A (setup of third *current number*)
- I.A (instruction to write value 1 on third *current number*)
- I.B (instruction to evaluate conditional expression *current number* > 1, which is false)
- I.B.1′ (instruction to write the value 1 on *factorial*)

Having completed the last 4 steps, we may finish the second I.B.1 instruction. We have computed 1! as being 1, and we erase any previous values written on *old factorial* and put the new value there.

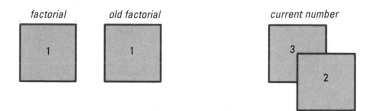

We can now perform instruction I.B.2. It says to find the product of *current number* and *old factorial,* which is the product of 2 × 1. We write that value on *factorial,* erasing any old values we find there:

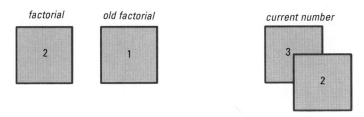

The instructions we have performed so far are listed:

- *I.   (setup of *factorial*)
- *II. (setup of *old factorial*)
- I.   (instruction to enter Compute Factorial)
- *I.A (setup of *current number*)
- I.A   (instruction to write value 3 on *current number*)
- I.B   (instruction to evaluate conditional expression *current number* > 1, which is true)
- I.B.1 (instruction to find the value of 2! and write that value on *old factorial*)
  - *I.A   (setup of second *current number*)
  - I.A   (instruction to write value 2 on second *current number*)
  - I.B   (instruction to evaluate conditional expression *current number* > 1, which is true)
  - I.B.1 (instructions to find the value of 1! and write that value on *old factorial*)
    (Instructions to compute 1!)
  - I.B.2 (instruction to find the product of 2 × 1 and write that value on *factorial*)

Having finished another performance of the Compute Factorial subalgorithm, we may throw away the most recent *current number.* We now need only finish the original performance of Compute Factorial. We finish the original step I.B.1 by writing the value of 2! on *old factorial.*

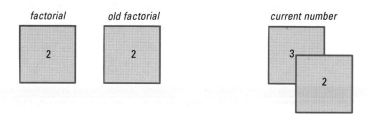

We can then discard the second piece of paper labeled *current number.*

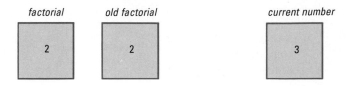

We then go on to do the last step in the subalgorithm, I.B.2. We find the product of *current number* and *old factorial* and write that value on *factorial:*

factorial 6   old factorial 2   current number 3

We have now finished performing the subalgorithm Compute Factorial. We have done the following steps:

- *I.   (setup of *factorial*)
- *II.   (setup of *old factorial*)
- I.   (instruction to enter Compute Factorial)
- *I.A   (setup of *current number*)
- I.A   (instruction to write value 3 on *current number*)
- I.B   (instruction to evaluate conditional expression *current number* > 1, which is true)
- I.B.1   (instruction to find the value of 2! and write that value on *old factorial*)
    - *I.A   (setup of second *current number*)
    - I.A   (instruction to write value 2 on second *current number*)
    - I.B   (instruction to evaluate conditional expression *current number* > 1, which is true)
    - I.B.1   (instruction to find the value of 1! and write that value on *old factorial*)
        - *I.A   (setup of third *current number*)
        - I.A   (instruction to write value 1 on third *current number*)
        - I.B   (instruction to evaluate conditional expression *current number* > 1, which is false)
        - I.B.1′   (instruction to write the value 1 on *factorial*)
    - I.B.2   (find the product of 2 × 1 and write that value on *factorial*)
- I.B.2 (instruction to find the product of 3 × 2 and write that value on *factorial*)

We can now complete the trace of the algorithm by performing steps II, III, IV, and V, saying, "The factorial of 3 is 6."

Exercise   3.1: Following the format given above, trace the instructions to compute the factorial of 4. Show the pieces of paper at each step and the instructions you perform. ∎

There are several important points to remember:

1. Every recursive algorithm must have a stopping point. As long as the person following the instructions gives a legitimate number (1 or greater), the recursion will stop when we try to compute the value of 1!. There must be something in every recursive set of instructions that will stop the instructions from referring to themselves forever. Any set of recursive instructions that does not have a stopping condition violates the definition of *algorithm*.

2. The first instruction that causes the recursion to happen is not completed until the recursive portion of the algorithm that it references is complete. This point is also true of any subsequent instructions that use recursion.

3. Recursion is implemented within the instructions by having an instruction reference a portion of the algorithm that includes that instruction.

Notice that we could have the factorial of every number up to the given number as output. Consider the following algorithm:

Setup

I. Label a piece of paper *factorial.*

II. Label a piece of paper *old factorial.*

Instructions

I. Compute Factorial
   Setup
   A. Label a piece of paper *current number.*
   Instructions
   A. Write the number whose factorial you are trying to calculate on the paper labeled *current number.*
   B. If the number on the paper labeled *current number* is greater than 1, then
      1. Use the subalgorithm Compute Factorial to find the value of (*current number* - 1)! and write that value on the piece of paper labeled *old factorial.*
      2. In your head, calculate the product of the number written on the piece of paper labeled *old factorial* and the number written on the piece of paper labeled *current number.* Erase the number written on the piece of paper labeled *factorial* and put the number you just calculated there.
      3. Say, "The value of."
      4. Say the value on *current number.*
      5. Say, "factorial is."
      6. Say the value on *factorial.*

else
    1'. Write the number 1 on the paper labeled *factorial.*
    2'. Say, "The value of."
    3'. Say the value on *current number.*
    4'. Say, "factorial is."
    5'. Say the value on *factorial.*

The additional instructions 3, 4, 5, and 6 are performed every time the factorial of some number greater than 1 is computed. The additional instructions 2', 3', 4', 5' are performed when the factorial of 1 is computed. Instructions II, III, IV, and V of the original algorithm were removed because their task is performed by the new instructions.

Exercise 3.2: Trace the above algorithm for the factorial of 3. ∎

3.2 How to Write Recursive Algorithms

Note that all recursive sets of instructions can be written nonrecursively, and most nonrecursive sets of instructions can be written recursively. Some problems are better suited to recursive solutions than others.

    Once you recognize that a problem might have a recursive solution, you need to identify the following things in order to write the algorithm:

1. When you want the recursive step to happen. In the case of the factorial algorithm, it was when the **current number** was greater than 1.
2. What you want to be different when the recursive portion of the algorithm is performed again. In the case of the factorial algorithm, **current number** was always 1 less than it had been in the previous reference to the recursive portion of the algorithm.

3.3 Another Recursive Example

Here is another problem that can be solved using recursion:

    You are given a list of 100 names. Find at which position the name "Benjamin Franklin" occurs, or report if the name does not occur at all.

The input to this problem consists of a list of 100 names and the name we are searching for, "Benjamin Franklin." The output is the position of the found name or the fact that it was not found at all. Below we have identified the two things needed to write a recursive solution to the problem:

1. The recursive step should happen when the end of the list has not been reached and the name "Benjamin Franklin" has not been found.

2. To make the recursive step different, the position of the name we are looking at on the list will be 1 more than it was previously.

One other point is important in this algorithm; we don't want to have an instruction to give directions for looking beyond the end of list. Here is a recursive algorithm to solve the problem:

FIND NAME

Setup

  I. Write the words *current place* on a piece of paper.

Instructions

  I. Write the number 1 on the paper labeled *current place*.

  II. Find Place
    A. If the name at *current place* in the list is not equal to "Benjamin Franklin,"
       then
          1. If the value written on *current place* is less than 100,
            then
               a. Add 1 to the value you currently find on the paper labeled *current place*. Erase the value on the paper labeled *current place* and write down the value you just computed.
               b. Do the subset of instructions Find Place again using the new value of *current place*.
           else
               c. Say, "Sorry, the name "Benjamin Franklin" is not on the list."
       else
         1'. Say, "The place where "Benjamin Franklin" is found is position," say the value on *current place*.

Figure 3.1 shows a trace of the algorithm with the following as the first five names on the list:

1. George Mann
2. Ryan Bechler
3. Benjamin Franklin
4. Betty Li Santi
5. Molly Tharp
   :
   :

Note that it is not necessary to set up a new piece of paper labeled *current position* each time the recursive portion of the instructions is performed because we do not need to remember previous positions.

Figure 3.1 **Trace of the algorithm to find a name in a list**

Step	Conditional expression	Memory	Output
1. Setup—I		*current place*	
2. Inst.—I		1	
3. Inst.—II		1	
4. Inst.—II.A	T	1	
5. Inst.—II.A.1	T	1	
6. Inst.—II.A.1.a		2	
7. Inst.—II.A.1.b. (recursive call)		2	
1′. Inst.—II		2	
2′. Inst.—II.A	T	2	
3′. Inst.—II.A.1		2	
4′. Inst.—II.A.1.a		3	
5′. Inst.—II.A.1.b (recursive call)		3	
1″. Inst.—II		3	
2″. Inst.—II.A	F	3	
3″. Inst.—II.A.1′		3	The place where *Benjamin Franklin* is found is position 3.

CHAPTER SUMMARY

This chapter introduced recursion, a style of writing algorithms in which one of the instructions invokes the entire set of instructions. Most programming languages support recursion.

SUPPLEMENTAL PROBLEMS

1. Identify the inputs, outputs, and constraints in the following problem. Restate the problem and write a recursive algorithm to solve it.

   You are given a list of numbers. The list is of unspecified length; however, the end of the list is indicated by -1, which should not be considered part of the list. Determine and report if the numbers are in order from smallest to largest.

2. Identify the inputs, outputs, and constraints in the following problem. Restate the problem and write a recursive algorithm to solve it.

   You are given a list of numbers. The list is of unspecified length, however, the end of the list is indicated by -1, which should not be considered part of the list. The numbers in the list should either be in the form smaller, larger, smaller, larger. . . or in the form larger, smaller, larger, smaller. Determine and report whether the list fits the criteria.

3. You have the following problem statement:

   You are given a list of five names. Find at which position the name "Linda Acosta" occurs and report it, or report if the name does not occur at all.
   A) Write a recursive algorithm to solve this problem.
   B) Trace the algorithm you just wrote with the following list of names: (1) Sue Smythe, (2) Susy Boyet, (3) Carmen Miranda, (4) Fred Zlotnick, (5) Betsy Ross.

4. Write a recursive algorithm to read in a list of names until an asterisk is reached, and then print them out backwards.

5. Write a recursive algorithm to sum the numbers from 1 to 100.

6. Someone wants to know how many three-digit numbers they can create from the three digits 1, 2, and 3 (for example, 111, 112, 113, 211. . .). Write a recursive algorithm to display all possible combinations.

7. Write a recursive algorithm to determine the number of combinations that can be made from any three different symbols.

8. (This problem is for mathematically minded students.) A *function* is a rule that for any input value gives a unique output value. Functions can be defined recursively. Here is one such definition: For any positive whole number n, let $f(n)$ be the number defined by the recursive rule:

$$f(n) = \begin{cases} 1 & \text{if } n = 1 \\ f(n - 1) + 2n - 1 & \text{if } n > 1 \end{cases}$$

a. Write a recursive algorithm to compute $f(n)$.

b. Use your algorithm to compute $f(1)$, $f(2)$, $f(3)$, $f(4)$, $f(5)$, and $f(6)$. Try to guess $f(1000)$ based on the pattern you see.

c. (For students who know the technique of proof by induction.) Prove that $f(n) = n^2$.

9. Some terms are naturally defined in a recursive way. For example, an ancestor is either your mother, your father, or one of their ancestors. Suppose you arrange all your known ancestors into a family tree:

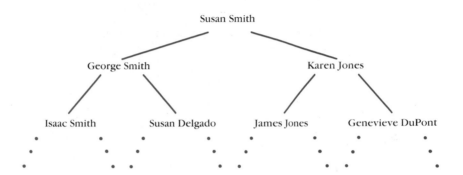

This tree may go back a different number of generations on each branch. Write a recursive algorithm that takes such a tree and produces a list—in any order—of the names in the tree.

C H A P T E R

4

Most problems that you will deal with using computers will have large and complex solutions. Once you have identified the inputs, constraints, and outputs of a problem, the next step before attempting to write the algorithm is to break the problem down into manageable subproblems. For each subproblem, you must then create a subalgorithm or procedure based on data manipulation, sequencing, selection, iteration, and recursion. That subalgorithm constitutes a solution to the subproblem. Before proceeding to the next subproblem, you should test that solution for correctness, convincing yourself that it will work in every possible instance. If you find that it does not work in a particular instance, you should pinpoint the errors in your solution and identify which instructions are causing the trouble. This is an extremely important step in problem solving. After you have corrected the faulty instructions, you should test your solution for correctness.

4.1 SUBPROBLEMS

A subproblem has its own logical inputs and outputs and its own beginning and end. For example, in doing laundry you generally sort the laundry first. This is a distinct step in itself, but a step that is important in doing laundry.

We often go through this process of breaking a common problem down into subproblems without really thinking about it. Think of how you go about giving people directions to where you live. If they are coming from a distant point, you try to direct them onto a major highway heading in the right direction. That is the first subproblem. Next you direct them to a major roadway in the vicinity of your house. Finally, you tell them what streets to take and what turns to make to arrive at your doorstep. You break the initial problem down into manageable subproblems.

There are three main ways of identifying subproblems within a problem.

DESIGNING THE ALGORITHM

1. Look at how data is manipulated in the problem. If you think of clothes as data, sorting laundry is one action you perform on that data. Washing is another. Drying is a third.

2. Write out clearly what you expect the final output of the problem to be. For example, in writing a paper, it is often useful to create an outline of everything you wish to write in order to organize your paper into manageable pieces and to identify your final goals for it.

3. Attempt to come up with a general solution to the problem and test it. Identify when in the general solution you have reached a subgoal or something you consider to be necessary for reaching the final solution. These points will tend to indicate the end of a subproblem. The problem of directing someone to your house is a good example of identifying subgoals.

There are two common ways of representing the decomposition of a problem. The first is a tree structure, as shown in Figure 4.1.

Figure 4.1   Tree structure

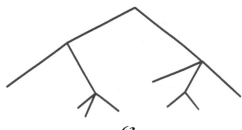

For example, a tree structure showing the decomposition of how to do laundry might look like the diagram in Figure 4.2. The second representation for the decomposition of a problem is an outline such as the one shown in Figure 4.3. We could outline the steps for doing laundry as shown in Figure 4.4.

Figure 4.2   **Tree structure for doing laundry**

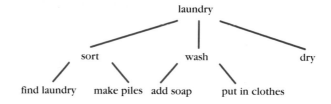

Figure 4.3   **Outline**

TITLE

I.
    A.
    B.
        1.
        2.
            i.
            ii.
            iii.
        3.
II.
    A.
        1.

Figure 4.4   **Outline for doing laundry**

LAUNDRY

I. Sort
   A. Find laundry
   B. Make piles

II. Wash
   A. Add soap
   B. Put in clothes

III. Dry

We will develop a solution for a problem using this new technique. Here is the problem:

A robot is inside a rectangular room of unspecified size. The room has a single door large enough for the robot to pass through. The robot is directly facing one of the walls. The robot can perform the following operations if instructed to do so:

- It can go forward one step.
- It can make a quarter turn to the left.
- It can make a quarter turn to the right.
- It can turn itself off.

The robot also has sensors that are constantly reporting to the operator

- If there is a wall immediately ahead of it
- If there is a wall immediately to its left
- If there is a wall immediately to its right
- If it is outside the room

You must give instructions for an operator of the robot. The operator must have explicit instructions on how to get the robot out of the room and have it turn off immediately by using only the operations and sensor readings given above. The instructions must work regardless of the robot's initial position in the room and regardless of the size of the room.

The input to this problem consists of a robot positioned in a room and the sensor readings of the robot. The output consists of the robot outside the room and turned off. The constraints of this problem are (1) that the robot must turn off immediately after it has left the room, (2) that the robot can only understand simple robot commands, and (3) that we must clearly tell the operator what commands to give the robot.

The room's layout and the robot's position in the room represent the data in this problem. Manipulating the data means moving the robot. Figure 4.5 shows possible ways of manipulating the data. The first solution seems like the easiest and most efficient. We can use it to formulate a general solution that can be broken into subproblems. Here is the general solution:

Given a robot somewhere in a room, direct the robot to a wall. Once the robot reaches a wall, it should be directed to go around the room until it reaches a door. Once it reaches a door, it should be directed to exit and then turn off.

We should test this solution for reasonableness. Figure 4.6 shows different scenarios in which the robot might be found. Notice that the general solution doesn't seem to work when the robot is already facing the door. We must change the general solution to accommodate this possibility:

> Given a robot somewhere in a room, direct the robot to a wall. If the robot should exit before reaching a wall, it should be immediately directed to turn off. Otherwise, once it reaches a wall, it should be directed to go around the room until it reaches a door. Once it reaches a door, it should be directed to exit and then turn off.

This general solution can be broken down into clear subproblems that we can solve. Figure 4.7 shows the current subproblems in outline form. The general solution itself begins to describe the subalgorithms that will solve these subproblems.

Figure 4.5   Manipulating position of robot in room

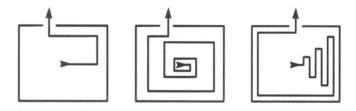

Figure 4.6   Test of general solution for robot problem

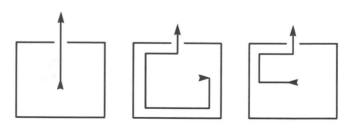

Figure 4.8 shows the general solution decomposed into subalgorithms. Notice that subalgorithm II or subalgorithm III may cause the robot to turn off. It is redundant to have this command twice in the algorithm because it is always the last step the robot performs. If we take it out of subproblem II, we can eliminate subproblem II entirely. Our new subproblems are given in Figure 4.9.

Figure 4.7   Subproblems in robot problem

    I. Direct the robot to a wall or out the door.

    II. What to do if the robot goes out of the room.

    III. What to do if the robot gets to the wall.

Figure 4.8   Robot subalgorithms

    I. Direct the robot to a wall.

    II. If the robot should exit before reaching a wall, it should immediately be directed to turn off.

    III. Otherwise, the robot should be directed to
       A. Go around the room until it reaches a door.
       B. Exit.
       C. Turn off.

Figure 4.9   Revised robot subalgorithms

    I. Direct the robot to a wall.

    II. If the robot doesn't exit before reaching a wall, it should be directed to
       A. Go around the room until it finds a door.
       B. Exit.

    III. Direct the robot to turn off.

Having broken down the problem this far, we can now begin to refine it in terms of robot instructions and the instructions that were introduced in Chapter 2. This process is called *stepwise refinement*. It is a common way of solving complex problems. Some of the resulting subalgorithms may themselves be too complex and need to be refined into further subalgorithms.

The first subproblem is to give instructions that will move the robot to the wall. Remember that if the robot's initial position is facing the door, these instructions will move the robot out of the room. Since we don't know the initial position of the robot in the room, we will need to use an indefinite iterative instruction. It will allow us to give instructions to the operator to direct the robot forward as many steps as are necessary to reach the wall or leave the room. The iterative instruction will contain an instruction directing the robot to take a step forward.

Recall that we have a choice between an iterative instruction that checks a conditional expression before entering the body of the loop and an instruction that checks a conditional expression after performing the body of the loop. Since the robot may already be at the wall, we should use an instruction that checks a conditional expression before entering the body of the loop. (We don't want the robot to try to step through the wall!) Since we are using a loop that checks a conditional expression first, the conditional expression for this loop will be **robot does not sense a wall in front and robot does not sense that it is out of the room**. Subalgorithm I has been refined as shown in Figure 4.10.

The first subalgorithm is refined enough to fit our solution criteria. We should now trace it in various situations and debug it if necessary. Figure 4.11 shows the situations we will use to trace this portion of the algorithm. Note that we need not trace the robot in every possible situation (that would be impossible since there is no limitation on the size of the room). We have chosen situations that are representative of all the situations in which the robot can be placed.

Figure 4.10   **First subalgorithm in robot problem**

I. While the robot has not sensed a wall in front of it and it is not out of the room,
   A. Direct the robot to take a step forward.

Figure 4.11   **Possible robot scenarios. Note: ○ = possible positions for robot in room, ∧ = robot facing direction of arrow.**

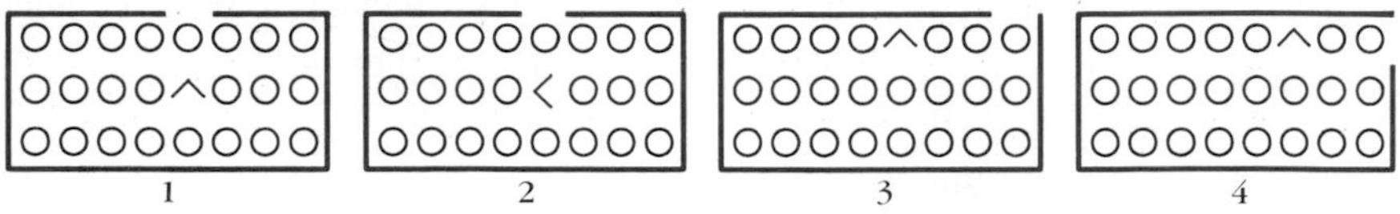

If the subalgorithm works correctly, it should take the robot either out the door or to a wall. A trace with scenario 1 of Figure 4.11 is given in Figure 4.12. The position of the robot in the room will be the data for the trace. The robot was successfully directed out of the room, so the subalgorithm works with scenario 1.

Exercise 4.1: Trace part I of the robot algorithm with scenarios 2 and 3. ■

Exercise 4.2: Having traced part I of the robot algorithm using scenario 3, it is unnecessary to trace it using scenario 4. Why? ■

Figure 4.12 **Trace of first subalgorithm with scenario 1**

Instructions	Conditional expressions	Memory
I.	T	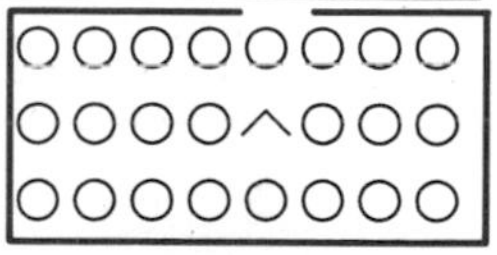
I.A		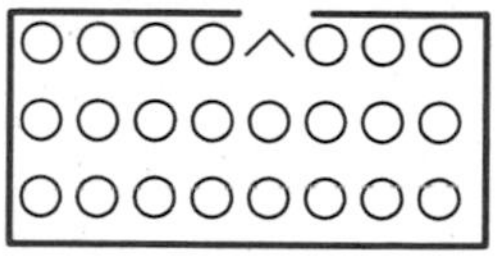
I.	T	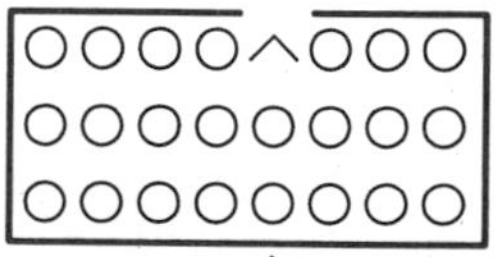
I.A		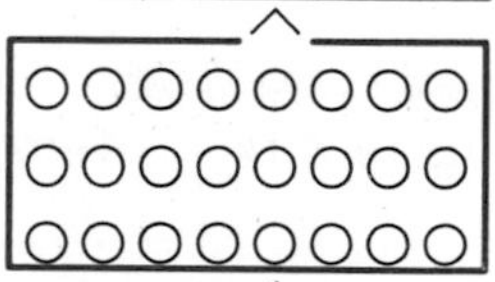
I.	F	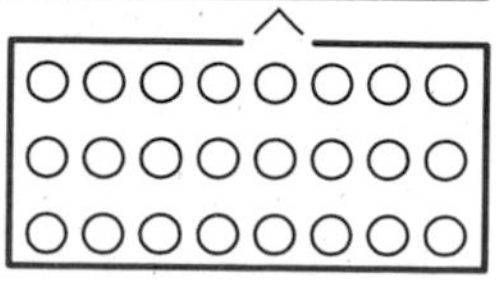

We now return to the refinement of our algorithm. The second subproblem depends on the possible outcomes of the first subproblem, which will leave the robot either sensing a wall in front of it or sensing that it is out of the room. The current subalgorithm checks to see if the robot has not exited. This would be equivalent to the conditional expression **not out of the room**. A specific subset of instructions will be performed if this is true; therefore, we need to use a single-option selection instruction. The actions within the selection instruction are those stated in the outline. The present state of the subalgorithm is given in Figure 4.13.

We will now refine steps A and B. We start with step A. To begin the robot on its journey around the room, we must make a tactical decision: The robot cannot perform the action of going around the room until it is directed to turn left or right. If it turns right, the wall will be to its left. If it turns left, the wall will be to its right. Many decisions that follow will depend on this choice. We choose to have the robot turn right. Because of this choice, the robot will have the wall on its left once it has turned right. Subalgorithm II with this refinement is given in Figure 4.14.

Since we don't know how far the robot will have to go to find the door, we need to use an indefinite iterative instruction. The conditional expression will check whether the robot has reached the door. How can we check for this possiblity with the robot sensors? Since the robot will have the wall to its left, the door will also be on its left. We have no way of directly checking for "there is a door on the left," but we can think of a door as the absence of a wall.

We must choose between the two types of iterative instructions. The input to this subproblem answers the question: Since the robot has a wall to its left at this point, some action must take place before there can be a door on the robot's left.

Figure 4.13   **First refinement of second subproblem**

II. If the robot does not sense that it is out of the room,
   then
         A. Direct the robot to go around the room until it reaches a door.
         B. Direct the robot to exit.

Figure 4.14   **Further refinement of subalgorithm II**

II. If the robot does not sense that it is out of the room,
   then
         A. Direct the robot to turn right.
         B. Direct the robot to go around the room until it finds a door.
         C. Direct the robot to exit.

An iterative instruction that checks the conditional expression after entering the loop is appropriate. Figure 4.15 shows the current state of subalgorithm II.B.

How do we get the robot to go around the room? We might direct it to take a step forward. But what if it reaches a corner? Or what if it starts at a corner? Consider the situation in Figure 4.16. We should check the condition that there is a wall directly in front of the robot before we instruct it to take a step forward. If there is a wall in front of the robot, we should instruct it to turn right and go along the next wall; otherwise, it should just take a step forward. We need some type of selection instruction. If we phrase it in this way, the multioption selection structure shown in Figure 4.17 is what we need.

Notice that within each option of the selection instruction we are directing the robot to take a step forward. This instruction occurs as the last step in both the **then** and the **else** clause. Consequently, we can remove the instruction from both

Figure 4.15   Current refinement of subalgorithm II.B

> B. Repeat
>
>> [do something to go around room]
>
>> until the robot does not sense a wall to its left.

Figure 4.16   Possible situation with robot at corner

Figure 4.17   Directing the robot around the room

> 1. If the robot senses a wall in front,
>   then
>   i. Direct the robot to turn right.
>   ii. Direct the robot to step forward.
>   else
>   i′. Direct the robot to step forward.

clauses and position it following the selection statement. This eliminates the need for the **else** clause. The resulting structure is given in Figure 4.18.

Notice that we could remove **Direct the robot to step forward** from both clauses in the selection instruction only because doing so did not affect the outcome of the algorithm. This is not always the case, so be careful in removing what seem like redundant instructions from multioption selection statements.

We have now completely refined subalgorithm II.B. Figure 4.19 gives the completed version of the subalgorithm. Since this is a fairly complex subalgorithm, we should test it to see whether it works. We will trace it with the scenarios we used to test subalgorithm I. When subalgorithm II.B has been completed, we expect the robot to have a door on its left. Note that we have omitted tracing the algorithm with scenario 1, because step II.B will not be performed for that scenario.

Exercise 4.3: Why won't the robot perform instruction II.B for scenario 1? ■

A trace of subalgorithm II.B with situation 2 is given in Figure 4.20. The trace is successful because the robot has the door on its left.

Figure 4.18   Directing the robot around the room

1. If the robot senses a wall in front,
    then
        i. Direct the robot to turn right.
2. Direct the robot to step forward.

Figure 4.19   Completed subalgorithm II.B

B. Repeat
    1. If the robot senses a wall in front,
        then
            i. Direct the robot to turn right.
    2. Direct the robot to step forward
    until the robot does not sense a wall on the left.

Figure 4.20   **Trace of subalgorithm II.B with scenario 2**

Instructions	Conditional expressions	Memory
II.B.1	F	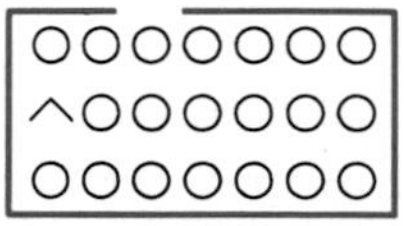
II.B.2.		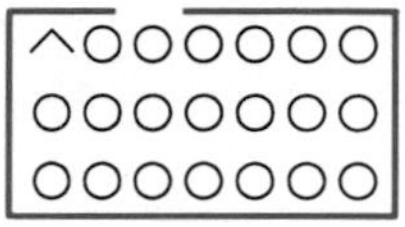
II.B	F	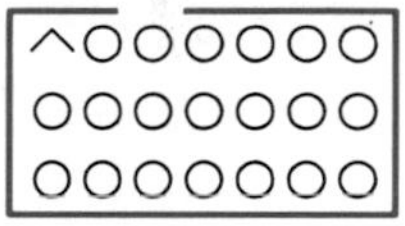
II.B.1	T	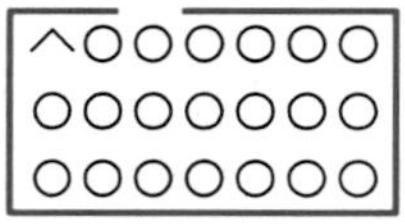
II.B.1.i		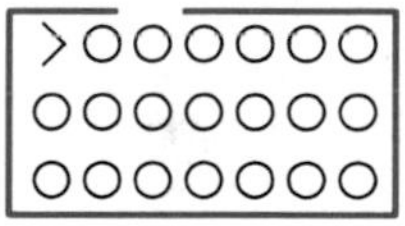
II.B.2		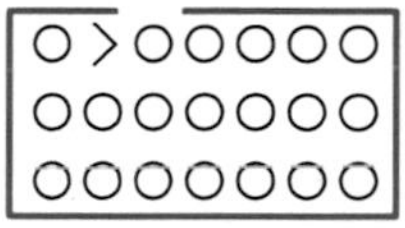
II.B	F	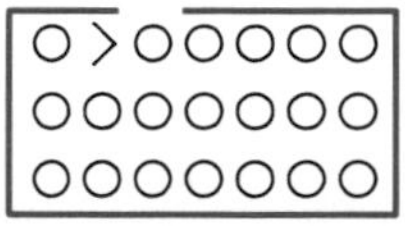
II.B.1	F	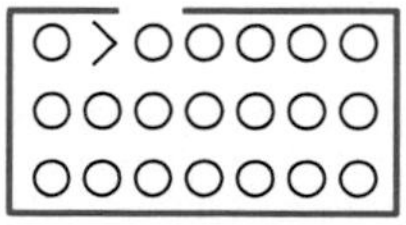
II.B.2		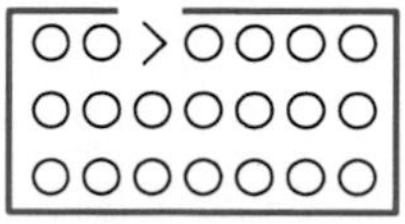
II.B	T	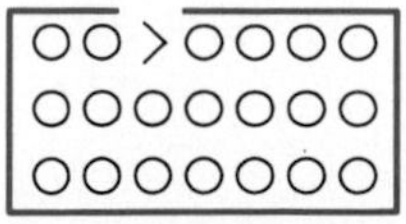

Figure 4.21   Trace of subalgorithm II.B with scenario 4

Instructions	Conditional expressions	Memory
II.B.1	F	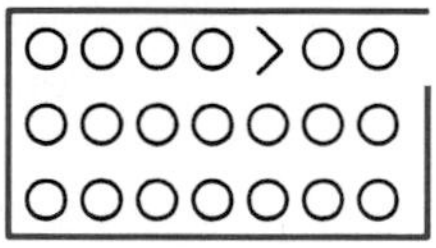 OOOO > OO OOOOOOO OOOOOOO
II.B.2		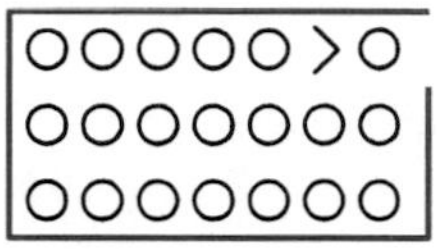 OOOOO > O OOOOOOO OOOOOOO
II.B	F	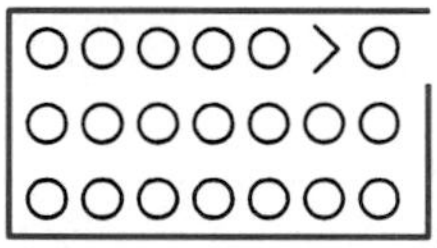 OOOOO > O OOOOOOO OOOOOOO
II.B.1	F	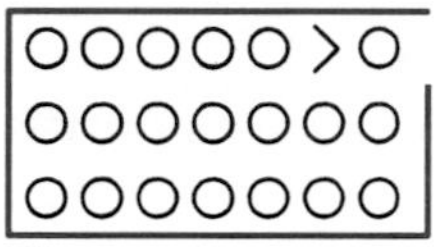 OOOOO > O OOOOOOO OOOOOOO
II.B.2		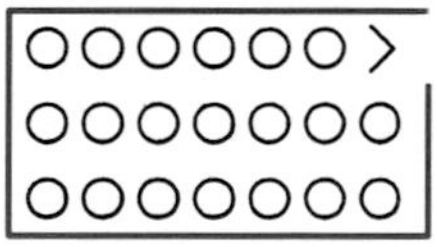 OOOOOO > OOOOOOO OOOOOOO
II.B	F	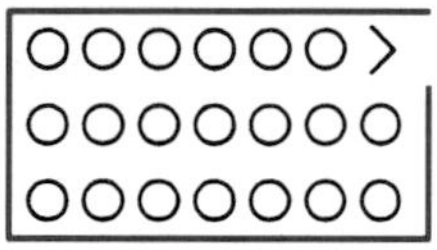 OOOOOO > OOOOOOO OOOOOOO
II.B.1	F	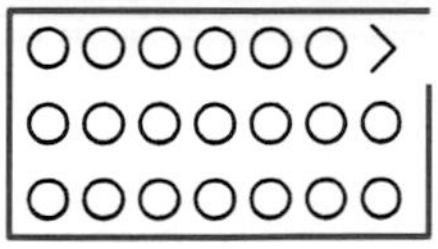 OOOOOO > OOOOOOO OOOOOOO
II.B.2 (At this point the robot leaves the room.)		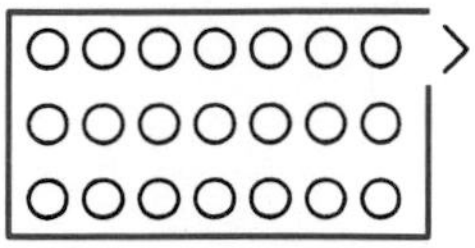 OOOOOOO > OOOOOOO OOOOOOO
II.B	T	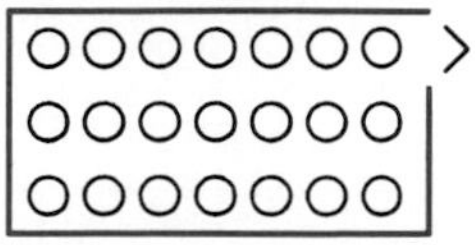 OOOOOOO > OOOOOOO OOOOOOO

Exercise 4.4: Trace subalgorithm II.B using scenario 3. ■

Figure 4.21 shows the final trace with scenario 4. The robot does not end up exactly as we predicted in the last trace. Remember that step II.C of the algorithm will direct the robot to exit, but in this case the robot has already exited. We must either fix this subalgorithm, or take its new possible output into account when we refine step II.C. We have chosen the latter course.

In order to have the robot exit the room only if it is not already out of the room, we need a simple selection structure, as shown in Figure 4.22. After performing step II.C, the robot is out of the room and is now ready to be turned off in step III. Notice that by checking each step as we went along, we avoided having errors embedded in the completed algorithm.

Part III of the original decomposition of the problem describes the final instruction of the algorithm. Whether the robot exited from the room as a result of step I or as a result of step II, it can now be directed to turn off. Figure 4.23 shows the complete algorithm.

Figure 4.22   Refinement of step II.C

C. If the robot does not sense that it is out of the room,
   then
      1. Direct the robot to turn left.
      2. Direct the robot to take a step forward.

Figure 4.23   Completed robot algorithm

I. While the robot has not sensed a wall in front of it and it is not out of the room,
   A. Direct the robot to take a step forward.

II. If the robot does not sense that it is out of the room,
   then
      A. Direct the robot to turn right.
      B. Repeat
         1. If the robot senses a wall in front,
            then
               i. Direct the robot to turn right.
         2. Direct the robot to step forward.
         until the robot does not sense a wall to its left.
      C. If the robot does not sense that it is out of the room,
         then
            1. Direct the robot to turn left.
            2. Direct the robot to step forward.

III. Direct the robot to turn off.

4.2 COMPLEX CONDITIONAL EXPRESSIONS

In writing a conditional expression for the robot algorithm, we used the words *and* and *not*. The word *and* allows us to combine two conditional expressions to evaluate to *true* or *false*. The word *not* changes the value of a conditional expression to its opposite (*true* to *false*, and *false* to *true*). These words, along with the word *or,* are called *boolean operators* in logic. They are a way of making conditional expressions more versatile. They have vague meanings in everyday English, but in computer science they have very specific meanings. When you use them to form a complex conditional expression you must observe their specific meanings. Each boolean operator is listed below, along with a description of how it may be used and the possible results of using it.

- *and* combines two conditional expressions. If both expressions are true, the complex conditional expression formed by using *and* evaluates to true. If either or both of the expressions are false, then the complex conditional expression formed by using *and* evaluates to false.

- *or* combines two conditional expressions. At least one, but possibly both of the conditional expressions must be true for the complex conditional expression formed with the *or* to be true. If both the conditional expressions are false, then the complex conditional expression formed with the *or* evaluates to false.

- *not* takes a single conditional expression. If the conditional expression is true, the complex conditional expression formed with the *not* is false. If the conditional expression is false, the complex conditional expression formed with the *not* is true.

Figure 4.24 gives a list of the basic compound conditional expressions.

Figure 4.24   **Truth tables**

Possible values		and	or	Possible value	not
T	T	T	T	T	F
T	F	F	T	F	T
F	T	F	T		
F	F	F	F		

Here are some examples of how boolean operators are used in conditional expressions. Assume that the following statements are true:

- John likes flowers.
- Mary likes trucks.
- June likes books.
- Fred likes the library.

Assume that the following statements are false:

- Joe likes cars.
- Susy likes lima beans.
- Harry likes ice cream.

Here is how the boolean operators work:

"Mary likes trucks *or* Susy likes lima beans" is *true* because one of the expressions surrounding the *or* is true—"Mary likes trucks."

"Joe likes cars *and* Susy likes lima beans" is *false* because both expressions surrounding the *and* are false.

"*not* Fred likes the library" is *false* because Fred does like the library.

"Susy likes lima beans *or* Harry likes ice cream" is *false* because neither statement is true.

"*not* Joe likes cars" is *true* because "Joe likes cars" is false.

"June likes books *and* John likes flowers" is *true* because both statements are true.

Although these statements are useful ways of grouping conditional expressions together, they are limited in that *and* and *or* combine only two conditional expressions, and *not* works with only one. For example, how can we check to see if it is true that

"John likes flowers *and* Mary likes trucks, *or* Joe likes cars"?

By building up a single conditional expression out of many conditional expressions using the boolean operators, we can expand the groupings. In the situation above for example, the *and* can be evaluated first to give us a *true* value (both conditional expressions surrounding the *and* are true). Then the *or* can be evaluated to give us a *true* value. (On the left side of the *or* we have a true value from the evaluation of the *and*. On the right side, we have the value false). Or the *or* can be evaluated first to give a *true* value (the expressions surrounding the *or* are true and false, therefore the complex expression is true). Then the expression formed with the *and* can be evaluated to give us a *true* value (both expressions surrounding the *and* are true).

But consider the following complex conditional expression:

"Joe likes cars *and* June likes books *or* John likes flowers."

Is this a true or a false statement? It depends, in this case, on whether we evaluate the *and* first or the *or* first. If we evaluate the *or* first, the entire conditional expression evaluates to *false*. If we evaluate the *and* first, the entire conditional expression evaluates to *true*. We can get around that problem by establishing an order of precedence—that is, by deciding beforehand that we will always evaluate certain operators before others. For example, we could say that whenever boolean operators are mixed in a compound conditional expression, *not* is always evaluated first, then *or*, then *and*. With this order of precedence, the above expression would then evaluate to *false*. (*True* or *true* is *true; false* and *true* is *false*.) Or we could say that we will evaluate the operators starting from the left and going to the right. With that order of precedence, the above expression would evaluate to true. (*False* and *true* is *false; false* or *true* is *true*.)

Exercise   4.4: Look back at the simple true and false statements given above to form conditional expressions. Assume that *not* is evaluated first, followed by *or*, followed by *and*. Evaluate the following expressions:

"Joe likes cars *or* John likes flowers *and* June likes books *or* Harry likes ice cream."

"Susy likes lima beans *and not* Joe likes cars *or* Fred likes the library."   ■

This is a difficult system to use, however, because it requires that we always refer to an order of precedence when we are building a complex conditional statement. In English, we use commas and extra words like *either* to indicate the order of precedence. For example, we could restate the first sentence above as follows:

"Joe likes cars, and either June likes books or John likes flowers."

In programming, we usually put parentheses around an expression when we want to indicate that it is to be evaluated first. For example:

"Joe likes cars *and* (June likes books *or* John likes flowers)."

The parentheses make it clear that the *or* is to be evaluated first, then the *and*.

This is a useful system to use when writing algorithms because we often form very complex conditional expressions.

4.3 GENERAL SOLUTIONS

When we solved the robot problem, we ended up with a general solution. We might have worked out a set of specific solutions for every situation the robot might have encountered, but that approach is time-consuming and often impossible. In how many different situations might the robot have found itself? The answer is an infinite number. A general solution is much more useful than any set of specific solutions.

Ours is not the only general solution to the robot problem, however. We chose one particular solution simply to show how an algorithm is developed. There are other possible solutions as there would be for any problem. The following section deals with general problem solving techniques to help you develop your own algorithms.

4.4 PROBLEM SOLVING

In solving the robot problem, we gave a general solution, which we broke into subproblems. We then refined the subproblems until we arrived at what we hoped was a correct solution. But you may be asking, "How did you arrive at the general solution in the first place?" or "How did you know where to decompose the problem into subproblems?" These questions cannot be answered in a straightforward way, because problem solving is a creative process that requires imagination and a great deal of thought.

Remember that a problem rarely has just one solution (although some alternatives are clearer or easier to implement than others). Also, realize that people solve problems in very individual ways using very different techniques.

Problem Restatement

One technique is to restate a problem in a different "language." Chapter 1 emphasized that you should restate a problem to understand it more clearly. Often a means to a solution becomes clearer if you can restate a problem verbally or pictorially or with an equation. The best way to restate a problem depends on the problem itself. You should attempt to restate problems in different languages and find the approach that best suits you and that best suits the particular problem you are trying to solve.

Delimiting the Problem

Often more than one restatement of a problem is useful. Restating a problem several times from several points of view often uncovers a possible solution. For example, look at the following problem:

> Taking public transportation, go from Oakland, California to San Francisco, California.[1]

This looks like a fairly straightforward problem that doesn't need to be restated for clarity. But we can restate it with different limitations to give us some ideas of how to solve it:

> Taking either a train, bus, airplane, helicopter, taxi, or ferryboat, go from Oakland, California, to San Francisco, California.

> Taking a train, bus, airplane, helicopter, taxi, and ferryboat, or any combination thereof, go from Oakland, California, to San Francisco, California.

> Taking public transportation, go from Oakland, California, to San Francisco, California, by way of Tokyo, Japan, or Mazatlan, Mexico.

These restatements, although constraining the problem unnecessarily, give us ideas about various routes we might take in solving the problem. By using our imagination we open up new perspectives. Some restatements of the problem seem ridiculous, like going from Oakland to San Francisco via Japan, but they may lead us to reasonable possibilities that we ignored because we were delimiting the possibilities too strictly (for example, assuming that we had to go from Oakland directly to San Francisco).

When you are trying to solve a problem, always look at extreme and varying constraints and possibilities that might affect your perspective. Do not avoid the outrageous or the ridiculous. For example, the first and second restatements of the problem listed all sorts of public transportation, including an airplane (San Francisco and Oakland are only about five miles apart). But that long list gave us several options that might not otherwise have occurred to us.

Limiting the possible ways of solving a problem is a serious block. Stretch your imagination beyond the everyday. Try the following exercise while keeping this point in mind.

Exercise   4.5: Consider the following problem:

> Sum ten numbers and announce their sum.
> Think of ten different ways to sum the numbers.   ■

---

1. If you are not familiar with these two cities, any other two will do.

Sometimes, however, the problem statement is not constrained enough. Consider the following problem:

Sum some numbers.

This problem statement does not tell us where to find the numbers or what to do with the sum when and if we arrive at it. The context in which a problem is presented might give us a better understanding of what was desired, but some problems are ambiguous, even in context. When you are dealing with ambiguities, always state what assumptions you are making and, if possible, verify that those assumptions are correct.

Exercise 4.6: Consider the following recipe:

To make a peanut butter and jelly sandwich you need (1) some bread, (2) some peanut butter, (3) some jelly. Once you have these ingredients, put some peanut butter on the bread. Put some jelly on the bread. Put the two slices of bread together. You are done.

What assumptions has the person who wrote the recipe made? List at least five.   ■

Looking at Possible Solutions

Often you can find a general solution if you look at several specific situations that might occur for a given problem. For example, to help solve the Oakland to San Francisco problem you might draw several routes on a map. In the robot problem, you might draw pictures showing the possible inputs (the positions of the robot and the door in the room):

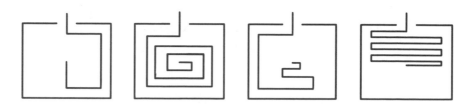

In the robot problem we might also draw various routes the robot would follow to get out of the room:

These sample diagrams give you some idea of what would happen with various techniques for getting the robot out of the room.

Another approach that often helps in problem solving is to write out what you expect the output to look like. For example, if you had to write an algorithm for balancing a checkbook at the end of the month and for producing a bank statement showing the deposits, the checks, and the final balance, you might write down the desired output as shown in Figure 4.25. If you wanted your output to look like that in Figure 4.25, you might outline this problem as

I. Add up checks.

II. Add up deposits.

III. Subtract checks from old balance and add deposits to get final balance.

If you created a different output, you might approach the problem differently.

Exercise 4.7: Create a different design for the output of the bank statement and create a different problem outline using your statement. ■

Finally, try to state the problem verbally to yourself or to someone else. Saying something out loud often stimulates ideas or makes things clearer. Discussing a problem with other people often triggers new ideas. Do not begin to criticize ideas until you have several to choose from and don't go off on a wild goose chase with the first idea that comes to you.

Figure 4.25   Sample output for checkbook problem

Old balance	XXX.XX
Checks	XX.XX
	X.XX
	XXX.XX
Check total	XXXX.XX
Deposits	XXXX.XX
	X.XX
Deposit total	XXXX.XX
Final balance	XXXX.XX

CHAPTER SUMMARY

1. The best way to solve complex problems is to:
   a. Find a general solution to the problem.
   b. Create an outline from your general solution.
   c. Use stepwise refinement to create a specific solution to each subproblem.
   d. Trace and debug each subalgorithm before going on to the next subproblem.

2. Complex conditional expressions are formed using the boolean operators *and, or,* and *not.*

3. This chapter also provided some general hints for problem solving, including:
   a. Restating a problem in several ways, using a different representation, and adding constraints
   b. Creating sample solutions
   c. Creating sample output

SUPPLEMENTAL PROBLEMS

1. Create a new algorithm for the robot problem with the following added constraints and desired output:

   > Constraints: The room may not have any doors.
   >
   > Output: The robot should turn off as soon as it leaves the room or when it discovers that the room does not have any doors.
   >
   > (Hint: How can you tell if the robot has gone around all four walls and has not found a door? You need to count.)

   Rebuild the outline (or tree) structure to help you solve the problem. *Do not* change just a few commands in the algorithm. It won't work!

2. You want to tell someone how to get to your house. Give clear instructions with three different options for where the person is starting from (for example, the local airport or the bus station). Break the problem down into subproblems using both the outline and tree forms.

3. Write an algorithm for preparing your favorite meal. Make sure that another person can understand it.
   a. Indicate all the conditional and iterative structures in your algorithm.
   b. Give an example of where a change in sequencing would change the outcome of your algorithm.

4. Consider each of the following statements and answer the question that follows it.

1. If I have tomatoes and some spices, then I can make spaghetti sauce.
   Q: I have some tomatoes. Can I make spaghetti sauce?
b. If the price of gasoline goes up or my car breaks down, then I won't drive anymore, else I'll keep driving.
   Q: What are the conditions under which I'll keep driving?
c. If I'm not paid more, then I'll quit, else I'll stay at my job.
   Q: If I'm paid more, what will happen?

5. Consider the following algorithm:

Setup

I. Label a piece of paper *first*.

II. Label a piece of paper *second*.

III. Label a piece of paper *third*.

Instructions

I. Write a number on the piece of paper labeled *first*.

II. Write a number on the piece of paper labeled *second*.

III. If the number on the paper labeled *first* is greater than the number on the paper labeled *second*,
   then
       A. Add 5 to *first*,[2] erase the value on *first* and write the new value there.
       B. Add 5 to *second*, erase the value on *second* and write the new value there.
       C. Multiply *first* times *second*, erase anything on *third* and write the new value there.
       D. Say the values on *first, second,* and *third*.
   else
       E. Add 5 to *second*, erase the value on *second* and write the new value there.
       F. Multiply *first* times *second*, erase anything on *third* and write the new value there.
       G. Add 5 to *first*, erase the value on *first* and write the new value there.
       H. Say the values on *first, second,* and *third*.

a. Trace the above algorithm.
b. Are there any instructions in the above **if-then-else** instruction that can be taken out and put before or after the **if-then-else** instruction? Which instructions? Why?

---

2. We shall just refer to each piece of paper simply by its label.

6. Write an algorithm to describe what you do at an automated teller machine. Your description should clearly indicate subproblems.

7. Write an algorithm to describe what the teller machine does when a person is using it. Your description should clearly indicate subproblems. List all the assumptions you make.

8. Write an algorithm to verify a person's password. The person should have at most 3 chances to enter his or her password.

9. Evaluate the following complex conditional expressions. Assume the following:

   ■ Fred is 38.

   ■ Barbara is 32.

   ■ Lydia is 24.

   a. (Fred's age is greater than Barbara's age) and (Barbara's age is less than Lydia's age).
   b. (Fred's age is greater than Barbara's age) or (Barbara's age is less than Lydia's age).
   c. (Lydia's age is less than Fred's age) or (Barbara's age is less than Fred's age).
   d. Not (Fred's age is less than Barbara's age).
   e. Not (((Fred's age is equal to Barbara's age) or (Lydia's age is greater than Barbara's age)) and (Lydia's age is greater than Fred's age)) or (Not (Barbara's age is greater than Fred's age)).

10. For each of the following conditional expressions, write a conditional expression which, when evaluated, will always have the opposite value of the given conditional expression.
    a. (x and y)
    b. (x or y)
    c. ((a and b) or (x and y))
    d. ((x and y) or b)
    e. (not (x or y))
    f. (not (x and y))

11. Write a new robot algorithm that enables the operator to count the number of doors in the room by directing the robot. Assume that the robot does not face a door at its starting position.

CHAPTER

5

In this chapter, we develop a number of problem examples and algorithms for their solution. We also trace the algorithms in order to debug them. The examples involve issues that are typical of those you might encounter in problems for computer solution. We occasionally interrupt the discussion to make a more general point, and we have intentionally included a few false starts to show how to refine and debug an incorrect solution.

The problems in this chapter are designed to be independent of each other. While each has been chosen to illustrate some particular points, you need not read all of them in sequence or in a single stretch. We do refer to most of them in later chapters, however.

5.1 THE SUPERMARKET PROBLEM

You are on your way to the supermarket to buy several items, and you're not sure you have enough cash to cover them all. You decide to keep track of the cumulative cost of your purchases as you put them into your shopping cart. To complicate matters, there is a 5% sales tax on nonfood items that you must take into account as you compute the running total. You can compute the sales tax using the formula $0.05 \times cost$, or you can simply compute the cost including tax for each item by using the formula $1.05 \times cost$.[1] Here's one statement of the problem:

You are given a list of grocery items, and for each item you have a price (in dollars and cents) and an indication of whether the item is food or nonfood.

1. $cost + 0.05 \times cost = 1 \times cost + 0.05 \times cost = (1 + 0.05) \times cost = 1.05 \times cost$.

CASE STUDIES
OF ALGORITHMS

You must provide the total cost of the items on your list, computed according to the following formula:

(total of food item costs) + (1.05 × total of nonfood item costs)

rounded to the nearest cent.

Does this problem statement accurately reflect the problem described above? No, it doesn't! The problem statement calls for a single amount as the output, but our description calls for a sequence of amounts, namely the partial totals computed after each item. In fact, you must have that output as you go along. Otherwise, if you have only $50 and the total cost comes to $67.93, you will exceed your limit before you know it. If you have partial totals, however, you will know when you are about to exceed your limit and will be able to act accordingly. We must revise the problem statement to reflect this observation:

You are given a list of grocery items, and for each item you have a price (in dollars and cents) and an indication of whether the item is food or nonfood. You must provide, for each item, the total cost of all the items on the list up to (and including) that item. This total is to be computed according to the formula

(total of food items so far) + (1.05 × total of nonfood items so far)

rounded to the nearest cent.

Now let's see whether the input and output agree with the original description. The phrase "you are given . . ." specifies the input, and phrase "you must provide. . ." specifies the output. We have this problem definition:

- Input: A list containing a sequence of name, cost, and food/nonfood indicator
- Output: A sequence of subtotals, computed according to the formula above
- Restrictions: Output rounded to nearest cent

Since there seem to be no ambiguities in the problem statement, we can develop an algorithm for solving this problem by thinking carefully and sequentially about how we would go about solving such problems in real life. Here's a possibility:

Setup

I. Label a scratchpad *Food Subtotal.*

II. Label a scratchpad *Nonfood Subtotal.*

III. Label a sheet of paper *Output.*

Instructions

I. On the scratchpad labeled *Food Subtotal,* write the number 0.00.

II. On the scratchpad labeled *Nonfood Subtotal,* write the number 0.00.

III. For each item on the list, do the following:
    A. If the item is a food item,
       then
          1. Add its cost to the number on the *Food Subtotal* scratchpad and replace the number on that pad with this sum.
       otherwise
          1'. Multiply the price of the item by 1.05, round this product to the nearest cent, and add this number to the number on the *Nonfood Subtotal* scratchpad. Then replace the number on the *Nonfood Subtotal* scratchpad with this sum.
    B. Add the numbers on the two *Subtotal* scratchpads. Write the sum on the *Output* sheet.

As you may have noticed, this algorithm has an error. We'll trace the algorithm with some sample input to exhibit the bug. Figure 5.1 gives the sample input data for this trace. What output should we expect? The problem statement indicates that our output will be a sequence of subtotals and gives a formula calculating them:

(total of food items so far) + (1.05 × total of nonfood items so far)

rounded to the nearest cent. According to this formula, our output should be as shown in Figure 5.2.

Figure 5.1 **Sample input for first trace**

```
Item 1  0.45  Nonfood
Item 2  0.45  Nonfood
Item 3  0.45  Nonfood
Item 4  0.45  Nonfood
```

Figure 5.2 **Expected output of trace**

0.00 + 0.45 X 1.05 = 0.4725	0.47
0.00 + 0.90 X 1.05 = 0.945	0.95
0.00 + 1.35 X 1.05 = 1.4175	1.42
0.00 + 1.80 X 1.05 = 1.8900	1.89

Now let's trace the algorithm and see what happens.

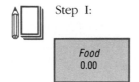

Step I:

```
Food
0.00
```

Step II:

```
Nonfood
0.00
```

Step III.A (first iteration): Do III.A.1'.

```
Food        Nonfood
0.00        0.47
```

Step III.B (first iteration):

> Output
> 0.47

Step III.A (second iteration): Do III.A.1′.

> Food
> 0.00

> Nonfood
> 0.94

Step III.B (second iteration):

> Output
> 0.47
> 0.94

Stop! We have already deviated from the expected output. If we continue the trace, we find that the algorithm yields the output shown in Figure 5.3.

What we have here is a rounding error. It is not true that

$$(1.05 \times 0.45) \text{ rounded} + (1.05 \times 0.45) \text{ rounded} = (1.05 \times 0.45 + 1.05 \times 0.45) \text{ rounded.}$$

Instead of using the formula given in the problem statement, we used what seemed to be an equivalent one. The problem statement gave us this formula:

(total of food items so far) + (1.05 × total of nonfood items so far)

rounded to the nearest cent. But the formula we actually used was this:

(total of food items so far) + (total of (1.05 × cost of nonfood
items rounded to the nearest cent) so far)

There are two lessons to be learned here:

1. When you're doing rounded or inexact calculations, the usual laws of arithmetic are not valid.
2. When you're given a formula, use it!

Figure 5.3   **Output of traced algorithm**

```
Output
0.47
0.94
1.41
1.88
```

To correct the algorithm, we must calculate the sales tax on the total of non-food items, rather than on each item separately. We replace steps III.A and III.B in the original algorithm with these steps:

A'. If the item is a food item,
   then
      1. Add its cost to the number on the *Food Subtotal* scratchpad and replace the number on the scratchpad with this sum.
   otherwise
      1'. Add its cost to the number on the *Nonfood Subtotal* scratchpad and replace the number on the scratchpad with this sum.
B'. Multiply the number on the *Nonfood Subtotal* by 1.05 and round the result to the nearest cent. Add this rounded result to the number on the *Food Subtotal* scratchpad and write the sum on the *Output* sheet.

Exercise 5.1: (a) Trace the corrected algorithm with the given input data to see that it gives the correct result. (b) Trace the corrected algorithm with the following input data:

Trace 2: sample input

```
Item 1   1.23   Food
Item 2   1.23   Nonfood
Item 3   0.77   Nonfood
```

Note that this algorithm is built on the basic building blocks: *sequencing, iteration,* and *selection.*

5.2 THE HAND OF CARDS PROBLEM

In this problem, you are to take five ordinary playing cards from a standard deck of 52 and place them in a particular order. For many card games, the most convenient way to hold a hand is to group the cards in suits and to order them by rank within each suit. For visual convenience, we'll alternate the red and black suits. We'll call diamonds lowest, clubs next, then hearts, and spades highest. Within each suit, we'll use the usual ace-high ranking:

two (lowest), three, four, five, six, seven, eight, nine, ten, jack, queen, king, ace

It turns out that the algorithm we'll get is essentially independent of this ordering. All that matters is that we specify some way of comparing cards (that is, saying which of two is greater). We need a precise problem statement, and here it is:

You are given five cards. You must arrange the five cards so that all the diamonds appear first (on the left), followed by all the clubs, then all the hearts, and then all the spades. Within each suit you must arrange the cards in ascending order: two, three, four, five, six, seven, eight, nine, ten, jack, queen, king, ace.

Exercise 5.2: Identify the input, output, and any constraints in this problem. ■

This a special case of the general sorting problem, which has received a good deal of attention from computer scientists. There are many algorithms for sorting under various circumstances. Before you read the solution below, try to write your own.

Exercise 5.3: Write an algorithm to solve the hand of cards problem stated above. ■

Here is one of many possible solutions. For convenience, we refer to the cards by number, calling the leftmost card the first, and the rightmost the fifth. The comments in brackets are not part of the algorithm. They explain how the algorithm works.

ALGORITHM FOR SORTING
A HAND OF FIVE CARDS

I. Compare the first two cards. If they are not in correct order, interchange them. [After this step, the first two cards are in correct order.]

II. Insert the third card in its proper place among the first two. [After this step, the first three cards are in correct order.]

III. Insert the fourth card in its proper place among the first three. [After this step, the first four cards are in order.]

IV. Insert the fifth card in its proper place among the first four.

This algorithm creates an ordered sequence by building larger and larger ordered subsequences from left to right. You could sort longer sequences by adding steps.

Two things about the algorithm require clarification: How do we compare two cards? And how do we insert a card into its proper place in an already sorted sequence? Each action demands a subalgorithm of its own.

We turn first to the algorithm for comparing two cards. Here the input is two cards, and the output is a declaration of which of the cards is the lesser (according to the order we specified in the problem statement).

Subalgorithm for Comparing
Two Cards

I. If the cards are of the same suit,
    then
        A. Compare the ranks of the two cards. The card with lower rank is the lesser card.
    else
        A′. Compare the suits of the two cards. The card with the lower suit is the lesser card.

The insertion subalgorithm is more complex. The input of this algorithm consists of an already-sorted sequence of cards and another card to be inserted in the correct place in that sequence. The output is the correctly expanded sequence. The algorithm must work for ordered sequences of various lengths: length 2, length 3, and length 4. Thus, we need some sort of indefinite iteration (see Chapter 2)—that is, some way of describing repetition without saying explicitly how many repetitions there will be. Here's one way to write the algorithm.

Subalgorithm for Inserting
a Card into Its Proper Place
in an Ordered Sequence

I. Mark the first (leftmost) card in the sequence with a paper clip.

II. Repeat step A below until the card to be inserted (which we'll refer to as the new card) has been inserted:
 A. If the new card is less than the card marked with a paper clip,
  then
  1. Insert the new card before (to the left of) the paper-clipped card.
  otherwise
  2. If the paper-clipped card is not the last card in the sequence,
   then
   i. Move the paper clip one card to the right.
   otherwise
   ii. Insert the new card after (to the right of) the paper-clipped card.

With these two subalgorithms, we have a complete algorithm for sorting a hand of cards. But is it correct? To find out, we'll trace it, using the "bottom-up" approach: First we'll trace each subalgorithm. If we're confident they both work, we'll trace the main algorithm. Let's start by tracing the subalgorithm for comparing two cards:

Trace 1: Input data: three of spades, jack of diamonds

We expect, as output, to find that the jack is less.

Step I: The suits are different. We do the **else** clause (step I.A′) and compare suits. Since diamonds are lower than spades, the jack of diamonds is the lesser card.

The result is what we expect.

Trace 2: Input data: seven of clubs, four of clubs

We expect, as output, to find that the four of clubs is less.

Step I: The suits are equal. We do the **then** clause (step I.A) and compare ranks. Since four is lower than seven, the four of clubs is the lesser card.

Again, the result is as expected.

Now let's trace the subalgorithm for insertion. Recall that this algorithm expects as input a sequence of at least two cards, already sorted, and a single card to be inserted into that sequence.

Trace 1: Input Sequence: king of diamonds, four of clubs, eight of hearts. Card to be inserted: jack of clubs

We expect, as output, the sequence in the order king, four, jack, eight.

Step I: Mark the king of diamonds with a paper clip.
Step II:
   Step II.A (first iteration): The jack of clubs is higher than the king of diamonds [according to our subalgorithm for comparing cards], so do the **otherwise** clause:
      Step II.A.2 (first iteration): the king of diamonds is not the last card in the sequence, so do the **then** clause:
         Step II.A.2.i (first iteration): Move the paper clip to the four of clubs.
   Step II.A (second iteration): The jack of clubs is greater than the four of clubs [again, according to our subalgorithm for comparison], so do:
      Step II.A.2 (second iteration): The four of clubs is not the last card in the sequence, so do:
         Step II.A.2.i (second iteration): Move the paper clip to the eight of hearts.
   Step II.A (third iteration): The jack of clubs is less than the eight of hearts, so do the **then** clause:
      Step II.A.1 (third iteration): Insert the jack to the left of the eight.

Now that we have inserted the new card, we stop the repetition of step II.A with an output sequence of king of diamonds, four of clubs, jack of clubs, eight of hearts. This output is what we expected.

Exercise 5.4: Trace this algorithm with a second set of test data to see whether it behaves correctly. Show the state of the cards at every step. You might choose a card to be inserted that should wind up being placed at the end. That would test a portion of the algorithm (step II.A.2.ii) that our trace did not test. ■

Now let's go on to the main algorithm. The input is five cards in any order.

Trace 1: Input sequence: three of spades, four of hearts, five of hearts, six of diamonds, seven of clubs

We expect as output six of diamonds, seven of clubs, four of hearts, five of hearts, three of spades.

Step I: Compare the three of spades with the four of hearts [using our comparison subalgorithm, which we are not tracing here]. They're in the wrong order, so interchange them. Our sequence is now

four, three, five, six, seven

Step II: Insert the five of hearts into its proper place in the sequence consisting of the four of hearts and the three of spades [using our insertion subalgorithm, which we are not tracing]. Our sequence is now

four, five, three, six, seven.

Step III: Insert the six of diamonds into its proper place among the cards which are now the first three cards. Our sequence is now

six, four, five, three, seven

Step IV: Insert the seven of clubs into its proper place among the first four cards. Our sequence is now

six, seven, four, five, three

Our output is what we expected.

Since our sorting algorithm is designed for exactly five cards, we would need to modify it somewhat if we wanted to sort, say, a bridge hand of 13 cards. Even so, the same general procedure would work for any number of cards. Moreover, our subalgorithm for insertion will work for an ordered sequence of any length because of the iterative construct built into the first step. We can use a similar form of iteration to rewrite the main sorting algorithm to accommodate a card hand of any size:

ALGORITHM FOR SORTING A HAND OF CARDS (SECOND VERSION)

I. Repeat step A below for every card, starting at the second card and including the last one.
   A. Call the card for which we're repeating this step the current card. Insert the current card into the (already-ordered) subsequence of cards beginning at the first card and ending with the card just to the left of the current one.

That's it. Not only is this version more general than the first version, it's also shorter. Notice, however, that the English we're using to refer to various cards is becoming nearly incomprehensible. We need a better way to specify exactly what we're talking about. We can borrow a notation from mathematics to make the meaning clearer: We'll use n to specify the number of cards in the hand (which can be any number we like) and we'll refer to the cards by their position numbers, calling the leftmost card in the hand card 1, the next one card 2, and so forth, calling the rightmost card card n. We'll also use a letter for the counting numbers 2, 3, 4,. . ., n, since we're repeating a step for each of those cards. We'll use card i, where i is a number between 2 and n, to stand for the card in the ith position. With that preamble, here's a restatement of the algorithm:

ALGORITHM FOR SORTING A HAND OF CARDS (THIRD VERSION)

I. Repeat step A below for every card from card 2 to card n. In each repetition, let i stand for the position number of the card for which the repetition is being done, so that i takes on the successive values 2, 3, 4,. . ., n.
  A. Insert card i in the (already sorted) subsequence of cards 1 through i - 1.

This sorting algorithm is known as *sorting by insertion*. In Chapter 7, we'll discuss another algorithm for sorting a sequence of items for which an order is defined. We still haven't tested this algorithm thoroughly, however. So:

Exercise 5.5: A single trace of a sorting algorithm is never enough. In fact, before we conclude that a sorting algorithm works, we should try test data

- In already-sorted order, since it's possible that our algorithm will somehow scramble an input sequence that by chance happens to be sorted
- In reverse sorted order, since this is, in a way, the worst possible case
- In random order

Make up sets of each type of test data and use them to trace the sorting algorithm. ■

5.3 THE LETTER-COUNTING PROBLEM

This is the problem from Section 1.2 of Chapter 1. In that section, we arrived at the following problem statement:

> You are given a sample of English text. You must produce a list consisting of 26 numbers, of which the *n*th number in the list is the number of times the *n*th letter of the Roman alphabet occurs in the text, in either upper- or lowercase form. Nothing else should appear on the list. Any nonletter characters in the text are to be ignored.

We develop an algorithm for this problem simply by thinking carefully and sequentially about the task. Here is one possibility:

ALGORITHM FOR COUNTING LETTERS IN TEXT

Setup

I. Label a sheet of paper *Letter Count.*

II. Label a sheet of paper *Output.*

III. Write the letters of the alphabet in order down the left side of the paper labeled *Letter Count.*

Instructions

I. Next to each letter on the sheet labeled *Letter Count* write the number 0.

II. For each character in the text that is a letter, do:
    A. Find the corresponding letter on the sheet labeled *Letter Count.* Add 1 to the number next to the letter. Erase the number next to the letter and replace it by this sum.

III. For each of the letters on the sheet labeled *Letter Count,* do:
    A. Copy the number next to that letter on the sheet labeled *Output* in order down the left side.

Let's trace this algorithm with some simple input. In Figure 5.4, to save space, we give the state of the **Letter Count** sheet in columns, with each column representing a version of the sheet after each successive step. Each column is headed by the letter that has been read in that step.

Next is a completely different algorithm for solving the same problem. Some readers may find this algorithm more natural, while others may find it strange.

Figure 5.4 **Trace of the letter-counting algorithm**

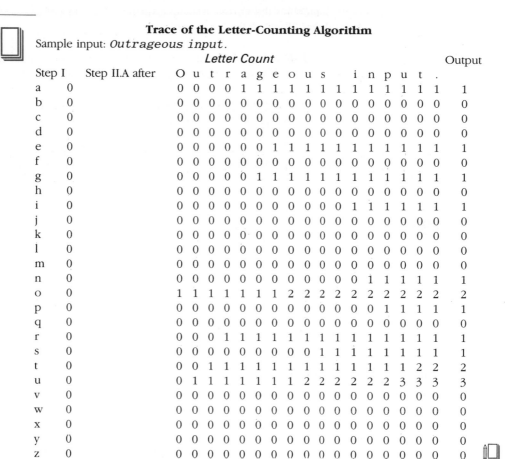

Trace of the Letter-Counting Algorithm

Sample input: *Outrageous input.*

Step I		Step II.A after	O	u	t	r	a	g	e	o	u	s		i	n	p	u	t	.	Output
a	0		0	0	0	0	1	1	1	1	1	1	1	1	1	1	1	1	1	1
b	0		0	0	0	0	0	0	0	0	0	0	0	0	0	0	0	0	0	0
c	0		0	0	0	0	0	0	0	0	0	0	0	0	0	0	0	0	0	0
d	0		0	0	0	0	0	0	0	0	0	0	0	0	0	0	0	0	0	0
e	0		0	0	0	0	0	0	1	1	1	1	1	1	1	1	1	1	1	1
f	0		0	0	0	0	0	0	0	0	0	0	0	0	0	0	0	0	0	0
g	0		0	0	0	0	0	1	1	1	1	1	1	1	1	1	1	1	1	1
h	0		0	0	0	0	0	0	0	0	0	0	0	0	0	0	0	0	0	0
i	0		0	0	0	0	0	0	0	0	0	0	0	1	1	1	1	1	1	1
j	0		0	0	0	0	0	0	0	0	0	0	0	0	0	0	0	0	0	0
k	0		0	0	0	0	0	0	0	0	0	0	0	0	0	0	0	0	0	0
l	0		0	0	0	0	0	0	0	0	0	0	0	0	0	0	0	0	0	0
m	0		0	0	0	0	0	0	0	0	0	0	0	0	0	0	0	0	0	0
n	0		0	0	0	0	0	0	0	0	0	0	0	0	1	1	1	1	1	1
o	0		1	1	1	1	1	1	1	2	2	2	2	2	2	2	2	2	2	2
p	0		0	0	0	0	0	0	0	0	0	0	0	0	0	1	1	1	1	1
q	0		0	0	0	0	0	0	0	0	0	0	0	0	0	0	0	0	0	0
r	0		0	0	0	1	1	1	1	1	1	1	1	1	1	1	1	1	1	1
s	0		0	0	0	0	0	0	0	0	0	1	1	1	1	1	1	1	1	1
t	0		0	0	1	1	1	1	1	1	1	1	1	1	1	1	1	2	2	2
u	0		0	1	1	1	1	1	1	1	2	2	2	2	2	2	3	3	3	3
v	0		0	0	0	0	0	0	0	0	0	0	0	0	0	0	0	0	0	0
w	0		0	0	0	0	0	0	0	0	0	0	0	0	0	0	0	0	0	0
x	0		0	0	0	0	0	0	0	0	0	0	0	0	0	0	0	0	0	0
y	0		0	0	0	0	0	0	0	0	0	0	0	0	0	0	0	0	0	0
z	0		0	0	0	0	0	0	0	0	0	0	0	0	0	0	0	0	0	0

ALGORITHM FOR COUNTING LETTERS IN TEXT (SECOND VERSION)

Setup

I. Label a box of 26 blank file cards *Letter Count*.

II. Label a sheet of paper *Output*.

III. Remove the file cards from the box.

Instructions

I. For each character in the text that is a letter, do:
    A. Search for the corresponding letter on a card in the box labeled *Letter Count.* If you find such a card,
        then
           1. Add 1 to the number on the card. Erase the number on the card and replace it by this sum.
        otherwise
           2. Write the letter on a new card and write the number 1 next to it. Put the card in the box behind any other cards already there.

II. For each letter in the alphabet, in alphabetical order, do:
    A. Search for the letter on a card in the box labeled *Letter Count.* If you find the letter,
        then
           1. Copy the number next to it on the next available line on the sheet labeled *output.*
        otherwise
           2. Write a 0 on the next available line on the sheet labeled *output.*

The idea of this algorithm is to count only those letters that actually appear in the text, and to count those letters in the order in which they appear. In step II, we use the information we've gathered to construct the output.

Exercise 5.6: (a) What would be the advantages and disadvantages of each of these algorithms if you had to carry them out by hand? (Hint: Which would be easiest for a very long input text? For a very short input text?) (b) Suppose you were asked to count the number of occurrences of each word in the text, rather than of each letter. Choose the algorithms you would modify to serve this purpose. Which one did you choose? Why? ■

5.4 THE GRADES PROBLEM

The grades problem is more complex than the previous ones. You are to develop a procedure for recording, totaling, and sorting the grades for a class of students. Since it is difficult to state the problem precisely, we will have to develop the statement in several steps.[2] Here is a first attempt at a problem statement:

---

2. Working through this problem will require patience and concentration. We present it to demonstrate certain considerations that arise only in solving large, complex problems. What we will do is repeatedly decompose the problem into subproblems. As you will see later on, one of the strengths of the Pascal programming language is that it has features designed to specifically accommodate this decomposition.

You are teaching a class. At the end of the semester, you want to produce a report with all the students' names, all the scores each student received, and the total of each student's scores. You want to organize this report in descending order by total score, so that the student with the highest total appears first, and the student with the lowest total appears last.

This is not an adequate problem statement. It leaves too many details unspecified or ambiguous. At a minimum, you need to know where the scores are available, and what the format of the report must be. There is also an ambiguity that is typical of problems that involve sorting: If two or more students have a given total, in what order should their records appear?

We will deal with these ambiguities by making some simplifying assumptions. You can assume that all the students' names are available on a class list and that all the scores for each student for the entire semester are available from informal records you've kept. The report should be tabular in form:

1. Student A   XX   XX   XX   . . .   XX   Total XXX
2. Student B   XX   XX   XX   . . .   XX   Total XXX
   . . .

You can report students with the same total in any order you please.

These additional specifications help. To see if they're enough, you should try to describe the input and the output of this problem. Possible descriptions are

- Input: A sequence of names, and for each name, a sequence of numbers.
- Output: A report consisting of a column of names, with each name followed by columns of numbers. The names are the same as those in the input sequence, but they are not necessarily in the same order. The columns of numbers after a name are the sequence of input numbers for that name, followed by one additional number, which is the sum of the preceding numbers for that name. The names and corresponding numbers are arranged so that the column of totals forms a decreasing sequence when read from top to bottom. The students' names should be numbered, starting at 1.

Despite the length of the output description, it is still inadequate. You also need to know the answers to these questions: How many students are there? How many scores are to be recorded for each student? What should you do if a student is missing one or more scores?

A realistic response to these questions is that you want an algorithm that will work for a class of any size, that there will be no more than 30 scores for each student, and that any missing score is to be replaced by the number 0. Thus, the final report will list the same number of scores for each student, with no more than 30 columns of scores and one column of totals.

With these details specified, you have enough information to begin formulating a solution. Since this problem is complex, you should not attempt to solve it in one piece but to break it into subproblems. With this in mind, here is an algorithm for solving the grades problem:

MAIN ALGORITHM FOR THE GRADES PROBLEM

Setup

I. Label a piece of paper *Interim Data*. Divide it vertically into columns with a wide column for names followed by 31 columns for numbers.

II. Label a piece of paper *Final Report*. Divide it in columns like *Interim Data*.

III. Label a piece of paper *Scratch*.

Instructions

I. Record all the input information (the names and the scores) on the sheet labeled *Interim Data*.

II. Compute the total scores for each student and record the results on *Interim Data*.

III. Sort the information by total score in descending order and write the results on *Scratch*.

IV. Write the final report on *Final Report,* using the information on *Scratch*.

Each of these steps is a subproblem, and you must describe each with a subalgorithm. There is no absolute rule for breaking problems down into subproblems, and you might find other ways for this problem that are equally satisfactory. Good guidelines are that each subproblem should be logically cohesive and that the subproblems should not be tightly coupled to each other. This means that the different subproblems should share a minimal amount of information.

Your next task is to write the subalgorithm for step I of the main algorithm. This subproblem logically divides into two parts, from which you can get

First Subalgorithm: Recording Scores (Sketch)

Instructions

I. Record the names of the students on *Interim Data*.

II. For each student, do:
   A. Record the grades for that student on *Interim Data*.

You can proceed from this point in two ways. One is to declare this subalgorithm complete and write two sub-subalgorithms to further describe these two steps. The other is to refine them here by rewriting this subalgorithm in more detail. The first choice is better when the steps are still sufficiently complex to warrant an algorithm each. In this case, you can use the second approach. An expanded version of this subalgorithm is

First Subalgorithm: Recording Scores (Expanded)

Instructions

I. For each student name on the class list, do:
    A. Write the name on *Interim Data* below any names that you may have already written.

II. For each student name on *Interim Data,* do
    A. For each score recorded for that student, do:
        1. Write that score in the next available column to the right of the student's name.

This expansion provides a complete subalgorithm for the first step of the main algorithm.

Exercise 5.7: Suppose you want line numbers to the left of the names and scores on *Interim Data.* Modify the subalgorithm to produce such a numbered list. (Hint: You will need to add a setup stage to the subalgorithm because you need some place to count names.)   ■

The next task is the subalgorithm for finding each student's total score. This task is straightforward, and we can write a subalgorithm for it directly:

Second Subalgorithm: Computing Total Scores

Setup

I. Label a piece of paper *Total.*

Instructions

I. For each student name on the class list, do:
  A. Write the number 0 on *Total* after erasing any number that may be there.
  B. For each score for this student, do:
    1. Add the score to the number on *Total*. Write the sum on *Total* after erasing the previous value written there.
  C. Write the number from *Total* on *Interim Data* in the thirty-first column to the right of the student's name.

If you carry out this subalgorithm, you will have all the data you need for your final report but not in the order you desire. The third step in the main algorithm is to sort the total scores and list them in descending order with the associated names. We have already given one algorithm for sorting; here is a second.

Third Subalgorithm: Sorting The Names and Scores

Instructions

I. Repeat the following steps:
  A. Find the student whose total score is the highest of all those on the list.
  B. Copy the entire line of information pertaining to that student from *Interim Data* to *Scratch*.
  C. Erase the line from *Interim Data*
  until there are no more lines left on *Interim Data*.

This is a variant of the algorithm known as *sorting by selection*. It works by repeatedly finding the largest total score and putting it on the output of the subalgorithm (which is the sheet labeled **Scratch.**) Finding the largest remaining score is itself a subproblem worth an algorithm of its own. We leave it up to you to provide it.

Exercise 5.8: Write a sub-subalgorithm to implement step I.A of the sorting subalgorithm. ■

In the next chapter, we describe a number of fundamental algorithms that often appear as parts of larger algorithms. Finding the maximum of a sequence of values is one of these fundamental algorithms.

To solve the grades problem, you need one more subalgorithm, and it's straightforward. It simply involves copying the data from *Scratch* to *Final Report,* adding a line number at the start of each line.

Fourth Subalgorithm: Final Report

Setup

I. Label a piece of paper *Line Number.*

Instructions

I. Write the number 1 on *Line Number.*

II. Repeat the following steps:
   A. Copy the value on *Line Number* to the next blank line on *Final Report,* followed by a period.
   B. Copy the first line of data on *Scratch* to *Final Report.*
   C. Erase the first line of data on *Scratch.*
   D. Add 1 to the number on *Line Number* and write the sum on *Line Number* after erasing the previous value.
   until no more lines of data remain on *Scratch.*

We have described a complete solution to the problem using six algorithms (one of which we left as an exercise). You might be tempted to combine all of them into one large algorithm. That is certainly possible, but it's not a good idea. Keeping the solution in pieces makes it easier to understand each piece. More important, it makes it easier to change the solution to adapt to changes in the problem. If our division of the problem into subproblems is logical, then most changes in the problem specification should only require changes to one of the subalgorithms. The following exercise illustrates this point:

Exercise   5.9: Here are several possible ways to change the problem. For each such change, (a) describe which subalgorithm(s) must be modified and (b) make the required modifications.

1. The final report must be in ascending order by total score, rather than descending order.
2. The final report should be in descending order, but if several students have the same score they must appear in alphabetical order by last name.

3. The data is not all simultaneously available. Rather, the scores for each home-work assignment or exam are reported at a given time for the entire class and must be recorded at that time. The totals can only be computed at the end of the semester.

4. The scores are not all of equal weight. The first, third, fourth, and tenth scores count double.

5. The individual scores should not be on the final report. For each student, only a line number, a name, and the total score should appear.

6. No scores should appear on the final report. Instead, each line should consist of a line number, name, and letter grade, assigned according to this table:

Total Score	Grade
265–300	A
225–264	B
190–224	C
155–189	D
0–154	F ■

Exercise   5.10: The algorithms we wrote require that all the data be copied three times. Such copying is laborious. If you number the lines on *Interim Data,* you can then avoid one copying task: When you sort the data, don't write the entire line on the *Scratch.* Instead, write only its line number. Use these line numbers to copy the data directly from the *Interim Data* to the *Final Report.* Modify the algorithm(s) to implement this scheme. (Hint: You can't erase the lines from *Interim Data* as you sort them because you will need the data later. Thus, you must somehow keep track of which line numbers have already been copied to *Scratch.*)   ■

5.5 THE HAND OF CARDS PROBLEM REVISITED

In this section, we describe a new algorithm for sorting a hand of five cards. The problem is the same one we discussed earlier, and the method of solution is essentially the same: We sort cards by inserting them into already-sorted subsequences. The difference lies in the way we describe the sorting process. We will assume that the subalgorithms for comparing two cards and for inserting a card into an already sorted subsequence will work as described on pages 93–94. Here's one description of the new algorithm:

ALGORITHM FOR SORTING A HAND OF FIVE CARDS

I. Sort the hand consisting of the first four cards.

II. Insert the fifth card in its proper place among the first four cards.

But, you may object, doesn't step I require that we know how to sort cards already? Isn't the reasoning circular? We can answer that objection by presenting an

ALGORITHM FOR SORTING A HAND OF FOUR CARDS

I. Sort the hand consisting of the first three cards.

II. Insert the fourth card in its proper place among the first three cards.

Before you object again, here is an

ALGORITHM FOR SORTING A HAND OF THREE CARDS

I. Sort the hand consisting of the first two cards.

II. Insert the third card in its proper place among the first two cards.

Finally, here is an algorithm for sorting a hand of two cards. Note that this one is different:

ALGORITHM FOR SORTING A HAND OF TWO CARDS

I. Compare the first and second cards. If the value of the first card is higher than that of the second,
    then
        A. Interchange them.

We need to generalize this algorithm and to express it more compactly. We don't want to write 51 algorithms to describe how to sort a deck of 52 cards. In fact, we don't even want to write four algorithms to describe how to sort five cards. We want one algorithm.

Notice that three of the four algorithms given above are essentially identical. And if we tried to write 51 such algorithms to sort a full deck, the first 50 would be essentially identical. They would look like this:

ALGORITHM TO SORT N CARDS

I. Sort the first $N-1$ cards using an algorithm to sort $N-1$ cards.

II. Insert the Nth card into the sorted subsequence of $N-1$ cards.

The last algorithm would be the algorithm for sorting two cards given above. This is a special case, and our simple description of it can hardly be improved upon. What we can do, however, is combine all these algorithms into a single algorithm. This algorithm will be self-referential—that is, it will refer to itself. Such algorithms are called *recursive*. (Recall the discussion of recursion in Chapter 3.)

RECURSIVE ALGORITHM FOR SORTING N CARDS

I. If N is 2,
    then
        A. Compare the first and second cards. If the value of the first card is greater than that of the second,
            then
                1. Interchange them.
    otherwise
        A'. Invoke this algorithm, with $N-1$ instead of N, to sort the first $N-1$ cards.
        B'. Insert the Nth card in the sorted subsequence of $N-1$ cards.

The recursion in this algorithm occurs in step I.A', where we say **invoke this algorithm, with $N-1$ instead of N** . . . You may think at first that recursion can't work because it seems to involve circular reasoning. Indeed, it's possible for a careless use of recursion to lead to a circular sequence of steps that will never end. To be valid, a recursive algorithm must exhibit these essential features:

■ Any given instance of the algorithm refers only to simpler cases of the algorithm, not to more complex cases or to the same case.

- The simplest instance of the algorithm is explicitly described, and is not recursive.

In our example, the simplest instance is the case of sorting two cards.

We will now trace this algorithm using the same set of input data we used to trace the card-sorting algorithm on page 96.

Trace input sequence: three of spades, four of hearts, five of hearts, six of diamonds, seven of clubs

We expect as output six of diamonds, seven of clubs, four of hearts, five of hearts, three of spades.

Step I:

| 5 | 3S, 4H, 5H, 6D, 7C |

N

Since N is 5, which is not 2, we do the **otherwise** clause. This means we invoke the same algorithm with four cards:

Step I.A′:
Step I:

| 4 | 3S, 4H, 5H, 6D |

N

Since this instance of N is 4, which is not 2, we do the **otherwise** clause. Thus, we're invoking the algorithm on its own behalf at a second level, this time with three cards:

Step I.A′:
Step I:

| 3 | 3S, 4H, 5H |

N

N is still greater than 2. We invoke the algorithm yet again:

Step I.A′:
Step I:

| 2 | 3S, 4H |

N

Now N is 2, so this instance of the algorithm uses the then clause of step I. Since all spades are greater than any heart, we interchange the first two cards:

Step I.A:
Step I:

| 2 | 4H, 3S |

N

This completes the algorithm for the case $N = 2$. What should we do next? The last thing we did before running the algorithm with $N = 2$ was step I.A' from the case $N = 3$. Looking back at the algorithm, we see that the next thing to do is step I.B' of the same case. This is the crucial step in understanding the trace: When an instance of the algorithm completes, we return (as always when a subalgorithm finishes) to the next step in the invoking algorithm: the next "unfinished business." So we go on with

Step I.B':   [3]   4H, 5H, 3S   Nth card is 5H

            N

This instance of the algorithm now finishes, and we return to step I.B' of the case $N = 4$:

Step I.B':   [4]   6D, 4H, 5H, 3S   Nth card is 6D

            N

This instance of the algorithm also terminates, and we return (finally!) to step I.B' of the original algorithm:

Step I.B':   [5]   6D, 7C, 4H, 5H, 3S   Nth card is 7C

            N

If you compare this algorithm for sorting cards with the third version of the algorithm given on page 97 you will see that the use of recursion has enabled us to do away with iteration. That algorithm had an iterative step, while this one does not. Is that an advantage? Not necessarily. The use of recursion in this example is slightly artificial. It results in a compact and (we think) elegant solution to the sorting problem, but the nonrecursive algorithm was perfectly satisfactory. For certain problems, however, a recursive algorithm is much more satisfactory than any other. The next example is such a problem.

5.6 THE TOWER OF HANOI

The Tower of Hanoi is the name of a famous puzzle that was popular as a novelty item in the nineteenth century. The puzzle consists of a board or block that has three pegs. On one of the pegs—assume it's the leftmost, as in Figure 5.5—several disks of different sizes are stacked in increasing order of size, with the smallest at the top. You must move all the disks to the rightmost peg subject to the following rules:

Figure 5.5   **The Tower of Hanoi puzzle**

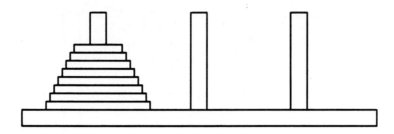

- You may move only one disk at a time.
- No disk may ever rest on a smaller disk.

The difficulty of the problem seems to depend on the number of disks on the left peg. Clearly, if there's only one disk on the left peg you can solve the puzzle in a single move. What we want, however, is a solution that will work no matter how many disks we start with.

You can use the center peg to hold disks temporarily. Suppose you start with only two disks on the left peg. In this case, you can solve the puzzle in three steps:

1. Move the smaller disk to the center peg.
2. Move the larger disk to the right peg.
3. Move the smaller disk to the right peg.

These moves are shown in Figure 5.6.

Exercise **5.11:** Solve the three-disk Tower of Hanoi problem, pictured below:

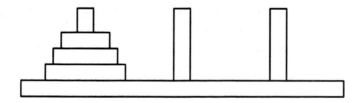

Figure 5.6   **Solution to the two-disk Tower of Hanoi**

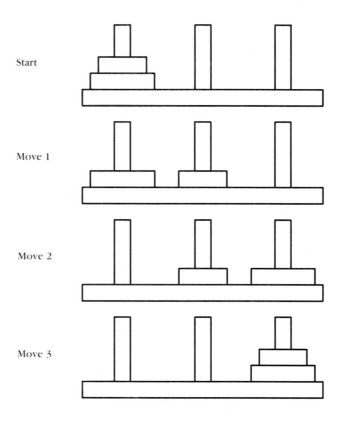

To solve this puzzle in generality, you must recognize the recursive nature of the problem: You can solve the N-disk problem by reducing it to the $(N-1)$-disk problem. For example, here's a description of a solution to Exercise 5.11, the three-disk problem:

1. Move the top two disks to the center peg as if you were solving the two-disk problem, except that the roles of the center peg and the right peg are interchanged.
2. Move the bottom disk to the right peg (which is empty).
3. Move the two disks from the center peg to the right peg as if you were solving the two-disk problem, except that the roles of the center peg and the left peg are interchanged.

This is a seven-move solution. Step 1 involves three moves, step 2 involves a single move, and step 3 involves three moves.

We can generalize this solution. Suppose we want to solve the N-disk Tower of Hanoi puzzle, where N is some unspecified number. If we know how to solve the problem with $N-1$ disks, we can solve the N-disk problem as follows:

SOLUTION TO THE N-DISK TOWER OF HANOI PUZZLE

1. Move the top $N-1$ disks to the center peg, as if you were solving the $(N-1)$-disk problem, except that the roles of the center peg and the right peg are interchanged.

2. Move the bottom disk to the right peg (which is empty).

3. Move the $N-1$ disks from the center peg to the right peg, as if you were solving the $(N-1)$-disk problem, except that the roles of the center peg and the left peg are interchanged.

This is almost, but not quite, a satisfactory algorithm. It doesn't quite explain what to do in the case $N=1$, the simplest case. We know how to solve that one, of course, but we haven't written it down. Reading step 1 of the algorithm with N replaced by 1 gives

1. Move the top zero disks to the center peg as if you were solving the zero-disk problem, except that the roles of the center peg and the right peg are interchanged.

This step doesn't make much sense. The most reasonable interpretation of it is to do nothing whatsoever. In fact, that would work, but we should express ourselves more precisely. Also, the language we use to describe the roles of the various pegs in steps 1 and 3 is a bit obscure. To make it more explicit, we need names for the roles the pegs play in each step. Let's call the peg where the disks start out the *Source* peg, the peg where we want them to end up the *Destination* peg, and the other peg the *Temporary* peg. Now we can write an algorithm for a precisely specified Tower of Hanoi problem:

RECURSIVE ALGORITHM FOR AN N-DISK TOWER OF HANOI PROBLEM WITH *SOURCE, DESTINATION,* AND *TEMPORARY* PEGS

I. If N is bigger than 1,
   then
       A. Perform the $N-1$ case of this algorithm with the same *Source* and with *Destination* and *Temporary* interchanged.

II. Move the top disk from *Source* to *Destination.*

III. If N is bigger than 1,
    then
        A. Perform the N − 1 case of this algorithm with the same *Destination* and with *Source* and *Temporary* interchanged.

Figure 5.7 shows the algorithm diagramatically for the case N = 3. Each box represents an instance of the algorithm. The boxes that involve only a single disk (N = 1) can be carried out directly. The others are carried out recursively according to the algorithm. Thus, the seven actual moves of disks are represented by the seven boxes labeled *1 disk*.

A common cause of confusion in tracing recursive algorithms like this one is a misunderstanding of the sequence in which the steps are carried out. Remember

Figure 5.7   Tower of Hanoi algorithm for N = 3

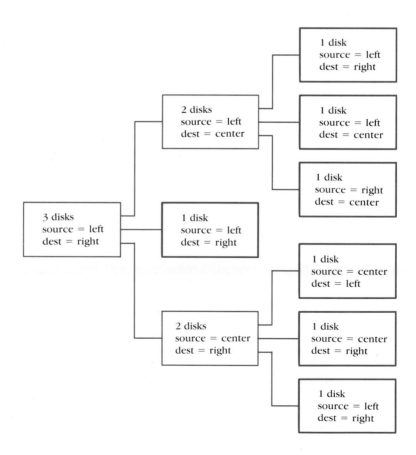

that when a main algorithm step invokes a subalgorithm, the next step of the main algorithm does not execute until the entire subalgorithm has finished. This is true even when the subalgorithm is a simpler case of the main one. In this case, we must also keep track of which pegs play the role of *Source, Destination,* and *Temporary* at each stage. As we trace the steps in the algorithm (for the case N=3), we will provide that information. We'll abbreviate *Source, Destination,* and *Temporary* with *S, D* and *T,* and refer to the three pegs as *L*(eft), *C*(enter) and *R*(ight). We start with S=L, D=R, and T=C.

Trace of Steps for N=3, Tower of Hanoi

	Level	**Step**	**N**	**Effect of step**
1.	1	1	3	Invoke N=2 case with S=L, D=C, T=R
2.	2	1	2	Invoke N=1 case with S=L, D=R, T=C
3.	3	1	1	Nothing
4.	3	2	1	Move disk L→R
5.	3	3	1	Nothing. Finish N=1
6.	2	2	2	Move disk L→C
7.	2	3	2	Invoke N=1 case with S=R, D=C, T=L
8.	3	1	1	Nothing
9.	3	2	1	Move disk R→C
10.	3	3	1	Nothing. Finish N=1
				Finish N=2
11.	1	2	3	Move disk L→R
12.	1	3	3	Invoke N=2 case with S=C, D=R, T=L
13.	2	1	2	Invoke N=1 case with S=C, D=L, T=R
14.	3	1	1	Nothing
15.	3	2	1	Move disk C→L
16.	3	3	1	Nothing. Finish N=1
17.	2	2	2	Move disk C→R
18.	2	3	2	Invoke N=1 case with S=L, D=R, T=C
19.	3	1	1	Nothing
20.	3	2	1	Move disk L→R
21.	3	3	1	Nothing. Finish N=1
				Finish N=2
				Finish N=3.

Although you may find this example confusing at first, it is well worth studying. Carefully follow the meaning of each step of the algorithm. You may find it helpful to draw a picture of the state of the disks at each step, or you may even want to build a simple model of a Tower of Hanoi and carry out the algorithm.

Exercise   5.12: (for mathematically minded students): (a) It takes one move (of a disk) to solve the Tower of Hanoi problem in the case $N=1$. It takes three moves in the case $N=2$, and seven moves in the case $N=3$. How many moves will it take in the case $N=4$? $N=5$? In general? (b) (For students who know the method of proof by mathematical induction): Prove your answer to part (a).   ∎

Note: We provide no summary for this chapter because the material it covers is illustrative rather than expository. Most of the ideas have been developed in earlier chapters.

CHAPTER 6

Anyone who does computer programming should master certain fundamental algorithms. These algorithms act as building blocks for more complex algorithms. Although the details of implementation differ from one programming language to another, these algorithms describe the basic procedures that computers are often asked to perform: switching, counting, accumulating, calculating, determining a minimum or maximum value, creating a list, searching a list, sorting a list, and merging two lists into one. In this chapter, we will discuss the first five fundamental algorithms. In Chapter 7, we will discuss other fundamental algorithms dealing with lists of data.

6.1 SWITCHING

Suppose we have two pieces of paper labeled *number1* and *number2*.[1] Suppose further that the value 10 is written on *number1* and that the value 20 is written on *number2.* We would like to switch the values. We need an algorithm that leaves the value 20 on *number1* and the value 10 on *number2.*

We must write an algorithm that simulates the switching of two values stored in a computer's memory. When a person is asked to switch two values, he or she seems to switch the two values simultaneously. But two actions cannot occur simultaneously in a computer. Hence, we must list the steps to be performed and put them in the proper sequence.

Consider the two pieces of paper shown in Figure 6.1. If we replace the value

---

1. When we refer to a value written on a labeled piece of paper, we will use the label written on the paper to identify it. Thus, instead of saying, "the value on the paper labeled *number1,*" we will say, "the value on *number1.*"

SOME FUNDAMENTAL ALGORITHMS

Figure 6.1   **The two pieces of paper as given**

Figure 6.2   **Value on *number2* replaced**

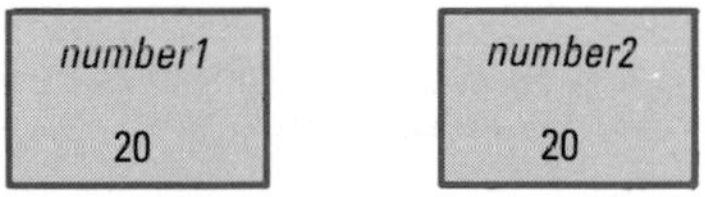

on *number1* with the value on *number2*, our papers appear as shown in Figure 6.2. We have lost the value 10, and we cannot write an instruction to retrieve it.

Exercise 6.1: Begin with the value 10 on *number1* and the value 20 on *number2*. What is the result of replacing the value on *number2* with the value on *number1*? ■

Simply replacing the value on one paper with the value on the other will not work. A value is lost. We need a third piece of paper to act as an intermediate holding place.

Let's label a third piece of paper *hold.* We can then copy the value on *number1* onto *hold.* The three pieces of paper appear as shown in Figure 6.3. Now we can replace the value on *number1* with the value on *number2,* leaving the three pieces of paper appearing as shown in Figure 6.4. We complete the switching process by replacing the value on *number2* with the value on *hold* as shown in Figure 6.5. Given two pieces of paper labeled *number1* and *number2,* the algorithm in Figure 6.6 switches the values written on those papers.

Exercise   6.2: (a) Write down all of the possible rearrangements of the instructions I, II, and III of the algorithm in Figure 6.6. (b) Trace the effects of each of the rearrangements of instructions determined in part a. Which rearrangements are impossible to perform? Which rearrangements are possible to perform, but do not switch the values?   ■

Figure 6.3   **After the value on *number1* is copied onto *hold***

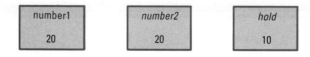

Figure 6.4   **After the value on *number1* is replaced by the value on *number2***

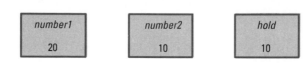

Figure 6.5   **After the switch is complete**

Figure 6.6 **Algorithm for switching two values**

Setup

    I. Label a piece of paper *hold.*

Instructions

    I. Copy the value on *number1* onto *hold.*

    II. Replace the value on *number1* with the value on *number2.*

    III. Replace the value on *number2* with the value on *hold.*

Note that we introduce each of the algorithms of counting, accumulating, calculating, and determining a maximum or minimum value in a concrete setting. The setting is not an integral part of the algorithm. It is merely meant to suggest how the algorithms can be implemented in a particular situation. Ultimately, you should be able to adapt each fundamental algorithm to the specific problem at hand.

6.2 COUNTING

Assume that you have to count the number of people who come to a dance. People are allowed to enter until your co-worker, who has been assigned the duty of picking up the collected entrance fees, arrives. You need an algorithm to determine an accurate count of the people who attend. There are 0 participants when the dance begins. While your co-worker has not yet arrived, you permit each person to enter and add 1 to the current number of participants to get the new number of participants.

Begin with two pieces of paper, one labeled **participants** and the other labeled **co-worker present.** Write the value 0 on **participants** and the value *false* on **co-worker present.** Wait for the first person to arrive. If the person is your co-worker, change the value on **co-worker present** to *true.* As long as the value on **co-worker present** is *false,* perform the following set of steps:

In your mind add 1 to the value on **participants.** Cross out the value on **participants** and replace it with the value you just calculated. Wait for the

Figure 6.7   **Counting algorithm**

Setup

I. Label a piece of paper *participants.*

II. Label a piece of paper *co-worker present.*

Instructions

I. Write the value 0 on *participants.*

II. Write the value false on *co-worker present.*

III. Wait for the first person to arrive.

IV. If the first person is your co-worker,
   then
      A. Change the value on *co-worker present* to true.

V. While the value on *co-worker present* is false, do the following:
   A. Look at the value on *participants.* In your mind, add 1 to the value on *participants.* Cross out the value on *participants* and write the value you just calculated on *participants.*
   B. Wait for the next person to arrive.
   C. If the person is your co-worker,
      then
         i. Change the value on *co-worker present* to true.

VI. Announce the value on *participants* to your co-worker.

next person to arrive. If the person is your co-worker, change the value on **co-worker present** to *true.*

Finally, you can announce the number of participants at the dance to your co-worker. Figure 6.7 formally displays our algorithm. Figure 6.8 shows a tracing form for the counting algorithm in Figure 6.7, assuming that the third person to arrive is your co-worker.

Exercise   6.3: Construct the tracing form for the algorithm in Figure 6.7 in the circumstance that your co-worker is the first to arrive.   ■

Exercise   6.4: Adapt the model of the counting algorithm given above to the following situation and rewrite the algorithm. You are given a jar full of

Figure 6.8 **Tracing form for counting algorithm**

Instructions	Conditional expression	Memory		Output
		participants	*co-worker present*	
I.		0	?	
II.		0	false	
III.		0	false	
IV.	F	0	false	
V.	T	0	false	
V.A		1	false	
V.B		1	false	
V.C	F	1	false	
V.	T	1	false	
V.A		2	false	
V.B		2	false	
V.C	T	2	false	
V.C.i.		2	true	
V.	F	2	true	
VI.		2	true	2

jelly beans. Determine the number of jelly beans in the jar. This problem should be a bit easier, since it has no constraint involving the presence of another person. You will, however, need to determine what condition will end the counting process. ■

6.3 ACCUMULATING

Let's change the scene now to a dance that is being given for the benefit of a local charity. Each person is asked to make a donation as she or he enters the auditorium, but no fixed donation is specified. Again, the arrival of your co-worker will signal you to stop admitting people. Your job is to keep a running total of the amount of money donated.

There are two kinds of input for this problem. The first kind is the amount of each person's donation. The second is your recognition of whether or not the person who arrives is your co-worker. The output is the total of the donations. A constraint is that no one will be admitted after your co-worker arrives.

This is a problem of accumulating. The algorithm for accumulating is similar to the algorithm for counting. You begin with 0 dollars. Each time a person arrives, you check to see if she or he is your co-worker. If not, you collect the person's donation and add the amount of that person's donation to the current total to get the updated total. Figure 6.9 gives a formal version of the algorithm. For example, suppose the first six people to arrive give donations of $10.00, $7.00, $3.50, $5.00, $10.00, $2.00. The piece of paper labeled *total* should appear as in Figure 6.10.

Figure 6.9   Accumulating algorithm

Setup

   I. Label a piece of paper *new donations*.

  II. Label a piece of paper *total*.

 III. Label a piece of paper *co-worker present*.

Instructions

    I. Write the value 0 on *total*.

   II. Write the value false on *co-worker present*.

  III. Wait for the first person to arrive.

  IV. If the first person is your co-worker,
       then
          A. Change the value on *co-worker present* to true.

   V. While the value on *co-worker present* is false, do the following:
      A. Ask for the person's donation.
      B. Record the amount of the person's donation on *new donation*.
      C. Look at the number on *total*. In your mind, add the value on *new donation* to the number on total. Cross out the value on *total* and write the value you just calculated on *total*.
      D. Wait for the next person to arrive.
      E. If the person is your co-worker,
         then
            i. Change the value on *co-worker present* to true.

  VI. Announce the value on *total* to your co-worker.

Figure 6.10 **Piece of paper labeled *total* after execution of algorithm**

Exercise 6.5: Assume that your co-worker is the third person to arrive and that the first two people give donations of $15.00 and $20.00. Construct the tracing form for the accumulating algorithm in Figure 6.9. ■

Exercise 6.6: How does the accumulating algorithm differ from the counting algorithm? ■

6.4 CALCULATING

When the benefit dance is over, someone asks you for the amount of the average donation. If you used the accumulating algorithm, the paper labeled ***total*** will give you the final total, but to calculate the average donation you also need to know how many people attended the dance. With those two figures, you could simply divide the total donations by the number of attendees and get the average donation. But you haven't been counting the people as they arrived. You will apparently have to use the algorithm for counting. Let's work through the complete solution of this problem.

The inputs for this problem are the same as the inputs for the accumulating problem. The output is the amount of the average donation. The constraint once again is that participants are allowed to enter only until your co-worker arrives.

You might be tempted at first to sketch out the algorithm as shown in Figure 6.11.

Figure 6.11   Possible algorithm for averaging

I. Determine the total of all donations.

II. Determine the number of participants.

III. Divide the total of all donations by the number of participants to get the average donation.

IV. Announce the average donation to your co-worker.

When you try to implement this algorithm, however, you soon uncover a bug. How can you count the number of participants if you wait until after you have calculated the total amount of the donations? All the people will have entered the auditorium. In fact, some of them may have left before the last donation is made. The bug is one of sequencing. You cannot accomplish your task by following the steps in the order given in Figure 6.11.

You can fix this bug by rewriting the algorithm in a way that will enable you to keep a running total of the donations and to count the participants simultaneously. The revised algorithm appears in Figure 6.12. A refinement of the revised algorithm is shown in Figure 6.13. If we use the same six people as in our previous example, two of our pieces of paper would look like those shown in Figure 6.14. If those were the only people to come to the dance, the average donation would be $37.50/6 or $6.25.

Exercise   6.7: Suppose four more people come to the dance and give donations of $5.00, $2.50, $10.00, and $6.00. Continue the diagrams in Figure 6.14 and calculate the average donation for a total of ten people.   ■

Figure 6.12   Revised averaging algorithm

I. Simultaneously determine the total of all donations and the number of participants.

II. Divide the total of all donations by the number of participants to get the average donation.

III. Announce the average donation to your co-worker.

Figure 6.13   Averaging algorithm

Setup

I. Label a piece of paper *donations.*

II. Label a piece of paper *new donation.*

III. Label a piece of paper *co-worker present.*

IV. Label a piece of paper *people.*

Instructions

I. Write the value 0 on *people.*

II. Write the value 0 on *donations.*

III. Write the value false on *co-worker present.*

IV. Wait for the first person to arrive.

V. If the first person is your co-worker,
  then
    A. Change the value on *co-worker present* to true.

VI. While the value on *co-worker present* is false, do the following:
    A. In your mind add 1 to the number on *people.* Cross out the number on *people* and write the value you just determined on *people.*
    B. Ask for the person's donation.
    C. Record the amount of the person's donation on *new donation.*
    D. Look at the number on *donations.* In your mind, add the value on *new donation* to the number on *donations.* Cross out the value on *donations* and write the value you just calculated on *donations.*
    E. Wait for the next person to arrive.
    F. If the person is your co-worker,
      then
        i. Change the value on *co-worker present* to true.

VII. Divide the value on *donations* by the value on *people* to get the average donation and announce that value to your co-worker.

Exercise 6.8: Assume that three people giving donations of $10.00, $17.00, and $20.50 arrive before your co-worker. Construct a tracing form for the algorithm in Figure 6.13 in this situation. ■

Figure 6.14   Pieces of paper after execution of averaging algorithm

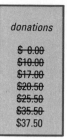

6.5 DETERMINING A MAXIMUM OR A MINIMUM VALUE

Now that you have calculated the average donation, someone else comes up to you and asks, "What was the maximum donation?" One algorithm for solving this problem is the following: When the first donation is given, its value is obviously the largest up to that time. When the second donation is given, its value must be compared to that of the first donation. The larger of the two is then the maximum donation. When the third donation is given, its value must be compared to that of the larger of the first two donations to determine the largest donation given so far. Each successive donation must be compared to the value of the largest of the preceding donations to determine the largest up to and including the current donation. When the comparison is performed for the last donation, the largest of all the donations is determined.

The inputs for this problem are the same as those for the average donation problem. The constraint is also the same. The output, however, is the amount of the largest donation. We can write this algorithm formally as in Figure 6.15.

Exercise 6.9: How would you modify the algorithm in Figure 6.15 to determine the minimum donation?   ■

Exercise 6.10: Assume that three people giving donations of $10.00, $20.00, and $15.00 arrive before your co-worker. Construct a tracing form for the algorithm in Figure 6.15 in this situation.   ■

Figure 6.15 **Algorithm to determine a maximum value**

Setup

   I. Label a piece of paper *largest.*

  II. Label a piece of paper *co-worker present.*

 III. Label a piece of paper *current donation.*

Instructions

   I. Write the value false on *co-worker present.*

  II. Wait for the first person to arrive.

 III. If the first person is your co-worker,
     then
       A. Announce that there have been no donations.
     else
      A'. Ask for the amount of the person's donation.
      B'. Record the person's response on *largest.*
      C'. While the value on *co-worker present* is false, do the following:
        1. Wait for a person to arrive.
        2. If the person is your co-worker
          then
            a. Change the value on *co-worker present* to true.
          else
           a'. Ask for the amount of the person's donation.
           b'. Record the response on *current donation,* replacing
             any previous value if one exists.
           c'. If the value on *current donation* is larger than the
             value on *largest,*
              then
                i. Cross out the value on *largest* and replace it
                  with the value on *current donation.*
      D'. Announce the value on *largest* to your co-worker.

CHAPTER SUMMARY

In this chapter we have discussed five algorithms that are often used as basic building blocks in computer algorithms: switching, counting, accumulating, calculating, and determining a maximum or a minimum value of a collection of data items.

You will find these algorithms quite useful when you attempt to solve the programming problems posed in Part II of this book.

SUPPLEMENTAL PROBLEMS

1. We wish to calculate the average weight of a single jelly bean in a jar of jelly beans.
   a. What are the inputs, outputs, and constraints of this problem?
   b. Write an algorithm to solve this problem for a jar of 500 jelly beans.
   c. Write an algorithm to solve this problem for a jar containing an unknown number of jelly beans.

2. Suppose that a jar contains some blue marbles, some red marbles, some white marbles, and some black marbles. We would like to calculate the number of marbles of each possible color and the percentage of marbles of each possible color.
   a. What are the inputs, outputs, and constraints of this problem?
   b. Write an algorithm to solve this problem.

3. Suppose that a teacher gives an exam. The range of possible scores is 0 through 100. The number of students taking the exam is unknown. We would like to know the average score on the exam.
   a. What are the inputs, outputs, and constraints of this problem?
   b. Write an algorithm to solve this problem.

4. We wish to calculate the average height of all of the participants at the dance described in Section 6.2.
   a. What are the inputs, outputs, and constraints of this problem?
   b. Write an algorithm to solve this problem.

*5. Write an algorithm to determine the minimum of three numbers without using an iterative construct.

*6. You are taking coffee orders for a group of 50 people. The coffee can be served black or with cream and/or sugar.
   a. Determine all possible ways in which the coffee can be served.
   b. Write an algorithm to calculate the number of people who have ordered coffee in each possible way.

*7. A standard piano has 88 different keys. You are given the sheet music for a certain composition. You wish to calculate the number of times each of the 88 keys would need to be pressed in order to play the composition. (You may want to write this algorithm informally because it requires 88 pieces of paper to keep track of the 88 possible key values.)
   a. What are the inputs, outputs, and constraints of this problem?
   b. Write an algorithm to solve this problem.

*8. Assume that you are collecting donations at a dance. You would like to calculate the average donation of all those people who arrive before 7:30 P.M. and the average donation of all of those people who arrive after 7:30 P.M. and before your co-worker arrives.

a. What are the inputs, outputs, and constraints of this problem?

b. Write an algorithm to solve this problem.

*9. The following formula gives what is called the *variance* of a set of data values, x_i's, where m is the average of the x_i's.

$$\frac{1}{n-1} \sum_{i=1}^{n} (x_i - m)^2$$

Which of the fundamental algorithms are needed to calculate the variance of a set of data values? How would you use those fundamental algorithms?

*10. Consider 10 classes of students. Each class contains 30 students. Each student has received grades in six subjects. We want to determine the class in which the average grade of the 5 best students is highest. Which of the fundamental algorithms are needed to solve this problem? When and to what data are those algorithms applied?

C H A P T E R

7

The fundamental algorithms discussed in Chapter 6 dealt with input data in a common way. Each piece of input data was manipulated and then became unimportant to the further workings of the algorithm. There are, however, a vast variety of computer programming problems that require each piece of data to be available to the algorithm until all of its steps have been completed. In those cases, one typical way to think of the collection of data items is in a list format. Hence, there are some fundamental programming algorithms that deal with lists of data items.

In this chapter, we discuss some of the fundamental algorithms used in conjunction with limited-size lists. We will first need to discuss the algorithm for creating a limited-size list. Then we will be able to discuss the algorithms for searching a list, sorting a list, and merging two lists into one list.

7.1 CREATING A LIST

Suppose that a friend of ours is planning a New Year's Eve party and wants us to create a list of at most 50 guests.

The algorithm for creating a list of limited size is a bit complicated. We must find a way of keeping track of the number of names on the list so that we can keep within the specified maximum of 50.

The inputs for this problem are the names of the guests. The output is the guest list. The constraint is that the number of names not exceed 50.

As each successive name comes to mind, we will add it to the bottom of the list and assign it a number. We must always know how many names are on the list to make sure that we don't exceed 50 names. Remember that to implement this algorithm, we need to describe all the steps to be performed so that eventually we will be able to write a complete set of instructions for a computer to follow. Figure 7.1 gives those instructions.

FUNDAMENTAL ALGORITHMS THAT INVOLVE LISTS

Figure 7.1   **Algorithm to create a limited-size list**

Setup

I. Label a piece of paper *Guest List* on top and write the numbers from 1 to 50 leaving a space next to each number for a name.

II. Label a piece of paper *Number of Guests.*

III. Label a piece of paper *another name to add.*

Instructions

I. Write the value 0 on *Number of Guests.*

II. Ask your friend if there is another name to put on the list.

III. Record the response on *another name to add.*

IV. While the value on *another name to add* is yes and the value on *Number of Guests* is less than 50:
     A. Look at the value on *Number of Guests.* In your mind, add 1 to that number. Cross out the value on *Number of Guests.* Write down the value you just calculated on *Number of Guests.*
     B. Ask your friend what name she or he would like to add to the list.
     C. Record your friend's response on *Guest List* next to the number indicated by *Number of Guests.*
     D. Ask your friend if there is another name to add to the list.
     E. Record your friend's response on *another name to add.*

V. Give the *Guest List* to your friend.

Note that step IV in Figure 7.1 will not be performed if 50 names were already on the list. We would probably want to have some sort of plan to handle the possibility of an error condition of more than 50 names to enter on the list. Remember that the condition in step IV is checked before we perform steps IV.A– IV.E the first time and then always after step IV.E is completed.

Exercise 7.1: Adapt the algorithm in Figure 7.1 to solve the following problem: A friend has asked you to do his grocery shopping for him. You will of course need a list. Write an algorithm to create the needed grocery list. ■

Exercise 7.2: Write a general algorithm for creating a list of limited size based on the algorithm in Figure 7.1. Here are some suggested substitutions to make your work easy!

Substitute	For
maximum allowed in list⟶	50
list ⟶	*Guest List*
item ⟶	*name*
items ⟶	*Guests* ■

7.2 SEARCHING A LIST OF LIMITED SIZE

Now our friend comes back to us and asks us to check to see if a particular name appears on the guest list. We must search through the list to see if the name is there. Since the names on the list appear in no particular order, we will have to start from the top and search through the names one by one until we find the particular name or until we have searched through all the names on the list.

In searching a list of limited size, the value on the piece of paper labeled *Number of Guests* plays an important role. We will refer to the individual items on the list by their position. In searching the list, we begin in the first position. We compare the name we are searching for with each name on the list until we either find a match or run out of names. We will know that we have run out of names when the next position to be checked is greater than the value on *Number of Guests.*

Now suppose we have our limited list in hand and the piece of paper labeled *Number of Guests.* Figure 7.2 gives the algorithm for the search procedure.

Figure 7.2   **Algorithm to search an unordered, limited-size list**

Setup

  I. Label a piece of paper *Found Desired Name.*

  II. Label a piece of paper *Position of the Name Being Checked.*

  III. Label a piece of paper *Desired Name.*

Instructions

  I. Write the value false on *Found Desired Name.*

  II. Write the value 1 on *Position of the Name Being Checked.*

  III. Write the name we are searching for on *Desired Name.*

  IV. While the value on *Found Desired Name* is false and the value on *Position of the Name Being Checked* is less than or equal to the value on *Number of Guests,* do the following:

    A. If the name on the *Guest List* in the position indicated by *Position of the Name Being Checked* is the same as the name on *Desired Name,*
      then
        1. Change the value on *Found Desired Name* to true.
      else
        1'. Look at the value on *Position of the Name Being Checked.* Add one to that value. Cross out the value on *Position of the Name Being Checked.* Write down the value you just calculated on *Position of the Name Being Checked.*

  V. If the value on *Found Desired Name* is true,
    then
      A. Announce that the *Desired Name* appears on the guest list.
    else
      A'. Announce that the *Desired Name* does not appear on the guest list.

Exercise 7.3: Suppose that you are given a guest list. Suppose also that you are asked to determine the position on the list of the name that is first among all of the names in alphabetical order. Searching the list for that name is analogous to finding the smallest or minimum value on the list. Recall the algorithm for determining a maximum or a minimum value, discussed without reference to list structures in Chapter 6 (pages 128–129). Write an algorithm to determine the position on the list of the name that is first in alphabetical order. When your algorithm is complete, the position it determined should be written on a piece of paper labeled *Position of Desired Name.* ■

If the guest list had 1,000,000 names instead of just 100, it could take a long time to search for a specific name. We could save time if we had a list that was in alphabetical order. Such a list is called an ordered list.
We can restate the task as follows:

Given a limited-size list of names in alphabetical order, determine whether a particular name appears on the list.

In searching an ordered list, we can be more efficient than we were in searching an unordered list. By *more efficient,* we mean that we can decide more quickly whether the desired name appears on the list. This is true because we can determine the fact that a name is not on the list when we compare it to a name that is after it in alphabetical order.

Exercise 7.4: The formal algorithm for searching an ordered, limited-size list is quite similar to the algorithm displayed in Figure 7.2. Revise that algorithm to take advantage of the fact that you can detect that the desired name does not appear on the list when the name being checked is after the desired name in alphabetical order. Do so by adding another condition to the **while** structure of the algorithm in Figure 7.2. ■

Exercise 7.5: Assume that a name consists of a last name, a first name, and a middle initial. Given two such names denoted by *Name #1* and *Name #2,* the task of determining if *Name #1* is before *Name #2* in alphabetical order requires careful attention. For example, if the last names are identical, the first names must be compared. If the last and first names are identical, the middle initials must be compared. Begin with two pieces of paper labeled *Name #1* and *Name #2* and a third piece of paper labeled *Before.* Write an algorithm that leaves the value *true* on the paper labeled *Before* if *Name #1* is before *Name #2* in alphabetical order and leaves the value *false* otherwise. This algorithm can be considered as a subalgorithm for the algorithm you wrote for Exercise 7.4. ■

We can be even more efficient in searching an ordered, limited-size list. In compensation for being able to reach a decision more quickly, we will find that the algorithm is a bit more complicated. This search does not consist of just a sequential check through the names in the list. To give you a more concrete example of how this algorithm works, we'll digress for a moment and look at the familiar problem of finding a specific word in a dictionary.

If you wanted to look up the word *programming* in a dictionary, you would not begin on the first page with *a* and search through every word until you reached the word *programming*. Instead, you would probably flip open the dictionary in the middle, say in the *m*'s and then decide to continue looking between the *m*'s and the *z*'s. By making that decision you have narrowed your search to half of the original list. You now flip to somewhere between the *m*'s and the *z*'s, say to the *r*'s. Since *p* is between *m* and *r,* you have now narrowed your search to a quarter of the original list after only two decisions. One more iteration of this procedure will narrow the search to one-eighth of the original list. (For the mathematically minded, note that we need to search through $(1/2^n)$th of the original list after *n* decisions.) You repeat this process until you finally find *programming*.

Let's apply this algorithm to our guest list, making it more precise. Remember that we have a piece of paper showing the **Number of Guests** on the list. We need to keep track of that part of the list to which we have narrowed our search. To do so, we need three more pieces of paper labeled **Start Search Position,** **End Search Position,** and **Middle Position.** The values on these three pieces of paper will change as we narrow down the search area.

At each stage we will need to determine a middle position to divide the search area in half. If there is an odd number of names in the search area, the middle position will be apparent. For instance, if there are seven names in the search area, the fourth name is in the middle position. An even number of names in the search area, however, will not have a single middle position. For example, if there are eight names in the search area, no single name is in the middle position. We need to choose one of the two names that are in the middle positions. Let's agree to choose the one closer to the beginning of the list. In other words, if there are eight names, we will choose the fourth one as the middle name. We can calculate the position of the middle name as follows: Add together the first and last positions $(1 + 8 \rightarrow 9)$. Divide by two $(9/2 \rightarrow 4.5)$. Round down if necessary $(4.5 \rightarrow 4)$. (Note that if the list has an odd number of names, rounding down will not be necessary.)

We then compare the name in the fourth position to the name for which we are searching. Suppose the name in the fourth position is before the name for which we are searching. We can then narrow our search area to positions 5 through 8. To calculate the middle position in this search area, follow the algorithm described above: Add together the first and last positions $(5 + 8 \rightarrow 13)$. Divide by two $(13/2 \rightarrow 6.5)$. Round down if necessary $(6.5 \rightarrow 6)$. Our calculation determines that we should compare the name in the sixth position with the name for which we are searching.

Exercise   7.6: Show the steps of the calculation to determine the middle position for a list of 11 names.   ■

Let's see how these calculations work in a specific example. We will trace through two examples of a search for the name *Carol Lennox* in a list of 20 names. The first list contains the name *Carol Lennox* and the second list does not. In searching the first list we expect our algorithm to end when we encounter the name *Carol Lennox*. In processing the second list, we need to determine a condition that assures us that the name does not appear on the list.

Figure 7.3 gives the first list of 20 names in alphabetical order. Since we must assume at the outset that we will have to search the entire list, we begin by writing the value 1 on the paper labeled **Start Search Position** and the value 20 on the paper labeled **End Search Position,** as shown in Figure 7.4. We begin narrowing down the search area by calculating the position of the middle name on our list of 20 and writing its value on the paper labeled **Middle Position** as shown in Figure 7.5.

Since we know that the name *Carol Lennox* must appear before the name *Jan MacDonald* if it appears on the list at all, we narrow the search to the part of the list before *Jan MacDonald.* So we change the value of **End Search Position** to 9, because the ninth name is the last one that could possibly be *Carol Lennox.* We then proceed to calculate a new **Middle Position,** as shown in Figure 7.6.

Since the name *Carol Lennox* must appear after the name *Evalyn Clark* if it appears at all, we narrow our search to the part of the current search area after *Evalyn Clark.* So we change the value of **Start Search Position** to 6. We then proceed to calculate a new **Middle Position,** as shown in Figure 7.7.

Figure 7.3   **An alphabetically ordered list of 20 names**

1. Linda Acosta
2. Elizabeth Baggan
3. Richard Bassein
4. Mildred Campbell
5. Evalyn Clark
6. Dennis Hansen
7. Kinley Karlsen
8. Carol Lennox
9. Barbara LiSanti
10. Jan MacDonald
11. Lydia Mann
12. Diane McEntyre
13. Marilyn Meikle
14. Janet Muther
15. Michele Pawlicki
16. Diane Resek
17. Nancy Roberts
18. Amy Sands
19. Elizabeth Stage
20. Fred Zlotnick

Figure 7.4   **Initial values of *Start Search Position* and *End Search Position***

Start Search Position 1	Middle Position ?	End Search Position 20

Figure 7.5   **After the first calculation of *Middle Position*. The names that correspond to these positions are 1. Linda Acosta, 10. Jan MacDonald, and 20. Fred Zlotnick.**

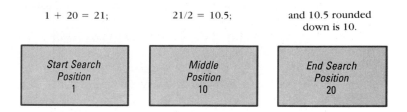

$$1 + 20 = 21; \qquad 21/2 = 10.5; \qquad \text{and 10.5 rounded down is 10.}$$

| Start Search Position 1 | Middle Position 10 | End Search Position 20 |

Figure 7.6   **After the second calculation of *Middle Position*. The names that correspond to these positions are 1. Linda Acosta, 5. Evalyn Clark, and 9. Barbara LiSanti.**

$$1 + 9 = 10; \text{ and } 10/2 = 5.$$

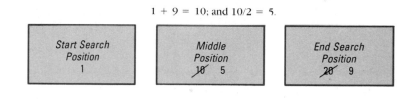

| Start Search Position 1 | Middle Position ~~10~~ 5 | End Search Position ~~20~~ 9 |

Figure 7.7   **After the third calculation of *Middle Position*. The names that correspond to these positions are 6. Dennis Hansen, 7. Kinley Karlsen, and 9. Barbara LiSanti.**

$$6 + 9 = 15; \qquad 15/2 = 7.5; \qquad \text{and 7.5 rounded down is 7.}$$

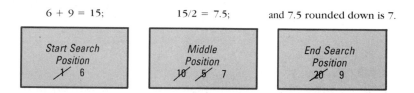

| Start Search Position ~~1~~ 6 | Middle Position ~~10~~ ~~5~~ 7 | End Search Position ~~20~~ 9 |

The name *Carol Lennox* must now appear after the name *Kinley Karlsen* if it appears on the list at all. So we change the value of **Start Search Position** to 8. We calculate a new value for **Middle Position,** as shown in Figure 7.8.

It may seem a bit magical, but we've found *Carol Lennox.* Her name appears in the middle position!

Figure 7.8

After the fourth calculation of *Middle Position.* The names that correspond to these positions are 8. Carol Lennox, 8. Carol Lennox, and 9. Barbara LiSanti.

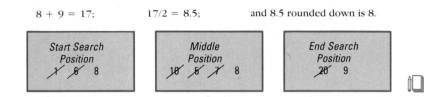

$8 + 9 = 17;$ $\qquad$ $17/2 = 8.5;$ $\qquad$ and 8.5 rounded down is 8.

We have just completed a trace in a situation in which the name we are looking for appears on the list. Now we will trace our searching process in a situation in which the name we are looking for does not appear on the list.

Let's search for the name *Carol Lennox* in a list that does not contain that name. We alter the original list of 20 people by substituting the name *Lisa Lemon* for the name *Carol Lennox* in the eighth position. Our algorithm would have proceeded as we have already traced, but now leaving us with the substitution of *Lisa Lemon* for *Carol Lennox* as shown in Figure 7.9.

To continue our search, we change the value of **Start Search Position** to 9, since the name *Carol Lennox* must appear after *Lisa Lemon* if it appears at all.

Figure 7.9

After the fourth calculation of *Middle Position* in revised list. The names that correspond to these positions are 8. Lisa Lemon, 8. Lisa Lemon, and 9. Barbara LiSanti.

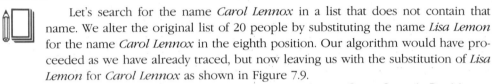

Figure 7.10

After the fifth calculation of *Middle Position* in revised list. The names that correspond to these positions are 9. Barbara LiSanti, 9. Barbara LiSanti, and 9. Barbara LiSanti.

$9 + 10 = 19;$ $\qquad$ $19/2 = 9.5;$ $\qquad$ and 9.5 rounded down is 9.

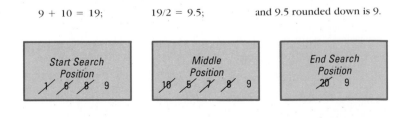

The calculation of our new **Middle Position** is shown in Figure 7.10. Since the name *Carol Lennox* must appear before the name *Barbara LiSanti,* we should change the value of **End Search Position** to 8. But notice that we now have the value of **Start Search Position** equal to 9 and the value of **End Search Position** equal to 8. This is impossible since the **Start** is beyond the **End.** This condition allows us to conclude that the name *Carol Lennox* does not appear on the list.

The complete algorithm is displayed in Figure 7.11. Notice that it is the most complicated of the fundamental algorithms we have explored so far.

The algorithm we have just described is an application of a general algorithm called *binary search.* It is called a binary[1] search because the search area is split into two segments in each step.

Exercise 7.7: Suppose when we averaged the values of **Start Search Position** and **End Search Position,** we rounded up to a whole number if necessary instead of rounding down. Trace the search through the original list with this modification. ∎

Exercise 7.8: Suppose that you are given the following ordered list of names:

1. Linda Acosta
2. Elizabeth Baggan
3. Richard Bassein
4. Mildred Campbell
5. Evalyn Clark
6. Barbara LiSanti
7. Lydia Mann
8. Diane McEntyre
9. Amy Sands
10. Fred Zlotnick

Create a tracing form for each of the following situations:

1. Using the algorithm you wrote to search an ordered, limited-size list (Exercise 7.4):
   a. Search for the name *Linda Acosta.*
   b. Search for the name *Diane McEntyre.*   *(continued on page 143)*

---

1. *Webster's Ninth New Collegiate Dictionary* defines *binary* as "consisting of two things or parts."

Figure 7.11   More efficient algorithm to search an ordered, limited-size list

Setup

I. Label a piece of paper *Start Search Position.*

II. Label a piece of paper *End Search Position.*

III. Label a piece of paper *Middle Position.*

IV. Label a piece of paper *Found Desired Name.*

Instructions

I. Write the value 1 on *Start Search Position.*

II. Copy the value already written on *Number of Guests* onto *End Search Position.*

III. Write the value false on *Found Desired Name.*

IV. Repeat the following steps until either the value on *Found Desired Name* is true or the value on *Start Search Position* is greater than the value on *End Search Position:*
   A. Use the subalgorithm displayed below to calculate the new value for *Middle Position.*
   B. If the name on *Guest List* in the position indicated by *Middle Position* is the same as the *Desired Name,*
      then
         1. Change the value on *Found Desired Name* to true.
      else
        1'. If the *Desired Name* is alphabetically before the name on *Guest List* in the *Middle Position,*
         then
           a. Change the value on *End Search Position* to 1 less than the value on *Middle Position.*
         else
           a'. Change the value on *Start Search Position* to be 1 more than the value on *Middle Position.*

V. If the value on *Found Desired Name* is true,
      then
       A'. Announce that the *Desired Name* appears on the *Guest List.*
      else
       A'. Announce that the *Desired Name* does not appear on the *Guest List.*

Subalgorithm to calculate *Middle Position*

I. Add together the values on *Start Search Position* and *End Search Position*.

II. Divide the result of step I by 2.

III. If the result of step II is not a whole number,
    then
       A. Round it down to the nearest whole number.

IV. Replace the value on *Middle Position* (if one exists) with the result of step III.

        c. Search for the name *Fred Zlotnick*.
        d. Search for the name *Carol Lennox*.

2. Using the binary search algorithm shown in Figure 7.11:
   a. Search for the name *Linda Acosta*.
   b. Search for the name *Diane McEntyre*.
   c. Search for the name *Fred Zlotnick*.
   d. Search for the name *Carol Lennox*.   ∎

Exercise   7.9: Count the number of algorithm steps performed in each of the situations in Exercise 7.8. Can you draw any conclusions?   ∎

7.3 SORTING A LIST OF LIMITED SIZE

We know that we can more efficiently search through a list if we know that the list is in order. Let's consider the problem of sorting a list of limited size—that is, rearranging the list elements to put them into a specific order.

Assume that we have a piece of paper labeled *Number of Guests* showing us the number of names on our guest list and the guest list itself. It is now our task to sort the list. It is clear that we need to manipulate the names on the list so that none of the names are lost and so that we leave each name in the appropriate position according to alphabetical ordering. We sketch the algorithm in Figure 7.12.

The sketch in Figure 7.12 certainly needs refinement, but first notice that it does a bit of extra work. If we perform the steps of the algorithm for all positions except the last one, then the name in the last position is the name that belongs there. In other words, we need not perform steps I.A and I.B for the last position.

Figure 7.12   **Sketch of sorting algorithm for *Guest List***

I. For each position on the list from the first position through the position numbered with the value on *Number of Guests,* do the following:
   A. Locate the name belonging in that position.
   B. Move the appropriate name into that position if it is not already there.

Figure 7.13   **Modified sketch of sorting algorithm for *Guest List***

I. For each position on the list from the first position through the position numbered 1 less than the value on *Number of Guests,* do the following:
   A. Locate the name belonging in that position.
   B. Move the appropriate name into that position if it is not already there.

Exercise   7.10: Explain why what we have said in the last paragraph is true. ■

We modify the algorithm sketch to take into account that we need not do any work for the last position. The modification is shown in Figure 7.13.

We use a piece of paper labeled ***Position Being Fixed*** to keep track of the position currently under consideration by the algorithm. This allows us to formalize the algorithm sketch as shown in Figure 7.14.

Now we must decide how to do step II.A, **Locate the name that belongs in *Position Being Fixed.*** When the value on ***Position Being Fixed*** is 1, we are locating on the list the name that is first in alphabetical order. We essentially need to locate the smallest element on the list. The subalgorithm required here is the same as the answer to Exercise 7.3.

When the value on ***Position Being Fixed*** is 2, we can ignore the name in position 1 because it is already in its appropriate place. We search through the positions numbered 2 through the value on ***Number of Guests*** to find the name that is second among all the names in alphabetical order. In other words, we locate the smallest list element among the elements in the positions numbered 2 through the value on ***Number of Guests.***

In general, when the value on ***Position Being Fixed*** is n, we can ignore the names in positions 1 through $n - 1$ because they are each already in correct position. We search through positions numbered n through the value on ***Number of Guests*** to find the name that belongs in position n.

Let's assume that step II.A leaves the position of the name that belongs in ***Position Being Fixed*** on a piece of paper labeled ***Position of Desired Name.***

Figure 7.14   **Formalized (but still rough) algorithm for sorting *Guest List***

Setup

I. Label a piece of paper *Position Being Fixed*.

Instructions

I. Write the value 1 on *Position Being Fixed*.

II. While the value on *Position Being Fixed* is less than the value on *Number of Guests,* do the following:
   A. Locate the name that belongs in *Position Being Fixed*.
   B. Move the appropriate name into *Position Being Fixed* if it is not already there.
   C. Replace the value on *Position Being Fixed* with 1 more than its current value.

There are two possible situations. Either the value on *Position Being Fixed* is the same as the value on *Position of Desired Name,* or it is different. If the two values are the same, then the name that belongs in *Position Being Fixed* is already there, and no more needs to be done for that position. If the two values are different, we need to move the name in *Position of Desired Name* to *Position Being Fixed.* Since we do not want to lose the name currently in *Position Being Fixed,* we will just use our fundamental switching algorithm on the names in *Position Being Fixed* and *Position of Desired Name.* Figure 7.15 contains a further refinement of the sorting algorithm.

It remains to refine step II.A. In general, suppose that the value on *Position Being Fixed* is n. How do we search through the positions numbered n through the value on *Number of Guests* to locate the name that is first among those names in alphabetical order? We can begin by guessing that the name in position n is the name we want and write the value n on *Position of Desired Name.* Then, for each position from $n + 1$ through the value on *Number of Guests,* we must compare the name in that position with the name in *Position of Desired Name.* If we find a name that is before the name in *Position of Desired Name,* we should change the value on *Position of Desired Name* to become the position we are currently checking. To keep track of these comparisons, we need another piece of paper labeled *Position Being Checked.* The completed algorithm is shown in Figure 7.16.

Figure 7.15   **Sorting algorithm including refinement of step II.B**

Setup

   I. Label a piece of paper *Position Being Fixed.*

   II. Label a piece of paper *Position of Desired Name.*

Instructions

   I. Write the value 1 on *Position Being Fixed.*

   II. While the value on *Position Being Fixed* is less than the value on *Number of Guests,* do the following:
      A. Locate the name that belongs in *Position Being Fixed* and leave its position number on *Position of Desired Name.*
      B. If the value on *Position Being Fixed* is not equal to the value on *Position of Desired Name,*
         then
           1. Use the fundamental switching algorithm to interchange the names in *Position Being Fixed* and *Position of Desired Name.*
      C. Replace the value on *Position Being Fixed* with 1 more than its current value.

Figure 7.16   **Completely refined algorithm to sort the *Guest List***

Setup

   I. Label a piece of paper *Position Being Fixed.*

   II. Label a piece of paper *Position of Desired Name.*

Instructions

   I. Write the value 1 on *Position Being Fixed.*

   II. While the value on *Position Being Fixed* is less than the value on *Number of Guests,* do the following:
      A. Locate the name that belongs in *Position Being Fixed* and leave its position number on *Position of Desired Name.*
      B. If the value on *Position Being Fixed* is not equal to the value on *Position of Desired Name,*
         then
           1. Use the fundamental switching algorithm to interchange the names in *Position Being Fixed* and *Position of Desired Name.*
      C. Replace the value on *Position Being Fixed* with 1 more than its current value.

Subalgorithm to Locate the Name That Belongs in *Position Being Fixed,* Leaving Its Position on the Paper Labeled *Position of Desired Name*

Setup

I. Label a piece of paper *Position Being Checked.*

Instructions

I. Copy the value on *Position Being Fixed* onto *Position of Desired Name.*

II. Add 1 to the value on *Position Being Fixed* and write the result on *Position Being Checked.*

III. While the value on *Position Being Checked* is less than or equal to the value on *Number of Guests,* do the following:
   A. If the name on the *Guest List* in *Position Being Checked* is alphabetically before the name on the *Guest List* in *Position of Desired Name,* then
      1. Replace the value on *Position of Desired Name* with the value on *Position Being Checked.*
   B. Replace the value on *Position Being Checked* with 1 more than its current value.

Switching Subalgorithm

Setup

I. Label a piece of paper *hold.*

Instructions

I. Copy the name on the *Guest List* in *Position Being Checked* onto *hold.*

II. Replace the name on the *Guest List* in *Position Being Checked* with the name on the *Guest List* in *Position of Desired Name.*

III. Replace the name on the *Guest List* in *Position of Desired Name* with the name on *hold.*

Let's illustrate this sorting process, sometimes called a *selection sort,* with an example. We will begin with the short list of five names shown in Figure 7.17. Figure 7.18 shows a partial tracing form for our algorithm working on the list shown in Figure 7.17.

Figure 7.17   Sample *Guest List* to sort

```
Guest List
1. Lydia Mann
2. Lisa Lemon
3. Fred Zlotnick
4. Linda Acosta
5. Barbara LiSanti
```

```
Number of Guests
5
```

Figure 7.18   Partial trace of the sorting algorithm shown in Figure 7.16

			Memory		
Instruction	Conditional expression	Number of Guests	Position Being Fixed	Position Desired Name	Position Being Checked
I.		5	1	?	?
II.	T	5	1	?	?
II.A Invoke the subalgorithm to locate the name that belongs in position 1.					
subalg I.		5	1	1	?
subalg II.		5	1	1	2
subalg III.	T	5	1	1	2
subalg III.A	T	5	1	1	2
subalg III.A.1		5	1	2	2
subalg III.B		5	1	2	3
subalg III.	T	5	1	2	3
subalg III.A	F	5	1	2	3
subalg III.B		5	1	2	4
subalg III.	T	5	1	2	4
subalg III.A	T	5	1	2	4
subalg III.A.1		5	1	4	4
subalg III.B		5	1	4	5
subalg III.	T	5	1	4	5
subalg III.A	F	5	1	4	5
subalg III.B		5	1	4	6
subalg III.	F	5	1	4	6

Subalgorithm is complete and has located the name that belongs in position 1. That name is currently in position 4. We return to the main algorithm. Note that the value of *Position Being Checked* becomes unpredictable.

Instruction	Conditional expression	Number of Guests	Memory		
			Position Being Fixed	Position Desired Name	Position Being Checked
II.B	T	5	1	4	?

II.B.1: Invoke the switching subalgorithm.

After the switch is completed the list appears as

    1. Linda Acosta
    2. Lisa Lemon
    3. Fred Zlotnick
    4. Lydia Mann
    5. Barbara LiSanti

We return to the main algorithm.

Instruction	Conditional expression	Number of Guests	Position Being Fixed	Position Desired Name	Position Being Checked
II.C		5	2	4	?
II.	T	5	2	4	?

II.A: Invoke the subalgorithm to locate the name that belongs in position 2.

Instruction	Conditional expression	Number of Guests	Position Being Fixed	Position Desired Name	Position Being Checked
subalg I.		5	2	2	?
subalg II.		5	2	2	3
subalg III.	T	5	2	2	3
subalg III.A	F	5	2	2	3
subalg III.B		5	2	2	4
subalg III.	T	5	2	2	4
subalg III.A	F	5	2	2	4
subalg III.B		5	2	2	5
subalg III.	T	5	2	2	5
subalg III.A	F	5	2	2	5
subalg III.B		5	2	2	6
subalg III.	F	5	2	2	6

Subalgorithm is complete and has located the name that belongs in position 2. That name is currently in position 2. We return to the main algorithm. Note that the value of *Position Being Checked* again is unpredictable.

Instruction	Conditional expression	Number of Guests	Memory		
			Position Being Fixed	Position Desired Name	Position Being Checked
II.B	F	5	2	2	?

Notice that no switching is necessary since the name that is second in alphabetical order is already in position 2. The list remains in the form

    1. Linda Acosta
    2. Lisa Lemon
    3. Fred Zlotnick
    4. Lydia Mann
    5. Barbara LiSanti

We return to the main algorithm.

Exercise 7.11: We have traced the subalgorithm to locate the name that belongs in a particular position in two distinct situations:

1. The name is already in its proper position.

2. The name is not already in its proper position.

Complete our trace of the sorting algorithm. ■

7.4 MERGING LISTS OF LIMITED SIZE

The last fundamental algorithm we are going to discuss is the algorithm for merging two ordered, limited-size lists into a single ordered, limited-size list. As an example, suppose we have created the two lists in Figure 7.19 and we want to combine those two lists into the list shown in Figure 7.20.

We need three pieces of paper labeled *Position in List 1, Position in List 2,* and *Position in Combined List.* We will use *Position in List 1* and *Position in List 2* to keep track of the next name in each list that we consider for placement on the combined list. We must be careful to notice when *Position in List 1* and/ or *Position in List 2* exceed *Number of Guests 1* and/or *Number of Guests 2,* respectively. *Position in Combined List* will indicate the next available space on the combined list.

We compare the name on *Guest List 1* in *Position in List 1* with the name on *Guest List 2* in *Position in List 2.* We place the name that is first in alphabetical order on *Combined List* in *Position in Combined List,* and we increment by 1 the corresponding *Position in List 1* or *Position in List 2.* After we have placed a name on *Combined Guest List,* we increment by 1 *Position in Combined List* to point to the next available position. If, as a result, either *Position in List 1* or *Position in List 2* (or both) becomes greater than *Number of Guests 1* or *Number of Guests 2,* respectively, we adjoin the remainder of the corresponding list to *Combined Guest List.* (No more merging is necessary.)

Figure 7.21 displays an algorithm for the merging of two ordered, limited-size lists.

Figure 7.19   Two ordered, limited-size lists

Guest List 1	Guest List 2
1. Bassein	1. Clark
2. Campbell	2. McEntyre
3. Mann	3. Zlotnick

Number of Guests 1	Number of Guests 2
3	3

Figure 7.20   **Combined list**

```
Combined List
1. Bassein
2. Campbell
3. Clark
4. Mann
5. McEntyre
6. Zlotnick
```

Figure 7.21   **Algorithm to merge two ordered, limited-size lists**

Setup

   I. Label a piece of paper *Position in List 1.*

  II. Label a piece of paper *Position in List 2.*

 III. Label a piece of paper *Position in Combined List.*

Instructions

   I. Write the value 1 on *Position in List 1.*

  II. Write the value 1 on *Position in List 2.*

 III. Write the value 0 on *Position in Combined List.*

 IV. While the value on *Position in List 1* is less than or equal to the value on *Number of Guests 1* and the value on *Position in List 2* is less than or equal to the value on *Number of Guests 2,* do the following:

    A. Replace the value on *Position in Combined List* with 1 more than its current value.

    B. If the name on *Guest List 1* in *Position in List 1* is before or the same as the name on *Guest List 2* in *Position in List 2,*

      then

        1. Put name appearing on *Guest List 1* in *Position in List 1* on *Combined List* in *Position in Combined List.*

        2. Replace the value on *Position in List 1* with 1 more than its current value.

      else

        1'. Put name appearing on *Guest List 2* in *Position in List 2* on *Combined List* in *Position in Combined List.*

        2'. Replace the value on *Position in List 2* with 1 more than its current value.

(continued)

Figure 7.21
Continued

V. While the value on *Position in List 1* is less than or equal to the value on *Number of Guests 1,* do the following:
  A. Replace the value on *Position in Combined List* with 1 more than its current value.
  B. Put the name appearing on *Guest List 1* in *Position in List 1* on *Combined List* in *Position in Combined List.*
  C. Replace the value on *Position in List 1* with 1 more than its current value.

VI. While the value on *Position in List 2* is less than or equal to the value on *Number of Guests 2,* do the following:
  A. Replace the value on *Position in Combined List* with 1 more than its current value.
  B. Put the name appearing on *Guest List 2* in *Position in List 2* on *Combined List* in *Position in Combined List.*
  C. Replace the value on *Position in List 2* with 1 more than its current value.

Let's use a tracing form to step through our example. Figure 7.22 contains all of the relevant information. In this example *P1* represents *Position in List 1*, *P2* represents *Position in List 2,* and *PC* represents *Position in Combined List.*

Exercise   7.12 Create a tracing form similar to the one in Figure 7.22 for the merging of the following two lists:

Guest List 1	*Guest List 2*
1. Elizabeth Baggan	1. Michele Pawlicki
2. Peter Pelican	2. Elizabeth Stage
3. Diane Resek	3. Henry Telfian
	4. Fred Zlotnick

Number of Guests 1	*Number of Guests 2*
3	4

Figure 7.22   Tracing form for the merging algorithm

Inst.	Conditional expression	Memory			Name in List 1	Name in List 2	Name put in Combined List
		P1	P2	PC			
I.		1	?	?	Bassein	?	
II.		1	1	?	Bassein	Clark	
III.		1	1	0	Bassein	Clark	
IV.	T	1	1	0	Bassein	Clark	
IV.A		1	1	1	Bassein	Clark	
IV.B	T	1	1	1	Bassein	Clark	
IV.B.1		1	1	1	Bassein	Clark	Bassein
IV.B.2		2	1	1	Campbell	Clark	
IV.	T	2	1	1	Campbell	Clark	
IV.A		2	1	2	Campbell	Clark	
IV.B	T	2	1	2	Campbell	Clark	
IV.B.1		2	1	2	Campbell	Clark	Campbell
IV.B.2		3	1	2	Mann	Clark	
IV	T	3	1	2	Mann	Clark	
IV.A		3	1	3	Mann	Clark	
IV.B	F	3	1	3	Mann	Clark	
IV.B.1′		3	1	3	Mann	Clark	Clark
IV.B.2′		3	2	3	Mann	McEntyre	
IV.	T	3	2	3	Mann	McEntyre	
IV.A		3	2	4	Mann	McEntyre	
IV.B	T	3	2	4	Mann	McEntyre	
IV.B.1		3	2	4	Mann	McEntyre	Mann
IV.B.2		4	2	4	?	McEntyre	
IV.	F	4	2	4	?	McEntyre	
V.	F	4	2	4	?	McEntyre	
VI.	T	4	2	4	?	McEntyre	
VI.A		4	2	5	?	McEntyre	
VI.B		4	2	5	?	McEntyre	McEntyre
VI.C		4	3	5	?	Zlotnick	
VI	T	4	3	5	?	Zlotnick	
VI.A		4	3	6	?	Zlotnick	
VI.B		4	3	6	?	Zlotnick	Zlotnick
VI.C		4	4	6	?	?	
VI.	F—The merging algorithm is complete.						

CHAPTER SUMMARY

In this chapter, we have discussed the fundamental algorithms pertaining to lists of data: creating a list, searching a list for a specific value, sorting a list, and merging two lists into one. We used the fundamental algorithm of switching (page 121) as a subalgorithm in the selection sort algorithm. We also suggested that the fundamental algorithm for determining a maximum or a minimum value (page 129) could be modified to search a list for its maximum or minimum element. Thus, we have seen two examples of how the fundamental algorithms can be combined to solve more complex problems.

SUPPLEMENTAL PROBLEMS

1. Describe how you can use some of the fundamental algorithms of chapters 6 and 7 (perhaps in combination) to solve the following problems. Assume that you are collecting donations at a dance.
    a. Find the average donation of the first half of the people who arrive and of the last half of the people who arrive. (You'll need to decide what *half* means if there is an odd number of participants in total.)
    b. Determine how many people contributed exactly the average donation.
    c. Determine how many people contributed more than the average donation and how many contributed less than the average donation.

2. Given a list of 20 names, write an algorithm that will switch the names so that the first name becomes the last and the last becomes the first, so that the second becomes the second from the last and the second from the last becomes the second, and so forth until the entire list has been reversed.

3. Generalize the algorithm for the preceding problem for a list of n names.

*4. Given a list of at most 20 names in alphabetical order, write an algorithm to solve the following problem:

> Eliminate any duplicate names from the list. For example, if the original list is
>
> 1. Linda Acosta
> 2. Linda Acosta
> 3. Barbara LiSanti
> 4. George Mann
> 5. Lydia Mann
> 6. Lydia Mann
> 7. Fred Zlotnick
> 8. Fred Zlotnick
>
> make the final list contain only

1. Linda Acosta
2. Barbara LiSanti
3. George Mann
4. Lydia Mann
5. Fred Zlotnick

*5. Write an algorithm to merge three ordered, limited-size lists into one ordered, limited-size list. Is there any way to use our algorithm for merging two ordered, limited-size lists?

*6. You are given two ordered, limited-size lists named **List 1** and **List 2.** Write an algorithm to merge the elements of **List 2** into **List 1. List 1** should remain an ordered list throughout the performance of the algorithm.

*7. You are given two ordered, limited-size lists named **List 1** and **List 2.** Write an algorithm that adjoins the elements of **List 2** to the end of **List 1** and uses our selection sort algorithm to sort the combined list.

*8. Create a tracing form for the work of the selection sort algorithm on the following guest list. What is the final form of the list?

Guest List	*Number of Guests*
1. Evalyn Clark	5
2. Mildred Campbell	
3. Ruth Timm	
4. Winifred Asprey	
5. Mildred Campbell	

*9. You are given two ordered, limited-size lists named **List 1** and **List 2.** Write an algorithm to merge the two lists into one ordered, limited-size list that contains no duplicates. Eliminate duplicates while you are merging the lists, not after the merging is complete.

*10. Consider our merging algorithm in Figure 7.21. Steps V and VI seem quite similar. Revise the algorithm using a subalgorithm that corresponds to the action of step V on an arbitrary list.

CHAPTER

8

8.1 COMPARING ALGORITHMS

Suppose we are given a problem, and we develop two different algorithms for solving it. Suppose further that both algorithms turn out to be correct; that is, both will solve the problem. Now we want to know which of the two is better. Before we can do that, we have to decide what we mean by *better*. We say, tentatively, that one algorithm is better than another if it is more efficient—that is, if it requires fewer steps for the same input. In this chapter, we discuss a way of measuring the efficiency of an algorithm. This measure is rough rather than exact, but it often lets us decide which of two algorithms will solve a particular problem more quickly.

Why Timing Is an Inadequate Measure

We are concerned here only with algorithms that can be implemented by computer programs. So one way we could compare two algorithms would be to write the two corresponding programs and then run both of them on several sets of sample input, timing the results. This method is actually used sometimes, but is usually unsatisfactory for a number of reasons.

One reason that timing a program is an inadequate measure of the efficiency of the underlying algorithm is that many irrelevant factors may influence the results. These factors include the choice of programming language, the choice of computer, and the choice of sample input. Decisions made by the programmers who implemented the algorithm may also influence the results. We want a measure that depends only on the algorithm itself, not on any particular implementation of it.

The method we use is mathematical. You won't need most of the ideas behind

COMPARING
AND ANALYZING
ALGORITHMS

this method in the rest of this book. (You will need them, though, if you go on with your study of computer science.) First we introduce the ideas behind the method and then describe the method itself.

An Example: Finding the Maximum

In Chapter 6 (page 128), we introduced an algorithm for finding the maximum value in a sequence of values. There we were trying to find the largest donation made at a dance. Figure 8.1 shows a variation of that algorithm. This version assumes that the sequence of values is available in a list of fixed size that has already been created.

How many times will each step in this algorithm be carried out? That depends on the sequence of input values. Step I will be carried out exactly once, regardless of the input sequence, but step II will be carried out as many times as there are values in the sequence minus 1. Even if we know the number of values in the sequence, we still can't tell how many times step II.A.1 will be carried out. That step might be performed as few as zero times (if the first value happens to be the maximum value), or it might be performed for every value after the first (if the values in the sequence happen to be in ascending order).

Exercise 8.1: Give two different input sequences of 10 items each for the algorithm in Figure 8.1. The first sequence should be one for which step II.A.1 is never carried out; the second should be one for which step II.A.1 is carried out nine times. ■

Figure 8.1   Finding the maximum value in a sequence of values

Setup

I. Label a piece of paper *Maximum Value.*

Instructions

I. Record the first value of the sequence on the piece of paper labeled *Maximum Value.*

II. Repeat the following step for each item in the list from the second through the last:

    A. If the current value from the sequence is larger than the value on *Maximum Value,*
      then

          1. Copy the current value on the piece of paper labeled *Maximum Value,* replacing the value previously written there.

Still, if we know how many values there are in the sequence, we can say something about the total number of steps that will be performed. For example, suppose there are 10 items in the list. We can then be certain that:

- Step I will be performed once.
- Step II will be performed nine times.
- Step II.A will be performed nine times.
- Step II.A.1 will be performed between zero and nine times.

In total, at least 19 steps will be performed and at most 28. If the list has 1,000 items, then we can conclude:

- Step I will be performed once.
- Step II will be performed 999 times.
- Step II.A will be performed 999 times.
- Step II.A.1 will be performed between 0 and 999 times.

The total number of steps performed will be between 1,999 and 2,998. Knowing how many items there are in the list provides enough information for us to estimate the total number of steps that will be performed, but not enough to determine the precise number. The precise number depends on the order of the values in the sequence as well as on the number of values.

Finding the maximum of a list of 10 numbers or the maximum of a list of

1,000 numbers are two versions of the same problem. They differ only in size. The same algorithm will work for finding the maximum value in a list of n values, where n is any possible list size. When we analyze that algorithm with a list of n items without knowing what number n is, we get the following result:

- Step I will be performed once.
- Step II will be performed $n-1$ times.
- Step II.A will be performed $n-1$ times.
- Step II.A.1 will be performed between 0 and $n-1$ times.

The total number of steps performed will be at least

$$(1 + (n - 1) + (n - 1) + 0),$$

which is $2n-1$, and at most

$$(1 + (n - 1) + (n - 1) + (n - 1)),$$

which is $3n-2$.

This is just the kind of measure we're looking for. In general, we'll consider problems in which we can assign some measure of size to the input data. (In the last problem, the size of the input was the number of items in the list.) Given that size, we want to determine the number of steps that will be performed in carrying out an algorithm for solving the problem.

Exercise 8.2: Modify the algorithm in Figure 8.1 to find the minimum of a sequence of values. Then determine the number of steps that will be performed. Are your results any different from the ones above? ∎

8.2 MEASURING COMPLEXITY

We have seen that knowing the size of the problem isn't enough for us to tell precisely how many steps will be required. Usually, we're content to settle for the answers to these two questions:

1. What is the worst case? In other words, for a problem of size n, what is the greatest number of steps that may be performed in carrying out the algorithm?
2. What is the average case? In other words, if we use the algorithm to solve many different problems, all of the same size n, how many steps will be performed on average for any one instance of the algorithm?

The answer we're looking for is some sort of formula or rule that will tell us, given the size *n* of some problem, the maximum number or the average number of steps that will be performed. Such a rule is what mathematicians call a function:

A *function* is a rule that, given one or more values, describes how to produce a single result value.

For example, the worst-case rule for the maximum-value algorithm is this: For an input of size *n*, multiply *n* by 3 and subtract 2 to get the maximum number of steps. In functional notation we can write this rule as follows:

$$\text{worst-case-max}(n) = 3n - 2.$$

If we can't figure out an exact formula for the maximum number of steps to be performed, we have to settle for a good approximation. We won't try to define *good approximation* precisely, but we'll give examples to illustrate the kind of approximations we mean.[1]

We haven't yet found a function to describe the average-case behavior of our algorithm. That turns out to be much harder than finding a function to describe the worst-case behavior. We'll postpone this analysis until we've developed some more techniques.

Counting Steps and Measuring Time

Ultimately, we are interested in some measure of the time it takes to carry out an algorithm. Unfortunately, knowing the number of steps that will be performed in carrying out an algorithm doesn't tell us how long it will take to carry it out, even if we do it by hand. Different steps may take different amounts of time. A single step in one algorithm might be expressed as several steps in another algorithm. For example, Figure 8.2 shows another way to write the maximum value algorithm.

Although this algorithm is expressed somewhat differently than the algorithm in Figure 8.1, the idea behind both algorithms is the same. An analysis of the algorithm given in Figure 8.2 yields the following results:

- Step I will be performed once.
- Step II will be performed once.
- Step III will be performed *n* times. (Performing this step means deciding whether the conditional expression **the value on *Position in List* is less than or equal to n** is true or false. This will be done for each of the values 2 through

1. The idea of good approximation can be made more precise by use of the mathematical notion of limits.

Figure 8.2 Finding the maximum of a sequence of *n* values

Setup

I. Label a piece of paper *Maximum Value.*

II. Label a piece of paper *Position in List.*

Instructions

I. Record the first value of the sequence on the piece of paper labeled *Maximum Value.*

II. Write the value 2 on the piece of paper labeled *Position in List.*

III. While the value on *Position in List* is less than or equal to *n,* do the following steps:
    A. If the value in the sequence at the position specified on *Position in List* is larger than the value on *Maximum Value,*
        then
        1. Copy the current value on the piece of paper labeled *Maximum Value,* replacing the value previously written there.
    B. Increment the value on *Position in List* by 1.

through *n,* a total of $n-1$ times, and one final time with **Position in List** equal to $n+1$, when the conditional expression becomes false.)

- Step III.A will be performed $n-1$ times (every time step III is done except the last).
- Step III.A.1 will be performed between 0 and $n-1$ times.
- Step III.B will be performed $n-1$ times.

This version of the algorithm will involve at least $3n$ steps, and at most $4n-1$ steps. This does not mean that it's any less efficient than the earlier version because each step may be faster. For example, step II of the algorithm in Figure 8.1 combines steps II, III, and III.B of the algorithm in Figure 8.2. All we can say is that the number of steps in both cases is roughly proportional to *n,* the size of the problem.

But what about the time taken to carry out each algorithm? If we examine the various steps in each algorithm, we see that performing each individual step once should take an amount of time that doesn't depend on *n.* (For example, it takes the same amount of time to compare two values of the sequence, regardless of whether the sequence has 10 or 10,000 items.) Since the amount of time taken by any of these steps is constant (it doesn't depend on *n*), the time each algorithm will take is also roughly proportional to *n.* Thus, whichever of these algorithms we use, finding the maximum of 5,000 numbers will take about five times as long as finding the maximum of 1,000 numbers.

From this analysis, we see how the time consumed by the algorithm varies as the size of the problem varies. Consequently we can predict roughly how an algorithm will behave on large problems once we know how it will behave on small ones. To illustrate this point, we'll compare two of the algorithms we introduced in Chapter 7: sequential search and binary search (pages 135 and 142). If your memory of binary search is a bit hazy, review that section before reading on.

Comparing Two Searching Algorithms

Recall that to search a list sequentially, we compare the item we're looking for to successive elements of the list, starting with the first element. We stop either when we find the item or when we reach the end of the list. If the list is arranged in order of increasing value, we can stop as soon as we reach an item in the list whose value is greater than that of the item we're looking for. This variation of sequential search is described in Exercise 7.4 of Chapter 7 (page 136). Figure 8.3 gives an algorithm for sequential search of an ordered list. This algorithm is essentially the same as the algorithm in Figure 7.2 placed in a general context. To modify it to search an ordered list, we have added the extra stopping condition in step IV.

We can analyze this algorithm as follows: steps I, II, and III are each done once. Step IV is done at least once, and it is done repeatedly until the search is over. In the worst case, step IV continues until we stop by reaching the end of the list, so step IV is done at most $n + 1$ times.[2] Step IV.A is done each time step IV is done except for the last time, so it's done exactly one time less than step IV. Step IV.A.1 is either never done or done once; if it's done at all, it causes step IV to stop iterating. Step IV.A.1′ is done either as many times as step IV.A, or perhaps one less time (if step IV.A.1 is done). Steps IV.A.1 and steps IV.A.1′ together contribute a number of steps equal to the number of times step IV.A is done. To summarize:

- Step I is performed once.
- Step II is performed once.
- Step III is performed once.
- Step IV is performed at least once, and at most $n + 1$ times.
- Step IV.A is performed each time step IV is done except the last time.
- Exactly one of step IV.A.1 and step IV.A.1′ is performed each time step IV.A is done.

If we call T the total number of times step IV.A is performed, then step IV is performed $T + 1$ times, and steps IV.A.1 and IV.A.1′ are performed a total of T times

2. As in the preceding example, the condition will always be evaluated one last time, giving the value *false*.

Figure 8.3 **Sequential search of an ordered list of *n* items**

Setup

I. Label a piece of paper *Found Desired Item.*

II. Label a piece of paper *Position of the Item Being Checked.*

III. Label a piece of paper *Desired Item.*

Instructions

I. Write the value false on the paper labeled *Found Desired Item.*

II. Write the value 1 on the paper labeled *Position of the Item Being Checked.*

III. Write the value we are searching for on the paper labeled *Desired Item.*

IV. While the value on the paper labeled *Found Desired Item* is false and the value on the paper labeled *Position of the Item Being Checked* is less than or equal to *n,* and the value in the sequence at the position indicated by *Position of the Item Being Checked* is less than or equal to the value on the paper labeled *Desired Item,* do the following:

  A. If the value in the sequence in the position indicated by *Position of the Item Being Checked* is the same as the value on the paper labeled *Desired Item,*
    then
      1. Change the value on the paper labeled *Found Desired Item* to true.
    else
      1'. Increment the value on the paper labeled *Position of the Item Being Checked* by 1.

between them. The total number of steps performed is thus $1 + 1 + 1 + T+1 + T + T$. Since T is in the range 0 to n, the total is at least 4 (if T is 0), and at most $4 + 3n$ (if T is n). The algorithm will stop after 4 steps if the item we're searching for is the first item on the list, and after $4 + 3n$ steps if the item is found at the end.

To figure out how many steps will be performed on the average, we can make certain "reasonable" assumptions. Since we have no way of knowing how likely it is that the item we are searching for is actually in the sequence (unless we have some special knowledge of the data), we'll simply ignore that issue and compute the average behavior only in the case where the desired item is in the sequence. And we'll assume that the item has an equal chance of being found in the first position, in the second position, in the third, . . . or in the last position. So the number of times step IV.A will be performed may be 1, or 2, or 3, . . ., or n—all with equal likelihood. (If the item is actually in the sequence, then step IV.A must be performed at least once.) To get the average, we simply average all the numbers between 1 and n:

$$\text{Average number of times step IV.A is done} = \frac{1 + 2 + 3 + \cdots + n}{n}.$$

We can use some mathematics to simplify the numerator in this fraction:

$$1 + 2 + 3 + \cdots + n = \frac{n(n + 1)}{2}.$$

Thus, the average number of times step IV.A is done equals

$$\frac{\dfrac{n(n + 1)}{2}}{n} \quad \text{or} \quad \frac{n + 1}{2}.$$

Steps IV.A.1 and/or IV.A.1$'$ are done, in total, the same number of times as step IV.A is done, and step IV is done once more. So the total number of steps on average is

$$1 + 1 + 1 + \left(\frac{n + 1}{2} + 1\right) + \frac{n + 1}{2} + \frac{n + 1}{2},$$

which simplifies to $4 + 3(n+1)/2$, or $5.5 + 3n/2$. Thus, the time to search an ordered list sequentially is, on average, roughly proportional to the number of items in the list.

Figure 8.4 gives an algorithm for binary search. This is essentially the same algorithm as the one in Figure 7.11 (page 142), placed in a general context. The analysis of this algorithm is somewhat complicated. We will content ourselves with a worst-case analysis, because—as we will see—for large problems even the worst case of binary search is dramatically faster than sequential search.

We start with the simple observation that steps I, II, and III are each performed exactly once. The key to this analysis is figuring out how many times step IV is performed, because step IV is the only iterative step in the algorithm. Each time step IV is done:

- Step IV.A is done exactly once.
- Step IV.B (testing for equality) is done exactly once.
- Step IV.B.1 is done zero or one time.
- Step IV.B.1$'$ is done zero or one time.
- Step IV.B.1$'$.a is done zero or one time.
- Step IV.B.1$'$.a$'$ is done zero or one time.

Figure 8.4   **Binary search of an ordered list of *n* items**

Setup

I. Label a piece of paper *Left Limit*.

II. Label a piece of paper *Right Limit*.

III. Label a piece of paper *Middle Position*.

IV. Label a piece of paper *Found Desired Item*.

Instructions

I. Write the value 1 on the paper labeled *Left Limit*.

II. Write the value *n* on the paper labeled *Right Limit*.

III. Write the value false on the paper labeled *Found Desired Item*.

IV. Repeat the following steps:
   A. Calculate *Middle Position* as follows: Add *Left Limit* and *Right Limit* and divide the sum by 2. If the answer is not a whole number, then round it down to the nearest whole number. Write that number on *Middle Position*.
   B. If the value in the sequence in the position indicated by *Middle Position* is the same as the *Desired Item*,
      then
         1. Change the value on the paper labeled *Found Desired Item* to true.
      else
         1'. If the *Desired Item* is alphabetically before the name in the *Middle Position* of the sequence,
            then
               a. Change the value on the paper labeled *Right Limit* to 1 less than the value on the paper labeled *Middle Position*.
            else
               a'. Change the value on the paper labeled *Left Limit* to be 1 more than the value on the paper labeled *Middle Position*.

Until either the value on the paper labeled *Found Desired Item* is true or the value on the paper labeled *Left Limit* is greater than the value on the paper labeled *Right Limit*.

In any one time through the loop, IV.B.1 and IV.B.1′ can't both be done, nor can IV.B.1′.a and IV.B.1′.a′ both be done. So the maximum number of steps that can be done each time through step IV is five: steps IV, IV.A, and IV.B once each, and steps IV.B.1′ and either IV.B.1′.a or IV.B.1′.a′. Thus, if we can count the worst-case number of times step IV is done, multiply that number by 5, and then add 3 for steps I, II, and III, we'll have an upper limit for the total number of steps.

The worst case of this search will occur when the item we're looking for isn't found. In that case, the loop will end when **Left Limit** becomes greater than **Right Limit.** Initially, **Left Limit** is 1, and **Right Limit** is n. Each time we go through the loop, either **Left Limit** will increase or **Right Limit** will decrease. We can count the number of times through the loop by examining the distance—the number of items in the sequence—between **Left Limit** and **Right Limit.** These items are the *search area,* that is, the places where the desired item might possibly be found. When **Left Limit** exceeds **Right Limit,** the size of the search area has been narrowed to zero, and the loop ends.

At the start, there are n items in the search area. After the first time through the loop, how many will there be? We have to look at two cases:

1. The desired item is less than the item in the middle position.

2. The desired item is greater than the item in the middle position.

In case 1, **Left Limit** remains unchanged and **Right Limit** is either $n/2 - 1$ (if n is even) or $n/2 - 1/2$ (if n is odd). The number of items left in the search area is less than $n/2$. In case 2, **Right Limit** remains unchanged, and **Left Limit** is either $n/2 + 1$ (if n is even) or $n/2 + 1\ 1/2$ (if n is odd.) In this case, the number of items left in the search area is at most $n/2$. For an example, refer to Chapter 7.

What happens on subsequent loops? Each time through the loop, at least half of the search area is eliminated. Thus, we are led to ask the following question:

Given a number n, suppose we repeatedly divide it by 2, discarding any fraction each time. How many times must we do that before the result is 0?

For example, suppose n is 100. Then we get

1. $100/2 = 50$

2. $50/2 = 25$

3. $25/2 = 12.5$, which rounded down is 12

4. $12/2 = 6$

5. $6/2 = 3$

6. $3/2 = 1.5$, which rounded down is 1

7. $1/2 = 0.5$, which rounded down is 0

After seven divisions, the search area will be reduced to 0.

Exercise 8.3: (a) Suppose you are playing a game in which a friend thinks of a number between 1 and 100 inclusive, and you have to guess it. After each incorrect guess, your friend tells you whether your guess was too high or too low. What strategy should you follow, and how many guesses will you need at most? (b) Suppose the rules are changed so that your friend can choose a number between 1 and 200 inclusive. How many guesses are required at most? ■

Since this process of repeatedly dividing a number in half comes up often, it's worth having the following definition:

Let *n* be any positive whole number. Then L(*n*) is the number of times *n* must be repeatedly divided by 2, discarding any fraction, until the result is 0.

Exercise 8.4 (for mathematically minded students): Show that L(*n*) is the same as the smallest power to which you must raise 2 to get a value larger than *n*. ■

The function we call L(*n*) is approximately the same as the logarithm base 2 of *n*.[3] The similarity is useful, because the behavior of logarithms is well understood. In particular, as we choose larger and larger values of *n*, L(*n*) also grows larger, but very slowly. Here are some sample values of L(*n*):

n	L(*n*)
10	4
100	7
1,000	10
10,000	13
1,000,000	20

We can now complete the analysis of binary search algorithm. The number of times step IV is done for a sequence of *n* items is at most L(*n*). So the total number of steps is no more than 5L(*n*) + 3. Thus, in doing a binary search of a sequence of a million items, you would have to go through the iterative part of the algorithm no more than 20 times, and you would have at most 103 steps to perform. In contrast, our sequential search algorithm could take as many as 3,000,004 steps.

---

3. To be precise: L(*n*) = 1 + [$\log_2(n)$], where [*x*] means "the greatest integer that is less than or equal to *x*."

8.3 LOGARITHMIC, POLYNOMIAL, AND EXPONENTIAL ALGORITHMS

Except for binary search, the algorithms we've analyzed so far have exhibited the same behavior: The time to execute the algorithm is roughly proportional to the size of the problem. Going from a problem of size n to a problem of size $n+1$ will (in the worst case) add a constant number of steps to the time required, and going from a problem of size n to one of size $2n$ will roughly double the time required.

Binary search behaves differently: Doubling the size of the problem only adds a constant number of steps and thus a fixed amount of time to the total time required. Think of the problem of guessing a number in the range 1 to 200. If your first guess is 100, then—after one guess—you've reduced the problem to guessing a number in the range 1 to 99, or in the range 101 to 200 (which is the same as between 1 and 100), or you've solved it. One guess divides the problem size in half. Algorithms with this kind of behavior are called *logarithmic*.

Other kinds of algorithms behave very differently. Figure 8.5 shows an algorithm to sort an unordered sequence of n items. It's a restatement of the selection sort from Chapter 7 (page 146).

Figure 8.5 **Sorting *n* items using selection sort**

Setup

   I. Label a piece of paper *Current Position*.

  II. Label a piece of paper *Location of Minimum*.

Instructions

   I. Write the number 1 on the paper labeled *Current Position*.

  II. While the number on *Current Position* is less than *n,* do the following steps:
     A. Carry out the subalgorithm in Figure 8.6 to find the location of the minimum item in the remainder of the sequence (positions *Current Position* + 1 through *n*) and record the answer on *Location of Minimum*.
     B. If the item at *Current Position* is greater than the item at *Location of Minimum,*
       then
         1. Exchange the item at *Current Position* and the item at *Location of Minimum.*
     C. Increment the number on *Current Position* by 1.

Our first attempt at analyzing the algorithm in Figure 8.5 leads to the following results:

- Step I is performed once.
- Step II is performed n times.
- Step II.A is performed $n - 1$ times.
- Step II.B is performed $n - 1$ times.
- Step II.B.1 is performed between 0 and $n - 1$ times.
- Step II.C is performed $n - 1$ times.

This gives between $4n - 3$ and $5n - 4$ steps, from which you might assume that the time is also roughly proportional to the size of the problem. That is incorrect. The difficulty is that step II.A does not take a fixed amount of time. The amount of time it takes varies each time it is performed according to the size of the problem. We won't do the details of the analysis here. However, since the subalgorithm in Figure 8.6 is very much like the algorithm in Figure 8.2 for finding a maximum, it's not surprising that the time this subalgorithm itself takes is proportional to n. Thus, step II.A is done about n times, each of which takes time proportional to n,

---

Figure 8.6 **Finding the position of the minimum of the sequence between positions k and n**

Setup

   I. Label a piece of paper *Position to Be Tested.*

   II. Label a piece of paper *Current Minimum.*

   III. Label a piece of paper *Position of Minimum.*

Instructions

   I. Write the number k on *Position of Minimum.*

   II. Write the number $k + 1$ on *Position to Be Tested.*

   III. While the number on *Position to Be Tested* is less than or equal to n, do the following steps:

      A. If the item at location *Position to Be Tested* is less than the item at location *Position of Minimum,*
        then
           1. Replace the value on *Position of Minimum* with the value on *Position to Be Tested.*

      B. Increment the value on *Position to Be Tested* by 1.

and the total time for this algorithm is in fact roughly proportional to n times n, or n squared.

If the running time of an algorithm is proportional to the square of the size of the problem, then doubling the size of the problem makes the running time 4 times as long, and multiplying the size by 10 multiplies the running time by a factor of 100. Algorithms that behave like this cannot be used for very large problems because they take too long.

In fact, there are much faster algorithms than selection sort for sorting large sequences of items. The best sorting algorithms known take a time to sort n items that is proportional to n times the logarithm of n, or equivalently $nL(n)$, where L is the function we defined in the previous section.

There are also algorithms whose running times are proportional to higher powers of n. Any algorithm that takes a time proportional to some power of the size of its problem is called a *polynomial time algorithm*. As you may know from mathematics, when we measure the relative values of polynomial functions for large values, the highest power term of the polynomial is all that is significant. Thus, an algorithm that has a running time for a problem of size n proportional to

$$n^3 - n^2 + n$$

would be described as an *n-cubed* algorithm. The n^3 term tells us all we need to know about how the running time varies with the size of the problem. A large enough substitution for n makes this point clear.

Not all algorithms are either logarithmic or polynomial, however. Many other kinds of behavior are possible. Consider the following problem:

Given an n-digit number x, find all of its factors (that is, all of the numbers that divide x).

Figure 8.7 shows a possible algorithm to solve this problem. Note that we measure the size of a number by the number of its digits, using the decimal system, rather than the value of the number. Thus, the numbers 8,798 and 2,234 are both of size 4. Using this measure (which turns out to be a reasonable one in studying the algorithms of arithmetic), our algorithm takes exponential time. That is, the number of steps for an input x of size n is about 10 to the nth power, since that's roughly how many numbers there are between 1 and x.

Exponential functions grow faster than any polynomial function. Their behavior is the opposite of logarithmic functions: Increasing the size of the problem by 1 multiplies the time required by some constant factor. Our algorithm will take about 10 times as long to factor a typical six-digit number as it will take to factor a typical five-digit number.

The algorithm we've given is not the fastest known method of factoring a number; it can be improved. But even the best methods known still take an amount of time that grows exponentially with the number of digits. Such algorithms are com-

Figure 8.7   **Finding the factors of the number *x***

Setup

I. Label a piece of paper *List of Factors.*

Instructions

I. Write the value 1 on *List of Factors* (because 1 is a factor of every number).

II. For each whole number between 2 and *x,* do the following steps:
 A. Divide *x* by the current number, noting the remainder.
 B. If the remainder is 0,
  then
   1. Append the current number to the *List of Factors.*

putationally intractable for large-size problems. That is, they take so long they can't actually be carried out. For example, suppose we wanted to factor a 20-digit number using the algorithm in Figure 8.7. Suppose further that our computer can carry out 10,000,000 divisions every second. Since a year has somewhat less than 32,000,000 seconds, in one century our computer can carry out something less than

$$100 \times 10,000,000 \times 32,000,000 = 32,000,000,000,000,000$$

divisions. This is, of course, an enormous amount, but it's not enough. It's not even 1 percent of the arithmetic we need done; our computer would have to work for more than 10,000 years to carry out this algorithm with a 20-digit number. And a 21-digit number would take 10 times as long!

Nobody knows a fast way to factor large numbers. This makes factoring very different from most of the other algorithms of arithmetic. For example, multiplying two *n*-digit decimal numbers using the algorithm you learned in grade school takes an amount of time proportional to *n* squared. That is quite practical. (If you had to, you could multiply two 20-digit numbers by hand in well under a day. A computer can do it in well under a second.) This difference points out the significance of the three categories of algorithms we've described:

- Logarithmic algorithms are practical even for problems of very large size.
- Polynomial algorithms are practical for problems of moderately large size.
- Exponential algorithms are impractical for all but the smallest problems.

8.4 THE MATHEMATICS OF ANALYZING ALGORITHMS

The idea behind the method we've been using is elementary. It amounts to counting: We count how many times each algorithm step is done. If we can't count precisely, we make reasonable assumptions and count approximately. Nevertheless, the analysis of even simple algorithms may call for some surprisingly sophisticated mathematics. To illustrate this point, we'll now do an average-case analysis of the maximum-value algorithm we presented in Figure 8.1.

In the section beginning on page 159, we determined that:

- Step I of the algorithm in Figure 8.1 is performed once.
- Step II is performed $n - 1$ times.
- Step II.A is performed $n - 1$ times.
- Step II.A.1 is performed between 0 and $n - 1$ times.

The only possible variation lies in step II.A.1. We must figure out how many times on average this step is performed. To compute such an average, we have to describe what the average input sequence looks like. We assume that if we look at many input sequences, on the average:

- The second value is larger than the first value half the time.
- The third value is larger than the first two values one-third of the time.
- In general, the kth value is larger than the first $k - 1$ values $1/k$th of the time.

This means that about half the time—when we're doing step II for the second element of the sequence—we'll perform step II.A.1. When we're doing step II for the third element, we'll do step II.A.1 about one-third of the time. When we do step II for each of the elements from the second through the nth, we'll do step II.A.1

$$\frac{1}{2} + \frac{1}{3} + \frac{1}{4} + \cdots + \frac{1}{n}$$

times on the average.

This sum is part of the harmonic series. It's not easy to evaluate it, or even estimate it, from scratch. In most college courses in the integral calculus, it is shown that

$$\frac{1}{2} + \frac{1}{3} + \frac{1}{4} + \cdots + \frac{1}{n}$$

is approximately equal to the natural logarithm of n for large values of n. The natural logarithm of n is about 0.7 times the function L(n) we introduced on page 167.

Putting this together, we can estimate the average number of steps to be executed for the algorithm in Figure 8.1 as

- 1 for step I
- $n-1$ for step II
- $n-1$ for step II.A
- $0.7 \times$ L(n) for Step II.A.1

or $2n-1 + 0.7$L(n). When n is a large number, the last term is insignificant, because L(n) is much, much smaller than $2n$.

CHAPTER SUMMARY

1. We are concerned with algorithms that can be applied to problems of different sizes. We measure how changing the size of the input changes the number of steps that have to be performed to carry out the algorithm. We can roughly translate *number of steps* into *elapsed time* if each step of the algorithm takes an amount of time that doesn't depend on the size of the input.

2. The method we use is to derive a function that, given the size of the input for the algorithm, yields the number of steps required. We may not be able to compute such a function in general, since the number of steps depends on many factors besides the size of the input. The most important approximate answers we want are functions that describe how many steps will be performed in the worst case and how many steps will be performed on average.

3. Three important classes of algorithms are
   - Those whose time is proportional to the *logarithm* of the input size
   - Those whose time is proportional to a *polynomial function* of the input size
   - Those whose time is proportional to an *exponential function* of the input size

SUPPLEMENTAL PROBLEMS

Questions 1 through 6 refer to the following table and algorithm.

Table for multiplying digits by 7

d	0	1	2	3	4	5	6	7	8	9
7d	0	7	14	21	28	35	42	49	56	63

Multiplying an *N*-Digit Number by 7

Setup

  I. Label a piece of paper *Number.*

  II. Label a piece of paper *Carry.*

  III. Label a piece of paper *Answer.*

Instructions

  I. Write the given *n*-digit number on *Number.*

  II. Write the number 0 on *Carry.*

  III. For each digit of the number on *Number,* starting at the right and moving left, do the following steps:
   - A. Look up the digit in the top row of the table given above and locate the corresponding number in the second row.
   - B. Add the number on *Carry* to this corresponding number.
   - C. Write the right digit of the sum from step III.B on *Answer* to the left of any digits that may be there.
   - D. Write the left digit of the sum (or 0 if the sum is less than 10) on *Carry,* replacing any number that is already there.

  IV. If the value on *Carry* is not 0,
   then
   - A. Copy it to *Answer,* placing it to the left of any digits that may be there.

1. Is the amount of time taken by each step of this algorithm independent of *n*? If not, which one(s) depend on *n*? (Remember, *n* is not the number we're multiplying, but the number of digits in that number.)

2. Suppose that you can carry out any one step of this algorithm in one second. How long will it take you to compute $2{,}059 \times 7$?

3. Assume that each step of this algorithm can be carried out in a fixed amount of time. Analyze the algorithm by determining how many steps, in the worst

case, must be carried out to multiply an n-digit number by 7. Which of the three categories of Section 8.3 does this algorithm fall into?

4. Analogous to this algorithm, we could write algorithms for multiplying an n-digit number by each of the digits 0 through 9. What must we change to produce such algorithms?

5. Assume you have written the ten algorithms described in problem 4. Use them as subalgorithms to write an algorithm for multiplying one n-digit number by another n-digit number.

6. Analyze the algorithm you wrote in answer to problem 5. For the purposes of the analysis, assume that you can add any two-decimal digits in a fixed amount of time.

*7. Write an algorithm for adding together two n-digit numbers. Analyze this algorithm for the worst case. What category does it fall into?

*8. Consider the problem of multiplying a number x by 7. Suppose we measure the size of this problem by the value of x itself rather than by the number of digits in x. Using this notion of size, what category does the above algorithm fall into?

*9. Analyze the sorting algorithm given in Figures 8.5 and 8.6.

*10. Analyze the recursive algorithm for sorting a hand of cards given in Chapter 5 (pages 106–110).

*11. Analyze the Tower of Hanoi algorithm given in Chapter 5 (pages 110–116).

CHAPTER

9

So far, much of our discussion has focused on defining problems and developing algorithms for their solution. We've emphasized these methods because describing the steps of an algorithm to the computer is one of two main aspects of writing a computer program. But in this chapter, we want to focus on the other main aspect—the description of the data our programs will use. Descriptions of data range from trivial to exceedingly complex.

9.1 DATA ABSTRACTION AND REPRESENTATION

If we think of the steps of an algorithm as operations that are being performed on something, then data is that "something."[1] Different types of data occur in real-life problems: text, numbers, sounds, pictures, gestures, and so on. Each type of data is manipulated differently. We do arithmetic on numbers. We interpret gestures. We replicate sounds. The computer has a limited way of representing data and a large but ultimately limited capacity for storing data. When we use a computer, we are restricted in the types of data and kinds of manipulations we can use to solve problems. Pascal and other programming languages are designed to make the transition from manual problem solving to solving problems with computers as easy as possible.

Exactly how the human mind represents information is still unknown. So we cannot expect the electronic mechanisms by which a computer represents information to constitute a model of the mechanisms of the human mind. The kinds of information that can be stored in a computer are limited by the characteristics of

---

1. Strictly speaking, the word *data* is the plural of the word *datum*. However, we follow the widespread practice of using the word *data* as a singular noun.

THE CONCEPT
OF DATA

the physical machine. Here we'll give only the briefest discussion of the machine and indicate why it doesn't concern us.

At some level, the computer represents all of its data as sequences of 0's and 1's.[2] Each 0 or 1 in such a sequence is known as a bit. Strictly speaking, each bit is not a 0 or a 1, but an electrical or magnetic state. These representations are invisible to the Pascal programmer. Pascal hides the details of how the computer represents the number -6, the letter Q or the character $>$, and allows you to think of them in more natural terms. For instance, the character Q is represented in many computer systems by the eight-bit sequence 01010001. In others, Q is represented by the eight-bit sequence 11011000, and in yet others by the six-bit sequence 010001. But a Pascal programmer on any of these systems will simply use the representation 'Q' (just like that, inside apostrophes) without knowing or caring how the computer will represent it internally.

Figure 9.1 shows different levels of abstraction that lie between the real-world data of your problem and the way that data is represented by a computer. We are concerned only with the first level of abstraction. So we need to know how to describe data in the programming language we are using and how to choose among the possible descriptions.

9.2 TYPES OF DATA ITEMS

Human beings can discern the type of a data item from a variety of representations. For instance, consider the following question:

2. This fact, which is almost completely irrelevant for the kinds of programs presented in this book, has prompted many comments of the sort "I can't learn to program—I was never good at math."

Figure 9.1   Levels of abstraction

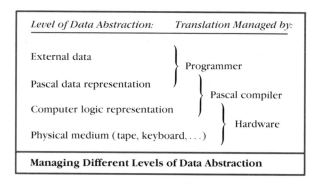

Level of Data Abstraction:	Translation Managed by:

External data

Pascal data representation

Computer logic representation

Physical medium (tape, keyboard, . . .)

Programmer

Pascal compiler

Hardware

Managing Different Levels of Data Abstraction

How much is 72 + forty-eight?

An English-speaking reader can interpret the sequence of characters that spell *forty-eight* as a number and from context know what to do with it to arrive at an answer of 120 (or, one hundred and twenty, if you prefer.) We can interpret the sequences of symbols '48,' 'forty-eight,' or even 'XLVIII' as referring to the same abstract concept. On the other hand, we recognize immediately that a question like

How much is 72 + forty winks?

is utter gibberish. The form the symbols take and our knowledge of language and other contexts enable us to detect the meaning of one question and the meaninglessness of the other.

Programming languages are not nearly so flexible. Recall that in Chapter 2 we made a distinction between constant data items that are written into the steps of algorithms and variable data items whose values are written on the labeled pieces of paper. We also discussed data items represented by expressions. Each language has specific rules for determining the type of each of these kinds of data items. We use the word *syntax* to refer to the rules that describe the proper form of programs written in a programming language.

We've recognized that data occurs in different types, but we haven't said exactly what we mean by *type*. The values that a data item can assume and the kinds of things you can do with that data item are what we mean when we talk about an item's type. Intuitively, we know that peoples' names are different from numbers. A numeric data item can only assume certain possible values. These values are different from the possible values that a data item representing a name can assume. In addition, the things we can do with numeric data are different from the things we can do with nonnumeric data. We can perform arithmetic operations (addition, subtraction, etc.) on numeric data items, but not on nonnumeric data items.

The Pascal programming language recognizes the standard types of data that occur most commonly in computer algorithms. Pascal also allows the programmer to describe his or her own data types and to build complex, structured data items. We build complex data items—data structures—just as we build complex algorithms: We combine a set of standard data types into a data structure according to a set of rules. Properly describing the data structures is just as important as properly describing the algorithms.

For example, an application for a bank loan requests several data items. Some items, such as income, are numeric; others, such as your name, are alphabetic. Some data items may simply consist of a choice from a list of options (for example, "Marital Status: __ single __ married __ widowed __ divorced __ other"). For the bank, a single application form constitutes a single, complex data item. Describing a data structure in a programming language can be a difficult task. But, as in designing algorithms, there are principles of structure that make the task manageable.

9.3 SOURCES OF DATA ITEMS

There are three possible sources of the data items used by computer programs. The simplest source is the instructions that comprise a program. We write constant data items into the program itself.

The second source lies outside the program. Recall instances in our algorithms in which a question was asked and the response was written on a labeled piece of paper. A data item whose value becomes known in this manner is called an *input data item*. By *input instruction* we mean an instruction to record a piece of data from a source outside the algorithm or program. Programming terminology for the action of an input instruction is *reading a data item.*

When a Pascal program performs an instruction to input a data item, there are usually two possible sources. Data can be supplied by the person running the program in the form of a stream of characters, or it can be prepared in advance in a machine-understandable format.

First, let's consider the case of data entered by the person who is running the program. Typically, that person, called the *user,* sits at a terminal and types in each data item as it is requested. In a well-written program, a message is printed on the terminal screen telling the user what data item is expected next. Such a message is called a *prompt.* The user responds to the prompt by typing in the data item. Programs that receive data in this way are called *interactive.*

Input data may also come from one or more files stored in the auxiliary or external storage facility of the computer. Programs that receive all of their input from files are *noninteractive* (or *batch*) programs.

The third source of data items is a computation performed as one of the steps of the program. For example, recall the fundamental algorithm of accumulating that we used to determine the total of all the donations given at a dance. It contained the following step:

> In your mind add the value on the paper labeled **new donation** to the value on the paper labeled **donations.** Replace the value on the paper labeled **donations** with the value you just calculated.

The updated value of the data item **donations** is computed by the program.[3]

9.4 ROLES OF DATA ITEMS

To illustrate the ways in which data items function in an algorithm or in a program, consider an electronic cash register that automatically computes sales tax. The purpose of the cash register is to make a record of each transaction (a receipt) and to compute and display the total owed. It uses an algorithm much like the one we developed for the supermarket problem of Chapter 5 (pages 86–91). Let's see what kinds of information the cash register uses and the sources of that information.

First, the clerk enters the price of each item the customer is buying along with a designation of the item's taxability. This information is input data since it is supplied from an outside source. The algorithm cannot be designed for any particular set of input data because each customer buys a different collection of things. It must work for any possible set of data items. The cash register does, however, expect certain kinds of data. The clerk has to press numeric keys for the prices in dollars and cents and a key that indicates whether the item is subject to tax.

The total owed is a data item computed by the algorithm. But the cash register needs more information to compute the total owed. The sales tax rate is needed. The clerk does not enter this value because it's the same for each customer. It is constant data and is built into the algorithm used by the cash register.

The various data items involved in the cash register's algorithm can play one of two roles: The first is as *output* from the cash register. The second is as a data item computed according to the algorithm but which is never output from the cash register. Data items playing this second role are called *temporary, scratch,* or *internal data.*

Let's first consider the output data items. Everything printed on the cash register receipt is output data, no matter what its source. The total owed, for example, is computed output. The input data (for example, prices) is copied onto the paper

---

3. By *computed* we don't necessarily mean that the data is numerical and arose from arithmetic calculations. It is data whose values are determined by the steps carried out in an algorithm. Here the computed output happens to be a numerical total. But an algorithm might take as input an English sentence and produce as output an alphabetical list of all the letters that appear in the sentence. That would also be computed output, since it was neither supplied as input nor built into the algorithm.

slip. Printing the input as part of the output is sometimes called *echo printing* and is commonly done when a permanent record of the input is needed. Most such registers also print the total amount of tax paid, a useful fact for tax records. This is computed output. In some stores, the register may also print the store's name or a message like *Thank-You.* This is a constant output; it appears the same on each receipt and is built into the algorithm.

As with input data, we have two choices for where to direct output data from a Pascal program. We can instruct the computer either to write the output data on the terminal screen or to write the output data in a file. The advantage of sending output data to a file is that it remains in machine-understandable format. We won't have to type it in again. Output to a terminal screen vanishes as soon as it scrolls off the top of the screen. Output on paper can be kept for reference. But, if we wanted to make output on paper into input for another program, we would need to type it again. We use files to keep output data in a machine-understandable format so that it may easily be used later as input data.

Now let's consider data items playing the role of scratch data. Some of the computed data never appears as output. Examples are the running totals of taxable and nontaxable goods. These data items change their values as the algorithm is carried out. We have already encountered such data items in earlier examples where we used labeled pieces of paper to keep track of their values. You can think of these items as the algorithm's personal business. It needs them to keep track of the point it has reached so far (What is my running total so far? or Where in this list of names will I next look for the name 'Carol Lennox'?), but they are not the concern of the user.

Figure 9.2 shows the flow of data values as the steps of an algorithm are performed.

9.5 DATA TRANSFER BETWEEN SUBALGORITHMS

We found in our discussion of the design of algorithms (pages 62–76) that problems logically decompose into subproblems, and their corresponding algorithms

Figure 9.2   **Flow of data values**

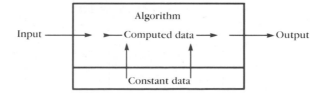

decompose into subalgorithms. Eventually our subalgorithms will become logical units of a Pascal program. We will want each logical unit to work properly and, as much as possible, independently of the other units. For example, if we were writing a program for creating and sorting a list, we would like to write two units of the program that do not depend on one another. One unit would create the list, and the other would sort the list. The sorting procedure, for example, should not be affected by the name used to refer to the list in the creation procedure. Once we have written a sorting procedure for a list of limited size, we would never need to write such a procedure from "scratch" again. We could use it, perhaps with minor changes, whenever we needed to sort a limited-size list.

For example, suppose we want to read in a list of names, alphabetize the list, and print out the alphabetized list. We need three subalgorithms corresponding to reading in the list, alphabetizing the list, and printing out the list. The three procedures are shown in Figure 9.3. Recall the fundamental algorithms for creating a list and sorting a list from chapter 7 (pages 133, 146). The number of items in the list is as crucial a data item as the content of the list itself. Let's refer to those two data items as *list* and *number* here.

Both the *list* and the *number* have no values before procedure *Read in List* does its job, but they should have well-defined values when *Read in List* is complete. Figure 9.4 illustrates the flow of data into and out of *Read in List*. *Read in list* has the ability to affect the values of *list* and *number,* as illustrated by the arrows entering and leaving *Read in List*.

Now consider the alphabetizing procedure. This procedure must be able to affect the *list*, but not the *number*. It must have the value of *number*, however,

Figure 9.3   **Three procedures corresponding to the three subalgorithms**

Figure 9.4   **Data flow diagram for *Read In List***

in order to alphabetize the *list*. The arrows in Figure 9.5 represent the ability of **Alphabetize List** to affect *list*, but not **number**. This is done by having only an arrow going into **Alphabetize List** for **number**.

Finally, consider the procedure **Print out List**. It will need the list itself to perform its job, and since the items on the *list* will be printed out one at a time, it should contain an iterative structure. Moreover, since the program will know the number of items in the *list*, this is a perfect case for definite iteration. Hence, **Print out List** also needs the value of **number**. It should not, however, be able to change the value of *list* or **number**, because its only job is to print out the items on the *list*. Hence, we have arrows going into, but not out of, **Print out List** for both *list* and **number** as shown in Figure 9.6. As Figure 9.7 shows, the list flows from **Read in List** to **Alphabetize List** to **Print out List**. But, **number** receives its value in **Read in List** and is only used by **Alphabetize List** and **Print out List**. Hence, **Read in List** should send the value of **number** to both **Alphabetize List** and **Print out List**. Figure 9.8 represents the complete data flow diagram for this problem.

Figure 9.5   **Data flow diagram for *Alphabetize List***

Figure 9.6   **Data flow diagram for *Print out List***

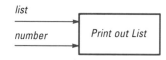

Figure 9.7   **Data flow diagram for data item *List***

Figure 9.8   **Complete data flow diagram**

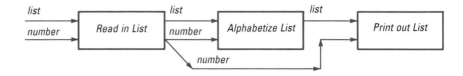

9.6 DATA AND MEMORY

When we traced algorithms earlier, we kept track of how the values changed at each stage of the algorithm. We used labeled pieces of paper to record those values. Algorithms carried out by computers must have data values available at each stage. Computers maintain these values in the portion of the hardware known as memory.

Although the memory hardware differs from one computer to another, all computer memories have certain characteristics in common. All consist of a sequence of numbered cells. The numbering usually starts at 0 and goes up to some number determined by the memory capacity of the computer.[4] The number of a memory cell is called its *address.*

The computer hardware refers to each data item stored in its memory by its address. This type of reference is extremely inconvenient for human beings. Fortunately, just as Pascal hides the internal representation of data, it also hides the computer's scheme for referring to data. Pascal programs use names to refer to data. These names are analogous to the labels we wrote on pieces of paper in our algorithms.

Different types of data occupy different amounts of space. Because computers store information in an encoded form, there may not be a direct correlation between the amount of space you need to write down a data item and the amount of space needed to record it in a computer memory. For example, in most computers every integer occupies the same amount of space in memory, regardless of how many digits its decimal representation contains.[5]

---

4. You may have heard computer memory sizes described in terms of the jargon words *bytes* and *K.* A byte is the amount of memory needed to store one character. This amount varies from one computer to another, but it is usually eight bits. The letter *K* stands for the number 1,024, which is 2 to the tenth power and is conveniently close to 1,000. Thus, a computer with a 64K memory has space to store $64 \times 1,024 = 65,536$ characters in its memory.

5. Each implementation of Pascal has an upper limit for the size of the integers that can be represented. For example, some computers cannot store an integer whose decimal representation contains 12 or more digits.

When we write a computer program to carry out an algorithm, we describe the data as well as the steps in the algorithm. In doing so, we must keep in mind the lifetime of the data values we are using. Some data items, like the tax rate in the cash register example, are always known to the algorithm. These values never change. But what about the values that change? After the algorithm has been carried out once, are the values from that instance saved? Do they become the starting point the next time the algorithm is carried out? Our cash register example does not use the previous customer's total as the next customer's starting point. Each time it must start with a total of $0.00.

Computer programs follow the same rule. Constant values are always known to the program because they are written into the instructions that constitute the program. The values of data items that are not constant must be provided each time the program runs. The memory component of the computer only holds the values of data items for a specific program while that program is executing. If you want to preserve values of nonconstant data items from one performance of a program to the next, you must save these values somewhere outside the program. The next time you need those values in the program, you must somehow make them available for the program to read. This is a situation where the use of files is appropriate. To preserve the values from one execution of a program, those values should be output to a file kept in the computer's external storage component. Then, the values can be read from that file in the next execution of the program.

Just as we don't need to know the details of the internal representation of data in the computer, we don't need to know how external storage works. (There are many kinds of external storage, such as tape, disk, punched cards, and so on. Their salient property is that they don't need continuous electrical power supplied to preserve the data values.) The important thing for the algorithm designer to know is precisely which data values come from which sources and what the life spans of those values are.

The analogy between storing data in a computer memory and recording it on paper, as we have done in our algorithms, isn't exact. Computer memories have some properties that are consequences of their electronic nature. In particular:

- If a memory cell has a recorded value and the computer writes a new value there, the new value replaces the previous one. The previous value is lost.
- A computer memory cell will maintain its value until the value is changed (by being overwritten) or, in most cases, until the electric current is turned off.

We've spoken of memory as having only the function of storing data values. In fact, memory must store something else as well: the instructions that make up your program. By now, you're probably impatient to learn how to write these instructions. Part II of this book is devoted to that subject.

CHAPTER SUMMARY

1. Several levels of abstraction lie between the real-world data used to solve a problem and the electrical representation of that data in a computer. As a programmer, you are concerned only with how to translate the real-world data into the formalism of Pascal.

2. All data items in a Pascal program have a *type*. A data item's type governs the possible values it can have and the ways in which it can be manipulated. Pascal recognizes standard data types and also enables the programmer to construct new types, including complex structured types.

3. Each data value used in an algorithm must come from one of three sources:

   ■ It may come from outside the algorithm. Such a data item is called an *input data item*.

   ■ It may be built into the algorithm. Such a data item is called a *constant data item*.

   ■ It may arise as a result of steps in the algorithm itself. Such a data item is called a *computed data item*.

4. Each data item must play at least one of the following two roles in an algorithm:

   ■ *Scratch* values, which keep track of the state of the algorithm
   ■ *Output* from the algorithm

5. Pascal provides a mechanism for transmitting data from one procedure to another to assist the programmer in writing independent procedures. It makes a distinction between data items whose values can be affected by a procedure and data items whose values cannot be affected by a procedure.

6. The data used by a computer program is stored in the computer's memory, which is part of the computer hardware. The hardware refers to different locations in memory by numerical addresses. Putting a value in a memory location erases the previous value in that location.

7. The data items that are part of a Pascal program exist only during the execution of the program. External storage devices are used to preserve data that is produced by a program or to prepare data ahead of time for entry to a program.

SUPPLEMENTAL PROBLEMS

1. Suppose we want to describe the dates of days in the twentieth century and the only data type available to us is the integer. Here are three possible ways to represent such dates:

   - As a single number representing the number of days that have elapsed from January 1, 1901,[6] to the given date

   - As a triplet of numbers representing the month number, the day number within each month, and the year number

   - As a pair of numbers representing the year number and the day number within that year

   a. Classify each representation as a structured or nonstructured data item.
   b. For each representation, find at least one application for which it is the most convenient representation of a date.

In each of the following problems:
   a. Identify each data item.
   b. Classify each data item as constant or variable.
   c. Identify the source of each data item.
   d. Identify the role of each data item.

2. The switching algorithm shown in Figure 6.1.

3. The counting algorithm shown in Figure 6.7.

4. The accumulating algorithm shown in Figure 6.9.

5. The averaging algorithm shown in Figure 6.13.

6. The algorithm to determine a maximum value shown in Figure 6.15.

7. The algorithm to create a limited-size list shown in Figure 7.1.

8. The algorithm to search an unordered, limited-size list shown in Figure 7.2.

9. The binary search algorithm shown in Figure 7.11.

10. The selection sort algorithm shown in Figure 7.16.

11. The algorithm to merge two ordered, limited-size lists shown in Figure 7.21.

6. The first day of the twentieth century.

P A R T

II

In this section, we introduce you to the computer programming language Pascal. The rules of Pascal that we present follow the standard established by the International Standards Organization (ISO). Although some implementations of Pascal deviate from or extend this standard, we deal only with Standard Pascal in this book.

Computers are machines that can carry out simple instructions (such as **move a number from here to there,** or **add two numbers together**). If a computer is to carry out complex instructions, those instructions must be encoded as a program. When you write a program in Pascal, it is translated into simple instructions for you by a translator. You, however, need to translate complex English instructions into those available in Pascal.

Learning to write a program is like learning to speak a new language with a new vocabulary, syntax, and semantics. If the computer is to do what you want it to do, you must give it precise instructions in a language it understands.

We assume that you will be programming as you use this portion of the book. First, though, we want to say a bit more about what a program is and how a computer processes a program.

WHAT IS A PROGRAM?

A computer program is a precise statement of an algorithm in a specialized language. Programming languages have syntax and semantics, just as natural languages do. The syntax of a programming language is a set of rules that describes how a sentence may be formed. The semantics of a programming language describe what each instruction tells the computer to do. The vocabulary of a programming language is smaller than that of a natural language, and the types

INTRODUCTION
TO PASCAL
PROGRAMMING

of instructions, or statements, that you can create with a programming language are limited.

Some of the vocabulary used in Pascal is similar to the vocabulary of English. But beware! This similarity often leads to carelessness. In Pascal, the meanings of words like *if* and *while* are not identical to their English counterparts. They may be used only in certain ways. Do not use the Pascal language as you would the English language. It does not work!

When you write computer programs, you may find that you have to use certain statements that seem trivial or unnecessary. But you cannot rely on the computer to figure out what you mean and then go ahead and do it. A computer understands only a limited set of instructions. To get the computer to solve a problem, you must describe every step precisely in the programming language you have chosen.

HOW THE COMPUTER PROCESSES
A PASCAL PROGRAM

Most computers process Pascal programs in two steps: In the first step, they translate the program into a type of machine code.[1] In the second step, they execute the translated code.[2]

---

1. Depending on the type of translator used, the program can be translated into either object code or intermediate code. Both types of code are incomprehensible to people.

2. Some computer languages, and occasionally Pascal, are translated interactively. This means that an instruction is translated and executed as soon as it is entered in the computer.

A given computer may have more than one method for translating a computer program. This translation is done by a program called a *translator*. The most common types of translators are compilers and interpreters. For our purposes here, the type of translator used is irrelevant.

When the computer translates a program, it attempts to catch any syntactic errors and certain semantic errors that may be in your program. If it comes across such errors, it will usually refuse to translate the program.[3] You must then correct your program and try to translate it again. Only if your program is syntactically correct will the computer translate it. You will be unable to read this translation, but you may try to have the computer execute it. Most syntactic errors are the result of typing mistakes or lack of familiarity with the language. Don't be discouraged when you make syntactic errors. They are easy to fix.

It is interesting to note that when you submit a program to the computer for translation, you are providing input data for use by another program because the translator is itself a program. It takes your program as input and produces a translation or error messages as output.

Once the computer has translated your program, it is ready for execution. During execution, however, your program may come to a halt. When that happens, it is said to have "halted," "crashed," "bombed," or "died." The most common reason for an error to occur at this point is the discovery of some semantic error that the computer could not recognize until the program was executed. Errors that halt the execution of a program are called *run-time* errors because they appear when your program is running.

Sometimes your program will run to completion but will produce incorrect output. Although you have written a syntactically and semantically correct program, you have failed to describe a correct algorithm, or you have misunderstood how a particular construct works. This type of error is called a *logic error*.[4] Logic errors are the hardest to uncover because you must trace the program or the algorithm it is implementing to find the error.

SUMMARY

1. A *program* is a precise statement of an algorithm in some computer language.

2. Computers process programs in two steps.

---

3. Some translators also attempt to identify your errors for you. The error messages are usually helpful but occasionally misleading.

4. The term *logic error* is used because it is assumed that the logic you are using to describe the algorithm is incorrect.

3. In the first step, they look for syntactic errors and certain semantic errors. If a computer detects errors, it will stop translating a program. If it detects no errors, the computer will complete translation of the program.

4. In the second step, the computer executes, or runs, the program.

5. A semantic error detected during execution is called a *run-time error*. Such an error will cause your program to halt or crash.

6. An error that causes a program to produce incorrect output is called a *logic error*. An error of this type is usually due to a mistake in your algorithm or your misconception of a Pascal statement.

7. Your program serves as input to the translator. The translation, or the error messages given, are the output of the translator.

CHAPTER

10

In Part I, we wrote several algorithms, most of which consisted of two parts: a setup part and an instruction part. A Pascal program consists of two similar parts, along with what is called a *header*. Figure 10.1 shows a sample Pascal program. Don't try to figure out what the program means at this point. Just notice how the parts are arranged. If you look at more complex programs, you will see that Pascal also has the facility to make it easy for you to break up your algorithms into sub-algorithms.

The first section of this chapter briefly describes the sequence of segments in a Pascal program. Later on, we will describe each segment in greater detail. It is a

Figure 10.1   Sample program, showing parts

```
program    ──────→ program simpleexample (input, output);
header
set up     ──────→ var number1,
section              number2,
                     number3: integer;
instruction ──────→ begin
section              write ('Number please?  ');
                     readln (number1);
                     write ('Second number please?  ');
                     readln (number2);
                     number3: = number1 + number2;
                     writeln ('  The sum of the numbers is  ',
                                    number3: 1)
                 end.
```

THE STRUCTURE OF A
PASCAL PROGRAM

rule of Pascal that the segments of a program must occur in the order in which they are described here. We shall refer to the parts of a program that break this rule or any other rule of Pascal as illegal.

10.1 THE GENERAL STRUCTURE OF A PASCAL PROGRAM

The first part of a Pascal program is the program header. The header identifies the program by name and specifies the sources of input and destinations of output used by the program. Every program requires a header.

All of the remaining parts of a Pascal program, except the period that indicates the end of the program, constitute what is called the *block*. The first part of a block is similar to the setup portion of an algorithm. The setup portion of a program may specify constant data that will be used in the execution of the program. It also may specify the type of a variable data item that can be made available to the program (see pages 177–179). It must also request the allocation of space for variable data that must be remembered throughout the execution of the program. The setup portion may contain all of the following items:

1. Constant definition section. Constants are data items whose values must remain the same throughout the program.[1]

2. Type definition section. These definitions specify different types of data that may be used by the program.

1. We are omitting a possible section of a Pascal program. That section describes **goto** labels, which are rarely used in Pascal.

193

3. Variable declaration section. These declarations give names to spaces in the memory component of the computer that the programmer wants reserved for any data items that are not constant.

The setup portion of the program and the sections that constitute it are not required in every Pascal program.

The second part of the block is similar to the instruction section of an algorithm. It describes subgroups of instructions and the main instructions of the program. This segment may consist of the following items:

1. Procedure and function declaration section. They correspond to the subalgorithms of an algorithm.
2. The word **begin**. This word indicates where the program will start execution.
3. The instructions of the program. The instructions are Pascal statements. They include the invocation of subalgorithms.
4. The word **end**. It indicates the end of the block.

The declarations of procedures and functions are optional in any program. The program block is followed by a period indicating the end of the program.

10.2 RESERVED WORDS AND IDENTIFIERS

Before explaining the basic parts of a program in depth, we must introduce the concept of a reserved word and the concept of an identifier.

Reserved Words

A *reserved word* is a word that has a particular and specific meaning when it is used in a Pascal program. Reserved words are often called *keywords* because they "key" the translator to what follows. You may not use a reserved word in any way other than that specified by the Pascal programming language. Reserved words are separated from other elements in a program by *delimiters*. Typical delimiters in Pascal are blank spaces, carriage returns, commas, semicolons, and parentheses.

Identifiers

Identifiers are names given by the programmer to identify things within the program. An identifier must start with a letter of the alphabet, which may be followed by any sequence of letters or digits. You may create an identifier of as many characters as you like, but the number of characters a translator recognizes varies, depending on how Pascal is set up or implemented on your machine.[2] No matter how many characters your translator recognizes, the remaining characters that make up the identifier must still conform to Pascal syntax. All identifiers in the text of this book (not in figures) will appear in italics.

Figure 10.2 shows a diagram that describes the syntax of a legal identifier. Syntax diagrams describe how to create elements of Pascal programs. Here's how to use the diagram: Start by following the arrow that enters the diagram from the left. The first thing you reach is a box with the word *letter* inside. When you reach a box, you have come to something that must be included in your identifier. In this case, you need a letter. You then follow the arrow going out of this box. This arrow splits into three arrows. You may follow any one of the three arrows, giving you the options of leaving the diagram (following the middle arrow), getting another letter to add to your identifier (by following the lower arrow), or getting a digit to add to your identifier (by following the upper arrow). You may continue adding letters or digits to your identifier as long as you wish. However, to finish the identifier you must eventually leave the diagram by the middle arrow.

In general, arrows going out of a box point to the possible items that may follow the item contained in the box. If you follow the path of an arrow going into a box, you must include what is in that box in your identifier. Figure 10.3a gives some legal identifiers. Figure 10.3b gives some illegal identifiers.

Figure 10.2   Syntax diagram for an identifier

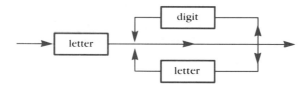

Figure 10.3a   Legal identifiers

```
average      program1    countwords
agetodrive   a           wordprocess
xyzn054t     a1b2c3       calculator
```
a

Figure 10.3b   Illegal identifiers

```
1stprogram      !thebestprogram!
program.1       the-most-wonderful-program
a bad program   a good program
```
b

2. For example, some translators only identify the identifier by its first eight characters.

Exercise 10.1: Why are the identifiers in Figure 10.3b illegal? ■

Exercise 10.2: Which of the following identifiers are legal? Why are the others illegal?

a. myprogram
b. agreatprogram!!!!
c. yrgnuhmai
d. 200thprogram
e. program54 ■

10.3 THE PROGRAM HEADER

The first item in a Pascal program is a program header. The program header starts with the reserved word **program.** It is followed by the identifier you are using to name the program. Next comes a left parenthesis followed by the sources of input and the destinations of output with which you wish the program to communicate. The sources of input and destinations of output are separated from each other by commas. The header ends with a right parenthesis followed by a semicolon. A Pascal program header might look like this:

```
program average (input, output);
```

Depending on how Pascal is implemented on the machine you are using, you may have to write the word **program** in uppercase letters or in lowercase letters, or it may not matter which you use.[3] All the reserved words in this book will appear in boldface.

You should try to think of a descriptive identifier when naming your program. The identifier should convey as much information as possible about what the program will do.

_____
3. We will show all reserved words in lowercase.

Exercise 10.3: Which of the identifiers in Figure 10.3a convey some information about what the program will do? ■

The translator must be able to distinguish the various components of the header. The reserved word **program** and the identifier naming the program must be separated by a space so that it is clear that one is a reserved word and the other an identifier. If no space is left, the translator will recognize the entire string of characters as an identifier. There may be blank spaces, as well as the required commas, between the names used to identify the sources and destinations of data. In fact, you may leave as many blank spaces and carriage returns between any two symbols (reserved words, parentheses, and so forth) as you like to enhance clarity or comprehension. They are only necessary, however, when the translator cannot differentiate two elements of a program. For example, a space is unnecessary between the identifier naming the program and the left parenthesis, because the translator knows that a left parenthesis cannot be part of an identifier.

The sources of input and destinations of output listed in the header can include three types of resources: standard input, standard output, and files. The words *input* and *output* are predefined Pascal identifiers. This means that they have predefined meanings in Pascal, but their meanings can be changed if the programmer wishes. The word *input* identifies standard input. The word *output* identifies standard output. The actual source and destination of data they respectively refer to depends on how Pascal is implemented on the computer you are using. Standard input usually refers to input from a keyboard. Standard output usually refers to a screen. Files (see Chapter 9, page 185), the third type of resource, may be used either as a source for input or as a destination for output. The name of a file used by a Pascal program must be a Pascal identifier.

Your program must state all the external sources and destinations of the data that it uses. This includes standard input, standard output, and files.

Figure 10.4 shows a syntax diagram describing the header statement. Here the items in the ovals must be used literally, just as they are written in the diagram. For example, the first part of a header must always be the reserved word **program**. The rectangular boxes indicate specific elements of the header that the programmer must fill in. For example, following the reserved word **program**, the programmer must choose an appropriate identifier to name the program.

Figure 10.4 **Syntax for a program header**

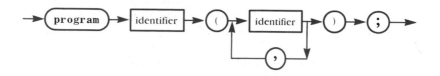

The following is a legal program header:

program inventory (input, output, books);

10.4 THE BLOCK

The first possible item in a block is the constant definition section, which specifies the data items that will remain unchanged throughout the execution of the program. If you define a constant in this section of your program, you associate an identifier with some constant value. You may then use that identifier in your program to represent the constant value. Doing so adds clarity to your program. If your program does not have any constant data items, you omit this section.

The second possible item in a block is the type definition section. Pascal has several predefined data types that allow you to request that memory may be set aside for those particular types of data. However, sometimes the programmer wishes to create a new type of data. The type definition section is used to create these new types of data. Each type definition specifies a particular structure in which data can be stored in memory. You omit this section if no additional data types are needed in a program.

The third possible item in a block is the variable declaration section. A *variable* is an identifier that refers to a space in memory that holds data that may be altered during the execution of a program. By referring to the name of a variable in your program, you refer to the value that is currently stored in the reserved space. This is analogous to the pieces of paper we used in Part I of this book. We may store and manipulate data within a program by declaring and using variables. Most interesting programs have variables. However, you omit this section if you write a program that does not use variables.

The fourth item in a block is the procedure and function declaration section. Procedures and functions correspond to the subalgorithms of a main algorithm. They are used to develop modular programs—that is, programs that are divided into sections that perform independent subtasks. Pascal was designed to encourage modular programming.

Procedures and functions encourage the use of stepwise refinement in programming solutions. In Figure 10.5, for example, the main program is similar to the general description of the algorithm. The procedures describe the more specific steps of the algorithm.

Just as subalgorithms may be refined into further subalgorithms, procedures and functions may be refined into subprocedures and subfunctions. In fact, a procedure is a kind of miniprogram that performs a more limited task than the main program. A function is a specialized type of miniprogram. Although procedures and functions are optional, they are usually required to make a program intelligible.

We shall refer to the last three parts of a block as *the main body of the program*. The main body of a program consists of the reserved word **begin**, followed by Pascal statements, followed by the keyword **end**. Different types of Pascal state-

Figure 10.5 Pascal program with an example of stepwise refinement

```
program        → program measurement (input, output);
header             {a program to convert inches to approximate}
                  {yards and feet and remaining inches}

constant       → const yard = 36;      {conversion for inches}
definition            foot = 12;      {conversion for inches}
section

variable       → var inchcount,        {the number of inches}
declaration         footcount,         {the number of feet}
section             yardcount: integer; {the number of yards}

procedure      →   procedure getnumber (var howmany: integer);
declaration            {gets the number of inches that the}
section                {user wishes to convert}

                   begin  {getnumber}
                     write ('How many inches are there?  ');
                     readln (howmany)
                   end;    {getnumber}

                   procedure converttofeet (var feet, inches: integer);
                       {converts inches to feet}

                   begin  {converttofeet}
                     feet: = inches div foot;
                     inches: = inches mod foot
                   end;    {converttofeet}

                   procedure converttoyards (var yards, inches: integer);
                       {converts inches to feet}

                   begin  {converttoyards}
                     yards: = inches div yard;
                     inches: = inches mod yard
                   end;    {converttoyards}

                   procedure printcalc (yardscount, footscount,
                       inchescount: integer); {prints answers}
```

(continued)

Figure 10.5
Continued

```
              begin  {printcalc}
                writeln(There are ',yardscount:2, ' yards and');
                writeln('there are ',footscount:2, ' feet and');
                writeln('there are ',inchescount:2,  ' inches');
                write('In the number of inches ');
                writeln('you described')
              end;   {printcalc}
```

main   → **begin** {main program}
program
```
                   getnumber(inchcount);
                   converttoyards(yardcount,inchcount);
                   converttofeet(footcount,inchcount);
                   printcalc(yardcount, footcount, inchcount)
              end.   {main program}
```

ments corresponding to instructions used in writing algorithms will be introduced later in this book. All statements in Pascal are separated from each other by semicolons. Semicolons used for this purpose are called *statement separators* and indicate to the translator that another instruction will follow.

In Pascal, execution begins with the statement that appears after the reserved word **begin** in the main body of the program. The statements between the keyword **begin** and the keyword **end** in the main body of the program are executed sequentially.

10.5 THE FINAL ELEMENT

The final element in a Pascal program is a period. The period follows the block and is used to indicate the end of the program.

We now have a general structure for a Pascal program. Figure 10.6 shows the syntax diagram for a program. Figure 10.7 shows the syntax diagram for a block.

Figure 10.6   **Syntax diagram for a program**

Figure 10.7   Syntax diagram for a block

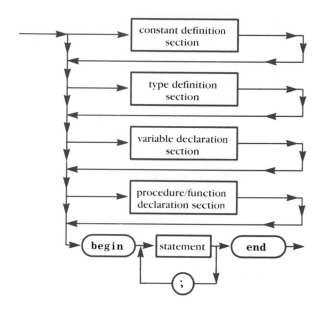

10.6 PROGRAM CLARITY AND DOCUMENTATION

Since programs have a long lifespan and are frequently altered by people other than the original programmer, the actions performed in a program should be described clearly and unambiguously. There are several ways to achieve this goal. One way is to break the program down into procedures so that each major action is precisely identified.

Figures 10.8 and 10.9 contrast two programs, one written with procedures, the other not. The main body of the program in Figure 10.8 conveys clearly the main subalgorithms used to solve the problem. The program in Figure 10.9 is just a long list of instructions. The general idea of what this program does and the algorithm it describes are hidden in the details of the program.

A second way to clarify the workings of a program is to document it carefully. Documentation should clearly explain the algorithm the program is describing and how the programmer has implemented that algorithm in Pascal. The main types of program documentation are:

A. Internal to the program
    1. Self-documenting identifiers
    2. Formatting
    3. Comments

B. External to the program
    1. User documentation
    2. Programmer documentation

Figure 10.8   Program with procedures

```pascal
program PatternMaker(input, output);
{This program allows the user to create a rectangle.}
{The user enters a character, followed by a }
{height and width. The program then creates a rectangle}
{using the respective character, height, and width.}

var    character: char;        {holds character for rectangle}
       height,          {holds height for rectangle}
       width: integer; {holds width for rectangle}

  procedure Instructions;
                  {a procedure to give instructions to the user}
  begin   {Instructions}
    writeln('Welcome to the PatternMaker Program');
    writeln('I hope that it is an enjoyable experience');
    writeln('for you. The program will allow you to');
    writeln('enter a character that will be used');
    writeln('to draw a rectangle.');
    writeln('The program will then');
    writeln('ask you for the dimensions of');
    writeln('your rectangle. Always remember');
    writeln('to follow your answers');
    writeln('with a carriage return.');
    writeln('  Good Luck Pattern Makers!!!!');
    writeln
  end;    {Instructions}

  procedure getch (var ch: char);
    {prompts user for character and reads it}

  begin    {getch}
    write ('Please enter character: ');
    readln(ch)
  end;     {getch}

  procedure getHW(var Hght, Wdth: integer);
    {a procedure to read in Height }
    {and Width for Rectangle}

  begin    {getHW}
    write('Please enter Height: ');
    readln(Hght);
    writeln;
```

```
        write('Please enter Width: ');
        readln(Wdth)
    end;    {getHW}


    procedure printrec(CH: char; Hght, Wdth: integer);
      {This is a procedure to print out a rectangle.}
      {It uses 2 nested repeat loops. The inside loop}
      {writes out a line of characters (keeps track of }
      {the width). The outside repeat keeps track of }
      {how many lines of characters (the height) have been}
      {printed out.}

    var counter1,              {keeps track of width}
        counter2: integer;   {keeps track of height}

    begin      {printrec}
      counter2: = 0;
      repeat                  {repeat loop to print out a certain}
        counter1: = 0;     {number of lines, described by Hght}
        repeat                          {repeat loop to print a}
          write(CH);                    {line of characters}
          counter1: = counter1 + 1   {the number of characters}
        until counter1 = Wdth;         {is described by Wdth}
        counter2: = counter2 + 1;
        writeln
      until counter2 = Hght
    end;      {printrec}

begin   {PatternMaker}
  Instructions;
  getch(character);
  getHW(height, width);
  printrec(character, height, width)
end.    {PatternMaker}
```

Internal Documentation

Algorithms are often complex and difficult to understand. As we have seen, a program is an implementation of an algorithm in a specific, predefined programming language, such as Pascal. Internal documentation should describe the various re-

Figure 10.9   Program without procedures

```
program PatternMaker(input, output);
{This program allows the user to create a}
{rectangle. The user enters a character, followed by a}
{height and width. The program then creates a rectangle}
{using the respective character, height, and width.}

var    ch: char;         {holds character for rectangle}
       height,           {holds height for rectangle}
       width: integer;  {holds width for rectangle}
       counter1,              {keeps track of width}
       counter2: integer;    {keeps track of height}

begin   {PatternMaker}
    writeln('Welcome to the PatternMaker Program');
    writeln('I hope that it is an enjoyable experience');
    writeln('for you. The program will allow you to');
    writeln('enter a character that will be used');
    writeln('to draw a rectangle.');
    writeln('The program will then');
    writeln('ask you for the dimensions of');
    writeln('your rectangle. Always remember');
    writeln('to follow your answers');
    writeln('with a carriage return.');
    writeln('  Good Luck Pattern Makers!!!!');
    writeln;
    writeln('Please enter character: ');
    readln(ch);
    write('Please enter Height: ');
    readln(height);
    writeln;
    write('Please enter Width: ');
    readln(width);
    counter2: =0;
    repeat
      counter1: =0;
      repeat
        write(ch);
        counter1: =counter1 + 1
      until counter1 = width;
        counter2: =counter2 + 1;
        writeln
    until counter2 = height
  end.    {PatternMaker}
```

finements of the algorithm as they occur. It should give a clear indication of what tasks the program is meant to accomplish and how it accomplishes them.

Descriptive identifiers provide one means of internal documentation. The programmer chooses identifiers to describe many elements of a Pascal program, including the program itself, the procedures, the variable data, and the constant data. Each identifier should suggest the purpose of what it is naming.

For example, if you create a procedure to alphabetize a list of names, you should choose a descriptive identifier like *alphabetize* rather than something like *x* or *thisisit*. The identifier *alphabetize* immediately suggests what task the procedure will accomplish.

Follow the same rule in naming data items. Naming a constant *taxrate* conveys more information than naming it *y* or *constant54*. Naming a variable *total* conveys more information than naming it *t*.

Exercise   10.4: In the program shown in Figure 10.10, all the identifiers appear in uppercase letters. Which give you some idea of what they are describing? Which do not? Explain your answers.   ■

A second way of building documentation into your program is through the format in which you present it. You can make the parts of a Pascal program identifiable by using indentation and blank lines in a consistent fashion. Although the manner in which a program is formatted is up to the programmer, the guidelines listed in Figure 10.11 have proved useful in a variety of programs. To see how we have applied these rules, you should look at the sample programs given throughout the book.

The third way of internally documenting a program is through the use of comments. Comments explain the algorithm your program is implementing. Comments must be surrounded by the symbols { and } or go between the symbols (* and *).[4] The translator does not attempt to translate anything that appears between these symbols. You may therefore put any type of comment you like between them. The only place comments are not allowed in a program is within a reserved word, a reserved symbol,[5] or an identifier. For example, you could never write a header like this:

```
pro{Joe's program}gram calcgrades(input,output);
```

We recommend that you put comments to the side of, or indented below or above, the elements of your program. The program in Figure 10.8 shows good examples of comments.

4. Either pair of symbols is fine. Some terminals do not have { and } as symbols. Hence (* and *) have also been provided as legitimate comment symbols.

5. In later chapters, we will introduce some symbols that are made up of two characters.

Figure 10.10   Program for Exercise 10.4

```pascal
program XYZ (input,output);

const MAXCOUNT = 50;
      IT = 'Do you have any more marbles? ';

var MYMARBLECOUNT,
    NUMBEROFMARBLES: integer;


    procedure HUH;

    var ANYMORE: char;

    begin
      NUMBEROFMARBLES:=0;
      writeln(IT);
      readln(ANYMORE);
      while ANYMORE = 'y' do
        begin
          NUMBEROFMARBLES:=NUMBEROFMARBLES + 1;
          writeln(IT);
          readln(ANYMORE)
        end
    end;

    procedure COMPARECOUNT;

    begin
      if MYMARBLECOUNT > NUMBEROFMARBLES
         then writeln('I have more marbles')
         else if NUMBEROFMARBLES > MAXCOUNT
                 then
                    writeln(' I can''t count that high')
                 else
                    writeln(' You have more marbles!')
    end;

begin
  MYMARBLECOUNT:=5;
  HUH;
  COMPARECOUNT
end.
```

Figure 10.11   Guidelines for formatting your program

- Separate sections by leaving blank lines between them.
- Indent procedure and function declarations more deeply than other sections.
- Line up **begin–end** pairs.
- Indent statements within **begin–end** pairs.

Here are the most useful ways to use comments for internal documentation:

1. To identify who worked on the program and when
2. To describe the purpose of the program
3. To describe the algorithm(s) used throughout the program
4. To clarify the purpose of identifiers that describe user-defined types, constants, and variables
5. To clarify the beginnings and endings of procedures, functions, statements, and the main body of the program

We will have more to say about the use of comments in later chapters. However, notice that internal documentation does not describe the meaning of Pascal statements. It is assumed that someone reading a program knows Pascal. What she or he doesn't know is the algorithm you are implementing in Pascal.

The Pascal program shown in Figure 10.12 makes use of all the types of internal documentation that we have mentioned. Note that most of the comments are set off in some way from the actual instructions to make them easy to spot.

External Documentation

External documentation serves two purposes: (1) It provides information to the users of the program and (2) it provides other programmers with a general view of the problem you have tried to solve, the algorithm you have implemented to solve it, and how you implemented the algorithm.

External documentation intended for users of the program is called *user documentation*. Its purpose is to tell users how to access the program on the computer they are using, what to do to start running the program, what to expect as the program executes (what they are required to type as input and what type of output will be given), and how to terminate execution of the program. The assumption behind user documentation is that the user knows nothing about programming.

External documentation intended for other programmers is called *programmer documentation*. Its purpose is to explain how your program works, what al-

Figure 10.12   Program with documentation

```
                    {Zlotnick, Mann, and LiSanti}
                    {Date Written: 9/27/84}
                    {revised: 9/8/85}
          program agetodrive(input, output);
             {This is a sample program. It takes as input the}
             {user's age, and states according to California }
             {law whether or not the user is able to drive.  }
             {The program consists of the main pieces:        }
                 {getage            }
                 {printresponse    }


          const legitimate = 16;   {the age you must be to drive}


          var age: integer; {a place to hold the user's age}


             procedure getage(var howold: integer);
                {a procedure to read in the user's age}

             begin    {getage}
               write('How old are you?   ');
               readln(howold)
             end;      {getage}


             procedure printresponse(howold: integer);
                    {prints response about whether or not user}
                    {is old enough to drive}

             begin {printresponse}
                   if howold< legitimate
                      then
                        writeln ('You are not old enough to drive.')
                      else
                        writeln ('You are old enough to drive.')
             end;    {printresponse}

             begin      {agetodrive}
                   getage(age);
                   printresponse(age)
             end.   {agetodrive}
```

gorithm your program is implementing, and how the procedures and functions interact. It should also indicate the various sources of data items, whether the items are variables or constants, where they are stored, and how they are transmitted from one part of the program to another. Finally, it should indicate where to find the program in the system and how to execute it. Figure 10.13 gives examples of user and programmer documentation for the program measurement that was given in Figure 10.5.[6]

Figure 10.13   Examples of user and programmer documentation

User Documentation for Program *Measurement*

Program *measurement* converts inches into yards, feet, and inches. The program may be executed by typing *measurement* at the prompt.

You will be expected to type in the number of inches when prompted, followed by a carriage return. The program will output the final result and will end execution automatically.

Programmer Documentation for Program *Measurement*

Program *measurement* converts inches into the equivalent yards, feet, and inches. It is written in Standard Pascal. It may be found in the directory ~imcs63/ programs/measurement.

The only data the user must input is the number of inches to be converted. It is read into an *integer* variable. The output consists of three integers representing yards, feet, and inches, respectively. The algorithm is as follows:

I. Get number of inches.

II. Convert inches to yards.
   A. Divide number of inches by 36 to get yards.
   B. Compute remainder when you divide inches by 36 and make that new value on inches.

III. Convert inches to feet.
   A. Divide number of inches by 12 to get feet.
   B. Compute remainder when you divide inches by 12 and make that new value on inches.

IV. Display number of yards, feet, and inches.

(continued)

---

6. Note that you may not understand the information telling where to find the program because the computer you are using may be very different from our computer.

Figure 10.13
Continued

The main procedures of the program are

1. *getnumber*, which corresponds to step I
2. *converttoyards*, which corresponds to step II
3. *converttofeet*, which corresponds to step III
4. *printcalc*, which corresponds to step IV

All the procedures must be executed in the order given.

CHAPTER SUMMARY

1. Pascal programs have the following structure:
   a. Header
   b. Block
   c. Period

2. A block is built of the following parts:
   a. Constant definition section
   b. Type definition section
   c. Variable declaration section
   d. Procedure and function declaration section
   e. The keyword **begin**
   f. A statement or statements separated by semicolons
   g. The keyword **end**

3. Reserved words and symbols have specific meanings in Pascal. They may not be used in any way other than that described by the Pascal language.

4. Identifiers are the names by which the programmer identifies various elements in a Pascal program. Pascal also has predefined identifiers. These identifiers already have a specific meaning, but the programmer may, if she wishes, change that meaning.

5. Documentation is a way of making a program more understandable and more usable. The types of documentation are:

   A. Internal to the program
      1. Self-documenting identifiers
      2. Formatting
      3. Comments

   B. External to the program
      1. User documentation
      2. Programmer documentation

COMMON ERRORS

Although we have not given you enough information to write a complete Pascal program, there are certain possible errors that are worth keeping in mind even at this stage. In general, possible errors will be listed at the end of every chapter.

- A misspelled keyword or mistyped symbol is a syntactic error—for example, putting a : where you need a =.

- A definition or declaration not given in the order specified in this chapter is a syntactic error. An example of such an error is putting the constant definition section after the variable declaration section.

- A missing keyword is a syntactic error. An example of such an error is omitting the keyword **program** in the program header.

- Beginning two identifiers with the same characters may be a syntactic or a logic error if your translator sees only a certain number of characters as significant. For example, a variable named *alphabet* may conflict with a procedure named *alphabetize* if the translator recognizes only the first eight characters.

- A missing or misplaced comment bracket may cause any type of error. The translator will consider any statements within brackets as part of a comment.

SUPPLEMENTAL PROBLEMS

1. Write a legal Pascal program header that identifies *input*, *output*, and a file named *frog* as sources and destinations of data.
2. Write a legal Pascal program header that identifies *output* as a destination of data.
3. Assume that the word *writeln* is a legal Pascal statement. Write a legal Pascal program.
4. Find the errors in the following program headers:

   ```
   porgram pickles(input,output);

   program !yeah! (input, output);

   program     hello    (in put, output);

   program hello input, output, files);

   program good-bye (input, files, output)
   ```

   (continued)

```
program great (output, input homework);
```

5. Which of the following program headers are legal? Which are not? Why are the illegal headers illegal?

```
program gotit (output, input, inventory);
```

```
program gotit (input, inventory, output);
```

```
gotit program (input, output);
```

```
program goforit (input, output, surf, ski, swim);
```

```
program whistle (song1 song2 song3 song4, output);
```

```
program problem (input, output).
```

```
program gone (whistle!, good-bye, input, output);
```

6. Which of the following are legal identifiers? Why are the illegal identifiers illegal?
   a. *goose*
   b. *begin*
   c. *C. Brown*
   d. *programghost*
   e. *program*

7. Assume that the word *writeln* is a legal Pascal statement. What is wrong with the following program?

```
program go (input, output);
  {a program to do something
    very exciting

begin    {main program}
  writeln
end.
```

8. Assume that the word *writeln* is a legal Pascal statement. What is wrong with the following program?

```
program wow (input, output);
  {another exciting program}
begin
  writeln
end;
```

9. Make lists of the keywords, identifiers, and reserved symbols in the following Pascal program. Assume *writeln* is a Pascal statement (you do not need to classify it).

```
program itworks (input, output, saveit);
  {a program for identifying things}
begin
  writeln
end.
```

10. Consider the following program. All the parts have been identified. What is wrong with the structure of this program?

constant → **const** x = 5;
definition
section

header → **program** messedup (input, output);

procedure → **procedure** gotit;
declaration   **begin**
section   writeln
              end;

variable → **var** two, three: integer;
declaration
section

main → **begin**
program   writeln
              end.

CHAPTER 11

Every useful computer program produces some sort of output. So we want some kind of statement that will produce output in every program we write. Moreover, every part of a program should contribute to the output in some way, although the effect may not be direct. (Output may also appear at the very start of a program: Most interactive programs start by greeting the user.)

11.1 LINE-ORIENTED OUTPUT

Line-oriented output includes character output displayed on a screen and output printed on paper. The output is displayed in lines, starting at the left and continuing to the right until one line terminates and the next one starts. (Other forms of output include graphic displays and output of data to external storage, which we deal with in Chapter 28.) Each line of output is made up of the printable characters available on our computer—in other words, the output resembles lines on a printed page.

In producing line-oriented output, we must control

- Which characters show up on each line
- When a line ends and a new one begins
- How each line is laid out (that is, where the spaces occur)

In this chapter, we are dealing with the simplest case: We want to produce a constant output, something that will appear the same every time the program is run. One way (not the only way!) we can do that is to incorporate the constant data to be displayed in the statement that produces the output.

PRODUCING OUTPUT FROM A PROGRAM

USING *write* **FOR OUTPUT OF STRING LITERALS**

Pascal performs output by means of *standard procedures*. A standard procedure can be thought of as a part of a program that is invisibly included in every program, so that you need not write it yourself. This is very convenient for producing output, since it means that the programmer does not have to deal with the peculiarities of the devices attached to one computer or another. In this section, we describe the standard procedure named *write*. We'll refer to lines of a program that use this standard procedure as *write statements*.

Here's a *write* statement that produces the constant output `Hello, world`. Note that we use single quote marks to indicate what the output should be, but they are not part of the output:

```
write ('Hello, world.')
```

Pascal interprets this statement as follows: The word *write* describes the type of action the statement is meant to produce. What appears inside the parentheses after the word *write* describes the output that is to be written. (The spaces before or after each parenthesis are optional.)

The description of the desired output can take many forms. In this case, we have a set of characters enclosed in single quotes (or apostrophes).[1] The quotes

---

1. When we speak of data enclosed in quotes, we will always be referring to single quotation marks. The double quotation mark `''` is not a special symbol in Pascal. You may use it, like any other character, as part of a string literal within single quotes: `'I said ''Hello.'' '`

enclose, but are not part of, the data to be written. Data enclosed in quotes is known as a *string* or a *string literal,* since it describes "literally" what you want the computer to display. The computer ignores any spaces that appear before or after the parentheses, but treats any spaces inside the quotes as spaces to be displayed. Such spaces are characters, just like the *H, e,* comma, and period. For example, the computer will treat all three statements in Figure 11.1 the same way as it treats the `write` statement above. However, it will treat the three statements in Figure 11.2 in different ways.

As a general rule, the characters enclosed in quotes are exactly the characters that are displayed. There is one exception, however. Assume that we want to display this output:

```
This isn't possible
```

How can we do it? We might try this:

```
write ('This isn't possible')
```

Do you see why this won't work? Pascal will interpret the apostrophe embedded in *isn't* as the closing quote mark of a literal: `'This isn'`. The characters immediately after that apostrophe, *t possible,* aren't enclosed in quotes. In effect, Pascal has appropriated the apostrophe for its own purposes.

Pascal provides a way around this problem: When you want a literal that contains an apostrophe, type two successive apostrophes with no intervening characters. When Pascal encounters two apostrophes in a row, it knows they're not intended to enclose a literal but to stand for a single apostrophe character inside a literal. For example:

```
write ('This isn''t possible')
```

Figure 11.1   **Three equivalent statements**

```
write('Hello, world.')
write    (       'Hello, world.'      )
write ( 'Hello, world.' )
```

Figure 11.2   **Three statements that give different results**

```
write (' Hello, world.')            { space before the H }
write ('Hello,world.')              { no space before the w }
write ('Hello,    world.')          { four spaces before the w }
```

We can use the same technique to handle an apostrophe that occurs at the beginning or the end of a literal. For example, suppose we want to display the line from Lewis Carroll's "Jabberwocky":

```
'Twas brillig and the slithy toves
```

This is how we can do it:

```
write ('''Twas brillig and the slithy toves')
```

And we can write an apostrophe at the end of a literal in the same way. To display

```
He said, 'I hunt for haddocks' eyes'
```

we can use this *write* statement:

```
write ('He said, ''I hunt for haddocks'' eyes''')
```

Pascal always recognizes the first quote it encounters as a delimiter—that is, a quote mark that is not part of the literal but instead indicates the start of the literal. Then it recognizes the two adjacent quotes as a single apostrophe character inside the literal. It recognizes a final quote (as in `''eyes'''`) as the end of the literal.

Now let's embed our first *write* statement in a complete Pascal program. Figure 11.3 shows a program that prints `Hello, world.` as its only output. This program will work; try it on your own computer. It may not work as you expect, however. After the program has finished running, the next thing most computers will display on your screen (if your output is being displayed on a screen) will appear on the same line as the program's output, after the period.[2] The statement

```
write ('Hello, world.')
```

Figure 11.3   **Program to display a string literal**

```
program howdy (output);
  { a program that prints the characters "Hello, world." }
begin   { howdy }
    write ('Hello, world.')
end.    { howdy }
```

2. Typically, the next thing to appear is the computer's prompt for another command.

instructs the computer simply to display the 13 characters enclosed in the quotes: *H, e, l, l, o,* comma, space (the space counts as a character), *w, o, r, l, d,* and period. We haven't told the computer to advance to the next line. A second example will illustrate our point: The program in Figure 11.4 will produce the same output as the preceding one.

Note that Pascal requires a semicolon between any two statements. The keywords **begin** and **end** are not statements but delimiters that describe where the body of the program starts and ends. Putting the *write* statements on separate lines does not make the program's output appear on separate lines. The format of your program (that is, how you lay out the statements) has no effect on the format of the output. Figure 11.5 gives yet another program that will produce the same output.

Where you break a line in writing a program is of no importance. You may break a line anywhere a space can legally occur, except between quotes (that is, inside string literals). Program *howdy3* is just as readable to a Pascal compiler as program *howdy1* or *howdy2*, but it's almost incomprehensible to a human. Proper spacing and line formatting of your program text are essential for your own benefit. But they have no effect on the format of the output.

You can keep track of what effect a *write* statement has by considering the cursor that is displayed on the terminal screen. The cursor always indicates where the next character is going to appear, both for characters you yourself enter and the characters the computer displays. The effect of a *write* statement is to display some characters starting at the current position of the cursor and to move the

Figure 11.4   Another program to display a string literal

```
program howdy2 (output);
   { another program that prints the characters "Hello, world." }
begin {howdy2 }
    write ('Hel');       { This writes the first 3 characters. }
    write ('lo, wo');    { This writes the next 6 characters. }
    write ('rld.')       { This writes the last 4 characters. }
end. {howdy2 }
```

Figure 11.5   A legal but badly formatted program to display a string literal

```
program howdy3 (output); { an ugly program that
prints "Hello, world." } begin {howdy3} write ('Hel'); write
('lo, wo'); write ('rld.') end. {howdy3}
```

cursor one position to the right after each character is displayed. (Printers and other hard-copy devices in effect have an invisible cursor or write pointer that keeps track of where the next character is to be displayed.)

11.3 CONTROLLING LINES

We also need some way of telling the computer when to end one line of display and begin a new line—what on a typewriter would be a carriage return. In Pascal, the standard procedure *writeln* (pronounced "write-line") serves that purpose. Figure 11.6 gives a version of program *howdy* in which the cursor is moved to the next line after the message has been printed. The difference between this program and the original *howdy* program is the presence of the *writeln* statement after the *write* statement. It means, now that the message has been printed, move the cursor to the start of a new line. Note that a semicolon is required after the first statement, because our program is now more than one statement long, and statements must be separated by semicolons.

Actually, Pascal simplifies the programmer's life by providing a way to combine the output to be displayed with the instruction to move to the next line, as follows:

```
writeln ('Hello, world.');
```

Anywhere you can say *write* you can say *writeln* instead. The effect is to produce all the output that a *write* statement would, and then move the cursor to a new line. Figure 11.7 shows a modified version of program *howdy2* that will produce exactly the same output as program *howdyline*.

The first *write* statement displays characters but leaves the cursor on the same line, waiting at the next unused location. Because of the standard rules of program sequence, the second *write* statement starts displaying output just after the first one ends. The *writeln* statement starts displaying output just after the second *write* ends, and then, after the period is printed, moves the cursor to the beginning of the next line. Even though the letters *ln* in the word *writeln*

Figure 11.6   **A program to print a message and advance to the next line**

```
program howdyline (output);
   { This program prints the characters "Hello, world." }
   { and then moves the cursor to the next line. }
begin { howdyline }
   write ('Hello, world.');      { Print message.}
   writeln                        { Go to next line.}
end. { howdyline }
```

Figure 11.7   Another program to print a message and advance to the next line

```pascal
program howdyline2 (output);
   { This is another program that prints "Hello, world." }
   { and then moves the cursor to the next line. }
begin { howdyline2 }
    write ('Hel');     { This writes the first 3 characters. }
    write ('lo, wo'); { This writes the next 6 characters. }
    writeln ('rld.')   { This writes the last 4, and }
                       { skips to the start of a new line. }
end. { howdyline2 }
```

appear before the item to be written, the cursor isn't moved to the next line until after the item has been written.

See if you can describe the output of the program shown in Figure 11.8. Be careful; we've laid a trap. Each *write* and *writeln* statement in this program will display a literal. The *write* statements will display the characters inside the quotes. The *writeln* statements will display the characters inside the quotes and will then move the cursor to the start of a new line. Since spacing after a *write* statement is not automatic, *after* and *noon* will be joined together. But so will *having* and *a*! Here's the output this program will produce:

```
Good afternoon, I hope
you are havinga nice day.
```

When splitting a constant output across several literals, programmers often forget to include a space in the boundary between words. To fix this program, we would rewrite it as shown in Figure 11.9. The difference between these two programs is simply the space after *having* in the literal 'you are having'. Since that space is inside the quotes, the computer prints it. Another way to fix this program would be to put a space before the *a* in 'a nice day', as shown in Figure 11.10.

Figure 11.8   A program with *write* and *writeln* statements

```pascal
program multiline (output);
   { This program produces output that you must deduce. }
begin { multiline }
    write ('Good after');
    writeln ('noon, I hope');
    write ('you are having');
    writeln ('a nice day.')
end. { multiline }
```

━━━━━━

Figure 11.9   **Corrected version of the program in Figure 11.8**

```
program multiline2(output);
  { This program produces a properly spaced two-line greeting. }
begin { multiline2 }
    write ('Good after');        { Part of the first line. }
    writeln ('noon, I hope');    { Rest of first line and  }
                                 { move to next line.       }

    write ('you are having ');   { Note a space between     }
                                 { "having" and '.          }

    writeln ('a nice day.')      { Finish and move to next line. }
end. { multiline2 }
```

━━━━━━

Figure 11.10   **Yet another way to fix the program in Figure 11.8**

```
program multiline3(output);
  { This program produces a properly spaced two-line greeting. }
begin { multiline3 }
    write ('Good after');        { Part of the first line. }
    writeln ('noon, I hope');    { Rest of first line and  }
                                 { move to next line.       }

    write ('you are having');    { No space between "having" }
                                 { and ', but a space        }
    writeln (' a nice day.')     { between ' and "a".        }
end. { multiline3 }
```

────────

Exercise   11.1: Describe the output of the following program:

```
program figureitout(output);
begin { figureitout }
    write('****');
    writeln('**');
    write('**');
    writeln('***');
```

(continued)

```
        writeln('****');
        write('***');
        writeln;
        writeln('**');
        write('*')
        writeln
end. { figureitout }  ■
```

Exercise 11.2: Describe the output of the following Pascal program:

```
program sampleoutput(output);
   { This program simply displays some text, but }
   { you have to figure out what it is. }
begin { sampleoutput }
        writeln('''The time has come'', the Walrus said');
        writeln('  ''to talk of many things:');
        writeln('Of shoes-and ships-and sealing wax-');
        writeln('  Of cabbages-and kings-');
        writeln('And why the sea is boiling hot-');
        writeln('  And whether pigs have wings.''')
end. { sampleoutput }  ■
```

Exercise 11.3: Write a complete Pascal program to display the following output exactly as it appears below. The spacing and special characters are as important as the letters:

```
'You are old, Father William,' the young man said,
  'And your hair has become very white;
And yet you incessantly stand on your head-
  Do you think, at your age, it is right?'  ■
```

11.4 USING *write* AND *writeln* WITH INTEGER EXPRESSIONS

Descriptions of the output you want displayed are placed between the parentheses of *write* and *writeln* statements. These descriptions may take many forms. The string literal is one form; another is an *integer expression*. An integer is a whole number written without a decimal point, and an integer expression is made up of integer values and arithmetic operations that you apply to those values. For example:

```
writeln ( 6 + 9 )
```

Here the expression inside the parentheses is not enclosed in quotes. That means that the expression will not be printed literally. Instead, it will be evaluated (by doing the addition), and the value will be displayed. The effect of the `writeln` statement will be to print the number 15 and then to move the cursor to the beginning of the next line. Contrast this with the following, slightly different statement:

```
writeln ( '6 + 9' )
```

Here the expression between the parentheses is a string literal because the characters are enclosed in quotes. The quotes tell Pascal that the desired effect is to print exactly what appears between them: the characters 6, space, +, space, and 9.

Figure 11.11 shows a short, but complete, Pascal program to illustrate the points we have covered so far. Try to figure out the output of the program before you read on. All the semicolons, quote marks, and parentheses in this program are essential. Which statements display literals and which display arithmetic expressions? The program in Figure 11.11 will produce the following output:

```
The sum 66+77 is          143
The sum of the numbers from one to six is          21
```

You may wonder where all those spaces before the numbers 143 and 21 come from. They certainly weren't requested in the `write` or `writeln` statements. They are present because integer expressions are displayed differently than string literals.

When a Pascal `write` or `writeln` statement contains a string literal in parentheses, the value of that literal—in other words, the exact characters between the

Figure 11.11   A program to display the value of an integer expression

```
program mathpractice(output);
{ Do a bit of arithmetic inside a writeln. }
begin { mathpractice }
    write ('The sum 66 + 77 is ');
    writeln ( 66 + 77 );
    write ('The sum of the numbers from one to six is ');
    writeln (1 + 2 + 3 + 4 + 5 + 6 )
end. { mathpractice }
```

quotes—is displayed. Literals are displayed exactly, character by character. When a *write* or *writeln* statement contains an integer expression between the parentheses, the value of that expression is displayed. Integer values are *not* displayed character by character. Instead, the computer allots a fixed number of spaces for displaying the value. (The number of spaces varies from one version of Pascal to another. Many versions of Pascal use ten spaces, and that is the convention we'll follow.) Within these spaces, the computer displays the value as a sequence of digits in the ordinary manner and right-justified—that is, it displays the value as far to the right as possible within the reserved space. If the integer value is negative, then a minus sign will appear just before the leftmost digit. The space taken up by the minus sign counts as one of the ten spaces. Thus, writing out the value of 66 + 77 causes the computer to print seven blank spaces followed by the digits 1, 4, and 3.

On most computer displays, every character (including the space) takes up the same amount of room on a line. You can think of a line as consisting of a fixed number of columns, or print positions. Most terminals have 80 columns on each line. In Figure 11.12, we show the output produced by the first two statements of the program in Figure 11.11. Below each character of output, we've indicated the column in the line where that character appears. Columns 1 through 19 are printed by the statement.

```
write ('The sum 66 + 77 is ')
```

Columns 20 through 29 are printed by the statement

```
writeln ( 66 + 77 );
```

This rule simply guarantees that, when an integer value is printed, there will be enough room for the largest integer value Pascal can represent.[3] It is useful in producing tabular output, such as columns of numbers. Still, the output looks a little strange, and you may want to avoid those blank spaces.

Figure 11.12   Output with columns indicated

```
|T|h|e|  |s|u|m|  |6|6|  | +|  |7|7|  |i|s|  |  |  |  |  |  |  |  |1|4|3|
 1 2 3  4 5 6 7  8 9 10 11 12 13 14 15 16 17 18 19 20 21 22 23 24 25 26 27 28 29
```

3. This value also varies from one version of Pascal to another, but a common largest integer is 2147483647, or one less than 2 to the thirty-first power.

Pascal provides a way to control the format of integer output. The method is simple: Instead of accepting some fixed width for the display of an integer, you can specify the width you want. To do so, you enter, after the integer expression in your *write* or *writeln* statement, a colon (:) character followed by an integer that specifies the width of the space. For example:

```
writeln ( 66 + 77:5)
```

The computer performs this instruction by producing the five characters—space, space, 1, 4, 3—and then advancing to the next line. The output looks like this:

　ˏ ˏ 143

(We use the ˏ character to indicate blank spaces.) You can leave spaces around the colon if you wish. The space allotted for printing a value is known as a *field,* and the number after the colon is known as the *field-width specifier.*

A number of rules govern the use of integer field-width specifiers. If, for example, you fail to specify enough space to accommodate the entire integer in the output, the computer will ignore your specification and will use the smallest number of columns that will permit all the digits (and, if necessary, a minus sign) to be displayed. Thus, the three statements shown in Figure 11.13 will all cause the computer to print just the three characters 1, 4, and 3. The three statements shown in Figure 11.14, however, will each produce different results.

If you don't know how many spaces your integer output will take up and you want to reserve exactly enough, use a field-width specifier of : 1. Thus, a field-width specifier is a request for a minimum number of columns. If more are needed, Pascal will allocate them. If the integer output is negative, it will be preceded by a minus sign, even if this requires more space than your width specifier requested.

Figure 11.13　*write* **statements that produce the same output**

```
write ( 66 + 77 :1);
write ( 66 + 77 :2);
write ( 66 + 77 :3);
```

Figure 11.14　*write* **statements that produce different output**

```
write ( 66 + 77 :4);
write ( 66 + 77 :5);
write ( 66 + 77 :6);
```

Exercise 11.4: Show the output generated by the three statements in Figure 11.14. ■

If you want to choose a field-width specifier that requests more than the usual width, you may do so. For example, the statement

```
write ( 66 + 77 :50)
```

will cause 47 blanks to be printed, followed by the number 143.

Exercise 11.5: What is the output of the following program?

```
program intformat (output);
{ Fooling around with field-width specifiers }
begin { intformat }
        writeln ( 9+85 :1 );
        writeln ( 9-85 :1 );
        writeln ( 9+85 :2 );
        writeln ( 9-85 :2 );
        writeln ( 9+85 :3 );
        writeln ( 9-85 :3 );
        writeln ( 9+85 :4 );
        writeln ( 9-85 :4 );
        writeln ( 9+85 :5 );
        writeln ( 9-85 :5 );
        writeln ( 9+85 :25 );
        writeln ( 9-85 :25 )
end. { intformat } ■
```

Field-width specifiers may be used with string literals as well as with integers. The effect is to add extra spaces to the left of the literal. This is sometimes referred to as *padding*. Thus, the effect of this statement

```
write ( 'Hi there':30 )
```

would be to display "Hi there" preceded by 22 spaces.

Let's review what we've covered so far. Pascal uses *write* and *writeln* statements to display line-oriented output. Each statement describes, within parentheses, the output to be displayed. We've seen two types of output so far, both constant outputs: string literals and constant integer expressions. The rules for displaying these types of output differ: a character-by-character rule for literals and a standard formatting rule for integer expressions. The programmer can override these rules by using field-width specifiers.

11.5 MORE ON *write* AND *writeln*

In fact, **write** and **writeln** statements can be used more flexibly than we have shown. Consider the program in Figure 11.15 and try to figure out what its output will look like.

This program produces only a single line of output because it contains only one **writeln**. It will give you the following output:

The sum of ∧∧∧∧∧∧7859 and ∧∧∧∧∧∧3001 is ∧∧∧∧∧10860

Everything inside quotes is reproduced exactly, while every integer expression is evaluated; the value is printed according to the appropriate formatting rule. The ∧ marks indicate the extra blanks caused by the standard formatting rule for integers.

It may seem strange that we need so many lines of program text to produce a single line of output, and in fact, we can produce this same line of output with a single Pascal statement instead of the six shown in Figure 11.15 by using **write** and **writeln** statements more flexibly. We can intersperse literals, integer expressions, and other types of expressions in those statements. The program in Figure 11.16 will produce an output that is identical to that of the **minimath** program. A single **write** or **writeln** statement will accept any number of output descriptions separated by commas and display the output corresponding to each, all on the same line. When you incorporate multiple output descriptions into a single **write** or **writeln** statement, you can use field-width specifiers for each one.

Figure 11.15   **Program minimath**

```
program minimath(output);
{ a little arithmetic }
begin { minimath }
    write ( 'The sum of ');       { first part of message }
    write ( 7859 );               { first summand }
    write ( ' and ');             { second part of message }
    write ( 3001 );               { second summand }
    write ( ' is ' );             { third part }
    writeln ( 7859 + 3001 )       { and the arithmetic }
end. { minimath }
```

Thus, to eliminate the extra spaces from the output of the program in Figure 11.16, we could rewrite the *writeln* statement like this:

```
writeln('The sum of ',7859:1,' and ',3001:1, ' is ',7859 + 3001:1)
```

The output will look like this:

```
The sum of 7859 and 3001 is 10860
```

The only spaces in this line of output are those that occur in the literals in the *writeln* statement.

To accurately describe the syntax of *write* and *writeln* statements, we first need the notion of an *expression*. Loosely speaking, we can say that an expression is anything that has a value. We are using *value* in its broadest sense, to include values of all types. So far we have encountered character and integer values; later, we will encounter other types of values. Figure 11.17 presents syntax diagrams for *write* and *writeln* statements.

Figure 11.16   Program minimath2

```
program minimath2(output);
begin { minimath2 }
  writeln('The sum of ',7859,' and ',3001,' is ',7859 + 3001)
end. { minimath2 }
```

Figure 11.17   Syntax diagrams for *write* and *writeln* statements

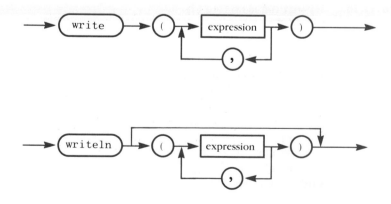

The syntax diagram describes the general form of a *write* or *writeln* statement, but it does not explain what a *write* or *writeln* statement means. In other words, it does not show the semantics of such statements—that is, the effect of executing them. We have described the semantics of these statements informally. Here is a more precise description:

> A write *statement performs the same action for each successive expression inside the parentheses. That action consists of evaluating the expression and displaying that value according to rules governed by the type of the expression. For character expressions, the rule calls for character-by-character display. For integer expressions, the standard rule calls for display as a sequence of digits, right-justified within a field of fixed width, preceded by a minus sign if the value of the expression is negative.*

> A writeln *statement performs all the actions of a* write *statement. In addition, when those actions have been completed, it moves the cursor to the start of the next line so that any future output begins on a new line. A* writeln *statement without any expression list in parentheses displays no output; instead, it simply advances the cursor to the start of the next line.*

We will postpone a description of the actions that *write* and *writeln* statements perform on other types of expressions until we encounter them.

We have omitted from the syntax descriptions the rules about where spaces may be inserted in a statement without changing its effect. In Pascal, these rules are the same for all statements:

> A *space may appear anywhere in a statement without changing the meaning of the statement except within a symbol. A symbol is an identifier, a reserved word, a number or a string literal, or any one of various special symbols (such as +). Moreover, a comment or a carriage return may appear anywhere a space may appear without affecting the meaning of the statement.*

Remember, there are many different ways of combining *write* and *writeln* statements to produce the same output. Figure 11.18 presents four programs, each of which produces the same output.

Figure 11.18   Four ways to display the alphabet

```
program alpha1(output);
begin { alpha1 }
     writeln('abcdefghijklmnopqrstuvwxyz')
end. { alpha1 }
```

(continued)

Figure 11.18
Continued

```pascal
program alpha2 (output);
begin { alpha2 }
        write ('abcdefghijklmnopqrstuvwxyz');
        writeln
end. { alpha2 }

program alpha3 (output);
begin { alpha3 }
        write ('abc', 'def', 'ghi', 'jkl');
        write ('mno', 'pqr', 'stu', 'vwx');
        writeln ('yz')
end. { alpha3 }

program alphahorrible (output);
begin { alphahorrible }
        write ('a'); write ('b'); write ('c'); write ('d');
        write ('e'); write ('f'); write ('g'); write ('h');
        write ('i'); write ('j'); write ('k'); write ('l');
        write ('m'); write ('n'); write ('o'); write ('p');
        write ('q'); write ('r'); write ('s'); write ('t');
        write ('u'); write ('v'); write ('w'); write ('x');
        write ('y'); write ('z');
        writeln
end. { alphahorrible }
```

CHAPTER SUMMARY

1. In Pascal, the standard procedures *write* and *writeln* produce line-oriented output.

2. These statements have, enclosed in parentheses, descriptions of the values that are to appear as output. There are many ways of writing output descriptions, including string literals and integer expressions.

3. The effect of *writeln* is to carry out all the actions of *write* and, in addition, force a carriage return after the specified output has been done. A *writeln* that does not contain output descriptions merely advances the cursor to the beginning of the next line.

4. The standard rule for displaying character data is character-for-character display of the output (on a terminal screen or printer). The standard rule for displaying integer data is as a sequence of digits, preceded by a minus sign if the integer is negative and right-justified within some fixed number of columns.

5. The width of the space allotted for output can be modified by the use of a field-width specifier after each output description. Field-width specifiers specify a minimum size to be reserved but will be overridden if more space is needed to display the data.

COMMON ERRORS

- Forgetting to double an apostrophe inside a literal
- Miscounting the number of quote marks at the beginning or end of a literal
- Misspelling *writeln* as *writeline*
- Omitting semicolons between statements
- Omitting commas between items inside parentheses, or placing a comma that is meant to be a separator inside quotes
- Using double quotes ('') rather than single quotes, or apostrophes ('), to delimit literals
- Forgetting to place spaces inside a string literal where they are needed to prevent two output items from running together
- Putting an integer expression inside quotes
- Omitting the quotes from a string literal

SUPPLEMENTAL PROBLEMS

1. Describe the output of the following program:

```
program mystery1 (output);
begin { mystery1 }
        write ('Life i');
        write ('s like a bo');
        write ('wl of jello: sweet, but ');
        writeln ('shaky.')
end. { mystery }
```

2. Which of these *write* and *writeln* statements are legal, and which are illegal? Explain the errors in the illegal ones.
   a. write ('6 + four')
   b. write (6 + 4)
   c. write '6 + 4'
   d. write (Hello world)
   e. write
   f. writeln

g. writeln ('The sum of six and four is, 6+4)
h. write (The sum of six and four is', 6+4)
i. writeln ('The sum of ', 'six and four is', 6+4)
j. write (' W h e r e   c a n   s p a c e s   g o ? ')
k. wr ite   (' Al mos t anywhere, but   not   quite .')
l. writeln(''''''')
m. writeln('''''''')
n. writeln ('97542 plus 803 = ' 97542 + 803)

3. What is displayed by each of the following statements? Where is the cursor at the completion of each statement?
   a. write ('Happy New Year!'   )
   b. write ('   Happy New Year!   ')
   c. write (111+222)
   d. writeln (333+444)
   e. write ('Twelve times eleven is NOT ', 12 + 11)
   f. write ('Sixty minus two hundred fifty is ', 60 − 250)
   g. writeln(',', ',', '   ,   ,   ,')
   h. writeln (1, 2, 'Buckle my shoe')
   i. writeln('1, 2, Buckle my shoe')
   j. write ('''s Gravenhage')
   k. writeln ('''', ' '' ', ' '''' ')

4. Describe the output of the following program:

```pascal
program mystery2(output);
begin { mystery2 }
        write ('One and one are', 1+1);
        writeln;
        writeln ('Two and two are', 2+2);
        writeln;
        write ('Four and four are', 4+4);
        writeln;
        writeln;
        writeln ('Eight and eight are', 8+8);
        writeln ('And one can go on, and on...');
        writeln
end. { mystery2 }
```

5. Write a Pascal program to print your own initials in block letters horizontally (appearing on the same set of lines across the screen). Build the block letters up out of *'s, or %'s, or your favorite character.

6. Write a Pascal program to print your own initials vertically in block letters. Make each letter appear on its side.

7. Write a Pascal program that uses no string literals and produces the following output, spaced as shown:

```
        2                 4
        6                 8
       10                12
       14                16
       18                20
```

There are 13 blanks before the 2, and 11 blanks between the 2 and the 4.

8. Write a complete, beautifully formatted and documented Pascal program to display the following output, spaced as shown:

```
'He said, ''I hunt for haddocks' eyes
   Among the heather bright,
And work them into waistcoat-buttons
   In the silent night.
And these I do not sell for gold
   Or coin of silvery shine,
But for a copper halfpenny,
   And that will purchase nine.'' '
```

9. The following program is supposed to print a verse of "Jabberwocky," but it has several errors. Correct them.

```pascal
program verse of Jabberwocky (output);
begin. { verse of Jabberwocky }
    write(Beware the Jabberwock, my son),
    write (''The jaws that bite, the claws that
       snatch'').
    writeline('Beware the Jubjub bird, and shun
       the frumious Bandersnatch!')
end; { verse of Jabberwocky }
```

10. What is the output of the following program?

```pascal
program playwithwidths(output);
begin
    writeln('abcdefghijklm':1);
    writeln('nopqrstuvwxyz':26);
    writeln(12:34, 34:12);
    writeln(5+6:7)
end.
```

CHAPTER 12

12.1 CONSTANTS

All of the data we used in the last chapter were constants. They included string literals like 'Hello, world', integer constants like 2001, and constant expressions like 6 + 9. In each case, we referred to the constant by its value or by the values of constants that made it up.

Sometimes it's clearer and more convenient to refer to constants by name rather than by value. For example, here's a complete program whose output you should now be able to deduce:

```
program song(output);
   { appropriate once a year for each of us }

begin { song }
      writeln('Happy birthday to you');
      writeln('Happy birthday to you');
      writeln('Happy birthday dear reader');
      writeln('Happy birthday to you')
end. { song }
```

All the output data items are constants—here, string literals. There's no need to include anything else in this program because we want it to do the same thing each time it runs. Suppose, however, that at some later date we decide to modify the program a bit by changing each occurrence of *you* to *thee*. That's easy enough:

CONSTANTS AND VARIABLES

```
program oldsong(output);
  { Appropriate once a year for each of us }

begin { oldsong }
        writeln('Happy birthday to thee');
        writeln('Happy birthday to thee');
        writeln('Happy birthday dear reader');
        writeln('Happy birthday to thee')
end. { oldsong }
```

We had to make only three changes because the literal we wanted to change occurred only 3 times. (For clarity, we also changed the name of the program, but we didn't have to.) But what if the literal we want to change occurs 300 times in a program? It would be tedious to go through the program and change the literal each time it appeared. Moreover, we might miss a few occurrences and end up with a faulty program.

The problem is that some constants aren't constant forever. Although a value may remain constant over many thousands of executions of a program, most programs have a long life span, and the value of the constant may change during this time. Back in Chapter 9, for example, we used the rate of the sales tax in one of our examples. If the state legislature decided to change the rate, we would have to alter each occurrence of its value in a program.

Pascal provides a solution to such problems. In a Pascal program, we can refer to constant data by name rather than by value. Here's an example:

```
program song2(output);
  { Appropriate once a year for each of us }

const   message1 = 'Happy birthday to you';
        message2 = 'Happy birthday dear reader!';
```

```
begin { song2 }
      writeln ( message1 );
      writeln ( message1 );
      writeln ( message2 );
      writeln ( message1 )
end. { song2 }
```

This program will produce exactly the same output as the first version of the song program. But there are important differences between them:

- Program *song2* has a section that doesn't appear in program *song*.
- In program *song*, the *writeln* statements contain string literals. In program *song2*, the *writeln* statements contain identifiers rather than literals.

An identifier is a name that the programmer makes up and then uses to refer to some object in the program. We discussed the rules for forming identifiers in Chapter 10. Many types of objects can be referred to by identifiers, including the whole program name or a constant.

In program *song2*, the section headed by the reserved word **const** is the constant definition section. (See Chapter 10.) After the word **const**, Pascal expects to find one or more constant definitions. A constant identifier is simply a name that you give a constant and to which you can refer later in the program. Thus, in *song2* the first constant definition gives the name *message1* to the literal 'Happy birthday to you!', and the second constant definition gives the name *message2* to the literal 'Happy birthday dear reader!'. When the Pascal translator encounters the reserved word **const**, it expects that everything that follows will consist of constant definitions until it reaches another reserved word that signals the start of a new section (in this case, **begin**).

When we want to change *you* to *thee* in program *song2*, we now have to make only a single change, the definition of *message1*:

```
program oldsong2(output);

const   message1 = 'Happy birthday to thee!';
        message2 = 'Happy birthday dear reader!';

begin { oldsong2 }
      writeln ( message1 );
      writeln ( message1 );
      writeln ( message2 );
      writeln ( message1 )
end. { oldsong2 }
```

This example uses names for string literals. You may also use names for numerical constants. These names can be used anywhere that numbers can be used. For example, consider this statement:

```
writeln('The basic workweek is ',  40:1,  ' hours.');
```

You can rewrite it using a name for the constant 40, like this:

```
const workweek = 40;  { Number of hours in workweek }
       . . .          { Later on in the program . . . }
writeln('The basic workweek is ', workweek:1, ' hours.');
```

Referring to constants by name enhances your program's readability. The significance of an explicit value (particularly a numeric value) embedded in the body of a program may not be apparent from the value or from the context to someone reading the program. Suppose you were working for a nationwide retail firm and were asked to modify a program written for use in another state so that it could be used in your state. You find the constant 0.05 in the body of the program. The context seems to indicate that 0.05 represents the rate of sales tax, but you're not sure. You could approach this job with more confidence if the program started out with this constant definition and then used the identifier *salestax* throughout:

```
const   salestax = 0.05;        { tax rate in Kentucky }
```

Values like 0.05, which have special significance in particular problems, are sometimes referred to as *magic numbers*. Unless you know what a magic number means in the context of a program, you will have a hard time trying to understand the program. You should always use a constant definition to make a meaningful identifier stand for a magic number and refer to the number by its identifier throughout the program.

We've encountered two reasons for using constant definitions:

- Ease of program modification
- Improved readability

Here are the rules for writing constant definitions. The syntax diagram describing these rules is shown in Figure 12.1.

The constant definition section consists of the reserved word **const** *followed by any number of constant definitions. A constant definition consists of an identifier followed by an = symbol, followed by an explicit value, followed by a semicolon. Legal values include both one or more characters enclosed in quotes, and numbers.*

We can summarize the semantics of a constant definition as follows:

The effect of a constant definition is to make each occurrence of a constant identifier equivalent to an occurrence of the constant value it represents.

Figure 12.1   **Syntax diagram for constant definition section**

12.2 DECLARING AND USING VARIABLES

All the sample programs we looked at in the last chapter would produce the same results every time they ran, because all the data in them is constant. Only if we change the input of a program from one execution to another will its output change.

When we describe the actions we want a program to perform on input data, we can't refer to the data by its value. There are two reasons: We don't know the values of the input data at the time we write the program, and these values will probably change each time the program is run. So we must refer to the input data by using identifiers. These identifiers stand for variables—data items whose value may vary during the program's execution. In Pascal, we can use variables for input data, temporary data, and output data. They are essential for any kind of input.

Variables, Memory, and Data Types

Pascal associates each variable identifier with a particular location in the computer's memory and treats every reference to that name as a reference to whatever value happens to be in that location at the time. Variables in programs correspond to the pieces of paper we used to record values in the algorithms in Part I.

The piece-of-paper analogy is not exact, however. A piece of paper can be used to record many different kinds of data. Each Pascal variable has a type, and the programmer must specify the type along with the name of the variable. A variable of a given type can only be used to record values of that type. Pascal uses the type specification to help detect programmer errors and to make decisions about the internal representation of the variable that are not the direct concern of the programmer.

Pascal has built-in knowledge of four types of data. They are known as *standard types,* and each of them has a predefined identifier:

- *char*. A type for variables whose value can be any character that you can type on the keyboard. At any given moment, a variable of type *char* holds the value of exactly one character.

- *integer*. A type for variables whose value can be any integer (whole number) within a range that depends on the particular implementation of Pascal.
- *real*. A type for variables whose values are numeric and might not be whole numbers.
- *boolean*. A type for variables whose values can only be *true* or *false*.

In the next few chapters we'll use only variables of types *char* and *integer*, which will suffice for the Pascal constructs discussed there.

Constants also have types. A single character between quotes, like '**x**', is a constant of type *char*. This is true even if the character is a digit: '**4**' is a *char* constant, not an *integer* constant. String literals consisting of several characters between quotes are not of any standard type. They have a structured type, which means a type that consists of several simple values. Integer constants are sequences of digits without quotes, possibly preceded by a + or − sign. When we write a constant value into a program, Pascal can deduce its type from its syntax (for example, the presence or absence of quotes), so we do not need to declare it.

Declaring Variables

Recall from Chapter 10 that Pascal programs have a section, called the variable declaration section, where we specify variable names and types.[1] This section can be more complex than the constant definition section, so we will describe it in several pieces:

> *The variable declaration section consists of the reserved word* **var** *followed by one or more variable declarations.*
>
> *A variable declaration consists of an identifier list followed by a colon, followed by a type identifier (the name of a type), followed by a semicolon.*
>
> *An identifier list consists of one or more identifiers. If it contains more than one, the identifiers are separated by commas.*

See Figure 12.2 for a syntax diagram that corresponds to these descriptions.

Suppose we're writing a program that needs three character variables to hold a person's three initials and two integer variables to hold her age and weight. Here are five different, equally valid ways to write the variable declaration section of such a program:

```
var    firstinit: char;          { for first initial }
       secondinit: char;         { for second initial }
       thirdinit: char;          { for third initial }
       age: integer;             { for storing age }
       weight: integer;          { for storing weight }      (continued)
```

1. Standard terminology deems that constants are *defined* while variables are *declared*.

var	firstinit,	{ for first initial }
	secondinit,	{ for second initial }
	thirdinit: char;	{ for third initial }
	age,	{ for storing age }
	weight: integer;	{ for storing weight }

var	age: integer;	{ for storing age }
	weight: integer;	{ for storing weight }
	firstinit,	{ for first initial }
	secondinit,	{ for second initial }
	thirdinit: char;	{ for third initial }

var	firstinit: char;	{ for first initial }
	age,	{ for storing age }
	weight: integer;	{ for storing weight }
	secondinit,	{ for second initial }
	thirdinit: char;	{ for third initial }

| **var** | firstinit, secondinit, thirdinit: char; { for 3 initials } |
| | age, weight: integer;   { for age & weight } |

Some of these versions are more desirable than others. It's good practice to put each variable declaration on a separate line, as in the first four examples. This allows you to place a comment to the right of each variable. Your comments should explain how each variable will be used in the program. It's also good practice to put variable declarations in some sensible order. For instance, the fourth version above is correct but rather silly because the first initial obviously has more in common with the second and third initials than it does with age and weight.

Remember that a variable declaration is not a step in the algorithm. It does not describe an explicit action to be carried out. Rather, it is a step in the setup, since it describes a place for a data item that will be used in the algorithm. Thus, the algorithm has no instructions that correspond to declarations. A variable declaration's meaning to Pascal is "here is the name of a data item, and here is its type."

Figure 12.2   Syntax diagram for variable declaration section

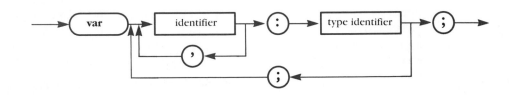

Assigning Values to Variables

When a variable is declared, it has no definite value. An identifier we use in the variable declaration section corresponds to a location in the computer's memory, and in general the contents of such a location are unpredictable when a program begins to execute. On some computers, the value will be whatever was left in this part of memory from the last program to use it. Other computers set every bit in their memories to zero before running a new program.

Since a variable's value is undefined at the start of a program, you should never use a variable before you have assigned a value to it. Here is a program that violates this principle:

```
program garbage(output);
    { This program attempts to display an undefined value }

var     mystery: char;

begin { garbage }                    { NEVER DO THIS!!! }
       writeln ( mystery )
end. { garbage }
```

Under most versions of Pascal, this program will write a single character, whose value is whatever happens to be in the memory space labeled *mystery*. Some implementations of Pascal will generate a run-time error when this program executes.

Another common error is to assume that *integer* variables start with a value of zero. A program written with this implicit assumption may work on one computer but may fail altogether when moved to a different computer.

We can give values to variables in a number of ways. The most direct method is the assignment statement. Assignment statements are instructions and appear in the instruction section of a program. The assignment statements in Figure 12.3 give values to the variables *firstinit*, *secondinit*, *thirdinit*, *age*, and *weight* that we declared earlier.

Figure   12.3   Examples of assignment statements

```
firstinit : = 'L';
secondinit : = 'M';
thirdinit : = 'Z';
age : = 65;
weight : = 143;
```

Figure 12.4   Syntax diagram for assignment statements

An assignment statement consists of a variable name followed by the symbol := (formed by a colon immediately followed by an equal sign) and then by an expression. The effect of an assignment statement is to evaluate the expression to the right of the := and give the resulting value to the variable named on the left of the :=. The symbol := is called the *assignment operator* and is usually read as "gets the value" or "becomes." Thus, the statement

```
age : =  65
```

is read "age gets the value 65." A syntax diagram for assignment statements is shown in Figure 12.4.

The variable before the := is often referred to as the *left side* of the assignment statement, while the expression after the := is referred to as the *right side*. So far we have used only constants for the right side, but much more complex expressions are permitted. In every case, however, an assignment statement must obey the following rule:

> *The type of the variable on the left side must be the same as, or compatible with, the type of the expression on the right side.*

We will discuss compatibility of types as we introduce the various types. The type *char* is not compatible with either the type *integer* or the type *real*. In our examples, the variables *firstinit*, *secondinit*, and *thirdinit* were each assigned a value of type *char*—a character inside quotes. Similarly, the variables *age* and *weight* were both assigned values of type *integer*.

Variables can appear as part of expressions. Consider these three statements:

```
firstinit : = 'A';
secondinit : = firstinit;
thirdinit : = secondinit;
```

When these statements have been executed, the three variables each have the same value, namely 'A'. Figure 12.5 shows what happens in memory as these three statements are executed. We'll use a question mark to indicate a memory location whose contents have not yet been assigned.

Figure 12.5   Trace of the execution of three assignment statements

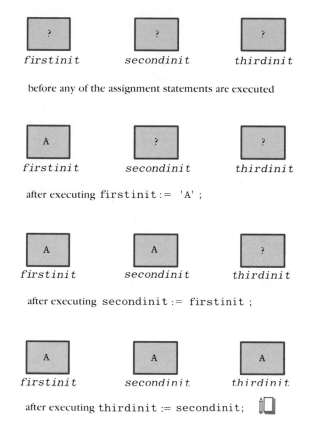

before any of the assignment statements are executed

after executing firstinit := 'A' ;

after executing secondinit := firstinit ;

after executing thirdinit := secondinit;

Here's an example using variables of type *integer*:

```
age : = 30;
weight : = age + 120;
writeln('Age = ', age:1, ' and Weight = ', weight:1);
```

The effect of the two assignment statements is to give *age* the value 30 and then to give *weight* the value 150. The *writeln* statement then displays:

```
Age = 30 and Weight = 150
```

Note that we use field-width specifiers with variables precisely as we used them with constant expressions, and that when we use a variable in a *write* or *writeln* statement it is the variable's current value that is displayed. Once a variable has been given a value, references to that variable are really references to its current value. The only exception is when a variable occurs on the left side of an assignment statement. In this case, the variable indicates where the value of the expression on the right side should be stored.

Exercise **12.1:** Suppose a program has the following variable declarations:

```
var     row:  integer;
        column:  char;
        x:  integer;
        y:  char;
```

Which of the following are valid assignment statements?

a. row : = '7';

b. row : = −291;

c. column : = '%';

d. x : = row;

e. x : = row + 291;

f. x : = y;

g. y : = '7';

h. y : = 7;

i. y : = column;   ■

Since a *char* variable can only hold the value of a single character, it's not legal to assign an entire string literal to such a variable. Thus, the following statement is not valid:

```
firstinit : = 'lmz';     {ERROR!}
```

In Standard Pascal, none of the four standard types is capable of storing the value of a string literal. This is because each of the four standard types is a simple type, capable of holding only a single value. A string literal actually consists of a sequence of *char* values. Pascal can manipulate several values at once by combining them in objects of structured type, but Standard Pascal specifies that the programmer must define his or her own structured types. Some implementations of Pascal have extended the standard by adding a fifth type named *string,* which can hold string literal values. Unfortunately, different versions of Pascal have added this extension in different, incompatible ways. We do not discuss string types in this book.

In Chapter 23, we describe how you can define your own structured data types for storing several characters in a single variable.

Exercise 12.2: What is the output of the following program?

```
program printvars (output);
  { a program that prints the values of some variables }

const   space = ' ';
        dash = '-';

var     letter1,
        letter2,
        letter3: char;
        value1,
        value2; integer;

begin { printvars }
        letter3 := 'l';
        letter2 := 'a';
        letter1 := 'C';
        value2 := 1212;
        value1 := 555;
        writeln (letter1, letter2, letter3, letter3,
          space, value1:1, dash, value2:1)
end. { printvars }  ■
```

Exercise 12.3: Suppose a program has the following variable declarations:

```
var     day,
        month,
        year: integer;
```

Use a tracing form to show the values of these variables as each of the following statements is executed:

```
        month := 1;
        day := month + month + month;
        month := day + day;
        year := 1900 + month + day  ■
```

Examples

Suppose we want to write a program that will ask the user to type a character—any character—on the keyboard. The program will print the character four times on one line, advance to the next line, and then stop. We need exactly one variable because the character that the user types will be the only thing to vary each time the program is run.

What identifier should we use for the variable? We could use *c*, or *q99*, or *elizabeth*, but none of these would convey any notion of how we were going to use the variable. Of course, Pascal doesn't care what name we choose, but other people will be reading your program as well. In fact, experience shows that programmers who go back to a program several weeks after writing it often have forgotten what some of their own statements mean. So it is essential that we use meaningful identifier names that give a clear indication of what role each identifier will play in the program.

A reasonable identifier for our program might be *typedchar* or *chfromuser* or *inputcharacter* or *repeatchar*. Let's use *typedchar*. Here's how we'd write the variable declaration section for our program:

```
var  typedchar: char;    {The user's typed character}
```

We can write the following algorithm to solve this problem:

Setup

I. Reserve a place named *Typed Char* to hold the user's input character.

Instructions

I. Tell the user to type a character.

II. Get the user's input character and save it in *Typed Char*.

III. Print the value in *Typed Char*.

IV. Print the value in *Typed Char*.

V. Print the value in *Typed Char*.

VI. Print the value in *Typed Char*.

VII. Move the cursor to the next line.

Even though we don't know what character the user will type, we can refer to it by a name. Thus, we can describe what actions we want to take with it.

Except for step II,[2] we can implement the algorithm with a Pascal program as follows:

2. Chapter 13 will explain the implementation of this step.

```
program echo4(input, output);
  { reads a typed character and displays it four times }

var      typedchar: char;         { user's input character }

begin { echo4 }
       write ('Type any character: '); { Prompt the user. }
         {Step II, omitted. Somehow get the user's }
         { character into the variable typedchar. }
       write ( typedchar );  { Print it once... }
       write ( typedchar );  { ...twice... }
       write ( typedchar );  { ...three times... }
       writeln ( typedchar ) { ...four, and go to next line. }
end.
```

It's very common for the same variable to occur on both sides of an assignment statement. You would write such a statement when you want to change a variable's value and the new value depends on the old value. Consider the following program fragment:

```
var counter: integer; { used to illustrate incrementing }
        . . .
    counter : = 99;           { initial value }
    writeln('The value of counter is now ', counter:1 );
    counter : = counter + 1;
    writeln('The value of counter is now ', counter:1 );
```

The output of this fragment consists of the two lines

```
The value of the counter is now 99
The value of the counter is now 100
```

To understand it, we'll trace the execution of these four statements.

Recall that when a program begins execution, the values of its variables are unpredictable. Thus, we start our trace like this:

counter

After the first assignment statement of our fragment, *counter* has the value 99:

counter

The first *writeln* statement displays this value. Then the statement

```
counter : = counter + 1
```

is executed. This statement follows the rule for all assignment statements: Evaluate the right side and assign its value to the variable on the left side. In this case, the value of the right side is 99 + 1 = 100, so the value 100 is assigned to *counter*. This value replaces the previous value, which is lost.

counter

The second *writeln* statement then displays the new value of *counter*.

Notice that the same variable holds a two-digit integer and a three-digit integer. Pascal represents integers internally in a manner that differs from our decimal notation. On most computers, the representation is based on the binary system. Consequently, the digits we use to write an integer usually do not correspond to the internal form of the integer. In the internal form, all integers take up the same amount of space.

A variable of type *char* is only large enough to hold a single character. The computer uses different internal representations for characters and integers. It represents characters according to a simple substitution code: Every character on the keyboard has a corresponding number in the code. The most common code used in minicomputers and microcomputers in the United States is the ASCII code. (ASCII stands for American Standard Code for Information Interchange.) Appendix A shows the ASCII correspondence between displayed characters and their internal codes.

Our next example is a program that asks the user to type three characters on a line and then displays the characters on the following line in reverse order. This program uses three variables, all of type *char*. An algorithm for this problem would be

Setup

  I. Reserve a space named *First Char* to hold a character.

  II. Reserve a space named *Second Char* to hold a character.

  III. Reserve a space named *Third Char* to hold a character.

Instructions

  I. Prompt the user to type three characters.

  II. Get the first character and record it on *First Char*.

  III. Get the second character and record it on *Second Char*.

  IV. Get the third character and record it on *Third Char*.

  V. Display the value of *Third Char*.

  VI. Display the value of *Second Char*.

  VII. Display the value of *First Char* and advance the cursor to a new line.

The following program implements this algorithm. The comments indicate which program step corresponds to which algorithm step. Again, we omit the program statements that perform input.

```
program reverse3chars(input, output);
  { Demonstrates use of char variables }

const prompt = 'Type three characters and press RETURN: ';

var     firstch,               { first character }
        secondch,              { second character }
        thirdch: char;         { third character }

begin { reverse3chars }
        write ( prompt );        { step I }
          {      Somehow do steps II, III, and IV.      }
          {      At end of these steps, the variables   }
          {      firstch, secondch, and thirdch         }
          {      have been given values.                }
        write ( thirdch );       { step V }
        write ( secondch );      { step VI }
        writeln ( firstch )      { step VII }
end. { reverse3chars }
```

Now instead of asking the user to type three characters just once, suppose we ask her to type them twice. Each time, we want the program to display the three letters in reverse order. How many variables do we need? We still need only three. Although we have to deal with six characters, we deal with only three at a time. After we display the first three characters in reverse order, we can reuse the space where they were stored for the next group of three characters. Whenever a value is stored in a memory location, any value that was there is overwritten.

```pascal
program reverse3charstwice(input, output);
  { demonstrates reuse of char variables }

const prompt = 'Type three characters and press RETURN: ';

var     firstch,                { first character }
        secondch,               { second character }
        thirdch: char;          { third character }

begin { reverse3charstwice }
        write ( prompt );         { first request }
          {     Somehow get three chars of input  }
          {     into firstch, secondch, thirdch.  }
        write ( thirdch );
        write ( secondch );
        writeln ( firstch )
        write( 'And once again, ',prompt);
          {     Again get three chars of input  }
          {     into firstch, secondch, thirdch. }
          {     This destroys their old values.  }
        write ( thirdch );
        write ( secondch );
        writeln ( firstch )
end. { reverse3charstwice }
```

CHAPTER SUMMARY

1. Although it's possible to refer to a constant value in a program by explicitly mentioning its value each time it occurs, it's usually advantageous to refer to such a value by name. Doing so makes program modification easier and makes programs more readable.

2. Named constants are defined in the constant definition section of the program. A *constant definition* consists of the name (an identifier), an equal sign, the value, and a semicolon. The constant definition section consists of the reserved word **const**, followed by one or more constant definitions.

3. When we write programs, we usually can't know at the time we write them the values upon which they will operate. Thus, we have to refer to these values

by *identifiers*. These identifiers are variables. Each variable refers to a space in the computer's memory. Any program that has input must use variables.

4. *All constants and variables in Pascal have a type.* The type of a variable describes what values the variable can have and what operations can be performed on it.

5. Variables are declared in the variable declaration section. A *variable declaration* consists of an identifier, a colon, a type identifier, and a semicolon. An alternative form allows you to declare several variables of the same type by listing a sequence of identifiers, separated by commas, before the colon.

6. Values can be assigned to variables with assignment statements. An *assignment statement* consists of a variable identifier followed by an assignment operator :=, followed by an expression. The type of the expression must be compatible with the type of the variable. The effect of an assignment statement is to evaluate the expression to the right of the := and assign this value to the variable.

7. When a variable identifier occurs in the instructions of a program, it stands for the current value of the variable, except when the identifier occurs on the left side of an assignment statement. The same variable can have different values at different moments during the program's execution.

COMMON ERRORS

- Putting the sections of the program in the wrong order. The constant definition section must precede the variable declaration section.
- Confusing the equal sign (which is used in a constant definition) with the colon (which is used in a variable declaration).
- Omitting a semicolon after a definition or declaration.
- Writing the word **const** more than once in the constant definition section, or writing the word **var** more than once in the variable definition section. The following fragment illustrates this error:

```
const   pi = 3.14159265;
const   greeting = 'Hi there!';
  { The second const is an error. }

var     total: integer;
var     initial: char;   { The second var is an error. }
```

- Misspelling the type name. Particularly common are *character* instead of *char*, and *interger* instead of *integer*.
- Using an equal sign instead of an assignment operator in assignment statements.

■ Forgetting to declare a variable name.

■ Writing an assignment statement in which the types of the left side and the right side are incompatible. A particularly common error is to assign a digit or digits in quotes to an *integer* variable, like this:

```
intvariable : = '3';
  { Error; the right side is of type char. }
```

SUPPLEMENTAL PROBLEMS

1. Which of the following constant definition sections are correctly specified? Correct the mistakes in the others.

```
a. const    greeting = 'Hello',
            farewell = 'Goodbye';


b. const    date = 'Jan 1, 1901';
            century = 20;
            moon = 'Full';


c. const    hour: 24;
            minute: 60;
            second: 60;


d. const    'This is simple' = message1;
            25 = fivesquared;
```

2. Describe the output of the following program:

```
program whoknows (output);
  { Deliberately confusing names }

const   one = 6;   { Real programs shouldn't do this. }
        two = 7;
        message = 'Here''s an arithmetic problem.';
        question = 'How much is ';
        answer = 'The answer is ';

begin

        writeln ( message );
        writeln ( question, one, ' + ', two );
        writeln ( answer, one + two )
end.
```

3. Consider the following code fragment:

```
var     num1, num2: integer;
          . . .
num1 : =  10;
num2 : =  20;
num1 : =  num2;
num2 : =  num1;
```

What are the values of *num1* and *num2* after these statements are executed? Write a program fragment that interchanges the values of *num1* and *num2*.

4. Consider the following code fragment:

```
var     num1, num2, num3, num4, num5: integer;
          . . .
num1 : =  10;
num2 : =  20;
num3 : =  30;
num4 : =  40;
num5 : =  50;
num1 : =  num2;
num2 : =  num3;
num3 : =  num4;
num4 : =  num5;
num5 : =  num1;
```

What are the values of *num1* through *num5* after these statements are executed? Write a program fragment that correctly rotates the values of *num1* through *num5*, so that *num1* gets the value 20, *num2* gets the value 30, *num3* gets the value 40, *num4* gets the value 50, and *num5* gets the value 10.

5. You need a program to solve the following problem: A user will type a letter of the alphabet, followed by a number. If the typed letter is a vowel, or if the number is odd, your program will type "Well done!" Otherwise the program prints out "You turkey!"
   a. Write an algorithm for this problem.
   b. Write an appropriate variable declaration section for this program, including useful comments to describe your variables. Do *not* attempt to write the whole program.

6. Which of the following variable declaration sections are correctly specified? Correct the mistakes in the others.

   a. **var**   left, center, right = integer;

   b. **var**   first: integer;
              second, third: integer;
              shortstop: integer;

c. **var**   ch1,
          ch2,
          int1,
          int2: char, char, integer, integer;

d. **var**   init1, init2: character;
          rows, columns: int;

e. **var**   init1: char;
          num1: integer;
          init2: char;
          num2: interger;
          message1 = 'Welcome to Pascalville'

7. Find and correct all the errors in the following fragment, which shows the beginning of a Pascal program:

```
program find-the-maximum;  (input, output);
   { This program finds the largest number }
   { in its input sequence. }

var      inputnum: integer;
         maximum: integer;

const    prompt: 'Enter the next number please';
         sentinel = 9999;

begin { find-the-maximum }
         sentinel := 1000;
         maximum = 0;
         inputnum := '0';
   . . .
```

8. Describe the output of the following program:

```
program example8(output);
   { computes values starting with a constant }

const    start = 5;

var      counter: integer;

begin { example8 }
         counter := start;
         writeln('Counter is ', counter:1 );
         counter := counter + counter;
         writeln('Counter is ', counter:1 );
```

```
            counter : = counter + counter;
            writeln('Counter is ', counter:1 );
            counter : = counter + counter;
            writeln('Counter is ', counter:1 )
      end. { example8 }
```

9. Write a program that prints the output

abracadabra

on a single line. Do not use any string literals. You may use single character constants, but not in **write** or **writeln** statements. Use no more than five variables.

10. The following program is supposed to print a children's rhyme, but it has errors. Correct them.

```
program mothergoose(output);

var     first-number = integer;
        second-number = integer;

const   first line : = 'buckle my shoe';
        second line : = 'shut the door';
        third line : = 'pick up sticks';
        fourth line : = 'lay them straight';
        fifth line : = 'a big fat hen';

begin { mothergoose }
        first-number = 1;
        second-number = 2;
        writeln(first-number, second-number, first line);
        first-number = 3;
        second-number = 4;
        writeln(first-number, second-number, second line);
        first-number = 5;
        second-number = 6;
        writeln(first-number, second-number, third line);
        first-number = 7;
        second-number = 8;
        writeln(first-number, second-number, fourth line);
        first-number = 9;
        second-number = 10;
        writeln(first-number, second-number, fifth line)
end; { mothergoose }
```

CHAPTER

13

We turn now to the means by which Pascal deals with line-oriented input from a terminal keyboard. The predefined identifier *input* must appear in the header of any program that expects the user to enter input data. *During the execution of a Pascal program, all of the data items that are needed by the program must be stored in the memory component of the computer.* When we write a Pascal instruction for the computer to input one or more data items, we must indicate where to store each item in memory. We do that by including in the instruction a list of the names of the variables corresponding to each item. When the instruction is executed by the computer, each data item is stored in memory in the space allocated to its variable.

Pascal has two standard procedures that are used to direct the computer to get input values for variables. Those procedures are *read* and *readln*.

The computer handles data typed by the user as a stream of characters. Each keystroke, including pressing the return key, counts as a character. The *read pointer* indicates the position in the input stream where the computer expects to read the next character. Every invocation of the *read* and *readln* procedures advances the read pointer. Since the read pointer never moves backward, individual data items are never read more than once.

Both the *read* and *readln* procedures begin by directing the computer to read values for each of the variables in its list. The computer does not perform any subsequent instructions until after the user has typed enough characters into the input stream to give values to each of the variables listed.

Typically, before a data item is to be read, the program displays a message on the screen describing what the user is to enter. This message is known as a *prompt* to the user. The user responds to the prompt by typing characters into the input stream. The prompt to the user is usually accomplished using *write* or *writeln*. The program then reads values from the input stream by using the procedure *read* or the procedure *readln*.

Execution of the *read* procedure leaves the read pointer pointing to the next

INPUT DATA FROM A KEYBOARD

character to be read. Execution of the *readln* procedure finishes by moving the read pointer just beyond the next carriage return character.

Let's discuss the details of the *readln* procedure first.

13.1 THE *readln* PROCEDURE

Consider the program shown in Figure 13.1.

Figure 13.1   Sample program using *readln* and a *char* variable

```
program onech(input,output);
        {a program to illustrate reading a value}
        {into a variable of type char.          }

var ch : char;
        {a variable to hold the character entered}
        {by the user.                            }

begin {onech}
        writeln('Enter your favorite character.');
        readln(ch);
        writeln(ch,' is a nice character!')
end. {onech}
```

The identifiers *input* and *output* in the program header indicate that the usual source of input and destination of output are to be used—that is, the terminal keyboard and the terminal screen. The **var** statement indicates that when the program is translated, the compiler will allot space in memory to store a *char* value known by the name *ch*.

When a user runs the program, the first statement executed by the computer prints the prompt Enter your favorite character. and moves the cursor to the beginning of the next line on the screen. The next statement, readln (ch), checks to see if there is anything in the input stream. Since it is empty, the program waits for the user to type something.

Assume that the user types a $ followed by a carriage return. When a carriage return is entered, it becomes part of the input stream. We denote the corresponding character ⏎. The input stream and the read pointer can be visualized as:

The computer reads the $, stores it in memory in the space allotted to *ch*, and moves the read pointer to point to the carriage return character.

The *readln* procedure finishes its job by moving the read pointer just beyond the carriage return character (where there currently is no character in the input stream).

The last statement of the program invokes the procedure *writeln*. The value stored in the variable *ch* is displayed on the screen followed by the literal constant is a nice character! Finally, *writeln* moves the cursor to the next line of the screen, and the program terminates.

We use the term *sample execution* to denote a figure that displays a sample situation as it appears on the terminal screen when a program is executed. Our convention is to italicize characters typed by the user. Figure 13.2 shows the sample execution of the program *onech* that we described above. Figure 13.3 shows a corresponding trace of what happens in memory.

The action of the computer when reading a value for an *integer* variable is quite different. The program *oneint*, displayed in Figure 13.4, is similar to the program *onech* except that it inputs and outputs an *integer* value.

Figure 13.2   Sample execution of the program *onech*

```
Enter your favorite character.
$ ⇦
$ is a nice character!
```

Figure 13.3   Memory trace of the program *onech*

ch	set up by **var** declaration
[?]	*ch* has unpredictable value.

ch	after *readln (ch)* is executed
[$]	

Figure 13.4   Program *oneint*

```
program oneint(input, output);
        {a program to illustrate reading a value}
        {into an integer variable.                }

var number : integer;
        {an integer variable to hold the number}
        {entered by the user.                   }

begin {oneint}
        writeln('Enter your favorite number.');
        readln(number);
        writeln(number, ' is great!')
end. {oneint}
```

When program *oneint* is compiled, space is allotted in memory for an *integer* variable known as *number*. The first invocation of *writeln* prints the prompt on the terminal screen. Since the input stream is empty, the computer waits for the user to type something. Assume that the user types the number 625 followed immediately by a carriage return. The input stream and read pointer can be visualized as:

Figure 13.5 shows the algorithm that both *read* and *readln* follow when they get a value for an *integer* variable from the input stream.

In our case, the condition in step I is *false,* since the character indicated by the read pointer is neither a blank nor a carriage return. The condition in step II is also *false,* since the character is not a + or a −. The condition in step III is *true,* since the read pointer is indicating the digit character 6. Thus, we proceed to the then clause and its repeat structure. The repeat structure advances the read pointer until it points to the carriage return character, which the computer recognizes as a nondigit.

Internally, the computer converts the three characters 6, 2, and 5 to its representation of the integer value 625.

To finish its job, the *readln* procedure moves the read pointer just beyond the carriage return character.

Finally, procedure *writeln* displays the value 625 and the literal constant is great! on the screen. It moves the cursor to the next line and the program terminates.

The sample execution and trace of memory changes for program *oneint* that we have just described is displayed in Figure 13.6. In our sample executions, ∧ indicates a blank space on the screen.

Figure 13.5 **Algorithm used by** *read* **and** *readln* **to input an** *integer* **value**

I. While the character indicated by the read pointer is a blank or a carriage return, do
   A. Advance the read pointer to the next character in the input stream.

II. If the character indicated by the read pointer indicates the sign of the number (+ or −).
   then
   A. Do whatever is necessary to obtain the correct internal representation.
   B. Advance the read pointer to the next character in the input stream.

III. If the character indicated by the read pointer is a digit (0–9),
   then
   A. Repeat the following until the character indicated by the read pointer is not a digit.
      1. (We need not be concerned with the details of what to do with each digit.)
      2. Advance the read pointer to the next character in the input stream.
   else
   A'. Stop execution of the program because the user has typed a nondigit character when an integer value is expected.

Figure 13.6 **Sample execution and trace of the program** *oneint*

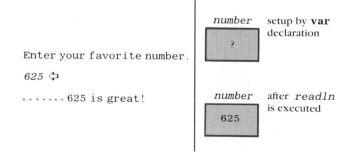

Note the seven blanks caused by procedure *writeln*. Remember that if we do not specify a field width in an instruction to write the value of an *integer* variable, the computer will print the value right-justified in a field that is some predetermined number of characters wide (see pages 223–224). We have assumed a field width of ten characters in our example.

Exercise   13.1: What would happen if the user typed just 625 and failed to type a carriage return? You might want to execute program *oneint* to see for yourself.   ■

Figure 13.7   **Syntax of a call to procedure *readln***

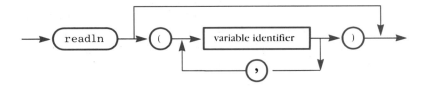

Figure 13.7 shows the syntax of a call to the standard procedure *readln*. The semantics of an invocation of procedure *readln* are

1. Get from the input stream and store in memory a value for each variable identifier listed and leave the read pointer pointing at the next character to be read.

2. Move the read pointer from its current position to just beyond the next carriage return character.

When no variable identifiers are listed in the instruction, the meaning of *readln* is simply "move the read pointer just beyond the next carriage return character." Note that in either case, the program cannot proceed until the user types a carriage return.

Now let's try a program that reads in and writes out a set of initials. We'll write the program two ways and show several sample executions. The first version, program *initials1*, appears in Figure 13.8. Procedure *readln* must get three characters from the input stream. After the computer reads those three characters, it must find a carriage return character so that it can move the read pointer just beyond it. The user must type at least three characters and a carriage return. If not, the execution of the program will "hang"—that is, no further instructions will be executed while it is waiting for more characters to enter the input stream.

Figure 13.8   **Program** *initials1*

```
program initials1(input, output);
      {a program to illustrate how Pascal reads}
      {character variables                     }

var init1, init2, init3 : char; {character variables}
                                {to hold initials}
begin {initials1}
      writeln('Enter your initials. ');
      readln(init1, init2, init3);
      writeln('Your initials are ', init1, init2, init3)
end. {initials1}
```

Figure 13.9 shows a sample execution and trace of the program *initials1*. Everything works fine so long as the user types all three initials on one line, followed by a carriage return. But suppose the user decides to type one initial per line. Figure 13.10 shows a sample execution and trace in this situation. What happened? Consider the input stream.

The computer must get three characters from the input stream. It gets 'b' for the first character and moves the read pointer as shown in Figure 13.11a.

The read pointer now indicates that a carriage return character is next. When a Pascal program's instruction is to read a *char* value and the read pointer is pointing to a carriage return character, the hardware stores a blank character in the type *char* variable and advances the read pointer to the next character in the input stream as shown in Figure 13.11b. Since the computer must still complete the instruction to input three characters, it reads the 'a' into *init3* and advances the read pointer as shown in Figure 13.11c. Finally, the computer moves the read pointer just beyond the next carriage return character as shown in Figure 13.11d.

Before the user gets to type in what he thinks is the third character, the computer has already read three characters and moved the read pointer beyond the next carriage return character. The computer then executes the final call to *writeln*.

Figure 13.12 shows yet another execution and trace. What happened to all those other letters? One might say that they have been "sent to computer heaven, never to return." Consider the input stream as shown in Figure 13.13a.

Figure 13.9   **First sample execution and trace of program** *initials1*

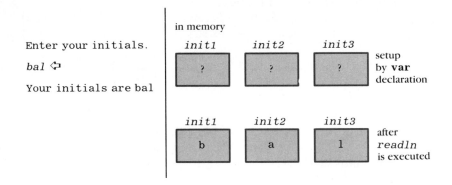

Figure 13.10   **Second sample execution and trace of program**
initials1

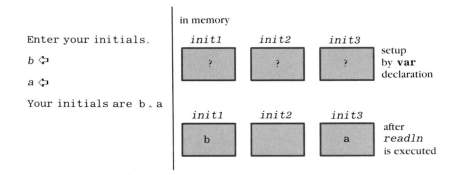

Figure 13.11   **Various positions of the read pointer**

The mission of **readln** was to get values for three character variables. The computer uses the first three characters, 'b', 'a', and 'l', leaving the read pointer at the 's' as shown in Figure 13.13b. The computer then moves the read pointer just beyond the next carriage return character, as shown in Figure 13.13c. The computer simply ignores **stmzqr**.

Figure 13.12   Third sample execution and trace of program *initials1*

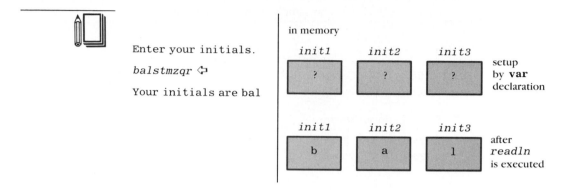

Enter your initials.

balstmzqr ⇦

Your initials are bal

Figure 13.13   Various positions of the read pointer

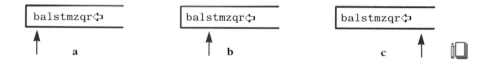

In general, *readln* directs the computer to read values until it has one value for each variable in its list. If the computer is trying to read a value for a variable of type *char* and the read pointer is pointing to a carriage return character, the computer will interpret the carriage return character as a blank. If it still needs to read values for variables in its list, it will continue reading characters in the input stream beyond that carriage return character.

Exercise   13.2: Consider each of the following as user input and

a. Draw the input stream.
b. Show a memory trace and the output produced by executing program *initials1*.
   (1) *ba* ⇦
   　　 ⇦
   (2) *b,1* ⇦
   (3) *b.a* ⇦   ■

Now consider program *initials2* shown in Figure 13.14. There are three separate calls to procedure *readln* in this program, one for each variable. Each *readln* gets one value of type *char*.

Figure 13.15 shows one sample execution and trace.

Exercise 13.3: Consider the sample execution and trace of program *initials2* given in Figure 13.15.

a. Draw the input stream.

b. Draw a diagram showing the various positions of the read pointer as each call to *readln* is executed. ∎

Figure 13.14   Program *initials2*

```
program initials2(input,output);
        {a program to illustrate reading in three character}
        {variables using three calls to readln              }

var init1,init2,init3 : char; {three character variables to}
                              {hold initials                }

begin {initials2}
      writeln('Enter your initials.');
      readln(init1);
      readln(init2);
      readln(init3);
      writeln('Your initials are ',init1,init2,init3)
end. {initials2}
```

Let us consider the actions of procedure *readln* when more than one *integer* variable is listed. Recall step I of the algorithm given in Figure 13.5. Since the computer simply skips over blanks and carriage returns when it is searching the input stream for an integer value, they are ideal characters to use to separate a sequence of integer values in the input stream. In contrast, separating a sequence of integer values with commas will not work. A comma can indicate the end of an integer value (see step III.A in Figure 13.5). However, the read pointer

Exercise   13.4: Consider each of the following as user input and

a. Draw the input stream.

b. Show a memory trace and the output produced by executing program *initials2*.

   (1) Enter your initials.

   b ⏎

   ⏎

   a ⏎

   1 ⏎

   (2) Enter your initials.

   ⏎

   ⏎

   b ⏎

   a ⏎

   (3) Enter your initials.

   b ⏎

   ⏎

   ⏎

   ⏎

   ⏎ ▪

Figure 13.15   Sample execution and trace of program *initials2*

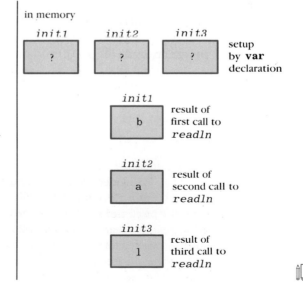

in memory

Enter your initials.

b ⏎

a ⏎

1 ⏎

Your initials are bal

init1   *init2*   *init3*

?   ?   ?   setup by **var** declaration

init1

b   result of first call to *readln*

init2

a   result of second call to *readln*

init3

1   result of third call to *readln*

will be left pointing to the comma. If a comma is encountered when the computer restarts the algorithm in order to read another *integer* value, the program will crash. The crash occurs because the conditions in steps I, II, and III are all false. Similarly, commas cannot be embedded within a single integer value. Pascal's syntax simply doesn't allow commas to be used to separate the digits of a single value. Figure 13.16 shows program *numbers1*, which inputs two *integer* values with a single invocation of *readln*. Figure 13.17 gives one sample execution and trace of program *numbers1*.

Everything seems to have gone as expected in this sample execution. Figure 13.18 shows the various positions of the read pointer in the input stream.

Exercise 13.5: Next are the beginnings of three sample executions of program *numbers1*. For each sample execution,

1. Draw the input stream.
2. Draw a diagram showing the various positions of the read pointer as the algorithm in Figure 13.5 is completed for each *integer* value read.
3. Show the output produced by program *numbers1*.

(continued on page 270)

Figure 13.16   Program *numbers1*

```
program numbers1(input,output);
        {a program to illustrate reading two integer}
        {values with a single call to readln        }

var num1,num2  : integer; {two integer variables to }
                          {hold input values        }

begin {numbers1}
        writeln('Enter two integers.');
        readln(num1,num2);
        writeln('Your numbers were');
        writeln(num1,num2)
end. {numbers1}
```

Figure 13.17   Sample execution and trace of program *numbers1*

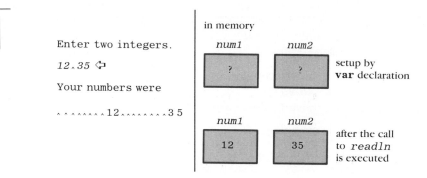

Enter two integers.

12.35 ⇦

Your numbers were

∧ ∧ ∧∧∧∧∧∧∧12∧∧∧∧∧∧∧∧∧3 5

in memory

num1   *num2*

setup by **var** declaration

? ?

after the call to *readln* is executed

num1   *num2*

12   35

Figure 13.18   Various positions of the read pointer

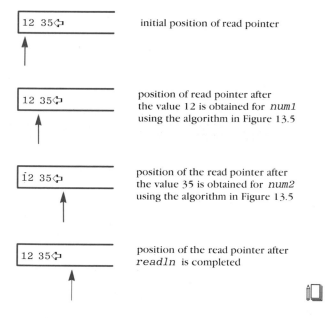

12 35⇦   initial position of read pointer

12 35⇦   position of read pointer after
                 the value 12 is obtained for *num1*
                 using the algorithm in Figure 13.5

12 35⇦   position of the read pointer after
                 the value 35 is obtained for *num2*
                 using the algorithm in Figure 13.5

12 35⇦   position of the read pointer after
                 readln is completed

Sample execution A:

```
Enter two integers.
12 ⏎
-35 ⏎
```

Sample execution B:

```
Enter two integers.
12_-35_46_89 ⏎
```

Sample execution C:

```
Enter two integers.
12 ⏎
⏎
45_-36_99 ⏎
```

∎

Exercise 13.6: Consider program *numbers2* shown in Figure 13.19 and answer the questions asked in Exercise 13.5.   ∎

Figure 13.19   Program *numbers2*

```
program numbers2(input,output);
        {a program to illustrate reading two integer}
        {values with two calls to readln            }

var num1,num2  : integer; {two integer variables to }
                          {hold input values         }

begin {numbers2}
      writeln('Enter two integers.');
      readln(num1);
      readln(num2);
      writeln('Your numbers were');
      writeln(num1,num2)
end. {numbers2}
```

Figure 13.20   **Syntax of a call to procedure** *read*

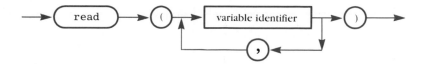

13.2 THE STANDARD PROCEDURE *read*

The syntax of a call to the standard procedure *read* is shown in Figure 13.20. Here we have only one option. A call to *read* must be accompanied by a list of variable identifiers separated by commas and enclosed in parentheses. The meaning of a call to procedure *read* is to get from the input stream and store in memory a value for each of the variables in the list.

The fundamental difference between *read* and *readln* occurs after the computer has obtained values from the input stream for each variable listed. Unlike *readln*, *read* does not direct the computer to move the read pointer beyond the next carriage return character. It leaves the read pointer pointing to the character just after the last one used to determine a value.

Figure 13.21 shows program *initials3*, which uses the *read* procedure. Figure 13.22 gives a sample execution of program *initials3*. And Figure 13.23 shows the various positions of the read pointer as the program is executed.

Figure 13.21   **Program** *initials3*

```
program initials3(input,output);
        {a program to illustrate reading character values}
        {using separate read's                           }

var init1,init2,init3:char; {three character variables to}
                            {hold the initials           }

begin {initials3}
      writeln('Enter your initials. ');
      read(init1);
      read(init2);
      read(init3);
      writeln('Your initials are ',init1,init2,init3)
end. {initials3}
```

Figure 13.22 **Sample execution and trace of program** *initials3*

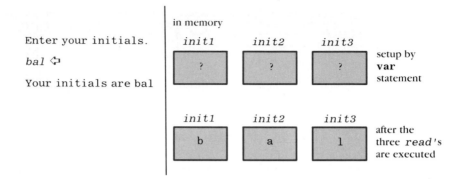

Figure 13.23 **Positions of the read pointer corresponding to the sample execution and trace in Figure 13.22**

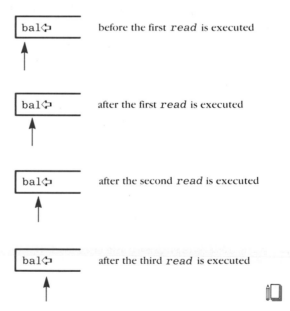

Exercise 13.7: Below are the beginnings of three sample executions of program *initials3*. For each sample execution,

a. Draw the input stream.

b. Draw a diagram showing the various positions of the read pointer as each call to *read* is executed.

c. Show the output produced by program *initials3*.

Sample execution A

```
Enter your initials.
b∧a∧1 ⏎
```

Sample execution B

```
Enter your initials.
b ⏎
al ⏎
```

Sample execution C

```
Enter your initials.
balstmqzr ⏎   ■
```

Next, consider the program *initials4* shown in Figure 13.24, which uses a single call to *read* for all three variables.

Although the Pascal code used in program *initials4* is different from the Pascal code used in program *initials3*, they will both deal with the input stream in exactly the same way. Both programs executed on the same user input will get the same values from the input stream and will leave the read pointer in the same position.

Figure 13.24   Program *initials4*

```
program initials4(input,output);
        {a program to illustrate reading three character}
        {variables with one call to read               }

var init1,init2,init3:char; {three character variables}
                            {to hold the initials     }

begin {initials4}
      writeln('Enter your initials.');
      read(init1,init2,init3);
      writeln('Your initials are ',init1,init2,init3)
end. {initials4}
```

Exercise 13.8: Show that what we have said in the last paragraph is true by repeating Exercise 13.7 using program *initials4*. ∎

Exercise 13.9: Consider the program *numbers3* and the two beginnings of sample executions shown in Figure 13.25. For each sample execution,

a. Draw the input stream.
b. Draw a diagram showing the various positions of the read pointer as the algorithm in Figure 13.5 is completed for each *integer* value read.
c. Complete the sample execution. ∎

Exercise 13.10: Repeat Exercise 13.9 for program *numbers4* shown in Figure 13.26. ∎

Figure 13.25 **Program *numbers3* and two sample executions**

```
program numbers3(input,output);
          {a program to illustrate reading two integer}
          {values with a single call to read          }

var num1,num2  : integer; {two integer variables to}
                          {hold input values        }

begin {numbers3}
        writeln('Enter two integers.');
        read(num1,num2);
        writeln('Your numbers were');
        writeln(num1,num2)
end. {numbers3}
```

Sample execution A

Enter two integers.
-729ˏ563ˏ14ˏ17ˏ99 ↵

Sample execution B

Enter two integers.
ˏˏˏˏ*298*ˏˏˏ ↵
364 ↵

Figure 13.26   Program *numbers4*

```
program numbers4(input,output);
        {a program to illustrate reading two integer}
        {values with two calls to read              }
var num1,num2  : integer; {two integer variables to }
                          {hold input values         }
begin {numbers4}
      writeln('Enter two integers.');
      read(num1);
      read(num2);
      writeln('Your numbers were');
      writeln(num1,num2)
end. {numbers4}
```

Remember that blanks and carriage returns may be used as delimiters to separate *integer* input values. However, when type *char* values are being read, blanks and carriage returns are read as individual *char* values. So, it is best not to try to read in both *char* and *integer* values with a single call to *read* or *readln*. Instead, use separate calls to *read* and *readln* for character variables and for *integer* variables.

The program *both*, shown in Figure 13.27, which reads *integer* values, uses both *read* and *readln*. Figure 13.28 shows two sample executions of program *both*.

Figure 13.27   Program *both*

```
program both(input,output);
        {a program to illustrate reading integer values}
        {using both read and readln                     }
var num1,num2,num3,num4,num5,num6: integer;
        {six integer variables used in this example}
begin {both}
      writeln ('Enter six integers.');
      read(num1,num2);
      readln(num3);
      read(num4,num5);
      readln(num6);
      writeln('Your numbers were: ');
      writeln(num1,num2,num3);
      writeln(num4,num5,num6)
end. {both}
```

Exercise 13.11: Explain how the values for the *integer* variables are obtained from the input stream in the sample executions of program *both* shown in Figure 13.27. Be sure to draw diagrams showing the various positions of the read pointer. ■

It's a bit more complicated to trace the interaction of *read* and *readln* when character data is being read. Figure 13.29 shows program *bothchar*, which is similar to program *both*. Figure 13.30 shows a sample execution of program *bothchar*.

Exercise 13.12: Show how the values for the character variables are obtained from the input stream in the sample execution of program *bothchar* shown in Figure 13.30. Be sure to draw diagrams showing the various positions of the read pointer. ■

Figure 13.28 Two sample executions of program *both*

Sample execution A

Enter six integers.
1ˌ2ˌ3ˌ4ˌ5ˌ6 ⇦
7ˌ8ˌ9ˌ10ˌ11ˌ12 ⇦
Your numbers were:
ˌˌˌˌˌˌˌˌˌˌˌ1ˌˌˌˌˌˌˌˌˌˌˌ2ˌˌˌˌˌˌˌˌˌˌˌ3
ˌˌˌˌˌˌˌˌˌˌ7ˌˌˌˌˌˌˌˌˌˌˌ8ˌˌˌˌˌˌˌˌˌˌˌ9

Sample execution B

Enter six integers.
10 ⇦
⇦
20 ⇦
30ˌ40ˌ50 ⇦
60 ⇦
70 ⇦
80ˌ90ˌ100 ⇦
Your numbers were:
ˌˌˌˌˌˌˌˌˌˌ10ˌˌˌˌˌˌˌˌˌˌ20ˌˌˌˌˌˌˌˌˌˌ30
ˌˌˌˌˌˌˌˌˌˌ60ˌˌˌˌˌˌˌˌˌˌ70ˌˌˌˌˌˌˌˌˌ80

Figure 13.29   Program *bothchar*

```
program bothchar(input,output);
        {a program to illustrate reading character }
        {values using both read and readln          }

var ch1,ch2,ch3,ch4,ch5,ch6:char;
        {six character variables for this example}

begin {bothchar}
        writeln('Enter six characters');
        read(ch1,ch2);
        readln(ch3);
        read(ch4,ch5);
        readln(ch6);
        writeln('Your characters were:  ',ch1,ch2,ch3,ch4,ch5,ch6)
end. {bothchar}
```

Figure 13.30   Sample execution of program *bothchar*

```
Enter six characters
abcdefgh ⏎
i ⏎
jklmnop ⏎
Your characters were:   abci⌃j
```

Exercise   13.13: Explain how values for the character variables are obtained from the input stream using the following as input data to program *bothchar*:

a. *a* ⏎
    b ⏎
    c⌃d⌃e⌃f ⏎

b. *a⌃b* ⏎
    1⌃2⌃5 ⏎
    4⌃3⌃2 ⏎ ∎

CHAPTER SUMMARY

1. The sequence of characters typed by a user as input to a program is called the *input stream*. Each keystroke counts as a character.

2. Pascal uses the standard procedures *read* and *readln* to get input data from the input stream into space allotted for variables in memory.

3. A *read pointer* manipulated by the procedures *read* and *readln* points to the next character in the input stream to be read.

4. The execution of procedure *readln* consists of these steps:
    A. Get and store in memory a value for each variable in its list.
    B. Move the read pointer just beyond the next carriage return character.

    If a list is not present, the execution of *readln* consists of just step B.

5. The instruction to invoke procedure *read* must include a list of variables. Its execution consists of getting and storing in memory a value for each variable in the list, leaving the read pointer just beyond the last character read.

6. When the computer reads a value for a variable of type *char*, the single character indicated by the read pointer is read. If that character happens to be a carriage return character, the computer stores a blank in the variable.

7. When the computer reads a value for a variable of type *integer*, the algorithm in Figure 13.5 is used. When the algorithm is complete, the read pointer is left pointing at the nondigit character that delimits the *integer* value.

COMMON ERRORS

- Using *read* instead of *readln* when inputting a single character. When this error is made, a subsequent call to *read* or *readln* for a *char* variable reads the carriage return and stores a blank.

- Embedding commas in an *integer* value or using commas to delimit *integer* input.

DEBUGGING HINTS

Output the value of each variable immediately after it is read. This process is called *echo-printing*. It enables a programmer to verify that data is being read as intended.

SUPPLEMENTAL PROBLEMS

1. Write a complete program to read in and print out today's date. Use three *integer* values to express the month, day, and year.

2. Write a complete program to ask the user how old she is, read the user's input, and print a message saying that the user's age is a great age.

    Here's a sample execution:

    ```
    Enter your age: 30 ⏎
    30 is a great age!
    ```

3. Write a program to prompt a user and read in his social security number. Assume that the number will be entered in the form:

    ```
    XXX-XX-XXXX ⏎
    ```

    You will need three *integer* variables and one *char* variable.

4. Someone has written the following program to read a phone number input as *XXX-XXXX*.

    ```
    program phone(input,output);
      {a program to read in a phone number}

    var dash : char; {to hold the dash typed between the }
                     {two numbers                        }
        prefix,      {to hold the beginning of the phone }
                     {number                             }
        postfix : integer;  {to hold the end of the }
                            {phone number           }

    begin {phone - main program}
      write('number please: ');
      read(prefix);
      read(dash);
      read(postfix);
      writeln('The phone number is',prefix:4,'-',postfix:4)
    end.  {phone - main program}
    ```

    Trace this program with the following inputs, explaining what happens in each case.

    a. ˄˄˄77-9025 ⏎
    b. ˄˄63-785-943 ⏎
    c. 678-˄9854˄ ⏎

    d. *67895ₓ-ₓ8* ⏎

    e. *9* ⏎
       3 ⏎
      -2578 ⏎

    f. *9* ⏎
       3 ⏎
     876 ⏎

5. The following program was written to read in an integer value representing a zip code and two character values representing a state code. It is expected that the zip code will be entered on the first line and that the state code will be entered on the second line. The program has an error. Find the error, explain why it is an error, and fix the program.

```
program stateinfo(input,output);
   {a program to read a zip code and a state code}

var zipcode : integer; {to hold the zipcode}
    statecode1,    {to hold the first character of the}
               {state code                          }
    statecode2 : char; {to hold the second character}
                   {of the state code               }

begin {stateinfo - main program}
  write('zipcode: ');
  read(zipcode);
  write('statecode: ');
  read(statecode1,statecode2);
  write('the zipcode ',zipcode:6,' is in the state');
  writeln(statecode1,statecode2,'.')
end. {stateinfo - main program}
```

6. Trace the code fragment given below with each of the following sets of input.

```
var x,y : char;
    z : integer;
   :
read(x,y,z);
readln(x)
   :
```

  a. *a* ⏎   b. *9567* ⏎   c. *z59tu* ⏎   d. *a* ⏎
    b ⏎   *t* ⏎   *s* ⏎   *9* ⏎
    c ⏎   *3* ⏎   *f* ⏎   *f* ⏎

  e. *a7* ⏎   f. *4n* ⏎
    t ⏎   *5* ⏎
           4 ⏎

7. Trace the given program with the following input.

```
program tracer (input, output);
  {a program for a tracing problem}

var let1, let2, let3 : char; {to hold three characters}

begin {tracer - main program}
  read (let1, let2, let3);
  read (let1);
  readln (let2);
  readln (let3)
end. {tracer - main program}
```

Here is the input:

Fred, ↵
Barbara, ↵
Lydia. ↵

8. Find the errors in the following program.

```
program errorprone (input, output);

const time = 'noon';
      letter = 'A';
      number = 17;

var let1, let2, let3 : char; {to hold three characters}
    num1, num2 : integer; {to hold two integer values}

begin {errorprone - main program}
  read (number, num1, num2);
  readln (let1);
  readln (let2, let3);
  let2 : = letter;
  letter : = time
end. {errorprone - main program}
```

9. Consider the following program, which was written to read in the first three characters of a person's name. Those three characters are to be typed on one line. The program has a logic error.

   a. If the user types in
      Larry ↵
      what will he need to type to make the program continue execution?

b. What does the user need to type to achieve reading the letters L, a, and **r** into the variables *firstlet*, *secondlet*, and *thirdlet*, respectively?

c. Fix the program to perform the task as originally intended.

```
program name(input,output);
  {a program to read in the first three letters of a }
  {person's name                                     }

var firstlet,   {to hold the first character }
                {of the user's name          }
    secondlet,  {to hold the second character }
                {of the user's name           }
    thirdlet : char;  {to hold the third character }
                      {of the user's name          }

begin {name - main program}
  write('Please enter your name: ');
  readln(firstlet);
  readln(secondlet);
  readln(thirdlet);
  writeln('The name begins ',firstlet,secondlet,thirdlet)
end. {name - main program}
```

10. Write a program to read in five letters typed on one line and then print them backward on the next line.

11. Write a program to do the following: Read in five integers, add five to each integer, and print out the calculated numbers.

CHAPTER

14

14.1 MODULAR PROGRAMS

In Chapter 4 (pages 62–75), we discussed the problem-solving technique usually described in computer science as stepwise refinement. The essential idea is to break a problem into subproblems. These subproblems may be refined into a solution, or into further subproblems if a subproblem is complex. When we have finished refining the problem, we have assembled a sequence of smaller steps that will accomplish the goal of a major task. These sequences of steps are subalgorithms and sometimes sub-subalgorithms.

The programming language statements that implement a given algorithm form a program. Statements that solve a specific subproblem or implement a particular subalgorithm should be grouped together into a logical unit of the program called a *program module*.

There are several reasons to use a modular style in writing computer programs:

1. The programmer can focus attention on a particular part of the problem during development of the program.

2. Individual segments of the program can be tested and debugged without the possible interference of other segments.

3. Program segments are more easily transported from one program to another.

4. When the same segment of code is needed in several places in a program, it need be written only once.

5. The completed program will be easier to read and hence easier to modify.

One kind of program module available in Pascal to a programmer is the *procedure*.

PROCEDURES AND THE FLOW OF DATA

The programs we have seen so far are simple. As we progress to programs that solve more complex problems, the usefulness of modularity in programs will become more apparent. When we discuss procedures in this chapter, however, we do so in the context of relatively simple programs. We do this to isolate the concept of using procedures from the details of a complex problem.

14.2 A SAMPLE PROBLEM

Consider the following problem: Write a computer program to simulate the game called "Guess My Number." The secret number should be built into the program. The computer will repeatedly prompt the user for guesses in the range from 1 to 100 inclusive. It should print a message commenting on each wrong guess (telling whether it is too high or too low) and terminate execution when the user's guess matches the secret number. The computer should also print the number of incorrect guesses the user made.

Algorithm Sketch

We can write a first sketch of an algorithm to solve this problem, as shown in Figure 14.1. The subalgorithms needed by our algorithm are shown in Figure 14.2.

Exercise 14.1: Trace the algorithm in Figure 14.1 using the subalgorithms in Figure 14.2. ∎

Figure 14.1   **First sketch of an algorithm for "Guess My Number"**

I. Give the user instructions.

II. Play the game.

III. Tell the user the number of wrong guesses.

Figure 14.2   **Subalgorithms for "Guess My Number" algorithm**

Subalgorithm to Give the User Directions

I. Print a greeting message.

II. Print an explanation of the game.

III. Print the upper and lower bounds for valid guesses.

Subalgorithm to Play the Game

Setup

I. Allocate a space in memory for the user's *guess*.

Instructions

I. Assign the value 0 to *total* of incorrect guesses.

II. Repeat the following:
   A. Ask the user to enter a guess.
   B. Read the response into *guess*.
   C. While the value of *guess* is less than the lower limit or the value of
      guess is greater than the upper limit, do the following:
      1. Print an error message.
      2. Ask the user to enter a guess between the lower and upper limits, inclusive.
      3. Read the user's response into *guess*.

D. If the value of *guess* is the secret number,
    then
        1. Print the congratulations message.
    else
        1'. Replace the value of *total* with one more than its current value.
        2'. If the value of *guess* is less than the secret number,
            then
                a. Print the too low message.
            else
                a'. Print the too high message.
until the value in *guess* is the secret number.

Subalgorithm to Tell the User the Number of Wrong Guesses

I. Print the value of *total* of incorrect guesses.

II. Print a goodbye message.

Using procedures we can write a program corresponding to the algorithm in Figure 14.1. The three steps constitute the subproblems to be solved and should correspond to three procedures in the program. We need to choose three names for the procedures. These names must be Pascal identifiers, and we should choose meaningful identifiers. We will give our procedures the names *instructions*, *playgame*, and *givescore*.

Analysis of Data

At this point we should analyze the data that our algorithm uses. Procedure *instructions* should print the constant values 1 and 100 to indicate to the user the bounds of valid input. Let's name those constants *min* and *max*.

The secret number is a constant value that procedure *playgame* must compare to each of the user's guesses. Let's name that constant *secret*.

Each of the user's guesses is an input data item used by procedure *playgame*. We referred to it as *guess* in our subalgorithm shown in Figure 14.2. If the user enters a *guess* that is out-of-bounds, the program should print an out-of-bounds error message. Procedure *playgame* needs to use the constants *min* and *max* to check the validity of each *guess*.

The total number of incorrect guesses is a computed data item named *total* in Figure 14.2. It is calculated in procedure *playgame* and output by procedure *givescore*. The data item *total* is the only one that must be transmitted from one procedure to another.

Using this analysis, we construct a data flow diagram for our algorithm, as shown in Figure 14.3. Notice that we have indicated the constant data item *secret*, used only by *playgame*, by writing its name inside the box for procedure *playgame*. We have indicated the variable data item *guess*, used only by *playgame*, by writing its name above a small box inside the box for procedure *playgame*. We will use this scheme to indicate constants and variables used by only a single procedure.

The other three data items are each used by more than one procedure and are indicated by arrows going into and out of the appropriate procedure box. Recall the discussion of data flow diagrams in Chapter 9 (pages 181–184).

Both procedure *instructions* and procedure *playgame* use the values of *min* and *max*, but neither needs to change them. Hence, arrows labeled *min* and *max* enter each procedure's box, but there are no such labeled arrows coming out.

The value of *total* is affected by the actions of procedure *playgame*. Thus, there are arrows labeled *total* both going into and coming out of the box for procedure *playgame*. In contrast, procedure *givescore* uses the value of *total* but should not be able to change that value. Hence, we only draw an arrow labeled *total* going into the box for procedure *givescore*.

Make sure that you understand what we have said about the diagram in Figure 14.3 before you continue reading.

There is a clear distinction between data values that are needed by only a single procedure and data values that are used by more than one procedure. Con-

Figure 14.3   Data flow diagram for "Guess My Number" algorithm

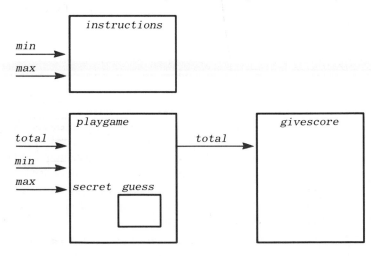

stant and variable data items that are used by more than one procedure must be defined or declared as we described in Chapter 12 (pages 234–250). Such definitions and declarations are called *global* and are placed after the program header and before the declaration of any procedure or function. The other data items that appropriately belong to only one procedure will be defined or declared *locally*— that is, within the particular procedure.

Procedure Calls and the Main Program

We are ready to write a skeleton of our program. Let's give the program the name *guessmynumber*. Our program should invoke the three procedures *instructions, playgame*, and *givescore* corresponding to the three algorithm steps shown in Figure 14.1. These three invocations constitute what is known as the *main program,* which is placed between **begin** and **end**.

A Pascal statement consisting of a procedure identifier alone constitutes an instruction to the computer to invoke that procedure. Such an instruction is known as a *procedure call*. The procedure identifier may be followed by a list of the data being transmitted to and/or from the procedure.

The word *argument* is commonly used to refer to a data item listed in a procedure call.[1] The list of arguments must be enclosed in parentheses, and arguments must be separated by commas. Arguments can be named or explicit constants, or variables, or expressions. For the moment, we use the word *expression* to indicate any legal argument. The syntax diagram for a procedure call is shown in Figure 14.4.

Figure 14.5 shows the skeleton of our program. Compare the three procedure calls to the data flow diagram in Figure 14.3. Notice that the constants we have defined and the variables that we have declared correspond to the labeled arrows in Figure 14.3. We have also put in special comments to indicate the position of global constant definitions and global variable declarations. Those comments are not standard, and we are simply using them for emphasis here.

Figure 14.4   Syntax diagram for a procedure call

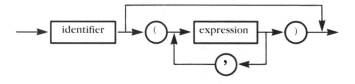

---

1. The term *actual parameter* is also used to refer to a data item listed in a procedure call.

Figure 14.5   **Skeleton of program *guessmynumber***

```
program guessmynumber (input, output);
  {a simulation of the Guess My Number Game}

{GLOBAL CONSTANT DEFINITIONS}
const  min = 1; {lower bound for secret number}
       max = 100; {upper bound for secret number}

{GLOBAL VARIABLE DECLARATIONS}
var  total : integer;   {total number of incorrect guesses}
                        {made by the user                  }
    .
    .
    .

begin {guessmynumber - main program}
   instructions(min, max);
   playgame(min, max, total);
   givescore(total)
end. {guessmynumber - main program}
```

Notice that the main program is clear and concise. The algorithm's structure is obvious. The smaller steps that need to be performed do not clutter up the main program. The data items that must be used by more than one procedure are also clearly shown.

The data items *secret* and *guess*, used only by procedure *playgame*, are not part of the global definitions and declarations. The structure of a procedure is very similar to the structure of a program. Procedure *playgame* will contain its own constant definition and variable declaration sections. It is there that we will define *secret* and declare *guess*.

Procedure Declarations

The main program does not show the smaller steps required to make our program perform properly. We need to state the smaller steps that constitute the procedures *instructions*, *playgame*, and *givescore* somewhere. The place to do that is within the procedure declarations. Recall from Chapter 10 that procedure and function declarations are placed between the global variable declarations and the main program.

Syntactically, procedure declarations resemble programs. This resemblance makes them seem like miniature programs embedded in a program. There are two points of difference, however: The first line of a procedure, called a *procedure header,* is not the same as a program header. The second syntactic difference is that the last punctuation mark at the end of a procedure is a semicolon instead of a period.

The Procedure Header

A procedure header begins with the reserved word **procedure**, followed by an identifier naming the procedure. The procedure identifier may be followed by a parameter list enclosed in parentheses. Parameters are the syntactic devices used to control the flow of data into and out of a procedure. Figure 14.6 shows the syntax diagram for a procedure header.

Individual program modules may either affect the value of a data item or just use the value of a data item without the possibility of changing it. Figure 14.7 displays the two possible types of access to a data item that a program module can have.

Pascal has two syntactic constructs that correspond to these two types of access to data items. Recall that space in memory must be allotted for each data item used by a program. The first syntactic construct, called a *value parameter,* allots a new space in memory for a data item and copies the value of the item into that space when a procedure begins execution. The module can then use the copy but cannot affect the original. The copy of the data item is erased when the module completes execution. In our data flow diagrams, this syntactic construct corresponds to a labeled arrow going into a procedure box with no arrow with the same label coming out.

The second syntactic construct, called a *variable parameter,* gives a second name to an already existing data item in memory. Thus, the argument correspond-

Figure 14.6   Syntax diagram for a procedure header

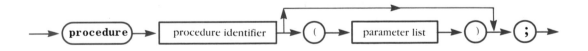

Figure 14.7   Two types of access to a data item available to a module

1. A module may need to know the values of certain data items to perform its task, or

2. A module may, as part of its task, affect the values of certain data items.

ing to a variable parameter must be a variable. The module can affect the value of the data item by referring to the second name. The second name is erased when the module terminates execution. In our data flow diagrams, this syntactic construct corresponds to labeled arrows for a particular data item going both into and out of a procedure box.

Recall the syntax diagram for a procedure header given in Figure 14.6. The parameter list of a procedure header is composed of the various parameters used by the procedure.[2] The syntax diagram for a parameter list is shown in Figure 14.8.

One sees immediately that there is a choice to be made: whether or not to use the reserved word **var**. This choice corresponds to the choice between a value parameter and a variable parameter. Variable parameter identifiers must be preceded by the reserved word **var** in the parameter list. The absence of **var** indicates that the following identifiers are value parameters.

The parameter identifiers are used as variable identifiers within the procedure. Thus, each parameter must be declared within the parameter list. A semicolon is used to separate parameters of different types and to separate variable parameters of a certain type from value parameters of the same type.

The data items in the argument list of a procedure call correspond to the parameters listed in the procedure's header. Recall that variable parameter identifiers are names that refer to corresponding arguments. Also recall that value parameter identifiers are names that refer to copies of corresponding arguments. The correspondence between arguments and parameters is determined by their order in the argument list and in the parameter list. Thus, the argument listed first corresponds to the parameter listed first. The second argument corresponds to the second parameter, and so on to the end of each list. There must be exactly as many arguments in the procedure call as there are parameters in the procedure header.

A complicated procedure header and a table describing its parameters is shown in Figure 14.9.

Let's write the procedure headers for our program *guessmynumber*. We need to refer to the procedure calls we wrote in Figure 14.5 and to the data flow diagram in Figure 14.3.

Figure 14.8   **Syntax diagram for a parameter list**

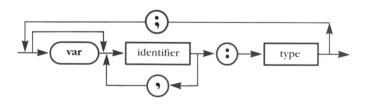

---

2. The term *formal parameter* is sometimes used to refer to what we have called a *parameter*.

Figure 14.9   Explanatory table for a complicated procedure header

```
procedure example (a,b:integer;  var c,d:char;  e:char;
                 var f,g,h:integer;  i,j:char);
```

Position	Value or variable	Identifier	Type
1	value	a	integer
2	value	b	integer
3	variable	c	char
4	variable	d	char
5	value	e	char
6	variable	f	integer
7	variable	g	integer
8	variable	h	integer
9	value	i	char
10	value	j	char

The procedure call that invokes procedure *instructions* is

```
instructions(min,max);
```

There are two arguments, *min* and *max*. The data flow diagram shows that both of these values are to be used by the procedure, but the procedure should not be able to affect them. Thus, *min* and *max* should correspond to value parameters. To reinforce the idea that procedures should be as independent as possible, we choose new identifiers for the value parameters. We use the identifier *lowerbound* for the parameter corresponding to *min* and the identifier *upperbound* for the parameter corresponding to *max*. The arguments *min* and *max* are both type *integer*. Hence, the corresponding value parameters, *lowerbound* and *upperbound,* should be declared as type *integer*.

We get this procedure header:

procedure instructions (lowerbound,upperbound: integer);

Note that if a procedure header is longer than one line, it can be written on several lines. You should place the parts of the procedure header that logically belong together as close to each other as possible.

Exercise 14.2: What is wrong with each of the following procedure headers for *instructions*?

a. **procedure** instructions (var lowerbound, upperbound:integer);

b. **procedure** instructions (upperbound, lowerbound:integer); ∎

The procedure call that invokes procedure *playgame* is

playgame(min, max, total);

The arguments *min* and *max* are again only to be used by *playgame*, and thus should correspond to value parameters. However, *total* represents a data item that has no predictable value before procedure *playgame* is invoked, but that should have a well-defined value after procedure *playgame* is executed. Hence, *total* should correspond to a variable parameter. We again choose new identifiers for the three parameters. Let *lower*, upper, and *numberwrong* correspond to *min*, max, and *total*, respectively. Notice that all three parameters should be type *integer*.

Exercise 14.3: Why must the variable parameter *numberwrong* be type *integer*? ∎

We have determined that the procedure header for procedure *playgame* is as follows:

procedure playgame (lower, upper: integer;
                    var numberwrong: integer);

Exercise 14.4: What is wrong with each of the following procedure headers for procedure *playgame*?

a. **procedure** playgame (**var** lower, upper: integer;
                        numberwrong: integer);

b. **procedure** playgame (**var** numberwrong: integer;
                        lower, upper: integer);

c. **procedure** playgame (upper, lower: integer;
                        var numberwrong: integer); ∎

The procedure call that invokes procedure *givescore* is

```
givescore(total);
```

The single argument *total* has a value that the procedure needs in order to print the score, but the procedure should not be able to change the value of *total*.

Exercise   14.5: Using the new identifier *score* for the parameter corresponding to the argument *total*, write the procedure header for procedure *givescore*. ∎

The Idea of a Block

A Pascal program can be considered as having three parts: the program header, the block, and the period. Thus, the block consists of everything in the program except the header and the period at the very end of the program. The idea of a block can also be used in conjunction with procedures. A Pascal procedure consists of three parts: the procedure header, the procedure's block, and a semicolon. The reason that we can use the word *block* in both cases is that both the program's block and the procedure's block are composed of the same kinds of sections: constant definition section, variable declaration section, procedure and function declaration section, and a main instruction section between the reserved words **begin** and **end**. Remember, though, that the last punctuation mark in a procedure is a semicolon, in contrast to the period used at the end of a program.

Figure 14.10 shows the syntax diagram for a procedure declaration.

Examples of Procedure Declarations

Since we have not yet discussed Pascal's instructions for selection and iteration, we cannot yet write all of Pascal instructions that form the procedures of program *guessmynumber*. However, we can sketch each procedure's block.

Procedure *instructions* simply prints directions for using the program. It needs no selection or iteration statements. The data that it needs to print correct directions has been "passed" to it from the main program through its param-

Figure 14.10   **Syntax diagram for a procedure declaration**

eters. It can refer to the values 1 and 100 that bound valid user input by the identifiers *lowerbound* and *upperbound*. We do not use the global identifiers *min* and *max* to emphasize the procedure's independence from the rest of the program.

Procedure *instructions* needs no other named constants or variables. It needs only an instruction section placed between **begin** and **end**.

Figure 14.11 shows our version of procedure *instructions*. Notice that we have placed a comment describing the purpose of the procedure just under the header. We have also commented the **begin** and **end** with the procedure's name. These comments are vital parts of the program's internal documentation.

Procedure *playgame* requires selection and iteration instructions. Hence, we will not write it completely. There are two data items used only by *playgame*: the constant **secret** and the variable *guess*. Thus, procedure *playgame* needs its own constant definition and variable declaration sections.

We sketch procedure *playgame* in Figure 14.12. We have chosen 39 to be the secret number. Once again, we have put in additional comments indicating the position of local constant definitions and the position of local variable declarations just to emphasize that we are introducing a new syntactic feature.

Since procedure *givescore* just prints a message indicating the number of incorrect guesses, we can write it completely. It receives the number of incorrect guesses through its parameter *score*. When we print the number of incorrect guesses, we should do so by outputting the value of *score*.

Figure 14.13 shows our version of procedure *givescore*. Notice that it needs no local constants or variables. Figure 14.14 shows what is called a *block diagram* for program *guessmynumber*.

Figure 14.11   **Procedure** *instructions*

```
procedure instructions(lowerbound,upperbound:integer);
   {explains the game to the user}

begin {instructions}
   writeln('Welcome to Guess My Number');
   write('I am thinking of a number between ');
   writeln(lowerbound:1,' and ',upperbound:1,'.');
   writeln('Please enter your guess when requested.');
   writeln('I will indicate whether your guess is');
   writeln('too high,too low,or correct!');
   writeln('After you have guessed correctly, I will');
   writeln('tell you how many incorrect guesses you made.')
end; {instructions}
```

Figure 14.12   Procedure *playgame*

```
procedure playgame (lower,upper:integer;
                        var numberwrong:integer);
   {This procedure simulates the game for the user.}

   {LOCAL CONSTANT DEFINITION SECTION FOR PLAYGAME}
const secret = 39; {the secret number that the user}
                   {is trying to guess}

   {LOCAL VARIABLE DECLARATION SECTION FOR PLAYGAME}
var guess : integer;    {to hold the user's guess}

begin {playgame}

{Here we expect to repeatedly prompt for and read}
{the user's guesses, compare each guess to the secret number,}
{output a message to tell whether the guess is high, low, or}
{correct, and keep track of the number of incorrect }
{guesses in the variable numberwrong.}

end; {playgame}
```

Figure 14.13   Procedure *givescore*

```
procedure givescore(score:integer);
   {tells the user how many incorrect guesses were made}

begin {givescore}
   writeln('You made ',score:1,' incorrect guesses');
   writeln('before guessing the secret number.')
end; {givescore}
```

Figure 14.14   Block diagram for program *guessmynumber*

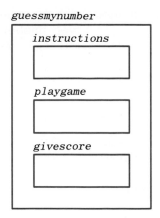

Parameters, Local Variables, and Memory

What happens in memory when a procedure is executed? We'll partially trace an execution of program *guessmynumber*, focusing on how data is managed.

 When the program begins execution, space is assigned in memory to the integer global variable *total*. Its value is unpredictable at this point, as we indicate with a ?.

The first statement of the main program invokes procedure *instructions*. *Control* has passed from the main program to procedure *instructions*. The constants *min* and *max* are arguments corresponding to the value parameters *lowerbound* and *upperbound*. Space is allotted in memory for *lowerbound* and *upperbound* to hold copies of *min* and *max*. We can picture the situation in memory as shown in Figure 14.15.

Procedure *instructions* then uses the values of *lowerbound* and *upperbound*. The calls to *write* and *writeln* listed in procedure *instructions* are executed in the order in which they appear. When procedure *instructions* terminates, the space in memory allotted to *lowerbound* and *upperbound* is withdrawn. The situation in memory is shown in Figure 14.16.

Figure 14.15   **Illustration of memory just after procedure *instructions* is invoked**

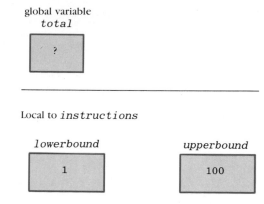

Figure 14.16   **Situation in memory just after termination of procedure *instructions***

Control returns to the main program. The next statement to be executed is the procedure call to *playgame*. The arguments *min*, *max*, and *total* in this invocation of the procedure correspond respectively to the value parameters *lower* and *upper* and the variable parameter *numberwrong*. Space is allotted in memory for *lower* and *upper*, and the values of *min* and *max* are copied into those locations. The identifier *numberwrong* becomes a second name for the global variable *total*. Procedure *playgame* also has a local *integer* variable *guess*, but the value of that location in memory is unpredictable when the procedure begins executing. The situation in memory at the start of procedure *playgame* is shown in Figure 14.17.

Suppose now that the user makes seven incorrect guesses before correctly guessing the secret number. Just before procedure *playgame* terminates, the values in memory should be as shown in Figure 14.18.

Figure 14.17   **Situation in memory just after procedure *playgame* is invoked**

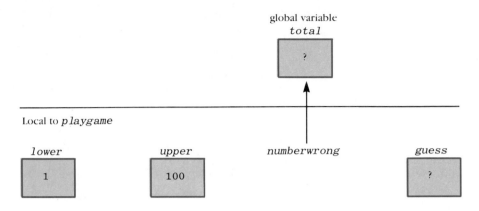

Control reverts to the main program after all memory allotments for procedure *playgame* are eliminated:

Finally, procedure *givescore* is invoked with the single argument *total*. In this invocation of procedure *givescore*, *total* corresponds to the value parameter *score* in the header of procedure *givescore*. Thus, space is allotted in memory for *score,* and the value of *total*, 7, is copied into that location. The situation in memory is shown in Figure 14.19.

Figure 14.18   **Situation in memory just before procedure *playgame* terminates**

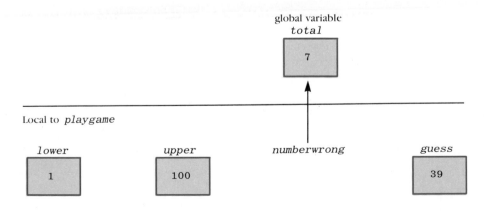

Figure 14.19   Situation in memory just after procedure *givescore* is invoked

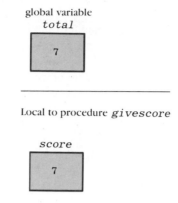

global variable
total

7

Local to procedure *givescore*

score

7

Procedure *givescore* then prints the value of *score* and says goodbye to the user. After *givescore* terminates, control reverts to the main program. The memory space allotted to *score* is withdrawn, leaving only the global variable *total* in memory:

global variable
total

7

Program *guessmynumber* then terminates.

A Structural Modification of Our Algorithm

We can revise the algorithm given in Figure 14.2 to increase its modularity. We do this by making subalgorithms corresponding to getting a valid guess and then testing the guess. Our revision of step II is shown in Figure 14.20.

Step II of the original algorithm corresponds to our procedure *playgame*. Syntactically, procedures can have their own locally declared procedures. The two subalgorithms shown in Figure 14.20 will be two subprocedures of procedure *playgame*. Let's name those procedures *getvalidguess* and *testguess*. We need to analyze the flow of data items into and out of the procedures *getvalidguess* and *testguess*.

The value of *guess* is determined by procedure *getvalidguess*. Procedure *getvalidguess* must also know the bounds for valid guesses. Procedure

Figure 14.20   Revised algorithm for step II

II. Play the game.
    A. Assign the value 0 to *total.*
    B. Repeat the following:
        1. Get a valid response into *guess.*
        2. Test the value of *guess* and update the value of *total.*
    until the value of *guess* is the same as the value of the secret number.

Subalgorithm to Get a Valid Guess

I. Ask the user to enter a valid guess.

II. Read the response into *guess.*

III. While the value of *guess* is less than the lower bound or the value of guess is greater than the upper bound, do the following:
    A. Print an error message.
    B. Ask the user to enter a guess between the lower and upper limits, inclusive.
    C. Read the response into *guess.*

Subalgorithm to Test *Guess* and Update *Total*

I. If the value of *guess* is the secret number,
    then
        A. Print the congratulations message.
    else
        A'. Replace the value of *total* with one more than its current value.
        B'. If the value of *guess* is less than the secret number,
            then
                1. Print the too low message.
            else
                1'. Print the too high message.

Figure 14.21   Data flow diagram for *getvalidguess*

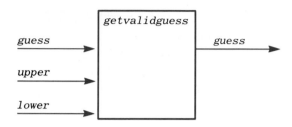

playgame knows those values as *lower* and *upper*. Thus, the procedure call to *getvalidguess* should be

getvalidguess(guess,lower,upper);

Procedure *getvalidguess* affects the value of *guess* but should not be able to affect *lower* or *upper*. Thus, Figure 14.21 shows the data flow diagram for *getvalidguess*.

The following procedure header reflects our data flow diagram and the procedure call statement. Note that we have chosen new names for the parameters so that there will be no confusion about our references.

procedure getvalidguess (**var** try:integer;
                                 low,high:integer);

Procedure *testguess* must know the values of *guess* and *secret* in order to compare them. It must also be able to update the value of *numberwrong* if the guess is incorrect. Thus, we can write the following procedure call to *testguess*:

testguess(guess,secret,numberwrong);

Procedure *testguess* should not be able to change *guess* or *secret*, but it should be able to change the value of *numberwrong*. Figure 14.22 shows its data flow diagram.

The following procedure header for *testguess* reflects its data flow diagram and procedure call. Again we have selected new names for the parameters.

procedure testguess(userguess,realanswer:integer;
                         var numwrong:integer);

Figure 14.23 shows a sketch of procedure *playgame* incorporating the subprocedures.

304

Figure 14.22   Data flow diagram for *testguess*

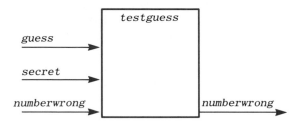

```
procedure playgame(lower,upper:integer;
                       var numberwrong:integer);
 {This procedure simulates the game for the user}.

const secret = 39;  {the secret number the user is}
                      {trying to guess            }

var guess : integer; {to hold the user's guess}

   procedure getvalidguess(var try:integer;
                             low,high:integer);
    {to get a guess between low and high, inclusive}
    {from the user                                }

   begin {getvalidguess}
    {Here we expect to repeatedly prompt for and read}
    {the user's guess until a valid guess is entered.}
   end; {getvalidguess}

   procedure testguess(userguess,realanswer:integer;
                        var numwrong:integer);
    {to test the user's guess and update number of}
    {incorrect guesses                           }

   begin {testguess}
    {Here we expect to compare userguess to }
    {realanswer and output a message about the}
    {guess being high, low, or correct. We    }
    {also increment numwrong if the          }
```

```
                   {userguess is incorrect.                    }
               end; {testguess}

        begin {playgame}
           .
           .
           .
           getvalidguess(guess,lower,upper);
           testguess(guess,secret,numberwrong);
           .
           .
           .
        end; {playgame}
```

Figure 14.24 shows a block diagram for program *guessmynumber* that reflects the modification of procedure *playgame*. Compare it to the block diagram in Figure 14.14.

Figure 14.24   Block diagram for modified program *guessmynumber*

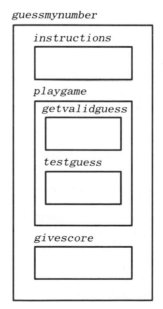

14.3 A MORE COMPLICATED EXAMPLE

Let's now consider a program to simulate a different game played by two players. The number of correct and incorrect responses made by each player will be calculated by the program. For each player, a percentage of correct responses out of the total number of responses will be calculated. The player who attains the higher percentage will be declared the winner. If both players attain the same percentage, the program will declare a tie.

An Algorithm for This Problem

Figure 14.25 shows an algorithm for our game simulation. The numbers of correct and incorrect responses made by player1 and player2, respectively, are named *right1*, *wrong1*, *right2*, and *wrong2*. The percentages of correct responses for each player are named *perc1* and *perc2*.

Procedures Corresponding to Our Algorithm

Steps II and IV are quite similar, as are steps III and V. You can imagine that the Pascal code used to implement those pairs of steps is similar to the point of being redundant. Besides forming logical units in a program, procedures help avoid re-

Figure 14.25   **Algorithm sketch for a two-player game**

Setup

   I. Allocate the following integer variables: *right1, wrong1, right2, wrong2, perc1,* and *perc2.*

Instructions

   I. Explain the game to both players.

  II. Let player1 play the game to determine values for *right1* and *wrong1.*

 III. Calculate player1's percentage using *right1* and *wrong1.* Record the value calculated on *perc1.*

 IV. Let player2 play the game to determine values for *right2* and *wrong2.*

  V. Calculate player2's percentage using *right2* and *wrong2.* Record the result on *perc2.*

 VI. Decide, on the basis of *perc1* and *perc2,* if there is a winner or a tie and announce the decision.

dundant coding. We should be able to write one procedure to simulate playing the game and invoke it twice (once for each player). Similarly, we should be able to write one procedure to calculate a percentage (steps III and V) and invoke it twice.

Let's name the procedures corresponding to steps I through VI. The procedure that implements step I will be *instructions*. We'll use the identifier *play* for the procedure that implements steps II and IV. We'll use the identifier *calculate* for the procedure that implements steps III and V and the identifier *decide* for the procedure that implements step VI.

The Data Flow between Procedures

Now we should analyze the data flow between procedures. None of the variable data items referred to in the setup portion of the algorithm are used by procedure *instructions*. The first time procedure *play* is invoked (step II), its actions determine the values of *right1* and *wrong1*. The first time procedure *calculate* is invoked (step III), it needs to use the values of *right1* and *wrong1* to determine the value of *perc1*. Step IV calls for the second invocation of procedure *play*, determining the values of *right2* and *wrong2*. Step V calls for the second invocation of procedure *calculate*, which will determine the value of *perc2* using the values of *right2* and *wrong2*. Procedure *decide* uses the values of *perc1* and *perc2*.

Figure 14.26 shows a data flow diagram reflecting what we have said in the last paragraph. We have omitted a box for procedure *instructions* because there is no data flowing from or to that procedure.

The Main Program and Procedure Calls

We are now in a position to write the main program and the global variable declarations for our two-player game simulation. Let's name the program *twocanplay*. Figure 14.27 shows a skeleton of the program. Notice that every data item that is passed from one procedure to another corresponds to a global variable. This must be the case because only global variables are allotted space in memory that is not withdrawn until the program terminates.

The Procedure Headers

We need to keep in mind that the arguments listed in the calls to procedure *play* correspond to data items whose values are affected by the procedure. Thus, the two corresponding parameters must be variable parameters.

Whereas each argument's identifier distinguishes the particular player in a pro-

Figure 14.26   Data flow diagram for our two-player game

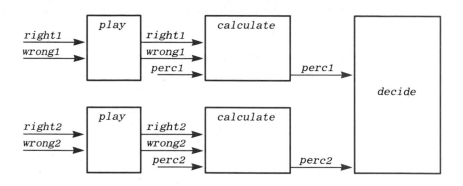

Figure 14.27   Skeleton of program *twocanplay*

```
program twocanplay(input,output);
   {simulation of a two-player game}

var right1,   {number of correct responses from player1}
    wrong1,   {number of incorrect responses from player1}
    perc1,    {player1's percentage of correct responses}
    right2,   {number of correct responses from player2}
    wrong2,   {number of incorrect responses from player 2}
    perc2 : integer;   {player2's percentage of }
                       { correct responses      }


      .
      .
      .

   {Procedure declarations go here.}
      .
      .
      .


begin {twocanplay - main program}
   instructions; {Note that this procedure call has no}
                 {arguments.                          }
   play(right1,wrong1);
   calculate(right1,wrong1,perc1);
   play(right2,wrong2);
   calculate(right2,wrong2,perc2);
   decide(perc1,perc2)
end. {twocanplay - main program}
```

cedure call to *play*, the corresponding parameter's identifiers should refer to a generic player's score. Procedure *play* should simulate the game for any player. It is the procedure call to *play* that indicates the particular player. Hence, the parameters of *play* are named *right* and *wrong* in the following procedure header:

procedure play (**var** right,wrong: integer);

Exercise   14.6: Write a procedure header for procedure *instructions* of program *twocanplay*.   ■

Procedure *calculate* should not be able to affect the values of the first two data items sent to it. It does, however, determine the value of the third data item. Choosing generic identifiers for the two value parameters and the one variable parameter, we write the following procedure header for *calculate*:

procedure calculate (numright,numwrong: integer;
                         var percent: integer);

Procedure *decide* is called with two arguments whose values should not be affected by the procedure. This is not a procedure that is called once for each player. Hence, generic identifiers for its parameters are inappropriate. We should use identifiers that make clear the correspondence between players and their percentages. The following procedure header suits our purposes:

procedure decide (score1,score2:integer);

Figure 14.28 gives a block diagram for program *twocanplay*.

Exercise   14.7: Add more detail to our skeleton of program *twocanplay* in Figure 14.27 by placing the procedure header and the **begin** and **end** for each of the procedures into the skeleton.   ■

Exercise   14.8: Given the following information, trace the effects on memory of an execution of program *twocanplay* as we did on pages 298–301 for program *guessmynumber:*

Assume that *player1* responds three times correctly and seven times incorrectly and that *player2* responds three times correctly and six times incorrectly.   ■

Figure 14.28   Block diagram for program *twocanplay*

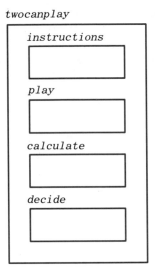

Figure 14.29   Program *showprecedence*

```pascal
program showprecedence(output);
   {just an example program to illustrate the precedence rule}

var number : integer;   {a global variable}

   procedure dosomething;

   var number : integer;   {a variable with the same}
                           {identifier declared locally}
   begin {dosomething}
      number := 10;
      write('In procedure dosomething number is: ');
      writeln(number:1)
   end; {dosomething}

begin {showprecedence - main program}
   number := 5;
   writeln('The value of number is ',number :1);
   dosomething;
   writeln('The value of number is ',number :1)
end. {showprecedence - main program}
```

14.4 THE QUESTION OF PRECEDENCE

We were very careful never to use the same identifier in two different blocks of a program in the two examples we have discussed in this chapter. By choosing distinct identifiers, we have avoided the problem of *precedence*—that is, if an identifier is used to name two distinct entities in a program, to which entity does it refer in any particular instance? Let's look at a simple example. Consider the program shown in Figure 14.29.

 Let's trace the effects on memory of an execution of program *showprecedence*. When the program begins execution, space is assigned in memory for the global variable *number*.

global variable
number

?

The first statement of the main program assigns the value 5 to *number*.

global variable
number

5

The *writeln* statement displays:

```
The value of number is 5
```

Procedure *dosomething* is called, and space is allotted in memory for its local variable *number*. At this point, both the local and global variables *number* exist in memory.

global variable
number

5

local variable
number

?

The first statement of procedure *dosomething* is number : = 10. Which *number* gets the value 10? The answer is the most local *number*. The global variable *number* is unaffected.

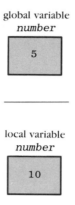

global variable
number

5

local variable
number

10

The *writeln* statement in procedure *dosomething* displays

In procedure dosomething number is 10

The *number* referred to in the *writeln* is also the most local *number*.

The procedure terminates, withdrawing all of the memory allotted to local variables. Only the global variable *number* is left in memory.

global variable
number

5

The last *writeln* statement in the main program of *showprecedence* displays

The value of number is 5

Using the same identifier for an argument in a procedure call and its corresponding parameter can also cause confusion. The parameter is more local than the argument. If the parameter is a value parameter, an assignment to it can be mistaken for an assignment to the corresponding argument, which won't work! Consider the program in Figure 14.30 as an example.

Figure 14.30   Program *showit*

```
program showit(output);
  {to show precedence problems with parameters}
var number : integer;   {a global variable}

  procedure doit(number:integer);
  begin {doit}
    number:= 20
  end; {doit}

begin {showit - main program}
  doit(number);
  writeln(number)
end. {showit - main program}
```

 The value output by program *showit* is completely unpredictable. The global variable *number* is assigned space in memory when the program begins execution.

global variable
number

Procedure *doit* is invoked. Its value parameter *number* is assigned space in memory, and the value of its corresponding argument, the global *number*, is copied into that memory location. Hence, both the global *number* and the local *number* have the same unpredictable value.

global variable
number

local variable
number

The assignment statement number := 20 gives the most local *number* the value 20.

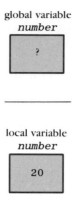

global variable
number

?

local variable
number

20

When procedure *doit* terminates, memory space is withdrawn from its local variables and value parameters, leaving

global variable
number

?

The still unpredictable value of *number* is displayed by the final *writeln* statement.

Exercise   14.9: Trace the effects on memory of the following program.

```
program allconfused(output);

var num1, num2 : integer;
    ch1, ch2 : char;

    procedure confuseit (var ch1:char;  ch2:char;
                         var num2:integer);

    var num1 : integer;

    begin {confuseit}
        ch1 := 'x';
        ch2 := 'y';
```

```
      num1 : = 100;
      num2 : = 200
   end; {confuseit}

begin {allconfused}
   num1 : = 10;
   num2 : = 20;
   ch1 : = 'a';
   ch2 : = 'b';
   confuseit(ch1,ch2,num1);
   writeln(num1,num2,ch1,ch2)
end. {allconfused}   ■
```

14.5 THE QUESTION OF SCOPE

We must also be concerned with the scope of an identifier in a Pascal program. By *scope,* we mean where in the program the identifier has meaning, or as we sometimes say, where an identifier is known.

In more complex programs, the question of the scope of an identifier is a crucial issue for procedure identifiers. The scope of a procedure identifier determines where a procedure may be invoked.

The scope of an identifier is defined in terms of the blocks of the program. The rule simply stated is

An identifier is known in its block of definition from its point of definition to the end of the block.

Consider the example block diagram and program skeleton shown in Figure 14.31.

The table in Figure 14.32 describes the block in which each procedure is defined. The table in Figure 14.33 shows the list of procedures that are *known* to each procedure—that is, the list of procedures that can be called by each procedure. Calls to a procedure must be within the scope of the procedure's identifier, that is, in its block of definition from its point of definition to the end of the block.

We should take note of when a procedure is not known to another procedure. For example, procedure *B* cannot call either of procedures *C* and *D* because *C* and *D* are declared in the same block as *B*, but after *B*. Thus, *B* does not know *C* and *D*. In fact, procedure *B* can only call procedures declared in its block or those declared in its block of definition (program *A*) above it. Hence, procedure *B* can only call procedures *B* and *E*.

Figure 14.31   **Program skeleton and block diagram for example program** *A*

```
program A(input,output);
 {global variable declarations}
    procedure B;
      {declarations for B}
          procedure E;
            {declarations for E}
          begin {E}
             :
          end;  {E}
    begin {B}
      :
    end; {B}
    procedure C;
      {declarations for C}
          procedure F;
            {declarations for F}
          begin {F}
             :
          end; {F}
          procedure G;
            {declarations for G}
          begin {G}
             :
          end; {G}
    begin {C}
      :
    end; {C}
    procedure D;
      {declarations for D}
          procedure H;
            {declarations for H}
              procedure I;
                {declarations for I}
              begin {I}
                 :
                end; {I}
          begin {H}
             :
          end; {H}
    begin {D}
      :
    end; {D}
begin {A — main program}
   :
end. {A — main program}
```

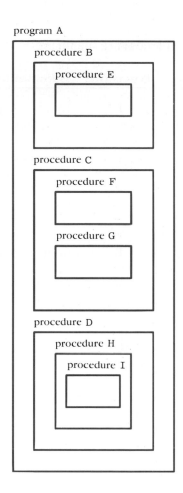

Figure 14.32   The block of definition for each procedure of program *A*

Procedure	Is defined in the block of
B	program A
E	procedure B
C	program A
F	procedure C
G	procedure C
D	program A
H	procedure D
I	procedure H

Figure 14.33   Scope of procedure identifiers

Procedure	Is known by (may be called by)
B	program A, procedure B, procedure E, procedure C, procedure F, procedure G, procedure D, procedure H, procedure I
E	procedure B, procedure E
C	program A, procedure C, procedure F, procedure G, procedure D, procedure H, procedure I
F	procedure F, procedure G, procedure C
G	procedure G, procedure C
D	program A, procedure D, procedure H, procedure I
H	procedure H, procedure I, procedure D
I	procedure I, procedure H

Exercise   14.10: Explain how what we have said in the last paragraph agrees with the information in Figure 14.33.   ■

Procedure *C* can call procedure *B* since *B* is declared in the same block as *C*, and above *C*. However, procedure *C* cannot call procedure *E*, since *E* is not declared in the same block as *C*. *E* is local to *B* and thus "hidden" from *C* by *B*. The scope of *E* ends when its block of definition, *B*, ends.

Program *A* can only call procedures *B*, *C*, and *D*. All the other procedures are local and are hidden from program *A*.

Figure 14.34 gives a complete list of the procedures that can be called by each procedure of our example.

Figure 14.34   Procedures that can be called by each procedure

Procedure	Can call
B	B, E
C	B, C, F, G
D	B, C, D, H
E	B, E
F	B, C, F
G	B, C, F, G
H	B, C, D, H, I
I	B, C, D, H, I

Exercise 14.11: Verify that the information in Figures 14.33 and 14.34 is not contradictory. ▪

CHAPTER SUMMARY

1. Procedures provide a means of modularizing Pascal programs.

2. Procedures correspond to subalgorithms.

3. A procedure call invokes a procedure. A procedure call consists of the procedure identifier, possibly followed by a list of arguments that is enclosed in parentheses.

4. The syntax of a procedure declaration is similar to the syntax of a program. Both a procedure and a program have a section called the *block*. The syntactic differences between a procedure and a program lie outside the block in the procedure header and the final punctuation mark.

5. Arguments and parameters are used to control the flow of data between program modules.

6. Data items declared or defined within a procedure are called *local*. Data items declared or defined in the program block are called *global*.

7. Global variables must be used to hold data items being transmitted between procedures. Local variables are allotted space in memory when the procedure begins execution. Space in memory is withdrawn from local variables when the procedure terminates.

8. There are two ways program modules can have access to data in Pascal:
   a. A module may need to know the value of a data item. This is accomplished by using a value parameter. We illustrate this in a data flow diagram as

   b. A module may, as part of its task, affect the value of a data item. This is accomplished by using a variable parameter. We illustrate this in a data flow diagram as

9. Parameters in a procedure header correspond by position to arguments in the procedure call.

10. A variable parameter is a locally known synonym for its corresponding argument. Hence, the argument of a variable parameter must be a variable.

11. A value parameter is allotted space in memory when the procedure is executed. That space is given the value of the corresponding argument.

12. Syntactically, one distinguishes between value and variable parameters in a parameter list by the absence or presence of the reserved word **var**.

13. If an identifier is used in more than one instance, the most local identifier has precedence.

14. The general rule that describes the scope of an identifier is

    An identifier is known in its block of definition from its point of definition to the end of the block.

COMMON ERRORS

■ Referring to a constant, variable, or procedure before it has been defined or declared is an error, because the translator has no meaning for the identifier that you are using.

■ Using a variable parameter when a value parameter is appropriate or vice versa.

■ The correspondence between an argument list and a parameter list may fail semantically in three ways:
   1. The number of arguments may be different from the number of parameters.
   2. The type of an individual argument may be different from the type of its corresponding parameter.
   3. The ordering of arguments may not correspond to the ordering of parameters.

■ Using a constant or an expression as the argument corresponding to a variable parameter. The argument of a variable parameter must be a variable.

■ Trying to access an identifier defined or declared locally in a procedure outside that procedure's block.

■ Trying to use the value of a local variable established in a previous call to the procedure. Space in memory for local variables is withdrawn when the procedure terminates. An identifier declared locally in a procedure loses its value every time the procedure terminates.

■ Trying to refer to a "more global" identifier when the same identifier is used locally. The most locally defined or declared identifier takes precedence.

DEBUGGING HINTS

To help trace the flow of control, output string literals at the beginning of each procedure indicating the procedure being executed. For example, the message, `Entering procedure decide` could be printed by inserting the following *writeln* statement just after the reserved word **begin** in procedure *decide*:

```
writeln('Entering procedure decide');
```

To check the effects of a procedure on the arguments listed in a procedure call:

- Output the values of arguments just before the procedure call.
- Output the values of corresponding parameters just after entering the procedure.
- Output the values of corresponding parameters just before exiting the procedure.
- Output the values of arguments just after the procedure call.

SUPPLEMENTAL PROBLEMS

1. Show sample output for the following program:

```
program showme(input, output);
   {a program for you to test whether you can}
   {follow the execution of a program}

   procedure aloha1;

   begin {aloha1}
     write('Isn''t this fun!!!');
     write('Hawaii here we come!!!')
   end;    {aloha1}


   procedure aloha2;

   begin {aloha2}
     writeln;
     write('Welcome to computer land');
     write('Beep beep bleep!!!');
```

```
             writeln
         end; {aloha2}

    begin    {main program}
       writeln;
       aloha2;
       aloha1;
       writeln;
       aloha2
    end. {main program}
```

2. Produce a table describing the parameters of the following procedure header:

   procedure problem2 (**var** a, b, c: char; **var** d, e: integer;
                       var f: integer; g: integer;
                       h, i, j: char;
                       var k: char);

3. Write the procedure header for a procedure named *problem3*, which has the following parameters:

Position	Value or variable	Identifier	Type
1	value	a	integer
2	variable	b	real
3	variable	c	char
4	value	d	integer
5	value	e	integer
6	variable	f	char
7	value	g	char
8	variable	h	real
9	variable	i	integer
10	variable	j	integer

4. The following pair, consisting of a procedure call and a procedure header, is semantically incorrect. Describe each of its flaws. Assume that the following variables have been declared:

   ```
   var ch1, ch2: char;
       int3, int4 : integer;
   ```

   call:

   ```
   procA (ch1, 'B', int3, ch2, 16, int4);
   ```

header:

```
procedure procA (var ch: integer;  cc: char;  x1: integer;
                 var cch: char;  var x2: integer;
                 x3:  char);
```

5. Trace the following program:

```
program parameters (input, output);
var a,b,c,d : integer; {four integer variables }
                       {to play with}

  procedure proceed(var e,f : integer; g: integer);
            {a procedure to play with parameters}
  var a : integer;  {a local variable with }
                    {the same identifier}
                    {as a global variable}
                    {. . . . .beware . . .}
  begin {proceed}
    a: =e + f;
    e: =a + g;
    f: =g + 1;
    g: =a + f
  end; {proceed}

begin {parameters}
    a: = 1;
    b: = 2;
    c: = 3;
    d: = 4;
    proceed(c,a,d); {Note the order of these arguments.}
    writeln(a: 2,b: 2, c: 2, d: 2)
end. {parameters}
```

6. Trace the execution of the following program. Be careful!

```
program problem6 (input, output);
var a: integer; {a variable to play with}

  procedure what (var c, d: integer);
      {a procedure to play with parameters}
  begin {what}
    c: =c + 1;
    d: =d * 2
  end; {what}
```

```
begin {problem6}
    a: = 3;
    what (a, a);
    writeln(a)
end. {problem6}
```

7. Make a list that describes the variables in the following program and where they can be used (the main program and/or procedures).

```
program nothing (input, output);
    {a program that doesn't do anything}

var   initial1,
      initial2,
      initial3: char;

    procedure donothing;

        procedure dosomething;

        var x, y, z: integer;

        begin   {dosomething}
        end;    {dosomething}

    begin   {donothing}
    end;    {donothing}

    procedure   what;

    var a, b, c: integer;

        procedure who;

        var n, o, p: char;

        begin   {who}
        end;    {who}

        procedure how;

        var s, t, u: integer;

        begin   {how}
        end;    {how}
```

```
        begin    {what}
          end;    {what}

      begin    {nothing - main program}
      end.     {nothing - main program}
```

8. Identify the procedures in program *nothing* and their scope.

9. Consider the following program. Which of the following statements about the program are true? Which are false? State reasons for your answers.

   a. Procedure *Instructions* could be called in the main program, after procedure *getch*.

   b. Procedure *getHW* may use the variable called *ch* if it wishes.

   c. Procedure *printrec* may call procedure *Instructions*.

   d. Procedure *getch* may use the variable called *counter1*.

   e. Procedure *getHW* must be called after procedure *getch* in the main program.

   f. Procedure *getHW* may call procedure *printrec*.

   g. Procedure *printrec* may use the variable *ch*.

   h. The variable *height* may be used anywhere in the program.

   i. Procedure *getch* could be referenced (called) by any procedure in the program.

   j. The main program can access any of the procedures, *Instructions*, *getch*, *getHW*, and *printrec*.

```
program PatternMaker (input, output);
{This is a program that allows the user to create a rectangle.}
{The user enters a character, followed by a }
{height and width. The program then creates a rectangle  }
{using the respective character, height, and width }

var   ch: char;       {holds character for rectangle}
      height,         {holds height for rectangle}
      width: integer; {holds width for rectangle}

  procedure Instructions;
              {a procedure using writelns to give}
              {instructions to the user}

  begin   {instructions}
    writeln('Welcome to the PatternMaker Program. ');
    writeln('I hope that it is an enjoyable experience');
    writeln('for you. The program will allow you to');
```

```
      writeln('enter a character that will be used');
      writeln('to draw a rectangle.');
      writeln('The program will then');
      writeln('ask you for the dimensions of');
      writeln('your rectangle. Always remember');
      writeln('to follow your answers with a carriage return.');
      writeln(' Good Luck Pattern Makers!!!!');
      writeln
   end;    {instructions}

procedure getch;
   {prompts user for character and reads in}

begin    {getch}
 write('Please enter character: ');
 readln(ch)
end;      {getch}

procedure getHW;
   {a procedure to read in Height and Width for Rectangle}

begin    {getHW}
   write('Please enter Height: ');
   readln(height);
   writeln;
   write('Please enter Width: ');
   readln(width)
end;    {getHW}

procedure printrec;
   {This is a procedure to print out a rectangle.}
   {It uses two nested repeat loops. The inside loop}
   {writes out a line of characters (keeps track of}
   {the width). The outside repeat keeps track of }
   {how many lines of characters (the height) have been}
   {printed out.}

var counter1,          {keeps track of width}
    counter2: integer; {keeps track of height}

begin     {printrec}
   counter2: = 0;
   repeat
     counter1: = 0;
     repeat
       write(ch);
```

```
        counter1: =counter1 + 1;
      until counter1 = width;
      counter2 : = counter2 + 1;
      writeln
    until counter2 = height
  end;    {printrec}

begin  {PatternMaker}
  Instructions;
  getch;
  getHW;
  printrec
end.    {PatternMaker}
```

10. Consider Figure 14.35 and:
    a. Construct a program skeleton like the one in Figure 14.31.
    b. Construct a block of definition table like the one in Figure 14.32.
    c. Construct a scope of procedure identifiers table as in Figure 14.33.
11. The following program does not use parameters to pass data from one procedure to another. It relies on the scope of variables. Modify the program so that the flow of all data items is controlled by arguments and their corresponding parameters.

Figure 14.35

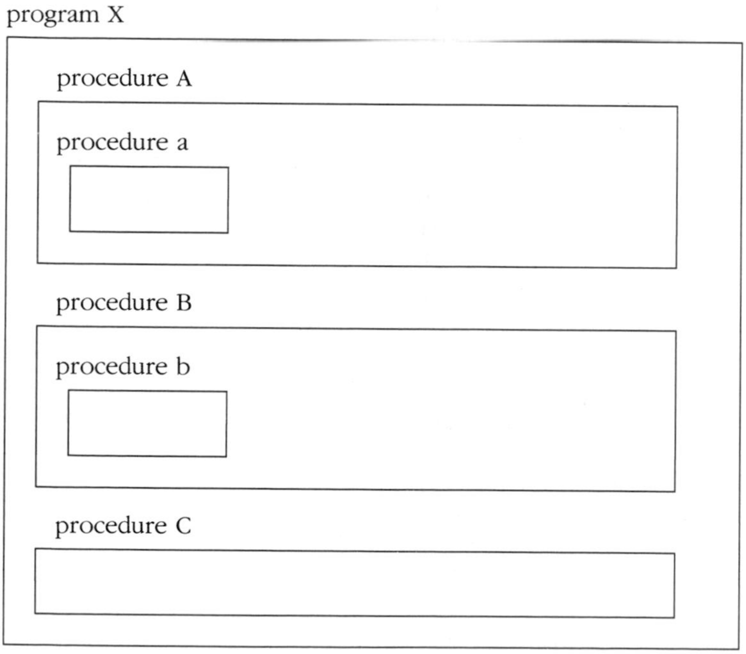

program X

    procedure A

        procedure a

    procedure B

        procedure b

    procedure C

```
program nonsense (input, output);

var onevariable,
    twovariable: integer;      {two variables of }
                               {the program}

    procedure first;
      { a subprocedure of nonsense}

    var firstvariable: integer;   {a variable of }
                                  {procedure first}

        procedure subfirst;
            {a subprocedure of first}

        var subvar: char;   {a variable of }
                            {procedure subfirst}

        begin  {subfirst}
           writeln('Please enter one character');
           read(subvar);
           firstvariable:= firstvariable + 1;
           twovariable := twovariable + 1;
           onevariable := onevariable + 1
        end;   {subfirst}
      begin  {first}
         writeln('Please enter one integer');
         read(firstvariable);
         twovariable := twovariable + 1;
         onevariable := onevariable + 1;
         subfirst
      end;    {first}


    procedure second;
        {a subprocedure of nonsense}

    var secondvariable: integer;   {a variable of }
                                   {procedure second}

        procedure subsecond;

        var minivar: char;
```

```
      begin    {subsecond}
          writeln('Please enter one character');
          read(minivar);
          twovariable := twovariable + 1;
          onevariable := onevariable + 1;
          secondvariable := secondvariable + 1;
          first
      end;    {subsecond}

   begin    {second}
       writeln('Please enter an integer');
       read(secondvariable);
       onevariable := onevariable + 1;
       twovariable := twovariable + 1;
       subsecond;
       first
   end;    {second}

begin   {nonsense, main program}
  writeln('Please enter two integers.');
  read(onevariable);
  read(twovariable);
  second;
  first
end.    {nonsense, main program}
```

CHAPTER

15

We have seen how input and output statements in Pascal enable a program to communicate with the user. To make more interesting programs, we need selection statements like those in Chapter 2 (pages 23–34). For example, we might want to write a program that would tell the user if he or she was old enough to drive. We would need to test the user's input in some way before we could make a decision. Pascal has three types of statements that perform one-time (as opposed to iterative) actions based on the outcome of some test.

Before we look at those statements, however, we need to see how values can be tested and what outcomes the testing will produce.

15.1 RELATIONAL OPERATORS

In Pascal, tests consist of *conditional expressions* that evaluate to either `true` or `false`. Conditional expressions are constructed of values whose type is `integer`, `real`, `char`, `boolean`, or programmer-defined, and what are called *operators*. Three types of operators are available in Pascal: relational, arithmetic, and boolean. In this chapter, we introduce some of the relational operators.

All the relational operators we refer to in this chapter compare two values. A relational operator is represented by a symbol (sometimes made up of more than one keystroke) between two values that are being compared. The two values and the operator make up a simple conditional expression.

CHOOSING ALTERNATIVES

The Operator Equals, =

The relational operator *equals* is represented by the symbol =. This operator checks the values on either side of it. If the values are equal, the conditional expression evaluates to *true*. If they are not equal, the conditional expression evaluates to *false*. Figure 15.1 shows some examples.

The comparisons in Figure 15.1 may seem rather trivial because we are comparing the values of two constants. But Pascal also lets us compare the value of a constant with the value of a variable or the value of a variable with the value of another variable. For example, if we have a variable of type *integer* named *age*, we can make the comparisons shown in Figure 15.2. If the value of the variable *age* is 16, both expressions will evaluate to *true*. If the value of *age* is any number other than 16, both expressions will evaluate to *false*.

We may also compare variables of type *char*. For example, if we have a variable of type *char* called *letter*, we can make the following comparison:

```
letter = 'a'
```

Figure 15.1   **Comparisons using =**

5 = 5	*true*, because the same number appears on both sides of the operator
'a' = 'a'	*true*, because the same character appears on both sides of the operator
3 = 6	*false*, because 3 and 6 are not equal
'd' = 'c'	*false*, because 'd' is not the same as 'c'

Figure 15.2 **Comparisons with variables**

$$age = 16$$

or

$$16 = age$$

Figure 15.3 **Illegal comparisons**

$$5 = 7 = 8$$

or

$$'a' = 'b', 'c'$$

If the value of the variable *letter* is 'a', the expression will evaluate to *true*. If the value of the variable *letter* is any other value (for example, 'b', 'z', '*', 'A'), the expression will evaluate to *false*.

We may also compare two variables. For example, if we have two variables of type *char*, *letter1* and *letter2*, we can make this comparison:

```
letter1 = letter2
```

Here, if the two variables have the same value—for example, 'a' and 'a'—the conditional expression will evaluate to *true*. If the two variables have different values—for example, 'a' and 'b'—the expression will evaluate to *false*.

Notice that we are comparing only those values that are of *compatible* type. Most types are only compatible with themselves.[1] Numeric values are the exception to this rule. All numeric values are of compatible type. Values of type *integer* may be compared to values of type *real*.

Notice, too, that we are comparing only two values in the above examples. The relational operators introduced in this chapter cannot compare more than two values. The comparisons in Figure 15.3, for example, are illegal.

Exercise 15.1: Which of the following comparisons are legal? Why are the others not legal? Are the legal comparisons *true* or *false*?

a. 8 = 9 = 10   c. 'd' = '1'

b. 8 = 25493   d. 'r' = x

---

1. This includes subranges of a type and subranges that have the same underlying ordinal type. (See Chapter 21.)

e. '124' = 124   i. 'f' = 'f'

f. 'A' = 'a'   j. 'B' = 'O'

g. 'c' = 'd'   k. 'c' = 'c' = 'c' = 'c'

h. 3.4 = 576   l. 'c' = 'c'   ∎

The Operator Not Equal, <>

The next relational operator, *not equal,* is represented by the symbol <>, which consists of a < immediately followed by a >. This operator is read as "not equal to." If the value to the left of the operator is not equal to the value to its right, the conditional expression will evaluate to *true*. If the two values are equal, the conditional expression will evaluate to *false*. Figure 15.4 shows some examples. Again, we can use this relational operator to compare variables as well as constants. This is true of all relational operators.

The Operator Greater Than, >

The relational operator *greater than* is represented by the character >. If the value to the left of the symbol is greater than the value to its right, the conditional expression will evaluate to *true*. If the value to the left of the symbol is less than or equal to the value to the right, the expression will evaluate to *false*. Figure 15.5 shows some examples.

Note that in Figure 15.5 we can evaluate a conditional expression that compares two characters. Every value of type *char* has an internal representation on the computer (a, L, *, 1 all qualify as type *char*: Any keystroke is considered a character). The two most common representations for characters on computers

Figure 15.4   **Comparisons using <>**

5 <> 7	*true*, because 5 is not equal to 7.
7 <> 7	*false*, because 7 is equal to 7.
'C' <> 'C'	*false*, because the character 'C' is the same as the character 'C'.
'b' <> 'a'	*true*, because the two characters are not the same.
'R' <> 'r'	*true*, because the computer sees the value of a capital letter as different from the value of a lowercase letter.
'7' <> 'd'	*true*, because the two values are not equal. Note: We can compare the two values because 7 is in quotes and is therefore considered to be of type *char*.

Figure 15.5   **Comparisons using $>$**

$5 > 5$	*false*, because 5 is equal to, not greater than, 5
$7 > -12$	*true*, because 7 is greater than -12
$'a' > 'b'$	*false*, because $'a'$ is not greater than (after) $'b'$ in the alphabet
$'g' > 'd'$	*true*, because $'g'$ is greater than (after) $'d'$ in the alphabet
$-13 > -14$	*true*, because -13 is greater than -14
$'*' > '!'$	?????
$'A' > 'a'$	??????

are called ASCII and EBCDIC.[2] Pascal guarantees that, no matter which representation is used, the lowercase letters a through z will be represented with a being less than z. The uppercase letters A through Z are also represented with A being less than Z. The digits 0 through 9 are contiguous with 0 being less than 9. Whether or not uppercase letters are considered less than lowercase letters depends on the representation used by your computer and is not guaranteed by Pascal. The internal representation of other symbols that are characters depends on the system your computer uses, and Pascal does not guarantee the order of that representation. For example, whether the character $*$ is greater than the character $?$ is not guaranteed by Pascal. Appendix A contains a chart of the ASCII representation.

Exercise   15.2: Complete the ??? comparisons in Figure 15.5 by trying them out on your computer.   ∎

The Operator Greater Than or Equal To, $>=$

The relational operator *greater than or equal to* is made of the character $>$ followed by the character $=$. If the value to the left of the symbol is greater than or equal to the value to the right of the symbol, the expression will evaluate to *true*. If the value to the left of the symbol is less than the value to the right of the symbol, the expression will evaluate to *false*. Some examples are shown in Figure 15.6.

---

2. EBCDIC is an acronym for Extended Binary Coded Decimal Interchange Code.

Figure 15.6   Comparisons using $>=$

$5 >= 5$	*true*, because 5 is equal to 5
$7 >= -12$	*true*, because 7 is greater than -12
$'a' >= 'b'$	*false*, because $'a'$ is less than (before) $'b'$
$'A' >= 'A'$	*true*, because $'A'$ is equal to $'A'$
$10.5 >= 270$	*false*, because 10.5 is less than 270
$'d' >= 'c'$	*true*, because $'d'$ is greater than (after) $'c'$

Figure 15.7   Comparisons using $<$

$4.4 < 6.7$	*true*, because 4.4 is less than 6.7
$'a' < 'b'$	*true*, because $'a'$ is less than (comes before) $'b'$
$-12 < -70$	*false*, because -12 is not less than -70
$'Z' < 'P'$	*false*, because $'Z'$ is not less than (before) $'P'$
$'a' < 'a'$	*false*, because $'a'$ is equal to, not less than, $'a'$

The Operator Less Than, $<$

The relational operator *less than* is referred to by the symbol $<$. If the value to the left of the symbol is less than the value to the right of the symbol, the expression evaluates to *true*. If the value to the left of the symbol is greater than or equal to the value to the right of the symbol, the expression evaluates to *false*. Notice that this operator evaluates exactly opposite to the way the $>=$ operator evaluates. Figure 15.7 shows some examples using the $<$ operator.

The Operator Less Than or Equal To, $<=$

The last relational operator presented in this chapter is *less than or equal to,* which is represented by the character $<$ followed by the character $=$. If the value to the left of the symbol is less than or equal to the value to the right of the symbol, the expression will evaluate to *true*. If the value to the left of the symbol is greater than the value to the right of the symbol, the expression will evaluate to *false*. Notice that the relational operator $<=$ evaluates exactly opposite to the way the relational operator $>$ evaluates. Examples using the relational operator $<=$ are given in Figure 15.8.

Figure 15.8   **Comparisons using $<=$**

`'a' <= 'a'`	*true*, because `'a'` is equal to `'a'`
`'c' <= 'd'`	*true*, because `'c'` is less than `'d'`
`560 <= 430`	*false*, because 560 is greater than 430
`4.5 <= 0.3`	*false*, because 4.5 is greater than 0.3

15.2 THE IF-THEN STATEMENT

We have just seen how relational operators are used in conditional expressions. Now we will see how conditional expressions are used in a selection statement. In Pascal, the single-option selection statement is the if-then statement.

The if-then statement works as follows: If a conditional expression evaluates to *true*, the statement within the **then** is executed. If the conditional expression evaluates to *false*, the statement in the **then** is skipped. Here is an example:

```
if age < 16
    then writeln('You aren''t old enough to drive')
```

In this example, the conditional expression **age** $<$ **16** is evaluated. If the value stored in *age* is less than 16—that is, if the conditional expression is *true*—the computer will execute the *writeln* statement following the reserved word **then** and will then go on to execute the next statement in the program. If the conditional expression evaluates to *false*, the computer will skip the *writeln* statement following the **then** and go directly to the next statement in the program.

Here's another example:

```
if answer = 'y'
    then writeln('Your answer was yes.')
```

Like the selection statement above, if the conditional expression evaluates to *true*, the *writeln* is executed and the next statement in the program is executed. Otherwise, the next statement in the program is simply executed. Figure 15.9 gives a syntax diagram for the if-then statement.

Figure 15.9   **Syntax diagram for the if-then statement**

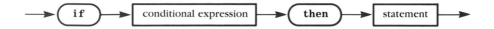

15.3 COMPOUND STATEMENTS

Note that the **then** part of an if-then statement has only one statement within it. Consider the following algorithm, which needs to be encoded in Pascal:

Ask the user if she wants instructions. If she answers *y* (for yes), you should give her instructions.

To solve this problem, we need to use an if-then statement with the instructions embedded within the **then**. Since we will need more than one statement to write the instructions, we are faced with a dilemma. Figure 15.10 provides a possible solution.

Since a procedure call is considered a single statement, the solution given in Figure 15.11 is a second possibility. Assume that procedure *instructions* has already been declared in the program. This is a much better solution to the problem.

If for some reason we don't want to use a procedure, Pascal has a special statement called a *compound statement* that allows a single statement to be replaced by several statements. Figure 15.12 gives the syntax diagram for a compound statement, and Figure 15.13 gives a solution that employs a compound statement. In Pascal, a compound statement may be used anywhere a single statement is allowed. When you are using compound statements, always indicate with comments which **begin** goes with which **end**.

Figure 15.14 gives a complete program using an if-then statement. Figures 15.15a and 15.15b show two sample executions of the program. (User input is in

Figure 15.10   **Possible way to give user instructions upon request**

```
               .
               .
               .
write('Do you want instructions?  ');
readln(answer);
if answer = 'y'
  then writeln('This is a question answer program.');
if answer = 'y'
  then writeln('When asked a question simply type a');
if answer = 'y'
  then writeln ('y or n followed by a carriage return');
               .
               .
               .
```

italics.) Figures 15.15a and 15.15b show that a different set of statements is executed depending on the user's input. If the user types in a *y* (or any sequence of characters beginning with a *y*), she will receive a message congratulating her on winning. If she types in any character other than a *y*, she will receive a thank-you message. No matter what the user types in, she will receive a good-bye message.

Figure 15.11   Second possible solution to the user instruction problem

```
                    .
                    .
                    .
    write('Do you want instructions?  ');
    readln(answer);
    if answer = 'y'
        then instructions;
                    .
                    .
                    .
```

Figure 15.12   Syntax diagram for a compound statement

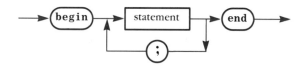

Figure 15.13   Third possible solution to the user instruction problem

```
    if answer = 'y'
        then
            begin  {if - then}
                writeln('This is a question answer program');
                writeln('When asked a question simply type');
                writeln('a y or n followed by a carriage return')
            end;     {if - then}
```

Figure 15.14   Sample program using if-then statements

```
program quiz(input, output);
  {a program to ask the user a question and give an answer}
  {based on the user's response                           }

var answer: char;   {to hold user's answer}

begin {quiz}
  write('Is the moon made of green cheese? ');
  readln(answer);
  writeln;
  if answer = 'y'
    then
        begin  {first if - then}
          writeln('Congratulations Ms. Mouse!');
          writeln('You Win!')
        end;  {first if - then}
  if answer <> 'y'
    then
        writeln('Thank-You Ms. Scientist!');
  writeln;
  writeln('Bye Quizzers!');
  writeln('See you next week on the 50-cent question!')
end.  {quiz}
```

Figure 15.15   Sample executions of program *quiz*

```
Is the moon made of green cheese? y ⏎

Congratulations Ms. Mouse!
You Win!

Bye Quizzers!
See you next week on the 50-cent question!
```
                            a

```
Is the moon made of green cheese? n ⏎

Thank-You Ms. Scientist!

Bye Quizzers!
See you next week on the 50-cent question!
```
                            b

15.4   IF-THEN-ELSE STATEMENTS

When we are testing a conditional expression, we often want one statement executed if the expression evaluates to *true* and another statement executed if it evaluates to *false*. In other words, we want the computer to perform one set of instructions or another depending on how the conditional expression evaluates. In the sample program given in Figure 15.14, we had to make a second test (**if** answer <> 'y') that was the opposite of the first test to determine what statements would be executed. It would be easier to add to the **then** of the if-then statement an alternative that would be executed only if the conditional expression evaluated to *false*. Pascal provides such a statement: the if-then-else statement. This statement is equivalent to the two-way selection statement introduced in Chapter 2 (pages 28–34).

The Syntax and Semantics of the If-Then-Else Statement

Figure 15.16 gives the syntax diagram for an if-then-else statement. The semantics are as follows:

- If the value of the conditional expression is *true*, the statement following the reserved word **then** is executed.

- Otherwise, if the value of the conditional expression is *false*, the statement following the reserved word **else** is executed.

Figure 15.17 shows the sample program given in Figure 15.14 modified to use the if-then-else statement. The execution of program *quiz2* will look just like the execution of program *quiz*. The *quiz2* program, however, takes less effort to write and is easier for the computer to execute (it does not have to make a second comparison).

Figure 15.16   **Syntax diagram for an if-then-else statement**

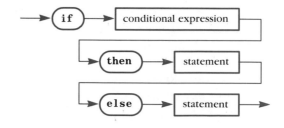

Figure 15.17   Sample program using an if-then-else statement

```
program quiz2(input, output);
   {a program to ask a user a question and give an answer}
   {based on the user's response                        }

var answer: char;   {to hold user's answer}

begin {quiz2}
   write('Is the moon made of green cheese? ');
   readln(answer);
   writeln;
   if answer = 'y'
      then
          begin  {if - then - (else)}
             writeln('Congratulations! Ms. Mouse!');
             writeln('You Win!')
          end    {if - then - (else)}
      else
          writeln('Thank-You Ms. Scientist!');
   writeln;
   writeln('Bye Quizzers!');
   writeln('See you next week on the 50-cent question!')
end.  {quiz2}
```

Notice that two if-then statements with opposite conditional expressions do not always translate exactly into an if-then-else statement. Let's look at two procedures, one that uses two if-then statements and one that uses a single if-then-else statement, to see how their outputs differ. Figure 15.18 shows a procedure with two if-then statements. Figure 15.19 shows a procedure with an if-then-else statement.

Figures 15.20a and 15.20b show two sample executions of procedure *print1*, and Figures 15.21a and 15.21b show two sample executions of procedure *print2*. Notice that both procedures seem to act identically when the user types in the correct number the first time. But when the user types in an incorrect number the first time with procedure *print1*, he is given one more chance to get the That's a good number message.[3] With procedure *print2*, however, the user has no chance of getting the That's a good number message.

_____

3. Note that this is an inappropriate way to do error checking. Iterative instructions, which give the user several chances to enter correct input, are better.

342

Figure 15.18 **Procedure using two if-then statements**

```
procedure print1;
   {a procedure to print an important message}

var number: integer;

begin {print1}
   write('Please input a number greater than 10:   ');
   readln(number);
   writeln;
   if number <= 10
         then
            begin {if - then, number <= 10}
               writeln('That number is too small.');
               writeln('One more try:   ');
               readln(number)
            end;    {if - then, number <= 10}
      if number > 10
         then
               writeln('That''s a good number! ')
end;   {print1}
```

Figure 15.19 **Procedure using an if-then-else statement**

```
procedure print2;
   {a procedure to print an important message}

var number: integer;

begin {print2}
   write('Please input a number greater than 10:   ');
   readln(number);
   writeln;
   if number <= 10
         then
            begin    {if - then - (else)}
               writeln('That number is too small.');
               writeln('Please try again: ');
               readln(number)
            end       {if - then - (else)}
         else
               writeln('That''s a good number! ')
end;   {print2}
```

Figure 15.20   Sample executions of procedure *print1*

```
Please input a number greater than 10:  112 ↩

That's a good number!
                          a

Please input a number greater than 10:  2 ↩

That number is too small.
Please try again: 12 ↩
That's a good number!
                          b
```

Figure 15.21   Sample executions of procedure *print2*

```
Please input a number greater than 10:  112 ↩

That's a good number!
                          a

Please input a number greater than 10:  2 ↩

That number is too small.
Please try again: 12 ↩
                          b
```

Now let's look at another example that uses just the if-then-else statement. Here is the problem statement:

John wants to know how many candy bars he can eat before it will affect his weight. Write a program to ask John how many candy bars he has eaten. Based on his response, give him one of the following messages: (1) `Still thin`, (2) `Plump, but okay`, (3) `Fat!` (4) `Jump for cover, he's going to explode`.

Note that this problem does not specify what inputs trigger a particular response. That decision is left to you. Figure 15.22 gives a possible solution. Notice the use of the if-then-else statements.

Figure 15.22   Sample program using if-then-else statements

```pascal
program eats(input, output);
  {a program to tell you the outcome of eating}
  {candy bars                                  }

var numofcb:integer;   {number of candy bars}
                       {consumed by user     }

begin  {eats}
  write('How many candy bars have you eaten?  ');
  read(numofcb);
  writeln;
  if numofcb < 5
     then writeln('Still thin')
     else if numofcb < 10
             then writeln('Plump, but okay')
             else if numofcb < 30
                     then writeln('Fat!')
                     else
                         begin  {else}
                           write('Jump for cover, ');
                           write('he''s going to ');
                           writeln('explode!')
                         end    {else}
end.      {eats}
```

Note two points in this example. First, we didn't need to test a conditional expression to get the last message. The computer will give that message if the user has said that he eats more than 29 candy bars.

Second, note that we used an if-then-else statement within an if-then-else statement. In fact, we did that twice. These are called *nested* statements. Nesting is common in Pascal programs. It can be done in if-then statements as well as in if-then-else statements.

Figure 15.23 gives a few sample executions of program *eats* shown in Figure 15.22. Note that no matter what input the user enters, he will get only one message.

Exercise   15.3: Show the output the user would get if he typed the following input:

a. *576438* ↩   c. *−17* ↩
b. *23* ↩   d. *9* ↩   ■

Figure 15.23   Sample executions of program *eats*

```
How many candy bars have you eaten?  3 ⟵

Still thin.


How many candy bars have you eaten?  113 ⟵

Jump for cover, he's going to explode!
```

Common Problems with If-Then-Else Statements

Whenever you use an if-then or if-then-else statement, keep these important points in mind:

1. If you put a semicolon directly before the **else** in an if-then-else statement, the translator will assume that the statement is just an if-then statement. It will then indicate an error when it tries to recognize the word **else** as the beginning of the next statement. Remember, semicolons are statement separators. Note that there is no semicolon before the keyword **else** in the syntax diagram for the if-then-else statement.

2. Beware of the "dangling **else**!" Consider the statements in Figure 15.24. Which **then** does the **else** go with? The general rule is: An **else** always goes with the nearest unmatched **then**. (Don't let the indentation mislead you!) The only way to get the **else** to go with the first **then** is to make it clear that the inside if-then is a complete statement without the **else**. This is done using the compound statement. The inside if-then statement is enclosed within a **begin-end** pair. Figure 15.25 shows how this is done. The arrangement shown there will associate the **else** with the **then** in the first if-then statement.

Figure 15.24   Program fragment showing a dangling else

```
if x > 5
    then if y > 5
            then write('hello')

        else write('bye');
```

Figure 15.25 **Program fragment showing how to eliminate a dangling else**

```
if x > 5
    then
        begin
            if y > 5
                then write('hello')
        end
    else write('bye');
```

15.5 THE CASE STATEMENT

The third type of conditional statement in Pascal is the **case** *statement.* The case statement is a specialized type of conditional statement. Consider the following problem:

A teacher is trying to calculate the number of low, medium, and high grades that she gave to a class on a quiz. The grades range from A to F, with A and B considered high, C and D considered medium, and F considered low. (The teacher has used no minuses or plusses.) Given a single grade, write a procedure to tabulate it in the proper range.

The possible inputs to this problem are the letters *A* through *D* and *F*. The output is the number of grades in each category. There are two constraints: (1) the grades *A* and *B* are considered high, the grades *C* and *D* are considered medium, and the grade *F* is considered low; and (2) there are no plusses or minuses given with grades. In this chapter we deal only with the problem of processing a single grade. Figure 15.26 shows one approach to this problem.

Figure 15.26 **Program fragment to process a grade**

```
if grade = 'A'
    then high: = high + 1
    else if grade = 'B'
            then high: = high + 1
            else if grade = 'C'
                    then medium : = medium + 1
                    else if grade = 'D'
                            then medium : = medium + 1
                            else low: = low + 1
```

Figure 15.27   Sample program fragment using a case statement

```
var grade: char;
            .
            .
            .
case grade of
  'A','B': high: = high + 1;
  'C','D': medium: = medium + 1;
  'F'    : low: = low + 1
end;   {case}
            .
            .
            .
```

This approach would be long and tedious however. Pascal has a special construct for testing to see if something is equal to any one of a list of values. That construct is the case statement. Figure 15.27 gives a possible solution to this problem using a case statement.

The lists of constants before the : on each line within the case statement in Figure 15.27 are called *labels*. Labels consist of constants of simple ordinal type, such as *char* and *integer*. Ordinal types are those in which it is possible to speak of the "next" thing in the type. For example, if the current integer is 5, the next integer is 6. Because of the character representation system on computers (ASCII and EBCDIC), items of type *char* are ordinal. You have not yet been introduced to any nonordinal types.

The variable following the reserved word **case** is called the *case expression*. The case statement causes the following sequence to happen:

I. The computer compares the case expression (in this example, the case expression is the variable *grade*) with the first label in the case statement.

II. If the value of the case expression is equal to anything in the first label, then
   A. The statement that follows the first colon will be performed, the remaining statements in the case statement will then be skipped, and the next statement in the program will be executed.
   else
   B. While a match has not been found and the **end** of the case statement has not been reached, do the following:
      1. Move to the next case label.
      2. If the case expression matches a member of the label, then
         i. Perform the statement following the label.

III. If no match is found before the end of the case statement is found (marked by the keyword **end**), this constitutes a run-time error. The computer may stop processing the program—that is, the program will crash.

If the teacher using this program types, say, an *E* by mistake, the program may crash. This is a serious flaw in the case statement; however, the case statement is still useful.

As we mentioned earlier, case statements are specialized selection statements. Compare the case statement given in Figure 15.27 to the nested if-then-else statements in Figure 15.26. You can see that the case statement is simpler than the nested if-then-else statements. The only disadvantage of using the case statement is that, given invalid input, the case statement may cause the program to crash.

Exercise   15.4: If invalid input is entered, what will be the output of the program fragment in Figure 15.26?   ∎

Here is another problem in which a case statement comes in handy:

You are to write a program that asks the user what month she was born in and displays the name of the birthstone for that month.

The input to this problem is some value indicating the month of the user's birth. The output is the name of the user's birthstone. The algorithm for this problem consists of a step to obtain the user's input, followed by several selection statements to display the name of the proper birthstone.

Figure 15.28 shows a procedure that will display the name of the birthstone when given the birth month. Note how we have protected the case statement to avoid the possibility of the program crashing if the user types incorrect input. This is always a good idea when using case statements.

Notice that in this example we were comparing an *integer, bmonth,* with *integer* case labels. Recall that we can compare only case expressions and labels of the same or compatible type. Remember: The labels of the case statement must be constants. The case expression may be an actual expression. For example, the *integer* expression

```
5 + number
```

would be a legal case expression (assuming that *number* is an *integer* value). Figure 15.29 gives the syntax diagram for the case statement. Figure 15.30 gives the syntax diagram for labels.

Note that the case statement requires an **end** *without* a matching **begin**. This is one of the few instances in Pascal where this occurs. You should always comment the **end** of the case statement to make it clear that it matches the keyword **case**, not the keyword **begin**.

Figure 15.28   Procedure *displaystone*

```
procedure displaystone(bmonth: integer);
  {a procedure to display the name of the birthstone}
  {of the user                                       }

begin      {displaystone}
   if bmonth > 0
      then
        if bmonth < 13
           then
             begin
               writeln('Your birthstone is ');
               case bmonth of
                  1: write('Garnet');
                  2: write('Amethyst');
                  3: write('Aquamarine');
                  4: write('Diamond');
                  5: write('Diamond');
                  6: write('Emerald');
                  7: write('Pearl');
                  8: write('Ruby');
                  9: write('Sardonyx');
                  10: write('Sapphire');
                  11: write('Opal');
                  12: write('Topaz')
               end;  {case}
               writeln
             end  {if - then}
           else  write('Incorrect input')
      else write('Incorrect input')
end;    {displaystone}
```

Figure 15.29   Syntax diagram for a case statement

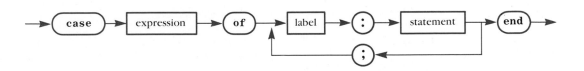

Figure 15.30 **Syntax diagram for a case label**

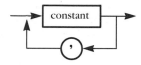

15.6 THE NULL STATEMENT

The null statement is a special statement in Pascal. The semantics of the null statement are as follows: When you see a null statement, consider it as you would a regular statement but do nothing.

The null statement is syntactically indicated by nothing where a statement should occur—for example, having a statement separator (a semicolon) without a preceding statement. In a case statement, the last case label, followed by a colon, followed by the keyword **end** (indicating the end of the case statement) indicates the null statement, since the syntax of a case statement requires a statement there. For example:

```
if x > 5
   then;
```

is a perfectly legal Pascal statement that does nothing. Misplaced semicolons often cause inappropriate null statements leading to logic errors. However, null statements are useful in case statements where every possible value of the case expression must be listed, but you want nothing to happen for a particular label. For example:

```
case numchoice of
   1: ;
   2: write('Hello');
   3: write('Goodbye');
   4:
end
```

is a perfectly legal and sometimes useful Pascal statement.

CHAPTER SUMMARY

1. *Selection statements* give the programmer a way of having a statement (or statements) executed conditionally. Three types of selection statements are available in Pascal: if-then, if-then-else, and case.

2. If the conditional expression in an if-then statement evaluates to *true*, the computer will execute the statement following the keyword **then**. If the conditional expression evaluates to *false*, the computer will move on to the next statement.

3. If the conditional expression in an if-then-else statement evaluates to *true*, the computer will execute the statement following the keyword **then**. If the conditional expression evaluates to *false*, the computer will execute the statement following the keyword **else**. After executing one statement or the other, the computer will move on to the next statement.

4. When the value of the **case** expression matches one member of a list in a label, the statement following the label will be executed. Then the computer will move on to the next statement following the case statement.

5. *Relational operators* are used to compare two values of compatible type. The following relational operators are used in Pascal:

=	equals	>=	greater than or equal to
<>	not equal	<	less than
>	greater than	<=	less than or equal to

6. Several statements may be grouped together using a *compound statement*. A compound statement may be used anywhere a single statement may be used. A compound statement is a set of statements bounded by the keywords **begin** and **end**. Statements within a compound statement are separated from each other by semicolons.

COMMON ERRORS

- A semicolon directly before the **else** in an if-then-else statement is a syntactic error. The translator will recognize the semicolon as the end of an if-then statement.

- A compound statement missing the keyword **begin** or the keyword **end** is a syntactic error.

- A case statement with the keyword **begin** directly following the keyword **of** is a syntactic error. Case statements have the keyword **end** without the matching keyword **begin**.

- Putting more than one statement after the keyword **then** and before the keyword **else** without using a compound statement is a syntactic error.

- A dangling **else** may cause a logic error.

- Leaving out the **begin** and **end** where you want a compound statement may be a logic error.

- Inserting a semicolon directly after the keyword **then** or the keyword **else** indicates that the statement following those keywords is a null statement. This may be a logic error in your program.

DEBUGGING HINTS

- Insert a *writeln* statement before the selection statement to indicate you have reached the statement.

- Insert *writeln* statements with matching arguments within each **then** and **else** pair. If a given output appears twice, you know that the **then**s and the **else**s are incorrectly matched.

- To check that each **begin** is matched with the appropriate **end**, insert matching *writeln* statements after the **begin** and before its respective **end**.

- Display the values involved in a conditional expression or **case** expression immediately before the expression is evaluated.

- Test your selection statements with a variety of inputs.

SUPPLEMENTAL PROBLEMS

1. Write a program that solves the following problem:

   The user wishes to input a character and find out whether it appears in the first 13 letters of the alphabet or in the second 13 letters.

2. Given the code fragment shown below, determine the output if the value of the user's input is
   a. *67* ↩   b. *2* ↩   c. *−908* ↩   d. *19234* ↩

   ```
   readln (answer);
   if answer > 100
      then
         writeln('Got it!')
      else
         if answer < 17
            then
               write('well, sort of. . . ');
   if answer >= 67
      then
         write('Good choice! ');
   if answer <> 2
      then
         writeln('Oh well!!!')
   ```

3. In the following piece of code, indicate which **if**s and which **then**s go with each **else**.

   ```
   if x > 5
      then write('Hello');
   ```

```
if y < 6
   then write('Sorry!')
   else if z < 7
           then if c >= 54
                   then write('Noodles!')
       else write('Who do I belong with??');
   if n > 5
       then
         begin
           if h <> 5
               then write('Pickles!')
         end
           else write('and I go with. . . ???');
```

4. Write three procedures that each solve the following problem. Use a different type of selection statement for each procedure.

   A person wishes to give an appropriate message to students who got the following scores: 40 or below, 41–60, 61–70, 71–80, 81–90, and 91–100. You may fill in the appropriate message.

5. Which type of selection statement is the best for the problem given in the preceding exercise? Why?

6. Write a program that takes three numbers as input and determines which is the largest.

7. Write a program to read in two numbers and determine which is larger or if they are equal.

8. Implement procedure *testguess* from program *guessmynumber* in Chapter 14 (pages 302–305).

9. Find the errors in the following procedure:

```
procedure messages (number: integer);
begin   {messages}
  if number > 5
      then
        write ('Thanks');
        write ('for entering a good number.')
      else
        if number < 5
            then
              begin
                write('Right on! ');
            else write ('Got 5!! ');
            else writeln('What''s going on here???')
end;    {message}
```

10. Write procedure *decide* for program *twocanplay* in Chapter 14 (pages 306–309).

11. Consider the program fragment given below. What is the output if the input is
    a. section = 1, chapter = 2
    b. section = 2, chapter = 2
    c. section = 3, chapter = 1
    d. section = 1, chapter = 0

```
case section of
   1:   case chapter of
           1:   writeln('Problem Definition');
           2:   writeln('Pieces of Algorithms');
           3:   writeln('Design of Algorithms')
        end;
   2:   case chapter of
           1:   writeln('Structure of a Program');
           2:   writeln('Producing Output');
           3:   writeln('Constants and Variables')
        end
end;
```

CHAPTER

16

16.1 INTRODUCTION

The first computers were designed to perform mathematical calculations, and the digital computers in use today operate on instructions and data that are coded internally into sequences of digits. Even computer users who are manipulating text rely on arithmetic operations. These users need not be concerned with what is going on inside the computer, as for the most part you need not concern yourself.

In this chapter, we begin our discussion of how to do arithmetic with Pascal. Recall that our second fundamental algorithm of counting required addition (pages 121–123).

Exercise   16.1: Describe six situations from Chapters 6 and 7 that require an arithmetic calculation.   ∎

16.2 ARITHMETIC AND PASCAL

Before we go into the details of how we instruct the computer to perform arithmetic on integers, we need to establish the meaning of a few terms.

The numbers on which we want the computer to perform the arithmetic are called *operands*. In the expression 5 + 10, for example, the operands are 5 and 10. In Pascal, we can perform five *binary operations* on integers: addition, subtraction, multiplication, division, and remainder. In the expression 5 + 10, the opera-

ARITHMETIC WITH INTEGERS

tion is addition. These operations are called *binary* because they are performed on two operands. The integer that is the answer after performing the operation is the *result*. In our example, the result is 15.

The Syntax of Integer Values

Integers fall into one of three classes: positive, negative, and zero. In Pascal, we indicate a nonnegative integer by a simple sequence of digits. We indicate a negative integer by a sequence of digits immediately preceded by a $-$.

The capacity of a computer to represent integers internally is limited. In fact, each model of computer is restricted to a largest possible positive integer and a smallest possible negative integer. Pascal has a predefined constant `maxint`, which has a value equal to the largest possible positive integer.

Exercise 16.2: Write and run a Pascal program to find the largest positive integer on the computer you are using. ■

The Unary Minus Operation

The $-$ that precedes a negative integer indicates that an operation is to be performed on a single operand. Such an operation is called a *unary operation;* this particular operation is called *unary minus*. Its action is simply negation. Hence -3 means: Do the operation of unary minus on the operand 3. The result of this operation is referred to as "negative three." We may want the unary minus operation to be performed more than once. It is legal in Pascal to write $- -3$, though $-(-3)$ is preferable. The parentheses indicate that the expression is to be evaluated from the inside to the outside. In other words, do unary minus to three, and then do it again to the result. In general, a $-$ may be placed in front of any arithmetic expression in parentheses and indicates doing the operation of unary minus to the result of that expression.

The Binary $+$, $-$, $*$, `div`, and `mod` Operators

To write *integer*-valued arithmetic expressions—that is, expressions that evaluate to an *integer* value—we use the unary minus operation and the binary operations of addition, subtraction, multiplication, and division. In Pascal, the symbol that denotes addition is $+$, and the symbol that denotes subtraction is $-$. The symbol that denotes multiplication is $*$. The symbols $+$, $-$, and $*$ are called operators.

Figure 16.1 gives a few examples of *integer*-valued expressions involving the operators $+$, $-$, and $*$. It is correct to write an expression such as $3 + -4$, but such expressions are easier to read if we use parentheses: $3 + (-4)$. We can, and should, use parentheses to clarify expressions. Remember, though, that parentheses come in pairs. For each left parenthesis, you must include a corresponding right parenthesis.

The division of one *integer* by another is a bit more complicated because the result may not be an *integer*. For instance, 7 divided by 2 is 3.5. But 3.5 is not an *integer,* and for the moment we are discussing only ways of obtaining integers as results. So we might say instead that the result of 7 divided by 2 is the quotient 3, with a remainder of 1, as shown in Figure 16.2.

Figure 16.1 *integer*-**valued expressions involving the operators** $+$, $-$, **and** $*$

$$-5 + 2 \qquad 7 - 3 \qquad 3 * 5$$
$$10 + 0 \qquad -49 - 12 \qquad (-6) * 21$$
$$-179 + 523 \qquad 100 - 144 \qquad 719 * 342$$

Figure 16.2 **Example of how a quotient and remainder are calculated**

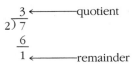

Hence, there are two *integer* answers for each problem of dividing one *integer* by another—the quotient and the remainder. The two Pascal operators involved in the *integer* division are **div**, used to determine the quotient, and **mod**, which is used to determine the remainder. In our example above, **7 div** 2 evaluates to 3, and **7 mod** 2 evaluates to 1. In Pascal, at least one space must separate the operators **div** and **mod** from each of their operands.

Figure 16.3 gives a few examples of **div** and **mod** and their corresponding results. Note that the following algebraic equation involving **div** and **mod** is always true:

$$((x \text{ } \mathbf{div} \text{ } y) * y + (x \text{ } \mathbf{mod} \text{ } y)) = x$$

Exercise   16.3: (a) Verify each of the examples in Figure 16.3 using a diagram similar to the one used for 7 divided by 2. (b) Write a program to check your answers to Exercise 16.3a.   ■

We may also perform these operations on *integer* variables and programmer-defined *integer* constants. To do so, we use expressions like *count* + 1 and *sum* + *newnumber*.

Operator Precedence

The binary operations of +, −, *, **div**, and **mod** work on a pair of operands to produce a result. Binary operations may be used in expressions that contain more than two operands, but arithmetic is performed on only two at a time. Often the result of one operation becomes an operand for another operation. Consider the following expression:

$$5 + 10 + 20$$

Figure 16.3   **Examples of expressions using div and mod**

a.	11 **div** 4	⟶ 2	11 **mod** 4	⟶	3
b.	0 **div** 5	⟶ 0	0 **mod** 5	⟶	0
c.	3 **div** 5	⟶ 0	3 **mod** 5	⟶	3
d.	−8 **div** 3	⟶ −2	−8 **mod** 3	⟶	−2
e.	−1 **div** 3	⟶ 0	−1 **mod** 3	⟶	−1
f.	−10 **div** −4	⟶ 2	−10 **mod** −4	⟶	−2

Which + is done first? In this particular case, it doesn't matter:

$$(5 + 10) + 20 \text{ is } 15 + 20 \text{ or } 35$$

and

$$5 + (10 + 20) \text{ is } 5 + 30 \text{ or } 35$$

Pascal always interprets such expressions from left to right. It first evaluates 5 + 10 as 15, and then takes 15 as the left operand of the next +, leaving 15 + 20 to be evaluated. In this expression, we have only + operators to deal with. But consider this expression:

5 + 7 * 2

Does this mean (5 + 7) * 2? Or does it mean 5 + (7 * 2)? Clearly, the order in which the operations are performed will affect the result. To avoid such ambiguity, Pascal has rules that govern operator precedence.

Pascal divides the operators into three groups, as shown in Figure 16.4.

To demonstrate how Pascal evaluates arithmetic expressions involving no parentheses, we first write a subalgorithm called Scan and Evaluate for a Group of Operators, as given in Figure 16.5.

With this subalgorithm written, it is easy to write the entire algorithm, as in Figure 16.6.

Figure 16.4   Pascal's groups of arithmetic operators for integers

> I. unary minus
> II. binary *, **div**, **mod**
> III. binary +, −

Figure 16.5   Algorithm to scan and evaluate for a group of operators

I. Repeat the following until no operators of the given group are left in the expression:
   A. Begin at the left end of the expression.
   B. Scan to the right until you encounter an operator of the given group.
   C. Perform the indicated operation and replace the operator and its operand(s) by the result.

We trace this algorithm on the following expression; the result of each operation is shown in parentheses.

5 + −7 **div** 3 ∗ 6 − −4 + 12 **mod** 5 − −−7

Figure 16.7 shows the trace of step 1. Step 1 is complete when all unary minus (group I) operations have been performed. Figure 16.8 shows step 2. Step 2 is complete when all group II operations have been evaluated. Figure 16.9 shows step 3.

Figure 16.6   **Algorithm to evaluate an *integer*-valued expression**

    I. Scan and evaluate for operator group I.

    II. Scan and evaluate for operator group II.

    III. Scan and evaluate for operator group III.

Figure 16.7   **Step 1 of the evaluation algorithm**

```
5 +  −7  div 3 * 6  −   −4  + 12 mod 5  −  −−7 {original expression}
5 + (−7) div 3 * 6  −   −4  + 12 mod 5  −  −−7
5 + (−7) div 3 * 6  −  (−4) + 12 mod 5  −  −−7
5 + (−7) div 3 * 6  −  (−4) + 12 mod 5  −  −(−7)
5 + (−7) div 3 * 6  −  (−4) + 12 mod 5  −  (7)
```

Figure 16.8   **Step 2 of the evaluation algorithm**

```
5 + (−2) * 6  −  (−4) + 12 mod 5  −  (7)
5 + (−12)  −  (−4) + 12 mod 5  −  (7)
5 + (−12)  −  (−4) +  (2)  −  (7)
```

Figure 16.9   **Step 3 of the evaluation algorithm**

```
(−7)  −  (−4) + 2  −  (7)
   (−3)  + 2  −  (7)
      (−1)  −  (7)
         (−8)
```

Note that we have used parentheses in the trace to show how each operator was evaluated. We could have used parentheses in the original expression. There are usually two reasons for using parentheses when writing an expression in Pascal: to make the expression easier to read by a human being and to override the usual rules of operator precedence.

Exercise 16.4: Trace the evaluation algorithm on each of the following expressions.

a. $10 + 2 \textbf{ div } 3 * 6 - 5 \textbf{ mod } 2 + 16$

b. $17 \textbf{ div } 3 * 2 + - 1 - 16 * - 2 * 3 + 1$

c. $- (7 + (6 \textbf{ div } (3 * (2 - (7 \textbf{ mod } 4))))) \quad \blacksquare$

16.3 USING ARITHMETIC EXPRESSIONS TO FORM *boolean*-VALUED EXPRESSIONS

Since arithmetic expressions represent values, we can combine them with relational operators to form *boolean*-valued expressions—that is, expressions that evaluate to either *true* or *false*. We can then use the *boolean*-valued expression as the condition being tested in an if-then or if-then-else statement.

For example, if *num* is an *integer* variable, consider the if-then-else statement in Figure 16.10. At this point, we need to worry about the precedence of the relational operators. Is the *boolean*-valued expression in Figure 16.10 equivalent to

$(num \textbf{ mod } 2) = 0$

or

$num \textbf{ mod } (2 = 0)$

Notice that $(num \textbf{ mod } 2) = 0$ makes sense because the value of $(num \textbf{ mod } 2)$ is an integer that can be compared to 0. On the other hand, $num \textbf{ mod } (2 = 0)$ does not make sense since the value of $(2 = 0)$ is *boolean (false)*, and a *boolean* value cannot be involved in a division operation.

Figure 16.10   Using an arithmetic expression to form a *boolean***-valued expression**

```
if num mod 2 = 0
    then writeln (num:1,' is even')
    else writeln (num:1,' is odd');
```

The relational operators have lower precedence than any of the arithmetic operators. Hence, num **mod** 2 = 0 is equivalent to (num **mod** 2) = 0. It makes sense that when two arithmetic expressions are to be compared using a relational operator, the two expressions should be completely evaluated first, before the comparison is performed. Pascal's rules governing the precedence of operators assures that this is precisely what happens. However, to increase the clarity of your program, we suggest that you use parentheses when both arithmetic and relational operators are involved in an expression.

Operator group IV consists of the relational operators. We must add step IV to the algorithm in Figure 16.6. An additional rule of Pascal is that an expression must be constructed so that when step IV of the evaluation algorithm is performed, only one relational operator remains to be evaluated. The resulting algorithm describes how to evaluate unparenthesized expressions involving the arithmetic operators for integers and the relational operators. That algorithm is shown in Figure 16.11.

boolean-valued expressions may also be used to control loop structures (as we will see in Chapter 17), making it possible to use arithmetic expressions to control the iteration of loops. They may also be used as the case expression.

16.4 ASSIGNING THE VALUE OF AN EXPRESSION TO A VARIABLE

Sometimes we need the value of an arithmetic expression to use as a piece of scratch data or as a piece of output data. Recall, for example, the algorithm we used to find the average donation at the charity dance (pages 125–128). Here, since we are discussing only integer arithmetic, we'll assume that the donations are made in terms of whole dollars. We need two scratch data items: the total of all donations and the number of donations. Each time a person gives a donation, we need to add the amount of the new donation to the previous total of donations, and we need to add 1 to the number of donations. In each case we need to hold on to the result of the arithmetic we perform.

There is also an output data item involved in this problem—the amount of the

Figure 16.11   Algorithm to evaluate expressions involving arithmetic operators for integers and relational operators

I. Scan and evaluate for operator group I.

II. Scan and evaluate for operator group II.

III. Scan and evaluate for operator group III.

IV. Scan and evaluate for operator group IV.

average donation. We calculate it by dividing the total of all donations by the number of donations.

In each case, we need to store the value computed in a variable. We use the Pascal assignment statement. The variable declarations and the assignment statements shown in Figure 16.12 are useful in implementing the average donation algorithm.

Consider the assignment statement:

```
numofdonations:=numofdonations + 1
```

Figure 16.12   Partial implementation of the average donation algorithm

```
var newdonation, {holds value of new donation}
    sumofdonations, {holds value of all donations}
    numofdonations, {holds num of donations}
    average:integer; {holds average of all donations}

        .
        .
        .

    sumofdonations:= 0;
    numofdonations:= 0;

        .
        .
        .

    sumofdonations:= sumofdonations + newdonation;
    numofdonations:= numofdonations + 1;

        .
        .
        .

    average:= sumofdonations div numofdonations;
```

Here 1 is added to the current value of the variable *numofdonations*, and the result is stored in the variable named *numofdonations*. The effect is to update the value of the variable *numofdonations*. The variable named on the left side of : = stands for the place where the value of the expression on the right side will be stored. It does not stand for the old value of the variable. This is the only circumstance in Pascal where the name of a variable does not stand for the value of that variable.

16.5 OTHER USES FOR ARITHMETIC EXPRESSIONS

Arguments listed in procedure calls that correspond to value parameters can be expressions of compatible type. For example, suppose we are writing a program to simulate a two-player game as discussed in Chapter 14 (pages 305–310). We need to calculate the percentage of correct responses out of all responses, knowing the numbers of correct and incorrect responses. Suppose variables named *right* and *wrong* hold the values of correct and incorrect responses, respectively. We can send the total number of responses as an argument by using the arithmetic expression

```
right + wrong
```

If *percent* is the variable identifier in which the calculated percentage is returned, we could use the following procedure call and procedure header:

```
procedure calculate (correct,total : integer;
                         var perc : integer);
         .
         .
         .
calculate (right,right + wrong,percent);
```

Arithmetic expressions can also be used as field-width specifiers. For example, the following *writeln* statement is syntactically correct:

```
writeln ( number : 2 * max)
```

The value of *number* is written in a field whose width is at least the value of 2 times *max*.

CHAPTER SUMMARY

1. In Pascal, five binary operations may be performed on two *integer* operands to produce an *integer* result. Those operations are addition, subtraction, multiplication, division, and remainder.

2. In Pascal, the unary minus operation may be performed on a single *integer* operand.

3. The symbols used in Pascal to indicate the binary operations of addition, subtraction, and multiplication are, respectively, $+$, $-$, and $*$. Pascal uses two operators in *integer* division: The operator **div** is used to calculate the *integer* quotient of two *integer* operands. The operator **mod** is used to calculate the *integer* remainder resulting from the division of one *integer* by another. The symbol $-$ before an *integer* expression in parentheses indicates the operation of negation.

4. The following *boolean*-valued expression is always *true*:

   ```
   ((x div y) * y + (x mod y)) = x
   ```

5. Pascal puts the relational operators and the operators for integer arithmetic into four groups:
   I. Unary minus
   II. Binary $*$, **div**, **mod**
   III. Binary $+$, $-$
   IV. Relational operators $<$, $<=$, $=$, $>=$, $>$, $<>$

6. In expressions that contain no parentheses, the algorithm for evaluation of the expressions is

   Step 1. Evaluate all operators of group I from left to right.
   Step 2. Evaluate all operators of group II from left to right.
   Step 3. Evaluate all operators of group III from left to right.
   Step 4. Evaluate all operators of group IV from left to right.

7. The use of parentheses overrides Pascal's built-in operator precedence and makes arithmetic expressions easier to read. Parenthesized expressions are evaluated from the most inner pair of parentheses outward.

8. Arithmetic expressions can be used as arguments corresponding to value parameters.

9. Arithmetic expressions can be used as field-width specifiers in *write* and *writeln* statements.

COMMON ERRORS

- Dividing by an *integer* constant or variable whose value is zero. This will cause a program to crash during execution.
- Incorrectly writing a fraction whose denominator is a product. For example, the integer quotient in algebraic notation

$$\frac{b}{2a}$$

is equivalent to b **div** (2 * a) in Pascal. The Pascal expression b **div** 2 * a is equivalent to the algebraic expression:

$$\left(\frac{b}{2}\right)a$$

- Juxtaposition cannot be used to indicate multiplication, which is possible in ordinary algebra. Pascal requires the * operator. Hence, b (b) is illegal in Pascal. The expression b*(b) is legal.
- Using an arithmetic expression as an argument corresponding to a variable parameter. The argument corresponding to a variable parameter must be a variable.

DEBUGGING HINTS

- Insert parentheses in unparenthesized expressions if those expressions yield invalid results.
- Use auxiliary variables to hold intermediate values determined by a complicated expression and display the values of those variables.
- Check to be sure that the value you are calculating and any intermediate values do not fall out of the range of $-maxint$ to $maxint$. Attempting to calculate values out of that range will cause erroneous results.

SUPPLEMENTAL PROBLEMS

1. Translate each of the following algebraic expressions into Pascal:
   a. $b^2 - 4ac$
   b. the quotient *(c/a)* − the quotient *(d/b)*
   c. the quotient *(a/bc)* − the quotient *(d/ef)*

    d. the remainder of *(ab/cd)*
    e. *x* + the remainder of *(c/x)*

2. Assume that *a*, *b*, *c*, *d*, and *x* are declared as *integer* variables. Write each of the following polynomials:
    a. without parentheses
    b. with parentheses
      i. $ax^2 + bx + c$
      ii. $ax^3 + bx^2 + cx + d$

3. Given the following values for *integer* variables *a*, *b*, *c*, and *d*, evaluate the following Pascal expressions:

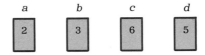

a	*b*	*c*	*d*
2	3	6	5

    a. a + b − c * d   b. −a **mod** c + b
    c. a **div** b * c + d   d. − a * b + c **mod** d
    e. b **mod** d + a **mod** c   f. a * − b + − c * d

4. Evaluate each of the following expressions using the values of *a*, *b*, *c*, and *d* given in problem 3.
    a. (((a + (b **mod** c) * d) **div** b) − c)
    b. a + b **mod** c * d **div** b − c

5. Write a program to determine if an *integer* input value is even or odd.

6. Write a program to determine if an *integer* input value is within 5 units of 17 on the number line.

*7. Assume that *x* has been declared to be an *integer* variable.
    a. What are the possible values of x **mod** 1?
    b. What are the possible values of x **mod** 2?
    c. What are the possible values of x **mod** 3?
    d. What are the possible values of x **mod** 4?
    e. What are the possible values of x **mod** n where n is a positive integer?

*8. Assume that the *integer* variable named *seconds* represents a certain number of seconds. Write Pascal expressions to convert the value of *seconds* to an equivalent number of hours, minutes, and seconds. Assume that we have already declared *integer* variables named *hours* and *minutes*.

*9. Write an entire program that inputs
    a. The current time of day in terms of a 24-hour clock and
    b. An elapsed time in hours, minutes, and seconds for a road race.
    Calculate the time, in terms of a 24-hour clock, when the race began.

*10. Read in a sequence of five digits as characters. Determine the integer value represented by the five characters, store it in a variable called *intval*, and print out the value of *intval*.

CHAPTER
17

We have now introduced Pascal constructs for subalgorithms (procedures) and selection (conditional statements). In this chapter, we introduce the Pascal statements for *indefinite iteration*. Such statements are often called *loops* because the instruction automatically causes the Pascal executor to "loop" back to a previous instruction.

17.1 A PROBLEM THAT REQUIRES INDEFINITE ITERATION

Pascal has two types of indefinite iterative statements. These iterative statements correspond to the algorithm constructs presented in Chapter 2 (pages 34–40). One iterative statement tests a conditional expression before possibly executing the steps contained in the loop. The other iterative statement executes the steps within the loop once before testing a conditional expression to see if iteration should continue.

Consider the following problem, whose solution requires indefinite iteration:

A person wishes to total a set of numbers. She does not know how many numbers she has to enter. She will indicate that she is done entering numbers by typing −999. The number −999 should not be included among the numbers to be totaled.

Because the user cannot specify how many numbers she has to enter, the algorithm that solves this problem requires an indefinite iterative instruction. Figure 17.1 shows an algorithm that solves this problem by using a loop that checks at the top. Figure 17.2 shows an algorithm that solves this problem by using a loop that checks at the bottom.

INDEFINITE
ITERATION

Figure 17.1

Figure 17.1   **Total algorithm using a loop that checks at the top**

Setup

   I. Allocate space in memory called *total* for the total of all numbers entered.

   II. Allocate space in memory called *number* to store the current number entered by the user.

Instructions

   I. Assign *total* the value 0.

   II. Ask for a number.

   III. Read the response into *number*.

   IV. While *number* <> − 999 do the following:
      A. Add *number* to *total* and store in *total*.
      B. Ask for a number.
      C. Read the response into *number*.

   V. Write "The total is", *total*.

17.2 **THE** while **STATEMENT**

The most commonly used iterative statement in Pascal is the **while** statement. Figure 17.3 shows the syntax diagram for the **while** statement. The **while** statement consists of two reserved words enclosing a conditional expression, followed

Figure 17.2   **Total algorithm using a loop that checks at the bottom**

Setup

   I. Allocate space in memory called *total* for the total of all numbers entered.

   II. Allocate space in memory called *number* to store the current number entered by the user.

Instructions

   I. Assign the value 0 to *total*.

   II. Repeat
      A. Ask the user for a number.
      B. Read the response into *number*.
      C. If *number* <> − 999
         then
            1. Add *number* to *total* and store in *total*.
      Until *number* = − 999.

   III. Write "The total is", *total*.

Figure 17.3   **Syntax diagram for a while statement**

by a statement. The statement is called the *body* of the **while** loop. This statement can be a simple statement or a compound statement. The **while** statement evaluates its conditional expression in order to decide what further action to take. The actions of the **while** loop—its semantics—are as follows:

- Evaluate the conditional expression. (The value will be either *true* or *false*.)

- If the value of the conditional expression is *true*, then repeat the following two steps until the value of the conditional expression becomes *false*:

   1. Execute the body of the **while** statement.

   2. Reevaluate the conditional expression.

Notice that the body of the **while** statement may be performed as few as zero times, or any number of times, before the computer executes the next statement.

If the conditional expression evaluates to *true*, then the whole body of the loop is executed before the conditional expression is reevaluated. If the conditional expression evaluates to *false*, the body of the loop is skipped and the next statement is executed.

Implementation of the Total Algorithm

Figure 17.4 shows a complete program implementing the algorithm shown in Figure 17.1. Notice that we need to use a compound statement to include more than one statement in the body of the **while** loop.

Figure 17.4   **Program implementing the total algorithm with a while loop**

```
program totaler (input, output);
   {a program to total a set of numbers}
   { - the end of the list of}
   {numbers will be indicated by -999}

const prompt = 'Please enter a number:   ';
                      {to prompt the user for a number}
         stop = -999;
                      {sentinel indicating no more numbers}

var total,            {to hold the total of all the numbers}
      number: integer;   {to hold the number the user }
                      {has just entered}

begin  {totaler}
{line 1}  total:= 0;              {Initialize total.}
{line 2}  write(prompt);
{line 3}  readln(number);            {Read in numbers}
{line 4}  while number <> stop do {and process until }
                                  {sentinel.}
              begin
{line 5}       total := total + number; {Calculate total.}
{line 6}       write(prompt);
{line 7}       readln(number)
              end;
{line 8}  writeln('The total is ', total:1);
{line 9}  writeln
end.   {totaler}
```

Notice in the program that, before the **while** loop is entered, the user is asked to enter a number. The conditional expression *number* <> *stop* is then evaluated. If the conditional expression evaluates to *true*, the body of the **while** loop is executed. This step will cause the number the user has entered to be added to the total. The procedure then asks the user for another number. Once the new number is recorded, the conditional expression at the top of the loop is evaluated again.

If the conditional expression *number* <> *stop* is tested and evaluates to *false*, the loop ends and execution continues at the statement following the **while** loop.

Figure 17.5 shows a trace of program *totaler* with the inputs *12, 78, − 70,* and *− 999*.

Important Pieces of the while statement

All **while** statements should be written using two implicit rules. The first rule is

*Always include at least one statement in the body of a **while** statement that is capable of changing the value of the **while** loop's conditional expression.*

Figure 17.5   **Trace of program *totaler***

Instruction	Conditional expression	Memory		Output
		number	total	
		?	?	
{line 1}		?	0	
{line 2}		?	0	Please enter a number:
{line 3}		12	0	
{line 4}	true	12	0	
{line 5}		12	12	
{line 6}		12	12	Please enter a number:
{line 7}		78	12	
{line 4}	true	78	12	
{line 5}		78	90	
{line 6}		78	90	Please enter a number:
{line 7}		− 70	90	
{line 4}	true	− 70	90	
{line 5}		− 70	20	
{line 6}		− 70	20	Please enter a number:
{line 7}		−999	20	
{line 4}	false	−999	20	
{line 8}				The total is 20
{line 9}				

If you do not follow this rule you may create what are known as *infinite loops* in your program.[1] Consider what would happen if a **while** statement's conditional expression evaluated to *true* the first time it is encountered and if there were nothing to change the value of that conditional expression within the loop. The loop's conditional expression would evaluate to *true* every time it was encountered, and the **while** statement would execute forever! Here are a couple of examples of infinite loops:

```
while 2 + 2 = 4 do        { What a bug!}
        writeln ('Two and two are still four.')

while x + 1 <> x do       { Another bad bug! }
        writeln ('No number equals itself plus one.')
```

In each of these examples, the conditional expression always evaluates to *true*. If executed, each fragment will print its output line an infinite number of times—or, more precisely, until something intervenes to stop the program. Here's a more subtle example:

```
while counter < maxvalue do        {a bad, bad bug}
        writeln(counter, maxvalue)
```

In this case, the conditional expression might evaluate to either *true* or *false*, depending on the values of *counter* and *maxvalue* when the **while** loop was encountered. If *counter* is not less than *maxvalue*, the body of the **while** loop will be skipped and all will be well. However, if *counter* is less than *maxvalue*, it will remain so forever because the only statement in the body of the **while** loop is a *writeln* statement. That statement can never change the value of the conditional expression, and the program will never leave the loop.

An infinite loop is usually a bug—and a particularly troublesome one. An infinite loop will mystify the user of a program. Moreover, on some computer systems shared by several users, an infinite loop in one program may make the entire system hang.

The second important rule concerning **while** loops is

*The values used in the **while** loop's conditional expression must be specified before the loop is entered.*

If this principle is not followed, it is unclear what will happen the first time the loop is encountered. For example, consider what might have happened in the *totaler* program if we had not read in a number from the user before testing the conditional expression *number <> stop*. We have no idea what value might

---

1. Under very rare circumstances you may decide to violate this principle, because infinite loops are sometimes useful. However, they are usually bugs.

be in *number*, and therefore we have no way of telling if the **while** loop will be executed or not. Since the user may actually have some numbers to enter, this error could be disastrous.

A Final Example

Consider the following problem:

Ask for two numbers from the user. Print every number, from the first number to the second number inclusive.

We don't know how many numbers there actually are, so we need an indefinite iterative structure. A general algorithm might be

I. Get numbers

II. Print range of numbers

We need two variables, one for each number to be read in, so the data flow diagram might look like Figure 17.6. For this example we will write just procedure *PrintRangeNums*. The algorithm for this procedure might be

A. While *firstnum* < = *secondnum*, do the following:
  1. Write out *firstnum* followed by a carriage return.
  2. Add 1 to *firstnum* and store in *firstnum*.

This algorithm can easily be translated into a Pascal procedure. Note that we use value parameters in this procedure because we don't have any reason to change the actual value of *num1* and because *num1* and *num2* are not used after procedure *PrintRangeNums*.

The Pascal procedure corresponding to the algorithm above is shown in Figure 17.7, procedure *PrintRangeNums*.

Figure 17.6   Data flow diagram for the example

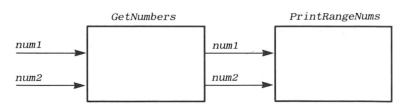

Figure 17.7   Procedure *PrintRangeNums*

```
procedure PrintRangeNums(firstnum, secondnum:integer);
  {a procedure to print the numbers from firstnum to  }
  {secondnum inclusive}

begin {PrintRangeNums}

  while firstnum <= secondnum do
     begin { body of while loop }
         writeln( firstnum );
         firstnum := firstnum + 1
     end { body of while loop }

end;   {PrintRangeNums}
```

In procedure *PrintRangeNums*, if the value of *firstnum* is less than or equal to that of *secondnum*, then the value of *firstnum* will be displayed and incremented until *firstnum* is greater than *secondnum*. If the value of *firstnum* is greater than that of *secondnum* the first time the **while** statement is reached, then the body of the **while** statement is not executed at all, and nothing will be printed. Notice that it assumes that *firstnum* and *secondnum* will have received a value from procedure *GetNumbers*.

Exercise   17.1: Trace procedure *PrintRangeNums*, assuming that the value of *firstnum* is 2 and that the value of *secondnum* is 6. What is the value of *firstnum* that is written out last? What is the value of *firstnum* in the computer's memory just before the procedure terminates?   ∎

17.3 THE repeat STATEMENT

The **repeat** statement is the second form of indefinite iteration available in Pascal. It corresponds to the loop that checks at the bottom. Figure 17.8 gives a syntax diagram for the **repeat** statement.

A **repeat** statement consists of the keyword **repeat** followed by one or more statements, followed by the keyword **until**, followed by a conditional expression. Note these points about the syntax of **repeat**:

■ If more than one statement appears between the keywords **repeat** and **until**, the statements must be separated by semicolons.

Figure 17.8   Syntax diagram for the `repeat` statement

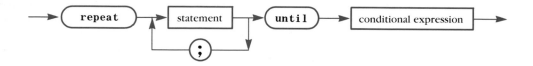

The keywords **begin** and **end** do *not* surround the statements in the loop because the statements to be repeated (known as the body of the **repeat** loop) are unambiguously set off by the keywords **repeat** and **until**.

- The conditional expression is the last part of the statement.
- Conditional expressions for **if**, **while**, and **repeat** statements are all formed in exactly the same way. All must evaluate to one of the two values *true* or *false*.

The effect of a **repeat** statement is to repeatedly execute its body (the statements between **repeat** and **until**) until the value of the conditional expression becomes *true*. The body of the **repeat** statement is always executed at least once; the conditional expression is not evaluated until after the body has been executed once and thereafter not until the body of the loop completes execution each time it is repeated.

An Example Using a `repeat` Statement

Figure 17.9 gives an implementation of the total algorithm given in Figure 17.2. This program will perform the same task as program *totaler*. There are some important differences, however, in the actual Pascal statements used.

One important difference is the type of logic used to formulate the conditional expressions for the two iterative statements. In **while** statements, the conditional expression is the condition for continuing; if the conditional expression evaluates to *true*, the body is executed and the condition is reevaluated. (It is sometimes referred to as the *entry condition*.) In **repeat** statements, the conditional expression is the condition for stopping; as soon as the conditional expression evaluates to *true*, the program moves on to the next statement. (It is sometimes referred to as the *exit condition*.)

Figure 17.9   Implementation of the total algorithm using a repeat
statement

```
program totaler2(input,output);
  {This is a program total of some numbers entered by the user.}
  {The user will indicate she is done by typing -999.}

const prompt = 'Please enter a number:   ';
                            {to prompt the user for a number}
      stop = -999;  {sentinel indicating no more numbers}

var total,           {to hold the total of all the numbers}
    number:integer;  {to hold the number the}
                     {user has just entered}

begin  {totaler2}
      total:= 0;                 {Initialize total.}
      repeat
        write(prompt);
        readln(number);
        if number <> stop
           then
              total := total + number
      until number = stop;
      writeln('The total is ',total:1)
end.   {totaler2}
```

Semantic Considerations When Using the repeat Statement

Like the **while** loop, the **repeat** loop is written with some implicit rules in mind. The first rule is

> *Always include in the body of a* **repeat** *statement at least one statement that is capable of changing the value of the* **repeat** *loop's conditional expression.*

If you ignore this rule, you can create an infinite loop using a **repeat** statement. The second rule is

> *The values in the* **repeat** *loop's conditional expression must be specified before the conditional expression is evaluated.*

Unlike the **while** loop, these values may be set within the body of the loop because the loop's conditional expression is not evaluated until the body of the loop is complete.

You should watch out, however, for the following type of error:

```
    . . .
repeat
   total : = 0;
   write ('number please: ');
   readln(number);
   total : = total + number
until total > maximum
    . . .
```

In this case, you probably do not want to assign *total* a value of 0 every time you enter the loop. You must carefully decide which statements you really want repeated.

Comparing **while** and **repeat** Statements

Figure 17.10 gives a version of the procedure shown in Figure 17.6, with the **while** loop replaced by a **repeat** loop. Notice that these two procedures are not equivalent.

The procedure in Figure 17.10 will display the value of *firstnum* and then increment that value until it is greater than the value of *secondnum*. If the value of *firstnum* is greater than the value of *secondnum* when the **repeat** statement is encountered, it will still print out the value of *firstnum* once and increment it once. Since we don't know if the value of *firstnum* is going to be less

Figure 17.10 **Procedure** *PrintRangeNum2*

```
procedure PrintRangeNums2(firstnum, secondnum: integer);
  {a procedure to print the numbers from firstnum to}
  {secondnum inclusive}

begin {PrintRangeNums2}
  repeat
      writeln( firstnum );
      firstnum : = firstnum + 1
   until firstnum > secondnum
end;   {PrintRangeNums2}
```

than or equal to the value of *secondnum*, this is a case in which a **while** loop is more appropriate than a **repeat** loop. If the initial values of *firstnum* and *secondnum* are 8 and 6, respectively, the **repeat** loop would print the value 8, which does not coincide with the problem statement.

Notice, however, that if we required the value of *firstnum* to be less than or equal to *secondnum*, using a **repeat** loop would be more appropriate, since we would know we wanted the body of the loop performed at least once.

Exercise   17.2: Trace the code in Figure 17.3 and Figure 17.10.

a. If the initial values of *firstnum* and *secondnum* are 4 and 6, respectively.

b. If the initial values of *firstnum* and *secondnum* are 6 and 4, respectively. ∎

In Figure 17.11, you can see flowcharts of the **while** and **repeat** statements. Note that the flowcharts differ in two fundamental ways: the point at which the entry to the body of the loop is made, and the value of the conditional expression that indicates that the body should be repeated.

Figure 17.11   Flowcharts for indefinite iterative statements

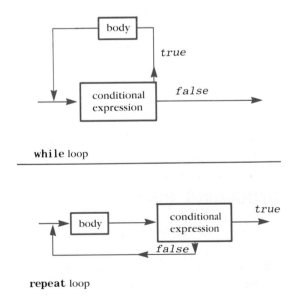

CHAPTER SUMMARY

1. The **while** statement is Pascal's indefinite iterative construct that tests conditions at the top of the loop. The body of a **while** statement can be executed as few as zero times. It is executed as long as the conditional expression is *true*.

2. The **repeat** statement is Pascal's indefinite iterative construct that tests conditions at the bottom of the loop. The body of a **repeat** statement is always executed at least once. It is executed as long as the conditional expression following the keyword **until** is *false*.

COMMON ERRORS

- Confusing the auxiliary keywords **then** and **do**. Thus, a student might write

  if condition **do** . . .   { a fairly common error }

  or, more rarely,

  while condition **then** . . .

- Inserting a semicolon after the keyword **do** in **while** statements. This has the effect of providing a null body to the loop.

- Omitting the keywords **begin** and **end** around the body of a **while** loop. This has the effect of making the first statement after **do** the body of the loop. This error is often obscured by spurious indenting, as in

  ```
  while counter < limit do
          readln (usernum);
          total : = total + usernum;
          counter : = counter + 1
  ```

  This is an infinite loop. Only the *readln* is in the body of the **while**.

DEBUGGING HINTS

- Insert a *writeln* statement at the beginning of the loop to identify an infinite loop.

- Display the value of the variables contained in the loop's conditional expression each time before it is evaluated. With the **repeat** loop, this requires one *writeln* statement. With the **while** loop, this requires two *writeln* statements.

- Insert a *writeln* as the last statement in the loop to ensure that everything you had intended is contained in the loop.

- Insert a *writeln* statement after the end of the loop to be sure that the body of the loop does not extend further than intended.

SUPPLEMENTAL PROBLEMS

1. Write a program to print triangles sized according to a user's input that look like this:

```
****
***
**
*
```

Notice that the width and the height of the triangle are identical.

2. Write a program to print rectangles sized according to the user's input. The rectangles should be filled and should look like this:

```
*******
*******
*******
```

3. Write a program to print rectangles sized according to the user's input. The rectangles should be hollow and should look like this:

```
********
*      *
*      *
********
```

The first and last rows should be full rows of *'s, and the intervening rows should have an *, an appropriate number of blanks, and another *.

4. Write a program to solve the problem stated in Chapter 15 (pages 346–347) to tabulate grades. Is it better to use a **while** or a **repeat** loop in this problem?

5. Write a program to compute the maximum and the minimum of a set of numbers entered by the user. The end of the numbers will be indicated by −9999.

6. Write a program to compute the maximum and the minimum of a set of numbers entered by the user. You should ask the user if he wants to enter any

numbers, and then ask him after every number if he has another number to enter. If no numbers are entered, the program should output that there is no maximum or minimum.

7. Convert the following program fragment that uses a **while** loop into a program fragment that uses a **repeat** loop. Make sure that the output is identical for both program fragments.

```
write('Please enter a value for counter: ');
readln(counter);
write('Please enter a value for finalcount: ');
readln(finalcount);
while counter > finalcount do
   begin
     write(finalcount:2);
     counter := counter - 1
   end
```

8. Convert the following program fragment that uses a **repeat** loop into a program fragment that uses a **while** loop. Make sure that the output is identical for both program fragments.

```
repeat
   write('Please enter a letter: ');
   readln(letter)
until letter = 'n'
```

9. Write a procedure to add up the values from n to m. The values n and m should be sent as parameters to the procedure, and the total should be sent back through a variable parameter.

10. Write a procedure to find the alternating sum of the numbers from n to m, where n and m are both sent as parameters. The result should be sent back as a parameter. For example, if $n = 5$ and $m = 10$, the alternating sum is $5 + 6 - 7 + 8 - 9 + 10$, or 13.

18.1 COMPOUND CONDITIONAL EXPRESSIONS

The problems we have presented so far have been somewhat simple because we wanted to illustrate specific points and because we were limited in the kinds of conditional expressions we could construct. In many real-world problems, the conditions that govern **if**, **while**, and **repeat** statements are complex. Here's a problem that uses a complex conditional expression and whose solution is helpful in many programs:

> You present a question to the user and ask for a response. The response should logically be either yes or no, so you instruct the user to type the letter *y* or *n*. If the user responds with any character other than *y* or *n*, you must remind him or her what a valid response is and repeatedly ask for another response until a valid answer is given.

This seems easy enough. We can write a straightforward algorithm and then try to implement it with a Pascal procedure. Figure 18.1 gives a possible algorithm. The difficulty in writing a procedure for this algorithm arises when we try to code the conditional expression in step IV. The condition we want to describe involves more than the relation of two values. It involves three values: the constants 'n' and 'y' and the value of the variable that holds the answer. We can write most of the procedure as shown in Figure 18.2, but, when you look at the figure, you can see that we must leave a hole in it for the moment.

What should we put in place of (?????????) in Figure 18.2? It should be some condition that will be *true* when *answer* is neither 'y' nor 'n' and that will be *false* when the answer is either of the two characters 'y' or 'n'. This can't be a condition of the sort we have encountered so far—that is, it can't be a condition that involves only two values. What we need is a compound conditional expression.

CONDITIONAL EXPRESSIONS AND *boolean* VARIABLES

Figure 18.1   **Algorithm for getting valid *y* or *n* input**

Setup

    I. Allocate space for a *char* variable to hold the user's answer.

Instructions

    I. Present the user with instructions.

    II. Ask your question.

    III. Read user's response into *answer.*

    IV. While *answer* isn't 'y' or 'n', do the following steps:
        A. Inform the user that the given answer is invalid and issue a reminder that only 'y' or 'n' is legitimate.
        B. Ask for another input.
        C. Read user's response into *answer.*

Recall that in Chapter 4 we discussed the role of the *boolean* operators 'and', 'or', and 'not' as they are used in algorithms. Corresponding operators are available in Pascal. You must be very careful when you use these operators to construct conditional expressions in Pascal because they cannot be used flexibly, as they are in English. For example, here are two sentences that mean the same thing in English:

The value of *ch* is not *y*, and the value of *ch* is not *n*.

The value of *ch* is not *y* or *n*.

Figure 18.2   **Procedure to check for valid *y* or *n* input**

```
procedure yesno(var answer:char);
  {repeatedly requests a response}
  {until a 'y' or 'n' is typed }

begin { yesno }
        write ('Answer y or n for ''yes'' or ''no'': ');
        readln(answer); { get answering char }
        while (?????????) do
            begin { while }
                write ('Invalid response.');
                write(' Please answer y or n:  ');
                readln (answer)
            end { while }
end;{ yesno }
```

Both sentences say the same thing about the value of *ch*, though they seem to be using two different operators. The first sentence can easily be translated into a conditional expression in Pascal:

```
(ch <> 'y') and (ch <> 'n')
        {using and to join two conditions}
```

The second sentence cannot be translated directly into Pascal. Here is a common erroneous attempt to do so:

```
ch <> ('y' or 'n') {This is WRONG! }
```

In Pascal, the reserved words **and** and **or** must be used between two conditional expressions. The erroneous construct above is an attempt to evaluate the conditional expression (`'y'` **or** `'n'`). Since `'y'` and `'n'` don't have *true* or *false* values, it is impossible to do so. In English, we can use the words *and* and *or* flexibly in various grammatical contexts. In Pascal, we can use the reserved words **and** and **or** only in a single context: as connectives between two conditional expressions. In other words, the expression immediately before the keyword **and** or **or** and the expression immediately after the keyword **and** or **or** must have a value that is either *true* or *false*.

Here is another mistake that is commonly made in constructing compound conditional expressions:

```
(ch <> 'y') or (ch <> 'n')
        {using or to join two conditions }
```

This is a correct Pascal expression. However, it always evaluates to *true*! It makes no difference what the value of *ch* is because *ch* can have only one value. Whatever that value is, either it is not equal to 'y' or it is not equal to 'n', because it can't possibly be equal to both 'y' and 'n'. There are three possible values of *ch* to consider in evaluating this conditional expression:

1. *ch* is equal to 'y'. If this is *true*, *ch* cannot be equal to 'n', so the conditional expression evaluates to *true*.

2. *ch* is equal to 'n'. If this is *true*, *ch* cannot be equal to 'y', so the conditional expression evaluates to *true*.

3. *ch* is equal to some other character. If this is *true*, *ch* cannot be equal to 'y' or 'n', so the conditional expression evaluates to *true*.

Usually, programmers who write expressions like this are translating an English expression of the form "*ch* isn't equal to 'y' or 'n'." But to translate that English sentence into proper Pascal, you must first rephrase it as "*ch* isn't equal to 'y' and *ch* isn't equal to 'n'." The corresponding Pascal conditional expression is

(ch <> 'y') **and** (ch <> 'n')

This expression will be *true* when *ch* has a value other than 'y' or 'n'.

You can deduce how compound conditional expressions will evaluate from the tables in Figure 18.3, which are known as *truth tables*. Notice that we have included the truth table for a third Pascal *boolean* operator, the keyword **not**. This operator is different from **and** and **or** because it takes only a single operand. We can use the operator **not** just before a conditional expression to indicate the negation—that is, the opposite—of the value of the conditional expression. The **and** and **or** tables are used as follows:

> *The values of the two conditional expressions surrounding the operator are used to select the row and column from that operator's truth table. We use the first value to select a row and the second value to select a column. The value found at the intersection of that row and that column is the value of the whole compound conditional expression.*

The **not** table is used as follows:

> *The value of the conditional expression on which the* **not** *is operating is used to select a row. The value in that row gives the value of the whole compound conditional expression.*

Figure 18.4 shows some compound conditional expressions. The expressions are preceded by a set of variable declarations that describe the types of the variables used.

Figure 18.3   Truth tables

or	T	F		and	T	F		not	
T	T	T		T	T	F		T	F
F	T	F		F	F	F		F	T

Figure 18.4   Sample compound conditional expressions

```
var     init1,
        init2: char;
        low,
        high,
        mid: integer;
```

The examples:

1. (init1 = 'a') **and** (init2 <> init1)
2. (init1 = 'a') **or** (init2 <> init1)
3. (low = mid) **or** (high = mid)
4. ((low = mid) **or** (high = mid)) **and** (low <> high)
5. (init1 = init2) **and** (low = high)
6. **not** (low = high)
7. **not** ((init1 = 'a') **or** (init2 = 'a'))
8. (**not** (init1 = 'a')) **or** (init2 = 'a')

Example 1 uses the **and** operator. The value of this expression is computed as follows:

■ The value of *init1* is compared to 'a'. If *init1* equals 'a', then the first conditional expression has the value *true*. Otherwise, it has the value *false*.

■ The value of *init2* is compared to the value of *init1*. If the values are unequal, then the second conditional expression evaluates to *true*; otherwise, it evaluates to *false*.

■ The values of those two conditional expressions are then used with the **and** truth table to find the value of the compound conditional expression.

For example, suppose the first conditional expression is *true* (that is, *init1* really does equal 'a'), but the second conditional expression is *false* (that is, *init2* happens to have the same value as *init1*). We deduce the value of the compound expression by looking at the first row (T) and second column (F) of the **and** table, and we find the value *F* there. The compound conditional expression is *false*, in accordance with our expectation of what **and** should mean in English.

If we consider example 2 with the same values for *init1* and *init2*, we see that the entry in the T row and the F column of the **or** table is T. This conditional expression has the value *true*, again in accordance with our usual interpretation of the English word *or*. Note, however, that the word *or* may be used with two quite different meanings in English: It may mean "one or the other, but not both," in which case its meaning is exclusive. Or it may mean "one or the other, or possibly both," in which case its meaning is inclusive. When we say "Sink or swim," we expect only one of the two to occur. When we say "Dr. Jones or Dr. Brown will be on duty," it's quite possible that both will be on duty. In Pascal, the keyword **or** always has the inclusive meaning. Thus, we see that the entry in the truth table for row T and column T is T. The **or** of two *true* expressions is *true*.

The operator **not** takes the value of the conditional expression that follows it and reverses it. Thus, example 6 above will evaluate to *true* whenever the condition *low = high* evaluates to *false*—that is, whenever *low* and *high* have different values. The conditional expressions

```
not (low = high)
```

and

```
low <> high
```

are really two different ways of saying the same thing. Both will evaluate to *true* when *low* is unequal to *high* and to *false* otherwise.

Sometimes we want to construct even more complex conditional expressions. For example, an income tax form might have an instruction like this:

> If you didn't itemize deductions, or if you itemized deductions and the total on line 38 was less than $3,000, then enter 0 on this line.

What two conditions are the operands of the *or* in this sentence? In other words, what two things are being asked such that if either is *true* we are to enter a 0? They are

1. You didn't itemize deductions.
2. You itemized deductions and the total on line 38 was less than $3,000.

One of these conditions is itself a compound condition. Notice that the full instruction contains a possible ambiguity. You might interpret it this way:

> If you either did or didn't itemize deductions, AND if the total on line 38 was less than $3,000, then. . . .

The meaning depends on which of the two boolean operators we give precedence to. Do we evaluate the *and* first and then the *or,* or the other way around? The English sentence gives us clues both through the punctuation and through the context: The first comma in the sentence helps us understand what is meant. Moreover, the second interpretation would make no sense, since everyone either did or didn't itemize deductions. (Even income tax forms aren't that badly written!) In Pascal, however, the context gives no help at all. We need a way to resolve such ambiguities as this:

```
if (itemize = 'n') or (itemize = 'y') and (line38 < 3000)
      then. . .
```

Since this expression can be interpreted in two ways, we use parentheses to group conditional expressions to indicate the meaning we intend. Here are the two possible ways to parenthesize the expression given above:

```
if (itemize = 'n') or ((itemize = 'y') and (line38 < 3000 ))
      then. . .
if ((itemize = 'n') or (itemize = 'y')) and (line38 < 3000 )
      then. . .
```

In Pascal, the rule that governs the use of parentheses in such cases is the same as the rule that governs the use of parentheses in arithmetic expressions: Every *boolean* operator inside the parentheses is evaluated first, and the resulting value is used as the operand for the *boolean* operator outside the parentheses. Thus, in the first fragment above, if *itemize* happens to have the value 'n', the conditional expression will evaluate to *true* no matter what the value of *line38* is. In the second fragment, if *itemize* has the value 'n' but *line38* has a value

Figure 18.5   **Completed procedure** *yesno*

```
procedure yesno(var answer:char);
   {repeatedly requests a response}
   {until a 'y' or 'n' is typed }

begin { yesno }
        write ('Answer y or n for "yes" or "no": ');
        readln(answer); {get answering char }
        while (answer <> 'y') and (answer <> 'n') do
           begin { while }
                write ('Invalid response.');
                write('Please answer y or n: ');
                readln (answer)
           end { while }
end; { yesno }
```

greater than or equal to 3000, the conditional expression will evaluate to *false*.

It is best to avoid highly complex conditional expressions because they tend to make a program confusing. Sometimes, of course, the logic of your algorithm will make it impossible to avoid complex conditional expressions. Later in this chapter, we introduce a new variable type that makes complex conditional expressions easier to use.

Now that we've seen how to build complex conditional expressions, we can finish the error-checking problem from Figure 18.2. Figure 18.5 shows a finished version of procedure *yesno*. Notice that if our algorithm had used a **repeat** loop rather than a **while** loop, the conditional expression we formulated would always have to evaluate to the opposite of the **while** loop's conditional expression:

```
(answer = 'y') or (answer = 'n')    { for until clause }
```

18.2 THE RELATIONAL OPERATOR in

We now introduce the last relational operator, **in**. The **in** operator is unique in Pascal: All the other relational operators in Pascal (=, <>, <=, <>, and >=) operate between two operands—that is, expressions—of compatible type. They are comparison operations. The operation performed by the **in** operator, however, is not a comparison, but a lookup. The first operand of **in** must be a constant, variable, or expression of some type. The second operand must be a set of objects of the same type. Although we will not discuss Pascal's notion of sets in full until Chapter 27, one special case—set constants—is relatively simple and extremely useful in the current context. Loosely speaking, *set constants* are lists of objects enclosed in brackets. There are restrictions on what kinds of objects may be listed inside the brackets, and those restrictions vary from one version of Pascal to another. Here we will use only sets of characters and sets of integers, such as the following:

```
['y', 'n']
['y', 'n', 'Y', 'N']
['a', 'e', 'i', 'o', 'u', 'y']
[1, 3, 4, 5]
[14, 19, 18]
```

The operator **in** works like this: A conditional expression is formed according to the syntax

```
expression in set-of-same-type
```

The value of the whole conditional expression is *true* if the expression it contains has a value that matches one of the items in the set, and *false* otherwise. For example,

```
answer in ['y', 'n']
```

will be *true* when *answer* has either value 'y' or value 'n', *false* if *answer* has any other value. (This is a valid expression only if *answer* has been declared to be of type *char* or of a type compatible with *char*).

The operator **in** serves as a powerful tool for forming conditional expressions. For example, suppose that, in a program that used procedure *yesno*, we didn't know if the user was going to type his response in uppercase or lowercase letters, but we would like to accept any of the four characters 'y', 'Y', 'n', 'N' as valid. We could write the conditional expression for the **while** loop as follows:

```
while (answer <> 'y') and (answer <> 'Y') and
        (answer <> 'n') and (answer <> 'N') do
    . . .
```

But this expression would be clumsy, error-prone, and difficult to read. We could achieve the same effect with this one:

```
while not (answer in ['Y', 'y', 'N', 'n']) do
    . . .
```

Similarly, if we want to test whether an integer typed by the user is between 10 and 15 inclusive, we can write

```
if inputnum in [10, 11, 12, 13, 14, 15]
    then. . .
```

Notice that the order in which we list the elements of the set is irrelevant. These two sets are the same:

```
['a', 'e', 'i', 'o', 'u', 'y']
['y', 'u', 'o', 'i', 'e', 'a']
```

The **in** operator is particularly useful in protecting against a type of run-time error that sometimes occurs with **case** statements. Recall that a **case** statement compares a value against a series of **case** labels. The matching **case** label determines which statement or which compound statement will be executed. However, the program might crash with a run-time error if no **case** label matches the value.

Figure 18.6 **Unprotected case statement**

```
case initial of
  'a':    writeln ('Able');
  'b':    writeln ('Baker');
  'c':    writeln ('Charlie')
end  {case initial of}
```

For example, the program fragment in Figure 18.6 will cause an error if *initial* is not 'a', 'b', or 'c'. We can protect against this type of error by having the computer execute the **case** statement only if we have some guarantee that the value of *initial* is one of the **case** labels. Figure 18.7 shows how we might do this.

18.3 THE PRECEDENCE OF OPERATORS

We have introduced all of the operators of the Pascal language with the exception of / (*real* division). Although we will encounter new meanings for some of them, we're finally in a position to describe the precedence of all Pascal's operators. In this section, we extend what was said about precedence in Chapter 16 (pages 359–362).

Recall that the precedence of operators means the order in which they will be applied in the absence of parentheses. In Chapter 16, we introduced the rules of precedence for the arithmetic operators and the simple relational operators. Pascal has a set of rules that describe the precedence of all its operators, including relational, boolean, and arithmetic. Figure 18.8 completes Figure 16.4 (page 360). The evaluation algorithm used in Chapter 16 (page 361) applies to this expanded group of operators.

Again, you can override Pascal's precedence rules by using parentheses. Any

Figure 18.7   Protected case statement

```
if initial in ['a', 'b', 'c']
   then
      case initial of
         'a':   writeln ('Able');
         'b':   writeln ('Baker');
         'c':   writeln ('Charlie')
      end {case initial of}
   else
      writeln ('Initial ', initial, ' is invalid')
```

Figure 18.8   Pascal's groups of operators

I.	unary minus, **not**
II.	*, /, **div**, **mod**, **and**
III.	+, −, **or**
IV.	=, <>, <=, >=, <, >, **in**

subexpression inside the parentheses is evaluated completely, according to the evaluation algorithm, before its value is used in evaluating the whole expression. Recall that parentheses can be nested to any level and that the parenthesized expressions are evaluated from the inside (most deeply nested parentheses) outward.

Figure 18.9 gives a set of variable declarations followed by unparenthesized expressions containing these variables. We'll evaluate each of these expressions. Expressions 1 and 2 are interpreted according to the precedence of **and** over **or** and the rule that you evaluate expressions from left to right. They are equivalent, respectively, to

1′. `((int1 = int2)` **and** `(int2 <> int3))` **or**
     `((int1 <> int2)` **and** `(int2 = int3))`

and

2′. `(int2 = int3)` **or** `((int2 = int4)` **and**
     `(int1 = int3))` **or** `(int1 = int4)`

The meaning of expression 3 seems to be fairly clear: It seems to be asking if either one of the two equalities holds. Actually, it isn't even a legal expression! The precedence table in Figure 18.8 indicates that the boolean operator **or** has a higher precedence than any of the relational operators, including =. So Pascal interprets expression 3 as if it were written:

3′. `int1 = (int2` **or** `int3) = int4`   `{ Wrong! }`

The parenthesized expression takes the **or** of two integers, which is an error. Also, parenthesized in that way, the conditional expression has two relational operators that share the same operand. As you will recall from Chapter 16, this is illegal in Pascal. The compiler will reject such an expression and will signal an error. The use of parentheses conveys the intended meaning of this expression:

`(int1 = int2)` **or** `(int3 = int4)`

Figure 18.9   Sample conditional expressions to evaluate

         var   `int1, int2, int3, int4: integer;`

The expressions:

1.   `(int1 = int2)` **and** `(int2 <> int3)` **or**
      `(int1 <> int2)` **and** `(int2 = int3)`
2.   `(int2 = int3)` **or** `(int2 = int4)` **and**
      `(int1 = int3)` **or** `(int1 = int4)`
3.   `int1 = int2` **or** `int3 = int4`

Unparenthesized compound expressions are usually very confusing. Moreover, they're dangerous. It's easy to write a legal expression whose meaning isn't what you intend and that will completely alter the meaning of your program. Instead of relying on the precedence rules for evaluating complex expressions, indicate your meaning with parentheses. But don't go too far. For example, there's never any need to put individual identifiers in parentheses. Too many parentheses clutter up your program and make it difficult to read.

18.4 *boolean* DATA

So far you have been introduced to two predefined data types, *integer* and *char*. We now introduce a third predefined type: *boolean*. *boolean* data items may have one of two values: *true* or *false*. These, you will recall, are the same as the possible values of conditional expressions. In fact, since compound conditional expressions can be so unwieldly, a principal use of *boolean* variables is to hold the values of conditional expressions.

boolean variables are declared in a syntax that is consistent with the syntax of other data declarations. The word *boolean* is a predefined type identifier. We declare several *boolean* variables in Figure 18.10. Such declarations announce to Pascal that there are three *boolean* variables, named *morenumbers*, *isundergrad*, and *seniorcit*. As always, these variables have unpredictable values until values are assigned to them. There are currently two methods we know for assigning values to *boolean* variables:

- By being positioned on the left side of an assignment statement
- By being passed as an argument to a variable parameter of a procedure that assigns a value to the corresponding parameter

Values cannot be assigned to *boolean* data from keyboard input.

Pascal represents *boolean* values by the predefined identifiers *true* and *false*. Note the difference between the following statements:

```
isundergrad : = true;     {OK; makes isundergrad true. }
isundergrad : = 'true';   { Incorrect!!! }
```

The first assignment statement sets the variable *isundergrad* to the value *true*. The second assignment statement is trying to set the variable *isundergrad* to

Figure 18.10   Variable declarations using *boolean* type

```
var      morenumbers,   {to be true if there's more data, . . .}
         isundergrad,    { if student is undergraduate, . . .}
         seniorcit: boolean;    { if student is over 65}
```

the string literal 'true', which is not a *boolean* value at all. Just as the sequence of digits 123 represents a single numerical value that is different from the three character values in '123', the identifier *true* represents a single *boolean* value that is different from the four character values in 'true'.

Exercise   18.1: Evaluate the following expressions.

a. **not** true = false

b. **not** true **or** false

c. **not** false **or** true

d. true **and** false **or** false **and** true   ∎

The Pascal Standard specifies that *boolean* values may be used in the standard procedures *write* and *writeln*. When a *boolean* expression is used in such a statement, the word **true** or the word **false** will be displayed. A field-width specifier may be used with a *boolean* expression, as in

var   isdigit: boolean;   { True if ch is 0–9. }
                . . .
writeln(isdigit: 6);

The effect of a width specifier is to pad the printed value by introducing blanks to the left of it.

The Pascal Standard does not permit the use of *boolean* variables as parameters in the standard procedures *read* and *readln*. That is why you cannot enter *boolean* values from the keyboard. Some implementations of Pascal do, however, allow such keyboard input and recognize the input strings *true* and *false* as *boolean* values (in lowercase or uppercase characters, or either.) Still, even if your implementation of Pascal supports such a feature, use it cautiously. The use of nonstandard features makes programs less portable.

As you will recall, *boolean* values appear as conditional expressions in **if**, **while**, and **repeat** statements. Such expressions may appear on the right side of assignments to *boolean* variables. Figure 18.11 gives two examples. Each of its assignment statements evaluates the right side to arrive at a *boolean* value. The first statement is equivalent to

if age >= 65
    then
        seniorcit := true
    else
        seniorcit := false

Figure 18.11   Program fragment showing conditional expressions in assignment statements

```
var     seniorcit,
        isundergrad: boolean;
        age: integer;
        class: char;
            . . .
    seniorcit := age >= 65;

    isundergrad := ( (class = 'f')  { freshman }
                or (class = 's')    { sophomore }
                or (class = 'j')    { junior }
                or (class = 'S') ); { senior }
```

The second statement is equivalent to

```
if (class = 'f')            { freshman }
   or (class = 's')         { sophomore }
   or (class = 'j')         { junior }
   or (class = 'S')         { senior }
  then
        isundergrad := true
  else
        isundergrad := false
```

The *boolean* assignment is more convenient than the **if** statement. Moreover, it expresses our intentions more clearly and directly because we're computing and assigning a value rather than performing something conditionally.

   boolean values may themselves appear in conditional expressions. These conditional expressions are evaluated in the usual manner.

```
if isundergrad and seniorcit
   then
        writeln('Wow! A late bloomer!')
```

will evaluate the **and** of the two *boolean* variables. Since **and** is *true* only if both its operands are *true*, the *writeln* will be performed only if both *isundergrad* and *seniorcit* have the value *true*.

   Similarly we can use *boolean* variables in conditional expressions that occur on the right side of assignments to other *boolean* variables. For example, if *oldman* has been declared of type *boolean* and *gender* of type *char*, then we can write

```
oldman := seniorcit and (gender = 'm')
```

This statement first evaluates the right side by computing the **and** of the variable *seniorcit* (which has a value of either *true* or *false*) with the expression (gender = 'm') (whose value will be *true* if the value of *gender* is 'm' and otherwise will be *false*). Thus, *oldman* will get the value *true* if both these values are *true* and otherwise will get the value *false*.

Exercise   18.2: Here's a fragment of a Pascal program:

```
var      isavowel: boolean;
         ch: char;
           .  .  .
         if (ch = 'a') or (ch = 'e') or
            (ch = 'i') or (ch = 'o') or
            (ch = 'u') or (ch = 'y')
           then
                 isavowel : = true
           else
                 isavowel = false
           .  .  .
```

Write an equivalent statement in the form of an assignment:

```
isavowel : = . . .
```

in which an appropriate *boolean*-valued expression occurs on the right side of the assignment operator.   ■

Exercise   18.3: What will be the output of the following fragment of a Pascal program?

```
var   firstnum,
      secondnum: integer;
      truthvalue: boolean;
         .  .  .
      firstnum : = −3;
      secondnum : = 9;
      truthvalue : = (firstnum * firstnum >= secondnum);
      writeln('It is ', truthvalue, ' that ',
              firstnum * firstnum : 1,
              ' is greater than or equal to ',
              secondnum : 1)
         .  .  .   ■
```

Figure 18.12 Procedure showing *boolean* variables in use

```
procedure setflags(ch: char; var islower, isupper, isletter,
                            isdigit, isspecial:boolean);
{This program gets a character in parameter "ch" and sets the}
{five flags to describe the character. This procedure}
{will only work with character sets in which the lower-}
{case letters of the alphabet are contiguous and the}
{uppercase letters as well—for example, ASCII, but not EBCDIC.}

begin { setflags }
      islower := (ch >= 'a') and (ch <= 'z');
      isupper := (ch >= 'A') and (ch <= 'Z');
      isletter := islower or isupper;
      isdigit := (ch >= '0') and (ch <= '9');
      isspecial := not ( isletter or isdigit )
end;   { setflags }
```

Figure 18.12 shows a procedure that assigns some useful values to booleans. Its purpose is to get a character from the keyboard and to set five *boolean* variables that collectively describe the character.

When procedure *setflags* is called, it gets a copy of its caller's argument in the parameter *ch*. It then compares that character value to the values 'a' and 'z' to determine if it is a lowercase letter. If the character value lies between those values, then the variable *islower* gets the value *true*, indicating that *ch* is a lowercase letter. Otherwise, *islower* gets the value *false*.

Similarly, *isupper* gets the value *true* if the typed character lies in the range 'A'-'Z' and *false* if it does not. The variable *isletter* gets the value *true* if either of *islower* or *isupper* is *true*, since a letter is either a lowercase letter or an uppercase letter. The variable *isdigit* gets the value *true* if the typed character lies in the range '0'-'9', and *false* if it does not.

The last statement of the procedure evaluates the negation of the **or** of the two variables *isdigit* and *isletter* and assigns the value it computes to *isspecial*. That means *isspecial* will get the value *true* precisely when *isdigit* and *isletter* are both *false*. So *isspecial* will be *true* whenever the user has typed a character that is not a letter or a digit, such as '+', '%', or ' ' (a blank).

Exercise 18.4: Assume that the following statements occur at the end of procedure *setflags*:

```
boolval1 := (isletter or isdigit) and (not islower);
boolval2 := isletter or (isdigit and (not islower));
boolval3 := isspecial or isdigit or isupper or islower;
boolval4 := isspecial and isdigit and isupper and
                islower;
boolval5 := not ( (not islower) or (not isupper));
```

What are the values of the five *boolean* variables on the left of these assignment statements if the character passed as an argument to *setflags* is

a. 'm'

b. 'G'

c. '+'

d. '8'   ■

Variables of type *boolean* can make your program more precise as well as clearer. Consider the following outline of an algorithm for the game of tic-tac-toe.

I. Repeat
    A. Get a move.
    B. Determine if there is a winner
  until there is winner or nine moves have been made.

II. If there has been a winner,
  then
    A. Indicate the winner.
  else
    B. Indicate a cat's game.

In this case, we leave the loop if there has been a winner or if nine moves have been made. Following the loop, we then check to see what type of message to give to the users. This is an excellent place for a *boolean* variable. If we set the *boolean* variable when we determine if there is a winner, we can use it again in step II. We could implement this algorithm as follows:

```
var winner: boolean;
    . . .
repeat
  getmove(player);
  determinewin(player, winner);   {Winner is set to true or}
  moves := moves + 1              {false in this procedure.}
until winner or (moves = 9);
```

```
if winner
then writeln('There''s a winner!')
else writeln('A cat''s game!!')
```

. . .

The use of the *boolean* variable makes the program more efficient as well as clearer.

CHAPTER SUMMARY

1. *Compound conditional expressions* can be constructed out of simple conditional expressions using the boolean operators **and**, **or**, and **not**. The meaning of these operators is described by the truth tables in Figure 18.3.

2. The relational operator **in** can often be used to express simply a condition that would otherwise require a compound conditional expression. Unlike the other relational operators, **in** does not perform a simple comparison, but a *lookup* in a set of values. If a value equal to the first expression is found in the set of values, the whole conditional expression evaluates to *true*.

3. You can use parentheses to control the order in which the operators are evaluated. In the absence of parentheses, the order of evaluation is governed by the set of precedence rules given in Chapter 16 (page 361). You can use a compound conditional expression anywhere you can legally use a simple conditional expression.

4. The type *boolean* is a predefined data type in Pascal that can be used to declare variables in the usual way. Variables of type *boolean* may have only the values *true* and *false*.

5. *boolean* variables may be used to hold the values of conditional expressions. The *boolean* operators **and**, **or**, and **not** may be used in combination with *boolean* variables to construct conditional expressions.

6. The values of *boolean* expressions may be written to standard output, using the procedures *write* and *writeln*. However, it is not possible to read values of *boolean* variables from standard input.

COMMON ERRORS

■ Assuming that relational operators have a higher precedence than *boolean* operators **and** and **or**. Such an assumption might result in an expression like this:

```
a = b or c = d
```

A semantically correct version of this expression will look like this:

(a = b) **or** (c = d)

- Assuming that the relational operator **in** has higher precedence than the *boolean* operator **not**.
- Writing the *boolean* values *true* and *false* as strings inside single quotes: `'true'` or `'false'`.
- Using **and** where you mean **or** and vice versa.

DEBUGGING HINTS

- Before evaluating the conditional expression, display the values of all the variables involved.
- Before evaluating a complex conditional expression, display the values of any expressions (arithmetic or *boolean*) involved.
- Display the value of the conditional expression.

SUPPLEMENTAL PROBLEMS

1. Write a procedure that prompts the user for one of the characters `'A'` through `'Z'` and then accepts a single character on a line as input. The procedure should repeatedly reject invalid characters and reprompt the user until he or she enters a valid character.

2. Write a procedure that reads typed input up to a `'$'` and counts the number of vowels in the input. Both uppercase and lowercase vowels should be counted.

3. Write procedure *playgame* and its subprocedures from program *guess-mynumber* from Chapter 14 (pages 286–294).

4. Assume the following values for the variables in the examples of Figure 18.4:

```
init1 = 'a'
init2 = 'b'
low = 23
mid = 34
high = 34
```

Evaluate each of the conditional expressions in Figure 18.4.

5. (An exercise in formal logic.) There is a *boolean* operator called *exclusive-or* (abbreviated *xor*) that is defined to give the value *true* if one of its op-

erands is true and the other is false, and to give the value *false* if both its operands are true or if both are false. We can show this in a truth table:

xor	T	F
T	F	T
F	T	F

There is no built-in operator in Pascal to compute the **xor** of two values. Write a procedure *xor*, that is passed two *boolean* value parameters and a single *boolean* variable parameter and returns the exclusive-or of the value parameters in the variable parameter.

6. Implement a procedure that checks the user's input to be in a specified range. The range should be a contiguous set of numbers. The minimum number and the maximum number of the range should be sent as parameters.

7. Write a program to simulate the game of craps.

8. Write a procedure to check an access code. The user should be given at most three chances to enter the access code correctly.

9. Assume the following data declarations:

```
var int1, int2, int3, int4: integer;
    bool1, bool2, bool3, bool4: boolean;
```

Which of the following are valid expressions? For each valid expression, give a completely parenthesized equivalent expression. For each invalid expression, explain why it's invalid.
a. bool1 **or** bool2 **and** bool2
b. bool1 **and** bool2 **or** bool2
c. int1 = int2 **and** int3 = int4
d. bool1 = bool2 **and** bool3 = bool4
c. bool1 **and** bool2 = bool3 **and** bool4
f. bool1 **and** int1 **in** [1, 2, 3, 4]

10. Write a procedure that receives a single number as an argument and returns three *boolean* values indicating if the number is divisible by 2, 3, and 5.

CHAPTER

19

The **while** and **repeat** statements perform indefinite iteration. The body of such a statement is repeated over and over based on the truth value of a conditional expression; it can—in principle—be performed any number of times. Some algorithms call for a different sort of iteration, one that performs some steps a specified number of times. The algorithm must count the number of times it has performed these steps to determine when the iteration must stop. This is *definite iteration*. Although you can perform definite iteration with **while** and **repeat** statements, they don't clearly express the underlying idea of counting. Pascal has a statement designed to implement definite iteration: the **for** *statement*. The full power of the **for** statement will become apparent only when we study the data structures known as *arrays* (Chapter 23). But we can show some of its uses here.

When **for** Statements Are Useful

Suppose we want to write a program that will read exactly 100 numbers typed by the user and print their sum. Clearly this problem involves iteration. We could write a procedure to read the numbers and compute the total using a **while** statement. Figure 19.1 shows such a procedure. A sample execution of this procedure would start off like this (the user's input is in italics):

```
Enter number 1:  346 ↵
Enter number 2:  9002 ↵
Enter number 3:  −623 ↵
  .  .  .
```

DEFINITE ITERATION

Figure 19.1   **Procedure** *getnumbers*

```pascal
procedure getnumbers(var total: integer);
  { reads 100 numbers and computes their sum }

const numnum = 100;

var     inputnum,              { holds the user's input }
        counter: integer;      { counts numbers read }

begin { getnumbers }
  counter := 1;
  while counter <= numnum do
    begin  { the body of the while }
        write('Enter number ', counter:1,':');
        readln(inputnum);
        total := total + inputnum;
        counter := counter + 1
    end   {of the body of the while }
end; { getnumbers }
```

There's a pattern of statements in procedure *getnumbers* that occurs so often that it becomes a programming cliché and warrants a construct of its own. This is the pattern:

```pascal
counter := 1;
while counter <= somelimit do
```

(continued)

```
        begin { while }
               .
               .    { some statements here }
               .
        counter : = counter + 1
    end { while }
```

In other words, we're using the **while** loop to count from 1 to *somelimit*, and at each step we're doing something and then incrementing our counter. The **for** statement is designed for such situations. Actually, there are two versions of the **for** statement: one to count forward and one to count backward.

The Syntax and Semantics of **for** Statements

Figure 19.2 shows the syntax of both versions of the **for** statement (or, as it's often called, the **for** loop). Since branched arrows point to the reserved words **to** and **downto** in the syntax diagram, one of the two words must be used at that point. The choice determines which way the **for** statement will count. The statement that follows the reserved word **do** may be either a simple or a compound statement. It is referred to as the *body* of the **for** loop.

The identifier called for in the syntax diagram must be the name of a variable. Known as the *loop control variable,* it plays the same role as the variable *counter* in the **while** loop. The loop control variable and the two expressions must all have the same or compatible type. (Although this type is often *integer*, it need not be. Pascal has very general notions about what counting is.) Figure 19.3 shows a version of procedure *getnumbers* that uses a **for** loop.

Figure 19.2   Syntax diagram of a for statement

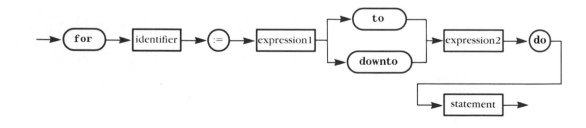

Figure 19.3   Procedure *getnumbers2*

```
procedure getnumbers2(var total: integer);
   {reads 100 numbers and computes their sum}

const    numnum = 100;

var      inputnum,                    { holds the user's input }
         counter: integer;           {counts numbers read }

begin { getnumbers }
   for counter := 1 to numnum do
           begin
                 write('Enter number ', counter:1, ': ');
                 readln (inputnum);
                 total := total + inputnum
           end { for loop }
end; { getnumbers }
```

This version of the procedure does the same writing, reading, and accumulating as the **while** loop in Figure 19.1. The **for** statement takes care of initializing *counter* to 1, incrementing it at the end of the body of the loop, and testing to see whether the loop is finished. Note that whereas initializing and incrementing are explicit in the **while** version, they are invisible in the **for** version. To understand how the procedure in Figure 19.3 works, we need a description of the semantics of the **for** statement. Here is a description for the first form of the **for** statement, which uses the reserved word **to** and counts forward:

I. Expression1 (see the syntax diagram, Figure 19.2) is evaluated.

II. Expression2 is evaluated.

III. If the value of Expression1 is less than or equal to the value of Expression2, then:
   A. The loop control variable is assigned the value of Expression1.
   B. The following steps are repeated until the value of the loop control variable is greater than the value of Expression2:
      1. The body of the **for** loop is executed.
      2. The loop control variable is incremented. If the type of the loop control variable is *integer,* it is increased by 1. Some other data types also have a natural notion of incrementing, as we will see.

IV. Control passes on to the next statement after the **for** loop.

To summarize: The body of the loop is executed once for each value of the loop control variable between the values of Expression1 and Expression2 inclusive. If the value of Expression1 is greater than the value of Expression2, then the body of the loop is skipped.

There are a number of semantic considerations you must be aware of when you use a **for** statement. You must remember to declare the loop control variable, just as you declare any other variable. The two expressions, which determine the limits of the loop control variable, can be of any desired complexity; they need not be constants or simple variables. However, they must both be of the same type as the loop control variable or of a compatible type. Figure 19.4 shows an example of a **for** loop in which the limits are integer expressions.

Exercise 19.1: Suppose the variables *rate*, *time*, and *error* are given the values

```
rate : = 300
time : = 60
error : = 3
```

What will be the output of the code in Figure 19.4? ■

Among the common errors in the use of **for** loops is this one:

```
counter : = 1;    { Superfluous! }
for counter : = 1 to . . . do
```

Here the first statement is unnecessary; it's done automatically by the **for** statement. Another common error is this:

```
for counter : = 1 to somethingorother do
   begin
        . . .
        counter : = counter + 1  { WRONG!!! }
   end
```

This is an error because *counter* is automatically being incremented at the bottom of the body of the loop. In fact, Pascal specifically forbids any statement in the

Figure 19.4   A for statement with complex expressions

```
writeln('Possible distances: ');
for dist : = (rate * time − error) to (rate * time + error) do
      writeln(dist:6)
```

body of the loop that will alter the value of the control variable.[1] The **for** statement itself controls the loop control variable.

The semantics of the second type of **for** statement, which uses the reserved
word **downto**, are similar. They differ only in the following respects:

- In step III, the body of the **for** loop will be performed when Expression1 has
a value that is greater than or equal to the value of Expression2.

- In step III.B, steps 1 and 2 are repeated until the value of the loop control
variable becomes less than the value of Expression2.

- In step III.B.2, the loop control value is decremented rather than incremented.
That is, its value is decreased to the next lower value.

In other words, one form of the **for** loop counts up, starting at a fixed value and
going on to some other value, executing the loop's body each count. The other
form does the same counting downward.

Figure 19.5 gives a silly version of the loop we encountered in Figure 19.1 as
a **while** statement and in Figure 19.3 as a **for** statement. This version also requests *numnum* numbers, but it asks for them backward. The only difference between this loop and the one in Figure 19.3 is that here the **for** statement starts
counter off at *numnum* and counts down to 1. The execution of the loop in
Figure 19.5 would start like this:

```
Enter number 100:  7462 ⏎
Enter number 99:  53 ⏎
Enter number 98:  291 ⏎
        .
        .
        .
```

Figure 19.6 gives a piece of Pascal code that might be useful at Cape Canaveral. In
this example, the last *writeln* statement is not part of the body of the **for** loop
and is not repeated. It is done after the last iteration of the **for** statement has been
completed.

Figure 19.5 **A downto version of a for statement**

```
for counter : = numnum downto 1 do
    begin { for }
        write ('Enter number ', counter:1, ': ');
        readln (inputnum) ;
        total : = total + inputnum
    end { for }
```

1. The effect of such a statement differs from one implementation of Pascal to another. Many
versions of Pascal will issue a compile-time error when such a statement is encountered.

Figure 19.6   **An example of a downto for statement**

```
for counter := 10 downto 1 do
        write ( counter:1, '...');
writeln('Blastoff!')
```

Exercise   19.2: Trace the execution of the code fragment in Figure 19.6. Show exactly what the output will be.   ■

19.2   COMPARING DEFINITE AND INDEFINITE ITERATION

Loosely speaking, definite iteration is based on counting while indefinite iteration is based on testing the truth of a conditional expression. But this distinction has some subtle implications. Consider the **while** loop shown in Figure 19.7. This fragment contains an example of very poor programming practice; we show it only to illustrate a point. What will this fragment do? It will print the numbers from 1 to 20 inclusive. Although the value of *limit* is set to 10 at the start, it is almost immediately reset to 20, and the condition

```
counter <= limit
```

is evaluated before each iteration. That means the values of *counter* and *limit* are inspected each time, and after the first time through the **while** statement the value of *limit* will be 20 and will stay at 20. (It is assigned this value 19 times!)

Figure 19.7   **A while loop with a misplaced statement**

```
limit := 10;
counter := 1;
while counter <= limit do
    begin { while }
        limit := 20; { This statement is misplaced! }
        writeln ( counter );
        counter := counter + 1
    end { while }
```

Figure 19.8   **A f or loop with a misplaced statement**

```
limit : = 10;
for counter : = 1 to limit do
    begin { for }
        limit : = 20;  { This statement is misplaced! }
        writeln ( counter )
    end { for }
```

The fragment in Figure 19.8 looks a lot like the fragment in Figure 19.7, but it uses a **for** loop. What will this fragment do? It will print the numbers from 1 to 10, not from 1 to 20. It's true that the value of *limit* will be 20 after the first time through the loop, but the semantics of the **for** statement obey the following rule:

> Evaluation rule: *The expressions that describe the limits of the* **for** *loop are evaluated only once. The values are stored (in unnamed locations) before the first execution of the body of the* **for***, and it is those values that are used to determine how many times the body of the loop will be executed.*

The consequence of this rule is that, at the moment the **for** statement is reached, it is possible to determine how many times the body of the statement will be executed. This is the characteristic property of definite iteration. The corresponding rule is not true for **while** or **repeat** loops; events that occur during some execution of the body of a **while** or a **repeat** loop may determine how many times the loop will be executed.

This rule gives you a good way to decide which iterative construct you should use: Use **for** statements to control iteration when the number of times the iteration should occur does not depend on anything that happens during the iteration. Use **while** and **repeat** statements when the number of times the iteration should occur may depend on something that happens during the iteration.

19.3 CONSIDERATIONS WHEN USING f or STATEMENTS

There is another subtle difference between apparently equivalent **while** and **for** loops. Figure 19.9 illustrates it with a code fragment that combines both types of statements. The first part of this fragment initializes *counter* to 1 and then writes each value of *counter* and increments it as long as *counter* has a value less than or equal to 10. The **while** loop will stop only when the condition

```
counter <= 10
```

Figure 19.9   Apparently equivalent while and for loops

```
counter : = 1;
while counter <= 10 do
    begin { while }
        writeln(counter);
        counter : = counter + 1
    end; { while }
writeln('Now the value of counter is ', counter:1);

for counter : = 1 to 10 do
        writeln(counter);
writeln('Now the value of counter is ', counter:1);
```

is *false*—in other words, only when the value of counter is 11. When the **while** loop is finished, the program will display

```
Now the value of counter is 11
```

Then it will execute the **for** loop. This sets the value of *counter* back to 1 and then writes and increments the value of *counter* 10 times. But what is printed next? We can't say! Different versions of Pascal will print different results (most will print either 10 or 11), but the Pascal rule is

> *The value of the loop control variable after the completion of a* **for** *statement is undefined.*

In other words, you can't assume that the loop control variable will have any particular value when the **for** loop is finished. The computer system you happen to be using may follow some definite behavior, but any program that depends on the value of the loop control variable after a **for** loop may execute differently on different systems.

Another semantic rule involving the loop control variable is this:

> *The loop control variable of a* **for** *loop must be declared in the same block in which the* **for** *loop occurs.*

This rule is not enforced by all Pascal translators, but you should adhere to it to guarantee the portability of your programs.

One error that occurs fairly often in using **for** loops is infuriatingly difficult to discover. It occurs when you put an extra semicolon in the wrong place, as shown in Figure 19.10. Notice that the only difference between this **for** loop and the one shown in Figure 19.5 is the semicolon after **do**. The consequences, how-

Figure 19.10   A common bug—an extra semicolon after do

```
for counter := 1 to numnum do;
    begin { for }
        write('Enter number ', counter:1, ':');
        readln(inputnum);
        total := total + inputnum
    end { for }
```

ever, are distressing. The body of this **for** statement consists of an empty statement—nothing. Recall the syntax diagram in Figure 19.2. Syntactically, the body of the **for** statement is the statement that appears after the word **do**. In Pascal, a null statement, which consists of no symbols at all, is legal. The Pascal compiler will interpret the semicolon in Figure 19.10 as delimiting a null statement and will take that statement as the body of the loop. It will not associate the succeeding compound statement, bracketed by **begin** and **end**, with the **for** and will execute that statement just once.

This error is difficult to spot because the semicolon is small and because it occurs at the end of a line where it seems natural. Moreover, many people believe that the translator will spot the error. It will not. The misplaced semicolon in this example is syntactically correct; it means something perfectly legal. It just doesn't mean what the programmer meant to write.

19.4 THE TYPES OF LOOP CONTROL VARIABLES

We mentioned earlier that the loop control variable in a **for** statement need not be of *integer* type. In fact, the data types known as *ordinal types* are permissible. Loosely described, *ordinal types* are those data types in which there is a meaningful notion of the "next value."[2] For example, integers are an ordinal type. For any *integer*, there's a well-defined notion of the next *integer*. In Chapter 20, we will encounter the type *real*, which is a non-ordinal type. Variables of type *real* represent numbers that may have fractional parts. A characteristic of such numbers is that there is no such thing as the "next" number after a given *real* number. (What would be the next number after 6.1753?) Thus, we are not allowed to construct **for** loops where the loop control variable is of type *real*.

The type *char* is an ordinal type. Each of the characters in the computer's character set is encoded internally by an integer, and this encoding gives rise to the notion of "next character." The standard character encoding in the United States is ASCII. In the ASCII encoding (sometimes called the ASCII character set),

---

2. In Chapter 21, we'll give a precise definition and describe some more ordinal types.

the lowercase letters are in alphabetical order with no intervening characters. The same is true for the uppercase letters. It is not true of the other character set widely used in this country, however—the encoding known as EBCDIC. The following perfectly legal **for** loop will print the lowercase alphabet on a machine with the ASCII character encoding (assume the variable *charvalue* has been declared of type *char*):

```
for charvalue := 'a' to 'z' do
        write (charvalue)
```

And the following **for** loop will print the uppercase alphabet backward on a machine with the ASCII character encoding:

```
for charvalue := 'Z' downto 'A' do
        write (charvalue)
```

Note the use of the **downto** form of the **for** statement. The value of 'Z' is greater (in both ASCII and EBCDIC) than the value of 'A', and the values of the loop control variable must be decremented, not incremented, to get from 'Z' to 'A'. The general notion of incrementing and decrementing for ordinal types is

> *A variable is incremented by replacing its value by the next successive value of the same type. A variable is decremented by replacing its value by the immediately preceding value of the same type.*

19.5 NESTED for LOOPS

It's often useful to write one **for** statement inside the body of another in what are referred to as *nested* **for** *loops*. They are particularly useful for manipulating the structures called multidimensional arrays (see Chapter 25), but they are useful in other situations as well. Here's a simple example. Suppose we want to draw rectangular forms filled with characters on the terminal screen. For example, here's a 4 × 9 rectangle filled with *'s:

```
* * * * * * * *
* * * * * * * *
* * * * * * * *
* * * * * * * *
```

If our goal is simply to draw a rectangle of known size, we can accomplish that with a few *writeln* statements. But if we want to ask the user to specify the dimensions of the rectangle, *writeln* statements alone will not suffice. Here is a sketch of an algorithm for this problem:

Setup

I. Reserve spaces named *numrows* and *numcols* for integer values.

Instructions

I. Get the user's input in *numrows* and *numcols.*

II. Draw the rectangle according to the values in *numrows* and *numcols.*

Step II needs further refinement. Since we don't know the dimensions when we write the program, we have to draw the rectangle one * at a time. We'll draw each row of the rectangle by iteratively writing *' s, and we'll draw the whole rectangle by iteratively drawing rows. We must be careful to advance the cursor to the next line once after each row. Step II can be refined like this:

II. Draw the rectangle by doing the following steps:
    A. For each value from 1 to *numrows,* do the following:
        1. For each value from 1 to *numcols,* do the following:
           i. Write an *.
        2. Advance to the start of the next line.

Exercise   19.3: Refine step I of the algorithm. Then draw a data flow diagram for the entire program.   ■

A complete program to print rectangles is shown in Figure 19.11. Pay particular attention to the procedure named `printrect`. Note carefully which statements constitute the body of each **for** loop.

The nested **for** statements in procedure `printrect` work like this: When the outer loop starts to execute, the loop control variable `row` gets the value 1. Then the inner loop runs to completion with `col` taking on each of the values from 1 to `numcols` inclusive. For each such value, the body of the inner **for** statement is performed: A single character is written. When the inner loop exits, the `writeln` is done. This finishes a row by moving the cursor to the next line. Then `row` gets the value 2, and the inner loop runs again in its entirety.

Exercise   19.4: Suppose a user who is running program `rectangles` enters the value 3 for `numrows` and 2 for `numcols`. Trace the execution of procedure `printrect` with those values.   ■

Figure 19.11   Program to print rectangular forms filled with ∗'s

```
program rectangles(input, output);
  { This program prints rectangular shapes of some character with a }
  { width and height specified by the user. It illustrates }
  { the use of nested for statements. }

const    rectchar = '*'; { Change the character if you }
                         { want a different filler. }

var      numrows,            { number of rows in rectangle }
         numcols: integer;       { and number of columns }

         procedure getdimensions(var height, width: integer);
           { asks user for dimensions of rectangle }
           { reads answers, then skips a line to set }
           { off the rectangle }
         begin    { getdimensions }
            write('How many rows do you want in the rectangle? ');
            readln(height);
            write('How many columns do you want? ');
            readln(width);
            writeln
         end;     { getdimensions }

         procedure printrect(nrow, ncol: integer);
           { prints the rectangle as required }
         var row,            { loop control variable for rows }
             col: integer;       { l.c.v. for columns }
         begin    { printrect }
            for row := 1 to nrow do
                begin    { Print one row. }
                    for col := 1 to ncol do
                        write( rectchar );
                    writeln       { End the row. }
                end    { Print one row. }
         end;      { printrect }

begin { main program - rectangles }
        getdimensions(numrows, numcols);
        printrect(numrows, numcols)
end. { rectangles }
```

Exercise   19.5

a. What will happen if the user types a negative value for *numrows*? What if the user types a positive value for *numrows* but a negative value for *numcols*?

b. What will happen if the *writeln* statement is moved inside the body of the inner **for** loop?

```
for row : = 1 to nrow do
    for col : = 1 to ncol do
        begin
            write ( rectchar );
            writeln { End the row. }
        end
```

c. Modify program *rectangles* to range-check the user's input: If the user enters values that are less than 1 or greater than 80, reject them as being out of range and prompt for new values until valid values are entered. Use an appropriate iterative construct.   ■

Exercise   19.6: The expressions that describe the initial and final values of the loop control variable in an inner **for** loop can depend on the current value of the outer loop's control variable. Use this fact to modify program *rectangles* to produce program *triangles*, which prints triangles of the following sort:

```
*
**
***
****
```

In each row, the number of *'s is the same as the row number.   ■

CHAPTER SUMMARY

1. The distinction between *definite* and *indefinite iteration* is that an indefinite iterative construct repeats some actions based on a condition, and the truth value of that condition may be changed by the repeated actions. A definite iterative construct repeats some actions based on counting, and the range of the count is fixed before the actions are begun.

2. The **for** *statement* is Pascal's construct for definite iteration. The body of a **for** statement is executed under the control of a loop control variable, which

counts up or down from one value to another. The values are fixed before the loop is entered and cannot be modified during the loop. It is possible for the body of a **for** statement to be executed zero times.

3. The **for** statement counts by using an auxiliary variable, called the *loop control variable*. This variable must be declared in the same block in which the **for** loop occurs. It can be of any ordinal type. The expressions that describe the limits of counting must be of the same or compatible type.

4. You may not change the value of the loop control variable inside the body of a **for** loop. The value of the loop control variable is undefined when the loop exits.

COMMON ERRORS

- Omitting the loop control variable and the assignment symbol in a **for** statement, so that the resulting construct looks like

  for 1 **to** 10 **do** . . .

- Inserting a semicolon after the keyword **do** in **while** or **for** statements. This has the effect of giving a null body to the loop.
- Omitting the keywords **begin** and **end** around the body of a **for** loop. This has the effect of making the first statement after the **do** the body of the loop. This error is often obscured by spurious indenting, as in

  for counter := 1 **to** limit **do**
          readln(usernum);
          total := total + usernum;

  Only the *readln* is in the body for the **for** statement.

- Attempting to modify the control variable of a **for** loop inside the body of the loop.
- Forgetting to declare the loop control variable of a **for** loop or declaring this variable in a scope larger than the block in which the **for** loop occurs.
- Using the value of a loop control variable outside the loop.

DEBUGGING HINTS

- Display the value of the loop control variable as soon as the loop is entered to check its value.

- Display the values of the two expressions that control the loop before the loop is entered.

- Insert a *writeln* as the last statement in the loop to ensure that everything you had intended is contained in the loop.

- Insert a *writeln* statement after the end of the loop to be sure that the body of the loop does not extend further than intended.

SUPPLEMENTAL PROBLEMS

1. Write a program to compute and print the average grade on an exam that is graded on the scale 0 to 100. The program should accept integers between 0 and 100 (inclusive) as input, rejecting any other values. It should accept exactly 30 input values. Do not include any out-of-range values in your calculations.

2. Modify the program you wrote for problem 1 to display the highest and lowest grade as well as the average. (Recall the fundamental algorithms for finding the minimum and maximum of a sequence of values in Chapter 6.)

3. a. Write a program that prints triangles sized according to the user's input like those in Exercise 19.7, but upside down:

```
****
***
**
*
```

   b. Write a program that prints rectangles sized according to the user's input like those printed in program *rectangles* (Figure 19.11), except that the rectangles should be hollow:

```
********
*      *
*      *
********
```

   The first and last rows should be full rows of *'s, and the intervening rows should have a *, an appropriate number of blanks, and another *.

4. Rewrite procedure *printrec* of program *rectangles* using **while** statements instead of **for** statements.

5. Rewrite procedure *printrec* of program *rectangles* using **repeat** statements instead of **for** statements. Make sure that your revised procedure produces the same output as the original for every possible input value typed by the user.

6. Sometimes you want to perform iteration based on counting, but you don't want to count every number. Rather, you may wish to count every other number or every tenth number. Some programming languages have special constructs to do this, but Pascal does not. You can accomplish the same effect using ordinary **for** statements.

   a. Write procedure *printoddsquares*, which prints the squares of the first 20 odd numbers. Use a loop that iterates only 20 times. (Hint: Use an extra variable. As the loop control variable takes on the values 1, 2, 3, . . ., 20, arrange for the other variable to take on the values 1, 3, 5, . . ., 39.)

   b. Write a procedure that is passed the three *integer* parameters *start*, *interval*, and *count*. The procedure should print *count* integers, starting at *start* and incrementing each time by *interval*. Use a **for** statement to perform the iteration.

7. Suppose the **downto** version of the **for** statement was not part of the Pascal language. Show how you can achieve the effect of a **for** . . . **downto** statement whose loop control variable is of type *integer* by using a **for** . . . **to** statement and an extra *integer* variable. Can you do the same with a **for** . . . **downto** statement whose loop control variable is of type **char**? Why or why not?

8. Modify program *rectangles* (Figure 19.11) as follows: Repeatedly print rectangles, starting with the dimensions provided by the user and decreasing the height and width of each rectangle by 1 each time. Thus, if the user enters a height of 10 and a width of 3, your program should print rectangles whose dimensions are 10 × 3, 9 × 2, and 8 × 1 and then terminate. Print a blank line after each rectangle.

9. Write a program that determines whether the character m or the character { comes first in your computer's character set. The program should then use **for** loops to print the characters between m and {, first in ascending order and then in descending order.

10. Write a program that allows the user to enter two numbers and then prints a multiplication table for all the numbers in the range between them. For example, if the user enters 98 and 102, the program should display

```
     |   98 |   99 |  100 |  101 |  102 |
-----|------|------|------|------|------|
  98 | 9604 | 9702 | 9800 | 9898 | 9996 |
-----|------|------|------|------|------|
  99 | 9702 | 9801 | 9900 | 9999 |10098 |
-----|------|------|------|------|------|
 100 | 9800 | 9900 |10000 |10100 |10200 |
-----|------|------|------|------|------|
 101 | 9898 | 9999 |10100 |10201 |10302 |
-----|------|------|------|------|------|
 102 | 9996 |10098 |10200 |10302 |10404 |
-----|------|------|------|------|------|
```

You should print row and column headers and separators as shown. Your program should not accept numbers that differ by more than 9 in order to keep the size of the table reasonably small. However, you should accept positive or negative input, and the user should be able to type the two numbers in any order.

CHAPTER

20

20.1 *real* DATA

The data type *real* is used for data items that represent numeric values that might not be whole numbers. The type name *real* comes from the term *real numbers* in mathematics, where it means all the numbers—positive, negative, and zero—that can be represented as decimals, including infinite decimals. In Pascal, data items of type *real* are ideally intended to represent any of the possible values that a real number may have. That isn't actually possible, however, since there are an infinite number of possible real numbers. Before we examine the consequences of that fact, let's see how we do arithmetic with values of type *real*.

20.2 ARITHMETIC WITH *real* VALUES

Most of the notation and ideas of *real* arithmetic are consistent with *integer* arithmetic. Figure 20.1 shows some data declarations, followed by some program fragments and comments that explain what the fragments mean.

The Symbols Used to Indicate *real* Operators

In Pascal, we use the symbols $+$, $-$, and $*$ to indicate the operations of addition, subtraction, and multiplication of *real* values, just as we do with *integer* values. This is not true of division, however, because the ideas behind *integer* division and *real* division are somewhat different. The **div** operator used for *integer*

THE TYPE *real*

Figure 20.1 **Declarations, expressions, and assignments with *real* values**

```
const   salestax = 0.065;          {6.5 % tax rate}
        commissionfactor = 0.22;   {22 % sales commission}

var     wholesale,                 {wholesale cost}
        markup,                    {markup over wholesale}
        retail,                    {retail price}
        commission,                {sales commission}
        price,                     {retail plus sales tax}
        profit: real;              {markup less commission}
              .   .   .
        retail := wholesale + markup;
                { Plus sign is used for adding reals as}
                {  well as integers.}
        commission := retail * commissionfactor;
                { same for multiplication symbol }
        profit := markup − commission;
                { same for subtraction symbol }
        price := retail + retail * salestaxfactor;
```

division always yields an *integer* result, with any remainder being ignored. We can find the remainder by using the **mod** operator (see pages 358–359). The notion of remainder is meaningless for *real* numbers, however, because any *real* number (except 0) exactly divides any other *real* number. The quotient of two *reals* is a *real*. We use the symbol / to denote division with a *real* result. Figure 20.2 gives an example of its use. Note that the precedence of the / operator is the same

425

Figure 20.2   **Example of the / operator**

```
distance : = 180.0;
time : = 3.2;
rate : = distance / time;
        {Rate will get the value 56.25.}
```

as that of the other multiplicative operators, as we indicated in Chapter 18 (see page 395).

It's possible to use the operator / between two expressions of type *integer*, as well as between two expressions of type *real*. It's even possible to have one operand of / be *integer* and the other be *real*. In every case, the result will be of type *real*. The fragment in Figure 20.3 shows the difference between **div** and /. Note, however, that the statement

```
intquot : = 9 / 4            { ERROR! }
```

is an error, because the type of the expression on the right side of the assignment operator : = is *real*, while the type of the variable on the left is *integer*. Since *integer* variables can't hold all the values that *real*s can represent, the translator will signal an error if you try to assign *real* values to *integer* variables.

Pascal allows you to mix *integer* and *real* operands when you use the arithmetic operators +, −, and *. However, the type of the result will always be *real*. Thus, if *hoursworked* is a variable of type *real*, the following statement is legal:

```
hoursworked : = hoursworked + 1
```

That statement is equivalent to this statement

```
hoursworked : = hoursworked + 1.0
```

On the other hand, if *numdays* is a variable of type *integer*, the following statement is not legal:

```
numdays : = numdays + 1.0 {assigns real value to integer}
```

Since one of the operands is of type *real*, the expression on the right of the assignment is of type *real*, and *real* values cannot be assigned to *integer* variables.

Figure 20.3 **The difference between** div **and** / **used with integers**

```
var     intquot: integer:
        realquot: real;

          .  .  .

        intquot := 9 div 4;      {yields integer value 2}
        realquot := 9 / 4;       {yields real value 2.25}
```

Pascal allows assignment statements in which a value of type *integer* is assigned to a variable of type *real*. Thus, the following assignment is legal:

```
var     int1,
        int2: integer;
        realval: real;

          .  .  .

        int1 := 83;
        int2 := 63;
        realval := int1 - int2; {gets value 20.0}
```

The reason Pascal permits such assignments is that every legal *integer* value is also a legal *real* value.[1] The reverse, however, is not true. The following assignment is not valid:

```
var     real1,
        real2: real;
        intval: integer;

          .  .  .

        real1 := 83.4;
        real2 := 63.3;
        intval := real1 - real2;          {Not legal!}
```

Since assigning a *real* value to an *integer* variable may result in a loss of accuracy, Pascal does not permit it. For example, the illegal statement above attempts to assign the value 20.1 to an *integer* variable. On occasion, you may want to "throw away the fractional part" and do the assignment anyway, but you can't do that simply by assigning a *real* value to an *integer* variable. (There is a way of doing it, as we'll see in Chapter 22.)

---

1. The computer's internal representations of an *integer* and the corresponding *real* are very different, however. Thus, if you assign an *integer* value to a *real* variable, Pascal silently converts the *integer* into a representation of the same value as a *real*. This process is sometimes referred to as *type coercion* or *type conversion*.

Expressions of type *`real`* and *`integer`* can be compared using the relational operators. As we mentioned in Chapter 15 (page 332), values of all numeric types can be compared with one another.

Figure 20.4 shows a short program that asks the user for some values and then computes the average value. The numbers may have fractional parts.

The program in Figure 20.4 will produce output that includes *`real`* values. Try running it. The answers will look strange. We'll explain later why this is so and how you can make the output look more like usual decimal notation. But this requires a preliminary discussion of the possible values of *`real`* data items. If you're familiar with scientific notation (sometimes called *exponential notation,* or *floating point notation*), you'll already know much of what we have to say in the next section. If you're completely unfamiliar with infinite decimals or with exponents, you may find it rough going. And if you are only interested in making *`real`* output look like standard decimal notation and don't want to understand the reasons for Pascal's conventions about displaying *`real`* data, just skip to page 433.

Exercise   20.1: Modify program *`average`* in Figure 20.4 as follows: Instead of asking the user how many numbers to average, have the program accept numbers until a value of 0 is entered. Then have it compute and display the average of all the numbers entered up to, but not including, the 0 value. Be sure your program will behave sensibly in the event the user enters 0 as the first input value!   ∎

An Aside: Scientific Notation

Data items of type *`real`* may have such values as 2.6, −99999.9999, 0.00005, and −3.14159265. For many purposes, you can consider such data items to be equivalent to ordinary decimal numbers. There are, however, some important differences between the two. Those differences are related to the limitations of the computer's hardware. The computer can represent only a finite number of different values for a data item. But an infinite number of possible decimals exists. In the case of integers, we solve the problem by limiting the range of values between *`maxint`* (which, on the authors' computer, is 2147483647) and −*`maxint`* (see page 357).

This solution won't work for *`real`*s, however. There is an infinite number of reals even between the *`real`* numbers −1.0 and 1.0. (That is true, in fact, between any two *`real`* numbers.) We have to restrict not only the allowed range but also the precision of the numbers we're allowed to represent. In decimal terms, that's like saying we can write numbers only to a fixed number of decimal places. Those restrictions leave us with a finite number of numbers that can be represented. For instance, if the restrictions specified a range of −1000 through 1000 and a maxi-

Figure 20.4   Program *average*

```
program average ( input, output );
   {This program asks the user how many numbers to average. It then asks}
   {for that many numbers, totals them up, and finally}
   {computes an average. }

var      numofnums: integer;        {number of numbers to average}

         procedure getnumofnums(var numnum: integer);
            {asks for and gets number of numbers}
         begin    {getnumofnums}
            write ( 'Enter the number of numbers to average: ');
            readln ( numnum )
         end;     {getnumofnums}

         procedure getnums(numnum: integer);
         {initializes total to 0, gets the input data,}
         {accumulates it, and computes the average}

         var count: integer;      {to count how many input}
                inputnum,         {to hold input}
                total,            {to accumulate input}
                average: real;    {where we'll compute average}

         begin    {getnums}
             total := 0.0;           {0.0 is the REAL number 0}
             for  count := 1 to numnum do
                  begin
                      write ( ' Enter number ', count:1, ': ');
                      readln ( inputnum );
                      total := total + inputnum
                  end; {for}
             average := total / numnum;
             writeln (' The average of these is ', average )
         end; {getnums}
begin    {average}
         getnumofnums (numofnums);
         if numofnums > 0
             then
                 getnums (numofnums)
end.     {average}
```

mum of three places to the right of the decimal point, the real numbers that satisfied those restrictions would be finite in number.[2]

We encounter much the same situation when we use a pocket calculator, which is a kind of computer. Pocket calculators have both limited range and limited precision. You can't enter more digits than the display can handle. This doesn't make calculators useless, but it means that you have to use them with care. For example, if you divide 1 by 3 mathematically, and then multiply the quotient (1/3) by 3, the arithmetic result is 1. But, since 1/3 is an infinite decimal, a pocket calculator can only approximate its value, 1/3, perhaps as 0.333333333. Then, when you multiply that value by 3, you get not 1 but 0.999999999. This is very close to the arithmetically correct answer, but it is not exact; it constitutes a representation error.

Pretty much the same thing happens when we try to do arithmetic with `real` data on a computer. Most computers use binary rather than decimal representation, so the representation errors are different. Still, the problems are analogous: Computers can store `real` numbers only up to a limited number of decimal places (or, more precisely, *binary places*).

The maximum number of binary places varies from one computer to another. The authors' computer, for example, can store `real` numbers to 56 binary places (56 digits after the binary point), which is roughly equivalent to 17 decimal places. That's a lot of decimal places. Very few computations, even scientific computations, need more accuracy than that.

The problem is, which 17 places do we use? If we use 17 places after the decimal point, we can't represent any numbers larger than 1. If we use 17 places before the decimal point, we lose the ability to represent fractions, and we might as well go back to integers. A compromise such as using 9 places before the decimal point and 8 after will be unsatisfactory in both respects; we may need to do a computation using the number of centimeters that light travels in a year (about 946045700000000000) or the number of seconds it takes light to travel one centimeter (about 0.0000000000333565).

In a sense, of course, the length of these numbers is artificial. Instead of measuring 946045700000000000 centimeters, we could measure 9460457000000000 meters, or 9460457000000 kilometers, or 9460457000 megameters, or 9460457 gigameters (billions of meters). They all indicate the same physical distance. The same is true of 0.0000000000333565 seconds, which we could write as 0.0333565 nanoseconds (billionths of a second). The point is that we need some way of keeping the number of trailing or leading zeroes from taking up the valuable digit space we need to represent what are called *significant digits*. Significant digits are any digits other than leading or trailing zeroes.[3] We might, for example, represent trailing zeroes by counting them and then writing 946045700000000000 as 9460457 × 100000000000. All we need to know about 100000000000 is that the number of zeroes is 11.

---

2. It wouldn't be fun to enumerate these numbers, though. There are 2001000 of them!

3. Thus, the 0 inside 9460457 is a significant digit.

Pascal uses a similar method of representation, but with a slightly different convention: The decimal point is shifted to the left as far as it can go up to the leftmost digit. Think of 946045700000000000 as 9.460457 × 100000000000000000. Since the number 100000000000000000 is the 17th power of 10, we can write it exponentially as 10^{17}. But, since most computer terminals can't handle superscripts, Pascal uses the letter *e* (for exponent) as a synonym for the phrase *times ten to the power.* (Some implementations of Pascal use lowercase *e* while others use upper-case *E*.) The number after the *e* is the power of 10 and is called the exponent. Here are some numbers written in decimal format, in scientific notation, and in Pascal exponential notation:

123456.0	1.23456×10^5	1.23456e+05
123.456	1.23456×10^2	1.23456e+02
−450009.2	$−4.500092 \times 10^5$	−4.500092e+05
999999999.99	9.9999999999×10^8	9.9999999999e+8
3.14159	3.14159×10^0	3.14159e+00

In accordance with mathematical convention, 10 to the zeroth power is 1.

How does Pascal represent numbers that are between 0 and 1? In the number 0.0000000000333565, we can't shift the decimal to the left to find a significant digit, so we have to shift it to the right. Think of 0.0000000000333565 as 3.33565/ 100000000000. The convention in exponential notation is to write a denominator of 10^{11} as 10 to a negative exponent: $0.0000000000333565 = 3.33565 \times 10^{-11}$. In Pascal exponential notation, we write that number as 3.33565e−11. The negative sign is not a minus sign for the number; it goes with the power of 10. We write −0.0000000000333565 as −3.33565e−11. Here the leading minus sign indicates that the number is negative, and the second minus sign goes with the exponent. Here are some examples of decimal, scientific, and Pascal exponential notations for numbers with negative exponents:

0.5	5.0×10^{-1}	5.0e−01
0.0005	5.0×10^{-4}	5.0e−04
0.00123456	1.23456×10^{-3}	1.23456e−03
−0.11111	$−1.1111 \times 10^{-1}$	−1.1111e−01

Some programming languages refer to reals as *floating point numbers,* indicating that the decimal point "floats" to the correct place with a power of 10 making up for its displacement.

Exercise 20.2: Write the following numbers in Pascal exponential notation:

45.006	28900.0	0.00347	0.5
−1.830	−0.00045	1000000000.0	0.25 ∎

If you use a `real` value with `write` or `writeln`, Pascal will display it in exponential notation unless you request otherwise.

The Syntax of `real`s

The simplest way to illustrate the syntax of `real` numbers is by example. Figure 20.5 shows several legal ways to write the two numbers 1/2 and −1/4:

Here's a description, in words, of the syntax of a `real` constant:

A `real` *constant consists of an optional sign (+ or −), followed by one or more digits, followed by an optional decimal point that, if present, must be followed by one or more digits, followed by an optional e or E that, if present, may be followed by an optional sign but must then be followed by one or more digits. At least one of the decimal point or the e or the E must occur. (Otherwise, the constant is an* `integer`.)

The syntax diagram in Figure 20.6 may clarify this somewhat complex description. Figure 20.7 shows some illegal `real` constants.

Figure 20.5   Different legal ways to write 1/2 and −1/4

1/2	−1/4
0.5	−0.25
5.0e−1	−2.5E−1
5E−1	−25e−2
+0.5	−25.0e−2
+5.0e−1	−0.025E+01
+5E−1	−0.25e+00

Figure 20.6   Syntax diagram for `real` constants

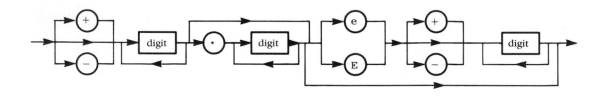

Figure 20.7   **Some illegal** **real** **constants**

```
.3       {no digits before decimal point}
-.5      {ditto}
e-01     {no digits before 'e'}
34.      {no digits after decimal point}
2.e4     {ditto}
```

Figure 20.8   **Several equivalent assignment statements**

```
realval := 1.0
realval := 1.0e0
realval := 1e+00
realval := 10.0e-1      {This is a silly way to write it.}
realval := 0.01e+02     {So is this.}
```

Any of the legal representations of a **real** number may be used to write constants in a program or to enter **real** input from a keyboard. All of the statements in Figure 20.8 are equivalent.

Displaying **real** Output

We can use field width specifiers to control the number of print positions a **real** value occupies when it is written out. However, the width specifier we described earlier doesn't provide all the control we need. We have to specify whether we want our output to be displayed in exponential notation or in decimal notation. (Exponential notation is far more compact for dealing with very large or very small numbers.) To select decimal notation we use a second specifier, which tells Pascal how many places to print to the right of the decimal. The syntax is shown in Figure 20.9. The first **integer** expression, if present, is the width specifier, and the second **integer** expression, if present, is the decimal specifier.

The semantics are as follows: If a width specifier is present, then it specifies the minimum number of print positions that will be reserved for displaying the output. If no decimal specifier is present, then the output will be printed in exponential notation and will always occupy at least seven positions, regardless of the value of the width specifier. The seven positions are

D. DeSDD

Figure 20.9   **Syntax diagram for outputting *real* numbers in decimal notation**

Here the *D*'s stand for digits, and the *S* stands for a + or − sign (the sign of the exponent). There will always be at least one digit before, and at least one digit after, the decimal point. If the specified width allows only an approximate value to be printed, the value will be rounded up or down. Thus, the statements

```
realval : = 647.791;
write ( realval:1);
```

will display the output

```
6.5e+02
```

The width specifier : 1 really says "use the minimum width," and the 5 after the decimal comes from rounding off 6.47791e+02 to fit. Note that a negative number is always preceded by a minus sign, regardless of the value of the width specifier. Thus,

```
realval : = −647.791;
write ( realval:1);
```

will display the output

```
−6.5e+02
```

Here an extra print position has been allocated for the leading minus sign.

The use of a decimal specifier *d* forces the output to be displayed in decimal notation. The value will be printed with exactly *d* digits to the right of the decimal point, rounded up or down if necessary, and all digits to the left of the decimal point will be displayed, along with a minus sign if needed. The total number of columns used by the displayed value will be at least the value of the width specifier, and possibly more if more are needed. Thus, the statements

```
realval : = 647.791;
write ( realval:1:1)
```

will display the output

```
647.8
```

Figure 20.10 shows a complete program that formats the value 4999.95 in several different ways. Try running that program, and see what output you get. On the authors' computer, the output is as shown in Figure 20.11. The spaces introduced into the output by the formatting request are indicated by a ∗.

Exercise 20.3: Show the output of the following program fragment:

```
writeln (245.37);
writeln (-6.02e1 :9:2);
writeln (0.0:1:0);
writeln (-28.95:1);  ■
```

The Inexactness of real Arithmetic (Optional)

Because the type *real* represents only a finite subset of all the real numbers, calculations using *real* values obey the laws of arithmetic only approximately and

Figure 20.10   Program to illustrate the formatting of reals

```pascal
program pricey (output);
    {demonstrate the consequences of using various choices}
    {of width and precision specifiers for formatting}
    {real output}

var     price: real;

begin
        price := 4999.95;
        writeln(price);            {exponential}
        writeln(price:10);         {exponential, limit to 10 positions}
        writeln(price:10:2);       {decimal, 2 decimals}
        writeln(price:10:3);       {decimal, 3 decimals}
        writeln(price:1);          {exponential, minimum width}
        writeln(price:0);          {exponential, minimum width}
        writeln(price:10:1);       {decimal, 1 decimal}
        writeln(price:10:0);       {decimal, no decimals}
        writeln('The price is $', price:1:2)
                        {decimal, 2 decimals, minimum width}
end.
```

Figure 20.11   Output from the program of Figure 20.10

The statement	Produces the output
`writeln(price);`	`ˏ4.99995000000000e+03`
`writeln(price:10);`	`ˏ5.000e+03`
`writeln(price:10:2);`	`ˏˏˏ4999.95`
`writeln(price:10:3);`	`ˏˏ4999.950`
`writeln(price:1);`	`5.0e+03`
`writeln(price:10:1);`	`ˏˏˏˏˏ5000.0`
`writeln(price:0);`	`5.0e+03`
`writeln(price:10:0);`	`ˏˏˏˏˏˏ5000`
`writeln('The price is $', price:1:2);`	
	`The price is $4999.95.`

ˏindicates a blank introduced by the formatting request.

can produce some subtly inexact results. A subfield of computer science called
numerical analysis studies the errors that arise in computations with *real*s (and
with their equivalents in other programming languages). Although we can't go into
the details of numerical analysis here, we can give a few examples.

Representation Errors

What is the output of the program shown in Figure 20.12? On the authors' computer, this program prints the word `Fuzzy`! On other computers, it may print the
word `Exact`! The reason is that our computer can handle only 17 significant
digits.[4] To compute the value

`1.0e+18 + 1.0`

our computer does the equivalent of the same alignment of decimal points that we
do manually:

$$\begin{array}{r} 1000000000000000000.0 \\ +1.0 \\ \hline 1000000000000000001.0 \end{array}$$

---

4. To simplify this discussion, we use decimal notation. Actually, as we have seen, the computer uses binary, not decimal, digits and has a binary point instead of a decimal point.

Figure 20.12   A program to illustrate inexact arithmetic

```
program realarith(output);
   {demonstrates the strange behavior of real arithmetic}
begin {realarith}
      if 1.0e+18 = (1.0e+18 + 1.0)
            then
                writeln('Fuzzy!')
            else
                writeln('Exact!')
   end. {realarith}
```

Then it saves the 17 most significant (leftmost) digits. Since these digits are identical with the first 17 digits of 1.0e+18, the computer can't distinguish between the two numbers. Other computers, which can preserve a greater number of significant digits, are able to distinguish between two numbers that differ in their first 19 digits. On such computers, the output of the program in Figure 20.12 is Exact!

Overflow and Underflow

Another example of inexact arithmetic concerns the phenomena of *overflow* and *underflow*. Overflow occurs when a computation produces a result that is larger than the largest number the computer can represent. For example, the largest real number our computer can represent is about 1.7e+38 (that's 17 followed by 37 zeros.) Suppose we tried to execute these statements:

```
var    verybig,
       verysmall,
       toobig: real;
         .  .  .
       verybig := 1.0e20;        {10 to the 20th power}
       verysmall := 1.0e-20;   {10 to the -20th power}
       toobig := verybig / verysmall;
                 {10 to the 40th power; toobig}
         .  .  .
```

The computer's attempt to perform the division here would result in overflow. Many Pascal implementations will detect the overflow, announce a run-time error, and halt execution. That is the best response, because if the program were to continue running, it would produce unpredictable results. Some computers treat the result of an overflow as if it were the largest legally representable value and continue with the program.

Underflow is a similar phenomenon. In any implementation of Pascal, there is

some smallest positive *real* number that can be represented. Conceivably, however, the result of some computation might be an even smaller positive number. For example, trying to compute

```
toosmall : = verysmall / verybig;
```

on the authors' computer with the previous values of *verysmall* and *verybig* will result in an underflow. Computers commonly deal with underflow in two ways: One is to halt execution and signal an error. The other is to substitute 0 for the result of the calculation. The 0 is "approximately correct" since an underflowing number is very close to zero. But the substitution may lead to some very strange results.

Exercise   20.4: Write programs to experiment with overflow and underflow on your version of Pascal. Determine

a. The highest power of 10 that your Pascal can represent as a *real*. (Hint: Initialize a *real* variable to the value 1.0. Then repeatedly multiply it by 10 and print the resulting value until the program crashes or gives nonsense results. In this case, exponential notation is probably the best form for the output.)

b. The lowest power of 10 that your Pascal can represent as a *real*.

c. The highest power of 2 that your Pascal can represent as a *real*.

d. The lowest power of 2 that your Pascal can represent as a *real*.

e. What action your Pascal takes when an overflow occurs.

f. What action your Pascal takes when an underflow occurs. ∎

A Mathematical Example (Optional)

In this section, we give an example of a simple mathematical application that uses *real*s. The problem is the computation of square roots by Newton's method. Newton's method is a technique for finding the approximate solutions of certain kinds of equations. It is commonly taught in first-year courses in the calculus. The application of this method to the problem of finding square roots works like this: Suppose we want to find the square root of the number **x**. Here's what we do:

1. Choose a first approximation for the square root of **x**. This can be a very rough approximation because the method will provide successively better ones. Call this first approximation *try*. We'll use the value of **x** itself for the initial value of *try*.

2. Repeatedly replace the value of **try** by the value

$$\frac{1}{2} * \left(try + \frac{x}{try} \right)$$

The values of **try** will get closer and closer to the square root of **x**. Stop when . . . well, when?

The problem is that we'll never get an exact value for the square root. In most cases, that value is an infinite decimal, which the computer can't represent. So we have to decide on an acceptable level of accuracy. Let's say that we'll quit when we get a value of **try** such that **try*try** differs from **x** by less than one ten-millionth of **x**.

When we write this condition in Pascal, we have to worry about whether **try*try** is going to be bigger than or smaller than **x**. Is our approximate value too big or too small? Actually, we would like to find the absolute value of the difference | **x − try*try** | . (In Chapter 22, we'll see how to do that. We'll also see that Pascal has a built-in facility for evaluating square roots.) For the moment, we'll just be careful about signs. Figure 20.13 gives a program that implements Newton's method for finding square roots.

Remember that **real** arithmetic produces inexact results. A common error in coding a program like this is to make the termination condition of the **repeat** something like

.
.
.

until x = try * try;

This might well lead to an infinite loop. In general, if you want to compare two **real** values, at least one of which is the result of computation, don't test for equality. Instead test to see if they differ by less than some small amount. The right value for that amount will depend on the computations.

Exercise 20.5: Enter program *newton* into your computer. Then

a. Modify the program so that it displays the value of **error** at the end of the **repeat** loop and also the value of **try*try**.

b. Modify the program so that it counts the number of times the **repeat** loop is executed and displays that count when the loop exits.

c. Modify the program so that the **repeat** loop tests for exact equality (**x** = **try*try**) , but ensure that it never loops more than 100 times. (Make sure

(continued on page 441)

Figure 20.13   Program *newton* for finding square roots

```
program newton(input,output);
  {This program demonstrates a mathematical application of the}
  { type real: the approximate calculation of }
  { square roots using Newton's Method.}

const    accuracy = 1.0e-7;          {one ten-millionth}

var      inputx: real;      {the user's number}

         procedure getx(var usersx: real);
         begin
             writeln('I can find square roots by Newton''s Method.');
             write('Enter the number whose square root you want: ');
             readln(usersx);        {prompt and get input}
             if usersx < 0
                 then     {No square roots of negative numbers!}
                         begin
                             writeln('You entered a negative value.');
                             writeln('I will ignore the sign.');
                             usersx := -usersx          {Make it positive.}
                         end {then}
         end;     {getx}

         procedure extractroot(x: real);
           {finds and displays the square root}
           {of its parameter}
         var      try,      {the approximating value to the root}
                  maxerr, {how much error to allow}
                  error: real;     {how much error so far}
         begin
             maxerr := x * accuracy;      {when to stop}
             try := x;    {first approximation}
             repeat
                 try := (try + x/try) / 2.0;       {next approx}
                 error := x - try * try;
                 if error < 0
                     then           {Make error positive for test.}
                             error := -error
             until error < maxerr;
             writeln('The square root of ', x:1:7,
                         ' is approximately ', try:1:7)
         end; {extractroot}
```

```
begin { newton }
        getx(inputx);
        extractroot(inputx)
end.  {newton}
```

Exercise 20.5 *(continued)*

that the number 100 is a named constant in your program!) Try the modified program with different input values, noting which ones terminate with exact equality and which do not. ■

CHAPTER SUMMARY

1. The type *real* is a predefined data type in Pascal. Variables of type *real* may have values that exactly represent some of the numeric values we usually write as decimals. The possible values of *real* variables depend on the particular implementation of Pascal.

2. Values of type *real* can be manipulated with the arithmetic operations of addition, subtraction, multiplication, and division. Real division is represented by the operator / (as opposed to the integer operator **div**) and always produces a result of type *real*. This is true even when the operands of / are of type *integer*.

3. Expressions using the operators +, −, *, and / can intermix operands of type *integer* and type *real*. If one or more of the operands is of type *real*, the entire expression will yield a *real* value.

4. To represent a wide range of *real* values, Pascal uses an internal representation similar to *scientific notation* (exponential, or floating-point, representation). The external (printed) representation of *real* values may take several forms, one of which is a form of scientific notation. You can control the printed form of *real*s by using width and precision specifiers.

5. Arithmetic with *real*s is approximate because not every number can be exactly represented as a *real* value. Programs written on the assumption that *real* arithmetic follows the normal laws of arithmetic may produce erroneous results.

COMMON ERRORS

- ■ Writing *real* constants in an invalid way—for example, omitting a digit before or after the decimal point
- ■ Assigning expressions of type *real* to variables of type *integer*
- ■ Trying to use *real* expressions with **div** and **mod** operators

DEBUGGING HINTS

- Insert parentheses in unparenthesized expressions if those expressions yield invalid results.

- Use auxilliary variables to hold intermediate values determined by a complicated expression and display the values of those variables.

- Check to be sure that the value you are calculating and any intermediate values do not fall out of the range of possible *real* values on your computer. Attempting to calculate values out of that range will result in erroneous results.

SUPPLEMENTAL PROBLEMS

1. Write a program that accepts as input an *integer* and displays the sum of the reciprocals of all the numbers from 1 to that *integer*. Thus, if the user enters the number 163, the program will compute

$$1/1 + 1/2 + 1/3 + 1/4 + \cdots + 1/163$$

and display this sum.

2. Write a program that will balance a checkbook. The program should read lines of input that consist of a character followed by a *real* value. The character should describe the type of transaction, and the value should be the amount of the transaction. The legal characters and their meanings are

 b   New balance. Ignore the old balance and make this amount the current balance. (This is useful as the first line of input.)
 c   Check. Subtract the corresponding amount from the current balance.
 d   Deposit. Add the corresponding amount to the current balance.
 q   Quit program. No amount is needed in this line.

After each transaction, display the current balance, printed to two decimal places. For example, assume the user types the following input:

b 400.00 ↩
c 123.45 ↩
c 21.95 ↩
d 350.00 ↩
c 10.65 ↩
c 100.00 ↩
q ↩

You should print output as follows (we show it intermingled with the input, as it would look on a terminal screen):

```
b 400.00 ↵
New balance is $400.00
c 123.45 ↵
New balance is $276.55
c 21.95 ↵
New balance is $254.60
d 350.00 ↵
New balance is $604.60
c 10.65 ↵
New balance is $593.95
c 100.00 ↵
New balance is $493.95
q ↵
Final balance is $493.95
```

3. Modify the preceding program to subtract a check charge of 75 cents for each check written.

4. Modify the program in problem 3 so that, when the user types **q**, the highest and lowest balances that were attained since the last **b** command are displayed.

5. Write a program that accepts as input the wholesale cost of an item, the retail price of that item, and the number of such items to be ordered, and then computes the total margin and percent margin for that item. Total margin is given by

```
(retail price – wholesale cost) * number of items
```

Percent margin is given by

```
((retail price – wholesale price) / wholesale price) * 100
```

Error check the input. For example, don't accept negative prices or a wholesale price of zero.

6. Write a program to compute grade point averages. Require that the user type one line of input per course in the following format: a number to indicate the number of units of credit for the course, followed by a single blank, followed by one of the characters A, B, C, D, or F, followed by one of the characters +, –, or blank, followed by a carriage return.

7. Write a program that accepts as input a *real* number x and, if x is not zero, computes $1.0/x$ and then multiplies the result by x. Your program should compare the product with the value 1.0 and print a message if $x * (1.0/x)$ is not equal to 1.0. Experiment with different input values.

*8. (For students who know the calculus.) Write a program to compute approximate derivatives of the functions $f(x) = x^2$ and $f(x) = 1/x$ at a value of x that is chosen by the user. Your program should compute the quotients

$$\frac{f(x + h) - f(x)}{h}$$

with h taking on small positive and negative values, such as 0.001, -0.001, 0.0001, -0.0001, 0.00001, -0.00001. Do the values you compute approach the exact values that you can compute using the calculus? Try using very small values of h, such as $1.0e-35$, or the value that you computed in Exercise 20.4b (page 438).

*9. Modify the program you wrote for problem 1 above to compute the sum in two different ways: as

$$1/1 + 1/2 + 1/3 + \cdots + 1/n$$

(where n is the number input by the user), and summed in the reverse order, as

$$1/n + 1/(n - 1) + 1/(n - 2) + \cdots + 1/1$$

Have your program display both sums. Are they always the same? (Experiment with different values of n, including some large values.) If they differ from some values of n, can you explain why? Which is more accurate?

*10. Write a program that accepts as input a **real** number x and computes the value of the exponential function e^x using the series

$$e^x = 1 + x + x^2/2! + x^3/3! + x^4/4! + \cdots$$

Have your program stop summing when the value of the next term of the series is less than epsilon, where epsilon is a small constant defined in your program.

*11. Sometimes a program must compute a value that is in the legal range of **real**s but whose computation requires intermediate values that are outside that range. For example, on many computers the value of 40! is larger than the largest representable **real**, but the value of 40!/(20! * 20!) is small enough to represent. The required value can occasionally be calculated by changing the order in which the calculations are done. Write a program that computes 40!/(20! * 20!) without overflowing.

CHAPTER 21

We have now presented most of the statement types and simple data types provided by Pascal. Much of the rest of this book describes ways to define your own types to represent data and the corresponding algorithms for manipulating data of those types. In this chapter, we show you how to define two classes of simple data types. These types are useful in their own right, and they'll also play a role in the definition of structured types later on.

21.1 SOME DEFINITIONS

We need to classify different kinds of simple data types. The terms *scalar type* and *ordinal type* are sometimes used to describe different data types. Unfortunately, there are several different and mutually contradictory conventions that cover the use of these terms. Some authors treat them as synonymous and others do not. Here we distinguish between scalar types and ordinal types by defining them as follows:

> A scalar type *is a data type that has an underlying order. Any two values of a given scalar type can be compared, and either the values will be equal, or else one will be greater than the other.*
>
> An ordinal type *is a data type that has an underlying order and for which it's meaningful to speak of the preceding value or the succeeding value.*

The distinction between these terms is slight; the only scalar type that is not also an ordinal type is the type `real`.

All of Pascal's predefined types are scalar. The ordering of the types `integer` and `real` is numerical. The ordering of the type `char` depends on the underlying

DEFINING ORDINAL TYPES

numerical representation of characters in the character set of your computer. The two values of the type *boolean* are ordered by the convention that *false* < *true*.

In Chapter 19, we mentioned that there is no notion of a next value for values of type *real*. Thus, *real* is not an ordinal type. By contrast, all the possible values of type *integer* can, in principle, be enumerated from $-maxint$ to $maxint$.[1] The values of types *char* and *boolean* can also be listed in order. Thus, *integer*, *char*, and *boolean* are all ordinal types. Two more kinds of ordinal types are *subrange* types and *enumerated* types.

21.2 SUBRANGE TYPES

Sometimes we want to restrict the values a variable can assume. For example, we may want to restrict the values of a variable of *integer* type to between 1 and 100, or to between -128 and 127, or to only positive values. Pascal allows us to define and name new types whose possible values are a subrange of existing ordinal types. We can then use those types in variable declarations, exactly as we use the names of the built-in types. In the next sections we explain how to do this and why it's useful.

---

1. In fact, the following single Pascal statement will do it:

```
for int := -maxint to maxint do
       writeln(int)
```

Defining Subrange Types

The part of a program or procedure in which new types are defined is the type definition section. This section consists of the reserved word **type**, followed by one or more type definitions, each followed by a semicolon, as shown in Figure 21.1. Each type definition consists of the name of the type (called the *type identifier*) followed by an equals sign, followed by a description of the type, as shown in Figure 21.2.

Because Pascal makes it possible to build a rich variety of data types, many type descriptions are possible. We will introduce the syntax of each type description as we introduce that data type. Subrange types are described by the following syntax: a constant value, followed by the symbol . . , followed by a second constant value. The symbol . . consists of two periods typed with no intervening space. Figure 21.3 shows a syntax diagram for subrange type descriptions. Figure 21.4 shows a sample type definition section in which six subrange types are defined.

The Semantics of Subrange Type Definitions

A number of semantic rules govern subrange type definitions. The two constants of a subrange type definition must be of the same ordinal type. (In the first three definitions of Figure 21.4, the ordinal type is *integer*, and in the next three, the type is *char*.) Moreover, the first constant must be less than or equal to the second constant in the underlying order. The constant may be written out explicitly, it may be an identifier that has been previously defined in the constant section,[2] or it may be a predefined identifier like *maxint*. Figure 21.5 shows a combination of constant and subrange type definitions. Figure 21.6 shows some invalid subrange types with explanations of the errors.

Figure 21.1   **Syntax diagram for a type definition section**

Figure 21.2   **Syntax diagram for a single type definition**

2. Recall from Chapter 11 that the constant section of a program or a procedure, if present, must always precede the type section, if present.

Figure 21.3   **Syntax diagram for a subrange type description**

Figure 21.4   **Examples of subrange type definitions**

```
type    grades  =  0..100;
        posnums = 1..maxint;
        balance = -1000 .. 1000;
        lowercase = 'a'..'z';
        uppercase = 'A' .. 'Z';
        digit = '0'..'9';
```

Figure 21.5   **Using a defined constant in a subrange type definition**

```
const   length = 20;

type    position = 1..length;
```

Figure 21.6   **Incorrect subrange type definitions**

```
type    reverseorder = 10..-10;        {wrong order}
        digit = 0..'9';                {mixed types}
        noexpr = maxlen..maxlen+3;      {no expressions}
        fractions = -0.9999..0.9999;    {reals are not ordinal}
        letters = 'A'..'Z','a'..'z';    {two ranges}
```

Exercise 21.1: In the following fragment of a Pascal program containing subrange type definitions, indicate which type definitions are incorrect and why.

```
program showsubranges(input, output);

const    bigval = 100;
         bigdigit = '9';

type     -bigval..bigval;
         range = 0..bigval;
         rangeplus1 = 1..bigval+1;
         pos = 1..length;
         lowerhalf : 'a'..'m';
         weird = 0..bigdigit;
         funnyalpha = 'Z'..'A';
         fahrenheit = 32   ..   212;    ■
```

Exercise 21.2: One of the following subrange type definitions will be legal on your computer, and one will not be. Determine which of them is legal and explain why they can't both be legal.

```
type     lowtoup = 'a'..'Z';
         uptolow = 'A'..'z';    ■
```

Like variable declarations and constant definitions, type definitions have a scope—that is, they are known only to a certain portion of the program. The scope rules for a type identifier are the same as for any other identifier in a Pascal program: A type identifier is meaningful from the point where it is defined until the end of the block in which it's defined. Within its scope, a type identifier has the same status as the names of the four predefined types. Thus, you can use a type identifier to declare variables. Figure 21.7 shows some examples of variable declarations that use some of the subrange types from Figure 21.4.

Variables declared with a subrange type identifier may have any value between the lower and the upper range of that type identifier, inclusive. Thus, the variable named *sociology* declared in Figure 21.7 can take on any of the 101 possible values 0, 1, 2, 3, . . ., 100. Similarly, the variable *firstinit* may take on all the values of the range *uppercase*, that is, all the values between 'A' and 'Z', inclusive. Attempting to assign *sociology* or *firstinit* values outside their respective ranges will cause an error and halt execution of the program.

Assuming the variable declarations in Figure 21.7, each of the fragments shown in Figure 21.8 will cause an error.

Figure 21.7   **Declarations of some variables of subrange types**

```
var     english,
        calculus,
        sociology: grades;
        firstinit,
        secondinit: uppercase;
```

Figure 21.8   **Fragments that will cause a run-time error**

```
sociology := 101; {out of range}

sociology := 99;
sociology := sociology + 2;      {99 + 2 out of range}

firstinit := '%';        {out of range}
```

Figure 21.9   **Subrange type declarations using anonymous types**

```
var     english,
        calculus,
        sociology: 0..100;
        firstinit,
        secondinit: 'A'..'Z';
```

The subrange *uppercase* can take on all the values between 'A' and 'Z', inclusive, and no others. In the ASCII character set, this range consists of only the 26 uppercase letters. In EBCDIC, it includes other characters because the alphabet is not contiguous in EBCDIC. Thus, the values specified by a subrange may depend on the implementation of Pascal.

It's possible to omit the type definition of a subrange type and still declare variables of that type. Such declarations are said to use *anonymous types*. They are made by writing the type description directly in the variable declaration instead of a type identifier. Thus, the variable declarations in Figure 21.9 are equivalent to those in Figure 21.7. We do not recommend this practice, however, because anonymous types make the program hard to read. Moreover, they are not legal in every context in which named types are legal. The exception arises from the following Pascal rule regarding the types of procedure parameters:

The type of a procedure parameter declared in the procedure header must be specified by a type identifier.

Note that this rule applies to parameters of functions as well as procedures. (See Chapter 22.) Figure 21.10 shows the correct and incorrect use of subranges as types of parameters.

The Uses of Subrange Types

Subrange types have two principal uses: to perform automatic range-checking of data and to specify the index types for the data structures known as *arrays*. (We'll discuss arrays and indexing in Chapter 23.) We have already encountered programs that check their input data for valid values (page 388). Sometimes we want to check the range of computed data as well; the subrange type provides a way of doing so.

Whenever a variable of subrange type is assigned a value, your program automatically checks the value to see if it is within the subrange specified by that type. When a value is out of range, you have no choice about what action to take. The program halts and signals an error. The purpose of declaring variables to be of a subrange type is to detect errors. There are two distinct classes of errors that you can detect this way: logical errors and noninteractive input errors.

Sometimes the logic of your algorithm implies that a value will be within a certain range. For example, if x is a positive *integer*, and if we compute the remainder of x when divided by 100 using the expression

```
x mod 100
```

the result will be between 0 and 99. To hold this value, we might declare a variable of type 0..99. If we happen to make a logical error and somehow assign a value to the variable outside this range, a run-time error will result. If, instead, we had declared the variable of type *integer*, the program might well run to completion and give erroneous results that could go undetected. Run-time errors that expose flaws in the logic of our programs are desirable. Undesirable errors are those that go undetected and produce incorrect results on which important decisions are based.

Figure 21.10   **Subrange types for procedure parameters**

Correct:
```
type       grades  =  0..100;
                . . .
           procedure printgrades( classgrade:  grades);
                    {valid procedure header}
```

Incorrect:
```
                . . .
           procedure printgrades( classgrade:  1..100);
                    {invalid procedure header}
```

It is often necessary to range-check input data for validity. The best method for doing so depends on the source of the input. We must distinguish between interactive and noninteractive input. *Interactive input* is typed by a user during a program's execution. *Noninteractive input* has been prepared ahead of time and is read from a medium such as tape, disk, or punched cards during a program's execution.[3]

You should not use subrange types to range-check interactive input. However, subrange types are an appropriate way to range-check noninteractive input. Figure 21.11 illustrates two ways to range-check a value between 0 and 100.

In the first example in Figure 21.11, an input value outside the range 0..100 will cause the program to halt. This is appropriate because the program can't ask the cards or the tape for a new value. The only alternative is to halt the program and determine why invalid data is present. That method is not appropriate for range-checking interactive input, however. We need some way of range-checking short of halting the program when the user accidentally enters invalid data. A user who has entered 30 valid values before entering an invalid value will not be happy when told to rerun the program and correct the error. We use program logic rather than subrange types to range-check interactive input, as in the second method shown in Figure 21.11.

Exercise   21.3: Refer to the two versions of procedure `getnumbers` in Figure 19.1 and Figure 19.3 (pages 407 and 409). Which variables, if any, can be declared using a subrange type in each of these procedures? What is the required subrange in each case?   ■

21.3 ENUMERATED TYPES

Enumerated types are types whose values are symbols made up by the programmer. The principal use of such types is to make a program more self-documenting. We define enumerated types according to the syntax shown in Figure 21.12. The identifiers within parentheses constitute the symbolic values of the type.[4] Figure 21.13 shows two examples of enumerated type definitions.

---

3. The term *batch processing* is sometimes used to describe programs whose input has been prepared in machine-readable form before the program begins execution.

4. These types are sometimes called *user-defined types,* since the user (actually the programmer, who is the "user" of the Pascal compiler) defines their values. We prefer the name *enumerated types,* since Pascal has many other types that can be defined by the programmer.

Figure 21.11   Two methods of range-checking input

To range-check noninteractive input:

```
const    low = 0;
         high = 100;
type     grades = low..high;
var      inputnum: grades;
    .
    .
    .
readln(inputnum);
```

To range-check interactive input:

```
var      inputnum: integer;
    .
    .
    .
write('Enter value between ',low:1,' and ',high:1, ': ' );
readln(inputnum);
while ( inputnum < low) or (inputnum > high) do
  begin {while}
    writeln('That value is out of range.');
    write('Enter value between ',low:1,' and ',high:1,': ');
    readln(inputnum)
  end {while}
```

Figure 21.12   Syntax diagram for an enumerated type definition

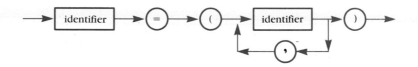

A variable that is declared to be of type *suit* can take on four possible values: the symbolic values *clubs*, *diamonds*, *hearts*, and *spades*. Assuming the type definitions in Figure 21.13, the declarations and statements shown in Figure 21.14 are legal.

Figure 21.13   Two examples of enumerated type definitions

```
type    suit = (clubs, diamonds, hearts, spades);

        fruit = (cantaloupe, casaba, honeydew, watermelon,
                 grapefruit, lemon, lime, orange, tangerine,
                 blackberry, blueberry, boysenberry,
                 raspberry, strawberry);
```

Figure 21.14   Examples of the use of variables of enumerated type

```
var    trumpsuit: suit;
       appetizer,
       dessert: fruit;

                 .
                 .
                 .

       trumpsuit := hearts;
       if appetizer = cantaloupe
           then
                 dessert := blueberry
           else
                 dessert := strawberry;
```

Note that the identifiers that constitute the values of an enumerated type are not enclosed in apostrophes. These values are not literals. The assignment

```
trumpsuit := 'hearts';   { ERROR! }
```

is an error, since the types of the left and right sides of the assignment are incompatible. The right side of the assignment is a string literal while the left side is a variable of type *suit*.

The definitions, declarations, and statements shown in Figure 21.15 are also correct. In Pascal, these definitions make as much sense as the definition in Figure 21.13. To a person reading the program, however, the definition in Figure 21.13 conveys much more information about the values of the variable *trumpsuit* than either of the definitions in Figure 21.15.

Enumerated types are ordinal types. The order of an enumerated type is the order in which the values are listed in the type definition. Thus, *clubs* are the lowest suit and *spades* the highest according to the definition in Figure 21.13.

Figure 21.15   **Alternative ways to define type** *suit* **with four values**

```
type    suit = 1..4;
var     trumpsuit: suit;

        .

        .

        .

        trumpsuit := 3;


type    suit = (snurgle, bargle, doogle, zorf);
var     trumpsuit: suit;

        .

        .

        .

        trumpsuit := doogle;
```

Since enumerated types are ordinal types, we can use them to define subrange types. Figure 21.16 shows some subranges of the type *fruit* from Figure 21.13.

Similarly, we can use the order of an enumerated type for comparisons using all the relational operators. Figure 21.17 gives some examples. We can also use variables of an enumerated type as loop control variables in **for** loops. The expressions that describe the lower and upper limits of the loop's execution must be of that enumerated type:

for dessert := cantaloupe **to** strawberry **do**
    . . .

The statements that constitute the body of this **for** loop will be executed 14 times, with *dessert* taking on each of the values *cantaloupe*, *casaba*, *honey-dew*, . . ., *strawberry* in succession.

Figure 21.16   **Subrange types of an enumerated type**

```
type    fruit = (cantaloupe, casaba, honeydew, watermelon,
                grapefruit, lemon, lime, orange, tangerine,
                blackberry, blueberry, boysenberry,
                raspberry, strawberry);
        melon = cantaloupe..watermelon;
        citrus = grapefruit..tangerine;
        berry = blackberry..strawberry;
```

Figure 21.17   Using enumerated type values with relational operators

```
var     dessert: fruit;
        acidic: boolean;
          .
          .
          .

        {Assume that dessert has been given some value of type fruit.}
        acidic := (dessert >= grapefruit);
        {Acidic will be true if the value of dessert}
        {is any one of the fruits after watermelon.}

if dessert in [honeydew, blueberry, raspberry]
    then
        writeln('One of my favorites.')
    else
        dessert := watermelon
```

The Semantics of Enumerated Type Definitions

The identifiers that constitute the values of an enumerated type must be unique to that type. In other words, the same identifier cannot be used as a value in two different enumerations with overlapping scope. Thus, the following definitions will cause an error:

```
type    bases = (first, second, third, home);
        timeunits = (hour, minute, second, millisecond);
```

The error is that the identifier *second* occurs in the list of values of both types. Similarly, no identifier or symbol that has a reserved meaning in Pascal can be used as a value of an enumerated type. Thus, the type definitions shown in Figure 21.18 are all illegal.

Pascal distinguishes between reserved words and predefined identifiers. It's legal, but generally disastrous, to redefine a predefined identifier. Thus, although the definitions shown in Figure 21.19 are legal, they should never be used in any program.

Like subrange types, enumerated types may be used anonymously to declare variables. Thus, the variable declarations in Figure 21.20 are legal, although we discourage the use of such shorthand.

One thing you cannot do with variables of enumerated type is use their values directly as input from, or output to, a terminal. This is a serious limitation. When

Figure 21.18 **Illegal enumerated type definitions**

```
type    odddigits = (1, 3, 5, 7, 9);
           {These values are integers; they can't be another type. }
        moreodds = ('1', '3', '5', '7', '9');
           {These are characters, not identifiers. }
        offense = (quarterback, halfback, fullback, center,
                   guard, tackle, end);
           {end is a reserved word in Pascal!}
```

Figure 21.19 **Enumerated type definitions that redefine predefined identifiers**

```
type    oosounds = (true, blue, stew, goo, pew);
           {In the scope of this definition, the identifier}
           {true is no longer a boolean value.}
        procnames = (read, readln, write, writeln);
           {In the scope of this definition, any attempt to}
           {use these as procedure identifiers will}
           {cause an error.}
```

Figure 21.20 **Anonymous enumerated and subrange types**

```
var    suit1,
       suit2: (clubs, diamonds, hearts, spades);
       redsuits: diamonds..hearts;
```

you try to write the value of such a variable, the identifier that stands for the value will not be displayed.[5] Pascal's internal representation of such values is not in character form, and they have no external representation. To get values for enumerated types as input, the programmer must ask the user for another type of value and then arrange to "convert" it—that is, interpret the input value as a value of the enumerated type. An example appears in Figure 21.21, where input values of type *char* are used to specify values of type *suit*. Notice that the **case** statement in Figure 21.21 is "protected" by the code that precedes it—that is, the **repeat** loop guarantees that the **case** won't be entered until the value of *suitinit* is one of the four characters that serve as the **case** labels.

---

5. That is, according to the Pascal Standard; some implementations of Pascal provide for the output of enumerated types by displaying the identifier, as written in the program, for the value. Since this is nonstandard, any program that uses such a feature is not portable.

Figure 21.21 Using character input to assign an enumerated type value

```pascal
procedure getsuit(var usersuit: suit);
{This program asks the user for a character and uses the value to}
{compute a value for the parameter usersuit.}

var        suitinit: char;           {for user's input}

begin    {getsuit}
    repeat
        writeln('Type ''c'' for clubs, ''d'' for diamonds,');
        write('''h'' for hearts or ''s'' for spades: ');
        readln(suitinit);
        if not (suitinit in ['c','d','h','s'])
            then
                writeln('That is not a valid input.')
    until suitinit in ['c','d','h','s'];
    case suitinit of
        'c': usersuit := clubs;
        'd': usersuit := diamonds;
        'h': usersuit := hearts;
        's': usersuit := spades
    end {case}
end; {getsuit}
```

Figure 21.22 gives an example of how values of enumerated type are used to display output values. Like the preceding example, this one uses a **case** statement. The **case** statement in Figure 21.22 doesn't need protection. Since *trumpsuit* has only four possible values, and since they are all present as **case** labels, no error can occur.

Figure 21.22 Using enumerated type values to display output

```pascal
write('The trump suit is ');
case trumpsuit of
        clubs:      writeln('Clubs.');
        diamonds:   writeln('Diamonds.');
        hearts:     writeln('Hearts.');
        spades:     writeln('Spades.')
end;       { case }
```

Exercise   21.4: What is the output of the following program?

```
program enumtype (output);
type    rank = (two, three, four, five, six, seven, eight,
                nine, ten, jack, queen, king, ace);
        picture = jack..ace;

var     card1,
        card2: picture;
        anyrank: rank;

        procedure showpic ( card: picture);
        begin
                case card of
                    jack:   write('J');
                    queen:  write('Q');
                    king:   write('K');
                    ace:    write('A');
                  end { case }
        end; { showpic }

begin
        if ace < two
          then
            card1 := king
          else
            card1 := jack;
        card2 := queen;
        for anyrank := ace downto five do
          if anyrank < card1
            then
                showpic(card2)
            else
                showpic(anyrank);
        writeln
end.
```

Note that procedure *showpic* has a parameter of type *picture* but is invoked
with an argument of type *rank*. This is legal, since the two types are compatible:
Type *picture* is a subrange of *rank*. ∎

CHAPTER SUMMARY

1. A *scalar type* is a type that has an underlying order. Therefore, it is meaningful to use relational operators between values of a scalar type.

2. An *ordinal type* is a type for which it is meaningful to speak of the preceding value or the succeeding value.

3. In Pascal, the simple types are scalar types. They include the four predefined types, any enumerated types defined by the programmer, and any subrange types of any ordinal type. All the scalar types in Pascal except the type `real` are ordinal.

4. A subrange of any ordinal type can be used to define a *subrange type*.

5. If a variable of subrange type is assigned a value outside the legal range, an error will result and the program will halt. This feature is useful in detecting errors in the design of a program and errors in noninteractive input. In general, however, variables of subrange type should not be used for interactive input.

6. *Enumerated types* are defined by listing the identifiers that are their values. These values are purely symbolic. They cannot include keywords, and they should not include predefined identifiers. The principal benefit of using enumerated types is to produce programs that are as self-documenting as possible.

7. Enumerated values do not have any external representation. Thus, they cannot be used directly for interactive input and output.

COMMON ERRORS

- Using colons instead of equal signs in type definitions.
- Omitting the parentheses around the value list of an enumerated type.
- Defining a subrange type of the form `1..limit` but using a value of zero for a variable of that type (especially in initializations).
- Confusing values of enumerated type with the string literals formed by using the value identifiers inside quotes. For example:

```
type    cheese = (cheddar, brie, gouda,
                  jarlsberg, mozzarella);
var     lunch: cheese;
        . . .
        lunch: = 'gouda'; { This is an ERROR. }
```

SUPPLEMENTAL PROBLEMS

1. The following program fragment will cause a run-time error. Explain why.

   ```
   type     lowerlet = 'a'..'z';

   var      ch: lowerlet;
            .
            .

   while ch in ['a'..'z'] do
           read(ch);
   ```

2. What is the output of the following program fragment?

   ```
   type     direction = (N, NE, E, SE, S, SW, W, NW);

   var      dir: direction;
            deg: integer;
            .
            .

   deg := 0;
   for dir := N to NW do
       begin
           writeln(deg:1, ' degrees');
           deg := deg + 45
       end
   ```

3. The following type definition section is invalid. Why?

   ```
   type     day = (sun, mon, tues, wed, thurs, fri, sat);
            weekend = (sat..sun);
   ```

   Write a correct type definition for a type to represent days of the week and a subrange type to represent weekend days.

4. Consider the following program skeleton:

```
program  kidsgame(input, output);
  { fragment of a program to play the game rock, paper, scissors }

type     move = (rock, paper, scissors); { possible moves }
         outcome = (win1, win2, tie);    { possible results }

var      player1move,             { holds 1st player's move }
         player2move: move;       { holds 2nd player's move }
```

```
    inputch: char;           { for both player's input }
    winner: outcome;         { holds result of game }

  procedure getvalidinput (var userchar: char);
  begin { getvalidinput }
    repeat
      readln (userchar);
      if not (userchar in ['r', 'p', 's'])
         then
            writeln('Illegal move: type ''r'', ''p'', or ''s'' ')
    until userchar in ['r', 'p', 's']
  end; { getvalidinput }

  procedure translate(userchar: char; var usermove: move);
  begin { translate }
         case userchar of
            'r':  . . .
            'p':  . . .
            's':  . . .
         end
  end; { translate }

  procedure whowins(move1, move2: move; var result: outcome);
  begin { whowins }
          . . .
  end; { whowins }

  procedure showresult( result: outcome);
  begin { showresult }
          . . .
  end; { showresult }

begin { kidsgame }
      writeln('Player 1, enter your move: ');
      getvalidinput(inputch);
      translate(inputch, player1move);
      writeln('Player 2, enter your move: ');
      getvalidinput(inputch);
      translate(inputch, player2move);
      whowins(player1move, player2move, winner);
      showresult( winner )
end. { kidsgames }
```

Complete this program by finishing procedure *translate* and writing the body of procedures *whowins* and *showresult*. Procedure *translate* should fill in the value of its variable parameter *usermove*, corresponding to

the character passed as the argument in *userchar*. Procedure *whowins* should fill in the value of **result** based on the two arguments, according to the traditional rules:

Rock beats scissors.
Scissors beats paper.
Paper beats rock.
Identical moves tie.

Procedure *showresult* should print a message describing the outcome of the game based on the value of its parameter **result**.

5. Rewrite the program in problem 4 without using enumerated types. Which version is easier to understand? Why?

6. There are six errors in the following program fragment. Correct them.

```
program mistakes(input, output);
type    liquid: 32 .. 212;
        length = 1 .. max;
        lower = 'a'..'z';
        upper = 'Z'..'A';
const   maximum = 20;
var     letter1: lower;
        letter2: upper;
        temp: liquid;
begin
        liquid := 0;
        letter1 := liquid;
        . . .
```

7. Consider the following program fragment:

```
        . . .
for i := 1 to 200 do
        writeln(i:1, ' squared = ', i*i:1);
        . . .
```

Suppose this is the only time the variable *i* is used in the program. What type should *i* be declared as?

8. The previous fragment is rewritten using a while loop:

```
        . . .
i := 1;
while i <= 200 do
```

```
begin
    writeln(i:1, ' squared = ', i*i:1);
    i := i + 1
end; { while }
    . . .
```

Again, suppose this is the only use in the program of the variable *i*. What type should *i* be declared as?

*9. Suppose you include the definition

type   boolean = (false, true);

in the global type definitions for a program. Is this legal? What are the consequences of such a definition?

*10. Suppose you include the definition

type   integer = −maxint..maxint;

in the global type definitions for a program. Is this legal? What are the consequences of such a definition?

CHAPTER

22

In Chapter 14 (pages 284–310) we discussed the use of procedures to write modular Pascal programs. When the purpose of a program module is to determine a single value, it is possible to achieve that action using a procedure with a variable parameter. However, because this type of action is frequently needed in programs, Pascal provides a second kind of program module whose sole purpose is to compute and return a single value. This kind of program module is called a *function*.

Pascal functions work in a way that is similar to the way mathematical functions work. You give a mathematical function one or more values as input, and it produces a value as output. For example, a common mathematical function is the "square" function $f(x) = x^2$. For each input value of x, the function $f(x)$ produces the output value x^2.

In Pascal, we pass input values to a function through value parameters. The value calculated by the function may be any scalar type.[1]

22.1 COMPARING PROCEDURES TO FUNCTIONS

Functions are similar to procedures in that they allow the programmer to refer to one or several lines of code by name. They are quite different, however, in an important respect. Procedures may return values through variable parameters. The values a procedure has returned are held in variables in its argument list. We must make use of those arguments after the procedure call in order to access the values determined by the procedure. Function calls, on the other hand, actually represent

---

1. In Chapter 30, we will learn about another type available in Pascal that can be the type of a value calculated by a function.

FUNCTIONS

values. They may be used in or as expressions of any scalar type. For example, if we had a function called *square*, we could make the statement

```
x:=square(y) + 5;
```

In this respect, *square (y)* is similar to a variable, except that its value is determined by the actions described in the declaration of function *square*.

To make clearer the difference between calling a function and calling a procedure, let's look at what would happen if we treated a function call like a procedure call and vice versa. We treat a function call like a procedure call in Figure 22.1. The code in Figure 22.1 is equivalent to the code in Figure 22.2. Since there is no statement in Pascal that corresponds to 25 (or, for that matter, to any number by itself on a line), the piece of code in Figure 22.2 is an error.

Now, let's see what would happen if we tried to use a procedure call as we should use a function call, as shown in Figure 22.3. The code in Figure 22.3 is equivalent to the code shown in Figure 22.4, which is quite illegal in Pascal.

Figure 22.1   Incorrectly using a function call

```
          .
          .
          .
      y:=5;                {Note; This is an}
      square(y);           {incorrect use of a}
                           {function.}
          .
          .
          .
```

Figure 22.2   Equivalent to the code in Figure 22.1

.
.
.
                    y: = 5;
                    25;
.
.

Figure 22.3   Incorrectly using a procedure call

.
.

```
procedure getanswer(var answer:char);
{a procedure to read in a char}

begin   (getanswer)
  write('Answer please?  ');
  readln(answer)
end;    {getanswer}
```

.
.
.

```
if getanswer(ans)  =  'x'  {an incorrect use}
        then...            {of a procedure call}
```

.
.
.

Figure 22.4   Equivalent to the code in Figure 22.3

.
.
.

```
if write('Answer please? '); readln(answer);  =  'x'
        then...
```

.
.
.

22.2 PROGRAMMER-DEFINED FUNCTIONS

When a programmer writes the Pascal code that declares a function, the function is referred to as *programmer-defined.*

An Example of a Programmer-Defined Function

Consider this problem:

> Mary wants to implement a test on the computer. She is going to ask five true-or-false questions. If a student answers all five questions correctly, she gets an A; for four correct answers, a B; for three correct answers, a C; for two correct answers, a D; and for one or no correct answers, an F. Write a function that performs this task for Mary.

The input to this problem is the number of correct answers a student has given. The output is a single letter grade. There are two constraints: The score must be less than or equal to five and greater than or equal to zero. Any score out of that range will receive a grade of I for incomplete. Hence, the student must receive a grade of A, B, C, D, F, or I. Since the input to this problem is the number of correct answers a student has given, we should expect to pass that number as an argument to the function.

Should the program module be able to alter the value of the argument? The answer to this question is no. The program should not alter the value of the variable representing the number of correct answers in any way. Thus, the argument must correspond to a value parameter. Actually, since functions are supposed to return only one value—namely, the value of the function—we should only declare value parameters for a function. By sending variable parameters, we would be giving the function the ability to return more than one value, and that is not the purpose of a function. In fact, sending arguments to variable parameters almost always contradicts the purpose of the function construct.

The output of this problem is a grade, so we want our function to return a value of type *char*. Since functions can be used in expressions, they must have a declared type, just as variables do.

Figure 22.5 displays our function *ScoreToLetter*. Assuming that *CharlieScore* is an *integer* variable that holds the score Charlie got on the quiz, we might use function *ScoreToLetter* as in Figure 22.6. The grade we see in the output depends on Charlie's score. For example, if *CharlieScore* has the value 4, we will get this output:

```
Charlie got a(n) B on the test.
```

Figure 22.5   **Function *ScoreToLetter***

```
function ScoreToLetter (numCorrect: integer) : char;
  {This function will change a score into a letter grade.}
  {It will do so using a case statement.}

begin   {ScoreToLetter}
  if (numCorrect < 0) or (numCorrect > 5)
    then ScoreToLetter: = 'I'
    else case numCorrect of
              5: ScoreToLetter: = 'A';
              4: ScoreToLetter: = 'B';
              3: ScoreToLetter: = 'C';
              2: ScoreToLetter: = 'D';
           1, 0: ScoreToLetter: = 'F'
         end    {case numCorrect}
end;     {ScoreToLetter}
```

Figure 22.6   **Invoking function *ScoreToLetter***

```
write('Charlie got a(n) ', ScoreToLetter(CharlieScore));
writeln(' on the test: ');
```

The Syntax of Programmer-Defined Functions

The Placement of Function Declarations in a Program

Function declarations can occur wherever procedure declarations can occur, and they can be intermixed with procedure declarations. Figure 22.7 is an example.

The Syntax of a Function Declaration

The function header starts with the keyword **function** followed by an identifier that names the function. The identifier may be followed by a parameter list enclosed in parentheses. The parameters may be either variable or value parameters. We strongly recommend, however, that you use only value parameters. If you need a variable parameter, you should probably use a procedure rather than a function. The right parenthesis enclosing the parameter list is followed by a colon, which is followed by a type identifier that describes the type of the function. The type of the function is the type of the value that the function will return. The type of the

Figure 22.7   Program *d*, showing intermixed procedure and function declarations

```
program d (input, output);
            .
            .
            .

    procedure x;
      begin {x}
            .
            .
            .
      end; {x}

    function y(num: integer): real;
      begin {y}
            .
            .
            .
      end; {y}

    procedure z;
      begin {z}
            .
            .
            .
      end; {z}

  begin   {d - main program}
            .
            .
            .
  end.    {d - main program}
```

function is followed by a semicolon, which ends the header. Figure 22.8 shows the syntax diagram for a function header.

The rest of the function declaration looks like a procedure declaration, except that the name of the function must appear on the left side of at least one assignment operator in the statement section of the function. It is crucial to the function since it is this assignment that gives the function call its value.

Recall that when an assignment statement is executed, its right-hand side is evaluated first. Hence, we will want to see the name of a function on the right-hand side of an assignment statement within the function declaration only when we intend that the function call itself. This is precisely the idea behind recursion. In a later section, we will see how Pascal implements recursive algorithms.

Figure 22.8   Syntax diagram for a function header

The Syntax of a Function Call

Functions are invoked just as procedures are invoked. A function call consists of the function identifier, possibly followed by an argument list enclosed in parentheses. The arguments must correspond both in number and type to the parameters in the header of the function declaration.

Two More Examples of Programmer-Defined Functions

Let's look at two more examples of programmer-defined functions. The first example involves a *boolean*-valued function, a common type of function. These programmer-defined functions tend to be short and are mainly used for clarity in programming. They look less like procedures than other types of functions. Consider the following problem:

We are trying to get characters from a user. The first character must be between *a* and *d* inclusive, the second character between *e* and *g* inclusive, and the third character between *h* and *j* inclusive. Write three procedures that get legitimate characters from the user.

The inputs to this problem are the three characters typed by the user. The output consists of three characters. The constraints are the limits described for each character. We will use a *boolean*-valued function to help us check the user's input for validity. Figure 22.9 shows a function and three procedures we can use to solve the problem.

Using function *valid* helps other programmers understand what we are doing. It frees them from the details of the possible **and**'s, **or**'s, **not**'s, less than's, and so forth that we would otherwise use in each **until** clause to find out if an answer is valid.

Our second example is a mathematical function. Here is the problem:

Mary wants a function that calculates an integer number to a given power. She wishes to use exponents equal to positive whole numbers only. Write a function that, given a number and a power, computes that number to the given power.

Figure 22.9 **Three procedures using function** *valid*

```
function valid(min,max,answer:char) :boolean;
  {a function to return true if answer is}
  {within limits, else will return false}

begin {valid}
  valid:= (answer >= min) and (answer <= max)
end;   {valid}

procedure getanswer1(var answer1:char);
 {a procedure to get the answer to}
 {the multiple choice question:    }
 {The moon is made of?}

begin    {getanswer1}
  repeat
    writeln('The question is: The moon is made of');
    writeln('    (a) Green Cheese');
    writeln('    (b) Swiss Cheese');
    writeln('    (c) Brie');
    writeln('    (d) Rock');
    readln(answer1)
  until valid('a','d',answer1)
end;    {getanswer1}

procedure getanswer2(var answer2:char);
 {a procedure to get the answer to}
 {the multiple choice question }
 {I like my hamburger with?}

begin    {getanswer2}
  repeat
    writeln('The question is:  I like my hamburger with');
    writeln('    (e) Cheese');
    writeln('    (f) Catsup');
    writeln('    (g) French Fries');
    readln(answer2)
  until valid('e','g',answer2)
end;    {getanswer2}
```

(continued)

Figure 22.9
Continued

```
procedure getanswer3 (var answer3:char);
{a procedure to get the answer to}
{the multiple choice question  }
{When I get hungry I eat?}

begin    {getanswer3}
  repeat
    writeln('The question is: When I get hungry');
    writeln('I eat?');
    writeln('   (h) Cookies');
    writeln('   (i) Tofu');
    writeln('   (j) Chocolate');
    readln(answer3)
  until valid('h','i',answer3)
end;    {getanswer3}
```

For example: $3^4 = 3 \times 3 \times 3 \times 3$. The exponent 4 indicates how many times the number should occur as a factor in the product. In general, we could say that

$$n^p = n \times n \times n \times n \times \cdots \times n$$

p factors

If we begin with 1 and multiply it p times by n, we will arrive at the desired result. This description of the solution indicates the use of a loop that iterates p times. The action performed by the loop is just a multiplication by n.

The inputs to this problem are two values: the number and the exponent. The output is the number raised to the given exponent. There are two constraints: The exponent must be a positive whole number value, and the number must be an integer. The function call should therefore have two arguments corresponding to two value parameters and should represent an *integer* value. The function is shown in Figure 22.10. Note that, in Figure 22.10, we needed an additional variable *subtotal* in function *powers*. This was necessary because we did not want to use the function's name, *powers*, on the right side of the assignment operator within the function's declaration.

We could now call the function as in Figure 22.11. Assume that *result* is an *integer* variable. We would get the following output:

```
2 to the 5th power is 32
```

Figure 22.10   Function *powers*

```
function powers (number, power: integer) : integer;
  {a function to compute the value of number}
  {to the given power by multiplying the given}
  {number by itself power times}

var index,                  {to use in for loop}
                            {to keep track of the}
                            {number of multiplications}
    subtotal: integer;      {to hold subtotal until done}

begin    {powers}
  subtotal := 1;
  for index := 1 to power do
    subtotal := subtotal * number;
  powers := subtotal
end;     {powers}
```

Figure 22.11   Example of a call to function *powers*

```
result:=powers (2, 5);
write('2 to the 5th power is ', result: 2);
```

Exercise   22.1: What output is produced by the following line of code?

```
writeln('3 to the −2nd power is', powers (3, −2): 2)    ■
```

Recursive Programmer-Defined Functions

We can consider the problem of raising a number to a power in another way that depends on a recursive definition. Instead of thinking that three to the fourth power is calculated by multiplying three with itself four times, consider thinking about it as shown in Figure 22.12.

Figure 22.12 **Thinking about 3^4 recursively**

Step #1 $3^4 = 3 * 3^3$ This is fine, but what is 3^3?

Step #2 $3^3 = 3 * 3^2$ This is fine, but what is 3^2?

Step #3 $3^2 = 3 * 3^1$ This is quite a bit better since we know that

Step #4 $3^1 = 3$

We can now work backward to get to the solution of the original problem. Since $3^1 = 3$, we can complete step 3 by calculating

$$3^2 = 3 \times 3^1 = 3 \times 3 = 9$$

Now, since $3^2 = 9$, we can complete step 2 by calculating

$$3^3 = 3 \times 3^2 = 3 \times 9 = 27$$

Finally, since $3^3 = 27$, we can complete step 1 by calculating

$$3^4 = 3 \times 3^3 = 3 \times 27 = 81$$

In general, for two positive integers representing the number and the power, we know the two facts shown in Figure 22.13. This approach to the problem is recursive because the number raised to a power is calculated by determining the value of that same number raised to (power $-$ 1). At each stage, we define a solution to a problem in terms of a similar problem that should be easier to solve. When we get to a stage where the number raised to a power can be calculated without reference to a similar problem involving a smaller power, we solve that problem. That stage occurs when the power is equal to 1. Then a number raised to the power 1 is simply equal to the number itself. We take that result and move backward to calculate the number raised to the power 2, then the number raised to the power 3, and so on until we get back to the original problem.

Before we can write a Pascal function that executes in exactly the manner we have just described, we need to restate in English the two facts given in Figure 22.13. To calculate a number raised to a power, follow the directions in Figure 22.14. Figure 22.15 shows the translation of the algorithm in Figure 22.14 into Pascal code; it comprises most of the function we desire. Notice that *recurspower* is a recursive function because it invokes itself in the **else** clause.

Figure 22.13 **Recursive definition of exponentiation**

$$\text{number}^{\text{power}} = \begin{cases} \text{number, if power} = 1 \\ \text{number} \times \text{number}^{(\text{power} - 1)}, \text{if power} > 1 \end{cases}$$

Figure 22.14   Recursive algorithm for exponentiation

> if the *power* is equal to one,
>   then *number* raised to the *power* is equal to the *number*,
>   else *number* raised to the *power* is equal to the
>   *number* times the *number* raised to (*power* − 1).

Figure 22.15   Recursive Pascal function to implement a recursive exponentiation algorithm

```
function recurspower (number, power : integer) : integer;
  {a function to compute the value of a number raised to}
  {given power recursively}
begin {recurspower}
  if power = 1
    then recurspower : = number
    else recurspower : =
             number * recurspower (number, power − 1)
end; {recurspower}
```

You will recall that any recursive function or procedure must have a stopping condition (page 56); otherwise, we would go on forever defining the solution to one problem in terms of another problem. There must be a point at which recursion stops and a result is calculated. That result can then be taken back through the sequence of intermediate problems to determine the result of the original problem.

Let's do a trace to see how Pascal executes our function *recurspower*. It is very similar to our recursive calculation of 3^4 above. Suppose we have the following statement, where *result* has been declared to be an *integer* variable:

```
result : = recurspower (3, 4);
```

To execute this assignment statement, we must evaluate the function call to the right of the : =. Hence, we invoke function *recurspower* for the first time with arguments equal to 3 and 4. We have the situation in memory as shown in Figure 22.16. Next, we execute the if-then-else statement. Since *power* is not equal to 1, we attempt to perform the assignment statement in the **else** clause. (See Figure 22.17.)

Figure 22.16 **Local to the first invocation of function** $recurspower$

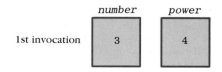

Figure 22.17 **Statement being executed in the first invocation**

$$recurspower \; := \; number \; * \; recurspower (number, \; power \; - \; 1)$$

$$\uparrow \qquad \qquad \underline{\qquad\qquad}$$

$$3 \qquad\qquad\qquad 3$$

On the right side of $:=$ we know the value of *number* (3), but we need to evaluate $recurspower$ (*number, power* $-$ 1) before we can multiply. Pascal simply suspends the first invocation of function $recurspower$ until it can complete this multiplication. Any program, procedure, or function that calls a procedure or function has its execution suspended until the invoked procedure or function terminates. In other words, Pascal preserves the situation in memory as is until it eventually returns to finish this assignment statement. At the moment, we need to focus on evaluating $recurspower$ (3, 3).

Our second call to the function causes the setup in memory shown in Figure 22.18. Remember that the variables set up for the first invocation of the function are still in memory. They have not been erased!

Once again we execute the if-then-else statement. Since *power* is not equal to 1, we attempt to perform the assignment statement shown in Figure 22.19. Since we cannot complete evaluation of the right-hand side of the assignment statement, we suspend the second invocation of function $recurspower$ until we calculate the value of $recurspower$ (3, 2).

We now make our third call to the function, causing the setup in memory shown in Figure 22.20. (Remember that the variables set up for the first two invocations are still there!)

In executing the if-then-else statement, *power* is once again not equal to 1. Hence, we attempt to execute the statement shown in Figure 22.21. Since we do not yet have a value for $recurspower$ (3, 1), we make our fourth call to the function, leaving the third invocation suspended. We get the setup in memory shown in Figure 22.22. (Remember, all variables set up for the first three invocations are still there.)

Finally, the value of *power* is equal to 1 when we execute the if-then-else statement in the fourth invocation. We proceed to execute the **then** section and

Figure 22.18   **The situation in memory just after the second invocation of function *recurspower***

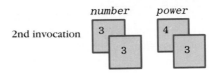

Figure 22.19   **Statement being executed in the second invocation**

$$\text{recurspower} := \text{number} * \text{recurspower}\,(\text{number},\ \underbrace{\text{power}\ -\ 1}_{2})$$
$$\underset{3}{\uparrow}$$

Figure 22.20   **The situation in memory just after the third invocation of function *recurspower***

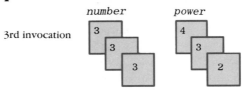

Figure 22.21   **Statement being executed in the third invocation**

$$\text{recurspower} := \text{number} * \text{recurspower}\,(\text{number},\ \underbrace{\text{power}\ -\ 1}_{1})$$
$$\underset{3}{\uparrow}$$

Figure 22.22   **The situation in memory just after the fourth invocation of function *recurspower***

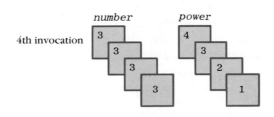

assign *recurspower* the value 3. Since we have completed execution of the if-then-else statement, the function's fourth invocation terminates, returning the value 3 for *recurspower* (3, 1) in the third invocation. Now the assignment statement left suspended in the third invocation can be completed, since the right-hand side is just 3 times 3, or 9. The value 9 is assigned to *recurspower*.

This completes the if-then-else in the third invocation of the function. Hence, the third invocation terminates, returning the value 9 for *recurspower* (3, 2) to the suspended assignment statement in the second invocation. The right-hand side of that assignment statement then evaluates to 3 times 9, or 27. The value 27 is then assigned to *recurspower*, completing the if-then-else and the second invocation of the function.

Hence, *recurspower* (3, 3) in the first invocation gets the value 27. The right-hand side of the assignment statement that was left suspended in the first invocation can now be evaluated as 3 times 27, or 81. The value 81 is then assigned to *recurspower*. The if-then-else and the first invocation of function *recurspower* are now complete.

The value 81 is returned to the statement that originally invoked the function. Finally, the variable *result* is assigned the value 81.

Even though the function *recurspower* seems to work well in our example, it has a serious flaw. If the value of *power* is less than 1 in the initial call to the function, we create a situation of infinite recursion because the stopping condition will never be satisfied. The function would call itself continually, with decreasing values of *power*, until it was interrupted by some outside mechanism. Most likely, the program would run out of space in memory, since space is allotted to two *integer* variables each time the function is invoked.

Assume that we had an *integer* variable called *result* and executed the statement:

```
result := recurspower (3, 0)
```

This would begin an infinite recursion. In the first invocation of the function, *power* would get the value 0. Since 0 is not equal to 1, the **else** clause would be executed, causing a call to function *recurspower* with arguments equal to 3 and −1. In the second invocation, *power* would attain the value −1. Since −1 is not equal to 1, the **else** clause would be executed. The function *recurspower* is called for the third time with arguments equal to 3 and −2. The value of *power* would never reach 1 because it would be decreasing.

Exercise 22.2: Revise function *recurspower* to remove the possibility of infinite recursion. Return the value 1 for powers less than 1. ∎

Remember that the hard part of recursive programming is stating your solution to the problem in terms of itself. This idea is embodied in the Pascal code when we see a function call itself. In this case, the **else** clause showed the function invoking itself: recurspower (number, power − 1).

Exercise 22.3: What happens when the following invocation to each version of function *bugrecurspower* is executed?

result := bugrecurspower (5, 2);

a. **function** bugrecurspower (number, power): integer;

       begin {bugrecurspower}

         if power = 1

           then bugrecurspower := number

           else bugrecurspower :=

              number * bugrecurspower (number, power)

     end; {bugrecurspower}

b. **function** bugrecurspower (number, power): integer;

       begin {bugrecurspower}

         if power <> 1

           then bugrecurspower :=

              number * bugrecurspower (number, power − 1)

           else bugrecurspower := 1

     end; {bugrecurspower} ■

22.3 PASCAL'S STANDARD PREDEFINED FUNCTIONS

Pascal has several predefined standard functions for calculating special values, much like the function keys on a pocket calculator. The use of predefined functions is similar to the use of programmer-defined functions. There is one striking difference, however. We are aware of the strict type matching between arguments and parameters in programmer-defined functions and procedures. Once we have given a type to a specific parameter, its corresponding argument must be of a compatible type. If, for example, we were to declare a parameter to be of type *integer* and its corresponding argument to be of type *real*, the compiler would give us a type-clash error that would prevent the program from being translated.

Moreover, the result of any programmer-defined function must be a specific scalar type. That type is given in the function header. Hence, calls to the function represent values of that specific type.

By contrast, several predefined functions may be called legally with either of two incompatible argument types. Furthermore, in some predefined functions the type of the value returned by the function varies according to the type of the argument. Figure 22.31 on page 489 displays the argument/result type information for all of the standard predefined functions.

The predefined functions logically fall into several groups.

The Predefined Functions to Calculate Squares and Square Roots

The first group of functions consists of the functions used to calculate squares and square roots. Your pocket calculator most likely has buttons marked x^2 and $\sqrt{}$. In Pascal, the two identifiers for those functions are *sqr* and *sqrt*. These two predefined functions exhibit what we've mentioned above about flexibility of the type of the argument and the result. The argument for either function may be *real* or *integer*. In the case of the squaring function, *sqr*, the type of the result matches the type of the argument. The result of the square root function, *sqrt*, is always *real*. In accordance with mathematical rules, the argument of *sqrt* must be nonnegative.

Figure 22.23 gives examples of the correspondence between standard algebraic notation and the Pascal syntax involving these two functions.

Figure 22.23   Comparison of algebraic notation to Pascal syntax

Algebraic notation	Pascal
$(16.1)^2$	`sqr(16.1)`
x^2	`sqr(x)`
$\sqrt{25}$	`sqrt(25)`
$\sqrt{x}$	`sqrt(x)`

The Predefined Functions to Round, Truncate, and Calculate Absolute Value

You are probably familiar with the idea of rounding off a decimal number. (When a student gets 94.25 points on an exam, is the score 94 or 95?) Pascal has two built-in methods to convert a *real* value to an *integer*. The first method is to round a *real* value to the closest *integer* value. That action is performed by the predefined function *round*. The second method is to simply chop off the digits to the right of the decimal point to create an *integer* value. That action, called truncation, is performed by the predefined function *trunc*. Each function requires a *real* argument and produces an *integer* result. Figure 22.24 gives examples of how these functions perform.

Exercise   22.4: The *round* function rounds a *real* number to the nearest *integer*. Write your own function to round the value of a *real* number to the nearest one-hundredth—that is, to two decimal places. (Hint: Multiply by 100.0.) ∎

Figure 22.24   Examples of *round* and *trunc*

```
round(  6.57)  ──────→   7   |   trunc (  6.57)  ──────→    6
round(  6.25)  ──────→   6   |   trunc (  6.25)  ──────→    6
round(-3.75)  ──────→  -4   |   trunc (-3.75)  ──────→   -3
round(-0.67)  ──────→  -1   |   trunc (-0.76)  ──────→    0
```

Exercise 22.5: Write a function to truncate a *real* number to two decimal places. (Hint: Multiply by 100.0.) ∎

The absolute value of a number is defined in mathematics as the positive distance of the number from the origin on the real number line. Less formally, it is the number's value with the sign ignored. Pascal's absolute value function is denoted by **abs**. Like the *sqr* function, its argument may be *real* or *integer*, and the type of its result matches the type of its argument.

The Predefined Trigonometric Functions

The next group of predefined functions is the group of trigonometric functions: *sin*, *cos*, and *arctan*. Pascal considers angular measurement in terms of radians. The result produced by each of these functions is *real*. Their arguments may be *real* or *integer*.

If *x*, *y*, and *z* are declared to be variables of type *real*, the function calls in Figure 22.25 are legal.

Since the designers of Pascal were aware that values of the other four trigonometric functions and two inverse trigonometric functions can be determined from the values of sine, cosine, and inverse tangent, they chose not to build any further trigonometric functions into the language.

The Predefined Logarithmic and Exponential Functions

The last group of numerical functions we discuss consists of the logarithmic and exponential functions. You may have noted the absence of an exponentiation operator in our discussion of *integer* and *real* arithmetic. It was the desire to avoid redundancy that led Pascal's designers to omit an exponentiation operator. Moreover, exponentiation is not one of the primitive operations performed by computer hardware. We can use the logarithmic and exponential functions to perform exponentiation.

Pascal's logarithmic function corresponds to the natural logarithm function of mathematics, that is, to the logarithm using a base e = 2.71828. . . . Its identifier is the same as is used in mathematics: *ln*. Also, in keeping with its mathematical meaning, its argument must be positive. Pascal's exponential function corresponds to the usual e^x in mathematics. Its identifier is *exp*. Both *ln* and *exp* may have a *real* or *integer* argument, and their results are *real*.

Figure 22.26 gives some examples of the correspondence between standard algebraic notation involving these two functions and Pascal's syntax.

Figure 22.25 **Example using the predefined trigonometric functions**

```
z := sin(x);
y := cos(x);
if (sin(x) + cos(x)) > 1.5
    then
        z := arctan(y);
```

Figure 22.26 **Comparisons of algebraic notation and Pascal syntax involving** *ln* **and** *exp*

Algebraic notation	Pascal
e^2	exp(2)
$\sqrt{e} = e^{1/2} = e^{.5}$	exp(0.5)
$e^{-1} = \dfrac{1}{e}$	exp(-1)
ln 3	ln(3)
ln 16.5	ln(16.5)
$\ln(e^x)$	ln(exp(x))
$e^{\ln(x)}$ $(x > 0)$	exp(ln(x))

Figure 22.27 gives the mathematical formula for determining the value of a number n raised to a power p using the natural logarithm and exponential functions. Note that since n will be an argument to the natural logarithm function, it must be positive.

Exercise 22.6

a. Translate the formula given in Figure 22.27 into Pascal.

b. Convert each of the following algebraic expressions into Pascal, using your answer for part a: 2^3, 3^4, 4^{-5}, $2^{0.75}$, and $6^{-0.33}$. ∎

Figure 22.27 **Exponentiation through natural logarithm and exponentiation with base e**

$$n^p = e^{(\ln n^p)} = e^{p(\ln n)}$$

The Predefined Functions That Deal with Ordinal Types

The next set of predefined functions is used to manipulate character values according to the computer's internal collating sequence. Recall our earlier discussion of ASCII and EBCDIC (page 334). For example, the ASCII character set contains 128 characters. The uppercase alphabet (A, B, . . ., Z) forms a contiguous set of characters. Hence, since A is character #65, B is character #66, C is character #67, . . ., and Z is character #90. The character number (#) is also known as the *ordinal position*.

Pascal has two functions that convert character arguments into their corresponding ordinal positions and vice versa. The function that takes a character as an argument and produces an *integer* result equal to its ordinal position is named *ord*. The function that does the reverse—that is, takes an *integer* representing an ordinal position as its argument and produces the corresponding character as its result—is named *chr*. Figure 22.28 gives examples of the actions of *ord* and *chr*.

The word *ordinal* means that there is no ambiguity in "what is next" or "what is just before." Two predefined functions that take advantage of this quality of the collating sequence are *succ* and *pred*, standing for *successor* and *predecessor,* respectively. Given a character argument named *ch*, succ (ch) is the next character in the collating sequence and pred (ch) is the character just before *ch* in the collating sequence.

Figure 22.29 gives examples involving all four of the functions described in this section.

In Chapter 21, we discussed programmer-defined ordinal types. The predefined functions *ord*, *pred*, and *succ* will work on those types as well. The predefined function *chr* works only with an integer argument to determine the corresponding character in the collating sequence.

Figure 22.28   Examples of *ord* and *chr* values in the ASCII system

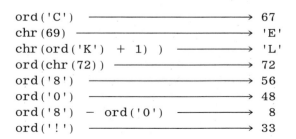

```
ord('C')                          ⟶ 67
chr(69)                           ⟶ 'E'
chr(ord('K') + 1) )               ⟶ 'L'
ord(chr(72))                      ⟶ 72
ord('8')                          ⟶ 56
ord('0')                          ⟶ 48
ord('8') - ord('0')               ⟶ 8
ord('!')                          ⟶ 33
```

To illustrate the actions of *ord, pred,* and *succ* on programmer-defined ordinal types, consider the following type:

```
type fruit = (banana, apricot, apple, cantaloupe, lemon,
              lime, orange, raspberry, grape, strawberry,
              pineapple);
```

Since ordinal positions begin with zero, our 11 identifiers of type *fruit* have ordinal positions 0 through 10. Figure 22.30 shows some examples of the results obtained when *ord, pred,* and *succ* are applied to the values of type *fruit*. Notice that pred(banana) and succ(pineapple) are undefined.

boolean-Valued Predefined Functions

Our last group of predefined functions consists of those functions that produce a *boolean* result. Two of them are usually used in conjunction with reading in values for structured data items or reading in values from external storage media.

Figure 22.29   **Examples using *ord, chr, pred,* and *succ* in ASCII**

```
pred('k')                    ⟶  'j'
succ('p')                    ⟶  'q'
pred(pred(pred('n')))        ⟶  'k'
succ(succ(succ('w')))        ⟶  'z'
pred('2')                    ⟶  '1'
pred(succ('3'))              ⟶  '3'
pred(chr(ord('d') + 1))      ⟶  'd'
succ(chr(ord('9') - 1))      ⟶  '9'
```

Figure 22.30   **Examples using *ord, pred,* and *succ* on values of a programmer-defined type**

```
ord(banana)        ⟶  0
ord(raspberry)     ⟶  7
ord(pineapple)     ⟶  10
pred(lime)         ⟶  lemon
pred(cantaloupe)   ⟶  apple
succ(strawberry)   ⟶  pineapple
succ(apricot)      ⟶  apple
```

They are *eoln* and *eof*, standing for "end of line" and "end of file" respectively. We will postpone our discussion of these functions until they are needed.

The last predefined function that produces a *boolean* result is called *odd*. Its argument is of type *integer*. The function *odd* returns the value *true* when its argument is *odd* and the value *false* when its argument is even. Hence, to find out if an *integer variable* named *number* is evenly divisible by 2 we could use the following *boolean*-valued expression:

not (odd(number))

Note that this expression is *true* if number is evenly divisible by 2 and *false* if it is not. Its argument must be of type *integer*. Its result is type *boolean*.

Exercise 22.7: Write your own function called *myodd* whose result is *boolean* and whose argument is *integer*. It should perform just as the predefined function *odd* performs. Use the following fact in constructing an algorithm for your function *myodd*:

If *n* is a variable having an odd value,

then *n* **mod** 2 is 1

else *n* **mod** 2 is 0 ∎

CHAPTER SUMMARY

1. Pascal has a special construct, known as a *function,* that represents a segment of code whose purpose is to calculate a single value.
2. Functions are similar to procedures, but there are three major differences:
   a. Since a function represents a value, its type must be specified in the function header.
   b. The declaration of a function must include at least one statement that assigns a value to the name of the function.
   c. Since a function is supposed to return a single value, it is rare that it will have any variable parameters.
3. Programmer-defined functions may represent a value of any scalar type.
4. Functions, especially *boolean*-valued functions, are often used to make programs easier to read.
5. Functions can perform *recursive calculations.* The recursion is indicated syntactically by a call to a function within its declaration. Recursive calculations must have some stopping condition.
6. Figure 22.31 summarizes information about Pascal's predefined functions.

Figure 22.31 **The argument/result types for the predefined functions**

Function	Argument	Result type
sqr	*real* or *integer*	*real* or *integer* matching argument type
sqrt	*real* >= 0 or *integer* >= 0	*real*
round	*real*	*integer*
trunc	*real*	*integer*
abs	*real* or *integer*	*real* or *integer* matching argument type
sin	*integer* or *real* (in terms of radians)	*real*
cos	*integer* or *real* (in terms of radians)	*real*
arctan	*integer* or *real*	*real* (in terms of radians)
ln	*integer* or *real*, > 0	*real*
exp	*integer* or *real*	*real*
ord	any ordinal type	*integer*
chr	*integer* (in range dependent on size of collating sequence)	*char*
pred	any ordinal type	same ordinal type
succ	any ordinal type	same ordinal type
odd	*integer*	*boolean*

COMMON ERRORS

- A statement consisting solely of a function call is an error. See Figures 22.1 and 22.2.

- Using the name of a function on the right-hand side of an assignment statement within the function declaration when the situation is not recursive. The error usually involves just the name of the function with no argument list. This error occurs frequently when a running total or a running product is involved. For example, consider this incorrect version of function *powers*:

```
function powers (number,power:integer) :integer;
   {a function to compute the value of number}
   {to the given power by multiplying the given}
   {number by itself power times}
```

```
        var index: integer;        {to use in for loop}
                                   {to keep track of the}
                                   {number of multiplications}


        begin   {powers}
          powers : = 1;
          for index : = 1 to power do
            powers : = powers * number {This is the erroneous}
                                       {use of the identifier}
                                            {powers.}

        end;    {powers}
```

■ Omission of a type declaration for the function in its header.

DEBUGGING HINTS

■ Check the effects of a function on its arguments just as you do for a procedure.

Display argument values before the function is invoked.

Display parameter values just after entering the function.

Display parameter values just before exiting the function.

Display argument values just after the function is invoked.

■ Check to make sure that a nonrecursive function's identifier does not appear in any expression within the declaration of the function.

■ To trace the flow of control, display string literals indicating entry into a function.

SUPPLEMENTAL PROBLEMS

1. Write a program that inputs a whole number of seconds and converts it to its equivalent in hours, minutes, and seconds.

2. Write a program that inputs a whole number of feet and converts it to its equivalent in miles, yards, and feet. (Note that 1 mile = 1,760 yards and that 1 yard = 3 feet.)

3. Write a program that inputs a whole number of centimeters and converts it to its equivalent in kilometers, meters, and centimeters.

4. Write a *boolean*-valued function named *isupper* that takes a character argument and returns the value *true* if the character is an element of the upper case alphabet, 'A'. . 'Z' and returns *false* if not. The answer to this problem depends on your computer's underlying representation of its character set.

5. Joe is writing a program to calculate the average of a set of exam scores. The range of possible scores is 0 to 100. His program will need to error-check each value as it is entered. Write a *boolean*-valued function named *invalid* that takes an *integer* argument, the exam score. Your function should return the value *true* if the score is not between 0 and 100 inclusive and should return the value *false* otherwise.

6. A mathematical calculation that may be done either recursively or nonrecursively is the factorial calculation. Refer back to Chapter 3 (pages 46–57) for a fuller discussion of the recursive algorithm. Here we give both mathematical definitions. In each case you are to
   a. Write an algorithm corresponding to the mathematical definition, and
   b. Write the Pascal function corresponding to the algorithm.

   I. Nonrecursive definition

   $$n! = 1\,(2)\,(3)\,(4) \cdots (n-2)\,(n-1)\,(n)$$

   In other words, n factorial is equal to the product of the integers 1 through n.

   II. Recursive definition

   $$n! = \begin{cases} n(n-1)! & \text{if } n > 1 \\ 1 & \text{if } n = 1 \end{cases}$$

7. A mathematical definition that requires double recursion is the definition of the nth Fibonacci number. Consider the mathematical definition below.
   a. Write an algorithm corresponding to the mathematical definition.
   b. Write the Pascal function corresponding to the algorithm.
   We will use $f(n)$ to denote the nth Fibonacci number.

   $$f(n) = \begin{cases} f(n-1) + f(n-2) & \text{if } n > 2 \\ 1 & \text{if } n <= 2 \end{cases}$$

8. a. Use the definition of the nth Fibonacci number given in problem 7 to write out the first ten Fibonacci numbers. This process should reveal a clear pattern.
   b. Write an iterative (nonrecursive) function to calculate the nth Fibonacci number.
   c. If you've done both problem 7 and problem 8b, compare the efficiency of your two functions with respect to execution time by printing the thirtieth Fibonacci number.

9. It is possible to write a recursive *real*-valued function that will return the value of any *integer* $(\ldots -3, -2, -1, 0, 1, 2, 3, \ldots)$ power of a number. The function must represent a *real* value since negative powers result in values between zero and one. Use the following mathematical definition to:

a. Develop an algorithm to calculate any *integer* power of a positive *integer*

b. Write a Pascal function to implement your algorithm

$$
n^p = \begin{cases}
1 \text{ if } p = 0 \\[2mm]
\dfrac{1}{n^{-p}} \text{ if } p < 0 \begin{array}{l} \{p \text{ less than zero }\} \\ \{\text{means } -p \text{ is }\hphantom{xx}\} \\ \{\text{greater than zero}\} \end{array} \\[4mm]
n * n^{p-1} \text{ if } p > 0
\end{cases}
$$

Note that there are three parts to this definition. In one case, no calculations are required ($p = 0$). In the other two cases, the definition depends upon itself.

10. Recall the discussion of Newton's algorithm for approximating square roots in Chapter 20. Revise the program given in that section so that it displays, for each approximation, the difference between Pascal's determination of the square root using *sqrt* and the approximation.

11. Write two functions *sqrreal* and *sqrinteger* that perform the squaring operation on their argument to produce the result. Your two programmer-defined functions will have both argument and result of the same type. *sqrreal* will have both argument and result of type *real*. *sqrinteger* will have both argument and result of type *integer*.

12. Write a function to round a *real* number to a specified nonnegative number of decimal places. Your function will have two arguments: the number to be rounded and the number of decimal places.

13. Write a function to truncate a *real* number to a specified nonnegative number of decimal places. Your function will have two arguments: the number to be truncated and the number of decimal places to remain.

14. The following is an algebraic definition of the absolute value function:

$$
|x| = \begin{cases}
x \text{ if } x >= 0 \\
- x \text{ if } x < 0
\end{cases}
$$

Write an absolute value function that takes a *real* argument and produces a *real* result. Use the algebraic definition above as the basis of your algorithm.

15. Write an entire program to determine the solutions to a quadratic equation. Use the quadratic formula to determine the solutions, that is:

If $ax^2 + bx + c = 0$,

$$
\text{then} \quad x = \frac{-b \pm \sqrt{b^2 - 4(a)(c)}}{2(a)}
$$

Hint: Remember that you will need to test the discriminant, $b^2 - 4(a)(c)$. If the discriminant is zero, you will obtain two real roots, both equal to

$-b/(2(a))$. If the discriminant is positive, you will obtain two unequal real roots. If the discriminant is negative, you will obtain two unequal complex roots:

$$\frac{-b}{2(a)} + \left(\frac{\sqrt{-(\text{discriminant})}}{2(a)} \right) i$$

and

$$\frac{-b}{2(a)} - \left(\frac{\sqrt{-(\text{discriminant})}}{2(a)} \right) i$$

Since Pascal does not have a predefined type to deal with the imaginary part of a complex number, the *i* displayed above in the complex solutions should be printed as a literal constant when your program prints complex solutions.

16. Write an entire Pascal program to read in a number and print it out in a wavelike format. For example, if the number is 12345, your program should produce output similar to the following:

```
                        12345
                          12345
                            12345
                              12345
                                12345
                                  12345
                                12345
                              12345
                            12345
                          12345
                        12345
                      12345
                    12345
                  12345
                12345
              12345
            12345
          12345
        12345
      12345
        12345
          12345
            12345
              12345
```

Hint: Use the predefined function *sin*.

17. Write a Pascal function whose argument is a character in the range between '0' and '9' inclusive and whose result is the *integer* value we usually associate with that character. (Hint: See the examples in Figure 22.28.)

CHAPTER 23

23.1 INTRODUCTION TO STRUCTURED TYPES

In Chapter 9 (pages 177–179), we discussed the idea that an individual data item can be simple—for example, a single number or a single character—or complex—for example, all of the information on an income tax return. Complex data items are composed of simple data items organized into a data structure.

The syntax of Pascal allows a programmer to define a rich variety of data structures for use in solving problems. We first discuss the data structures used to represent fixed maximum-size lists. Such a data structure is referred to as a *one-dimensional array,* and the type of a variable representing such a data structure is called an *array type.*

23.2 DEFINING ONE-DIMENSIONAL ARRAY TYPES

Consider a data structure that holds a person's name. We use the simple type *char* to allocate memory space for a single character. Hence, a fixed-size list of items, each of type *char*, could represent a person's name. To define such a fixed-size list, we must decide on the maximum number of characters we will need. (This is standard practice. You may have seen computerized lists that cut off the ends of names that exceed a certain length.) Let's agree to allow 20 characters for the name. Such a list of characters is called a *string.* Imagine 20 boxes in memory, arranged sequentially as shown in Figure 23.1.

If we think of variables of simple types as homes in which a single data item can live, we can regard the structured type we have shown in Figure 23.1 as a

ONE-DIMENSIONAL ARRAYS

blueprint for an apartment building where 20 items all of type *char* reside. We need a way to refer to a specific or individual apartment. The individual items in this structure are referred to by using what is called an *index* or a *subscript*. In Figure 23.1, we show the subscripts as *integer* values from 1 to 20.

To use a structured data type, you must go through the two-stage process shown in Figure 23.2. We need an identifier to define this new structured type. Let's use *charstring*. In Figure 23.3, the type definition section of our program defines the type *charstring*. Note that we use a constant *maxname* to define a subrange type *nameindex*.

The definition of *charstring* consists of the identifier *charstring* followed by an =, followed by the reserved word **array**, followed by [, followed by a range of subscripts (indicated by the subrange type identifier *nameindex*), followed by], followed by the reserved word **of**, and finally followed by the type

Figure 23.1   **A blueprint for a data structure to hold a person's name**

$$[1] \quad [2] \quad [3] \quad [4] \quad \cdot \ \cdot \ \cdot \quad [16] \quad [17] \quad [18] \quad [19] \quad [20]$$

Figure 23.2   **The two stages used to set up variables of structured type**

1. Define the type.
2. Declare variables of that type.

for each item of the structure, *char*. The type of each item in the structure is called the structure's *base type*. The type that describes the range of subscripts is called the *index type*. In general, any ordinal type may be used for the index type. The reserved word **array** indicates that all of the elements of the structure are of the same type.

The syntax diagram in Figure 23.4 shows the generic structure of a one-dimensional array type definition.

The subrange type identifier can be replaced by the subrange itself. Thus, we could have defined type *charstring* as in Figure 23.5, where we have defined a type, but we have not yet declared a variable of this type. We have created a blueprint from which the computer can build variables of this array type.

23.3 DECLARING VARIABLES OF ARRAY TYPE

We can declare a variable of type *charstring* as follows:

var name : charstring;

This statement has the effect of allocating space in memory and identifying it by name. We can picture the array in memory with its identifier as in Figure 23.6.

Figure 23.3 Definition of array type *charstring*

```
const maxname = 20;
type nameindex = 1 .. maxname;
     charstring = array [nameindex] of char;
```

Figure 23.4 Syntax diagram for a one-dimensional array type definition

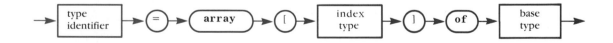

Figure 23.5 An array type definition using a subrange to define the subscript range

```
const maxname = 20;
type charstring = array [1..maxname] of char;
```

Figure 23.6 **Illustration of the effect on memory of declaring the variable** *name* **of type** *charstring*

Once we have defined a new type identifier, the syntax of declaring variables of that type is the same as the syntax of declaring variables of simple type.

23.4 ASSIGNING VALUES TO ARRAY ELEMENTS

Whenever we want to refer to a specific element in a one-dimensional array, we must give the name of the variable together with a single subscript enclosed in square brackets. *name* is a variable of type *charstring*. Hence, *name*[14] is a variable of type *char* and refers to the 14th element in the array *name*. Figure 23.7 shows some examples of assignments to array elements.

Exercise 23.1: Describe the effect on memory of the assignment statements in Figure 23.7. ■

As with simple variables, the values of array elements are unpredictable just after space in memory is allocated to them. Some computer systems fill these array elements with blanks, while others leave miscellaneous leftovers in them. To be safe, it is best to fill the entire array of characters with blanks before attempting to do anything with it. Figure 23.8 displays a procedure for filling an array of type *charstring* with blanks.

Figure 23.7 **Examples of assignments to array elements**

```
name[1] := 'b';
name[2] := 'a';
name[3] := 'r';
name[4] := name[1];
name[5] := name[2];
name[6] := name[3];
name[7] := name[2];
```

Figure 23.8 **Procedure** `blankfill`

```
procedure blankfill (var nm:charstring);
  {a procedure to fill an array of type charstring }
  {with blanks                                      }

const blank = ' '; {used to put blank into each position}
var index:integer; {used as array subscript}

begin {blankfill}
  for index: = 1 to maxname do
    nm[index]: =blank
end; {blankfill}
```

Exercise 23.2: Why must *nm* be a variable parameter in procedure *blankfill* displayed in Figure 23.8? ■

We use a **for** loop since we know that there are exactly 20 spaces to blank out. In fact, **for** loops and arrays seem to be made for each other, and the loop control variable in a **for** loop is often used as the subscript in an array. As the loop control variable changes value during iterations of the loop, every element of the array is referenced in succession. For instance, when *index* is 5, we assign the value *blank* to the fifth position in the array, as shown in Figure 23.9.

Figure 23.9 **Situation in memory just after the fifth array element is assigned the value *blank***

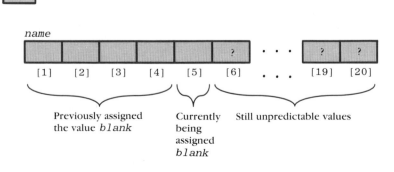

23.5 READING VALUES INTO ARRAY ELEMENTS

We can read values directly into array elements. For example the user, after being prompted to enter her name, types her name followed by a carriage return.

```
Please enter your name: Elizabeth ⏎
```

We need to read one character at a time into the element of the array in the appropriate position. We need to stop reading when we reach a carriage return or fill up the array. We need to be sure that the values used to access elements of the array are not greater than 20. Using a subscript out of the range of subscripts described in the index type of the array causes a run-time error. In this example, the range of possible subscripts is

```
1..maxname
```

where *maxname* is the constant value 20. Thus, any attempt to use a subscript less than 1 or greater than 20 will cause the program to crash.

When we get to the carriage return or run out of space in the array, we want to move the read pointer to the beginning of the next input line. To help us locate the carriage return that marks the end of an input line, Pascal has a predefined function called *eoln*, which stands for *end of line*. This is a *boolean*-valued function that has the value *true* if the character indicated by the read pointer is a carriage return and that otherwise has the value *false*. Because this value is determined by the next character to be read, it is standard practice to check the value of *eoln* before reading the next character. This practice avoids reading the carriage return character. Figure 23.10 shows an algorithm for reading a user's name into an array of characters.

We use procedure *blankfill* to achieve step I of the algorithm. We can use the predefined function *eoln* in the conditional expression that controls the **while** loop in step III. Figure 23.11 shows procedure *readstring*, a translation of the algorithm in Figure 23.10 into Pascal.

Exercise 23.3: Trace procedure *readstring* of Figure 23.11 on the following input:

Barbara Ann Teresa Li Santi ⏎ ∎

Figure 23.10 Algorithm to read a user's name into an array of characters

Setup

I. Declare an integer variable named *index* to use as the array subscript

Instructions

I. Fill the array with blanks.

II. Assign the value 1 to *index*.

III. While the next character to be read is not a carriage return and the value of *index* is less than or equal to the size of the array, do the following:
   A. Read a character into the array in the position indicated by *index*.
   B. Replace the value of *index* by 1 more than its current value.

IV. Move the read pointer to the beginning of the next input line.

Figure 23.11 Procedure *readstring*

```
procedure readstring (var username: charstring);
 {a procedure to correctly read characters into}
 {an array of type charstring                   }

var index: integer;   {used as array subscript}

begin {readstring}
  blankfill (username, maxname);
  index: =1;
  while (not eoln) and (index <= maxname) do
    begin {while}
      read(username[index]);
      index: = index + 1
    end; {while}
  readln   {move read pointer down}
end; {readstring}
```

Figure 23.12 **Procedure** *bugreadstring*

```
procedure bugreadstring (var username:charstring);
{a procedure with a bug}

var index:integer;  {used as array subscript}

begin {bugreadstring}
  blankfill (username,maxname);
  index:=1;
  while not eoln do
    begin {while}
     read(username[index]);
     index:=index +1
    end; {while}
  readln {moves read pointer down}
end; {bugreadstring}
```

Exercise 23.4: Consider procedure `bugreadstring` displayed in Figure 23.12. Trace procedure *bugreadstring* on the following input:

Elizabeth Catherine Marie ↵

What is the value of *index* just before the procedure crashes? ∎

23.6 WRITING OUT ARRAY ELEMENTS

Having used *blankfill* to fill the array with blanks and *readstring* to read characters into the array, we can now write a procedure to print the name we have read in. We'll show you two procedures, the second of which is preferable. Assume we have read *Elizabeth* into an array of type *charstring*. Consider first the procedure *writeout* displayed in Figure 23.13.

Here's the output produced by procedure *writeout*:

```
Elizabeth ∧∧∧∧∧∧∧∧∧∧∧
```

This procedure seems straightforward enough, but do we really want those 11 blanks to be printed after the name? What if we also wanted to read in and print

out Elizabeth's last name? We would rather have it printed just to the right of her first name, not 11 spaces to the right:

`Elizabeth Baggan`

instead of

`Elizabeth`^^^^^^^^^^^`Baggan`^^^^^^^^^^^^^^^

    If we calculated the position in the array of the last nonblank character to be printed, we could use that number instead of *maxname* as the final value for the loop control variable. Figure 23.14 shows a second procedure we'll call *writestring*. This procedure needs a function that we'll define shortly; we'll call this function *length*. A call to function *length* with the array as its only argument is used as the final value for the loop control variable.

Figure 23.13   **Procedure *writeout***

```
procedure writeout (n: charstring);
 {a procedure to write out all 20 characters in the string}

var index: integer; {used as array subscript}

begin {writeout}
  for index := 1 to maxname do
    write (n[index])
end;  {writeout}
```

Figure 23.14   **Procedure *writestring***

```
procedure writestring(thename: charstring);
 {prints a string without trailing blanks}

var index: integer; {used as array subscript}

begin {writestring}
  for index := 1 to length(thename) do
    write (thename [index])
  end; {writestring}
```

Exercise 23.5: Why is a value parameter, as opposed to a variable parameter, used in the procedure **writestring** shown in Figure 23.14? ■

Now what about this function **length**? We will develop an algorithm for function **length** and then write the Pascal code. Our input will be a fixed-size list of 20 characters. Our output will be an **integer** in the range from 0 to 20.

What we want to know is the position of the last nonblank character in the array. Beware: Beginning in position 1 and searching for the first blank does not always work. Consider the case in Figure 23.15, where one author's last name could be determined to have a length equal to 2 if we began in position 1 and searched for the first blank character.

Instead, our algorithm should begin in the last position and scan back through the array, skipping blanks until it arrives at a nonblank character. The position of that nonblank character is the length of the string. Note that we must worry about the possibility of encountering an entirely blank array. In the event that the whole string is blank, we must avoid trying to check position 0 because that would cause the program to crash. The algorithm in Figure 23.16 describes the backward scan. We can easily convert this algorithm into the function displayed in Figure 23.17.

Figure 23.15 **An example to test the algorithm for function** *length*

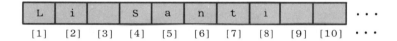

$$
\begin{array}{cccccccccc}
\text{L} & \text{i} & & \text{s} & \text{a} & \text{n} & \text{t} & \text{i} & & \\
[1] & [2] & [3] & [4] & [5] & [6] & [7] & [8] & [9] & [10]
\end{array}
\quad \cdots
$$

Figure 23.16 **Algorithm for function** *length*

Setup

I. Declare an integer variable named *index* to use as the array subscript.

Instructions

I. Assign *index* a value equal to the last possible subscript.

II. While the character in position indicated by *index* is blank and *index* is greater than 1, do the following:
   A. Replace the value of *index* with 1 less than its current value.

III. If the character in the position indicated by *index* is blank,
   then length of string is 0
   else length of string is the value of *index*.

Figure 23.17 **Function** *length*

```
function length (string:charstring) : integer;
 {a function to compute the length of a character string}

var curpos:integer; {to mark the current position}

begin {length}
  curpos: =maxname;
  while (string[curpos] =' ') and (curpos>1) do
    curpos: =curpos-1;
  if string[curpos] =' '
    then length: =0
    else length: =curpos
end; {length}
```

Exercise 23.6: What is wrong with the function *buglength* shown in Figure 23.18? (Hint: Trace it on a string containing only blank characters.) ∎

Exercise 23.7: Using procedures *blankfill*, *readstring*, and *write-string*, and function *length*, write a program that prompts a user to enter her first and last names on separate lines and then echo-prints the user's name on a single line with one blank space separating the first name from the last name. Figure 23.19 shows a sample execution. ∎

Figure 23.18 **Function** *buglength*

```
function buglength (string:charstring) : integer;
 {a buggy version of function length}

var curpos:integer; {to mark the current position}

begin {length}
  curpos: =maxname;
  while (string[curpos] =' ') and (curpos>1) do
    curpos: =curpos-1;
  length: =curpos
end; {length}
```

Figure 23.19   A sample execution for exercise 23.7

```
Please enter your first name followed by a
carriage return, followed by your last name
and another carriage return.

Barbara ⏎
Li.Santi ⏎

Your name is Barbara . Li . Santi
```

23.7 OTHER POSSIBLE ARRAY SUBSCRIPTS

It is sometimes inappropriate to use subscripts ranging from 1 to the size of the array. Pascal allows the programmer to choose more appropriate index types.

Integer Subscripts Other Than 1 . . *max*

Consider a program designed to calculate the number of players attaining each possible score in a golf tournament. Golf scores are given in terms of *par*—the expected number of strokes to finish the course. A score of exactly par corresponds to 0. A score four strokes under par corresponds to −4. A score three strokes more than par corresponds to 3. Suppose that the worst score for the tournament is 7 and the best is −5. The following array could be used to tabulate the number of players attaining each score.

```
type golfarray = array[-5 .. 7] of integer;
var golfscores : golfarray;
```

For example, golfscores[-3] represents the number of players attaining a score of 3 strokes under par.

Next consider a program designed to calculate the number of students earning the possible grades of 0 through 100, inclusive, on an exam. The following array could be used to tabulate the number of students earning each possible grade.

```
type gradearray = array[0 .. 100] of integer;
var examgrades : gradearray;
```

For example, examgrades[75] represents the number of students earning a grade of 75 on the exam.

Using Programmer-Defined Enumerated Types as Subscripts

Programmer-defined enumerated types can be used to make array subscripts more meaningful. Since array subscripts are not often read in or printed out, the standard restrictions governing programmer-defined enumerated types are not troublesome.

Consider the following example:

```
type produce = (orange, apple, banana, peach, nectarine);
     price = array [produce] of real;
     pounds = array [produce] of integer;

var perpound : price;
    totpounds : pounds;
    totaldue : real;
    fruit : produce;

begin
  totaldue := 0.0;
  for fruit := orange to nectarine do
    totaldue := totaldue +
                totpounds[fruit] * perpound[fruit]

end.
```

It is clear from the Pascal code that we are computing a bill for a certain number of pounds each of oranges, apples, bananas, peaches, and nectarines.

23.8 CASE STUDY: SORTING AN ARRAY

Problem Statement and General Algorithm

Let's look at an array whose elements are of the simple type *integer*. We want to write a program to read a set of exam scores into the array, to sort the array into descending order, and to print out the sorted array. We'll use an array with space for 100 exam scores. The user is to indicate the end of data by entering a negative score to act as a sentinel. The input is a list of up to 100 *integer* values. The output will be the list sorted into descending order. An algorithm to solve this problem could have three main parts, as shown in Figure 23.20.

Data Flow Diagram and Main Program

The list itself and the number of items in the list are data that will be transmitted between the procedures that correspond to the three major tasks described in Figure 23.20. Let's name the list *scores* and the number of items in the list *numscores*. We use a named constant *maxscores* to represent the size of the array, 100. Figure 23.21 shows the flow of data items between the three main procedures.

Figure 23.20   **Sketch of an algorithm to input, sort, and output exam scores**

I. Read in the list of scores.

II. Sort the list of scores.

III. Write out the sorted list of scores.

Figure 23.21   **Data flow diagram for exam score sorting problem**

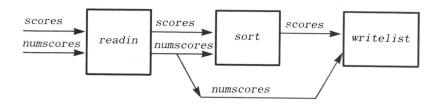

Now let's sketch the main program. Figure 23.22 contains our sketch of the main program.

Reading in the Data to Create a List

The first order of business is to read in scores until either a negative value is entered or until the array is filled. If the user tries to enter more scores than the data structure can handle, the program should print an error message and go on to process the full array.

Exercise   23.8: Write an algorithm for procedure *readin*. It should assume that we have passed it an array of at most 100 integers, an *integer* variable representing the number of scores entered, and an *integer* value representing the size of the array. The algorithm is to determine values for the array elements and for the number of scores. Refer to the algorithm for procedure *readstring* given in Figure 23.10. ∎

The data flow diagram in Figure 23.21 shows that procedure *readin* affects the values of both *scores* and *numscores*. Hence, they should both correspond to variable parameters in procedure *readin*.

Figure 23.23 gives one possible version of procedure *readin*.

Sorting the List

Now let's turn to procedure *sort*. You may want to refer back to Chapter 7 for an algorithm to sort a list of fixed size. Our data flow diagram in Figure 23.21 indicates that this procedure will affect the value of array *scores*, but only needs

Figure 23.22   Sketch of program *processcores*

```
program processcores (input,output);
   {a program to read in up to 100 integer test scores,}
   {sort the scores into descending order, and print out}
   {the sorted list}

const maxscores = 100;
     {maximum number of scores this program}
     {can process                           }

type testindex = 1 .. maxscores;
     {type for array subscripts}
     testarray = array [testindex] of integer;
     {type for array to hold test scores}

var scores : testarray;
     {array to hold test scores}
     numscores : integer;
     {number of scores actually input}
     response : char;
     {to hold user's response to "any data?"}

begin {processcores}
   writeln('Do you have any data?');
   readln(response);
   if response in [ 'y', 'Y']
       then
           begin {then}
              readin(scores,numscores);
              sort(scores,numscores);
              writelist(scores,numscores)
           end {then}
       else
           writeln('Good bye then.')
   end. {processcores}
```

to use the value of *numscores*. Hence, our procedure must have a variable parameter corresponding to *scores* and a value parameter corresponding to *numscores*.

Figure 23.24 displays the Pascal code for the selection sort algorithm. Notice that parts of the algorithm that used the while construct are implemented with **for** loops.

Figure 23.23   Procedure *readin*

```
procedure readin (var examscores: testarray; var num:integer);
  {This procedure creates the list of examscores for user input.}
  {It returns both the list and the number of scores in the list}
  {to the main program through variable parameters.}

var curpos:integer; {used as subscript for array}

begin {readin}
  writeln('Please enter your scores one per line');
  writeln('Signal the end of data with a negative number');
  curpos:=1;
  readln (examscores[1]);
  while (curpos<maxscores) and (examscores[curpos]>0) do
    begin {while}
      curpos:=curpos+1;
      readln(examscores[curpos])
    end; {while}
  if examscores [curpos]>=0
    then
      begin {then}
        writeln('array is filled');
        num:=curpos
      end   {then}
    else
      num:=curpos-1
end; {readin}
```

Exercise   23.9: Write a procedure named *switch* that interchanges the values of its two variable parameters. ■

Exercise   23.10: Rewrite our procedure *sort* so that it uses the procedure *switch* that you wrote for Exercise 23.9. Make procedure *switch* local to procedure *sort*. ■

Exercise   23.11: Write procedure *writelist*. It should be similar to procedure *writeout* in Figure 23.14. ■

Figure 23.24   Procedure *sort*

```
procedure sort (var exscores : testarray; numsc : integer);
   {sorts an array of type testarray into descending order}
   {using the selection sort algorithm}

var fixpos, {to hold position being fixed}
    compos, {to hold position being compared}
    desirepos : integer; {to hold position of}
                         {array element that }
                         {should be in fixpos}
    temp : integer; {to hold a value during switch}

begin {sort}
   for fixpos := 1 to (numsc - 1) do
      begin {for fixpos}
         desirepos := fixpos;
         for compos := (fixpos + 1) to numsc do
            if exscores [compos] > exscores[desirepos]
               then desirepos := compos;
         if fixpos <> desirepos
            then
               begin {switch}
                  temp := exscores[fixpos];
                  exscores[fixpos] := exscores[desirepos];
                  exscores[desirepos] := temp
               end {switch}
      end {fixpos}
end; {sort}
```

23.9 COMPARING CHARACTER STRINGS

A Programmer-Defined Function

We now have a structure capable of holding a complete word as a logical unit. What if we want to compare two words?

Recall that both ASCII and EBCDIC represent lowercase letters of the alphabet in order. In other words, 'a' < 'b' is a *true* expression and 'd' < 'b' is a *false* expression. Thus, if we have two character string variables of the same type, we can write an algorithm to decide if one word precedes the other in alphabetical order. For simplicity, we will assume that all the letters in our character arrays are lowercase.

We begin with the first letter of each word. If the letters are different, we can decide which word is first in alphabetical order. If the first letters of both words are the same, we check the second letter of each word. We then continue to compare the corresponding letters in the two words until we find two letters that are not the same. If all the corresponding letters match, we conclude that the two words are the same.

Exercise   23.12: Write an algorithm to decide whether or not word#1 is before word#2 in alphabetical order.   ■

Exercise   23.13: Assume the following definitions and declarations:

```
const    maxwordlength = 15;
type     wordindex = 1.. maxwordlength;
         wordstring = array [wordindex] of char;
var      word1, word2: wordstring;
```

Use the algorithm you wrote for Exercise 23.12 and the definitions and declarations given above to write a *boolean*-valued function *before*. *before* should have two value parameters of type *wordstring* corresponding to *word1* and *word2*. *before* should return the value *true* if its first parameter represents a word that is alphabetically before the word represented by its second parameter, and should return the value *false* otherwise.   ■

Packed Arrays

Pascal provides a variation of the *array* called the *packed array* structure.[1] This structure makes it possible to compare two character string variables of the same packed array type by using the relational operators $<$, $>$, $<=$, $>=$, $=$, and $<>$. Consider, for example, two variables *word1* and *word2* declared as shown in Figure 23.25.

To decide if *word1* is before *word2*, we could simply use the relational operator $<$ to form the following *boolean* expression:

```
word1 < word2
```

---

1. All arrays are automatically packed arrays on most byte-addressable systems, making use of this feature unnecessary.

Figure 23.25 **Declaration of two packed array-type variables**

```
const   maxwordlength = 15;
type    wordindex = 1..maxwordlength;
        pwordstring = packed array [wordindex] of char;
var     word1, word2: pwordstring;
```

This expression is *true* if *word1* is before *word2* in alphabetical order.

Although this is a useful feature, it has one disadvantage. A single element of a packed array (in this case, a single letter of a word) cannot be used as an argument corresponding to a variable parameter. For example, assuming once more the definitions and declarations in Figure 23.25, the following statement is illegal :

```
read(word1[1]); {illegal}
```

The Standard Procedures *pack* and *unpack*

Pascal does, however, provide a way to compare entire character string variables and to use their individual elements as arguments. As we have seen, a packed array enables us to make comparisons, and an array enables us to use individual elements as arguments in procedure calls. Pascal has two predefined procedures, *pack* and *unpack*, to allow us to accomplish both actions. The purpose of *pack* is to pack the contents of an array into a packed array. The purpose of *unpack* is to unpack the contents of a packed array into an array.[2]

To see how *pack* and *unpack* work, consider the definitions and declarations in Figure 23.26.

Figure 23.26 **Declarations for one array and one packed array**

```
const   maxwordlength = 15;
type    wordindex = 1.. maxwordlength;
        wordstring = array [wordindex] of char;
        pwordstring = packed array [wordindex] of char;
var     word: wordstring;
        pword: pwordstring;
```

2. The packed array and the array must have the same base type.

The following call to procedure *pack* copies the contents of the array *word* into the packed array *pword*.

```
pack(word, 1, pword)
```

The argument, 1, in the second position indicates the position in the array *word* of the character to be copied to the first position in the packed array *pword*. For example, the procedure call

```
pack(word, 5, pword)
```

would not copy the first four characters of *word* into *pword*.

In general, the three arguments to standard procedure *pack* are

1. The array to be packed
2. The position of the first character in the array to be copied into the packed array
3. The packed array receiving the copies of the characters of the array

Let's assume that we have a program that uses two array variables of type *wordstring*. We write a *boolean*-valued function *after* that has two parameters of type *wordstring* and returns the value *true* if the first parameter is after the second in alphabetical order. We use the standard procedure *pack* and two local variables of type *pwordstring*. We will simply pack each parameter and compare the packed arrays. Figure 23.27 displays the function *after*. The function *after* is useful in a program that sorts a list of names into alphabetical order.

Figure 23.27   Function *after*

```
function after (w1, w2: wordstring): boolean;
   {returns true if w1 is after w2 in alphabetical order}

var   pw1, pw2: pwordstring;
         {to hold packed copies of w1 and w2}

begin {after}
   pack(w1, 1, pw1);
   pack(w2, 1, pw2);
   after := pw1 > pw2
end; {after}
```

The syntax for a call to procedure *unpack* is as follows:

```
unpack(pword, word, first)
```

where *pword* is a packed array to be unpacked into array *word*, and *first* is the position in *word* where the first character of *pword* is to be copied. Procedure *unpack* is useful in a situation where an individual element in a packed array must be used as an argument corresponding to a variable parameter.

Exercise 23.14: Write an entire program that reads in the first and last names of two people. Your program should decide which name is first in alphabetical order and should print a message to the user proclaiming its decision. ■

23.10 ASSIGNMENTS TO ARRAY-TYPE VARIABLES

The assignment operator can be used in a powerful way in conjunction with array-type variables. Suppose we make the following declaration, where *charstring* is defined as in Figure 23.5.

```
var name1, name2: charstring;
```

We can assign all 20 character values in *name1* to *name2* as follows:

```
name2 := name1;
```

Such assignments are allowed between any two variables of the same type. When the type is a structured type, the entire contents of one structured variable can be assigned to another variable of the same type.

String literals are implicitly packed arrays of characters. Assume that the two variables *first* and *last* are declared as follows:

```
type  packedcharstr = packed array [1..20] of char;
var   first, last: packedcharstr;
```

The assignment statements shown in Figure 23.28 are legal. Note that according to Standard Pascal this type of assignment of a string literal is allowed only to a packed array-type variable. In some implementations of Pascal, all arrays of characters are automatically packed arrays that can be assigned the value of a string literal. Some implementations of Pascal allow assignment of shorter character

Figure 23.28 **Assignments of string literals to packed arrays of characters**

```
first := 'George^^^^^^^^^^^^^^^^^';

last := 'Washington^^^^^^^^^^^';
```

strings to longer character string variables. The shorter string is "padded" to the right with blank characters to make it as long as the longer string. Thus, the following assignments are possible in some implementations and have the same effect as those in Figure 23.28.

```
first := 'George';
last := 'Washington';
```

Many implementations of Pascal have an additional predefined type named, *string* that is similar to an array of characters.

CHAPTER SUMMARY

1. An *array* is a list of data items that are all of the same base type.

2. To use an array-type variable, we should
   a. Define a type for the array structure
   b. Declare variables of that type
   The syntax required to define a one-dimensional array type is shown in Figure 23.4. Once we have defined an array type, we can declare a variable of that type just as we declare a variable of simple type.

3. We refer to the individual elements in an array-type variable by using *subscripts* in the following manner:

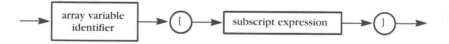

The index type of array-type variables may be defined as any subrange of a predefined or programmer-defined ordinal type.

4. The relational operators $<$, $<=$, $=$, $>=$, $>$, and $<>$ may be used to determine the alphabetical order of variables of type **packed array** of characters. (Some Pascal implementations pack all arrays of characters automatically, making it possible to compare two variables of type **array** of characters.)

5. Pascal permits assignments between two variables of the same array type. Since string literals are implicitly packed arrays of characters, they may be assigned to appropriately sized packed array variables.

6. The standard procedure *pack* is used to copy the values stored in an array-type variable to a packed array-type variable of the same base type. The standard procedure *unpack* is used to copy the values stored in a packed array-type variable to an array-type variable of the same base type.

COMMON ERRORS

■ The most frequent error in programs using array-type variables is the attempt to reference an array element with a subscript that is outside the defined range of subscripts. For example, assume we have declared the variable *name* to be an array of 20 characters. If we attempt to reference *name*[21], we will cause a run-time error, usually described as "subscript out of range."

■ Using a type identifier rather than a variable identifier to refer to an array is a syntactic error. This error is shown in Figure 23.29.

■ Using the variable identifier for an array-type variable to refer to an individual array element.

■ Assignment between two array-type variables that were not both declared with the same type identifier.

DEBUGGING HINTS

■ To determine why subscripts are out of range or why incorrect values are stored in arrays, display the values of both array elements and their subscripts with statements such as:

```
writeln('score[',index:1,']is ',score[index])
```

Insert such statements into all loops manipulating arrays.

Figure 23.29 **A common error using the type identifier instead of the variable identifier**

```
type   charstring = array [1.20] of char;
var    name: charstring;
   .            .
   .            .
   .            .
   charstring [1] := 'b';           {This is Illegal!!!}
```

SUPPLEMENTAL PROBLEMS

1. Count the number of occurrences of the word *the* in a paragraph. Use a line consisting of only a carriage return to mark the end of the paragraph.

2. Make an alphabetical list of all the letters that occur in a single line of input.

3. Perform the following statistical analyses on a set of *integer* values:
   a. Determine the largest value.
   b. Determine the smallest value.
   c. Determine the range of values (highest to lowest).
   d. Determine the average value.
   e. Determine the median value. (This requires sorting the values.) The median value is the middle value. If n is the number of values, then
     (i) if n is odd, the middle value is in position $(n+1)/2$.
     (ii) if n is even, the middle value is the average of the value in position $(n/2)$ and the value in position $(n/2) - 1$.
   f. Determine the standard deviation of the values. If there are n values, k is the average value determined in part d, and x_i denotes the ith value, the following formula gives the standard deviation:

$$\sqrt{\frac{1}{n-1} \sum_{i=1}^{n} (x_i - k)^2}$$

4. Read in a string of characters. Present the user with the following menu of possible manipulations of the string:
   a. Leave the string unchanged.
   b. Reverse the order of all characters in the string.
   c. Encode the string by replacing each alphabetical character with the next alphabetical character. (Replace z with a.)
   d. Decode the string by replacing each alphabetical character with the preceding alphabetical character (Replace a with z.)
   Allow the user to choose from the menu. Perform the action indicated by the user and print the resulting string.

5. Write a procedure to implement the binary search algorithm described in Chapter 7 (page 142–143) on a list of *integer* values. The procedure should have three value parameters corresponding, respectively, to the list, the number of items in the list, and the value being searched for. It should also have two variable parameters: one *boolean* parameter to return *true* if the value is found and *false* if not, and one *integer* parameter to return the position of the value being searched for in the list.

6. Write a procedure to merge two sorted lists of *integer* values into a single sorted list according to the algorithm described in Chapter 7 (page 151–152). The procedure should have four value parameters corresponding to the two

initial lists and the number of items in each list. It should also have two variable parameters corresponding to the combined list and the number of items in that list.

7. Write a program to encode sentences. The letters `'a'..'z'` should correspond to the letters `'nbfgrtzxopklcedmhjyuiqsvwa'`. The user should be able to type in a sentence and have the encoded version appear. (Hint: Use an array with subscript range `'a'..'z'` to hold the encoding letters.)

8. Write a program to decode sentences. The program should use the same code as the one you used in problem 7. The user should be able to type in an encoded sentence and have the decoded version appear.

9. Write a program that reads a line of input text and determines which of the lowercase letters `'a'..'z'` is in the line. Use an array with `['a'..'z']` as the index type and *boolean* as the base type.

10. (For the mathematically minded.) Use two one-dimensional array variables to represent two vectors in 3-space. Write a program to calculate both the dot product and the cross product of the two vectors.

C H A P T E R

24

The one-dimensional arrays we discussed in the preceding chapter are like limited-size lists in appearance. Each entry is accessed by means of a single subscript. Often, however, we want to record or refer to information that is not in list form. Consider the multiplication table in Figure 24.1.

To deal with such a table, we need a two-dimensional data structure. Other examples of nonlist formats that require two-dimensional data structures are such familiar game boards as chess, checkers, and tic-tac-toe; tax tables; baseball scoreboards; and any table that records information in terms of two attributes. Consider the following problem:

Milton's Candy Store keeps an inventory based on the type of candy and price of candy. There are three types of candy: hard, chewy, and gooey. There are four price ranges for candy: cheap, moderate, expensive, and extravagant. Create a diagram to help Milton keep track of his candy stock.

Figure 24.1   5-by-7 multiplication table

	1	2	3	4	5	6	7
1	1	2	3	4	5	6	7
2	2	4	6	8	10	12	14
3	3	6	9	12	15	18	21
4	4	8	12	16	20	24	28
5	5	10	15	20	25	30	35

MULTIDIMENSIONAL ARRAYS

Tabulations of this type (and more complicated versions) are often used in business and research. Figure 24.2 gives a diagram for the problem above. To keep track of his candy inventory, Milton can simply put a number in the appropriate box. Figure 24.3 gives an example.

With this type of tabulation, Milton could easily see that his stock includes five cheap hard candies and no expensive chewy candies. The two-dimensional format makes it much easier for Milton to keep track of his stock than a list format would.

Figure 24.2   Diagram for Milton's candy stock

	cheap	moderate	expensive	extravagant
hard				
chewy				
gooey				

Figure 24.3   A table indicating Milton's current candy stock

	cheap	moderate	expensive	extravagant
hard	5	0	2	1
chewy	17	0	0	0
gooey	4	3	7	6

24.1 TWO-DIMENSIONAL ARRAYS

Pascal provides an easy means of creating such two-dimensional arrays. Actually, it enables us to create data structures with a multidimensional format (for example, a board for three-dimensional tic-tac-toe).

As with a one-dimensional array, we must create a blueprint or type for a two-dimensional array before we can put it to use. Consider again the multiplication table in Figure 24.1. To find the product of two numbers (if r times $y = z$, then z is the product), we must locate the row and the column that correspond to the two numbers and then locate the intersection of the row and the column. Since we will be accessing a position in the array by two subscripts, we need to define the array type to have two index types.

The Pascal format used to define a two-dimensional array is similar to the format used to define a one-dimensional array, except that we must specify two index types within the square brackets. Figure 24.4 shows a sample definition for a data structure that could hold our 5×7 multiplication table. Notice that the specifications of the two index types within the brackets are separated by a comma. The syntax diagram for defining any array type is given in Figure 24.5.

Let's set up a variable to use this type and see how we assign values to the places in a two-dimensional array. Our variable declaration will be identical in structure to those we have made before, except that we'll use a new type, *multtable*. Figure 24.6 shows a variable declaration.

We can now assign values to the variable we have declared. When we want to refer to a place in our array, we specify one subscript for row and one subscript for column. For convenience, we follow traditional mathematical notation, in which a row is specified first, then a column. Pascal assumes the subscripts will appear in the order in which we declare them. Therefore, when specifying a position in the array, we must make sure that the first subscript fits within the first index type in the type definition and that the second subscript fits within the second index type

Figure 24.4   **Type definition for a multiplication table**

```
const minsize = 1;    {the minimum subscript for a table}
         maxsizerow  = 5;{the maximum row subscript for a }
                         {multidimensional array}
         maxsizecol  = 7;{the maximum col subscript for a}
                         {multidimensional array}

type multtable=array[minsize..maxsizerow,
                     minsize..maxsizecol] of integer;
                     {a two-dimensional array}
```

Figure 24.5   **Syntax diagram for defining an array type**

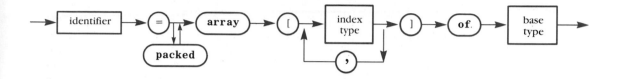

Figure 24.6   **Variable declaration section using** *multtable*

```
var table1 : multtable;    {a table to hold all possible}
                {combinations of the values n × m      }
```

in the type definition. And, we must separate the two subscripts with a comma. For example, if we wanted the box indicated by the third row and the second column to be 6 (3 × 2 = 6) we would write the following:

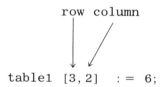

```
table1 [3,2]   : = 6;
```

Or we could assign the box indicated by the second row and the fifth column the value 10 (2 × 5 = 10) as follows:

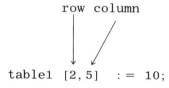

```
table1 [2,5]   : = 10;
```

Figure 24.7 shows how *table1* would look after these assignment statements.

Exercise   24.1: Assume that the subscripts represent the numbers being multiplied. Fill in the diagonal of *table1* that goes from position 1,1 to position 5,5 with the correct product, using assignment statements. ■

Figure 24.7   Variable `table1` **after assignment statements**

	1	2	3	4	5	6	7
1	?	?	?	?	?	?	?
2	?	?	?	?	10	?	?
3	?	6	?	?	?	?	?
4	?	?	?	?	?	?	?
5	?	?	?	?	?	?	?

For a second example of a two-dimensional array type definition, let's go back to Milton's Candy Store. Milton wants a data structure that has three rows and four columns. We need to define a type that fits that format.

We'll give our data structure the name *invent*. For index types we can define enumerated types that correspond to Milton's categories. Figure 24.8 shows the definition of the enumerated type and the array type.

We now have a Pascal type to describe the array shown in Figure 24.2. Milton can now declare variables of this type to hold information about his candy stock. For example, if he has two candy stores, he might make the variable declaration shown in Figure 24.9. Note that we cannot make the following assignment statement:

```
candy[cheap, moderate] := 50;   {ERROR!}
```

Figure 24.8   Type definition for Milton's candy inventory

```
type  consistency = (hard, chewy, gooey);
        {attribute to categorize candy}
      price = (cheap, moderate, expensive, extravagant);
        {attribute to categorize candy}
      invent = array [consistency, price] of integer;
             {a structure to hold inventory that }
             {is categorized by two fields}
```

Figure 24.9   Variable declaration for Milton's Candy Store's inventory

```
var uptownstore,            {to hold inventory for Milton's}
      downtownstore: invent;  {candy stores}
```

This is an error because we declared the index type for the first subscript to be of type *consistency*. Therefore, *cheap* is an illegal first subscript.

If we want to initialize all the values in a multidimensional array or to look at each value in the array, we can use **for** loops. Let's assume that Milton is just setting up his candy stock. We should start with a 0 in each position in the array. To do so, we could make the following series of assignment statements:

```
candy[hard, cheap] := 0;
candy[hard, moderate] := 0;
candy[hard, expensive] := 0;
candy[hard, extravagant] := 0;
                 .
                 .
                 .
```

and so on. Although this would be an onerous task, it would reveal a pattern. For the first four assignment statements we hold the row at *hard* and increment the column through the index type *price*. An algorithm for initializing the first row of our array might be as follows:

I. Set *row* to *hard.*

II. For every *column* from *cheap* to *extravagant,* do the following:
    A. Place the value 0 in the box indicated by *invent* [*row,column*].

We could apply the same basic algorithm to initialize the remaining rows of the array. For each row, we would increment the column through each value in the type *price*.

We could then combine our algorithms into something like the following:

I. For every *row* from *hard* to *gooey,* do the following:
    A. For every *column* from *cheap* to *extravagant,* do the following:
        1. Place the value 0 in the box indicated by *invent* [*row, column*].

Let's translate this algorithm into a procedure we'll call *initinventory*. We'll send the procedure a variable of type *invent* as an argument in order to make the procedure more general. Figure 24.10 shows the procedure. We could now create a procedure to allow Milton to enter inventory concerning his candy stock into the array.

Note that if two arrays are of the same type, we can assign one the value of the other. For example, if we wanted Milton's uptown store to start with the same inventory as the downtown store, we could make the following assignment statement:

```
uptownstore := downtownstore
```

In Pascal, any variable may be assigned the value of another variable of the same type.

Figure 24.10 **Procedure *initinventory* for Milton's Candy Store**

```
procedure initinventory (var table:invent);
    {This procedure initializes a variable of type}
    {invent to 0 in every space. It uses two nested}
    {for loops. The first for loop holds the row constant}
    {while the column is incremented. The row is then}
    {incremented and the same procedure is followed until}
    {everything is initialized.}

var row: consistency;
        {holds the place value of row in the for loop}
    col: price;
        {holds the place value of column in for loop }

begin    {proc. initinventory}

    for row := hard to gooey do        {for every row}
        for col := cheap to extravagant do {go through every}
            table[row,col] := 0            {column and set}
                                          {element to 0}
    end;      {proc. initinventory}
```

24.2 OTHER MULTIDIMENSIONAL ARRAYS

The type definition of other multidimensional arrays is the same as the type definition of one- and two-dimensional arrays, except for the number of index types specified. We might define a three-dimensional array and a four-dimensional array as follows:

```
type dim3 = array [1..5, 2..4, 1..3] of real;
                {an example of a three-dimensional array}
     dim4 = array ['a'..'d',1..3,2..3,'x'..'y'] of char;
                {an example of a four-dimensional array}
```

Variables of these types would typically be declared as follows:

```
var board1,
    board2: dim3;
    matrix: dim4;    {examples of multidimensional var}
                              {declarations}
```

and would be accessed by specifying a value for each subscript. Figure 24.11 shows the common representation for a complex structure such as *board1*. Figure 24.12 shows a complex structure such as *matrix*.

To access a certain place in *matrix*, we would have to specify four subscripts. A statement might look like this:

```
matrix['a',2,3,'y']:= 'r';
```

This would cause an `'r'` to be placed in the section marked `'y'`, in the box marked 3, in column 2, in row `'a'`.

Figure 24.11   Common representation for a three-dimensional array

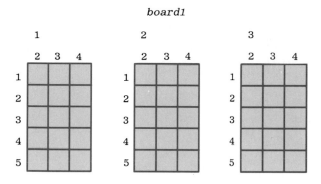

Figure 24.12   Common representation for a four-dimensional array

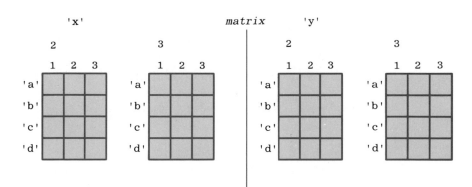

Multidimensional arrays of this sort are often used for cross-tabulating. For example, you could use such an array to categorize people according to these five attributes: age, place of birth, number of years of schooling, income, and tax bracket.

CHAPTER SUMMARY

1. *Multidimensional arrays* are useful for storing information that is best described by more than one attribute.

2. The number of dimensions of an array is described by the number of index types.

3. The particular spot being accessed in the array is described by subscripts, one for each dimension of the array.

COMMON ERRORS

■ Omitting a subscript needed to describe a position of the array is a syntactic error.

■ Presenting subscripts in an order that does not match the order in which they are presented in the definition of the variable's type is a syntactic error.

■ Any error commonly made when using one-dimensional arrays.

SUPPLEMENTAL PROBLEMS

1. Create a data structure to hold a student's class schedule for two years. Include the following means of selection: year, semester, day, hour. Make a type declaration and a variable declaration, and draw a picture to represent your variable.

2. You are given the following type definition:

```
type bigarray = array [1..3,'a'..'d','c'..'d',
                       4..6,1..2] of char;
```

Draw a picture of what a variable of the type would look like.

3. You are given the following type definition and variable declaration:

    ```
    type testarray = array ['a'..'c',10..15,4..9,
                                  10..15,'1'..'7'] of integer;
    var firstarray, secondarray: testarray;
    ```

    Which of the following are correct Pascal assignment statements and which are not? If a statement is not correct, explain why.
    a. `firstarray : = secondarray;`
    b. `firstarray['b',9,10,10,'6']: = 20;`
    c. `secondarray['c',10,5,11,4] : = 6;`
    d. `secondarray['c',10,7]: = firstarray['c',10,7];`
    e. `firstarray['c',10,4,10,1,'1']: = 6;`

4. Write a program that will enable Milton to keep track of his candy inventory. Use the structures defined in this chapter. The program should allow him to do the following:
    a. Enter his initial inventory. If he does not enter an amount for a certain type of candy, its value should be 0.
    b. Add to or subtract from any given number in his inventory as many times as he wishes.
    c. Check the current inventory of any given candy.
    d. Print his final inventory and leave the program.

5. Create a multiplication table that will show all the possibilities for the formula $n \times m$, where m and n can have the values of any number from 1 through 12. Print out the table.
    a. Write a program to solve this problem without using an array.
    b. Write a program to solve this problem using an array.

6. Create a type for a 12-by-12 multidimensional array. Write a procedure that will assign the values of $n \times m$ to a variable of that type where n goes from 6 to 17 and m goes from -3 to 8.

7. We want to create a 12-by-12 multiplication table that holds the following values: $R \times S$ where R goes from some whole number x to some number $x + 11$ (for example, 1..12, 2..13) and S goes from some whole number y to some number $y + 11$. Write a procedure that accepts as parameters the values x and y and fills in a multiplication table for the user.

8. Write a program to keep track of a game of three-dimensional tic-tac-toe. The program should take moves from two players. It should report a winner as soon as there is one; otherwise, it should report a tie. Any three in a row should be a winner. This includes having three in a row on different levels. For example, having pieces in position 1,1 on level 1, position 1,1 on level 2 and position 1,1 on level 3 would be three in a row. Diagonals through all three levels should also be allowed.

9. Expand the program written for Milton's Candy Store to allow Milton to find out how many candies he has that can be classified by a single attribute (for example, "hard candies").

10. Someone wishes to classify books by the following attributes:

    price: cheap, reasonable, expensive

    type: mystery, science fiction, romance, nonfiction

    condition: poor, fair, fine, great

    Create a data structure for this classification. Write a procedure to go through this data structure and report the number of books that are in great condition.

11. (For students who know matrix algebra.)
    a. Define a data type suitable for storing $n \times n$ matrices of **real** values.
    b. Write a procedure which takes two values of the type defined in 11a, computes their matrix product, and returns it in a variable parameter of the same type.

CHAPTER

25

We have seen that the array is a structure that can hold several pieces of data of the same type. So far we have used it to hold only elements that are of a simple data type: *real*, *integer*, *char*, or *boolean*. The array is capable, however, of holding more complex data types: In fact, it is capable of holding arrays as elements.

25.1 AN EXAMPLE: A LIST OF NAMES

Let's create an array in which every element is itself an array. Remember that all the elements of any array must be of the same type.

The following problem can be solved by using an array built of arrays:

Read in names from the user until you have five names or until the user types in an asterisk as the first character in a name. Print the names.

The input to this problem is up to five names followed by an asterisk. The output is a list of the names typed in, not including the asterisk.

In Chapter 23 (pages 499–500), we wrote procedure *readstring*, which takes an argument that is an array of characters and reads in the characters one at a time until either *eoln* is *true* or until the array is full. We'll use the data structures declared there and the procedures *readstring*, *blankfill*, and *writestring*. We'll use a constant *endmarker* for the asterisk.

To implement a solution using the structures with which we are already familiar, we would need the following variable declarations:

```
var name1,                {to hold 5 separate names}
    name2,
```

ARRAYS OF ARRAYS

```
name3,
name4,
name5 : charstring;
```

Figure 25.1 shows a procedure to read in names. Our procedure to print names would be similar.

These procedures would be awkward, especially if we had to deal with 20 or 100 names. We can solve the problem more easily with an array of arrays.

First, we must specify the type of elements we want in our array, because our array will not be made up of elements of a predefined type. Since we want every element in the array to contain a name, we use our definition of *charstring*:

```
const maxname = 20;      {max length of a string}
type charstring = array[1..maxname] of char;
                  {a blueprint for a character string}
```

Now we can declare an array that has as its elements arrays of type *charstring*. Since we want space for five names, we define a constant *maxlist* equal to five. Here are the additions to the constant and type definitions:

```
const maxname = 20;         {max length of a string}
      endmarker = '*'; {to indicate no more names}
      maxlist = 5;      {max number of names in a list}

type charstring = array[1..maxname] of char;
                  {a blueprint for a character string}
     list = array[1..maxlist] of charstring;
                  {a blueprint to hold a list of names}
```

Figure 25.1   Procedure to read in up to five names

```
procedure getnames (var nameA, nameB, nameC,
                         nameD, nameE :charstring);

{a procedure to read in up to five names, or stop}
{if an asterisk is typed as the first character}
{of a name}

begin    {getnames}
   write('name? ');
   readstring(nameA);
   if nameA[1] <> endmarker
      then
         begin  {to get nameB}
            write('name? ');
            readstring(nameB);
            if nameB[1] <> endmarker
               then
                  begin {to get nameC}
                     write('name? ');
                     readstring(nameC);
                     if nameC[1] <> endmarker
                        then
                           begin  {to get nameD}
                              write('name? ');
                              readstring(nameD);
                              if nameD[1] <> endmarker
                                 then
                                  begin
                                     write('name?');
                                     readstring(nameE)
                                  end
                           end  {to get nameD}
                  end  {to get nameC}
         end  {to get nameB}
end;   {getnames}
```

We have created a blueprint structure for an array in which each element is an array of type *charstring*. Figure 25.2 shows our blueprint. Now we can declare a single variable of type *list* to hold up to five names:

var names : list; {a list to hold names}

Each element of the array we have declared is of type *charstring* and can be passed to procedure *readstring*. We refer to the first element in the array as *names*[1], just as we refer to the first element in any array. We can send this first element as an argument to procedure *readstring* in the following way:

readstring(names[1]);

Procedure *readstring* will treat this specific element of *names* as a variable of type *charstring* and will read a name into it, just as we intended.

Now that we have an index for referring to each element in the array, we can use a **while** loop to read in the various names. In the **while** loop we will increment *index* every time we get a new name. Figure 25.3 shows an updated version of procedure *getnames*.

Exercise   25.1: Write a procedure to print out a list of names. You can assume that procedure *writestring* is available.   ■

Figure 25.2   Representation for an array of arrays

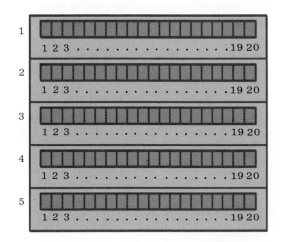

Figure 25.3   **Updated version of `getnames`**

```
procedure getnames (var emptylist : list);
  {a procedure to read in names until the maximum number}
  {is entered or until an asterisk is typed as the first}
  {character of a name}

var index: integer;        {to go through emptylist}
                           {as we fill it}
    done : boolean;        {to indicate no more names}
                           {will be entered}
begin   {getnames}
  done : = false;
  index : = 1;
  while (index <= maxlist )and (not done) do
    begin    {while loop}
      write('name please: ');
      readstring(emptylist[index]);
      if emptylist[index][1] = endmarker
        then done : = true;
      index : = index + 1
    end {while}
end; {getnames}
```

The array of arrays makes our task easier because we can go through the list simply by changing the subscript.

In procedure *getnames*, we look at the first character of an element of the array of type *list* when we check for an asterisk. This is an example of how an individual element within an array of arrays is accessed. Here is a general rule that is useful in dealing with complex data structures in Pascal:

> *When describing a specific component of a complex data structure, always start with the general part of the component and work down to the specific.*

Refer again to Figure 25.2. Assume that we want to look at the first letter of the fourth name on the list. The name of the variable is the most general part of the data structure because it describes the complete data structure. So we first put down the name of the variable:

names

Next we want to get at a specific array of type *charstring* within the structure. Since the array *names* is made up of elements of type *charstring*, describing one of the strings will give us a more specific description. Since we want the fourth element, we augment our description as follows:

names[4]

The final step is to refer to the actual character we want to access in the array of arrays. *names*[4] is of type *charstring*. To access a single character in an array of type *charstring*, we can simply add a subscript to describe the character we want. Since we want the first character, we complete our description as follows:

names[4][1]

We can treat our description as a variable of type *char*. For example, we can make the following assignment statement:

names[4][1] := 't'

Since *names* is of type *list*, *names*[4] is of type *charstring*, and *names*[4][1] is of type *char*. If the type *charstring* is a packed array, we can compare the first and second elements in the array of arrays by writing

if names[1] = names[2]
  then . . .

We can always compare two characters by writing

if names[3][1] = names[5][4]
  then . . .

The syntax for defining a type that is an array of arrays is identical to the syntax for declaring an array of simple type. In place of the simple type identifier we used earlier, we use the type identifier that describes a complex data structure. We must define that complex data structure before we can use it in the definition of another type.

The syntax and semantics for declaring a variable of the new type are identical to the syntax and semantics for declaring a variable of any other type. The syntax for accessing the newly declared structure is simply to give its name. If we want to describe specific elements of the variable, we start by describing the whole variable and then access its component data structures. If that is not specific enough, we go on to describe the data structure that makes up the component structure we are currently describing.

25.2 A CASE STUDY

We are going to develop the data structures for the grade problem given in Chapter 5 (pages 100–106). You should look back to that chapter to refresh your memory of the problem statement and the algorithm we developed.

The inputs to this problem are

1. Up to 20 names
2. Up to 30 grades per name

The outputs are

1. A list consisting of
   a. Each student's name
   b. Each student's scores
   c. Each student's total score

The names should be ordered by total score, with the highest score listed first.

We can use arrays to hold all this information. We need the following data strucures:

1. An array to hold 20 names.
2. An array to hold 20 sets of scores. There will be 30 scores in each set. Each score will be a *real* number.
3. An array to hold 20 total scores.

A question arises, however: How do we keep a student associated with his or her scores or with his or her total score? Often, in cases like this, a *key* is used. A key is a set of characters or a number that uniquely describes a single person. Anything that belongs to that person has the key attached to it to identify to whom it belongs. Your social security number is an example of such a key. In this case we use the array subscripts as keys. Therefore, the student whose name is in a particular position in the first array will have his or her scores in the same position in the second array, and his or her total score in the same position in the third array.

This requires us to define the three major arrays with the same index type. Since there will be at most 20 students, all of these arrays should be defined with index type 1..20.

The constant and type definitions and the variable declarations in our main program might look like those shown in Figure 25.4.

Exercise 25.2: Given the definitions and declarations in Figure 25.4, what is the type of each of the following expressions?

a. names [20] [2]

b. names

c. grades [2] [30]

d. grades [6] ■

The positions described by a single subscript in the parallel arrays refer to the same student. Figure 25.5 gives a pictorial representation of the situation. This method of organizing pieces of information can often be found in similar forms in database management systems. Database management systems are specialized computer programs that access and manipulate large amounts of data in different ways.

You should now be in a position to implement the algorithm given in Chapter 5 (pages 102–105). The most difficult part of the implementation is keeping track of which score belongs to which student when sorting the scores into descending order.

Exercise 25.3: Write procedures to implement the algorithm given in Chapter 5. ■

Figure 25.4   Definition and declarations for the grades problem

```
const maxstring = 20;   {max length of char string}
      maxlist   = 20;   {max length of lists}
      maxscores = 30;   {max number of scores}

type  charstring = array[1..maxstring] of char;
                          {to hold a name}
      namelist = array[1..maxlist] of charstring;
                          {to hold a list of names}
      scores = array[1..maxscores] of real;
                      {to hold a single person's scores}
      scorelist = array[1..maxlist] of scores;
                      {to hold scores of students}
      totalscores = array[1..maxlist] of real;
                      {to hold totals}

var names: list;        {to hold names of students}
    grades: scorelist;  {to hold scores of students}
    totals: totalscores; {to hold the totals of each}
                          {student's scores}
```

Figure 25.5 **Pictorial representation of arrays**

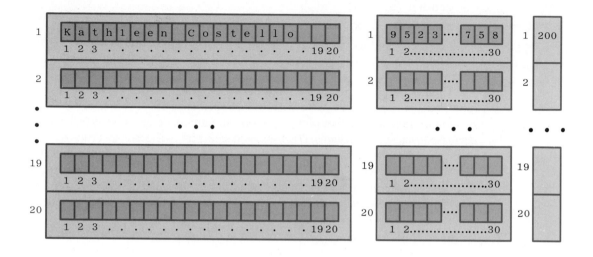

25.3 MORE COMPLEX ARRAYS OF ARRAYS

Arrays of arrays may be multidimensional as well as one-dimensional. For example, if you were representing an apartment complex by a multidimensional array going from 1 to 4 and from `'a'` to `'d'`, you might want every element of your array to be of type *charstring* so that you could represent each occupant's name. The constant and type definitions for such an array might look as follows:

```
const maxname = 20;       {max length of names}
      maxstories = 4;     {max stories in apt building}
      minapts = 'a';      {min apts per story in apt}
                          {building}
      maxapts = 'd';      {max apts per story}

type charstring = array[1..maxname] of char;
                  {to hold char string}
     building = array[1..maxstories,minapts..maxapts]
                                    of charstring;
                  {to define building with occupants}
```

The variable declaration might be this:

```
var SunnyApts : building;
               {your first apt. complex}
```

To access any name in the array, you could use an identifier such as this:

```
SunnyApts[1,'d']
```

This identifier would describe a data structure of type *charstring*. To get at a specific character in a name, you could use an identifier like this:

```
SunnyApts[1,'d'][19]
```

Arrays of arrays are not limited to having a base type of one-dimensional arrays of a simple type. The base type may be an array of one- or multidimensional arrays that themselves consist of simple or more complex types.

Let's go a step further with our apartment complex example. We might have several apartment complexes of identical structure but in different areas. Let's say that we want to refer to the areas with enumerated types. We could make the definitions and declarations shown in Figure 25.6 to represent our holdings. We could then describe any building in our holdings as shown in Figure 25.7a. We could describe a specific tenant in a specific building as shown in Figure 25.7b. If, for some reason, we wanted to describe a letter in a specific occupant's name, we could use the scheme shown in Figure 25.8.

Figure 25.6 **Definitions and declarations for a variable to hold apartment complex information**

```
const maxname    = 20;   {max len of char string}
      maxstories = 4;   {max number of stories in apt.}
                        {buildings}
      maxapts    = 'd'; {max number of apts. per story}

type where = (uptown, downtown, midtown);
                        {to describe where different}
                        {apt. complexes are}
     charstring = array[1..maxname] of char;
                        {to hold a string of char}
     building = array[1..maxstories,'a'..maxapts]
                        of charstring;
                        {to describe a building}
     complexes = array[where] of building;
                        {to describe a set of buildings}

var ManageCo : complexes;
                        {a structure to hold info about}
                        {apt. complexes}
```

Figure 25.7 **(a) Describing a building and (b) describing a name**

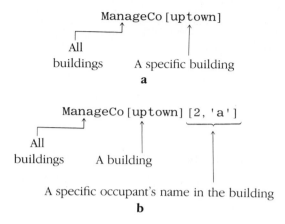

a

b

Figure 25.8 **Describing a character**

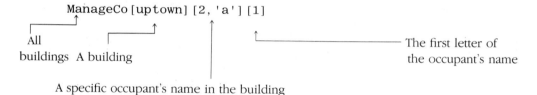

Note that the following is illegal because it skips the step that describes which building we should look in to find apartment 2a:

```
ManageCo[2,'a']
```

CHAPTER SUMMARY

1. *Arrays of arrays* are useful for creating lists and other complex data structures. They permit easy manipulation of multiple variables of the same type. They provide a natural way of describing real-life relationships between objects.

2. An array of arrays is defined in the same way as an array whose elements are of a simple type. The only difference is that the type identifier for the base

type describes a complex type rather than a simple type. Variables of this type are declared like variables of any other type.

3. To access the variable, you give the variable identifier. To access specific elements in the variable, you add additional subscripts in square brackets to the right of the variable name. Each addition of a subscript refers to a component of the variable described before it.

COMMON ERRORS

- Any of the standard errors committed with arrays of a simple data type.
- If you omit a subscript or add an extra subscript, you will access a piece of the variable other than the one you want to access.

SUPPLEMENTAL PROBLEMS

1. Given the definitions and declarations given for the variable *ManageCo* of type *complexes* (Figure 25.6), use variable identifiers to describe
   a. The person who lives in uptown building, apartment 1C
   b. The midtown building
   c. The second letter of the name of the person who lives in the downtown building, apartment 3C
2. Draw a picture to describe the variable *ManageCo* used in Figure 25.6.
3. Create a data structure to hold a deck of 52 standard playing cards. Each card should be represented by an array of two integers. One *integer* should indicate the suit, and the other *integer* should indicate the number. Write a procedure to shuffle the cards.
4. A program is needed to play five-card poker. There may be up to four players. Write the constant and type definitions needed to hold the players' hands of cards. Use an array of arrays.
5. Jane's Game Company is keeping track of five chess games. Define and declare constants, types, and variables that can be used to represent the five boards (the boards are 8 squares by 8 squares) and the two players playing each game. Refer to the grading program on page 539 as an example.
6. The following constant and type definitions and variable declarations are given:

```
const maxstring = 20;
      maxboard = 10;
```

```
type charstring = array[1..maxstring] of char;
      board = array[1..maxboard] of charstring;

var board1 : board;
```

Give an example of a variable identifier you could send to procedure *readstring*.

7. Assume that the declarations and definitions below are given. Which of the following references to parts of variable *gameSet* will lead to an error? Why? What is the type of each of the legal references?

a. *gameSet*
b. *gameSet* [4,3]
c. *gameSet* [4,2] [1]
d. *gameSet* [7] [4,3] [9]

e. *gameSet* [25] [7] [3] [1]
f. *gameSet* [5] [1,1]
g. *gameSet* [g] [6,6] [6]

```
const maxlen = 20;
      maxboard = 5;
      maxgames = 20;

type  scores = array[1..maxlen] of char;
      board  = array[1..maxboard, 1..maxboard]
                                    of scores;
      game   = array[1..maxgames] of board;

var   gameSet : game;
```

8. Write a procedure that, given the shuffled deck created in problem 3, sorts the deck of cards by suit and rank. The highest suit should be spades, followed by hearts, diamonds, and clubs. The highest rank should be king; the lowest, ace.

9. Develop a data structure to represent the titles of courses taken by a college student who attends college for eight semesters and is allowed to take a maximum of six courses in any one semester.

10. Write a program to make a list of all the words in a paragraph.

11. Suppose you have declared the variable *grades* as in Figure 25.4.
    a. Write a procedure to compute the average grade for each of the 30 assignments.
    b. Write a procedure to compute the average score for the entire class for all the assignments (in other words, the average value of all the real numbers that represent grades on assignments).

12. Assume the type *complexes* is defined as in Figure 25.6. Write a function that takes a variable of type *complexes* and returns the length of the largest occupant name in any apartment.

CHAPTER 26

As we have seen, Pascal enables the programmer to group data items of the same type together in arrays. Pascal also provides a data structure that enables the programmer to group together data items of different types. That data structure is called the *record*.

26.1 DEFINING AND DECLARING RECORDS

Let's start with a simple example: a person's first name, last name, and middle initial. Assuming a maximum of 20 characters each for the first name and the last name, we could use two character strings of length 20 to represent them. We can represent an initial by a simple *char* variable. So what we need is a data structure that will group together three data items, two arrays of 20 characters and one *char* value. This is a perfect place for a record-type data structure.

Just as we do with arrays, we first create the blueprint for the new data structure by defining a type, *namerec*. We allocate memory for a variable, *name*, of this type with a variable declaration. Figure 26.1 shows the definitions and declarations.

The logical units that comprise a record are called the *fields* of the record. The identifiers *last*, *first*, and *midinit* are the field identifiers for the fields of any variable of type *namerec*.

Figure 26.2 pictures the variable *name* in memory. Figure 26.3 gives the syntax diagram for defining a record structure. Notice that this is the second time we have encountered a construct that has an **end** but no **begin**. (See the **case** statement on page 349.) We comment the **end** of a record definition with the type identifier being defined.

RECORDS

Figure 26.1 **Definitions and declarations to declare a record-type variable to hold a person's whole name**

```
const maxnamelength = 20;
                    {maximum number of characters}
                    {in a first or last name}
type namestr = array[1..maxnamelength] of char;
                    {to hold a first or last name}
     namerec = record
                    last, first : namestr;
                    midinit : char
               end; {namerec}

var name : namerec;
                    {to hold one person's last name,}
                    {first name, and middle initial}
```

Figure 26.2 **Illustration of the variable *name* in memory**

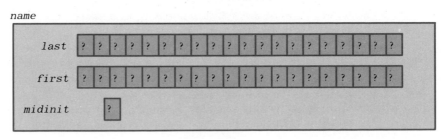

547

Figure 26.3 **Syntax diagram for defining a record type**

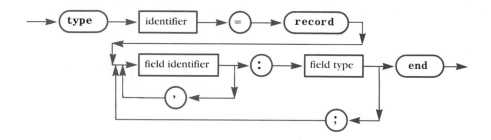

26.2 ACCESSING THE FIELDS OF A RECORD-TYPE VARIABLE

Assume that we have written a procedure named *readnamestr* that is just like procedure *readstring* of Chapter 23 except that its variable parameter is of type *namestr*. We could read a last name, first name, and middle initial into our variable *name* in two ways. One method is shown in Figure 26.4. Here we are using what is called *dot notation* to access an individual field of the variable. The general syntax required when using dot notation is described in Figure 26.5. Notice that the variable identifier appears in the variable declaration and the field identifier appears in the type definition of the record.

Below is a sample execution of the statements in Figure 26.4.

```
Please enter last name:
Mills ↩
Please enter first name:
Mary ↩
Please enter middle initial:
C ↩
```

Figure 26.6 shows the situation in memory created by this execution.

The second way to read values into the variable *name* is to use Pascal's **with** statement. Figure 26.7 shows what the code would look like. The syntax diagram for the **with** statement is shown in Figure 26.8. The important points are these: The record variable identifier is named at the beginning of the **with** statement, and only field identifiers are required within the body of the **with** statement.

Figure 26.4   **Examples of using dot notation to access fields in a record**

```
write('Please enter last name: ');
readnamestr(name.last);
write('Please enter first name: ');
readnamestr(name.first);
write('Please enter middle initial: ');
readln(name.midinit);
```

Figure 26.5   **Syntax necessary when using dot notation**

Figure 26.6   **Situation in memory after sample execution of the code in Figure 26.4**

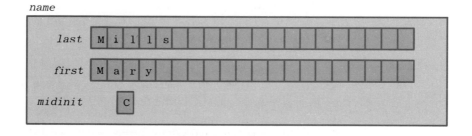

Figure 26.7   **Using the with statement to access fields in records**

```
with name do
  begin
    write('Please enter last name: ');
    readnamestr(last);
    write('Please enter first name: ');
    readnamestr(first);
    write('Please enter middle initial: ');
    readln(midinit)
  end; {with name do}
```

Figure 26.8 **Syntax diagram for the wi th statement**

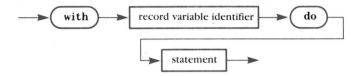

Every identifier that is a field name for the record variable specified between the keywords **wi th** and **do** refers to that field in the record type variable. Other identifiers are unaffected by the **wi th** statement. Thus, if *player1* and *player2* are variables of type *namerec*, the reference to *last* in the following statement would be unambiguous.

```
with player1 do
  begin
    .
    .
  readnamestr(last);
    {stands for player1. last}
    .
    .
  end; {with player1 do}
```

Since this Pascal construct allows only one statement after the reserved word **do**, we often use a compound statement in conjunction with the **wi th** statement. It is good style to label the end of the compound statement, as we have in Figure 26.7.

We can also directly assign values to the record one letter at a time, using a subscript to indicate a particular position in a field that is actually an array structure. As with any array of characters that might not be completely filled, we should initialize it before we use it. Figure 26.9 shows how we could do it by using dot notation.

Exercise 26.1: Rewrite the code in Figure 26.9 using a **wi th** statement.
■

Note that we refer to data by going from the general to the specific. *name* is the general identifier for the variable, and *last*, *first*, or *midinit* narrows our reference down to the *last*, *first*, or *midinit* field of *name*. With the

Figure 26.9 **Using assignment statements to assign individual characters to the fields of variable *name***

```
{fill first name field with blanks}
for index := 1 to maxnamelength do
        name.first[index] := ' ';

{fill last name field with blanks}
 for index := 1 to maxnamelength do
        name.last[index] := ' ';

name.first[1] := 'M';
name.first[2] := 'a';
name.first[3] := 'r';
name.first[4] := 'y';


name.last[1] := 'M';
name.last[2] := 'i';
name.last[3] := 'l';
name.last[4] := 'l';
name.last[5] := 's';
name.midinit := 'C';
```

fields *last* and *first*, if we choose to use subscripts, each subscript narrows our reference to a specific character in that particular field of the variable *name*.

Exercise 26.2: Assign your own name to the variable *name* one character at a time

   a. Using dot notation
   b. Using the **with** statement ■

26.3 RECORDS WITHIN RECORDS

Now suppose we want to build a data structure to contain not only a person's name, but also the person's birthday. We should think about the design of such a structure from the "top down." We begin by envisioning a place in memory reserved for the data about that one person, as shown in Figure 26.10.

The information divides into two logical units: the person's name and the person's birthday. We could add this level of detail to our picture of the situation in memory, as shown in Figure 26.11.

We can refine our design of the data structure by concentrating first on the name and then on the birthday. We have already done all the work necessary to refine the name. It consists of a last name, a first name, and a middle initial. Let's use the same design for the data structure representing the person's name that we used in Figure 26.1—that is, character strings of length 20 for the last and first names and a single character for the middle initial. Our picture is now as shown in Figure 26.12.

To refine the birthday data, we break it down to month, day, and year. We could easily use the type *integer* to represent the day and the year, and we could use an *integer* to represent the month also. But let's add a little more interest by using a character string of length 3. We will use the typical three-character abbreviations for the months: jan, feb, mar, . . ., dec.

Figure 26.10   Space in memory for information about one person

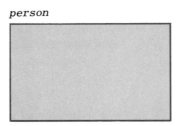

Figure 26.11   The two logical units of information about one person

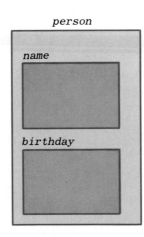

Figure 26.12   Refinement of the name information field

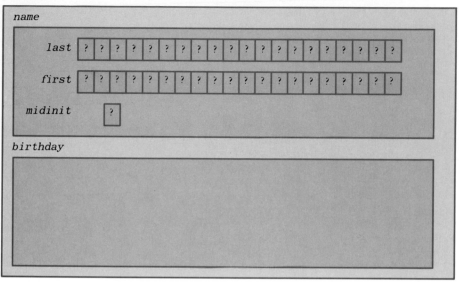

Figure 26.13 shows a completed version of the diagram of our data structure.

We can now write the Pascal code to implement our data structure. Similar to the manner in which we declare procedures above the main program, we'll need to add details to the code above the generalities.

To accommodate the logical units name and birthday we define a new record type *personrec* having two fields, *name* and *birthday*. We'll use *namerec* for the type of field *name* and *birthrec* for the type of field *birthday*, as shown in Figure 26.14.

We must define *namerec* and *birthrec*. We know that we'll use strings of two different lengths. We'll use *namestr* and *monthstr* to refer to the two different string types. We add the necessary code above what we've already written, as shown in Figure 26.15.

Now all we have to do is add the code to define the types *namestr* and *monthstr*. We use the constants *maxnamelength* and *maxmonthlength* to define *namestr* and *monthstr*, thus completing our definition of *personrec*. Note where we position the new code. Finally, we declare a variable *person* of type *personrec* and enter appropriate comments, as shown in Figure 26.16.

Remember that we go from the general to the specific in referring to fields in record-type variables. If we begin with the variable *person*, we have two field choices: *name* and *birthday*. Hence, the syntactic constructs *person.name* and

Figure 26.13   Completely refined structure to hold information about one person

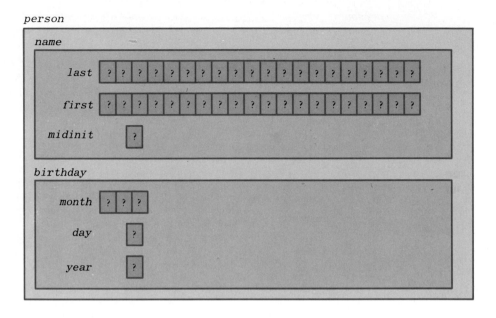

Figure 26.14   Definition of type *personrec*

```
type personrec = record
                   name : namerec;
                   birthday : birthrec
                 end; {personrec}
```

Figure 26.15   Refinement of types *namerec* and *birthrec*

```
type namerec  = record
                   last, first : namestr;
                   midinit : char
                 end; {namerec}
     birthrec = record
                   month : monthstr;
                   day, year : integer
                 end; {birthrec}
     personrec = record
                   name : namerec ;
                   birthday : birthrec
                 end; {personrec}
```

person.birthday are legal. Now *person.name* is an identifier for a variable of type *namerec*. Its three fields are referenced as *person.name.last*, *person.name.first*, and *person.name.midinit*. Similarly, *person.birthday* is an identifier for a variable of type *birthrec*. Its three fields are referenced as *person.birthday.month*, *person.birthday.day*, and *person.birthday.year*.

Assume that we have written two procedures named *readnamestr* and *readmonthstr* to read in variables of types *namestr* and *monthstr*, respectively. We'll write Pascal code to read name and birthday information into the variable *person* in two ways, as shown in Figure 26.17: using dot notation exclusively and using a **with** statement exclusively.

Figure 26.16 **Definitions and declarations needed to declare a variable of type** *personrec*

```
const maxnamelength = 20;{the maximum number of characters}
                         {in a last name or a first name}
      maxmonthlength = 3;{the maximum number of characters}
                         {used to represent a month}

type namestr    = array[1..maxnamelength] of char;
                     {type for an array}
                     {to represent a name}
     monthstr   = array[1..maxmonthlength] of char;
                     {type for an array}
                     {representing a month}
     namerec    = record {to represent a person's last name,}
                     {first name, and middle initial}
                     last, first : namestr;
                     midinit : char
                  end; {namerec}
     birthrec   = record {to represent the month,}
                         {day, and year of a birthday}
                     month : monthstr;
                     day, year : integer
                  end; {birthrec}
     personrec  = record {to represent the name and}
                         {birthday of a person}
                     name : namerec;
                     birthday : birthrec
                  end; {personrec}
var person : personrec;  {a variable to hold name and}
                         {birthday information about a}
                         {person}
```

Figure 26.17   Two ways to read data into variable *person*

Dot notation

```
write('Please enter last name: ');
readnamestr(person.name.last);
write('Please enter first name: ');
readnamestr(person.name.first);
write('Please enter middle initial: ');
readln(person.name.midinit);
write('Please enter birth month: ');
readmonthstr(person.birthday.month);
write('Please enter birth day: ');
readln(person.birthday.day);
write('Please enter birth year: ');
readln(person.birthday.year);
```

Using **with** statements

```
with person do
  begin
      with name do
          begin
            write('Please enter last name: ');
            readnamestr(last);
            write('Please enter first name: ');
            readnamestr(first);
            write('Please enter middle initial: ');
            readln(midinit)
          end; {with name do}
      with birthday do
          begin
            write('Please enter birth month: ');
            readmonthstr(month);
            write('Please enter birth day: ');
            readln(day);
            write('Please enter birth year: ');
            readln(year)
          end  {with birthday do}
    end; {with person do}
```

Exercise 26.3: Complete the following code to read values into the fields of variable *person*.

a. **with** person **do**
   begin
      write('Please enter last name: ');
      readnamestr(------------);
      write('Please enter first name: ');
      readnamestr(------------);
      write('Please enter middle initial: ');
      readln(------------);
      write('Please enter month of birth: ');
      readmonthstr(------------);
      write('Please enter day of birth: ');
      readln(------------);
      write('Please enter year of birth: ');
      readln(------------)
   end; {with person do}

b. **with** person.name **do**
   begin
      write('Please enter last name: ');
      readnamestr(------------);
      write('Please enter first name: ');
      readnamestr(------------);
      write('Please enter middle initial: ');
      readln(------------)
   end; {with person.name do}

   with person.birthday **do**
   begin
      write('Please enter month of birth: ');
      readmonthstr(------------);
      write('Please enter day of birth: ');
      readln(------------);
      write('Please enter year of birth: ');
      readln(------------)
   end; {with person.birthday do}   ■

26.4 ARRAYS OF RECORDS

An Example Problem

We can use the data structure developed in the preceding section to develop a more complex data structure. Consider the data structure needed to solve the following problem:

Write a program to

a. Allow the user to enter a maximum of 50 names with corresponding birthdays

b. Print out the list of birthdays with corresponding names in chronological order by month and day

The Development of a Data Structure for the Problem

The data structure we designed on pages 551–555 was a record of information about just one person. For this problem, we'll need a data structure representing a fixed-size list of 50 such records. We'll need an array of 50 elements in which each element is the record structure described in Figure 26.16 on page 555. This array should be relatively easy to implement in Pascal. We'll add a constant *maxlistsize* to the constant definition section. We'll define a new type for the list itself and add its type definition below the definition of *personrec*. Finally, we'll need a variable to hold all the data. Figure 26.18 shows all the needed definitions and declarations. We can envision the variable *list* as shown in Figure 26.19.

26.5 A WARNING ABOUT AVOIDING TYPE IDENTIFIERS

Pascal allows us a shortcut alternative to define and declare the data structure used on pages 551–555. First, we'll display the code in Figure 26.20, and then we'll tell you its disadvantages. Compare it to the code in Figure 26.16.

Note that we have eliminated the programmer-defined type identifiers *namestr*, *monthstr*, *namerec*, *birthrec*, and *personrec*. Although our record fields do have types, the types have no names and are thus called *anony-*

Figure 26.18   **Definitions and declarations to represent a list of at most 50 people's names and birthdays**

```
const maxnamelength = 20;{the maximum number of characters}
                         {to represent a name}
      maxmonthlength = 3;{the maximum number of characters}
                         {used to represent a month}
      maxlistsize = 50;  {maximum size of the list}
                         {of people}

type  namestr   = array[1..maxnamelength] of char;
                         {type for an array}
                         {to represent a name}
      monthstr  = array[1..maxmonthlength] of char;
                         {type for an array}
                         {to represent a month}
      namerec   = record {to represent a person's}
                         {last name, first name,}
                         {and middle initial}
                      last, first : namestr;
                      midinit : char
                  end; {namerec}
      birthrec  = record {to represent the month, day,}
                         {and year of a birthday}
                      month : monthstr;
                      day, year : integer
                  end; {birthrec}
      personrec = record {to represent the name}
                         {and birthday of a person}
                      name : namerec;
                      birthday : birthrec
                  end; {personrec}
      datalist = array[1..maxlistsize] of personrec;
                         {type for variable to}
                         {represent a list of people}
var list : datalist; {a variable to hold name}
                         {and birthday information}
                         {about up to 50 people}
```

Figure 26.19   Illustration of the list in memory

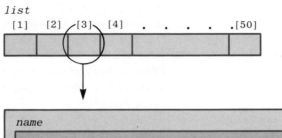

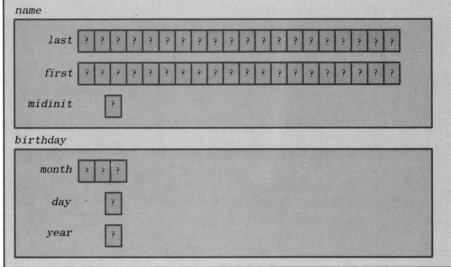

Figure 26.20   Shortcut declaration of variable *person*

```
const maxnamelength = 20;
      maxmonthlength = 9;

var person:record
          name:record
              last,first:array[1..maxnamelength] of char;
              midinit : char
            end; {record name}
          birthday:record
              month : array[1..maxmonthlength] of char;
              day,year : integer
              end {record birthday}
        end; {record person}
```

mous types. The code is certainly more compact, but the density of details makes it difficult to read. This is a stylistic disadvantage.

The second disadvantage is functional. To pass a unit of data as a parameter, that unit of data must have an associated type identifier. If we declare the variable **person** in the shortcut way above, only individual characters or integers could be used as arguments in procedure call statements. We could never use the logical units of data: last name, first name, birth month, name, or birthday as arguments in procedure calls, since there are no type identifiers for their corresponding parameters. To allow for more flexibility in the further coding of the program, it is better to have type identifiers for each programmer-defined type. One might consider this as a modularization of the data structure, which coincides with the modularization of the program achieved by using procedures with parameters.

CHAPTER SUMMARY

1. Pascal uses the *record* data structure to group together data items of possibly different types into a logical unit.

2. As with arrays, we should first define a type for the record data structure and then declare a variable of that type.

3. The various logical units that comprise a record are called *fields*. For each field, a field identifier is specified in the type definition for the record.

4. There are two ways to access the various fields of a record:
   a. Using dot notation, as follows:

   record variable identifier . field identifier

   b. Using the **with** statement:

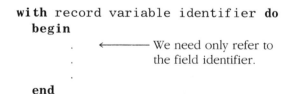

```
with record variable identifier do
   begin
          .    ←———— We need only refer to
          .          the field identifier.
          .
   end
```

5. The individual fields of a record may be of any predefined or programmer-defined types.

6. The base element type of an array may be a record type. Hence, we can use arrays of records.

COMMON ERRORS

■ It is an error to use a type identifier on either side of the dot. For example, consider the type definitions in Figure 26.16. All of the following are incorrect:

```
personrec.name
personrec.namerec
namerec.last
namerec.first        {All of these are incorrect}
namerec.namestr      {because they use type}
birthrec.day         {identifiers.}
person.birthrec.day
person.namerec.last
```

■ Using the relational operators to compare two variables of record type is a syntactic error. Relational operators can compare only expressions of simple type or of compatible types of packed arrays of characters.

DEBUGGING HINTS

■ Write a procedure that displays the values of all the fields in a record. Invoke this procedure before and after the record is manipulated.

SUPPLEMENTAL PROBLEMS

1. a. Write a procedure named *printinitials* to print the first, middle, and last initials of the name stored in the variable *person*. Your procedure should have a value parameter of type *namerec*.
   b. Write the procedure call to invoke the procedure *printinitials*.

2. a. Write a function *monthnum* to convert a three-character string representing a month into a corresponding *integer* in the range 1 to 12 inclusive. Function *monthnum* should take a single parameter of type *monthstr* and return an *integer* value in the range 1 to 12 if its argument is one of the possible abbreviations for a month. Function *monthnum* should return 0 if the three-character string is not one of the abbreviations for a month.
   b. Write a function called *age* whose purpose is to compute the age of a person given the person's birth date and the current date. It should have two value parameters of type *birthrec* representing the birth date and the current date. It should return an *integer* value ,that is the person's age. As an error-checking device, have the function return the value 0 and print an error message if the birth date is after the current date.

3. a. Modify the types of parameters used in procedures *readstring*, *writestring*, and *blankfill* and function *length* of Chapter 23 to create six new procedures *readnamestr*, *readmonthstr*, *blanknamestr*, *blankmonthstr*, *writenamestr*, and *writemonthstr* and two new functions *lengthname* and *lengthmonth* to correspond to the types *namestr* and *monthstr*.

   b. Write an entire program using the procedures modified in problem 3a and the types *namerec* and *birthrec* to read in a person's name and birthday and write it out with trailing blanks suppressed.

4. a. Write a procedure named *printdigitbirth* to print the birthday stored in the variable *person* in the format XX/XX/XX where *X* is a digit (0–9). For example, if the birthday is April 28, 1953, your program should print 04/28/53. Your procedure should have a value parameter of type *birthrec*.

   b. Write the procedure call to invoke the procedure *printdigitbirth*.

5. Using the data structure developed on page 559, write a program to solve the problem posed in that section.

6. Assume that two variables *name1* and *name2* have been declared as type *namerec* (see Figure 26.1).

   a. Write an algorithm that uses the last name, first name, and middle initial to decide if *name1* is before *name2* in alphabetical order.

   b. Write a *boolean*-valued function *before* that takes two parameters of type *namerec* and returns *true* if the first parameter represents a name that comes before the name represented by the second parameter in alphabetical order.

7. Using the function you wrote for problem 6b, write a procedure to sort an array of type *datalist* (see Figure 26.18) into alphabetical order.

8. a. Develop a data structure to represent the entire academic transcript of a college student.

   b. Write the procedure(s) necessary to read information into the structure you developed for problem 8a.

9. Develop a data structure to represent information about an apartment complex. There are five buildings in the complex. In each building there are ten apartments labeled A through J. For each apartment, you must represent the names of the people living in the apartment, the date they moved in, and the rent they pay.

*10. a. Develop a data structure to hold the following information about a company's employees: name, home address, home phone number, social security number, hourly wage rate, number of hours worked per week.

   b. Write a program to input the information listed above about a single employee and print that employee's pay check.

*11. Write a program that simulates the game of tic-tac-toe between two players.

*12. Write a program that simulates the game of three-dimensional tic-tac-toe between two players.

*13. Write a program to play the game of life. The game of life is a simulation of the births and deaths in a community. It is played on a 10-by-10 board of squares. Each square on the board is either vacant or occupied by a living being. Each square has a certain number of neighbors. The diagram below has *x*'s in the eight possible positions of neighbors for the center square.

x	x	x
x		x
x	x	x

Corner squares have a maximum of three possible neighbors. Squares on the border of the board but not in a corner have a maximum of five possible neighbors. The rules governing births and deaths on the board are as follows:

■ A birth occurs in a vacant square if it has three living neighbors.

■ A death occurs in a square housing a living being due to
  ■ Overcrowding if it has four or more living neighbors, or
  ■ Loneliness if it has less than two neighbors

Read in the positions of living beings in the initial generation. Calculate the succeeding five generations by the rules given above. For each generation, print the board and the number of births and deaths.

*14. a. Using programmer-defined enumerated types, develop a data structure to represent a standard deck of 52 cards.
  b. Write a program to simulate the shuffling of the deck and the dealing of 13 cards to each of four players.
  c. Write a function to calculate the point value of a hand of 13 cards in a bridge game.

CHAPTER 27

In addition to arrays and records, Pascal permits the creation of another kind of structured type: the *set*. Sets are a very handy feature of Pascal not offered by most other programming languages. The idea underlying sets in Pascal comes from mathematics. If you are familiar with the mathematical notion of sets and the operations on sets, some of the material in this chapter will be familiar to you. A word of caution, however: Pascal's idea of sets is not identical with the mathematical notion.

27.1 THE IDEA BEHIND SETS

Like arrays, sets have a base type. We can construct a variable whose type is **set of** *char*, or **set of** 1..100, or more generally **set of** ordinal type.[1] Two sets are of the same type if they have the same base type. For example, consider the declarations in Figure 27.1. Of the four variables, *chset1* and *chset2* are of the same type, and the various operations on sets (which we will describe later in this chapter) can be performed between them. The variables *scores* and *ranks*, however, are of different types—different from each other and different from *chset1* and *chset2*.

To illustrate what the values of such variables might be and how we can use them, let's look at an example. Here is a problem whose solution we can readily describe with the use of sets:

The Letter Occurrence Problem: Read in a line of text from the user, then report to the user which letters of the alphabet occur in the line of text.

---

1. Certain restrictions on the possible base types for sets exist in some versions of Pascal. We'll discuss them later in this chapter.

SETS

Figure 27.1

Figure 27.1   Defining set types and declaring set variables

```
type    charset = set of char;
        hundredset = set of 1..100;
        tenset = set of 1..10;
var     chset1,
        chset2: charset;
        scores: hundredset;
        ranks: tenset;
```

The output for this problem will be some collection of letters of the alphabet. In most cases, we can expect it to consist of fewer than 26 letters. It may consist of the entire alphabet if the user types something like

```
The quick brown fox jumps over the lazy dog
```

which contains every letter. On the other hand, if the text contains only numbers and special characters, the answer will consist of no letters at all. The answer to a problem of this sort has the following characteristics:

- The answer consists of a collection of values. We call these values *elements*.
- The elements of the answer are derived from some fixed range of values—in this case, the 26 letters of the alphabet.
- The elements of the answer are in no particular order, even though there is an underlying order in the fixed range of values (in this case, alphabetical order).

- The answer exhibits no notion of multiplicity. A value either will or won't be part of the answer. If it does occur in the answer, it will occur only once, even if it occurs more than once in the text.

- The answer may consist of any collection of values, ranging from the whole underlying range to no values at all.

What data structure can we use to represent this kind of answer? One possibility is to use an array of 26 characters:

```
type    letarray = array[1..26] of char;
var     answerlet: letarray;
```

The idea would be to fill *answerlet*[1] with the first letter of the alphabet that is to appear in the collection, to fill *answerlet*[2] with the second letter, *answerlet*[3] with the third, and so on. Unused entries would have blanks. Indeed, in many programming languages something like this is the best you can do. But it wouldn't be very appropriate because many of the characteristics listed above are not reflected in any property of arrays. For instance, an array might have some letters occurring twice. You would have to take care to avoid such duplication.

A more clever use of arrays would be as follows:

```
type    letarray = array['a'..'z'] of boolean;
var     answerlet: letarray;
```

In the ASCII character set, this array consists of 26 *true*'s or *false*'s, indexed by the letters 'a' through 'z'. Variable *answerlet* consists of the 26 elements *answerlet*['a'], *answerlet*['b'], *answerlet*['c']..., *answerlet*['z'], and each of these is a *boolean* value. At a given location in the array, indexed by some letter, the value of that location would be *true* if we wanted that letter to belong to the collection, and *false* if we did not want it to.

Actually, this isn't a bad data structure for our problem. It's logically equivalent to the data structure we propose, which is

```
type    letterset = set of 'a'..'z';
var     answerlet: letterset;
```

Although there are few conceptual differences between the two data structures, the set structure allows us to use Pascal's powerful battery of set operations. Moreover, the set structure is more space-efficient for technical reasons because it requires less memory to represent the same information.

Now for a definition. In mathematics, a set is "a well-defined collection of objects." This is too general for Pascal, because the computer can't represent the infinite sets that mathematicians use. In Pascal,

A set is a finite collection of objects of the same ordinal type.

A point about notation: In mathematics, the convention is to enumerate the elements of a set inside curly brackets. But, since Pascal preempts the use of curly brackets to delimit comments, the elements of a set are written inside square brackets.

In speaking of collections of objects, we consider only two possibilities: Either an object (of the correct type) is in the collection, or it isn't in the collection. We don't count multiple occurrences of the same object. Thus, the set of letters that occur in the text

have a banana.

is `['a', 'b', 'e', 'h', 'n', 'v']`. That `'a'` occurs five times in the text while `'v'` occurs only once is of no interest to us. Similarly, if we are told to remove an object from a set of objects of some type, we can remove it only once, and then only if it's there.

Now back to our problem. To solve it, we need to describe how sets are constructed. Although we have explained how to declare variables of set type, we have not explained how to give any values to those variables. We start by writing a top-level algorithm for the problem. Those portions of the algorithm that we cannot yet implement in Pascal will be typed in uppercase letters. Then, as we develop the needed tools, we'll fill in the details of the Pascal code. Since the method of solution depends somewhat on the character set, we assume in the rest of this chapter that characters are represented according to the ASCII standard.

The idea behind our algorithm is to start with a set of letters consisting of no letters at all. Such a set, known as the *empty set,* is a perfectly legal set value for any set type. Then we'll scan the characters of input text one at a time. Each time we find a letter, we'll add it to our set. (We won't worry about whether the letter is already in the set. If it is already there, we'll add it again anyway. This will not make it appear twice in the set.)

ALGORITHM FOR FINDING THE SET OF LETTERS IN A LINE OF TEXT

I. INITIALIZE A SET TO THE EMPTY SET.

II. Read a line of text into an array.

III. For each character in the array, do
    A. If the character is a letter,
       then
          1. ADD THE LETTER TO THE SET.

IV. PRINT THE LETTERS THAT ARE IN THE SET.

Figure 27.2 shows the sketch of a program to implement this algorithm. The parts of the algorithm we haven't yet explained how to code have been replaced

FIGURE 27.2   First attempt at program *lettersintext*

```
program lettersintext(input, output);
   {reads in a line of text, and displays}
   {the letters of the alphabet that}
   {have been used in that line}
const    linelength = 80; {typical length of a screen line}

type     line = array[1..linelength] of char;
         letterset = set of 'a'..'z';

var      inputline: line;          {holds the typed input line}
         len: integer;             {gets the length of typed line}
         typedletters: letterset; {the letters that were typed}

         procedure readstring(var inputdata: line);
         {This familiar procedure is omitted. See}
         {Chapter 23 }

         procedure makeletterset(inputtext: line;
                                     var outputset: letterset);
         {constructs set outputset consisting of the letters}
         {that occur in inputtext}
         var     index: 1..linelength;
         begin {makeletterset}
             INITIALIZE SET outputset TO THE EMPTY SET;
             for index := 1 to linelength do
                 if inputtext[index] IS A LETTER
                   then
                         ADD inputtext[index] TO outputset
         end; {makeletterset}

         procedure showset(letters: letterset);
         {displays the letters that are elements of letters}
         begin {showset}
             DISPLAY THE LETTERS IN letters
         end; {showset}

begin    {lettersintext}
         readstring ( inputline );
         makeletterset ( inputline, typedletters );
         showset ( typedletters )
end.     {lettersintext}
```

by text written in uppercase. To fill in the skeleton procedures, we need to know how to manipulate sets. As we describe the set operations in the next section, we'll write the missing parts.

27.2 OPERATIONS ON SETS

Set Assignment

Two Pascal set variables are of the same type if they have the same base type. If *set1* and *set2* are sets of the same type, then we can perform certain operations on them. For example, as always with two variables of the same type, we can assign one set value to the other:

```
set1 := set2     {copies value of set2 to set1}
```

The right side of such an assignment need not be a variable. As with any assignment statement, the right side need only be an expression of compatible type to the left side. One form of such expressions is a constant. We have already seen how to write set constants: Enumerate the elements, separated by commas, inside square brackets. But it would be tedious to have to write

```
typedletters := ['a', 'b', 'c', 'd', 'e', 'f', 'g', 'h',
        'i', 'j', 'k', 'l', 'm', 'n', 'o', 'p', 'q',
        'r', 's', 't', 'u', 'v', 'w', 'x', 'y', 'z']
```

Not only would this Pascal statement be tedious to write, but anyone reading it would have to make sure that all the letters were there and that the syntax was correct. Fortunately, in writing set constants we can use subranges to indicate an entire range of values:

```
typedletters := ['a'..'z']
```

This statement is equivalent to the previous one, but it's shorter and clearer, and it's easier to write. We can also, if we choose, use several subranges, such as

```
typedletters := ['a'..'e', 'm'..'p']
```

This is equivalent to the more verbose assignment

```
typedletters := ['a','b','c','d','e','m','n','o','p']
```

Note that all the subranges must fall within the base type of the set. Thus, a statement such as

```
typedletters := ['a'..'e', 'A'..'E']    {ERROR!}
```

is an error, since the characters `'A'` through `'E'` are not part of the base type `'a'..'z'`. The set `['a'..'e', 'A'..'E']` is a perfectly legal constant of type **set of** *char* but not of type *letterset*.

In specifying subranges for sets, we need not restrict ourselves to constant limits. Consider the following program fragment:

```
type    letterset = set of char;
var     ch1, ch2: char;
        range: letterset;
          .
          .
        readln(ch1, ch2);
        if ch1 < ch2
            then
                range := [ch1..ch2]
            else
                range := [ch2..ch1]
```

This fragment reads two characters and then assigns the set range the value consisting of all the characters from the lesser one to the greater inclusive.

Finally, a set consisting of no letters at all is perfectly legal. It is written

```
typedletters := [];     {the empty set}
```

The empty set provides one of the missing pieces in our program: It is the initialization called for in the first line of procedure *makeletterset*. The empty set is a set constant with a peculiar property: Its type is compatible with every set type. Thus, it can be assigned to, or compared with, or otherwise made to operate with, sets of every legal type.

The assignment operation can be carried out on most types of Pascal objects. Four operations, however, are peculiar to objects of set type: union, intersection, set difference, and testing for membership. We'll now explain what these operations mean and how they're written in Pascal (which lacks the special characters used to describe these operations in mathematics). Then we'll describe several operations for comparing sets.

Set Union

The union of two sets (of compatible type) is a set that consists of all the elements that are in either (or both) of the original sets. In other words, a value of the base type is an element of the union of *set1* and *set2* if it is an element of *set1*, or an element of *set2*, or both. For example, suppose we have the type definitions, variables, and assignments shown in Figure 27.3. Then the union of *set1* and *set2* is the set [2, 3, 4, 5, 6, 8]. Note that, as always with sets, an element occurs only once. In mathematical notation, the union of *set1* and *set2* is written this way:

$$set1 \cup set2$$

Since the symbol $\cup$ isn't available on most keyboards, Pascal uses the symbol +. Thus, the Pascal representation for the union of *set1* and *set2* is *set1* + *set2*. If we execute the statements

```
set1 := [2,4,6,8];
set2 := [2,3,4,5,6];
set3 := set1 + set2;     {union of sets}
```

the value of *set3* will be [2, 3, 4, 5, 6, 8]. This works for sets of any type, so long as they are of the same or compatible type.[2] Consider the fragment in Figure 27.4. We can use the operator + between two sets of type *letterset* or between two sets of type *tenset*. The following expression is illegal because the two operands of the + operator have incompatible types.

```
nums1 + lets2              {ERROR: type clash}
```

Figure 27.3   **Sample set values**

```
type      tenset = set of 1..10;
var       set1,
          set2: tenset;
             .  .  .
          set1 := [2,4,6,8];
          set2 := [2,3,4,5,6];
             .  .  .
```

2. Two set types are compatible if their base types are compatible. Recall that two ordinal types are compatible if one is a subrange of the other or if both are subranges of a common type.

Exercise 27.1: What will be the values of the sets *lets3* and *nums3* after the union operations of Figure 27.4 are performed? ∎

To construct sets using set union, we start with an empty set—that is, a set with no elements. Then we add elements one at a time by repeatedly taking the union of that set with a set that contains the single element we want to add. We can use this method to write procedure *makeletterset*, which was one of the skeleton procedures in program *lettersintext*. Figure 27.5 shows the refinement of procedure *makeletterset*.

Note carefully the statement

```
outputset := outputset + [inputtext[index]]
```

The two sets of brackets in the expression [*inputtext*[*index*]] have two different meanings. The outer brackets mean "the set whose only element is the character *inputtext*[*index*]," just as the expression [*x*] by itself means "the set whose only element is *x*." The inner brackets indicate that *index* is a subscript, not an element of a set. The meanings of these two uses of square brackets in Pascal can always be determined by context and by the types of variables involved.

We still don't know how to tell if a character is a letter, and we have ignored the question of uppercase and lowercase letters. Although our set can contain only

Figure 27.4   Examples of set union

```
type     letterset = set of 'a'..'z';
         tenset = set of 1..10;
var      lets1,
         lets2,
         lets3: letterset;
         nums1,
         nums2,
         nums3: tenset;

           . . .

         lets1 := ['a', 'e', 'i', 'o', 'u'];
         lets2 := ['a', 'b', 'c', 'd', 'e'];
         lets3 := lets1 + lets2;           {+ is set union}
         nums1 := [1, 3, 5, 7, 9];
         nums2 := [1, 2, 3, 4, 5];
         nums3 := nums1 + nums2;           {another set union}
```

Figure 27.5 **Refined procedure** `makeletterset`

```
procedure makeletterset (inputtext: line;
                              var outputset: letterset);
{constructs set outputset consisting of the letters}
{that occur in inputtext}
var       index: 1..linelength;
begin {makeletterset}
    outputset := [];
    for index := 1 to linelength do
        if inputtext [index] IS A LETTER
           then
              outputset := outputset + [inputtext [index]]
end; {makeletterset}
```

lowercase letters, the user is likely to type some uppercase letters, and we would like to include their lowercase equivalents. To deal with these two matters we need to refine the procedure further. We do so by writing two functions: Function *isletter* will take a character as an argument and will return a *boolean* value that is *true* if the character is a letter (either upper- or lowercase) and that is *false* if the character is not a letter. Function *lower* will take a character as its argument and will return its lowercase equivalent if it is an uppercase character; it will return the original character if it is not. Figure 27.6 shows versions of these functions that will work for the ASCII character set, followed by a final version of procedure *makeletterset*.

Set Intersection

The intersection of two sets (of compatible type) is a set that consists of all the elements common to both of the original sets. In other words, a value of the base type is an element of the intersection of *set1* and *set2* if it is an element of both *set1* and *set2*. For example, if *set1* and *set2* are both of type

type tenset = **set of** 1..10

and *set1* is [2, 4, 6, 8] while *set2* is [2, 3, 4, 5, 6], then the intersection of *set1* and *set2* is the set [2, 4, 6]. Only the elements 2, 4, and 6 are in both *set1* and *set2*. In mathematics, the intersection of *set1* and *set2* would be written as follows:

$$set1 \cap set2$$

Figure 27.6 **Functions** *isletter* **and** *lower* **and complete procedure**
makeletterset

```
function isletter(ch: char): boolean;
{returns true if ch is a letter, false otherwise}
begin {isletter}
    isletter := ch in ['a'..'z','A'..'Z']
end; {isletter}

function lower(ch: char): char;
{returns ch, converted to lowercase if possible}
{Works by adding ord('a') - ord('A') to ord of the}
{uppercase letter. The difference ord('a') - ord('A')}
{is the distance from an uppercase letter to its}
{lowercase equivalent.}
begin {lower}
    if ch in ['A'..'Z']
        then
            lower := chr( ord(ch) + ord('a') - ord('A') )
        else
            lower := ch
end; {lower}

procedure makeletterset (inputtext: line;
                                 var outputset: letterset);
{constructs set outputset consisting of the letters}
{that occur in inputtext}
var     index: 1..linelength;
begin {makeletterset}
    outputset := [];
    for index := 1 to linelength do
        if isletter(inputtext[index])
            then
                outputset := outputset + [lower(inputtext[index])]
end; {makeletterset}
```

But since the symbol ∩ isn't available in most computer character sets, Pascal uses the symbol * to indicate set intersection. This symbol also denotes multiplication of both *real*s and *integer*s, but the types of the operands will always make the meaning of * clear. Thus, if we had a variable *set3* of type *tenset*, we could write

```
set1 := [2,4,6,8];
set2 := [2,3,4,5,6];
set3 := set 1 * set2
```

Figure 27.7   Examples of set intersection

Assume the definitions and declarations of Figure 27.4.

. . .

```
lets1 : = ['a', 'e', 'i', 'o', 'u'];
lets2 : = ['a', 'b', 'c', 'd', 'e'];
lets3 : = lets1 * lets2;       {* is set intersection}
nums1 : = [1, 3, 5, 7, 9];
nums2 : = [1, 2, 3, 4, 5];
nums3 : = nums1 * nums2;        {another set intersection}
```

This gives *set3* the value $[2, 4, 6]$. The semantic rules for intersection of sets are the same as those for union: You can take the intersection of any two sets of the same or compatible type, as in Figure 27.7, but you can't take the intersection of two sets of different type. Thus, an expression of the sort

```
nums2 * lets1          {ERROR: type clash}
```

is an error because the two operands of the intersection operator are of incompatible types.

Exercise 27.2: What will be the values of the sets *lets3* and *nums3* after the intersection operations in Figure 27.7 are performed? ∎

Exercise 27.3: Suppose we have assigned the following set values:

```
nums1 : = [1, 3, 5, 7, 9];
nums2 : = [2, 4, 6, 8, 10];
nums3 : = [1, 2, 3, 4, 5, 6];
```

Compute the following set values:

```
nums1  *  nums2
nums1  *  nums3
nums2  *  nums3
(nums1  +  nums2)  *  nums3
```

(continued)

```
(nums1  *  nums2)   *  nums3
(nums2  +  nums3)   *  nums1
(nums2  *  nums3)   +  nums1   ■
```

To illustrate the use of set intersection, let's extend our letter occurrence problem as follows: In addition to reporting which letters occur in the text, we must report separately which vowels occur in the text. Although we could solve this problem with a procedure similar to *makeletterset*, set intersection provides a much simpler method. After computing the set *typedletters*, we can take its intersection with the set `['a', 'e', 'i', 'o', 'u', 'y']`. This intersection will consist exactly of the letters that are in both sets, that is, the letters in *typedletters*, which are also vowels. Figure 27.8 shows a revised version of the main program of *lettersintext*, which includes the code for this extended problem. Note that the set that is the intersection of *typedletters* and the set of vowels is not explicitly assigned to a variable. It simply appears as an expression, passed as an argument to procedure *showset*. This is perfectly reasonable so long as we have no further use for this set. Note also that we mention the constant set of vowels explicitly. It would be convenient if we could write a constant declaration of the form

```
const   vowels = ['a','e','i','o','u','y'];          {ERROR!}
```

However, it is not legal. Constants of set type are not permitted. We could achieve almost the same effect by declaring a variable named *vowels*, of type *letterset*, and assigning it a value just once:

```
var     vowels: letterset;
          . . .
begin {lettersintext}
        vowels := ['a','e','i','o','u','y'];

          . . .
        showset(typedletters * vowels)
end. {lettersintext}
```

Figure 27.8   Extended main program *lettersintext*

```
begin    {lettersintext}
         readstring ( inputline );
         makeletterset ( inputline, typedletters );
         writeln('The letters in the input line are');
         showset ( typedletters );
         writeln('The vowels in the input line are');
         showset ( typedletters *['a','e','i','o','u','y'])
    end.    {lettersintext}
```

Exercise 27.4: Modify the main program shown in Figure 27.8 to print only the letters from the first half of the alphabet (**a** through **m**) that occur in the typed text, rather than all the letters. ■

Set Difference

Set difference, like union and intersection, allows us to construct set values, but in a different way. We can start with a set that has more elements than we want and then remove those we don't want, leaving a set with the desired value. Here's a definition:

> *The difference,* set1 − set2, *of two sets of the same type is a set that consists of all objects of the base type that are in* set1 *and are not in* set2.

Note that (like ordinary subtraction) set difference is not a symmetric operation: set1 − set2 isn't the same set as set2 − set1.

Exercise 27.5: Describe in words the difference between set1 − set2 and set2 − set1. ■

Let's look at some examples. Suppose we have

```
set1 := [2,4,6,8];
set2 := [2,3,4,5,6];
set3 := set1 - sct2
```

Now *set3* has the value [8], because 8 is the only element of *set1* that is not also an element of *set2*. If we construct

```
set4 := set2 - set1
```

then *set4* has the value [3,5], because 3 and 5 are the elements of *set2* that are not elements of *set1*.

Exercise 27.6: Assume we have assigned the following set values:

```
nums1 := [1,3,5,7,9];
nums2 := [2,4,6,8,10];
nums3 := [1,2,3,4,5,6];
```

Compute the following set values:

a. `nums1 − nums2`

b. `nums1 − nums3`

c. `nums2 − nums3`

d. `(nums3 − nums2) − nums1`

e. `nums3 − (nums2 − nums1)`

f. `nums2 − (nums1 + nums3)`

g. `(nums2 − nums1) + nums3`

h. `[] − nums1`

i. `nums2 − []` ∎

To illustrate the value of set difference, let's modify the letter occurrence problem once again. Suppose that this time, in addition to showing those letters that occur in the line, we want to show those letters that don't occur. Figure 27.9 shows the change in the main program of *lettersintext* that will accomplish the job easily (with the ASCII character set). The expression passed as the argument in the last call to showset,

```
['a'..'z'] - typedletters
```

is the difference of two sets. A letter will be in this difference if it is in `['a'..'z']` and it isn't in *typedletters*.

Our program is incomplete because we haven't yet seen how to write procedure *showset*, which displays the contents of a set of lowercase letters. The operation of testing for membership, which we describe next, will enable us to fill in that procedure.

Figure 27.9   Changing *lettersintext* to show the letters not typed

```
begin    {lettersintext}
         readstring ( inputline );
         makeletterset ( inputline, typedletters );
         writeln('The letters in the input line are');
         showset ( typedletters );
         writeln('The letters not in the input line are');
         showset ( ['a'..'z'] − typedletters )
end.     {lettersintext}
```

Testing Set Membership

Testing for set membership is accomplished with the operator **in**. We encountered **in**, in a limited context, back in Chapter 18. (See, for example, Figure 18.7.) We used it earlier in this chapter to test whether a character is a lowercase letter. In both contexts, the set that we were testing was a constant set. Now we'll lift that restriction.

The **in** operator is unique in Pascal because its two operands are always of different types. The set membership operation is written as follows:

```
expression1 in expression2
```

where *expression2* must be a set of some base type, and where *expression1* must represent a value of that type.

Before we use **in** to write procedure *showset*, we should note that we can't use this naive method of displaying the contents of a set:

```
writeln(typedletters)    {This is WRONG!}
```

Alas, we cannot write an expression of set type with *writeln*. In general, *writeln* takes as its arguments only expressions of simple type. In fact, the only way to find out what elements are in a set is to try each of the possibilities—that is, to test each value of the base type of the set for membership. We illustrate this with procedure *showset* in Figure 27.10. Now we have filled in the last missing piece of our program.

Exercise 27.7: Assemble all the pieces of program *lettersintext* to form a complete program. ∎

Figure 27.10 **Displaying the contents of a set**

```
procedure showset(letters: letterset);
{Displays the letters that are the elements of letters.}
{Assumes ASCII, or at least that 'a' - 'z' are contiguous.}
var     chindex: char; {ranges over all values 'a' to 'z'}
begin {showset}
    for chindex := 'a' to 'z' do
        if chindex in letters
            then
                write(chindex);
    writeln
end;    {showset}
```

The Precedence of Set Operators

We said that the right-hand operand of the **in** operator can be any expression of set type. Thus, we can write

```
element in (set1 + set2)
```

in place of

```
(element in set1) or (element in set2)
```

We can write expressions of any desired complexity. In forming such expressions, the precedence of the operators +, −, and * when they are interpreted as set operators is the same as when they are interpreted as arithmetic operators. That is, * has the highest precedence, and + and − are of equal precedence and are evaluated left to right. The operator **in** has lower precedence than any of these. (See Figure 18.8 on page 395.)

Set Comparison

We can use certain operations to compare sets just as we can to compare numbers or characters. The comparisons are different, however, because sets have no underlying order. For instance, consider the following two sets of numbers between 1 and 20:

[2, 5, 11, 19]   and   [9, 10, 11, 12]

We can't meaningfully say that either of these sets is larger than the other. However, if we consider these two sets of numbers

[2, 5, 11, 19]   and   [2, 3, 5, 7, 11, 13, 17, 19]

we see a relationship between them. There is a sense in which the second set is larger than the first: Every element of the first set is also an element of the second, and some numbers that are not elements of the first set are elements of the second. This relationship prompts the following definition:

> *If set1 and set2 are set of the same type, we say set1 is a subset of set2 if every element of set1 is also an element of set2.*

Consider the sets shown in Figure 27.11. With these values, *s1* is a subset of *s4*. So is *s2*. *s3* is a subset of *s1* and also of *s4*. *s4* is a subset of the union of *s1* and *s2*. *s5* is not a subset of any of the other sets listed, nor are any of the other sets subsets of *s5*. Each of the sets is a subset of itself (as is true for every set). The empty set [] is a subset of every set.

Figure 27.11   **Sets to illustrate the subset relationship**

```
type      tenset = set of 1..10;
var       s1, s2, s3, s4, s5: tenset;
          . . .
s1 := [1, 3, 5, 7];
s2 := [2, 4, 6, 8];
s3 := [1, 3, 5];
s4 := [1, 2, 3, 4, 5, 6, 7, 8];
s5 := [1, 4, 5, 9, 10];
```

In mathematical notation, we would write

$$set1 \subseteq set2$$

to indicate that *set1* is a subset of *set2*. Since the symbol $\subseteq$ does not exist in most computer character sets, Pascal uses the symbol <= for subset. This symbol is used in a syntax identical to the syntax for its use between expressions of scalar type. Thus, the expression

```
setexpression1 <= setexpression2
```

is a conditional expression yielding a *boolean* value that is *true* if the first set expression is a subset of the second and *false* otherwise. For example, using the values of *s1* through *s5* from Figure 27.11, the following conditional expressions all evaluate to *false*:

```
s1 <= s2
s2 <= s1
s5 <= s4
s4 <= s5
```

On the other hand, the following conditional expressions all evaluate to *true*:

```
s1 <= s4
s2 <= s4
s3 <= s1
s4 <= s1 + s2    {+ means union}
s1 * s2 <= s3
```

The last expression needs an explanation: Recall that multiplicative operators have a higher precedence than relational operators, so this expression is interpreted as if it were parenthesized:

```
(s1 * s2) <= s3
```

The set *s1 * s2* is the intersection of the sets [1, 3, 5, 7] and [2, 4, 6, 8]. This is the empty set, since *s1* and *s2* have no elements in common. The empty set is considered a subset of every set.

Pascal also allows sets to be compared using the operand >=. The expression

```
set1 >= set2
```

always has the same value as the expression

```
set2 <= set1
```

The test for equality between sets is done with the symbol =, as you would expect, and yields the value *true* if its operands are sets with the same elements and *false* otherwise. We can also use the operator <> to test for set inequality. As with objects of other types, these operators can only be used between sets of the same or compatible type.

27.3 LEGAL TYPES OF SETS

We have not said exactly which ordinal types are permitted to be the base types of sets, because, unfortunately, the possible legal base types are not specified as part of the formal description of Pascal. Different versions of Pascal have different rules. For example, one of the most useful set types is this:

```
type    charset = set of char:
```

That is, *charset* is the set type whose base type is *char*. However, some implementations of Pascal do not permit *char* as a base type.[3] The most we can say is this: Consult the manual for your local version of Pascal.

There is one universal restriction on base types: They must form a contiguous subrange of some ordinal type. Thus, the following are incorrect set type declarations:

```
type    upperlower = set of 'A'..'Z', 'a'..'z'; {ILLEGAL}
        daysofweek = (sun, mon, tue, wed, thu, fri, sat);
        weekend = set of (sun, sat);              {ILLEGAL}
```

3. Usually such restrictions have to do with the number of possible values of the base type. For example, the first implementation of Pascal was done on a computer on which, for reasons dictated by the design of the hardware, the largest sets that could be easily and efficiently implemented were limited to 59 elements. The character set on that computer had 64 values. Thus, the type "**set of** *char*" was not implemented.

In the first case, the ranges leave out some characters between the 'Z' and the 'a' in ASCII. In the second case, the enumerated type *daysofweek* is perfectly correct, but the set type *weekend* has a base type that is a noncontiguous subtype. On the other hand, the following are legal in ASCII:

```
type    lettersplus = set of 'A'..'z';
        daysofweek = (mon, tue, wed, thu, fri, sat, sun);
        weekend = set of sat..sun;
        weekdays = set of mon..fri;
        days = set of daysofweek;
```

In ASCII, the type *lettersplus* includes more than just the upper- and lower-case letters. It includes the characters

ABCDEFGHIJKLMNOPQRSTUVWXYZ[\]^_'abcdefghijklmnopqrstuvwxyz

which form a contiguous subrange of the type *char*. Since the enumerated type *daysofweek* has been rearranged, the subrange *sat..sun* is contiguous and legal, as is *mon..fri*. Finally, the type *daysofweek* is a perfectly good ordinal type and suitable for the base type of a set.

CHAPTER SUMMARY

1. *Sets* are a structured type in Pascal. They are useful for representing collections of items from some ordinal type. A set of some ordinal type may have as values any one of the possible collections of that type. The items in a set are called its elements. There is no multiplicity of elements in a set. That is, an element either is or isn't in a set, but if it is there, it's there only once. There is no order to the elements in a set.

2. *Set constants* can be written by enumerating the elements of the set between square brackets separated by commas. You can use subranges to avoid enumerating all of a contiguous subset of values. You may not declare constants of set type in the constant section of a program or procedure.

3. The operation of *set union,* written with the operator +, constructs a new set value from two other set values. The union of two sets is the set whose elements are those values of the base type that are elements of either one or the other, or both, of the original sets. You may only take the union of two sets of the same or compatible type.

4. The operation of *set intersection,* written with the operator *, constructs a new set value from two other set values. The intersection of two sets is the set whose elements are those values of the base type that are elements of both of the original sets. You may only take the intersection of two sets of the same or compatible type.

5. The operation of *set difference,* written with the operator $-$, constructs a new set value from two other set values. The difference of two sets is the set whose elements are those values of the base type that are elements of the first set but not elements of the second. You may only take the difference of two sets of the same or compatible type.

6. The operator **in** takes two operands of different types. The first operand must be an expression of a type that is a legal base type for a set, while the second operand must be a set of that type. The value of an expression constructed with the **in** operator is of type *boolean* and is *true* if the first operand is in the set and *false* otherwise.

7. There are four comparison operators that can be used between sets of compatible type. They are

   ■ =, which tests for equality of set values and works the same as for values of other types

   ■ <=, which yields the value *true* if its first operand is a subset of its second operand and *false* otherwise.

   ■ <>, which tests for inequality of set values and works the same as for values of other types

   ■ >=, which yields the value *true* if its second operand is a subset of its first operand and *false* otherwise

8. It is not possible to display the contents of a set by using an expression of set type as an argument to *write* or *writeln*. The only way to display the contents of a set is by testing each member of the base type in turn, using **in** and displaying those values that are indicated to be members.

COMMON ERRORS

■ Writing [a, b, c, d, e] when you mean ['a', 'b', 'c', 'd', 'e'], or some other instance of identifiers used as constants

■ Writing a..z instead of 'a'..'z' in describing the base type of a set whose base type is a subrange of the type *char*

■ Attempting to define named set constants in the constant section of a program or procedure

■ Using the **in** operator between two sets to test for the subset relationship

DEBUGGING HINTS

■ For each set type, write a procedure like *showset* that displays the contents of sets of that type. Use calls to these procedures to trace the values of set variables as they change during your program's execution.

SUPPLEMENTAL PROBLEMS

1. Suppose you have the following sets of *char*:

```
ch1 := ['!', '@', '#', '$', '0'..'9'];
ch2 := ['0'..'9', 'A'..'Z'];
ch3 := ['A'..'Z', 'a'..'z']
```

What is the value of each of the following expressions?
a. ch1 − ch2
b. ch2 − ch1
c. (ch3 + ch2) * ch1
d. (ch3 * ch2) + ch1
e. 'X' in ch1
f. ch2 * ch3 <= ch1

2. Suppose you have the following sets of integers:

```
ch1 := [1..5, 9, 11];
ch2 := [1, 3, 7..11];
ch3 := [2, 4, 6, 8, 10];
```

Write set expressions using only these sets and the operators +, *, − to construct each of the following sets:
a. [1, 3, 5, 7, 9, 11]
b. [1..11]
c. [2, 4]
d. [5, 7]
e. [6]

3. Consider the following procedure:

```
type    charset = set of char;
          .

          .

          .
```

(continued)

```
procedure getuntil(stoppers: charset; var ch: char);
begin
    repeat
        read(ch)
    until ch in stoppers
end; {getuntil}
```

Suppose a program has the procedure call

```
getuntil( ['.', '?', '!'] );
```

Explain carefully the effect of this procedure call.

4. Joe works three days and has one day off. Sally has five days on and two days off. They both start work periods today. Write a program using sets that lists by number the days they both have off in the next 365 days. (Today is day number 1, tomorrow is day number 2, and so on.)

5. Write a program that reads two lines of input and then reports to the user
   a. Which letters of the alphabet occurred in the first line but not in the second
   b. Which letters of the alphabet occurred in the second line but not in the first
   c. Which letters of the alphabet occurred in both lines

6. The cardinality of a set is the number of elements in the set. Suppose the type *intset* is defined by

   ```
   type    intset = set of min..max;
   ```

   where *min* and *max* are integer constants. Write function *card* that takes a parameter of type *intset* and returns an *integer* that is the cardinality of its parameter.

*7. The Sieve of Eratosthenes is a classical algorithm for computing prime numbers. If your implementation of Pascal allows sets whose base type is 2. . *MAX*, you can list all the primes up to *MAX* by writing a program to implement the sieve, as follows:

Setup

I. The variable *numset,* a set of 2..*MAX*.

II. The variable *nextnum,* an integer.

Instructions

I. Initialize *numset* to [2..*MAX*].

II. Initialize *nextnum* to 2.

III. While *numset* is not empty, do the following:
  A. If *nextnum* is in *numset,* then
    1. Display the value of *nextnum.*
    2. Remove *nextnum,* and all multiples of *nextnum* up to *MAX,* from *numset.*
  B. Increment *nextnum* by 1.

Implement this algorithm in a program.

*8. Write a program to implement the Sieve of Eratosthenes without using sets. Is it harder or easier to write? To understand?

CHAPTER

28

28.1 THE KINDS OF FILES AVAILABLE IN PASCAL

Internal and External Files

Pascal is capable of using files kept on the computer's auxiliary storage devices as sources of input data, destinations of output data, and temporary places for large amounts of scratch data. Files for input and output data are classified as external files because they are external to the program itself. Files used for input may exist both before and after execution. Output files, which are usually created by executing a program, should continue to exist after execution is terminated. Files for scratch data are called *internal* or *temporary files* because they are internal to the program's execution environment and thus have a temporary life span. They are created by the program during execution and are removed when execution terminates.

The words *input* and *output* in the program header indicate the standard source and destination of data items. In this chapter, we'll discuss how to use files as a source of input and as a destination for output when you are dealing with noninteractive input and output of data. Any Pascal program can use both interactive and noninteractive transmission of data.

FILES

Textfiles and Structured Files

Two kinds of files are available in Pascal. The first is called a *textfile*. The unit of information in a textfile is a single character. Reading from and writing to textfiles is very similar to reading from standard input and writing to standard output. The descriptions we gave in Chapters 11, 13, and 20 regarding how *read*, *readln*, *write*, and *writeln* work with *integer*, *char*, and *real* values are valid when textfiles are used. The second kind of file is called a *structured file*. Its unit of information is any type other than *char*. Hence, its unit of information may be a structured type, such as an array or a record.

The units of information in a textfile correspond to variables of type *char*. Why are files whose unit of information is anything but a single character all thrown together into a single classification? Why aren't files whose unit of information is a single *integer* or a single *real* or a single *boolean* value given any distinction?

For the most part, the distinction given to textfiles stems from the desire to have alternative sources of input and output that work just as standard input and output work. When users type input for *integer* or *real* variables to be read during execution of a program, they type the familiar character string representations of numeric values. Pascal translates those character strings into machine-understandable representations. The contents of a textfile "look" just like the sequence of characters the user types. The characters in textfiles are arranged in lines. By using the computer's editing facility, a user can easily check the accuracy of the character representation of the data in a textfile by inspecting its contents.

Structured files, by contrast, cannot be so easily inspected because the values in those files are stored in their machine-understandable representations. Since no translation process is needed to transport these values from external storage to memory, the computer can read and write these values quickly. Moreover, the binary representation of a numeric value takes up less space than the equivalent character representation in external storage. We have a trade-off between hardware efficiency (in terms of time and space) and the programmer's ease of dealing with the data representation. The programmer has little trouble moving from the use of standard input and output to the use of text files. Dealing with structured files, however, demands a further level of abstraction because the programmer cannot view the computer's representation of the data.

28.2 FEATURES COMMON TO ALL PASCAL FILES

All files used by Pascal are sequential files. As an analogy, think of the magnetic recording tape used in audio cassettes. To find the song of your choice on the tape, you must scan past the songs that come before it. The songs are arranged in a sequence and you must search through the sequence to locate the one you want.

Pascal does *not* use random-access files. Such files are accessed like a long-playing record album. When you want to play your favorite song, you look up its position on the record, put the correct side of the record up, and set the needle to the correct band. You can access any song without having to search through previous songs. Some other programming languages do use random-access files.

The name of each file used by a Pascal program is an identifier and must follow the syntax rules for an identifier given in Chapter 10. The name of each external file used by a program must be listed in the program header. The syntax diagram for the program header is shown in Figure 28.1. The first identifier is the name of the program. The identifiers separated by commas within the parentheses are the sources of input data and destinations of output data. By contrast, the names of internal or temporary files are not listed in the program header.

All files, whether internal or external, textfiles or structured files, must be declared as variables. The syntax for defining file types in the type definition section is shown in Figure 28.2. Here the file identifier is the name of the file and the type identifier is the type of a unit of data in the file. There is a predefined type for textfiles. It is simply *text* and means **file of** *char*, indicating that the type is a file and that the unit of information in the file is a single character.

> *When any file is used as an argument to a procedure or function, the corresponding parameter must be a variable parameter.*

Figure 28.3 shows how to deal with two textfiles called *infile* and *outfile* in the program header and in the variable declaration section of the program. Notice that a temporary textfile called *tempfile* is also included in the variable declaration section.

Figure 28.1   Syntax diagram for a program header

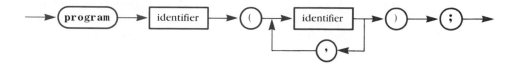

Figure 28.2   Syntax diagram for defining a file type

Figure 28.3   Internal versus external textfiles

```
program   demotextfiles (input, output, infile, outfile);
          .
          .
          .
var infile, outfile, tempfile : text;
          .
          .
          .
```

Figure 28.4 shows *infile2* and *outfile2* as structured files whose unit of data is a record.

You cannot use a single file simultaneously for both input and output. For example, you cannot read in information from the first ten units of a file and then try to write a unit of information after the tenth unit. Nor can you simply add a unit of data at the beginning, at the end, or in the middle of a file. To perform either of these operations, you have to recreate the entire file. At any given time, a Pascal file can be used only as a source of input or as a destination for output.

When you want to use a file for input, you must begin reading in its units of data from the beginning of the file. (This is like rewinding a cassette tape.) A read pointer is associated with a file used for input, similar to the read pointer discussed in Chapter 13. When you are preparing a file to be read, you must position the read pointer at the first unit of data in the file. To do so, you use the standard procedure *reset*. *reset* takes one argument, the name of the file, as shown in Figure 28.5.

When you want to use a file for output, you must position the associated *write pointer* at the beginning of the file before you can do any writing to the file. If there is any data in a file being prepared for output, all of that data is erased when you move the write pointer to the beginning of the file. The Standard Pascal procedure for moving the write pointer to the beginning of the file is *rewrite*. Its syntax is shown in Figure 28.6.

You access temporary files during program execution just as you access external files. You must *reset* temporary files before you can obtain data from them, and you must *rewrite* them before you can send data to them. Moreover, all statements that deal with data going to and coming from files must mention the name of the file.

Figure 28.4   **Declarations for internal and external structured files**

```
program   demostructfiles (input, output, infile2, outfile2);
             .
             .
             .

const maxnamelength = 20;

type string = array [1..maxnamelength] of char;
     student = record {student}
                     last, first : string;
                     gradyear : integer
                  end; {student}
     studentfile = file of student;

var infile2, outfile2, tempfile : studentfile;
             .
             .
             .
```

Figure 28.5   **Syntax of a call to *reset***

Figure 28.6   **Syntax of a call to *rewrite***

28.3 TEXTFILES

As we mentioned, Pascal reads from and writes to textfiles with code similar to the code for reading from and writing to standard input and output. Hence, the standard procedures *read*, *readln*, *write*, and *writeln* can be used in conjunction with textfiles. The only syntactic modification is that the name of the file must appear as the first argument in calls to these procedures. The standard identifiers *input* and *output* are optional arguments when those procedures are reading from the standard source of input or writing to the standard destination of output. Figure 28.7 shows modified syntax diagrams for calls to those standard procedures.

As we have seen (page 499), the predefined function *eoln* allows us to write Pascal code for conditional statements that depend on whether or not the next character to be read is the end-of-line marker (usually the carriage return). When we are checking for end-of-line in standard input, we use the *boolean*-valued function *eoln* without a parameter, as shown in Figure 28.8.

Figure 28.7 **Syntax of calls to *read*, *readln*, *write*, and *writeln***

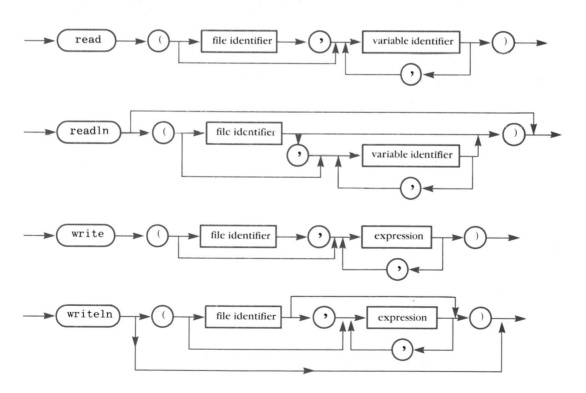

Figure 28.8   **Using *eoln* with standard input**

```
while not eoln do
            .
            .
            .
```

Figure 28.9   **Using *eoln* with a textfile**

```
while not eoln(infile) do
            .
            .
            .
```

To use the *eoln* function while reading from a file, we need to give the file name as a parameter. For instance, if we are reading in data from a textfile called *infile*, we could use the Pascal statement shown in Figure 28.9.

An Interactive Program versus a Noninteractive Program

Programs that read from and write to files may not interact with the user at all. Data may be transferred from memory to auxiliary storage devices and from auxiliary storage to memory during execution without any intervention by the user.

Let's write a couple of programs to show the contrast between these two situations:

1. The data input and output are interactive—that is, the user types input on the terminal keyboard and sees output on the terminal screen.
2. The data input and output are noninteractive—that is, input data comes from a file and output data goes to a file.

The program for the first situation, shown in Figure 28.10, is a standard program to read in a set of numbers and to write out the average of those numbers. A sample execution of this program is shown in Figure 28.11. Note how the user actually directs the program either to continue executing or to calculate the average and terminate.

In writing a similar but noninteractive program to deal with input from and output to a file, we cannot ask the user whether or not there is more data to be entered after each item is processed. The program, without any interaction with a

Figure 28.10   Program *interact*

```
program interact (input, output);
  {This program averages a set of numbers}
  {using interactive input and output.}

var response: char; {to hold user's response}
                    {about existence of data}

  procedure greeting (var resp: char);
   {to greet the user and find out}
   {if there is any data}
  begin {greeting}
    writeln('Welcome to the average program!');
    write('Please enter y if you have any data ');
    readln (resp)
  end; {greeting}

  procedure process;
   {to process data entered by the user}

  var sum,  {to hold the sum of all the data}
      counter: integer; {to hold the count of numbers}

    procedure getandsumup (var total, cnt: integer);
       {to read in data and keep a running}
       {sum and count of items}
    var moredata: char; {to determine if }
           {there is more data to be entered}
         num: integer; {to hold an individual data item}

    begin {getandsumup}
      repeat
        write('Please enter a single');
        write(' data item followed by a');
        writeln(' carriage return. ');
        readln(num) ;
        total : = total + num;
        cnt : = cnt + 1;
        write ('Enter y if there is more data ');
        readln(moredata)
      until not(moredata in ['y', 'Y'])
    end; {getandsumup}
```

(continued)

Figure 28.10
Continued

```
        begin {process}
          sum : = 0; {initialize running sum to 0}
          counter : = 0; {initialize counter to 0}
          getandsumup (sum, counter);
          write('The average of the numbers you entered is ');
          writeln(sum/counter: 1: 2)
        end; {process}

      begin {interact}
        greeting (response);
        if response in ['y','Y']
          then
            process
          else
            writeln('Sorry you have no data!')
      end. {interact}
```

Figure 28.11   Sample execution of the program *interact*

```
Welcome to the average program!
Please enter a y if you have any data y ⏎
Please enter a single data item followed by a carriage return
10 ⏎
Enter y if there is more data y ⏎
Please enter a single data item followed by a carriage return
20 ⏎
Enter y if there is more data y ⏎
Please enter a single data item followed by a carriage return
5 ⏎
Enter y if there is more data y ⏎
Please enter a single data item followed by a carriage return
10 ⏎
Enter y if there is more data n ⏎
The average of the numbers you entered is 11.25
```

user, must detect the absence of further data items—that is, the end of the input file. To avoid dividing by 0, the program should also be able to detect if no data items are present in the file.

Pascal has a predefined function to locate the end of a file of input data. That function is called *end of file* and denoted *eof*. Once again, we must indicate the

Figure 28.12   Using *eof* to test for the end of *infile*

$$\textbf{while not } \text{eof(infile) } \textbf{do}$$
$$\cdot$$
$$\cdot$$
$$\cdot$$

name of the file we are reading as an argument in any call to *eof*. The syntactic construct shown in Figure 28.12 is commonly used in a program that reads data from a file. The name of this file is *infile*.

If the next character to be read is the end-of-file marker, the function *eof* returns the value *true*. Otherwise, it returns the value *false*. When *eof* is *true*, the value returned by *eoln* is undefined.

We now have all the code we need to write a program for the second situation described above—that is, where data input and output are noninteractive. Let's write another program to calculate an average. This time, however, we'll use the computer's text editor to put the input data into a file named *infile*. Our program will calculate the average of the numbers in *infile* and will then send the average as output data to the file *outfile*. A user executing this program from a terminal will type the appropriate command to execute the program. The next thing the user will see on the terminal screen will be a message indicating termination of the program. The program is shown in Figure 28.13. Note that this program is somewhat shorter than the program *interact* because there is no need to support interaction with the user.

Figure 28.13   Program *noninteract*

```
program noninteract(infile,outfile);
  {a program to illustrate file input and output}

var infile, {file holding input data}
    outfile: text; {file to hold output data}
    sum, {to hold running sum of data items}
    counter: integer; {to hold the number of data items}

  procedure process (var total,cnt: integer);
    {to read in data, compute running sum, and compute count}
  var num: integer; {to hold an individual data item}

  begin {process}
    reset(infile);
```

(continued)

Figure 28.13
Continued

```
              total : = 0;
              cnt : = 0;
              while not eof (infile) do
                begin
                  while not eoln(infile) do
                    begin
                      read(infile,num);
                      total : = total + num;
                      cnt : = cnt + 1
                    end; {while not eoln}
                  readln(infile)
                end {while not eof}
              end; {process}

            procedure ansout(tot,count:integer);
              {a procedure to print out the average}
              {or inform the user of no data}
            begin  {ansout}
              rewrite(outfile);
              if count = 0
                then writeln(outfile, 'There is no data.')
                else writeln(outfile, tot/count:1:2,' is the average.')
            end; {ansout}

          begin    {main program, noninteract}
            process(sum,counter);
            ansout(sum,counter)
          end.    {noninteract}
```

Exercise   28.1: Let ⏎ indicate a carriage return character and * indicate the end of file marker. Assume that the contents of *infile* are as shown in Figure 28.14. Trace the program *noninteract*. ∎

The main difference between the two programs we have described in this section is that the first program calls for the interaction with a user, whereas the second program calls for reading from and writing to files. In the first program, we are continually prompting the user for both the actual data and for a signal to determine the end of the data. In the second program, we use Pascal's facility to detect the end-of-file marker to determine that there is no more data. Syntactically, the difference in reading from and writing to files is that the name of the file is required as the first argument in a call to *read*, *readln*, *write*, or *writeln*. The second program must also *reset* the input file and *rewrite* the output file.

Figure 28.14   **Sample contents of *infile* for Exercise 28.1**

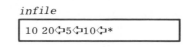

Exercise   28.2: Write a program to count the number of characters in a textfile.   ■

Exercise   28.3: Write a program to count the number of nonblank lines in a textfile.   ■

28.4 STRUCTURED FILES

To deal with structured files, we must first change our mental image of what a file is. Textfiles are filled with characters organized into lines. A structured file has no such line orientation. Hence, the familiar Pascal procedures *readln* and *writeln* and function *eoln* are neither valid nor relevant. It is an error to use them in conjunction with a structured file.

A Model of a File

Think of a structured file as a sequence of data items on an external storage medium. The type of each data item is determined by the programmer and is declared in the program. If we use □ to denote a unit of data in a file (remember our analogy to magnetic audio cassette tape), we can imagine a lineup of data items like the one shown in Figure 28.15.

Figure 28.15   **Model of a structured file**

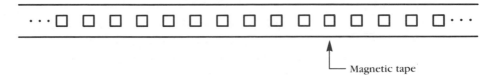

Magnetic tape

We must add two things to our picture. They are the end-of-file marker and a pointer to the data item that is being read or written.

The computer's memory has a copy of the data item in the file indicated by the pointer. That copy is called the *file window* and is denoted by the file name followed by the ^ character. For example, if a file is named *outf*, then its window is named *outf* ^ . The file window is a variable in memory that has the same structure as a single data item in the file. The file window variable is automatically declared when you declare the file variable. There is one file window associated with each file declared in a program. The computer "sees" an individual data item in the file through the file window. The file window variable associated with an input file is undefined until that file is *reset*. The file window variable associated with an output file is undefined until the program assigns it a value. In Figure 28.16, we add these two concepts to our picture of a file, using * to denote the end-of-file marker.

As we move through a file reading or writing data items, we are in a sense "sliding" the file window along the file. At any one time, only one data item from the file is in the window.

Writing to a Structured File

Let's see what happens when we write to a structured file. We'll use an example coded in Pascal so that you'll see the syntactic constructs at work. We want to create a file of our friends' birthdays that will remain on an external storage device of the computer after execution of our program. Since the life span of this file extends beyond the termination of execution of the program, it should be an external file. Its name will therefore appear in the program header. The name of the file must be an identifier in the program and thus must conform to the rule for forming

Figure 28.16   The file window

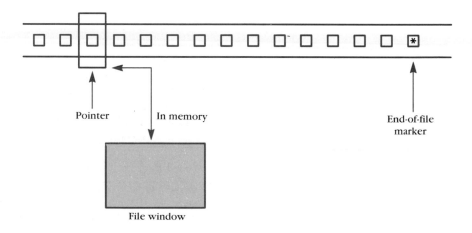

File window

identifiers. Let's call the file *birthdata* and name the program *createfile*. The program header will look like this:

program createfile (input, output, birthdata);

Our program will produce the file *birthdata* as output. That file will then be available to us in machine-understandable format whenever we next want to use it. The input data will come interactively from the user.

We use the data structure developed on pages 558–559 to hold the list of names and corresponding birthdays in memory. The program will sort the list into alphabetical order and write it, one record at a time, into file *birthdata*. Figure 28.17 shows the Pascal code used to define the data structure. Since *personrec* is the type identifier for one entire record of information, it should be the type for a single data item in a file of type *birthfile*.

Figure 28.17 **Definitions and declarations for program *createfile***

```
const maxnamelength = 20;
         {maximum number of characters}
         {in a first or a last name}
      maxmonthlength = 3;
         {maximum number of characters}
         {used to represent a month}
      maxlistsize = 50;
            {maximum number of items}
            {possible in a list}
type namestr = array[1..maxnamelength] of char;
        {to hold a first or last name}
      monthstr = array[1..maxmonthlength] of char;
        {to hold the name of a month}
      namerec = record {to hold one person's name}
                    last,first: namestr;
                    midinit: char
                end; {namerec}
      birthrec = record {to hold one person's birthday}
                    month : monthstr;
                    day,year : integer
                 end; {birthrec}
      personrec = record {to hold one person's name and}
                        {birthday}
                     name : namerec;
                     birthday : birthrec
                 end; {personrec}
      datalist = array[1..maxlistsize] of personrec;
            {to hold all information in a list}
```

(continued)

Figure 28.17
Continued

```
birthfile = file of personrec;
         {type for the external file}
var list : datalist; {the variable holding all info}
    numberinlist : integer; {number of items in the list}
    birthdata : birthfile; {the variable representing}
                           {the external file}
```

Exercise   28.4: Write a program that will:

a. Read all the names and corresponding birthdays into memory
b. Sort the list by month and day of birth   ∎

Let's assume that the parts of the program dealing with data entry and sorting the array have been written. We will concentrate on the procedure used to create the output file *birthdata*. Let's call that procedure *sendtofile*. It needs both *list* and *numberinlist*, but it should not be able to change them. We should also send it the file as an argument, which it will change. The procedure call for our main program and the corresponding procedure header appear in Figure 28.18.

Figure 28.18   Procedure call and header for *sendtofile*

```
sendtofile(list,numberinlist,birthdata)

procedure sendtofile(birthlist: datalist;
                     num: integer;
                     var birthf: birthfile)
```

 Recall that in order to prepare a file for writing, we must use procedure *rewrite* to move the write pointer to the beginning of the file and to erase any data being held in the file. At this point, we have in memory the entire list and a file window that contains unpredictable values and is associated with the first record in the file. We must also have a corresponding *integer* variable to indicate the position in the list of the data item to be copied into the file. Let's call it *index*. The situation in memory is shown in Figure 28.19.

To put a single element of the array into the file, we follow these steps:

l. Assign *birthlist*[index] to the file window variable, *birthf* ^.

Figure 28.19   **Situation in memory just after the call to *rewrite***

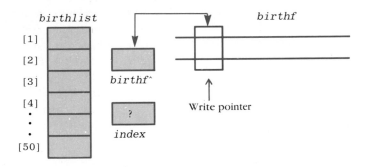

II. Transfer data from the file window variable in memory to the associated data item position in the file.

III. Slide the file window down to the next position in the file.

IV. Increment *index*.

The picture in Figure 28.20 describes the situation after we have carried out these steps for the first list element.

Figure 28.20   **After the first array element is copied into the file**

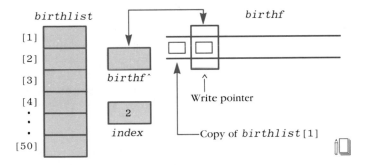

We'll have to repeat the above steps for every item in the array from position 1 to position *numberinlist*. To do that, we'll use a **for** loop. We can accomplish step I with a single assignment statement:

```
birthf^ := birthlist[index]
```

To carry out steps II and III we need another Pascal predefined procedure. The Standard Pascal procedure *put* accomplishes both steps for us:

```
put (birthf)
```

In general, the *put* procedure transfers the contents of the file window variable to the file and slides the file window down to the next available place for a data item in the file. We can think of the *put* procedure as just "putting" something into the file. With this much code in hand, we can write the entire procedure to output the list of names and birthdays to a file. Figure 28.21 gives the procedure *sendtofile*.

Remember that the **for** loop takes care of incrementing *index* for us. We must be sure to place the call to *rewrite* outside the loop, or else the contents of the file will be erased each time an item is put in the file. Upon termination of execution or if the file is *reset*, the computer places the end-of-file marker in the file.

Standard Pascal has a shortcut method of writing to a structured file that avoids the concept of the file window. In fact, the shortcut we will describe for structured files is the real meaning of a call to the standard procedure *write* for both textfiles and standard output. We showed you the longer method first to stress the manipulation of data that actually occurs. The shortcut makes it possible to accomplish these two statements:

```
birthf^ : = birthlist[index];
put (birthf);
```

Figure 28.21   Procedure *sendtofile*

```
procedure sendtofile (birthlist : datalist;
                      num : integer;
                      var birthf : birthfile);
{a procedure to copy the contents of an array}
{of type datalist into a file of type birthfile}

var index : integer;
    {used to subscript the array}

begin {sendtofile}
  rewrite(birthf);
  {Note that rewrite is called once and is outside the loop.}
  for index : = 1 to num do
    begin
      birthf^ : = birthlist [index];
      put (birthf)
    end {for}
end; {sendtofile}
```

by the single statement:

```
write(birthf,birthlist[index]);
```

Reading from Structured Files

Suppose we want to inspect our newly created file. We cannot use the computer's text editor to inspect the file; it's a structured file and hence in machine-understandable format. So let's write a quick Pascal program to print the contents of the file. We simply want to output each data item in the file to standard output. Each data item must pass through the computer's memory. Hence, we'll read each data item from the file into memory and write each data item from memory to standard output. There is no way to go directly from the file to standard output. Just after *reset* is executed, we have the picture shown in Figure 28.22.

Note that we have no need to place the entire list of data items in memory. We need only to pass the data items from the file to memory one at a time. The file window variable serves as the intermediate holding place for each data item.

A procedure to accomplish this task will give you a model that you may find useful later on. Let's call the procedure *printoutfile*. Its only parameter will be a variable parameter corresponding to the file. Remember that parameters of file type must be variable parameters. We'll use the following procedure header:

procedure printoutfile(**var** outfile : birthfile);

To prepare the file for reading, we use the standard procedure *reset*. Our first step is this:

```
reset(outfile);
```

Figure 28.22   Just after the file is *reset*

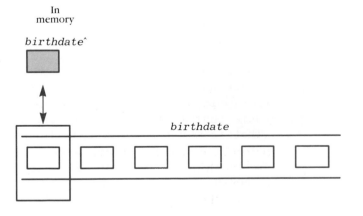

The effect of this statement is to move the read pointer to the beginning of the file and to get the contents of the first data item of the file into the file window. Thus, after the call to *reset* is executed, *outfile^* contains a copy of the first data item in the file.

From this point on, our general algorithm for processing each item in the file could be

I. Send the contents of the file window to standard output.

II. Slide the file window down so that *outfile^* contains a copy of the next data item in the file.

We repeat these two steps until we have moved the file window to the end-of-file marker. We accomplish step I by performing *write*'s or *writeln*'s to standard output. We can refer directly to the file window variable as *outfile^*. To do step II, we use yet another Standard Pascal procedure, which is accomplished by

```
get(outfile)
```

This procedure gets the next data item to be read into the file window.

We now have all the code to write procedure *printoutfile*, which is shown in Figure 28.23. We leave the details of procedures *writenamestr* and *writemonthstr* to you.

We used the file window variable *outfile^*, in the procedure *printoutfile*. If we had wanted to assign that value to another variable of type *personrec*, we could have done it with an assignment statement. For example, if *pers* is a variable of type *personrec*, we could write the following two Pascal statements:

```
pers := outfile^
get(outfile)
```

Figure 28.23   **Procedure *printoutfile***

```
procedure printoutfile (var outfile : birthfile);
{a procedure to send the contents of}
{a file of type birthfile to standard output}
begin {printoutfile}
  {Note that we want to reset the file only once.}
  {That is why the reset call is outside the loop.}
  reset (outfile); {gets first data item into window}
  while not eof(outfile)  do
    begin
```

```
        with outfile^.name do
          begin
            writenamestr(first);
            write(' ',midinit,' ');
            writenamestr(last)
          end; {with outfile ^.name do}
        with outfile^.birthday do
          begin
            write('  ');
            writemonthstr(month);
            writeln(' ',day:1,', ',year:1)
          end; {with outfile^.birthday do}
        get(outfile)
      end{while not eof(outfile) }
  end; {printoutfile}
```

These two statements have the effect of moving the contents of the file window into variable *pers* before moving the file window down. As was the case with the standard procedure *write*, the two statements above represent the real meaning of a call to procedure *read* when either a textfile or standard input is being read. In Standard Pascal, those two statements can be shortened to

```
read(outfile,pers)
```

Case Study: Updating a Structured File

As we mentioned on page 593, Pascal files can either be read from or written to at any given moment—but not both! Consider the problem of inserting a record into an ordered file. It is not possible to somehow move the write pointer to the proper position in the file and insert a new record. The reason it is not possible has to do with Pascal's *rewrite* procedure. Remember that we must prepare a file for writing by first calling *rewrite* and that a call to *rewrite* erases any data held in the file. Any data items put into the file after calling *rewrite* will therefore be the only data items in the file. The only way to change the contents of a Pascal file is to recreate the entire file.

Suppose we want to enlarge an ordered file by inserting new data items in appropriate positions. Take our file of names and corresponding birthdays, for example, which we ordered by the month and day of a person's birthday. We want to insert several new data items into the file. Here is a situation in which temporary files are useful, especially if we do not know how many data items are in the file and how many are to be inserted.

We can create a temporary file each time we want to insert a new data item into the external file. The data items in the temporary file will consist of all the data items in the external file, with the addition of one new data item in its proper place.

We can create a temporary file by following these three steps:

I. While an item in the file window is not after the new item, copy items from the external file into the temporary file one at a time.

II. Put the new data item into the temporary file.

III. Copy the remaining data items of the external file into the temporary file.

When the temporary file is complete, we *rewrite* the external file, erasing its contents, and copy the data items of the temporary file, one by one, into the external file. This may seem like a long process for inserting just one data item, but it works well in all situations. Sometimes we can speed up the process if we have more information.

If, for example, we knew how many data items we planned to insert before we began to enlarge the file, we might be able to use an array to hold all the new data items in memory at once. Then the following steps would solve our problem:

I. Read all of the new data items into an array.

II. Sort the array.

III. Merge the array and the original file into a temporary file.

IV. Rewrite the original file.

V. Copy the elements of the temporary file into the original file.

Another consideration is the size of the computer's memory component. Files are kept on the computer's external storage facilities quite separate from the computer's memory component. If we use temporary files, as described above, we don't have to worry about the size of the computer's memory because a copy of only one item from each file (in the file window) is in memory at any one time. If we use an array, we must have enough memory available to hold all the new data items.

Using temporary files is relatively slow because of the time it takes to transfer data items between an external storage device (usually magnetic tape or disk) and the computer's memory. The solution to this problem thus involves a trade-off between space and time. If we have lots of space available, and if we want the program to run quickly, we can use a data structure that will hold all of the new items in memory at once. If the amount of new data is very large, however, and if we don't have a large amount of computer memory available, we can use the slower method of creating one temporary file for each new item.

CHAPTER SUMMARY

1. The files with which Pascal interacts can be categorized in two ways:
   a. Some files are *external* while others are *internal* or *temporary*. The life span of an external file may be independent of the duration of execution of the program. An internal file, however, exists only during execution of the program. The names of external files appear in the program header. The names of internal files do not.
   b. Files are of two varieties with respect to the composition of an individual data item. *Textfiles* use a single character as their unit of data. *Structured files* use any valid predefined or programmer-defined type (except `char`) as their unit of data.

2. All the files with which Pascal interacts are sequential. In this respect, they are similar to magnetic recording tape.

3. All files must be declared as variables.

4. Files *cannot* be used for both input and output in a given situation. When a file is to be used for input, it must be prepared for reading by using the standard procedure `reset`. When a file is to be used for output, it must be prepared for writing by using the standard procedure `rewrite`.

5. Associated with each file is a *file window* variable. Data items are transferred into the computer's memory from the file through the file window, which is essentially a copy in memory of a data item in the file.

6. The `reset` procedure moves the file window to the first item in the file, putting a copy in memory.

7. The `rewrite` procedure erases any previous contents of the file and moves the file window to the beginning of the file, ready to write the first data item to the file.

8. The `boolean`-valued predefined function `eof` is used to detect the end of a file when reading from either a textfile or a structured file.

9. File variables used as arguments must correspond to variable parameters.

10. The `get` procedure is used in reading a structured file. It moves the file window one position, putting a copy of the next data item in memory.

11. The `put` procedure is used in writing to a structured file. When all information constituting a data item is assembled in the file window variable, execution of the `put` procedure makes that data item part of the file and moves the file window down to the next available position where a data item can be written in the file.

12. The file window variable may be avoided syntactically as follows:

   a. The two statements   x : = f^;
                                 get (f)
   are equivalent to   read (f, x).

b. The two statements   `fˆ : = x;`
                                 `put (f)`
    are equivalent to   `write (f, x)`.

13. Input from and output to textfiles is line-oriented and thus similar to input from and output to standard input and output. The difference when using *read*, *readln*, *write*, *writeln*, or *eoln* is that the name of the file must appear as the first argument. The standard identifiers *input* and *output* are optional arguments for those procedures when reading is from the standard source of input and when writing is done to the standard destination for output.

14. Temporary files are especially useful in programs for updating the contents of an external file.

COMMON ERRORS

■ A call to the *reset* procedure immediately followed by a call to the *get* procedure causes the first data item in a file to be skipped. The *reset* procedure puts a copy of the first data item of a file into the file window variable.

■ When reading from and writing to textfiles, the first parameter, which is the file identifier, is often forgotten because the process is so similar to reading from and writing to standard input and output.

■ Assigning one file variable to another file type variable is illegal. File variables are not identifiers for data in the computer's memory. Thus, an assignment of one to another is not possible.

■ The *reset* procedure should be called only once before reading from a file. If a procedure's purpose is to read and process a single data item from a file, that procedure should not contain a call to the *reset* procedure. If it did, the file would be *reset* each time the procedure was invoked, making only the first data item of the file available to the program.

■ Procedures *reset* and *rewrite* cannot be called with the standard identifiers *input* and *output* as arguments.

DEBUGGING HINTS

■ Write a procedure to display the contents of a file. Invoke this procedure before and after the file is manipulated.

■ Display the values of file items as they are read into memory.

SUPPLEMENTAL PROBLEMS

1. Write a procedure to move the contents of a file of type *birthfile* into an array of type *datalist* in memory. (See Figure 28.17 on page 603 for the type definitions.) Your procedure header should have three variable procedures corresponding to the file, the list, and the number of elements in the list. If there are more than 50 data items in the file, your procedure should print an error message, stop reading the file, and send the filled array back to the calling program.

2. Write an entire program to inspect and change data in a file of type *birthfile*.

3. a. Write an algorithm using temporary files to delete data items from an ordered file.
   b. Write a program using temporary files that allows a user to delete data items from the file of type *birthfile*.

4. a. Expand the discussion on pages 609–611 of using temporary files to enlarge an ordered file into a detailed algorithm.
   b. Write a program that allows a user to enlarge a file of type *birthfile* by appending new records at the end of the file.

5. a. Write an algorithm using temporary files to update items in an ordered file. By *update,* we mean insert, delete, or change data items.
   b. Write a program using temporary files that allows a user to update data items in the file of type *birthfile*.

6. Write a program to merge two ordered files named *birth1* and *birth2* whose items are type *personrec* into a single ordered file named *birth*.

7. Write a program to generate a concordance of the words in a textfile. The concordance should be stored in a structured file whose elements are records consisting of a word and a set of line numbers on which the word occurs. The structured file should be ordered alphabetically.

8. Write a program that takes a textfile as input and generates a structured file of records as output. There should be two fields in each record, the first containing a word and the second containing the number of times the word occurs in the file. The structured file should be ordered by two keys. The records should first be ordered numerically by the number of times a word occurs. Then among the records of words occurring the same number of times, the records should be ordered alphabetically.

9. Write a program to simulate the recording of births at a county record office. The information stored for each birth must include the child's name, the child's sex, the father's name, the mother's maiden name, the date of birth, the time of birth, and the place of birth. Assume that the county maintains one file for each month ordered by the day of the month and the time in a particular day. Your program should solve the problem of maintaining that file.

10. Write a program to maintain the accounts receivable files for a credit card company. There are two kinds of files. One file contains information about each account that has an outstanding balance. There is only one record for each account number. Each record in this file should include two fields. The first field contains an account number of type *integer*, and the second field contains the outstanding balance of type *real*. The second type of file is a transaction file containing information about payments made for certain accounts. There may be multiple records for a single account number if more than one payment has been made for that account. The two fields in each record of this file represent the account number and the amount of the payment. Both files are ordered numerically by account number.

11. Write programs to allow a teacher to maintain an electronic gradebook. The grades should be stored in a structured file. It should be able to hold 30 grades for each student. Allow the teacher to initialize the file by reading the names of the students from a textfile. After the file is initialized, the program should allow the teacher to record and change grades for each assignment in the file.

CHAPTER

29

29.1 THE NEED FOR DYNAMICALLY ALLOCATED DATA

All the programs we've written so far have had the following characteristic in common: For each of the data items we needed, we could declare corresponding variables at the time we wrote the program. As we were planning each program, we could think about each of the data structures we would need, define appropriate types, declare variables of those types, and use them in procedures and functions and in the main program. Sometimes, however, it's impossible to know in advance how many variables of a given type we'll need to solve a problem.

One strategy for coping with such a situation is to allocate for each possible type the largest possible array made up of elements of that structural type. True, we will have wasted space if we don't use every location in the array during execution of the program. But no great harm will have been done. Indeed, that is the only strategy available in some programming languages. The trouble is that we may run out of memory along the way. If we have several different data types whose space needs we don't know when we write the program, we have to guess how many of each we'll need to set as a reasonable maximum.

For example, suppose the program you wanted to write was a Pascal compiler. A compiler needs to keep track of many different tables, such as a list of type definitions and their meanings, a list of procedure and function declarations, a list of the parameters and parameter types of each procedure or function, a list of the data declarations, and so forth. You might set as reasonable maximums 50 different type definitions, 1,000 data declarations, 200 procedures, 200 functions, 50 constant definitions, and so on. But then a programmer who wanted to write a program with 51 constant definitions would be out of luck, even if the program called for only 3 procedures. On balance, this strategy makes for a poor use of available memory.

POINTERS AND
DYNAMIC DATA

Fortunately, Pascal offers an alternative strategy: *dynamic storage allocation*. With this strategy, variables are created and space is allocated for them during execution of the program.

29.2 POINTERS

Pascal allows us to allocate space for variables in the variable declaration sections of our programs. When this is done, a specific space in memory is set aside and the identifiers we have chosen become synonymous with those spaces. Since space in memory for dynamically allocated data is not reserved before execution begins, we cannot refer to it directly by name. Instead, Pascal provides us with an indirect reference through a special variable type called a *pointer*. When we request a space for a piece of data during execution of our program, a pointer variable will store the location of the new space in memory. Figure 29.1 shows a pictorial representation of both static and dynamic variables. Note that two memory spaces are involved in the dynamically allocated data structure: the pointer and the actual memory space to hold the data.

The data structures we are dynamically allocating must be of some type. When we define the type of a pointer variable, we need to know the type of the item it will point to. Figure 29.2 shows examples of type definitions for pointers and variable declarations using these types. The definition of the type *personptr* means that data items of type *personptr* are pointers that must refer to records of type *person*. The character ˆ before the identifier *person* should be read as *pointer to*. Note that we have declared three variables of type *personptr* but no variables of type *person*. We have declared no variables of type *person* because we will only request space for such variables when we need them.

Figure 29.1   Static versus dynamic data storage in memory

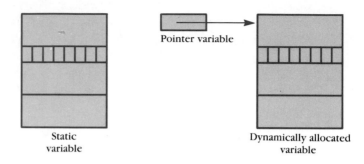

Static
variable

Pointer variable

Dynamically allocated
variable

Figure 29.2   Type definitions and variable declarations using pointers

```
const maxlen = 20;

type   personptr = ^person;   {a pointer to a person record}
       classptr = ^class;     {a pointer to a class record}

       string = packed array[1..maxlen] of char; {useful}
       person = record    {an arbitrary record}
                    name: string;
                    age: integer,
                    sex: (male, female);
                    plink: personptr
                end;    {person record}

       class = record     {another, for variety}
                    instructor: string;
                    department: string;
                    number: integer;
                    clink: classptr
                end;    {class record}

var    personp1,
       personp2,
       personp3: personptr;

       classp1,
       classp2: classptr;
```

The variables *personp1*, *personp2*, and *personp3* are each capable of storing a reference to a record of type *person*.[1] Like all variables, however, they have no value when they are declared. The same is true of all pointer variables. There are as yet no records of type *person* or of type *class*. Figure 29.3 pictures the situation after the definitions and declarations of Figure 29.2 have been made. Notice that in Figure 29.3 the pointers do not yet point to a data structure. In fact, their value is unpredictable because we have not yet given a value to any of the pointers—in other words, we can't tell where they are pointing.

Creating a Dynamic Data Structure

We are now ready to create a dynamic data structure. Typically, dynamic data structures are made with records. This is true because they will need to contain two types of data to be useful. We can create records during execution time by means of the predefined Pascal procedure *new*. This procedure takes a single argument, which must be a variable of pointer type. Using the definitions and declarations in Figure 29.2, we can use any variable of type *personptr* or *classptr*. An example, using a variable of type *personptr* is

Figure 29.3   **Situation after making the type definitions and variable declarations given in Figure 29.2**

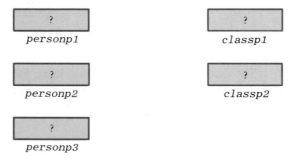

? means value of the pointer variables is undefined.

1. You may wonder how a pointer refers to a record. What exactly are the values stored in pointers? The value of a pointer is the address of the corresponding value in the computer's memory. If you find this a more concrete way to think about pointers, then by all means do so. The notion of a reference is more abstract and allows us to ignore the way a particular computer's memory addresses are constructed.

```
new (personp1)
```

Using the predefined procedure *new* with the argument *personp1* has two effects:

1. A record of type *person* is allocated
2. A reference to that record is stored in the pointer variable *personp1*.

Invoking procedure *new* will always assign a value to the pointer variable that is the argument of *new*. The effect of *new* is pictured in Figure 29.4.

Figure 29.4   **Effect of procedure** *new*

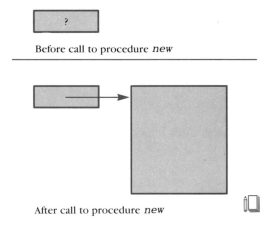

Before call to procedure *new*

After call to procedure *new*

Once a pointer has been given a value by procedure *new*, we can use that pointer to refer to the newly allocated record. In fact, the only way we can refer to the record or its fields is through the value of a pointer. The syntax for making such references is as follows:

`pointervariable^`	refers to the whole record
`pointervariable^.field`	refers to a field in the record

The character ^ appears after the pointer variable to distinguish this use of the symbol from its use in defining types, where it comes before the type identifier (as in Figure 29.2). You can think of the symbol ^ as meaning "the record stored at the location." The ordering of the symbol ^ and the pointer identifier don't agree with English, but we can read the following identifiers as:

`pointervariable`	"the location where a record of some type is stored"

`pointervariable^`	"the record stored at the location addressed by *pointervariable*"
`pointervariable^.field`	"the field in the record stored at the location addressed by *pointervariable*"

The following analogy is useful:

221B Baker Street	"the location of a certain home"
221B Baker Street^	"the home at that location"
221B Baker Street^.den	"the room called the den in the home at that location"

Thus, the procedure call `new(personp1)` creates a record that can be referred to as *personp1^*.

The fields of dynamically allocated records can be assigned, printed, and otherwise manipulated like the fields of statically allocated records. The various fields of *person1^* are *personp1^.name*, *personp1^.age*, and *personp1^.sex*.

Here is a code fragment that allocates a *class* record and fills it with values:

```
         .
         .
         .
new(classp1);     {allocates a class record, ref by classp1}
classp1^.instructor : = 'Sally Ride       ';
classp1^.department : = 'Astronautics     ';
classp1^.number : = 199;
         .
         .
         .
```

Exercise   29.1: You are given the following type definitions and variable declarations:

```
type    string = packed array[1..maxlen] of char;
        date =  record
                   month: string;
                   day: 1..31;
                   year: 1900..1999
                end; {date record}
        event = record
                   description: array[1..10] of string;
                   when: date
                end; {event record}

        eventp = ^event;

var     evt: eventp;
```

Suppose *evt* has been given a value by procedure *new*. What are the types of the following data items?

a. evt

b. evt^

c. evt^.when

d. evt^.when.day

e. evt^.when.month[1]

f. evt^.description

g. evt^.description[2]

h. evt^.description[2][5] ∎

Here are some valid Pascal statements that manipulate fields of dynamically allocated records:

```
new(personp1);
readstring(personp1^.name);     {Read name.}
readln(personp1^.age);          {Read age.}
ageplus1 := personp1^.age + 1;  {Compute age + 1.}
writeln(personp1^.name[1]);     {Write 1st letter of name.}
write(personp1^.age:1, ' is a fine age.');
                 {Field-width specifiers are OK as always.}
```

We can also assign records referenced by pointers the values of records of the same type, but first we must allocate those records. Here is a code sequence that assigns, not pointers, but the records the pointers point to:

```
        . . .
new(personp1);   {Allocate a record.}
new(personp2);   {Allocate another one!}
personp1^.name := 'Coretta King          ';
personp1^.age := 58;
personp1^.sex := female;
personp2^ := personp1^;   {Copy one record to another.}
        . . .
```

This code allocates two records. The first is referenced by *personp1*, and the second is referenced by *personp2*. The first three assignment statements fill the contents of the first record. The fourth assignment statement is a record assignment; it copies the contents of the first allocated record to the second, thereby creating two records with the same contents, as shown in Figure 29.5.

Figure 29.5 **Effect of** `personp1ˆ := personp2ˆ`

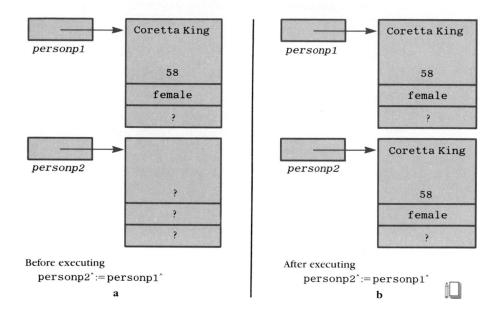

Before executing
   personp2ˆ:=personp1ˆ
   a

After executing
   personp2ˆ:=personp1ˆ
   b

Exercise 29.2: Assume the type definitions of Exercise 29.1, and the following variable declarations:

var evtp1,
     evtp2: eventp;

Both *evtp1* and *evtp2* have been assigned values by calls to procedure *new*. What is the effect of each of the following assignment statements?

a. `evtp1 := evtp2;`
b. `evtp1ˆ := evtp2ˆ;`
c. `evtp2ˆ.date.year := evtp1ˆ.date.year + 2;`
d. `evtp1ˆ.description := evtp2ˆ.description;`
e. `evtp2ˆ.dateˆ.month := evtp1ˆ.description[4];` ■

Assigning Values to Pointer Variables

There are only three ways to assign values to pointer variables in Standard Pascal:

■ By using the standard procedure *new*

- By assigning to one pointer variable the value of another pointer variable of the same type
- By assigning a pointer variable the special value **nil**

It's not possible to make a pointer variable refer to a data structure that is static—that is, a data structure that is defined in the variable declarations section.

We can assign pointer variables just as we assign variables of other types. If a pointer references (points to) a record, and we assign the pointer's value to another pointer of the same type, both pointers will reference the same area of memory. Thus, the code

```
        .
        .
        .
new(personp1);
personp1^.name := 'Garry Kasparov        ';
personp1^.age := 21;
personp1^.sex := male;
personp2 := personp1;
        .
        .
        .
```

allocates a single record, fills it with values, and creates a second reference to it. Both *personp1* and *personp2* point to the same space in memory, as shown in Figure 29.6.

Figure 29.6   **Assigning a pointer variable the value of another pointer variable of the same type**

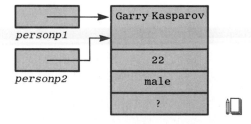

Notice that assigning pointers isn't like assigning records; we don't make a second copy of the data in the record. Also note that since *personptr* and *classptr* are different types, an assignment statement of the form

```
personp3 := classp2;        {ERROR: type clash}
```

is illegal.

Recall that the value of a pointer is unpredictable before it is used. Since pointers are made to point to space in memory; it's possible that they point to crucial parts of memory (like where the program instructions are stored). Using the memory spaces they reference may have disastrous results.

To guard against such disasters, Pascal provides a special value that can be assigned to any pointer variable so that it does not refer to any space in memory. That value is represented by the reserved word **nil**. It's a good idea to assign the value **nil** to any pointer variable that does not yet point to a dynamically allocated space in memory. This value is not assigned automatically; you must assign it in the program instructions.

29.3   LINKED LISTS

We still haven't solved our original problem—namely, being able to allocate data when we need to during execution of the program. Although we have replaced the names of data structures with the names of references to data structures, we still need to know what data structures we will need at the time we write a program because we need a pointer variable for every dynamically allocated data structure. The solution to this problem is simple: When we allocate a new data structure, we allocate a new pointer variable as part of that structure. This pointer variable may reference yet another data structure. That is why pointers usually point to record variables. At least two fields are needed, one for the data and one for the pointer.

If you look back at Figure 29.2, you can see that the type *person* has a field of type *personptr*—the field *plink*. Note the order of the definitions and declarations in Figure 29.2. The definition of the type *personptr* as a pointer to a *person* record appears before the definition of the record type *person*. Although this is an exception to the Pascal rule that objects must be defined before they are used, it is perfectly legal.

> *A pointer type can be defined before the type of the object it references. This is the only circumstance in Pascal in which a nonstandard type can be referred to before it is defined.*

Each time we allocate a *person* record, we will be allocating, as part of the record, a reference to another record: the field *plink*. Note that the definition of the pointer type must come before the definition of the record type. The types of fields in a record must be defined before the record itself is defined, and we want one of the fields of the record to be of the pointer type.

The ability of record types to refer to other records of the same type is a very useful property. As we will see, it enables us to create data structures of great flexibility and to manipulate those structures in ways that would be difficult with the other data structures we have discussed. For example, by using the single pointer variable we declared above, we can create several records, as shown in Figure 29.7. The effect of these four statements is to allocate four records of type

Figure 29.7   **Creating a dynamic data structure**

```
              . . .
   new ( personp1 );  {Allocate a record.}
   new ( personp1^.plink );  {Use its pointer}
                             {to allocate another.}
   new ( personp1^.plink^.plink );  {Use ITS pointer}
                                    {as well!}
   new ( personp1^.plink^.plink^.plink);
                             {This can go on . . .}
          . . .
```

person linked to each other as shown in Figure 29.8. In fact, we can use a single statically allocated pointer to create as many dynamically allocated records as we like. Moreover, we can relate those records to one another in an interesting and useful way. This type of linked structure is called a *linked list.*

29.4 MANIPULATING LINKED LISTS

The ability to construct and manipulate linked lists allows us to implement many algorithms that would otherwise be difficult to implement. However, the syntax for creating linked lists given in Figure 29.7 is clumsy. If, for example, we were to allocate 20 records this way and wanted to refer to the *age* field in the seventh one, we would have to write the reference as

```
personp1^.plink^.plink^.plink^.plink^.plink^.plink^.age
```

To use linked lists effectively, we usually need at least one auxiliary pointer variable. This pointer variable points to the head of the list—that is, to the first item—

Figure 29.8   **Dynamically allocated data structure**

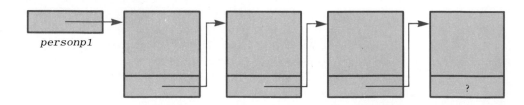

personp1

like the pointer *personp1* in Figure 29.8. Sometimes it's also useful to maintain a pointer to the tail of the list, as in Figure 29.9. We can now use these auxiliary pointers to build and manipulate linked lists.

Building Linked Lists

Here's a problem we can solve easily with pointers and linked lists:

> Read in a list of names until a blank name is typed (a carriage return on a line by itself). Then print the names in the reverse of their order of entry.

We could solve this problem with an array if we knew what the maximum number of names would be. But let's assume that our list is as long as our computer can handle. We won't specify any maximum size. Here's an algorithm for the problem:

I. Initialize a list pointer to **nil.**

II. Read a name.

III. While the name just read wasn't completely blank, do:
   A. Allocate a name record and put the name in it.
   B. Insert the name record at the front of the list.
   C. Read another name.

IV. Traverse the list from start to finish, printing each name as you encounter it.

Steps I through III build the list. Step III.B, by inserting new records at the front of the list, reverses the order of input.

Step IV prints the names. We'll see in a moment how we traverse a list from start to finish.

Figure 29.9   **Tail pointer**

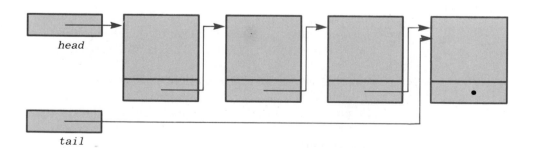

Figure 29.10   Program *namelist*

```
program namelist(input, output);
 {This program illustrates the use of pointers and}
 {linked lists by creating a list of names, inserting the}
 {names into the list at the head, and then printing}
 {them out from head to tail. The effect of creating}
 {the list in this manner is that the names are printed}
 {in reverse order to their order of input.}

const  maxlen = 30;     {max length of a name}

type   string = packed array[1..maxlen] of char;
                        {for names}
       nameptr = ^namerec; {pointer to a name record}
       namerec = record
                   name: string;
                   link: nameptr
                     {link to next structure in list}
                 end;   {namerec}

var    inputname: string; {to hold typed name}
       head: nameptr; {pointer to head of list}

procedure readstring( var nm: string);
  {We omit this—you've seen it before. It fills}
  {nm with blanks, then reads a string into it.}

function length(nm: string) : integer;
  {You've seen this before too; returns length of nm.}

procedure buildlist(var listhd: nameptr);
  {Reads input data and builds a list using local}
  {procedure inserthd. The parameter listhd}
  {ends up pointing to the list. Stops when a}
  {blank name is read.}

var tempptr: nameptr; {for allocating records}
    len: integer;     {length of input name}

  procedure inserthd( var headoflist: nameptr;
                      ptr: nameptr);
    {Is passed a pointer to the head of the list}
    {and a pointer to a namerec. Inserts the}
    {namerec at the head of the list and moves the}
    {head pointer to reflect the change}
```

```
begin {inserthd}
  ptr^.link := headoflist;
     {Make new rec point to what head pointed to}
  headoflist := ptr
     {and make head point to new record.}
end;  {inserthd}


begin {buildlist}
  readstring( inputname ); {Get first name.}
  len := length( inputname );
  while len > 0 do
    begin
      new(tempptr); {Allocate a record.}
      tempptr^.name := inputname;
              {Put name in it.}
      inserthd(listhd, tempptr);
              {Insert it into the list.}
      readstring(inputname);
              {Get next name.}
      len := length(inputname)
    end {while}
end; {buildlist}

procedure printlist(listhd: nameptr);
  {traverses the list pointed to by listhd}
  {and prints the name in each record}
            {TO BE FILLED IN . . .}

begin {namelist—main program}
  head := nil;
  buildlist(head);   {Put the names in list.}
  printlist(head)    {Print the names out.}
end. {namelist—main program}
```

First, let's concentrate on building the list. Figure 29.10 gives the Pascal code for steps I through III.

The procedure *inserthd*, which inserts records at the head of the list, is very simple. It has only two executable statements. Let's trace it. The list is empty the first time this procedure is called because we initialized the value of *head*, the list head pointer, to **nil** in the first line of the main program. Before we called *inserthd*, we created a *namerec* and placed the first name typed by the user in the record's *name* field. (See Figure 29.11.)

Figure 29.11 **Inserting the first record in the list**

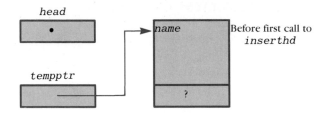

When we call *inserthd*, we pass *listhd* as an argument to the variable parameter *headoflist*. We also pass *tempptr*, which points to the newly allocated record, as an argument to the value parameter *ptr*. The steps in *inserthd* are

ptr^.link := headoflist

which will give the *link* field in the record the value **nil**, and

headoflist := ptr

which makes the pointer *listhead* point to the newly allocated record. The picture is as shown in Figure 29.12.

Figure 29.12 **Inserting the first item as the head of the list**

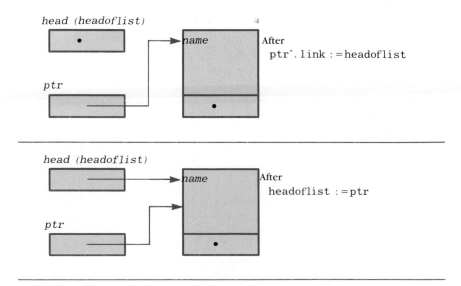

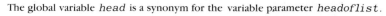

The global variable *head* is a synonym for the variable parameter *headoflist*.

The second and subsequent times we call *inserthd*, the effect is to insert a new record at the head of the list:

```
ptr^.link := headoflist
```

and to make the head of the list be the new record:

```
headoflist := ptr
```

Figure 29.13 shows the effect of these statements. The order of the two statements in *inserthd* is important. The procedure won't work if the order is reversed. The reason is that when we execute the statement

```
headoflist := ptr
```

we lose the reference to the record the head was pointing to.

Figure 29.13   Inserting a new record at the head of the list

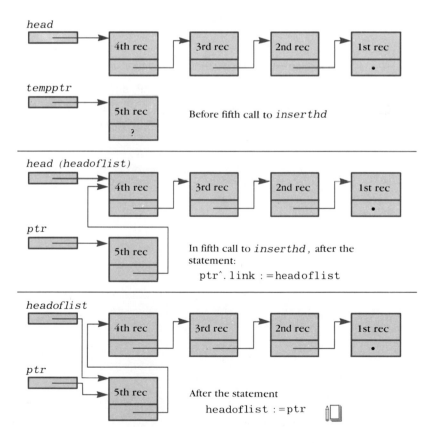

Exercise 29.3: Draw a picture to illustrate how reversing the order of the statements in procedure *inserthd* would cause reference to the list to be lost. ■

Now back to procedure *printlist*. It is an example of *list traversal*. Traversing a list means sequentially accessing the entries in the list. List traversal is a fundamental list-processing algorithm because it's the only way to access all the elements of a list. When we want to access the *n*th element of an array, we can do so directly by using the value *n* as an index. But when we want to access the *n*th entry in a list, we have to find that entry by starting at the head and following *n* links. The algorithm for list traversal is simple:

I. Assign an auxiliary pointer the value of the list header.

II. While the auxiliary pointer isn't **nil,** do:
   A. Assign the auxiliary pointer the value of the link field in the record it's pointing to.

Typically, the reason for traversing a list is to perform some operation on each element of the list (as we will in *printlist*), or to locate a particular entry. To complete our algorithm for procedure *printlist*, we need to insert a step before step II.A in the preceding algorithm:

I. Assign an auxiliary pointer the value of the list header.

II. While the auxiliary pointer isn't **nil,** do:
   A. Print the name in the record pointed to by the auxiliary pointer.
   B. Assign the auxiliary pointer the value of the link field in the record it's pointing to.

With this algorithm, we can write procedure *printlist*, as shown in Figure 29.14.

Figure 29.14 Procedure *printlist*

```
procedure printlist(listhd: nameptr);

var      ptr: nameptr;   {auxiliary pointer}

begin {printlist}
    ptr : = listhd;        {step I}
    while ptr <> nil do {step II}
        begin
            writeln(ptr^.name); {step II.A}
            ptr : = ptr^.link    {step II.B}
        end {while}
end; {printlist}
```

Exercise 29.4: Trace procedure *printlist* with the list shown below:

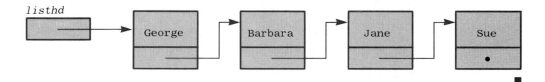

Many of the algorithms for manipulating linked lists can be written more simply by taking advantage of recursion. This is because linked lists are recursive in nature. We can give this recursive definition of a linked list:

A linked list is a data structure which is either empty, or consists of a record followed by a linked list.

This definition suggests that we think of the link field of a list record as the head of a sublist. Using this idea, we can write a recursive version of procedure *printlist*. Such a procedure is shown in Figure 29.15.

Other Ways to Build Lists

There are two other commonly used ways to build lists. One is to add records at the end of the list so that when we traverse the list we encounter records in the same order in which they were read.

The second method is useful for keeping records in some order other than

Figure 29.15   **Recursive procedure to print a list**

```
procedure printlist2 (ptr: nameptr);

begin {printlist2}
  if ptr <> nil
    then
      begin
        writeln(ptr^.name);
        printlist2(ptr^.link)
      end {if then}
end; {printlist2}
```

the order of input, such as alphabetical or numerical order based on a field in the record. We insert a new record after all the records (if any) that must precede it in order and before all the records (if any) that must follow it. (This procedure is analogous to inserting a card catalogue entry into a card drawer in alphabetical order.) We'll develop algorithms and programs to build lists according to each of these two methods.

A record may be added at the end of a list in at least two ways. One of them emphasizes a common pitfall. Here's the algorithm, with the pitfall, for that method:

I. Initialize a list pointer to **nil.** We'll use this pointer to mark the head of the list.

II. Read in a name.

III. While the name is not completely blank, do:
    A. Allocate a name record and put the name in it.
    B. Insert the name record at the end of the list pointed to by the list pointer by doing the following steps:
        1. Assign an auxiliary pointer the value of the list head pointer (so the auxiliary pointer is either **nil,** or is pointing to the first record on the list).
        2. While the auxiliary pointer is not **nil,** do:
            i. Assign the auxiliary pointer the value of the link field in the record it's pointing to. (This has the effect of "walking" along the list.)
        3. Make the value of the link field in the last record we found be the value of the temporary pointer used to allocate our new record.
    C. Read in a name.

IV. Traverse the list from start to finish, printing each name as you encounter it.

Figure 29.16   An attempt at writing procedure *inserttl*

```
procedure inserttl ( listhd: nameptr; ptr: nameptr);
  {Gets a pointer to a (dynamically allocated) namerec.}
  {Appends the namerec to the end of the list headed by}
  {listhd.}

var      auxptr: nameptr;   {We'll need an extra ptr.}

begin    {inserttl}
    auxptr := listhd;           {step III.B.1}
    while auxptr <> nil do      {step III.B.2}
        auxptr := auxptr^.link; {step III.B.2.i}
    ????????????????            {Can't implement III.B.3!}
end;     {inserttl}
```

When we set about writing a program to implement this algorithm, we discover that almost all of it is identical to program *namelist* above. All we need to change is procedure *inserthd*, rewriting it to become procedure *inserttl*. (This ease of modificiation illustrates again the power of procedures!) In procedure *inserttl*, we must implement step III.B and its substeps. Figure 29.16 shows how we could try to do that. Unfortunately, we can't do it in this way. The problem is that we need to access the pointer field of the last record in the list (so we can add the new record). But we don't have a reference to the last record—we've gone past it. And we have another problem. The first time we insert a record, the pointer field we want to assign to isn't a field in a record at all; it's the list-head pointer *head*. Figure 29.17 illustrates both problems. One possible solution is to make two changes to the algorithm: First, treat the very first addition of a record as a special case. Second, use yet another pointer, a *trailer pointer,* which will always point one record behind the auxiliary pointer. When we find the last record in the list, the trailer pointer will be a reference to that record and will allow us to modify the link in the record it references. Figure 29.18 illustrates this idea.

Here's a modified version of the algorithm using the trailer pointer. We show only step III.B, since nothing else has changed:

B. Insert the name record at the end of the list pointed to by the list pointer by doing the following steps:
  1. If the value of the list-head pointer is **nil,**
      then
          i. Assign the list-head pointer the value of the pointer used to allocate the record.
      else
          Do the following steps:
          i′. Assign an auxiliary pointer the value of the list-head pointer (so

the auxiliary pointer is pointing to the first record on the list).

iii. While the auxiliary pointer is not **nil** (which it will not be the first time, since we're in the else clause), do:

a. Assign a trailer pointer the value of the auxiliary pointer.

b. Assign the auxiliary pointer the value of the link field in the record it's pointing to. (This has the effect of "walking" along the list.)

iii'. Assign the link field in the record pointed to by the trailer pointer the value of the temporary pointer used to allocate our new record.

Figure 29.19 shows procedure *inserttl* after we implement this version of step III.B.

This algorithm for adding records at the end of a list is considerably more complex than the algorithm for adding records at the head. A simpler way to add records at the end is to maintain an extra, statically defined pointer that points to the tail of the list. Then, after the list has at least one entry, we'll always have a pointer to the record whose link we want to modify—namely, the tail pointer. But we'll still have to take special action to insert the first record.

An algorithm follows for a program that, like the preceding one, reads a list of names and then prints them in the same order as they have been read.

Figure 29.17   Problems with code given in Figure 29.16

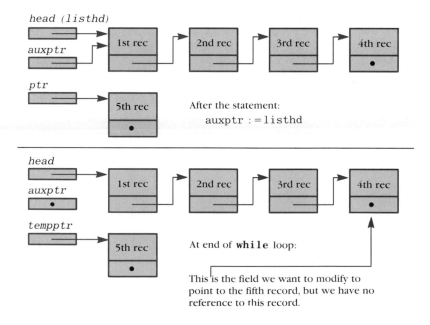

Figure 29.18   Position of the trailing pointer

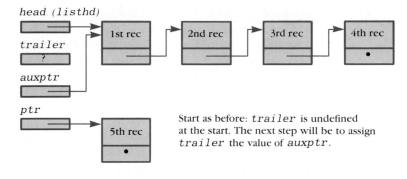

Start as before: `trailer` is undefined at the start. The next step will be to assign `trailer` the value of `auxptr`.

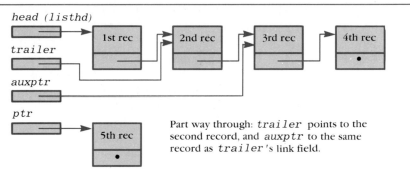

Part way through: `trailer` points to the second record, and `auxptr` to the same record as `trailer`'s link field.

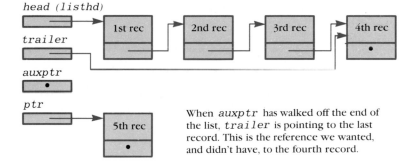

When `auxptr` has walked off the end of the list, `trailer` is pointing to the last record. This is the reference we wanted, and didn't have, to the fourth record.

Figure 29.19   Procedure *inserttl*

```
procedure inserttl( var listhd: nameptr; ptr: nameptr );
   {Is passed a pointer to a name record. Inserts}
   {the name record at the end of the list, which is}
   {headed by head.}
var    auxptr,                        {For walking . . .}
       trailptr: nameptr;            {. . . and following}

begin  {inserttl}
   if listhd = nil                    {step III.B.1}
     then
        listhd := ptr
     else
        begin
           auxptr := listhd;        {step III.B.1.i}
           while auxptr <> nil do
             begin                    {step III.B.1.ii}
                trailptr := auxptr;
                auxptr := auxptr^.link
             end;          {while}
           trailptr^.link := ptr {and III.B.1.iii}
        end      {else}
end;      {inserttl}
```

I. Initialize a list-head pointer and a list-tail pointer to **nil**.

II. Read in a name.

III. While the name read in isn't completely blank, do:
   A. Allocate a name record and put the name in it.
   B. Insert the name record at the end of the list by doing the following steps:
      1. If the value of the tail pointer is **nil,**
         then
            i. Assign both the head and tail pointers to point to the newly allocated record.
         else
            i'. Assign the link field in the record currently referenced by the tail pointer to point to the newly allocated record.
            ii'. Assign the tail pointer to point to the newly allocated record.
   C. Read in a name.

IV. Read the list from start to finish, printing each name as you encounter it.

The order of steps III.B.1.i′ and III.B.1.ii′ is crucial! Once we have done step III.B.1.ii′, we have lost the reference to the record whose link we need to update. Therefore, we must do that update first. Figure 29.20 shows how to implement this algorithm in a procedure. By doing a little extra bookkeeping, we've made the algorithm much simpler. Figure 29.21 illustrates the use of this method when the list already has four entries.

Figure 29.20   Procedure *inserttl2*

```
{We need to add the following to}
{our global data declarations:}
        tail: nameptr;


procedure inserttl2( var listhd, listtl: nameptr;
                     ptr: nameptr );
{Is passed the head and tail pointers as var parameters,}
{and a pointer to a name record as a value parameter.}
{Inserts the name record at the end of the list.}
begin {inserttl2}
   if listtl = nil              {If list is empty . . .}
     then
       begin
         listhd := ptr;  {both head and tail . . .}
         listtl := ptr    {. . . point to first rec}
       end        {then}
     else
       begin
         listtl^.link := ptr;    {link into list}
         listtl := ptr           {advance tail ptr}
       end        {else}
end; {inserttl2}


{In the main program, we must}
{initialize not one but}
{two pointers:}
head := nil;
tail := nil;
```

Figure 29.21 Using procedure *inserttl2*

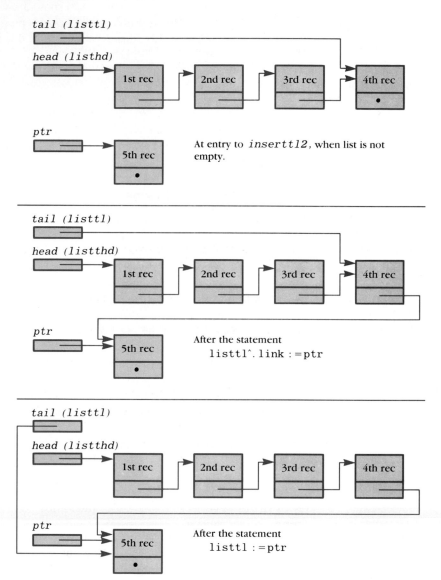

tail (listtl)

head (listhd)

| 1st rec | 2nd rec | 3rd rec | 4th rec |

ptr

5th rec

At entry to *inserttl2*, when list is not empty.

tail (listtl)

head (listthd)

| 1st rec | 2nd rec | 3rd rec | 4th rec |

ptr

5th rec

After the statement
listtl^.link := ptr

tail (listtl)

head (listthd)

| 1st rec | 2nd rec | 3rd rec | 4th rec |

ptr

5th rec

After the statement
listtl := ptr

Building Ordered Linked Lists

Recall that this method is for inserting elements into the list in order (alphabetical or numerical). The method of inserting list records in order is a way of "sorting on the fly." Although it is a useful method, it's not as efficient (in terms of total instructions executed and processing time used) as sorting an array would be. Still, it has the advantage of leaving the existing portion of the list in order after every record insert.

Rather than write an algorithm for inserting records of a particular type in an ordered list, we'll write a more general algorithm. We'll assume that we're reading records of some sort and that the record type has some field that we will use to order the records. Such a field is known as a *key* (see Chapter 25, page 538).

I. Initialize a list-head pointer to **nil.**

II. While there are records to be read, do:
    A. Read a record.
    B. If the record is the first (that is, the value of the list head pointer is **nil**),
        then
            1. Make the list-head pointer point to it.
        else
            1'. Find the correct place to insert the record by doing the following steps:
                i. Assign an auxiliary pointer variable the value of the list-head pointer.
                ii. While the auxiliary pointer isn't **nil** and the key field in the record pointed to by the auxiliary pointer is less than the key field in the new record, do:
                    a. Advance the auxiliary pointer to the next record.
                iii. If the auxiliary pointer is **nil,**
                    then
                        a. Add the new record at the tail. (You've walked all the way to the end of the list.)
                    else
                        a'. Insert the new record before the record pointed to by the auxiliary pointer. (You've found the first record whose key is larger than the key of the record you're inserting.)

Figure 29.22   Insertion into the middle of the list

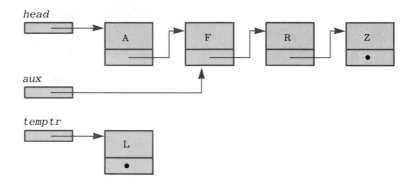

We run into trouble, however, when we try to implement this algorithm with an insertion procedure. We've met the problem before: We have a pointer to the record after the place we want our new record to go, but we need a pointer to the record before the place we want to make the insertion. Last time we solved this problem with a trailing pointer, which followed one step behind. This time, we'll use another solution: We'll always look ahead one record before advancing our pointer, so we'll know ahead of time when to insert our record. Figure 29.22 shows this solution in the case where the record to be inserted falls somewhere within the middle of the list.

There are two cases in which special care must be taken:

■ The key of the record to be inserted is less than any key in the list so far, and thus the new record must be inserted at the head. We can detect this case because *head^.key* will be greater than the key of the new record.

■ The key of the record to be inserted is greater than any key in the list so far, and thus the new record must be inserted at the tail. We will discuss this case in more detail below.

Exercise   29.5: Draw pictures to show the pointers that must be modified to make the insertion in these two special cases.   ■

Here's a corrected version of step II.B.2 of our algorithm, the step that searches for the correct insertion point in the case of a nonempty list:

2. Find the correct place to insert the record by doing the following steps:

      i. If the key of the record to be inserted is less than the key of the first record in the list,

        then

          a. Insert the new record at the head of the list.

        else

          a'. Initialize an auxiliary pointer to point to the first record in the list.

          b'. While the link field in the record referenced by the auxiliary pointer isn't **nil** and the key of the record referenced by that link field is less than the key of the new record,

            i. Advance the auxiliary pointer to the next record.

          c'. (At this point, the auxiliary pointer is pointing to the record before which we must insert the new record. That's what we wanted.) Insert the new record after the record pointed to by the auxiliary pointer.

Sentences like those in step II.B.2.i.b' are very difficult to understand. That's why we use pictures to explain algorithms to programmers and Pascal to explain them to computers.

We'll assume the following type declarations in writing a Pascal implementation of this algorithm:

```
type keytype = . . .        {some type}
     dataptr = ^datarec;
     datarec = record
                  key: keytype;
                  link: dataptr;
     {possibly other fields . . .}
                 end;
```

The key can be a data item of any scalar type; as you'll see, the algorithms for manipulating the lists don't depend on the type of the key.

Figure 29.23 shows an implementation of this algorithm fragment. Be careful: There's a subtle bug in this code. We've left it in because it's so common that if you don't become aware of it here you may build it into your own code. Notice the "double indirection" involved in the expression *auxptr^.link^.key*. This is the Pascal translation of the unwieldy phrase "the key of the record referenced by that link field." The bug lies in the conditional expression of the **while** statement. Although the conditional expression

(auxptr^.link <> **nil**) **and** (auxptr^.link^.key <= ptr^.key)

is perfectly legal, it may cause a run-time error. That will happen, for instance, if the record to be inserted must go at the end of the list. When *auxptr^.link* becomes **nil** (which it will when we get to the end of the list), the conditional expression is evaluated. You expect the conditional expression to be *false* so that the **while** will terminate and you can insert the record at the end. However, the program may first evaluate the whole conditional expression. The expression

(auxptr^.link <> **nil**)

evaluates to *false*, as you expected. But most implementations of Pascal then try to evaluate the expression

(auxptr^.link^.key <= ptr^.key)

and here the error occurs. Since *auxptr^.link* is **nil**, it doesn't refer to any record at all, and the reference *auxptr^.link^.key* is meaningless because there is no such key field. This is a "reference through a **nil** pointer," which is a fatal run-time error and will cause your program to crash.

Figure 29.23   A buggy procedure to insert an element in key order into a list

```
procedure insertordr(var listhd: dataptr; ptr: dataptr);
  {Is passed a pointer to the list head as a var}
  {parameter, and a pointer to a data record as a}
  {value parameter. Inserts the data record in}
  {order in the list.}

var     auxptr: dataptr;          {for walking}

begin {insertordr}
  if listhd = nil
    then
      listhd := ptr
    else if listhd^.key > ptr^.key
          then
            begin
              ptr^.link := listhd;
              listhd := ptr
            end {else if}
          else
            begin
              auxptr := listhd;
              while (auxptr^.link <> nil) and
                    (auxptr^.link^.key <= ptr^.key) do
                      auxptr := auxptr^.link;
              ptr^.link := auxptr^.link;
              auxptr^.link := ptr
            end {else}
  end;     {insertordr}
```

Whenever your program attempts to make a reference through a pointer that is currently **nil***, a fatal run-time error will occur and your program will crash.*

Why does Pascal bother to evaluate the second expression? After all, in a compound expression of the form *expr1* **and** *expr2*, if *expr1* evaluates to *false* the whole compound conditional expression will evaluate to *false* regardless of the value of *expr2*. But Standard Pascal does not specify how such an expression should be evaluated. When a compound conditional expression is evaluated, it is possible that evaluation will stop when either the value of the first expression is known or when every component has been evaluated. To fix the bug, we have to guarantee that *auxptr^.link^.key* won't be referenced if *auxptr^.link* is **nil**. There are a number of ways to do this. Perhaps the simplest way is to use a *boolean* variable to keep track of the **while** conditional. Figure 29.24 gives a solution.

Exercise 29.6: There is a clever trick for inserting a record into an ordered list without using a trailer pointer or looking ahead an extra record. The trick is this: Locate the record that should follow the new record. Insert the new record after that record, so that it's in the wrong place by one slot. Then exchange the contents of the two misplaced records. (You can use a temporary record variable to do this.)

1. Implement this method in a procedure.
2. When is this a good idea? When it is a bad idea? (Hint: The amount of work done by the computer in assigning a pointer doesn't depend on the type of the pointer. The amount of work done in assigning records is, for most computers, proportional to the size of the record.) ∎

The procedure in Figure 29.24 is somewhat complex. Just as we did with procedure *printlist*, we can write a recursive version of procedure *insertordr*. Such a procedure is shown in Figure 29.25.

This procedure is much simpler than the nonrecursive version because we don't need to use extra variables to keep track of where we are in the list and whether or not we're done. In general, recursive algorithms will often provide the simplest solutions to problems that involve recursive data structures.

Exercise 29.7: Write a recursive version of procedure *inserttl* (Figure 29.19 on page 638) that adds records at the end of a list. ∎

Figure 29.24   **A procedure to insert elements in a list**

```
procedure insertordr (var listhd: dataptr; ptr: dataptr);
   {Is passed a pointer to a data record. Inserts}
   {the data record in order in the list that is}
   {headed by head.}

var     auxptr: dataptr;          {for walking}
        keepgoing: boolean;       {true when we haven't}
                                  {yet found insert point}
begin {insertordr}
   if listhd = nil               {if list is empty}
     then
        listhd := ptr            {then make this the first}
                                 {element of the list}
      else if listhd^.key > ptr^.key
             then                {if this is smallest}
               begin
                 ptr^.link := listhd; {then insert at head}
                 listhd := ptr
               end {else if}
             else         {must search for right spot}
               begin
                 keepgoing := true;   {assume not there yet}
                 auxptr := listhd;
                 while keepgoing do
                    begin
                      if auxptr^.link = nil {don't look}
                        then {further 'cause we're at end}
                          keepgoing := false
                        else
                          if auxptr^.link^.key <= ptr^.key
                             then
                               auxptr := auxptr^.link {advance}
                             else {also don't look further}
                               keepgoing := false {found spot}
                    end; {while}
                 ptr^.link := auxptr^.link;        {Insert it.}
                 auxptr^.link := ptr
               end           {else}
   end;      {procedure insertordr}
```

Figure 29.25   A recursive procedure to insert elements into a list

```
procedure insertordr(var listhd: dataptr; ptr: dataptr);
  {Is passed a pointer to a data record. Inserts}
  {the data record in order in the sublist that is}
  {headed by listhd. listhd may be the true head of}
  {the list, or a link field in a list record.}

begin {insertordr}
  if listhd = nil                    {if sublist is empty}
    then
      listhd := ptr                  {then make this the first}
                                     {element of the sublist}
    else if listhd^.key > ptr^.key
              then                   {if this is smallest}
                begin
                  ptr^.link := listhd; {then insert at head}
                  listhd := ptr
                end {else if}
              else          {Search recursively for right spot.}
                insertordr(listhd^.link, ptr)
end;      {procedure insertordr}
```

Searching Linked Lists

In addition to building lists, there are two other operations that are commonly performed on lists: Searching a list for a specified entry and deleting an entry. We'll look at list searching first. It's very simple—in fact, the list traversal procedure *printlist*, which we've described above, contains most of the essential ideas. The algorithm, stated somewhat informally, is as follows:

I. Initialize an auxiliary pointer to the value of the list header.

II. While the key field pointed to by the auxiliary pointer is not the key you're searching for and there's another record, advance the auxiliary pointer to point to the next record.

III. If the auxiliary pointer points to a record whose key is what you're searching for, you've found the correct record. Otherwise, it's not there.

This algorithm is readily implemented in Pascal. To indicate whether the search has succeeded or failed, we'll write a function that returns a pointer value. That value will be a reference to the relevant record if the search has succeeded, and

nil if it has failed. Note that since the condition for continuing the search in step II above is a compound condition, we have to be careful in coding it to avoid references through a **nil** pointer. We'll use records with names as keys, although, as usual, doing so is irrelevant as far as the algorithm's structure is concerned. Figure 29.26 gives function *searchlist*.

Exercise 29.7

a. Write a program to build a list of name records and then request a name and search for it in the list. The program should report whether or not it has found the name.

b. Suppose the list you're searching is an ordered list. Write a more efficient

Figure 29.26 **A function to return the place of a name in the list or nil if the name is not found**

```
function searchlist(listhd: nameptr;
                              name: string): nameptr;
   {Takes a string as parameter. Searches the list}
   {headed by listhd looking for a record with the}
   {corresponding string. Returns a pointer to the}
   {record if successful, a nil value otherwise.}

var   auxptr: nameptr;    {as usual}
      done: boolean;      {search conditional}

begin {searchlist}
  done : = false;
  auxptr : = head;
  while not done do
    if auxptr = nil
      then
        done : = true
      else if auxptr^.name = name
              then
                done : = true
              else
                auxptr : = auxptr^.link;
    searchlist : = auxptr  {Always return this.}
  end;   {searchlist}
```

algorithm for searching such a list. (Hint: How will you know when to stop searching?) Write a function *searchorderedlist* to implement this algorithm. ■

Deleting Records from Lists

Deleting an item from a list is relatively straightforward. All we need to do is make the link that points to that item point to the next item. But what happens to the deleted item? If we're not careful, it will remain in memory with no references to it. That is a waste of memory. If we want to free its storage for another purpose, we must arrange to do so. If we want to keep the deleted item, perhaps to insert in another list or some other type of structure, we must keep a reference to it. Figure 29.27 shows the deletion of an item from the middle of a list.

To free dynamically allocated memory, Pascal has a standard procedure named *dispose*. In a sense, *dispose* is the opposite of *new*. It takes an argument that is a pointer to a record and releases the memory used by the record to the pool of available memory for further requests by *new*. (This pool of memory is referred to as the *heap*.) It would be convenient if an argument passed to *dispose* also had its value changed to **nil**, but Pascal doesn't do that. Thus, you may inadver-

Figure 29.27   **Deletion of an item in the middle of a list**

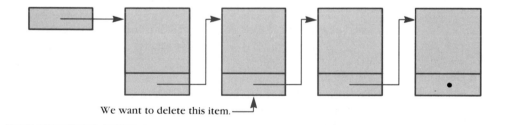

We want to delete this item.

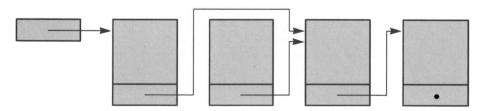

Now it's deleted, but unless we save a reference to it we
can't reclaim the storage.

tently refer to a deleted item in memory even after you've disposed of it. To do so is always a bug! Here's the syntax of a call to *dispose*:

```
dispose(pointervariable)
```

Here's how the trouble might arise:

```
var   ptr1: ^type1record;
      ptr2: ^type2record;
         . . .
      dispose(ptr1);      {Deallocates it; ptr1 still }
                          {has its old value.}
      new(ptr2); {Allocates a type2record. It}
                     {most likely uses the SAME storage}
                     {that the recently disposed}
                     {type1record used.}
      ptr1^.field := . . .   {A BAD bug. This writes}
                          {into memory that is undefined}
                          {with unpredictable results.}
```

This bug is illustrated in Figure 29.28.

Here's a good rule to follow: After you dispose of a record with *dispose*, always give the pointer that was referencing it the value **nil**. Unfortunately, even this safeguard may not be enough because an even more subtle bug may arise in this fashion:

```
new(ptr1);
ptr2 := ptr1;     {Both reference the same region.}
      . . .
dispose(ptr1);    {The region is returned to heap, but}
                     {ptr2 still points to it!}
```

In this case, we have disposed of a region of memory we are still using! We shouldn't have used *dispose* in this case, because we still have a pointer pointing to it. We must be very careful when disposing of dynamically allocated memory spaces.

Figure 29.30 shows a procedure for searching a list for a record and, if it is found, deleting it from the list and disposing of it. The record is identified by its key field. To delete the record, we need to manipulate the record before it by using a trailer pointer, or by looking ahead one record, or by using a clever trick. Let's see what happens when we look ahead one record. Since we cannot look ahead at the first record, we have to treat its deletion specially. Let's trace this procedure. Suppose we have a linked list of *namerecs* with the data shown in Figure 29.29.

Figure 29.28   A possible bug when using *dispose*

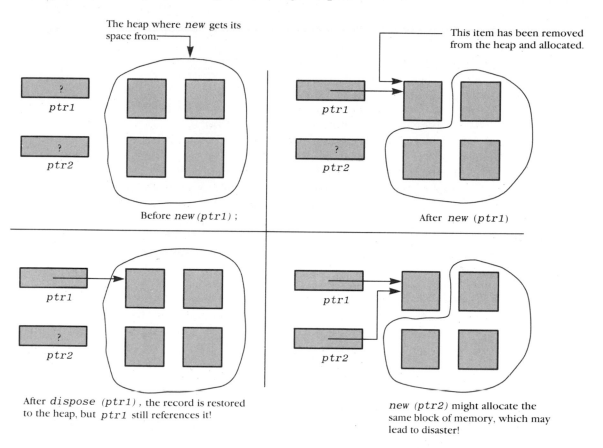

The heap where *new* gets its space from.

Before *new(ptr1)*;

This item has been removed from the heap and allocated.

After *new (ptr1)*

After *dispose (ptr1)*, the record is restored to the heap, but *ptr1* still references it!

new (ptr2) might allocate the same block of memory, which may lead to disaster!

Figure 29.29   Sample situation for procedure *searchanddestroy*

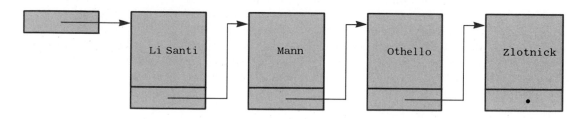

Li Santi   Mann   Othello   Zlotnick

Figure 29.30   Procedure *searchanddestroy*

```
procedure searchanddestroy(var listhd: nameptr;name: string);
  {Looks for a record with the key}
  {field name. If found, unlinks it}
  {and disposes of it.}

var   auxptr: nameptr;  {for searching list}
      saveref: nameptr; {for disposing}
      found: boolean;   {for compound conditional}
begin {searchanddestroy}
  if listhd^.name = name {if first record}
    then
      begin
        saveref := listhd;       {Save a reference to it}
        listhd := listhd^.link; {This unlinks it.}
        dispose( saveref );      {This frees the space.}
        saveref := nil
      end   {then}
    else
      begin
        auxptr := listhd;          {Start looking at head.}
        found := false;
        while (auxptr^.link <> nil) and (not found) do
            {search for name}
                if auxptr^.link^.name = name
                  then found := true     {Found it!}
                  else auxptr := auxptr^.link;
                                        {Keep looking.}
        if found
          then    {It was found.}
            begin
              saveref := auxptr^.link; {Save ref to it.}
              auxptr^.link := auxptr^.link^.link;
                                      {Unlink it.}
              dispose(saveref);   {Free up space.}
              saveref := nil
            end   {then}
      end   {else}
end;      {searchanddestroy}
```

We'll trace a call to *searchanddestroy* with a *name* argument that contains the name "Othello."

At the start of the procedure, *listhd* references the record with the name "Li Santi," *name* is the string "Othello," and the three local variables *auxptr*, *saveref*, and *found* are all undefined.

1. **if** listhd^. name = name **then**

   listhd^.name has the value *Li Santi*, which isn't equal to *Othello*, so the condition is *false*. The **then** clause is skipped. The next statement executed is in the **else** clause:

2. auxptr : = listhd

   Now *auxptr* is pointing to the same record as *listhd*—that is, the first record of the list. We'll use *auxptr* to walk the list.

3. found : = false

   We want *found* to be *false* as long as we haven't found the matching record.

4. **while** (auxptr^. link <> **nil**) **and** (**not** found) **do**

   auxptr. *link* is the *link* field in the record pointed to by *auxptr*. It isn't **nil**, it's a reference to the second record in the list. Moreover, since **not** *found* is *true* (because we made *found false* in step 3 above), the whole condition is *true*. So we execute the body of the **while**, which consists of a single if-then-else statement.

5. **if** auxptr^. link^. name = name **then**

   This is where we look ahead. Although *auxptr* is pointing to the "Li Santi" record, the link in that record is pointing to the next record. So the value of *auxptr^. link^. name* is *Mann*. It is not equal to *Othello*, so the condition is *false*. The body of the **if** is not executed, and we go to the next statement, in the **else**.

6. auxptr : = auxptr^. link

   Now *auxptr* refers to the second record in the list. We go back to the **while** clause.

7. **while** (auxptr^. link <> **nil**) **and** (**not** found) **do**

   auxptr^.link still isn't **nil**. The value of *found* hasn't changed. We execute the body of the **while** once again.

8. **if** auxptr^. link^.name = name **then**

This time, *auxptr^.link^.name* is equal to *name*: *auxptr^.link* is the pointer in the "Mann" record, and it references a record whose name is indeed "Othello." So we do the next statement.

9. **found** : = **true**

We skip the **else** clause and go back to:

10. **while** (auxptr^.link <> **nil**) **and not** found **do**

This time, although *auxptr^.link* is still not **nil**, *found* has the value *true*. So **not** *found* is *false*, the whole condition is *false*, and the body of the **while** is skipped. The next statement to be executed is

11. **if** found **then**

This condition is *true*, so we do the body of the **if**, which consists of four statements.

12. saveref : = auxptr^.link

This is the first time we use *saveref*. It now references the same record that *auxptr^.link* does, the record with "Othello."

13. auxptr^.link : = auxptr^.link^.link

This is the statement that actually removes the record from the list. It says: Take the pointer value in the "Othello" record *(auxptr^.link^.link)* and copy it to the pointer in the "Mann" record *(auxptr^.link)*. The "Mann" record now points to the "Zlotnick" record.

14. dispose(saveref)

This takes the the "Othello" record from reserved memory.

15. saveref : = **nil**

This sets *saveref* to **nil** so that we can not access the "Othello" record.

Exercise   29.8: Draw the pictures that describe the trace given above. ∎

Notice that most of the work here is in searching the list for the specified record. Once we have found it, unlinking it is easy.

Exercise   29.9: Trace the above procedure, using the same list (1) with an input parameter equal to "Li Santi" and (2) with an input parameter equal to "Hamlet". ∎

29.5 POINTERS AS PARAMETERS

We refer to a list by a pointer that references the first element of the list. If we pass a list header as a value parameter to a procedure, a copy of the pointer is made that refers to the same list as the original pointer. However, the procedure has full access to the original list. The effect is to pass the list as a variable parameter.[2] We have taken advantage of this feature repeatedly in this chapter. For instance, the lists we built or modified in procedures were available outside those procedures. But this feature also poses a danger because it's possible to modify structures in a procedure that are not explicitly made available to that procedure. For this and other reasons, some computer scientists have expressed reservations about programming languages that allow programmers to manipulate pointer variables directly. Although the power and flexibility provided by pointers seem to outweigh the dangers, remember that using pointers indiscriminately may impair the modularity of your program, making it easier to introduce bugs and harder to trace the flow of data.

29.6 ARRAYS AND LISTS

There are a number of similarities between arrays and linked lists. Indeed, in some circumstances it's possible to implement an algorithm with either an array or a linked list, and it's not always clear which choice is better. Let's compare the two types of structures to see their relative strengths and weaknesses.

The principal feature arrays and lists have in common is that both are linear arrangements of identical structures. That is, in either case it's meaningful to speak of the first, second, . . ., nth element, and all the elements are of the same type. If you need a data structure with only this characteristic, then either will do. In such a case, you will base your choice on considerations of efficiency, space, personal taste, and program readability.

The principal advantage of arrays over lists is that arrays provide random access. You can access (refer to, modify, or use) any element in an array as easily as you can access any other element. A second advantage is that an array has elements of some base type indexed by elements of some index type. If there is a close logical relationship between the value of an index and the item stored at that index, an array makes that relationship evident in the program. For example, if you want to count the number of each type of character in an input stream, a file, or a string, you can use an array of this sort:

---

2. In fact, this is how variable parameters are implemented. When you declare that a procedure or function parameter is a variable parameter, the compiler arranges to pass the address of the actual parameter to the procedure or function. This address behaves just like a pointer variable. All this occurs invisibly as far as the programmer is concerned, but the similarity of behavior between pointer parameters and variable parameters is not accidental.

```
type      charray = array[char] of integer;
var       charcount: charray;
```

Then you can store the number of *x*'s in *charcount*`['x']`, the number of %'s in *charcount*`['%']`, and so forth. There is no corresponding relationship in lists.

Another advantage of arrays is their space efficiency. To store 1,000 records of some sort in an array requires 1,000 times the space taken up by one record. To store 1,000 records in a list also requires 1,000 times the space required by one record. However, the record sizes must be augmented by the space required for the pointer fields. In most applications, this won't present any problem. But in some applications it may make the difference between a program that fits and a program that is too big to run.

The principal advantage of lists is the flexibility of their size and our ability to manipulate them. When we can't predict the number of items we'll need at the time we write the program, only a linked list will suffice. A linked list is also necessary if we must be conscientious about using only as much space as we need.

Another aspect of list flexibility is less obvious, although we've taken advantage of it several times in this chapter. The sequence relationship between list records is dynamic. That is, it's relatively easy to change the order of elements in a list, to insert or delete items, and to move items from one list to another. To delete an item from an array, however, or to insert an item in the middle, we have to shift many of the values. With a list we merely change a couple of pointer values.

This flexibility suggests a second meaning for the word *dynamic*. The size, and thus the shape, of a linked list viewed as a single data structure changes during program execution. In the next chapter, we'll see other types of dynamic data structures with more complex shapes that also change during execution.

CHAPTER SUMMARY

1. Pascal makes it possible to create variables during program execution. Such variables have no names, however, which means that the only way we can refer to them is by using pointers that refer to these variables.

2. Pointers to data items of different types are themselves different data types. Two pointers are of the same type only if they have been declared as pointers to the same type of data.

3. Dynamic variables are created by invoking the Standard Pascal procedure *new*. That procedure allocates space for a variable and assigns the address of the allocated space to a pointer variable that is passed as an argument to *new*.

4. If a dynamically allocated record contains a field that is itself a pointer to that type of record, then we can use that field to allocate another record, and so forth. We can thus use a single, statically allocated pointer variable to point to an entire sequence of records. Such a sequence is a linked list that can contain an unlimited number of items.

5. The fundamental algorithms for manipulating linked lists include several ways to build lists (inserting new records at the head, at the tail, or in order based on a key field); to traverse the records of a list; to search for an item in a list; and to delete a record from a list.

6. When inserting a record into the middle of a linked list, we must modify the link field in the record that will come before the record to be inserted. Consequently, we must maintain a pointer to that record and look ahead to the next record to determine the correct insertion point.

COMMON ERRORS

- Declaring pointers incorrectly, particularly by misplacing the ^ character.
- Declaring a pointer type after a record type that includes a field of the pointer type.
- Assigning a pointer when you intend to assign the record being pointed to, or vice versa.
- Referencing a field through a **nil** pointer. This error is particularly common when, in traversing a list, you use the link field in the last record rather than the link field in the preceding record.

DEBUGGING HINTS

- Trace the buggy code by drawing pictures showing all pointers and the records to which they point.
- Print out the value of a particular field in a record referenced by a pointer.
- Traverse the entire linked list, printing out the values contained in each record.

SUPPLEMENTAL PROBLEMS

1. Assume you have the following definitions and declarations:

```
type    link = ^object;
        ptr = ^thing;

        object = record
                 data: char;
                 next: link
                 end; {object}
```

```
         thing = record
                    info: integer;
                    following: ptr
                 end; {thing}


var      p,
         q: link;
         r,
         s: ptr;
```

Which of the following statements are valid? Describe what's wrong with the invalid statements and describe the effect of executing the valid ones.

a. p : = q;
b. q^ : = r^;
c. r^ : = s^;
d. q^ : = p;
e. p^. info : = 1985;
f. q^. info : = 'a';
g. p^. next : = q;
h. s^. next : = q^. next;
i. s^. following : = q^. next;
j. r^. next : = s;
k. s^. next^ : = s^;

2. Write a procedure that traverses a linked list in which each record contains a field of type *integer* and that deletes all records in which the *integer* field is not in increasing order relative to the preceding record. (The first record of the list is automatically acceptable.) Make any necessary declarations and definitions. Assume that a list of the type you define already exists.

3. Assume that you have two separate lists of the same type headed by the two pointers *base* and *start*. Write a procedure that appends the list that begins with *start* to the end of the list that begins with *base*. The list should not be copied, but instead linked onto the end.

4. When we read characters from a line-oriented source (a textfile or the keyboard), we usually store them in an array. An alternative is to store them in a linked list of characters constructed of records like this:

```
type     chlink = ^chrec;
         chrec = record
                    ch: char;
                    next: chlink
                 end; {chrec}
```

What advantage does this method provide over an array? What disadvantages?

5. Rewrite procedure *readstring* to read lines of text from the source named *input* and to store them in a list as described in problem 4.

6. Rewrite procedure *writestring* to write lines of text to the destination named *output*, taken from a list as described in problem 4.

7. Write a program to do the following:
   a. Ask the user for a word and store that word in a linked list of characters.
   b. Write a procedure that takes the word and a line of text stored in a linked list of characters and deletes the word from the line of text.

8. Write a program to do the following:
   a. Ask the user for two words and store each word in a linked list of characters. Call the first word *old*. Call the second word *new*.
   b. Ask the user for a line of text and store the text in a linked list of characters.
   c. Write a procedure that takes the two words *old* and *new* and the list and finds the first occurrence of *old* in the line and replaces it with *new*.

*9. Write a program that reads a textfile and creates an alphabetized ordered list of the words that occur in it, along with a count of the number of occurrences of each word. The program should then print the words and counts. Convert all input text to lowercase.

*10. Extend the program in problem 9 so that, for each word, you maintain a linked list of all the line numbers on which that word occurs. Then display the words with a list of line numbers for each.

The study of data structures is worth a course of its own. In this chapter, we give you a brief look at some of the questions that such a course might address. We start by examining queues and stacks—two dynamic structures that can be implemented using linked lists. Then we'll briefly look at linked structures whose shapes are different from a list.

30.1 QUEUES

A *queue* is a data structure in which items are added and deleted, subject to the restriction that items are always deleted in the order they were added. A queue is sometimes called a *FIFO structure*; FIFO is an acronym for *first in, first out*. Figure 30.1 illustrates a queue.

There are many different situations whose behavior can be modeled by a queue. One such common situation is a line in a bank. A customer joins the line at the end, and when a teller becomes available, the customer at the front leaves the line. Another is the flow of traffic past a tollbooth. Yet another might be a

Figure 30.1   A queue structure

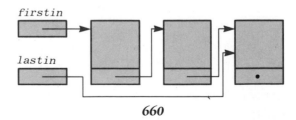

OTHER DYNAMIC
DATA STRUCTURES

command line typed on a terminal: Many computer systems allow users to enter several commands on a single line and then carry them out in sequence. To do this, the system may build a queue of commands.

In many systems, such as the bank line or the tollbooth, items in a queue are added or deleted asynchronously. That is, there is no relationship between the frequency with which new items arrive in the queue and the frequency with which items are removed. In such cases, the size of the queue can grow and shrink unpredictably. For this reason, a linked list is a good choice for a data structure to represent the queue.

All that we need do to use a linked list as a queue is to restrict the choice of algorithms we use to process the list. We must always add items at one end of the list and delete items from the other end. It turns out to be easy to add items at the end of the list, maintaining a tail pointer, and to delete items from the head. To *enqueue* (add an item to the queue), we simply use procedure *inserttl2* (see Figure 29.20, page 640). To *dequeue* (remove an item from the queue) requires a simple procedure, which we leave as an exercise.

Exercise 30.1: Write procedure *dequeue*, which has three parameters: a pointer variable, which will be returned as a pointer to the dequeued record; and head and tail pointers, which delimit the queue. The procedure should remove the dequeued item from the queue and should update the head and tail pointers accordingly. Make sure that, if the queue is empty, procedure *dequeue* returns the value **nil**. ■

Exercise 30.2: It's possible to write a function whose type is a pointer type. Why is it a stylistic mistake to write *dequeue* as a function rather than as a procedure? (Hint: What kinds of parameters must the head and tail pointers be?) ■

Exercise 30.3: Suppose your program must manage a queue of records, but you know that there will never be more than *MAXQUEUE* records in the queue. Can you use an array of records to represent the queue? Write algorithms and corresponding procedures to enqueue items to and dequeue items from such a data structure. ∎

30.2 STACKS

A *stack* is a data structure in which items are added and deleted, subject to the restriction that items are always deleted in the reverse order in which they were added. A stack is sometimes called a *LIFO structure;* LIFO is an acronym for *last in, first out.*

The name *stack* comes from the LIFO behavior of physical stacks of objects. The analogy universally cited in computer science texts is a stack of trays in a cafeteria: The tray last added to the stack will be the next tray removed. Possibly because of this analogy, stacks are sometimes referred to as *pushdown stacks.* The term *push* is used for adding an item to a stack, and the term *pop* for removing an item. Figure 30.2 illustrates a stack.

Like queues, stacks are an appropriate model for the behavior of many phenomena.[1] Some of these phenomena arise in programming. An important example is the order in which procedure calls are processed. If procedure *A* calls procedure *B*, and *B* calls *C*, and *C* calls *D*, then the procedures exit in the reverse order: *D* first, then *C*, then *B*, then *A*. Internally, Pascal programs use a stack to remember where a program should resume executing when a procedure call exits.

Another example involves the programming technique known as *backtracking.* Backtracking is useful for solving problems that involve exploring different

Figure 30.2   A stack

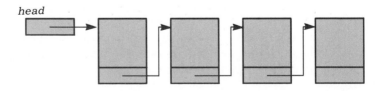

head

1. Including the "IN" tray on the desk of at least one of the authors.

alternatives, many of which may lead to dead ends. For example, suppose you needed a program to solve maze problems. One strategy that uses backtracking is to keep track of each place where you are presented with a possible choice. To start, you always choose the left-most path. Each time you reach a dead end, you go back to the most recent decision point that still has an unexplored path and choose the next unexplored path to the right of the one you backed out of.

To implement a backtracking strategy, you can use a stack to keep track of all the places where you make a choice. Each time you encounter a new decision point, you push the information about that point (where it is, how many paths it has, which one you chose) onto a stack. Each time you reach a dead end, you look on the stack for a place to restart your search. And each time you exhaust all the possibilities of a decision point, you pop it off the stack and go back to the previous decision point.

Stacks can be implemented with linked lists or with arrays. In many circumstances, stacks will grow in a predictable way with a clear maximum size, and an array is a suitable structure. Other problems may have stacks whose maximum size is unpredictable. For such problems, a linked list is the best choice of data structure for a stack.

Figure 30.3 shows two procedures for pushing items onto or popping items off of a stack. The stack is implemented as a list, and items are always added at or deleted from the head of the list.

Figure 30.3   **Procedures *push* and *pop* for a stack implemented as a list**

```
procedure push(rec: link; var hd: link);
  {Pushes the record pointed to by rec onto}
  {the list headed by hd.}
begin { push }
        rec^.link : = hd;
        hd : = rec
end; {push}

procedure pop (var rec: link; var hd: link);
  {Pops a record off the stack headed by hd}
  {and returns a pointer to it in rec. If}
  {the list is empty, returns the value nil.}
begin { pop }
        rec : = hd;
        if hd <> nil
            then
                    hd : = hd^.next
end; {pop}
```

Exercise   30.4: Suppose your program must manage a stack of records, but you know that there will never be more than *MAXSTACK* records in the stack. Write procedures *push* and *pop* to implement a stack as an array of records.   ■

In Chapter 29, we gave an example of a program that read a list of names and then printed them out in reverse order (pages 628–629). That program manipulated its list as a stack of names.

30.3 NONLIST STRUCTURES

The use of pointers allows us to create dynamic data structures of very general shapes. Figure 30.4 shows four different kinds of data structures that can be built using pointers as links: the doubly linked list, the circular list, the binary tree, and the directed graph. Each of these structures is useful under appropriate circumstances. Trees and graphs are particularly important, and a good deal of research has gone into studying the best ways to represent and manipulate such structures. We can't cover that material here. As a brief introduction to this type of data structure, we'll discuss some of the algorithms for manipulating doubly linked lists.

Doubly Linked Lists

The idea behind the doubly linked list is simple: Each item in the list has two pointers, one to its successor and one to its predecessor. The structure is shown in Figure 30.4a.

The motivation for constructing doubly linked lists arises from a problem we encountered in the last chapter. It occurs when we search lists for a particular item. When we find what we're looking for, we often need to update the pointer of the preceding item. But we have no way to access the preceding item unless we have used a trailer pointer or we've looked ahead one item. The bookkeeping and coding for such a search can become onerous. And there are other circumstances when we would like to be able to move in either direction along a list.

If our list is doubly linked, it is a simple matter to find an item's predecessor. The price for this is the extra work needed to build the list as doubly linked in the first place. Although we won't describe all the algorithms you need for manipulating doubly linked lists in this chapter, we illustrate their use by means of a procedure for building such a list. Figure 30.5 shows the relevant data structure definitions. Figure 30.6 pictures a doubly linked list before and after the insertion of a record. Note which pointers have to be "shifted" to make the insertion.

Finally, Figure 30.7 shows a procedure for building a doubly linked list in key order. The main difficulties in this procedure involve searching for the correct

Figure 30.4 Nonlist dynamic data structures

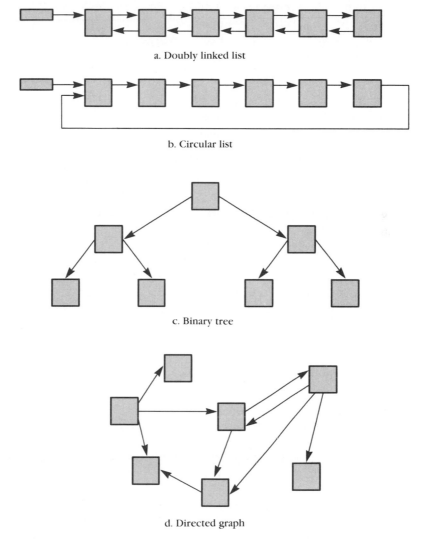

a. Doubly linked list

b. Circular list

c. Binary tree

d. Directed graph

insertion point and dealing with the special cases where the item is to be inserted at one of the ends of the list.

Exercise 30.5: Write **procedure** deletedouble(key: integer) to search a doubly linked list for a record with a particular key. If the record is found, the procedure should delete it from the list and free the storage space it occupies. ∎

Figure 30.5   Data structure definition for a doubly linked list

```
type    itemptr = ^item;
        item = record
                key: integer;          {for simplicity}
                  .
                  .
                  .
                                       {other fields in record}
                next,                  {forward pointer}
                previous: itemptr      {backward pointer}
              end;
```

Figure 30.6   Inserting a record into a doubly linked list

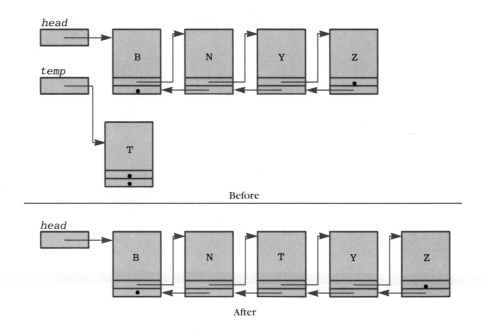

Figure 30.7   Procedure to construct a doubly linked list

```
var     head: itemptr;              {list header}
        . . .
procedure builddouble ( newrec:itemptr );
{The parameter "newrec" is a pointer to an item}
{record to be inserted, in key order, into}
{the doubly linked list headed by "head".}

begin    {builddouble}
    auxptr : = head;
    if auxptr = nil {list is empty}
        then
            begin
                head : = newrec;
                newrec^.next : = nil;
                newrec^.previous : = nil
            end    {if auxptr = nil}
        else
            begin {Search for correct place to insert.}
                keepgoing : = true;
                while keepgoing do
                    begin
                        if auxptr^.next = nil
                            then
                                keepgoing : = false
                            else if auxptr^.key > newrec^.key
                                then
                                    keepgoing : = false
                                else
                                    auxptr : = auxptr^.next
                    end; {while keepgoing}
    {The "shifting of arrows" happens here:}
                    if auxptr^.key > newrec^.key
                        then
                            begin    {found bigger key}
                                newrec^.next : = auxptr;
                                newrec^.previous : = auxptr^.previous;
                                if auxptr^.previous <> nil
                                    then
                                        auxptr^.previous^.next : = newrec;
                                auxptr^.previous : = newrec;
```

(continued)

Figure 30.7
Continued

```
                    if head  =  auxptr
                         then         {Insert at head.}
                              head  : =  newrec
                end {if-then found bigger key}
          else {There's no bigger key.}

          begin    {Insert at end.}
              newrec^.previous  : =  auxptr;
              newrec^.next  : =  nil;
              auxptr^.next  : =  newrec
          end { else }
       end {else, auxptr <> nil}
 end;     {builddouble}
```

CHAPTER SUMMARY

1. A *queue* is a data structure in which items are added and removed dynamically but are always removed in the same order they were added. A queue is sometimes called a *FIFO structure*. In many cases, the best way to implement a queue in a Pascal program is to use a linked list, in which items are always added to one end of the list and removed from the other end.

2. A *stack* is a data structure in which items are added and removed dynamically but are always removed in the reverse order of their arrival. A stack is sometimes called a *LIFO structure*. In many cases, the best way to implement a stack in a Pascal program is to use a linked list, in which items are always added to and removed from the same end of the list.

3. A *doubly linked list* is a variation of a linked list in which each item has pointers to its predecessor as well as its successor. Such a list is useful in applications where it's necessary to search in either direction from a given list item.

COMMON ERRORS

- Trying to dequeue an item from an empty list or pop an item off an empty stack

- Forgetting to initialize to **nil** the backward-pointing link in the first record added to a doubly linked list

DEBUGGING HINTS

- If you have implemented a queue as an array, print the values of the indices that indicate the start and end of the queue as you enqueue and dequeue items.
- If you have implemented a stack as an array, print the value of the index that indicates the top of the stack as you push items onto, or pop items off of, the stack.

SUPPLEMENTAL PROBLEMS

1. Write a program that uses a stack to read a line of input and print it backward.
2. Write a program that uses a stack of stacks to read a file of text and print the lines in reverse order (last line first), with each line printed backward.
3. Recursion makes use of a stack in a manner that is invisible to the programmer: When a procedure calls itself, the values of the caller's copies of the parameters and local variables are pushed onto a stack. When the called procedure exits, these values are popped off the stack and restored. By managing a stack explicitly in your program, you can write any recursive function or procedure nonrecursively.

   For example, consider the function f given by recursive definition

   $$f(n) = \begin{cases} 1 & \text{if } n = 1 \\ 3 \times f(n-1) - 1 & \text{if } n > 1 \end{cases}$$

   Here is a nonrecursive algorithm for computing $f(n)$:

Setup

I. Reserve space for a stack of records. Each record has two integers: a value N, and a space for $f(N)$.

Instructions

I. If $n = 1$,
   then
      A. Return the value 1.
   else
      A'. Repeat the following steps:
         1. Push the value of n onto the stack in the field N.

        2. Subtract 1 from *n*.
    until *n* = 1.

B′. Store the value 1 in the *f(N)* field on the topmost record of the stack.

C′. Repeat the following steps:

    1. Pop the top record off the stack. Store its *f(N)* value in *Temp*.

    2. Multiply the value in *Temp* by 3, and subtract 1 from the product. Store the result in the *f(N)* value of the topmost element on the stack.

    until the stack has only one record.

D′. Pop the last record off the stack and return the value in its *f(N)* field.

Write a nonrecursive function implementing this procedure. Is the best data structure for the stack in this problem an array or a linked list?

*4. Write a nonrecursive procedure to solve the Tower of Hanoi problem of Chapter 5.

5. Write a procedure that reads a linked list of names and creates a doubly linked list with the same names in the reverse order.

6. A *circular list* is a data structure like a linked list, with the difference that no record has a **nil** pointer. Rather, the link field of the last record points to the first record. Write a function to search a circular list of records for a particular key value. If the record is found, the function should return a pointer to it; otherwise, the function should return the value **nil**.

*7. The Bottleneck Bridge has only a single westbound tollbooth. Every weekday morning, rush hour traffic starts to arrive at 6:00 A.M. Between 6:00 and 6:15, cars arrive at the rate of 5 per minute. Between 6:15 and 6:30, cars arrive at the rate of 8 per minute. Between 6:30 and 7:00, cars arrive at the rate of 12 per minute. Between 7:00 and 8:00, cars arrive at the rate of 15 per minute. Between 8:00 and 9:00, cars arrive at the rate of 6 per minute, and from 9:00 to 10:00, cars arrive at the rate of 1 per minute. No traffic travels west after 10:00. The toll collector can collect tolls from 7 cars each minute.

a. Write a program that simulates the flow of traffic past the tollbooth. Your program should build a queue with a record for each car. Store the time of the car's arrival (to the nearest minute) in the record for that car. Have your program print out the maximum length of the queue, the maximum time any car waited in the queue, and the average wait time for all cars that traveled across the bridge that day.

b. Modify the program from problem 7a so that the user can input the number of tolls per minute that can be collected. Then experiment with different values to see how the maximum size of the queue changes as you vary this value.

CHAPTER

31

In this chapter, we discuss a number of unrelated topics that, for the most part, have to do with little-used features of Pascal.

31.1 goto STATEMENTS AND LABELS

When we talk about the *flow of control* of a program, we mean the sequence in which the program's statements are executed. We've seen many Pascal constructs that affect the flow of control, including conditional statements like if-then, if-then-else, and **case**, and iterative statements like **for**, **while**, and **repeat**. Function and procedure calls also affect the flow of control.

The **goto** statement is used to make an unconditional transfer of control to a specified statement. The syntax of a **goto** statement is as in Figure 31.1.

Labels are a way of naming, or labeling, a particular Pascal statement. You may recall that a part of the structure of a program or procedure is the label declaration section (page 193). We have not made use of this section in our programs up to this point. Now we will.

A **label** consists of a number in the range 1 to 9999. Once a **label** has been declared, it can be written before a statement, followed by a colon. Figure 31.2 illustrates the declaration and use of a label and a **goto** statement that transfers to that statement.

Like every other object in Pascal, a label has a scope—that is, a portion of the program in which it is meaningful. The scope rule for a **label** is the same as for an identifier: A **label** is defined from the point where it's declared to the end of the program unit (procedure, function, or program) in which it was declared. Like identifiers, labels may be masked by identical labels within a program subunit. For example, consider the situation in Figure 31.3. In this fragment, there are two labels named 50, one of which is local to procedure *useslabels*. Within this

OTHER TOPICS

Figure 31.1   **Syntax diagram for a** goto **statement**

Figure 31.2   **Declaring a label and using a** goto **statement**

```
program usegotos(input, output);
label   240;     {Makes 240 possible target of a goto}
        .
        .
        .

        if errval > 0
          then
            goto 240;
        .
        .
        .

240:    writeln('Error number ', errval:1, ' has occurred.');
        .
        .
        .
```

procedure, any reference to **label** 50 means the local label, while outside the procedure references to **label** 50 mean the global label.

Note that it's possible to use a **goto** to transfer control from inside a procedure to outside that procedure. (The **goto** 99 statement of Figure 31.3 would do that, for example.) Such a transfer is known as a *nonlocal* goto. Nonlocal gotos are almost always a bad idea, although they may be useful on rare occasions. In fact, many computer scientists have criticized the inclusion of the **goto** statement in the Pascal language.

The reason **goto** statements are frowned upon is that they make a program difficult to understand. They obscure the flow of control, especially if they are used liberally. The result is known as "spaghetti code." Compare the two functionally equivalent sets of statements in Figure 31.4. The if-then-else form is clearly easier to read and expresses the logic of the algorithm better.

Figure 31.3   Example of a local label masking a global label

```
program showlabels(input, output);
label 99, 50;

          .
          .
          .

        procedure useslabels;
        label 50;         { This local 50 masks out }
                          { the globally defined 50. }
        begin {useslabels}
              .
              .
              .

          if somethingorother
              then
                    goto 99; {goes to global label}
                            {99, the only 99 there is}

              .
              .
              .

          if somethingelse
              then
                  goto 50; {goes to local 50}
              .
              .
              .

            50: writeln(. . .);
        end; {useslabels}
```

```
begin {showlabels}
        .

        .

        .
        goto 50:           {goes to global 50}
        .

        .

        .
50:     writeln(. . .);
        .

        .

        .
99:     writeln(. . .)
end. {showlabels}
```

───────

Figure 31.4   Two-way selection with and without goto **statements**

```
        if a > b                    if a <= b
           then                        then
              goto 50;                    c := c + d
           c := c + d;               else
           goto 60;                     e := e + f
50:        e := e + f
60:        . . . {next statement}
```

If you want statement A to be unconditionally followed by statement B, then you should code statement B immediately after statement A. If, based on the current state of the program, you want to choose the next statement to be executed, then the conditional and iterative statements we mentioned above are sufficient. The only justification for using a **goto** statement would be if it more clearly expressed the intention of the algorithm. We believe that you should use a **goto** in only one circumstance: To make a premature exit from a program when the program has detected some sort of error from which it cannot recover. In Figure 31.5, we show a fragment of a program to illustrate how a **goto** might be useful in this situation.

The idea of this code is that no further useful work can be done after procedure *testchar* discovers that the value of *ch* is invalid. The best thing to do is to end the program immediately, with an indication of why it's not running to completion. In Figure 31.5, we write an error number. Presumably there are several places in the program where a test for a fatal error condition will occur, and at each such place a different value is assigned to *errornum*. Then a **goto 99** occurs. It has the effect of writing the error message and ending the program.

Figure 31.5   **Using a `goto` statement to exit a procedure early**

```
program moregotos(input, output);
label    99;
var      errornum: integer;        {holds error number}
         .
         .
         .

         procedure testchar;
         var      validchar: set of char;
         .
         .
         .

         if not (ch in validchar)
           then
             begin
               errornum := 17;
               goto 99
             end;
         .
         .
         .

begin {moregotos}
         errornum := 0;  {initially, no error}
         .
         .
         .

99:      if errornum > 0
           then
             writeln('Abnormal termination due to error ',
                     errornum:1)
end. {moregotos}
```

Ordinarily, when a procedure has been entered, there's no way to leave it except the normal flow of control through the **end** symbol. In cases where premature exit from a procedure is the only sensible way to proceed, a **goto** enables the program to leave the procedure immediately.

31.2 VARIANT RECORDS

In some circumstances, it's useful to have a record type that can contain several different types of data but where the different fields will never all occur simultaneously. For example, suppose we want to write a system to produce a company's payroll. One part of this system might consist of a program that reads a file of records and (based on the contents of the file) calculates each employee's pay for a given period. It may be that employees are paid in several ways: Some may be salaried, some may be hourly, and some may be paid by commission. To deal with these possibilities, we might make a record definition of the sort shown in Figure 31.6.

This record definition has all the information we need for a simplified payroll system. (Real payroll systems need much more information, such as year-to-date tax withholding figures, other deductions, union dues, and so forth.) However, for any given employee, there are many fields in the record that will not be used. For example, a record for a salaried employee has no need for the *hourlyrate*, *hours*, *commrate*, and *commsales* fields. Similarly, an hourly employee's record has no need for the *salary*, *commrate*, or *commsales* fields. This situation causes a number of problems.

One problem is waste of space. A value of type **real** can take up as much space as 8 characters in a typical computer. Thus, four unused fields of type **real** will waste 32 characters worth of space (32 *bytes*). If you have a file of 10,000 payroll records for salaried employees, you'll be wasting 320,000 characters worth of file storage space by using such a record structure. More complex record types will produce even greater waste.

Another problem is that such records create opportunities for errors. A record for an employee who's paid by commission will ordinarily have no use for fields like *salary* and *hours*. However, those fields are there. It's not obvious to someone looking at the record definition that there's a relationship between the value of the field *emptype* and the meaningfulness of the other fields in the record. A programmer who modifies such a program may misunderstand the record structure and use fields that haven't been assigned a value.

To deal with these problems, Pascal has a type of structure known as a variant record. Variant records are record types that do not contain all the fields in every

---

Figure 31.6   Possible structure of *payrec* record

```
type    paytype = (salaried, hourly, commission);
        string = packed array[1..maxlen] of char;
        payrec = record
                    empname: string;        {employee's name}
                    emptype: paytype;       {type of pay}
                    salary: real;           {weekly salary}
                    hourlyrate: real;       {hourly pay rate}
                    hours: real;            {hours worked this week}
                    commrate: real;         {commission percent}
                    commsales: real         {amount subject to comm.}
                 end; {payrec}
```

record. The choice of which fields are present is based on the possible values of some ordinal type. The idea is best explained with an example. Figure 31.7 shows a variant record that implements the ideas of the record in Figure 31.6.

Note the construct within the record that looks like a kind of **case** statement. This is a second, logically related, use of the reserved word **case** in Pascal. Its syntax is quite different from that of the **case** statement, however. The portion of the record definition following the word **case** is known as the variant part of the record. The syntax and semantics of the variant part of a record require some explanation.

Following the word **case** must be the name of an ordinal type, or (more commonly) the declaration of a variable of an ordinal type. If such a variable exists, it is known as the *tag field*. In Figure 31.7, the field named *emptype* is the tag field. After the type name, the reserved word **of** must occur. Then, each of the possible values of the ordinal type must be listed. Every value must occur. Each value must be followed by a colon, followed by a parenthesized list of the field definitions that apply to that value. Thus, the meaning of the record definition in Figure 31.7 is as follows: Records of type *payrec* consist of a string (the *empname* field), a field of type *paytype* (*emptype*), and some other fields. The other fields differ, depending on the value of *emptype*. If a record's *emptype* field has the value *salaried*, then it has only one more field, which is named *salary* and is of type *real*. If a record's *emptype* field has the value *hourly*, then the record has two more fields of type *real*. If *emptype* has the value *commission*, then the record also has two other fields of type *real*, but they are not the same two fields as for *hourly* records.

Figure 31.7   **Variant record structure for *payrec***

```
type    paytype = (salaried, hourly, commission);
        string = packed array[1..maxlen] of char;
        payrec = record
                    empname: string;    {employee's name}
                    case emptype: paytype of {type of pay}
                      salaried:
                         ( salary: real); {weekly salary}
                      hourly:
                         ( hourlyrate,     {hourly pay rate}
                           hours: real);   {hours worked this week}
                      commission:
                         ( commrate,    {commission percent}
                           commsales: real )
                             {amount subject to commission}
                 end; {payrec}
```

There are three special points to be noted about this syntax. First, *no* **end** keyword corresponding to the **case** is needed. The compiler can deduce where the end of the variant part is, since you must mention every possible value of the tag field type. Second, it may be that for some value of the tag type you might want a variant part consisting of no records. In that case, you must provide a parenthesized list with nothing in it:

```
case emptype: paytype of
  salaried: ();          {no fields for this variant}
  hourly: (hours, hourlyrate: real);
  commission: (commrate, commsales: real)
```

Third, the variant part of a record must always come as the last part of the record structure. You may not define any fields after the variant part of the record.

The fields of variant records are referred to using the same syntax as other records. Thus, we can declare

```
var     rec1,
        rec2: payrec;
```

When these records are declared, their tag fields have no value, and it's not meaningful to describe their variant part. We could assign them values like this:

```
rec1.emptype := salaried;
rec1.salary := 568.0;

rec2.emptype := hourly;
rec2.hours := 37.5;
rec2.hourlyrate := 9.85;
```

We only assign values to those fields that are meaningful for the record. It is legal, but meaningless, to do something like this:

```
rec1.type := salaried;
rec1.commsales := 8392.46;     {inappropriate field}
```

By *legal,* we mean that the compiler won't signal an error and the program will run. The effect of the assignment is unpredictable, however, because of the way variant records are implemented. The fields for the different cases of the variant part all share the same area of storage. Thus, assigning a value to the field named *hours* may change the apparent value of the field named *salary*. Protecting against errors like the one shown above is the responsibility of the programmer.

On rare occasions, it's useful to have variant records without a tag field—perhaps to investigate the way your compiler allocates storage. For example, consider the program shown in Figure 31.8.

Figure 31.8   Using a variant record without a tag field

```
program peekinmemory(output);
{Investigate the correspondence of chars and integers.}
type charint = (chtype, intype);
     word = record
                case charint of
                    chtype: (ch: char);
                    intype: (int: integer)
             end; {word}
var wd: word;
begin {peekinmemory}
      wd.ch := chr(1);
      writeln(wd.int:1)
end. {peekinmemory}
```

The fields *ch* and *int* of a *word* record share space, but *ch* typically will take up less space and might therefore occur in the middle of *int*. The value of *int* that is displayed will depend on how the two fields overlap.

31.3 PACKED RECORDS

We've seen the use of the reserved word **packed** to modify the type definition of arrays. It's also possible to define packed record types. The syntax of such declarations, the reasons for making them, and the corresponding restrictions are very similar to those for arrays.

A packed record is defined by including the reserved word **packed** before the reserved word **record** in the type definition. Figure 31.9 shows an example that uses the variant record type from the previous section.

The advantage of packed records is that in some implementations of Pascal they take up less space than the corresponding unpacked records. (But unlike packed arrays of characters, it's not possible to compare packed records according to a sequence.)

The principal disadvantages are twofold. First, corresponding to the saving in space is a loss of speed when referring to the individual fields of the record. Second, it's not permitted to pass the subfields of a packed record as variable parameters to a procedure. Nor is it possible to pass a subcomponent of a subfield of such a record as a variable parameter. Thus, if a packed record contains as one of its fields an array, individual elements of the array are not allowed as variable parameters even if the array is not specifically declared to be packed.

On many implementations of Pascal, particularly on minicomputers and microcomputers, the keyword **packed** has no effect because the unpacked and packed

Figure 31.9   Defining *payrec* as a packed record

```
type    paytype = (salaried, hourly, commission);
        string = packed array[1..maxlen] of char;
        payrec = packed record
                    empname: string;     {employee's name}
                    case emptype: paytype of {type of pay}
                      salaried:
                        ( salary: real); {weekly salary}
                      hourly:
                        ( hourlyrate,       {hourly pay rate}
                          hours: real);     {hours worked this week}
                      commission:
                        ( commrate,    {commission percent}
                          commsales: real )
                              {amount subject to commission}
                  end; {payrec}
```

forms of a structure are identical. Before using packed records, make sure that the advantage you seek to gain is real and is worth the trouble.

31.4 PROCEDURES AND FUNCTIONS AS PARAMETERS

It's very common for a procedure or a function to invoke another procedure or function. You can usually decide at the time the program is being written what procedures or functions will be invoked when. Under rare circumstances, however, it may be possible only during run time to decide which procedure or function should be invoked in a particular circumstance. To deal with this possibility, Pascal allows the identifiers that name procedures and functions to be themselves passed as parameters to other procedures and functions.

To illustrate the idea, suppose we're writing a program to play some board game, such as chess, go, or Reversi. A typical feature of such programs is that at each move, they search ahead some (usually small) number of moves, looking at possible board configurations, evaluating them, and deciding which sequence is the best. A procedure to choose the next possible move would repeatedly generate board positions, evaluate them according to some criteria, and use the evaluations to make a decision. It might look something like Figure 31.10.

In this fragment, function *evaluate* is some unspecified function that is passed a board position and returns some sort of value. However, in many games the criteria for evaluating the board change during the game. Thus, in chess a

---

Figure 31.10   **Part of a procedure for evaluating game positions**

```
procedure choosemove (position: board; var nextmove: move);
{chooses the best move from the current board position}

var move value: integer;

begin {choosemove}
        .

        .

        .

    movevalue := evaluate (position);
        .

        .

        .
end; {choosemove}
```

program might have one set of rules for position evaluation during the opening, a second set of rules during the middle game, and a third set during the endgame. To implement these three sets of rules, we might write three separate functions. In such a case, how would we code procedure *choosemove*?

One possibility would be to replace each call to function *evaluate* with a sequence of the following sort:

```
case gamestage of
        opening: movevalue := openeval (position);
        midgame: movevalue := mideval (position);
        endgame: movevalue := endeval (position)
end; { case }
```

This sequence isn't too bad if the number of calls to *evaluate* is small. However, it requires that procedure *choosemove* know the value of *gamestage*, which it might not otherwise need to know. Moreover, if we later decide to divide the game into two stages, or four, this part of the program will have to change. Finally, it's verbose. We may have to use this sequence or a similar one many times in procedure *choosemove*.

An alternative is to think of the procedure that will evaluate the board position as a kind of variable that can take on any one of the three values *openeval*, *mideval*, or *endeval*. Actually, it's impossible in Pascal to have an ordinary variable whose values are procedures or functions. (It's possible in some other programming languages.) However, we can have a formal parameter to a procedure or function whose values are procedure or function names. Thus, we can pass the name of the function to be used in evaluating the position as a parameter to *choosemove*. We would code the procedure heading for *choosemove* like this:

```
procedure choosemove( function eval(pos: board): integer;
                      position:board; var nextmove:move);
```

In this procedure heading, there's a new type of parameter: a function parameter. It looks like a function header within the procedure header.[1] The meaning of this parameter is that, when procedure *choosemove* is invoked, it will be passed an argument that is a function name. Furthermore, that function will take a single argument, of type *board*, and will return a value of type `integer`. Wherever the parameter *eval* occurs in the body of *choosemove*, the name of function *eval* should be replaced by the name passed as an argument. Thus, suppose *choosemove* contains the line

```
movevalue := eval(position);    {**}
```

If we wanted to invoke procedure *choosemove* during the opening of the game and thus use function *openeval* for evaluating the board, we might write

```
choosemove(openeval, currpos, currval)
```

Then the line marked {**} will cause function *openeval* to be invoked with parameter *currpos* and the result returned in *movevalue*. Function *openeval* must agree in type and parameter types with the formal function parameter *eval*. Furthermore, the scope of function *openeval* must include the call to procedure *choosemove*. Note that the identifier *pos*, which occurs in the function parameter's formal header, has no other purpose. It is merely a placeholder. It is there to describe the type of the parameter that functions passed as arguments to *choosemove* must have.

Just as we can pass function names as parameters, so we can pass procedure names. A procedure that takes another procedure as a parameter might have a header like this:

```
procedure useprocs(procedure dummy(var1, var2: integer) );
```

This would be invoked with a statement like

```
useprocs(procname);
```

procname would have to be the name of a procedure that takes two arguments of type `integer`. Parameters of this sort are (not surprisingly, but confusingly) known as *procedure parameters*. There are four kinds of parameters that can be declared in Pascal: procedure, function, variable, and value parameters.

---

1. In describing the syntax of procedure and function parameters, we follow the ISO Standard. This syntax differs from the other widely accepted standard, Jensen and Wirth. In fact, this is the only syntactic point of difference between these two standards.

There is a restriction on the functions and procedures that can be passed as arguments to other procedures and functions: The procedures and functions being passed can themselves have only value parameters. Many implementations of Pascal impose the further restriction that you may not pass any of the standard procedures or functions as arguments.

31.5   FORWARD DECLARATIONS OF PROCEDURES

We've seen that a procedure can invoke itself recursively. Recursion may also take a more subtle form: Procedure *A* may invoke procedure *B*, and procedure *B* may invoke procedure *A*. Such a pair of procedures is said to be *mutually recursive*. We might have three or more mutually recursive procedures.

Mutual recursion turns out to be quite useful in a number of circumstances. But when we try to code two mutually recursive procedures, we encounter a difficulty: Which should occur first in the program text? The problem is that if *A* occurs first, it can't refer to *B*, while if *B* occurs first, it can't refer to *A*.

One possible solution is to make one of the procedures local to the other. This way, each is within the other's scope. This solution is often sufficient, but sometimes it won't work. It won't work, for example, if procedures *A* and *B* must each be invokable by some other procedures, and thus must have a broader scope. Moreover, nesting may not reflect the logic of the problem accurately even when it solves the problem. Nesting of procedures should mirror the locality of algorithms and should not be used just for convenience.

The solution that works in general involves *forward declaration* of procedures. Forward declaration announces the existence of a procedure whose actual declaration occurs at a later point in the program. Figure 31.11 illustrates a forward declaration of procedure *A*.

The first line of Figure 31.11 contains the procedure header of procedure *A* followed by the statement consisting of the single reserved word **forward**. This statement takes the place of the procedure's body (definitions, declarations, and statements). Later, when procedure *B* invokes procedure *A*, the identifier *A* is known, as are the number and type of *A*'s parameters. Thus, the compiler can check the correctness of the line invoking *A*. The actual definition of *A* occurs later. Note an important point: The full procedure header for *A* occurs only once, at the forward declaration. When the definition of the body of *A* occurs, it is preceded by an abbreviated header consisting only of the reserved word **procedure** followed by the procedure name, followed by a semicolon. The parameters are not mentioned; they have already been described.

A similar rule holds for functions: Forward declarations of functions are allowed. When they occur, the full function header (including the type of the function) occurs only once, at the forward declaration. The body of the function, which occurs later, is preceded by an abbreviated header consisting of the reserved word **function**, the function name, and a semicolon.

Figure 31.11   Example of a forward declaration of a procedure

```
procedure A(val: integer; var result: integer); forward;
                              .
                              .
                              .

procedure B(ch: char);
begin {B}
        {statements of B}
                              .
                              .
                              .
        A(somevalue, someresult);
                              .
                              .
                              .

end; {B}

procedure A;
begin {A}
        {statements of A}
                              .
                              .
                              .
        B(somechar);
                              .
                              .
                              .

end; {A}
```

CHAPTER SUMMARY

1. The **goto** *statement* is used in Pascal to unconditionally transfer control to a specified, labeled statement. A statement label consists of an *integer* in the range 1 to 9999 followed by a colon. A **goto** statement can transfer to a label outside of the block in which it occurs, as long as the label's scope includes the **goto** statement. **goto** statements should only be used when no other control structure effectively describes the required flow of control.

2. Variant records are a form of record structure in which not every field of the record occurs in each variable of the record type. They are useful when a record type needs many fields, and the nature of the problem implies that not all the fields will be needed in each record of that type.

3. The variant part of a record is described using syntax that resembles a **case** statement. Each value of the ordinal type that describes the possible variants must occur in the variant part.

4. Any structured type can be declared using the reserved word **packed**. The effect of declaring records to be packed is similar to the effect of declaring arrays to be packed: It does not change the meaning of the program. Individual fields of packed records may not be passed as arguments corresponding to variable parameters.

5. It is possible to pass the names of procedures or functions as parameters to other procedures or functions. This allows a program module to choose, during execution, which other module to invoke. Procedures and functions passed as parameters can themselves have only value parameters.

6. To facilitate mutually recursive program modules, Pascal allows the forward declaration of procedures and functions. When a forward declaration is made, the full procedure or function header is written only once, at the forward declaration. The actual declaration of the procedure or function is preceded by a simplified header.

COMMON ERRORS

- Using a **goto** statement to branch to a label whose scope does not include the **goto**—for example, trying to branch into a procedure from an enclosing block

- Using a label without declaring it

- Omitting some of the values of the tag type in the variant portion of a variant record

- Forgetting to define a tag field in a variant record

- Failing to indicate the parameters of a function or procedure parameter in the header of the module for which it is a parameter

- Putting a dummy header in a forward procedure declaration, or putting a full header in the actual declaration of a forward procedure or function

SUPPLEMENTAL PROBLEMS

1. Rewrite the following code fragment without using **goto** statements or labels.

```
label    100;
const    limit = 20;
var      n,
         sum: integer;
              .
              .
              .
```

```
            n : = 1;
            sum : = 0;
100:        sum : = sum + n;
            n : = n + 1
            if n <= limit
                then
                        goto 100;
            writeln(sum);
```

2. Consider the following skeleton of a program, which shows procedure headers:

program skeleton(input, output);

procedure A; **forward**;

procedure B;

      procedure C; **forward**;

      procedure D;
      begin { D }
         . . .
      end; { D }

      procedure E;
      begin { E }
         . . .
      end; { E }

      procedure C;
      begin { C }
         . . .
      end; { C }
begin { B }
   . . .
end; { B }

procedure A;
begin { A }
   . . .
end; { A }

For each of the procedures *A*, *B*, *C*, *D*, and *E*, list
a. The procedures that they may call
b. The procedures that may call them

APPENDIX

APPENDIX A   ASCII Character Set

0 nul	1 soh	2 stx	3 etx	4 eot	5 enq	6 ack	7 bel
8 bs	9 ht	10 nl	11 vt	12 np	13 cr	14 so	15 si
16 dle	17 dc1	18 dc2	19 dc3	20 dc4	21 nak	22 syn	23 etb
24 can	25 em	26 sub	27 esc	28 fs	29 gs	30 rs	31 us
32 space	33 !	34 "	35 #	36 $	37 %	38 &	39 '
40 (	41)	42 *	43 +	44 ,	45 -	46 .	47 /
48 0	49 1	50 2	51 3	52 4	53 5	54 6	55 7
56 8	57 9	58 :	59 ;	60 <	61 =	62 >	63 ?
64 @	65 A	66 B	67 C	68 D	69 E	70 F	71 G
72 H	73 I	74 J	76 K	77 L	78 M	78 N	79 O
80 P	81 Q	82 R	83 S	84 T	85 U	86 V	87 W
88 X	89 Y	90 Z	91 [	92 \	93]	94 ^	95 _
96 '	97 a	98 b	99 c	100 d	101 e	102 f	103 g
104 h	105 i	106 j	107 k	108 l	109 m	110 n	111 o
112 p	113 q	114 r	115 s	116 t	117 u	118 v	119 w
120 x	121 y	122 z	123 {	124		125 }	126 ~	127 del

APPENDIX B   Rules of Style

The following appendix contains some things to keep in mind when writing a program. Remember, most programs go through several revisions, which are often not made by the original author. Your program should therefore be a way of communicating the algorithm you employed to another programmer.

Internal Documentation

Documentation is the easiest way to convey information about your program to others. There are five ways in which you should utilize documentation:

1. To identify general information about the program—when it was written, who wrote it, what it was written for, when it has been updated and by whom

2. To identify the goal of the program and each of its procedures—not how they are implemented, but what task they are supposed to accomplish

3. To identify the algorithm used to implement the program and the subalgorithms used to implement each procedure and function

4. To identify the uses of identifiers that describe constants, types, and variables

5. To keep track of beginnings and endings of statements and sections of the program

Presentation

The translator that processes your Pascal program does not notice spaces, carriage returns, or blank lines between symbols and identifiers. You could, if you wished (assuming the computer didn't have any limitations), place all your Pascal statements on one line. Unfortunately, humans are not as good as the translator at processing Pascal programs. You should place blank spaces and blank lines in your program in such a way that the following things are clear:

1. Where a new section of the program or its procedures or functions begin. For example, there should be a clear distinction between the type definition and variable declaration section in the program and in the procedures.

2. Where a statement begins and ends.

3. When a statement or statements are within another statement.

4. Which **begin** goes with which **end**. We highly recommend that you line them up.

Several styles of using blank spaces and blank lines have been shown throughout the text. Any system that follows the above criteria will be useful, as long as it is consistently used.

Meaningful Identifiers

One of the nicer features of Pascal is the fact that identifiers can be real names. You should use this fact in naming all identifiers. Keep in mind the following things when naming identifiers:

1. They should, as much as possible, describe what they represent.
2. If possible, don't give two identifiers the same name at different levels in your program.
3. It is fine for two or more procedures or functions to use the same identifiers to name parameters, if it is highly likely that the parameters will be accepting the same data structure.
4. *Never* give a parameter the same name any of its corresponding argument.

Modularization

Due to the ability to have functions and procedures as well as subfunctions and subprocedures the Pascal language helps in the development of modular programs. Procedures and functions should always be used, when appropriate, in writing a program. Always consider the following rules when writing a program:

1. Every subproblem breakdown in your solution should have a corresponding function or procedure.
2. Procedures and functions should be local to other procedures and functions whenever possible.
3. General procedures used throughout the program should be identified as such.

In keeping with the idea of modularization also remember the following rules:

1. Identifiers should be declared or defined locally whenever possible.
2. It is best to avoid giving two identifiers the same name.

Errorchecking

All programs should have errorchecking. If it is possible that the user or some other external source of data might provide incorrect input, errorchecking should attempt to inform the user of the incorrect data and keep the program going until completion if possible.

Example

The following is a sample program that attempts to use the general rules of style examined in this appendix.

```
{Li Santi, Mann, & Zlotnick}
{September 29, 1985}
{for: appendix B}
program alpha (input,output);
{purpose:  to alphabetize a list of fixed size}
{algorithm:
    I.    Initialization of list.
    II.   Read in items.
```

```
            III.  Alphabetize list.
            IV.   Print list.}

const wordsize = 30;    {maximum length of item in list}
      listsize = 10;    {maximum number of items in list}

type string = array [1..wordsize] of char;
                          {string to hold item in list}
     list = array [1..listsize] of string;
                          {list to hold items}

var howmanyitems: integer;  {number of items in list}
    items:list;      {the list of items}

  procedure initialize(var things:list);
    {sets all arrays in things to blanks}

  var initindex,            {to keep track of current
                             position in current array}
        initcount:integer;  {to keep track of current array}


  begin    {initialize}
    for initcount := 1 to listsize do
        for initindex := 1 to wordsize do
          things[initcount][initindex] := ' '
  end;    {initialize}

  procedure readitems (var things:list; var numitems:
                          integer);
  {reads in items until a carriage return alone is typed}
  {returns number of items read}
  {alg:   I.  Set numitems to 0.
          II. Repeat
                 A.  Prompt for item.
                 B.  Read item.
              Until item is all blanks
          III.Set numitems to one less so as not to
              include blank typed.}

  procedure readstring(var thing:string);
    { a procedure to correctly read characters into }
    { an array of type string}
    {alg:   I.  Initialize index.
            II. While index isn't greater than length
                of string and it is not eoln do
                   A.  Read a character.
```

```
              B.   Increase index by 1.}

     var readindex: integer;   {used as array subscript}

        begin {readstring}
           readindex := 1;
           while (not(eoln)) and (readindex <= wordsize) do
            begin {while}
             read(thing[readindex]);
             readindex := readindex +1
            end; {while}
           readln {move read pointer down}
        end; {readstring}

      begin  {readitems}
        numitems := 1;
        repeat
          write('Item please: ');
          readstring(things[numitems]);
          numitems := numitems + 1
        until (things[numitems - 1][1] = ' ') or
              (numitems > listsize);
        numitems := numitems - 1
      end;  {readitems}

procedure sort(var things:list; numitems:integer);
  {a procedure to sort the items in a list}
  {alg:  selection sort:
      I.  For every position from the first
          to the last - 1 do
          A.  Find the lowest value from the
              current position on.
          B.  Put that value in the current
              position.}

var current,      {current place looking for lowest
                    value}
    min,          {current place of lowest value}
    next: integer;{current place being compared}

  function before(n1,n2: string): boolean;
      {a boolean-valued function that returns the value}
      {true if string "n1" is before string "n2" in }
      {alphabetical order}
      {alg:   I.   pack "n1" into a packed array-type variable }
      {            "pn1"                                        }
      {       II.  pack "n2" into a packed array-type variable }
```

```
{           "pn2"                                              }
{     III.  use the relational operator ">" to compare }
{           "pn1" to "pn2" and assign this value to the}
{           identifier for the function "before"        }
type packedstring = packed array[1..wordsize] of char;
var pn1,pn2 : packedstring;
    {arrays to hold packed copies of the values of strings}
    {"n1" and "n2", which are the parameters}

begin {before}
    pack(n1,1,pn1);
    pack(n2,1,pn2);
    before := pn1 > pn2
end; {before}

procedure switch(var currplace, newplace: string);
    {a procedure to switch two items in the list}
    {alg:   I.   Save item currplace in temp spot.
            II.  Move newplace into currplace spot.
            III. Move temp into newplace.}

var temp: string;   {to hold the value of a character}
                    {that is switching places}

begin   {switch}
    temp := currplace;
    currplace := newplace;
    newplace := temp
end;    {switch}

begin    {sort}
 for current := 1 to (numitems - 1) do
   begin    {current place in list, for}
     min := current;
     for next := (current + 1) to numitems do
         begin   {place being checked in list, for }
           if before(things[min], things[next])
               then
                   min := next
         end;    {place being checked in list, for}
     if min <> current
           then switch(things[current],things[min])
   end    {current place in list, for}
end;    {sort}

procedure printlist(things:list; numitems:integer);
    {a procedure to print all items in list}
```

```
{alg:   I.  For every element in list array do
              A. While not at end of item do
                  1.  Write character.
                  2.  Get next character.
              B. Write a carriage return.}

    var printindex,           {current position in list}
        printcount: integer;    {current position in item}

            function length (item: string) : integer;
            {a function to compute the length of a string}
            {alg:   I.  Set curpos at end of array.
                    II. While still get a blank and not
                        at first position in array do
                        A. Decrement curpos.
                   III.If curpos is blank we must be at pos
                       1 and array must be empty so
                          then set length to 0
                          else set length to curpos.}

        var curpos: integer; {to mark the current position}

        begin {length}
           curpos : = wordsize;
           while (item[curpos] = ' ') and (curpos > 1) do
               curpos : = curpos - 1;
           if item[curpos] = ' '
               then length : = 0
               else length : = curpos
        end; {length}

  begin    {printlist}
   for printindex : = 1 to numitems do
     begin {going through list, for}
       for printcount : = 1 to
       length(things[printindex]) do
           write(things[printindex] [printcount]);
       writeln
     end     {going through list, for}
  end;      {printlist}

begin    {alpha, main program}
   initialize(items);
   readitems(items, howmanyitems);
   sort(items, howmanyitems);
   printlist(items, howmanyitems)
end.      {alpha, main program}
```

APPENDIX C   Reserved Words, Standard Identifiers, and Syntax Diagrams

Reserved Words

and	end	nil	set
array	file	not	then
begin	for	of	to
case	function	or	type
const	goto	packed	until
div	if	procedure	var
do	in	program	while
downto	label	record	with
else	mod	repeat	

Standard Identifiers

Standard Constants:

false	*true*	*maxint*

Standard Types:

integer	*boolean*	*real*	*char*
text			

Standard Files:

input	*output*

Standard Functions:

abs	*arctan*	*chr*	*cos*
eof	*eoln*	*exp*	*ln*
odd	*ord*	*pred*	*round*
sin	*sqr*	*sqrt*	*succ*
trunc			

Standard Procedures:

get	*new*	*pack*	*page*
put	*read*	*readln*	*reset*
rewrite	*unpack*	*write*	*writeln*

Syntax Diagrams

program

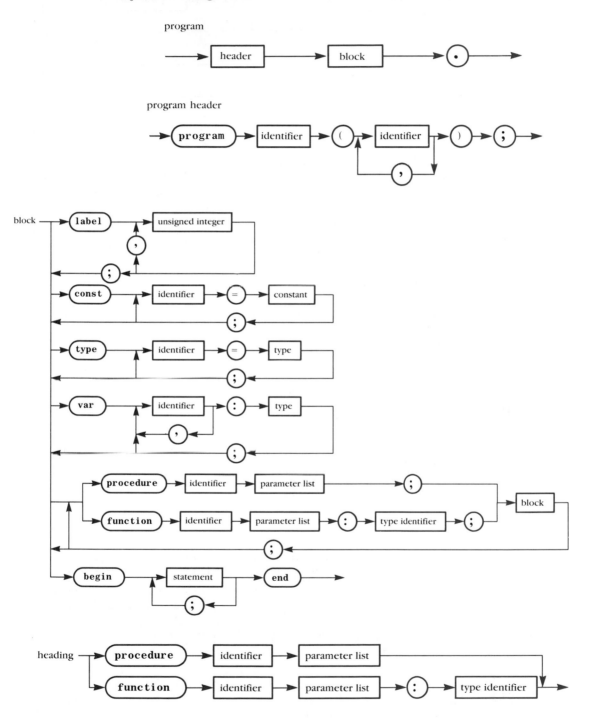

parameter list

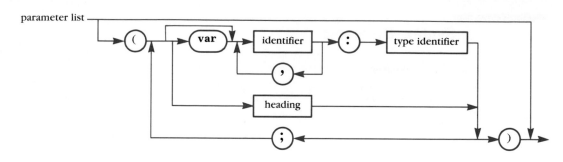

type

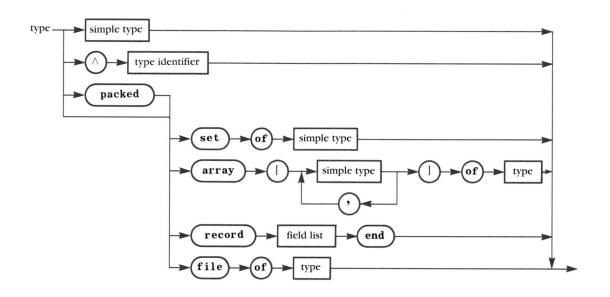

field list

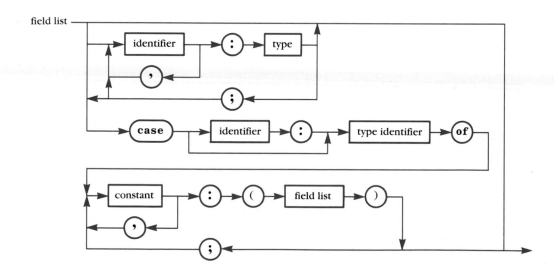

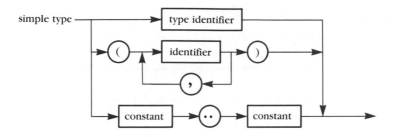

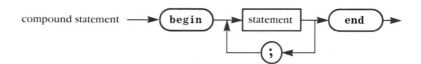

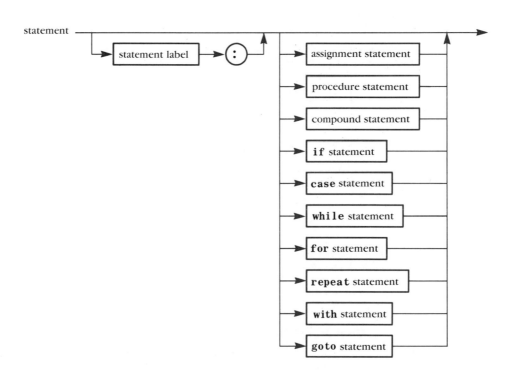

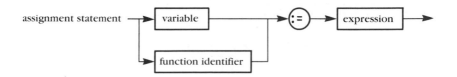

procedure statement

```pascal
program numbers3(input, output);
        {a program to illustrate reading two integer}
        {values with a single call to read           }

var num1, num2  : integer; {two integer variables to}
                           {hold input values        }

begin {numbers3}
        writeln('Enter two integers. ');
        read(num1, num2);
        writeln('Your numbers were');
        writeln(num1, num2)
end. {numbers3}
```

if statement

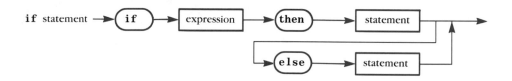

case statement

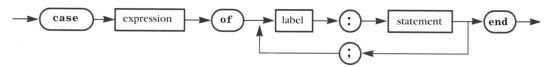

case statement

```pascal
if num mod 2 = 0
    then writeln (num: 1, ' is even')
    else writeln (num: 1, ' is odd');
```

while statement

repeat statement

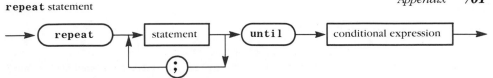

for statement

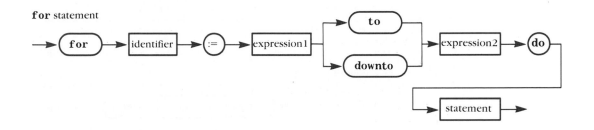

with statement

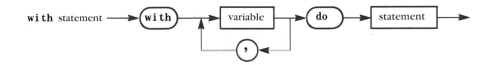

goto statement

expression

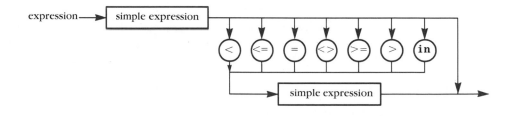

simple expression

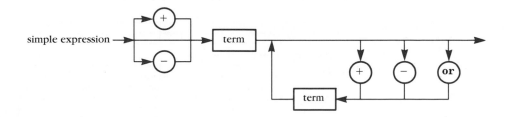

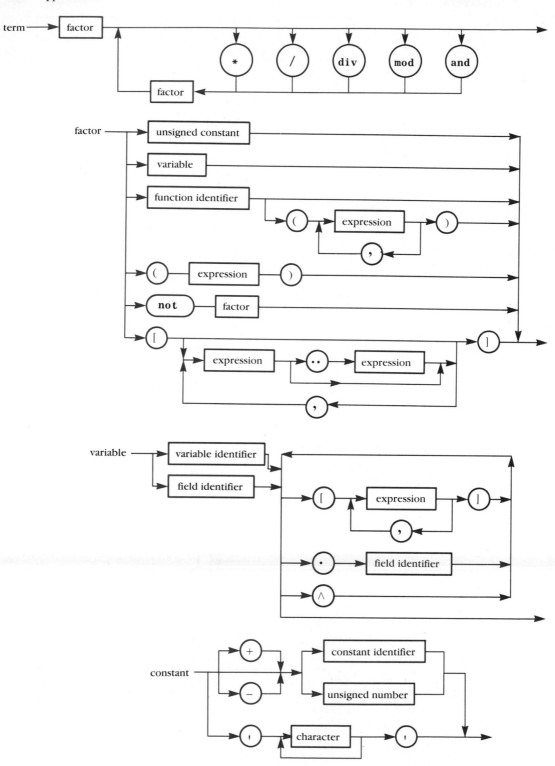

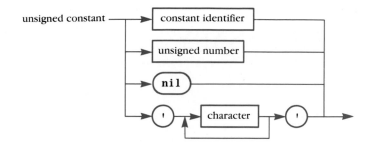

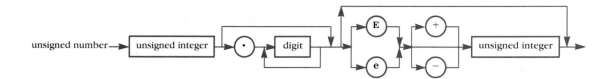

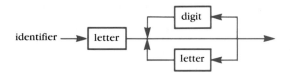

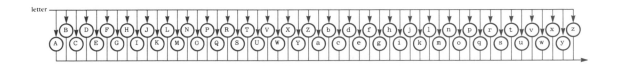

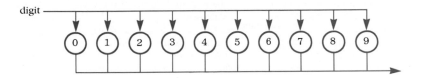

GLOSSARY

algorithm a precise, finite sequence of steps that solves a specific problem

ambiguities characteristics of a problem statement that can be interpreted in more than one way

anonymous type a type created without a type identifier

argument a data item appearing in an invocation of a procedure or a function; also called an actual parameter

arithmetic operators symbols used to indicate arithmetic operations: $+, -, *, /,$ **div**, and **mod**

array a data structure corresponding to a fixed size, linear or matrix arrangement of data items

ASCII a system for coding characters into binary representations; acronym for American Standard Code for Information Interchange

assignment statement a statement that assigns the value of an expression to a variable

auxiliary (external) storage a physical component of the computer; used to store data between runs of programs

base type the type of individual elements in an array or a set

batch a method of running computer programs that is not interactive; all data is supplied with the program

binary having two parts

binary number system the number system used internally by most computers; using the two digits 0 and 1

binary operation an operation that takes two operands

binary search a method of searching an ordered list for a single item in which the portion of the list being searched decreases by a factor of two at each stage

bit a binary digit, either 0 or 1

block the major component of either a Pascal program or a Pascal procedure, the other two components being a header and a final punctuation mark

block diagram a diagram showing the various blocks of a Pascal program

body of a loop the statements in a loop that form the unit that is iterated

boolean a predefined type in Pascal whose possible values are *true* and *false*

boolean expression an expression that evaluates to one of the boolean values, *true* or *false;* also called a conditional expression

boolean operator an operator whose operands are *boolean* and that produces a *boolean* result

byte the smallest addressable unit in a computer's memory unit, usually 6 or 8 bits

case expression the expression whose value determines the action to be chosen by the *case* statement

case statement a Pascal statement providing multiway selection by means of equality comparisons

case statement labels the various possible values of the *case* expression that correspond to the possible actions of the *case* statement

circular list a linked list in which the last element points to the first element

code a set of program statements

comments documentary phrases placed in a program. In Pascal, comments are placed either between { and } or between (* and *)

compatible types two or more types that can be used interchangably without causing a type-clash error

compound conditional expressions conditional expressions involving the *boolean* operators **and, or,** and **not**

computed data a data item whose value is determined by performing the steps of the algorithm

conditional expression an expression whose value is of type *boolean*

constant data a data item whose value cannot change while performing the steps of an algorithm

constant definition section the section of a Pascal program or procedure where identifiers are equated to the values they represent

constraints restrictions imposed on the solution of a problem

cursor a character, usually a box or an underscore, showing where the next character to be typed on the keyboard will appear on the screen.

dangling else an *else* clause nested inside of the **then** clause of an if-then statement

data information used by an algorithm or program

debug determine and fix the errors in a computer program

default rule a rule that is in effect in the absence of any other rules

definite iteration the performance of a set of steps some number of times that is determined before the performance begins

delimiters things that indicate the end of one item and the beginning of the next

dequeue to remove an item from a queue

documentation various forms of written discussion about the method of solution of a problem carried out by a computer

dot notation one method used to indicate a desired field in a **record**, consisting of a **record** variable identifier, followed by a period, followed by a field identifier

doubly linked list a linked list in which each element contains pointers to both the preceding element and succeeding elements

dynamic storage allocation allocation of space in memory to variables during execution of a program

EBCDIC a system for coding characters into binary representations; acronym for Extended Binary Coded Decimal Interchange Code

echo printing a method of verifying data input by immediately printing each data item after it is read

empty set a set having no members; in Pascal indicated by [ ]

enqueue to add an element to a queue

entry condition a condition that must be satisfied to enter a loop

enumerated type an ordinal type whose values are identifiers chosen by the programmer

evaluate determine the value of

execution the performance by a computer of the instructions of a program

exit condition a condition that must be satisfied to exit a loop

exponential (scientific, floating-point) notation a notational system in which numbers are expressed in terms of a mantissa and an exponent for a given base, usually 10

expression a syntactic construct that represents a value

external documentation program documentation that is not written in the program itself; includes user and programmer documentation

external files files in the computer's auxiliary storage component that exist beyond the execution of a program

field of a record one of the logical units of which **records** are composed

field width the number of print positions in which a value will be printed

field width specifier an integer-valued expression that determines a field width

FIFO short for "first in, first out"; used to describe a dynamic data structure that is processed in that way

file window a place in the computer's memory unit that contains a copy of the current element of its associated file

flow of control the determination of which statement in a program will be the next executed

formatting the positioning of program statements with respect to each other; also the arrangement of output on a screen or page

function a Pascal program module used to determine a single value

global known everywhere in the program

header the first line of a program, procedure, or function in Pascal

identifiers names chosen to identify elements of a Pascal program, such as data items and program modules

indefinite iteration the performance of a set of steps some number of times that is determined by a conditional expression

index a value used to indicate a single item in an array

index type the type of the possible values used to indicate individual items in an array

initialize give a beginning value

input the data from an outside source upon which an algorithm or program works

input instruction *read, readln,* or *get* in Pascal; an instruction to obtain a data value from an outside source during execution of a program

input stream the collection of characters typed by a user as input, including carriage returns

integer expression an expression that evaluates to an *integer* value

interactive used to describe a program whose input data is partially or totally entered by a user during execution

internal documentation comments and identifiers within a program that describe the method of solution implemented by the program

internal files files whose life-spans are only a single execution of a program

iteration the process of doing something repeatedly

k 1024; short for 2 to the 10th power

key the part of a data item that determines its order with respect to the other data items in its structure or some value by which a data item may be found

LIFO short for "last in, first out"; used to describe a type of dynamic data structure accessed in that way

line-oriented output output that is configured in terms of lines and line breaks

linked list a form of dynamic data structure in which one element points to only one other element

list traversal the process of reviewing the elements of a linked list from the beginning of the list to its end

local known only to a particular segment of a program

logic error an error in a program caused by a fault either in the algorithm or the implementation of the algorithm, but not due to incorrect syntax

loop a set of instructions that are performed repeatedly

loop control variable the variable determining the number of iterations of a *for* loop

machine code the translation of a Pascal program into a machine-understandable form

main program the part of a Pascal program corresponding to the first level of algorithm refinement; found physically at the bottom of the program between the reserved words **begin** and **end,** followed by a period

memory the component of the computer where data and the instructions that comprise a program are stored during execution

modular programs programs that are constructed from logical units of code that are as independent as possible

multioption selection an algorithmic device to provide for a choice between several courses of action

nested statements statements that are the component parts of other statements

noninteractive input input whose source is one or more files

null statement a statement indicating that no action is to be taken

operators symbols that indicate *boolean,* arithmetic, or comparison operations

ordinal position an integer value corresponding to the position of an item in an ordered set

ordinal type a type for which there is no ambiguity concerning the predecessor or successor of a particular item

output data whose values are transmitted to the program's environment by the program

padding filling in with blanks

parameter list the list of data items in a **procedure** or **function** header that correspond to data being transferred to and/or from the **procedure** or **function** when it is invoked or terminated

pointer the Pascal construct used to implement dynamically allocated data structures; a reference to a place in memory

pop the action of removing an item from the top of a stack

predefined function a function provided by the implementors of a version of Pascal

predefined identifiers identifiers given meaning by the implementors of the Pascal language

precedence of an identifier the rule describing how the scope of an identifier can be masked by a more locally declared identifier of the same name

procedure a Pascal program module representing a logical segment of an algorithm

procedure call an instruction to invoke a procedure

procedure and function declaration section the segment of a Pascal program or procedure in which procedures and functions are declared

procedure header the first line of a procedure, containing its name and parameter list

program a set of statements conforming to the syntax of a programming language that implements the steps of an algorithm to solve a problem

program modules the logical units of a program that implement logical units of an algorithm to solve specified subproblems

program skeleton a diagram showing the nesting of a program's procedures and functions

programmer-defined function a function written by the programmer

programmer documentation documentation of a program that is separate from the program itself and is intended to describe the program's purpose and structure to another programmer

prompt a message written on the screen asking the user for input data

push the action of adding an item to the top of a stack

queue a dynamic data structure characterized by "first in, first out" behavior

random-access file a file whose individual items can each be directly accessed in any order

read pointer an indicator of the next character to be read in the input stream for interactive input or of the next item to be read from a file

reading data physically transferring data from an external source into the computer's memory

record the data structure available in Pascal to group together data items of different types

recursion a method of solution of a problem that is defined in terms of the solution to the same problem in a simpler circumstance

relational operators operators used to determine relationships between two operands; $<$, $<=$, $<>$, $=$, $>=$, $>$, and **in**

repeat loop an indefinite iterative construct in Pascal that checks its exit condition after executing the body of the loop

reserved word a word that has specific meaning in a programming language and may not be redefined by the programmer

run-time error a program error that occurs during execution

running a program causing a computer to perform the instructions that comprise a program

sample execution a description of exactly what happens when a program is run with some sample data

scalar type a type in which all items have a definite order

scope the segment of a program where an identifier has meaning

scratch data data that is needed by the algorithm to accomplish its task but that is never output

selection a process of choosing between alternative courses of action

self-documenting identifiers identifiers that are chosen to indicate their purpose in the program

semantic errors errors in coding the program due to misunderstanding of the actions represented by certain program constructs

sequence the order in which instructions must be performed

sequential file a file in which all data items preceding a particular data item must be read before that item can be read

set in general, a collection of objects; in Pascal, a finite collection of values of the same ordinal type

set constants a collection of constant values of the same ordinal type enclosed in [and] and separated by commas

set difference the set of elements remaining when the elements of one set are removed from the second set

set intersection the set of elements common to two sets

set union the totality of elements that are members of either of two sets

simple data item a data item representing a single value

single-option selection the algorithmic construct used to implement a choice between going on to the next step or doing an extra action before going on to the next step

stack a dynamic data structure characterized by "last in, first out" behavior

Standard Pascal the Pascal programming language as described by the International Standards Organization

standard types types made available by Pascal: `char, integer, real, boolean, text`

stepwise refinement the process by which a problem's solution is developed from the problem statement to a precise detailed sequence of instructions

string a `packed array` of characters

string literal a constant consisting of a `packed array` of characters

structured data item a data item composed of various parts

structured file a file whose unit of data is not a single character

subproblem a logical unit or task that must be accomplished to solve a problem

subrange type a type whose values are a contiguous set of values of an ordinal type

subscript a value indicating a specific element in an array; synonymous with index

syntax the rules governing the formation of statements

syntax diagram a diagram describing the formation of a syntactic construct

syntax error an error in forming program statements; caused by not conforming to the syntax of the language

tag field the field of a variant `record` that specifies which of several possible structures that record has

textfile a file whose unit of data is a single character

trace the process of performing the steps of an algorithm or program by hand

trailing pointer a pointer indicating an element in a linked list just before the element pointed to by another pointer

translator a computer program that translates a program written in a high-level language (like Pas

cal) into a machine-understandable format

truth tables diagrams describing the results of logical operators on their operands

type of a variable the kind of data item represented

unary operation an operation performed on only one operand

user the person who executes a program

user documentation a description explaining to a user how to use a program

value parameter the syntactic construct used to transmit a value to a `procedure` or `function` and protect that value from being affected by that `procedure` or `function`

variable an identifier that represents a place to hold data in memory

variable data data that may change value during the performance of an algorithm or program

variable declaration section the section of a Pascal program or procedure where variables are given names and types

variable parameter the syntactic construct used in Pascal to allow a `procedure` to use and affect a data item

write pointer for a file an indicator of where the next item will be written in a file

INDEX